Innovation in Business and Enterprise:
Technologies and Frameworks

Latif Al-Hakim
University of Southern Queensland, Australia

Chen Jin
Zhejiang University, China

BUSINESS SCIENCE REFERENCE

Hershey · New York

Director of Editorial Content:	Kristin Klinger
Director of Book Publications:	Julia Mosemann
Acquisitions Editor:	Lindsay Johnston
Development Editor:	Julia Mosemann
Publishing Assistant:	Sean Woznicki
Typesetter:	Deanna Zombro
Production Editor:	Jamie Snavely
Cover Design:	Lisa Tosheff
Printed at:	Yurchak Printing Inc.

Published in the United States of America by
Business Science Reference (an imprint of IGI Global)
701 E. Chocolate Avenue
Hershey PA 17033
Tel: 717-533-8845
Fax: 717-533-8661
E-mail: cust@igi-global.com
Web site: http://www.igi-global.com/reference

Library of Congress Cataloging-in-Publication Data

Innovative in business and enterprise : technologies and frameworks / Latif Al-Hakim and Chen Jin, editors.
    p. cm.
 Includes bibliographical references and index.
 Summary: "The focus of the book is on managing innovation through bridging gaps created from theories, relative advantages or competitiveness, social differences, and innovation capability and performance"--Provided by publisher.
 ISBN 978-1-61520-643-8 (hardcover) -- ISBN 978-1-61520-644-5 (ebook) 1. Business enterprises--Technological innovations. I. Al-Hakim, Latif, 1946- II. Jin, Chen, 1968- III. Title.

 HD2351.I556 2010
 658.4'063--dc22

                                     2009044408

British Cataloguing in Publication Data
A Cataloguing in Publication record for this book is available from the British Library.

All work contributed to this book is new, previously-unpublished material. The views expressed in this book are those of the authors, but not necessarily of the publisher.

Table of Contents

Section 1
Theory and Practice

Section 2
Innovation Capability and Performance

Section 3
Social Aspects of Innovation

Detailed Table of Contents

Section 1
Theory and Practice

Chapter 1

Geoff Bamberry, Charles Sturt University, Australia

This chapter investigates the concept of innovation in cumulative causation theory and highlights the links of characteristics of the theory and their influences on innovation processes. The range of cases provided in this chapter paths the way to bridging the gap between the theory and practices on innovation.

Chapter 2

Amy C. Hutchins, IBM Corporation, USA
Brian D. Goodman, IBM Corporation, USA
John W. Rooney, IBM Corporation, USA

This chapter emphasises the importance of dealing with the technology and innovation as management program and presents IBM's Technology Adoption Program (TAP) as an example. The chapter demonstrates through three brief case studies how to mitigate the common plagues of development projects.

Chapter 3

J.R. Ortt, Delft University of Technology, The Netherlands

The chapter underlines the managerial relevance of the pre-diffusion phases for high-tech products. The study indicates that the resources devoted to research and development in different fields of expertise may have increased but the length of individual technological trajectories has not shortened accordingly.

Based on the study of 160 Chinese organisations, this chapter constructs a theoretical framework to explore the links between the types of innovation, the types of organizational change and levels of learning. The study hypothesises that deepest scope of change may take place even if lowest level of innovation happens in a Chinese organizations.

Chapter 5

This chapter empirically tests the impact of market and entrepreneurial orientations on the innovation decision. The study shows that company's performance is not conditioned by the decision of innovating or imitating, but is rather determined by the company's proactivity and focus on customers.

Chapter 6

This chapter explores the antecedents of ICT usage in new product development (NPD). The study employs case study methodology and finds that the most significant antecedents for sustained user-involvement in NPD with ICT tools are strategic emphasis, competencies and the type of ICT champion.

Section 2
Innovation Capability and Performance

Chapter 7

This chapter investigates the European Innovation Scoreboard database and use clusters analysis to verify how different countries are positioned and to determine which factors distinguish the country innovative capacity. The results point to the existence of four groups of countries.

The chapter challenges the context of entrepreneurship competences and management capabilities needed for innovation. This study explores the crucial capabilities to start an innovative business and discuss the capabilities have to be developed to sustain innovation and business growth.

This chapter deals with the innovation capability of large firms and explains the obstacles that firms face with respect to developing radical innovations. It identifies the practices leading firms have developed and established a radical innovation mechanism.

The chapter presents a framework for a conceptual evaluation of the performance of industrial product innovation activities and presents the results of research involving seven large companies in Sweden. Key success factors are discussed.

Section 3
Social Aspects of Innovation

Chapter 11

The chapter investigates the impact of labour relations on a firm's innovative output and finds that active practices of human resource management contribute positively to innovative output. In addition, firms that retain high levels of highly qualified personnel are more likely to introduce products that are new to the market.

The central argument of this chapter is that IC assists social enterprises to harness knowledge that leads to innovation for the pursuit of social and commercial activities. The study proposes an IC conceptual framework. The framework's implications for the development of effective innovation-based strategies in social enterprises are also discussed.

The chapter investigates how corporate social responsibility, individual and organizational level factors predict the innovation climate. The study analyse the results of large-scale survey received from 4632 respondents from Estonian, Chinese, Japanese, Russian and Slovakian enterprises.

This chapter introduces a collaborative conflict resolution model with a focus on cultural diversity and innovation. The chapter emphasises the correlations between collaborative conflict process at its best and innovation within diverse teams and organizations.

The chapter argues that many foreign multinational enterprises focus on legal compliance and charity in their corporate social responsibility (CSR) programs in China. This chapter describes a few innovative CSR initiatives being utilized within an industrial association and within partnerships between local non-government organizations.

Section 4
Innovative Systems

This chapter studies the output of implementing innovation systems in two diverse industries; a small micro manufacturing firm and a domestic building construction firm. The chapter finds that there are common factors that aided and inhibited innovation in each industry.

This chapter explores the reasons for the fragmentation of innovation system of Oil India Limited (OIL), a national oil company operating mainly in the northeast India. This fragmentation is evident from several issues such as stagnating oil production, technological obsolescence, continued impact of natural calamities and conflicts in the region and prolonged dependence on central government funding.

The aim of this chapter is to provide a systematic comparison of nanotechnology innovation systems (NanoSI) at the national level in Europe and Japan. The chapter addresses strengths and weaknesses, major drivers and barriers to a detailed understanding and smooth functioning of NanoSI.

Foreword

Computers, the Internet, nanotechnology and biotechnology have changed the world forever. While computers and the Internet have cut the distance between the producer and supplier and the innovator and consumer, they have also changed business processes themselves. In a similar vein, nanotechnology and biotechnology have enabled rapid innovation in many industries ranging from healthcare to aerospace through to the future of our very living. The advent of such disruptive technologies and devices have brought tremendous amount of tangible benefits to the population at large. However, several questions arise which include, but not limited to: Can innovation be induced? Can we learn from others' experience on innovation? How can nation states foster innovation? How does one build an innovative organization? How would diversity facilitate innovation? What kind of tools would aid innovation? What are the human resource challenges and work environment practices that could foster innovation? How can innovation be taken through its life cycle so that productization and commercialization become possible?

The book on *Innovation in Business and Enterprise: Technologies and Frameworks* is timely and appropriate. It addresses a number of the issues raised above – from theory that explains the basis and urge for innovation to frameworks that can foster innovation. Factors that contribute to innovation at organization levels have also been brought out, along with papers on tools that can facilitate and compress the innovation cycle. Mechanisms for building innovation at the national level, the processes and the interactions among the social, cultural and technological aspects have also been brought out in this book through case studies on several disciplines. These case studies have all been drawn from a number of countries, thereby providing a plethora of viewpoints on processes that encourage innovation and their long-term sustainability. The impact of human resource and their management is critical to creating a nation of innovation and so are mechanisms to foster entrepreneurship and inculcate a culture of continued learning. The topics are as interesting and exciting as the papers themselves.

This book on *Innovation in Business and Enterprise: Technologies and Frameworks* will be an excellent resource for educators and researchers and is a valuable addition to every library. I therefore commend the efforts of Prof. Hakim and the contributing authors in creating this wonderful book and dedicating it to the scientific and business communities.

V. Lakshmi Narasimhan, PhD
East Carolina University
Greenville, NC

Lakshmi Narasimhan is presently a Professor of Software Engineering in the Department of Computer Science at East Carolina University, USA. He has published over 180 papers in the areas of Software Engineering, Information security and Information Engineering. In particular, his research interests are in computer architecture, parallel and distributed computing, software testing, data mining, Software process, asset management systems and Standards, and information management & fusion. His papers have appeared in such archival journals as the various IEEE Transactions and IEE Proceedings. He has also been the technical chair of two other conferences and has been on the technical panel of over 60 leading International Conferences. He has consulted to a number of industries and educational institutions on various IT and Software Engineering projects, including Boeing Aerospace and DoD. Prof. Narasimhan is a Senior Member of the IEEE, ACM, Fellow of ACS, IEAust and IEE (UK). He is a Technical Member of various Standards bodies such as, ISO, ANSI and IEEE.

Preface

INTRODUCTION

Sustainable market growth of an organisation lies in its capability to create new ideas that have a market value. Innovation is defined as "the successful exploitation of new ideas" (Amabile, Conti, Coon, Lazenby, & Herron, 1996; DTI, 2003). Innovation, by definition, means "something that is new or significantly improved, done by enterprise to create added value either directly for the enterprise or indirectly for its customers"(BCA, 1993). For organisations, innovation is essential for long-term stability and sustainable performance (Cottam, Ensor, & Band, 2001). For consumers, innovation means higher quality and better value for goods and services. Tony Blair, the UK former Prime Minister, emphasises that innovation "is absolutely essential to safeguard and deliver high-quality jobs, successful business, better products and services for our consumers and new, more environmentally friendly processes" (DTI, 2003). The common dimension of innovation diffusion is the source of the newness in organization, market, technology, product and the process (Kim & Galliers, 2004).

Adopting ideas innovated by competitors may stimulate business improvement but will seldom result in anything other than one step toward closing the gap with competitors; innovation is a uniquely human activity and it is difficult to translate the tacit knowledge associated with the implementation of innovative ideas, system, technology or practice. The tacit knowledge of people creating and implementing the original innovation cannot be copied. Even copying successfully 'innovation' requires by itself innovation, that is, requires creative ideas. The term 'innovation' is associated with the term 'creativity'. Creativity implies coming up with, or bringing ideas to life, while innovation means successful implementation of the creative idea. Creativity can be created by individuals and forms a necessary condition for innovation. Innovation, on the other hand, occurs in organisational context and forms a managerial process that requires "specific tools, rules and discipline" (Davila, Epstein, & Shelton, 2006).

The process in which innovation is communicated through social system channels over time is referred to as diffusion (Rogers, 1995). Roger (1995) develops the diffusion of innovation theory (DOI) and specifies five variables that determine the rate of innovation adoption. These variables are relative advantage, compatibility, complexity, trialability and observability (pp. 15-16).

Research on innovation has been concerned with a wide range of areas related to products and services among them innovation in organizations (Damanpour, 1992), innovation in marketing (Atuahene-Gima, 1996), technological innovation diffusion (Bradford & Florin, 2003; Rogers, 1995), process innovation (Davenport, 1993), innovation for information systems (Allen, 2000; Kim & Galliers, 2004) and ecology (Rennings, 2000). The Organisation for Economic Co-Operation and Development (OECD) identifies five type of innovation within business and enterprise (OECD, 1997):

1. New product development or qualitative change to an existing product –good or service);
2. Process innovation
3. Opening of a new market
4. Development of new sources of supply, (for raw material or other input).
5. Creative changes in industrial organisation.

Recently research on innovation has widened into two interrelated directions:

- Consideration of social networks (Taatila, Suomala, Siltala, & Keskinen, 2006) and social responsibility (MacManus 2008) on innovation;
- Developing pathways that take advantages of both internal and external (other firms) innovation. This development in innovation is referred to as 'open innovation' (Chesbrough, Vanhaverbeke, & West, 2006).

The focus of the book is on managing innovation through bridging gaps created from theories, relative advantages or competitiveness, social differences, and innovation capability and performance. Bridging gaps is recognised by academics and practitioners as a vital matter to develop and implement innovation. There is also a strong tradition among the researchers on innovation of using empirical studies in the form of survey and multiple cases studies to determine factors, test hypotheses and propositions affecting or dealing with gaps. This feature makes the book a valuable resource for academic professionals, practitioners as well as postgraduate students dealing with innovation processes.

THE STRUCTURE OF THE BOOK

This book is comprised of eighteen chapters organised into four sections; theory and practice, capability and performance, social aspects of innovation, and innovation systems.

Section 1: Theory and Practice

This section features six chapters demonstrating attempts for bridging gaps between theories and practices. In the first chapter of this section, Professor Bamberry from Charles Stuart University (Australia) investigates the concept of innovation in cumulative causation theory and highlights the links of characteristics of the theory and their influences on innovation processes. The range of cases provided in this chapter paths the way to bridging the gap between the theory and practices on innovation. These characteristics and influences are then used as a basis for reporting empirical research into the nature of innovation in manufacturing and processing in an Australian rural region, and the usefulness of the theory for explanatory purposes is evaluated.

Technology adoption is based on principles of Diffusion of Innovation (DOI) theory. In the second chapter, "Lowering the center of gravity of enterprise IT", Hutchins, Goodman and Rooney from IBM Corporation provide a successful practical path to technology adoption. They emphasise the importance of dealing with the technology and innovation as management program. IBM's Technology Adoption Program (TAP) describes one such innovation management discipline demonstrating through three brief case studies how to mitigate the common plagues of development projects. While the issues with technology and innovation management are obviously wide and varied, this chapter focuses on the need for a formal initiative to manage innovation. Similarly, fully understanding the workings of a program such as TAP is of considerable scope. The benefit to the reader is the focus on driving the decision making around technology to the users – the community – as a core section of making decisions.

The third chapter of the 'Theory and Practice' section is authored by Ortt from Deft University of Technology, The Netherlands. Chapter 3 of the book underlines the managerial relevance of the pre-diffusion phases for high-tech products. These phases last from the first demonstration of a technological principle to the start of the large scale production and diffusion of products based on that principle. Based on fifty-three cases of high-tech products, invented between 1837 and 1998, the study shows that the pre-diffusion phase's length varies considerably per case. No proof for the shortening of these phases over time is found. The study indicates that the resources devoted to research and development in different fields of expertise may have increased but the length of individual technological trajectories has not shortened accordingly.

Based on the study of 160 Chinese organisations, Wei Sun and Ruth Alas construct a theoretical framework to explore the links between the types of innovation, the types of organizational change and levels of learning. On the basis of survey results, the authors of Chapter 4 find out there are close connections between the three aspects: innovation type, change type and learning type. The study finds that the highest level of innovation is accompanied by deepest change, but the lowest level of innovation may not be necessarily accompanied by lower level change, i.e. deepest scope of change may take place even if the lowest level of innovation happens in a Chinese organization.

In an attempt to answer the question; "what makes companies to be more productive and profitable?" Pérez-Luño, Valle-Cabrera and Wiklund empirically test the impact of market and entrepreneurial orientations on the innovation decision. They conducted a survey comprising 304 companies. Results of Chapter 5 show that proactivity is the most important determinant in the decision of whether to innovate or imitate. The study shows that a company's performance is not conditioned by the decision of innovating or imitating, but is rather determined by the company's proactivity and focus on customers.

Involvement of users in new product development is needed more than ever due to the technological and the social progression in recent years. Usage of ICT tools is one approach forwarded in literature discussing user-involvement. Chapter 6 entitled, "Usage of ICT tools in new development: creating user involvement" by Jespersen and Buck explores the antecedents of ICT usage in new product development (NPD). The study employs case study methodology and utilizes five groups of factors: innovative climate, strategic emphasis on ICT tools, ICT champions, competencies and performance expectations. The case findings demonstrate that the most significant antecedents for sustained user-involvement in NPD with ICT tools are strategic emphasis, competencies and the type of ICT champion.

Section 2: Innovation Capability and Performance

This section is comprised of four chapters dealing with the innovation performance and innovation capabilities at the national and organisational level. The first chapter of the second section (Chapter 7) deals with the factors and dimensions of national innovation capacity. Natário, Couto, Tiago and Braga investigate the European Innovation Scoreboard database and use clusters analysis to verify how different countries are positioned and to determine which factors distinguish the country's innovative capacity. The results point to the existence of four groups of countries. The factors identified point to aspects related to the institutional efficiency, the societies' cultural values associated with the level of hierarchy or "power distance" and with aspects such as the level of population with tertiary education and the percentages of expenses with research and development applied by the companies.

In the second chapter, Omar and Lewrick challenge the context of entrepreneurship competences and management capabilities needed for innovation. The authors build their arguments in step with actual practice, analyzing data from over 200 innovative companies which have been created under the formal requirements of a regional business plan competition during the last 10 years. This study explores the crucial capabilities to start an innovative business and discuss the capabilities have to be developed to sustain innovation and business growth.

Large firms are generally good at managing incremental innovations, yet they often lack the capabilities that are conducive to developing and deploying radical innovations. In Chapter 9, Shah, Ortt and Sholten deal with the innovation capability of large firms and explain the obstacles that firms face with respect to developing radical innovations. The authors collect data among three large enterprises; Shell, Nokia and IBM, and identify the practices these firms have developed and established a radical innovation mechanism that allows them to circumvent the obstacles for tapping into radical innovation.

Chapter 10 authored by Cedergren, Wall and Norström presents a framework for a conceptual evaluation of the performance of industrial product innovation activities by considering three categories of activities: Planning, Implementation, and Sales and Delivery. In this chapter the results of research involving seven large companies in Sweden, with the objective of improving the understanding of what is required to be successful when developing complex industrial products, are presented. Key success factors are discussed.

Section 3: Social Aspects of Innovation

This section includes five chapters dealing with various social aspects of innovation. The first chapter of this section (Chapter 11) investigates the impact of labour relations on a firm's innovative output. Zhou, Dekker and Kleinknechi from Erasmus University of Rotterdam, The Netherlands find that active practices of human resource management such as job rotation, performance pay, high qualification levels of personnel, as well as making use of employees with long-term temporary contracts contribute positively to innovative output. Furthermore, firms that retain high levels of highly qualified personnel are more likely to introduce products that are new to the market.

Very little research has investigated the role of intellectual (IC) capital in innovation processes in social enterprises. The central argument of Chapter 12 is that IC assists social enterprises to harness knowledge that leads to innovation for the pursuit of social and commercial activities. This chapter is authored by Eric Kong from the University of Southern Queensland (Australia). The chapter contributes to the literature by theoretically arguing that intellectual capital can be utilized in innovation processes in social enterprises. The study proposes an IC conceptual framework, which helps social entrepreneurs to visualize IC and its components in their organizations. The framework's implications for the development of effective innovation-based strategies in social enterprises are also discussed.

Chapter 13 "Factors predicting the innovation climate" by Übius and Alas from Estonian Business School, Estonia investigates how such factors as corporate social responsibility and individual and organizational level factors predict the innovation climate. The study analyses the results of large-scale survey received from 4632 respondents from Estonian, Chinese, Japanese, Russian and Slovakian enterprises. The results of the empirical study shows that both facets of corporate social responsibility - the firm performance concerning social issues and the firm respects the interests of agents, individual and organizational level factors predict the innovation climate, but it differs according to different countries. The study develops models to explain how corporate social responsibility, individual and organizational level factors predict the innovation climate in Estonian, Chinese, Japanese, Russian and Slovakian electric-electronic machine, retail store and machine-building enterprises.

Chapter 14 entitled, "Advancing the potential of diversity for innovation" by Nancy Erbe, California State University (USA) introduces a collaborative conflict resolution model with a focus on cultural diversity and innovation. The chapter presents the optimal criteria for amulticultural process identified in evaluative research conducted in four parts of the world: the Balkans, Cameroon, Nepal and Ukraine. It aims to demonstrate the correlations between collaborative conflict process at its best and innovation within diverse teams and organizations.

The final chapter of this section (Chapter 15), "Managing corporate social responsibility as an innovation in China" by Maria Lam, Malone University (USA) argues that many foreign multinational enterprises focus on legal compliance and charity in their corporate social responsibility (CSR) programs in China. This chapter describes a few innovative CSR initiatives being utilized within an industrial association and within partnerships between local non-government organizations. It also explores institutional incentives for managing the process by using the social movement theory. The chapter concludes that the key barriers for the strategic approach of CSR are the apathetic attitude of many executives toward CSR and the shortcomings of the institutional framework in China.

Section 4: Innovation Systems

This section features three chapters dealing with the application of the innovation systems. The first chapter of this section (Chapter 16), "Study of SMS innovation in two Queensland industries" authored by David Thorpe and Steven Goh two different types of industries; a small micro manufacturing firm and a domestic building construction firm. This chapter studies the output of implementing innovation systems in these both diverse industries and finds that there are common factors that aided and inhibited innovation in each industry.

In Chapter 17, Dhodapkar, Gogoi and Medhi study the innovation system linkages in Indian hydrocarbon sector. This chapter elaborates the concept of innovation system, that is, the formal or informal linkages between the policy makers, industry, academic and research institutions, etc. and its relevance for organizational effectiveness. Using creative and visual thinking tools, authors explore the reasons for the fragmentation of innovation system of Oil India Limited (OIL), a national oil company operating mainly in the northeast India. This fragmentation is evident from several issues such as stagnating oil production, technological obsolescence, continued impact of natural calamities and conflicts in the region and prolonged dependence on central government funding.

The final chapter of this book "Nanotechnology innovation systems – A regional comparison" is authored by Nazrul Islam from Cardiff University Innovative Manufacturing Research Centre (UK). The aim of this chapter (Chapter 18) is to provide a systematic comparison of nanotechnology innovation systems (NanoSI) at the national level in Europe and Japan. Having carried out a detailed analysis on the primary data, relevant attributes of nanotechnology innovation infrastructure have been identified and similarities and disparities between European and Japanese NanoSI have been explored. The chapter addresses strengths and weaknesses, major drivers and barriers to a detailed understanding and smooth functioning of NanoSI.

Latif Al-Hakim
University of Southern Queensland, Australia

Chen Jin
Zhejiang University, P. R. China

REFERENCES

Allen, J. P. (2000). Information systems as technological innovation. *Information Technology & People, 13*(3), 210-221.

Amabile, T. M., Conti, R., Coon, H., Lazenby,, J., & Herron, M. (1996). Assessing the work environment for creativity. *Academy of Management Journal*, 1154-1184.

Atuahene-Gima, K. (1996). Market orientation and innovation. *Journal of Business Research, 35*(2), 93-103.

BCA. (1993). *Managing the Innovation Enterprise*. Melbourne: Business Council of Australia.

Bradford, M., & Florin, J. (2003). Examining the role of innovation diffusion factors on the implementation success of enterprise resource planning systems. *International Journal of Accounting Information Systems, 4*(3), 205-225.

Chesbrough, H. W., Vanhaverbeke, W., & West, J. (2006). *Open innovation: researching a new paradigm*. New York: Oxford University Press.

Cottam, A., Ensor, J., & Band, C. (2001). A benchmark study of strategic commitment to innovation. *European Journal of Innovation Management, 4*(2), 88-94.

Damanpour, F. (1992). Organizational size and innovation. *Organization studies, 13*(3), 375.

Davenport, T. H. (1993). *Process innovation: reengineering work through information technology*. Boston, MA: Harvard Business School Pr.

Davila, T., Epstein, M., & Shelton, R. (2006). Design for Innovation. *Leadership Excellence, 23*(2), 15.

DTI. (2003). *Competing in the Global Economy: the Innovation Challlege*. London: Department of Trade and Industry.

Kim, C., & Galliers, R. D. (2004). Toward a diffusion model for Internet systems. *Internet Research, 14*(2), 155-166.

OECD. (1997). *The Oslo Manual: Proposed Guidelines for Collecting and Interpreting Technological Innovation Data*. Paris: Organisation for Economic Co-Operation and Development.

Rennings, K. (2000). Redefining innovation—eco-innovation research and the contribution from ecological economics. *Ecological Economics, 32*(2), 319-332.

Rogers, E. M. (1995). *Diffusion of innovation*. New York: The Free Press.

Taatila, V. P., Suomala, J., Siltala, R., & Keskinen, S. (2006). Framework to study the social innovation networks. *European Journal of Innovation Management, 9*(3), 312.

Acknowledgment

We are very grateful to the authors who deserve our heartfelt thanks for their contribution, patience, and cooperation throughout the long and complex process of compiling this book. We would also like to acknowledge our deepest appreciation to the reviewers for their time, effort and valuable comments. Their contribution was an essential ingredient necessary to improving the content and presentation of the book's chapters. A special note of thanks to the staff at IGI Global who provided the necessary process, templates, reminders, and project management of the entire process from our first proposal to this final publication. In particular we wish to express our thanks to Julia Mosemann, as well as all other editors and IGI staff who participate in managing the publication of this book.

Finally, we dedicate this book to Jin's mother Yijia Zhao and to his son Getai Chen and to Latif's five grandchildren; Sahra, Mustafa, Ibrahim, Yasamin and Ali.

Latif Al-Hakim
Chen Jin
Editors

Section 1
Theory and Practice

Chapter 1
Cumulative Causation as Explanatory Theory for Innovation

Geoff Bamberry
Charles Sturt University, Australia

ABSTRACT

While numerous theories have been used to explain innovation, one found to be useful in recent years is cumulative causation. Its major focus on incremental and evolutionary change, the path dependent nature of change, and its circular and cumulative effects, make it particularly useful in helping to explain innovation. In this chapter the literature on cumulative causation theory is reviewed to highlight links between these characteristics of the theory and innovation, as well as influences such as problem solving, learning by using and doing, collaboration, specialisation and the clustering of industry in certain locations. These characteristics and influences are then used as a basis for reporting empirical research into the nature of innovation in manufacturing and processing in an Australian rural region, and the usefulness of the theory for explanatory purposes is evaluated.

CUMULATIVE CAUSATION AS EXPLANATORY THEORY FOR INNOVATION

While a number of theories have been used to explain how innovation occurs and develops within organisations, one that has been found to be useful in recent years is cumulative causation. Although it had its origins in the late nineteenth and early twentieth century writings of Veblen (1899) and Young (1928), it was expanded in the mid-twentieth century by writers such as Myrdal (1944; 1957) Hirschman (1958), Kaldor (1966; 1970, 1972) and others to discuss economic growth in developing countries. In the latter part of the twentieth century it was refined to explain a range of economic, geographic and social issues. Its major focus on incremental change, its path dependent nature, and its cumulative effects, combined with its use in explaining technological change, make it particularly useful in helping to explain innovation.

DOI: 10.4018/978-1-61520-643-8.ch001

One of the advantages of cumulative causation as an explanatory theory is that it is a "multi-causal" approach, avoiding emphasis on any single factor, and drawing attention to complex interactions between variables (O'Hara 2008, 376). Similarly, Argyrous (1995, 113) points out that its methodology differs from that of traditional explanatory approaches such as neoclassical theory in that "rather than unidirectional causality from independent to dependent variables, each variable interacts with the others in a mutually dependent way."

Berger (2008, 358-359) draws attention to the writing of Kapp 1961, 188) who warned against attributing primary causation to economic factors alone, arguing that all relevant factors, as well as the reciprocal relationships between cause and effect, needed to be taken into consideration. Berger (2008, 359) goes on to argue that "the relevant factors can, of course, only be determined empirically in a given situation." However, Berger and Elsner (2007, 535) caution that the various factors are reciprocally interlinked in an "uneven and complex manner," and that these links are "in constant flux and mutually overlap." They argue that policymakers need to simultaneously take account of variables such as institutions, education and technology.

In the following section, the literature on cumulative causation theory is reviewed to highlight the aspects relating to technological change and innovation. Key factors and influences identified in the literature are used as a basis for reporting empirical research into the nature of innovation in regional manufacturing and processing, and the usefulness of the theory for explanatory purposes is evaluated.

THE CONCEPT OF INNOVATION IN CUMULATIVE CAUSATION THEORY

Innovation has been described within a cumulative causation framework in terms of "technical progress," being "a very complicated process emerging from the learning activities of human beings, and the application of this learning activity to production" (Pasinetti 1981, 67). Pasinetti saw innovation as not simply a matter of new inventions, but also involving other activities in the workplace such as re-organising old methods of production, making better use of materials, improving the quality of products, applying new methods of production, producing new products, finding new resources and discovering new sources of energy.

Innovation has also been described as a process of solving problems that emerge in the workplace. As solutions to particular problems are incorporated into work practices and diffused into the economy, they generate new problems that need to be solved (Argyrous 1995, 110). Innovation also emerges from "learning by using and doing," where advances in scientific knowledge are not enough on their own to achieve technical progress, but need to be followed up with "repeated application of particular engineering principles" to refine new techniques and processes (Kaldor 1972, 184; Targetti 1992, 166). Ricoy (1988, 732) refers to this as "the accretion of experience." In solving problems and seeking better ways to operate, workers often develop new tools, generating their own capital equipment. Examples of this in the Australian machine tool industry have been described by Argyrous (1995, 104). Toner (2000, 23) highlights the learning aspects of innovation, particularly where technological innovation becomes incorporated into vocational training, and is further diffused into industry as a form of "public knowledge."

Cumulative causation theory incorporates the idea that innovation through the development of new technology is an incremental or evolutionary process that depends on past developments (Argyrous and Sethi 1996, 487). O'Hara (2008, 376) points out that the acquisition of knowledge and technical skills, together with the associated development of economies of scale, "affect the path of development in complex and multifarious ways." While it is accepted that there are occasions when major technological break-throughs occur, these are thought to be relatively infrequent, and that most innovation in industry is an incremental, path dependent process where more complex developments are only possible after earlier, less complex innovations have been discovered and put into practice.

Rosenberg (1976, 29) observed that in the past, technological change was often a very gradual process, pointing out that the optimisation of an invention could take many decades, as was the case with the steam engine. Setterfield (1997, 366) argues that "cumulative causation represents an effort to refocus growth theory on the problems of creating productive resources over time (rather than allocating given production at a point in time), treating the heritage of the past as the only truly given variable in the system." This view is supported by De Ridder (1986, 45) in his comment that "at any moment capital endowment is a product of history, and not some gift of nature."

In arguing that economic development tends to be "path dependent," it has been observed that chance historical events can have long-run cumulative consequences (Porter 1998; Martin 1999, 69-70; Lowe and Miller 2001, 186). O'Hara (2008, 376) describes the cumulative effect of change as one where "the variables tend to operate as positive feed-back processes, magnifying the combined impact of the interactions through historical time." An example of this described by Wickham and Hanson (2002) is the Tasman Bridge disaster in Hobart in 1975, resulting in the need for vehicle ferries until the bridge could be repaired. This chance event had the long-term influence of stimulating the development of the light shipbuilding industry in Hobart. Research into the Australian wine industry showed that winery managers with a history of working overseas, or who had worked for a company that exported, were more likely than other managers to involve their companies in exporting (Wickramasekera and Bamberry 2003a, 26). An overseas example of the influence of history on industry development

was observed by Feldman (2001) in his study of biotechnology and information technology clusters in the United States. Thirlwall (1987, 327) commented that "the present and the future cannot be understood without reference to the past."

The comprehensive history of the Riverina rice industry by Lewis (1994) indicates clearly how 'accidents of history' led to the establishment of the Ricegrowers' Co-operative at Leeton, and the consolidation, over time, of the rice-processing industry there. This in turn helped establish Leeton as a centre for food processing in the Murrumbidgee Irrigation Area. A study of the wine industry in two major wine-producing regions in New South Wales has drawn attention to the significance of a firm's history, particularly at the regional stage of its market development, for its future growth (Argyrous & Bamberry 2009, 74). Owen's (1993) survey of Australian manufacturers draws attention to the influence of the 'history' of the people who established the enterprises she studied. Some writers have gone as far as arguing a case for "history friendly" models of economic growth (Malerba et al, 1999; Matthews, 2002).

Early cumulative causation theorists such as Young (1928, 533) tended to view innovation as "change," arguing that it is "progressive and propagates itself in a cumulative way." He believed that a state of continuous change occurs in industry as a result of external "adventitious" elements, as well as the internal daily operations of manufacturing enterprises, with all significant developments, including inventions, changing the nature of industry and causing reactions in other parts of industry. Rosenberg (1976, 110) has pointed out that "technology is much more a cumulative and self-generating process than the economist generally recognises."

Another pioneer of cumulative causation theory, Myrdal, (1968, 1870) argued that "over a period of time, a change in any one of a range of socio-economic conditions will tend to generate change in other conditions." He saw the secondary changes in this process generally operating in the same direction as the primary changes in terms of the improvement or deterioration of economic development. Dosi (1988, 1130) also observed that innovation can be cumulative in nature, arguing that in-house technological innovation is often augmented by "contributions from other firms and from public knowledge." Toner (1998, 96) argues that the cumulative effect of such changes occurs because "an initial expansion of economic activity induces successive (diminishing) rounds of income, employment and output expansion through input-output multipliers."

Cumulative causation writers have drawn attention to the significance of collaborative relationships in the innovation process. For example, Brusco (1989, 260), observing these relationships in the industrial districts of Italy, described the process as one where "a single idea goes through all phases of its development in a continuous confrontation between clients and sub-contractors," the relationship being one that is "extraordinarily rich and complex, full of reciprocal stimulation." Similar collaboration has been observed between individual workers, or between sections of a single firm, as workers seek to solve problems emerging from the day-to-day operations of the enterprise. Some writers have commented that successful innovation is becoming more dependent on what they refer to as "the associational capacity of the firm," including securing co-operation between firms in the supply chain (Cooke & Morgan 1998, 9, in Beer et al 2003, 39).

Some innovations can occur as a result of the collaboration of a number of firms in a particular industry. This was observed in a study of the wine industry in New South Wales, where an innovative collaborative approach was used to establish a joint venture by a group of five small-to-medium sized wineries under the name Penmara Wines to market their wines in national and international markets. This innovation allowed the new enterprise to achieve economies of scale by producing outputs well beyond the capacity of the individual wineries, and to achieve scale

economies in marketing (Argyrous & Bamberry 2009; Penmara Wines website). In another study of the Australian wine industry, it was found that wineries collaborating with distributors to establish strong networks were able to enhance their competitiveness in overseas markets (Wickramasekera and Bamberry 2001, 96).

A number of writers have incorporated specialisation as a key element of cumulative causation, indicating that innovation through problem solving can lead to the establishment of a specialised division in the firm, often using its own inventions of capital equipment. Young (1928, 531) argued that the economical use of specialised capital equipment generally requires a level of demand beyond that of a single, broadly-based industrial firm. To achieve economies of scale in the use of the equipment often requires demand from several firms. Consequently, over time, these specialised divisions may be 'hived off' to create new enterprises that can seek additional customers beyond the 'parent' firm. This process has been described as "vertical disintegration" (Vassilakis 1987, 762; Sweeney 1987, 11). The hived-off specialised divisions are often sources of innovation that are important for economic growth, because they "embody continually improving technologies, which improves the efficiency and quality of user industries" (Toner 2000, 28).

The new enterprises are usually established close to their parent companies, often relying on these companies for a high proportion of their work in the initial stages of growth (McKinsey, 1993; Argyrous, 1993; 2000). Over time, the new enterprises obtain work from other companies, and become more independent. This often results in the development of linkages between vertically integrated industries in the supply chain (Swann et al 1998, 3; Roberts 2000, 38; Toner 2000, 28). Related enterprises operating in close proximity begin to generate industry clusters, stimulating the development of business and social networks, the production of intermediate goods, the transfer of knowledge, the growth of pools of specialised labour, and the development of shared educational and training facilities (Porter 1996, 87; Martin 1999, 68). Such characteristics contribute to increasing returns to scale, and give the firms and locations involved a competitive advantage over others (Myrdal 1957, 27; Kaldor 1970, 148; Porter 1998, 13; Martin 1999, 77).

The significance of such geographic factors in the development and diffusion of technological innovation has been incorporated into cumulative causation theory. O'Hara (2008, 376) argues that geography is just as important as history, because not only do changes over time influence the evolutionary path of development, they differ from place to place, resulting in differences in growth and development. Storper and Scott (1992, 14) observe that "technical innovations are often place bound, as the stocks of human knowledge and human capital upon which technological changes are based, tend to be concentrated in specialised labour forces, which themselves are highly localised." The development of a specialised labour force was observed in a study of the information technology clusters in Silicon Valley and on Route 128 by Kenny and von Burgh (1999). Industry concentration of this type is sometimes aided by the presence of research laboratories, universities, and other institutions, (Martin, 1999, 79). Lowe and Miller (2001, 185) have observed that firms within a cluster develop relationships which depend on close proximity and trust, facilitating transactions, and improving productivity and innovation. However, as Beer et al (2003, 4) point out, some regions are able to generate or attract innovation and change for the better, while others lack this capacity.

Martin (1999, 80) has referred to the interdependence of firms in technological innovation as being "geographically constrained" in its initial stages, resulting in new ideas becoming available to local workforces in the early stages of their diffusion. This can sometimes give a locality or region competitive advantage over others. Porter (1998) also commented on the importance of industries being in close geographic proximity for technological innovation, particularly 'supporting' industries, where related firms can develop synergies in their operations. Linkages with related industries can lead to the sharing of common technologies as well as providing advantages in making use of common basic inputs or intermediate goods, together with common logistics services. Marceau et al (1997, 157) describe them as "networks of strongly interdependent firms, knowledge-producing agents and customers linked to each other in a value-adding production chain." The operation of linkages has been described in reports of earlier research undertaken in the Riverina Region of New South Wales (Bamberry 2006 a&b).

RESEARCH METHODOLOGY

The methodology for the empirical research reported in this chapter was based on a qualitative study involving the collection and analysis of data from fourteen in-depth interviews of manufacturers and processors located in the Riverina Region of New South Wales, and in most cases, site inspections. The interviews lasted for approximately one hour, and most were recorded and transcribed for further analysis. Where necessary, statistical information obtained from interviews has been updated with data from the firms' websites. The qualitative nature of the research has the advantage of allowing for a closer inspection of processes of change over time, particularly those involving interactions between people (Ticehurst and Veal 2000, 95; Kerlinger and Lee 2000, 589). The case studies gave interviewees the opportunity to discuss factual information and to express points of view and personal explanations of events, relationships and trends (Taylor and Bogdan 1984; Patton 1990, 172).

Manufacturing was chosen as a focus for the research because of its significant role in cumulative causation as described by key exponents of the theory such as Nicholas Kaldor. He saw endogenous growth, a major characteristic of circular and cumulative causation, as being stimulated mainly by manufacturing. Kaldor (1966) argued on the basis of research undertaken in twelve countries that the growth of manufacturing led to the growth of a country's gross domestic product, making it the engine of growth. He also identified the significance of increasing returns in manufacturing, together with the circular and cumulative effects of technological developments, arguing that as new products emerged, they stimulated demand, which in turn led to further technical progress (Pressman & Holt, 2008, 369).

In addition, manufacturing has been found to be a major source of innovation in Australia. As Toner (2000, 22-24) points out, it is the source of much of the research and development for product and process innovation, import replacement and export expansion, being three times more likely than other industries to engage in innovation. He also draws attention to its role in the production of capital goods, which are particularly significant for economic growth, providing resources for other manufacturers, and stimulating the development of technological service industries such as computer software.

Despite its decreasing proportion of GDP in the Australian economy, down from 18.6 percent in 1978 to 13 percent in 2000 (Beer et al 2003, 108) it remains a significant sector in terms of the levels of income and employment generated, and as O'Connor et al (2001, 44) point out, it has achieved increased levels of productivity through capital investment in new technologies. While the sector's contribution has decreased significantly in the urban areas of Australia, its contribution has stabilised or increased in many rural regions, particularly those engaged in the manufacturing or processing of products based on the outputs of the agricultural sector, or in the production of capital goods for that sector. Beer et al (1994, 59) argue that these changes "appear to be gaining momentum," indicating

that "regional cities are emerging as a much more significant geographic location for manufacturing industry in Australia."

The Riverina Region was selected for the study as it has a significant manufacturing sector involved in the processing of a large output of agricultural commodities, and producing equipment and capital goods for the agricultural sector (Bamberry & Wickramasekera, 1999). The region, as delineated by the Australian Bureau of Statistics and the New South Wales Government, is located in south-western New South Wales, extending along the Murrumbidgee River from the Snowy Mountains in the east to near its junction with the Murray River in the west. It has a total area of over 63,000 square kilometres, approximately 120 kilometres north to south and approximately 500 kilometres east to west. It is a diverse region, ranging from the eastern alpine forests of the Kosciusko National Park, through horticultural farms, pine forests and native hardwood forests of the mountain foothills, through broadacre grain and sheep grazing farms of the slopes, through the more intensive irrigated rice and horticultural farms of the irrigation areas, to the sheep grazing plains in the west. The region also has a long history of manufacturing, mainly in the processing of its primary production output. It has a total population of just over 150,000, Wagga Wagga being the largest urban centre with a population of about 62,000, and Griffith the second largest urban centre with a population of about 28,000.

Cases were selected from manufacturers/processors, mainly food and beverage manufacturing based on the processing of the region's agricultural and horticultural products, but also including engineering and fabrication of metal products, particularly those manufacturing capital goods for the processors. Several wineries were selected because viticulture and winemaking have become major industries in the Riverina Region, and because the winemaking industry has a record of being innovative in both the areas of production and marketing (Wickramasekera & Bamberry, 2001;

2003a & b). For purposes of comparison, other sub-sectors chosen included fruit and vegetable processors as well as grain and pulses processors. The engineering firms were selected as examples of enterprises known to be manufacturing equipment and capital goods for the range of food and beverage processors. However, for purposes of contrast, two manufacturers who did not appear to have any specific 'need' to be located in the region were chosen. These were Celair-Malmet, a firm producing airconditioners, heaters and hospital equipment, and Precision Parts, a firm producing automotive parts, where their location in Leeton and Wagga Wagga respectively appeared to be 'accidents of history.'

FINDINGS

Innovation through Problem Solving

Much of the innovation reported in the interviews arose from problem solving and "learning by doing" on the shop floor, or in small research and development divisions. One of the cases showing evidence of this was A&G Engineering at Griffith, founded by Ron Potter in 1963 when he was working as a winemaker for a small winery. Through collaboration, the firm built up its production of specialised capital goods to meet the particular needs of the local wine industry. Over a number of years, A&G developed the highly specialised spinning cone technology, which grew out of seeking a solution to the problem of removing sulphur dioxide from bulk-stored wine. Solving this problem resulted in the application of this process to flavour extraction from foods and beverages. A great deal of the flavour is often lost in the processing of primary products, particularly in processes involving heating. The spinning cone technology enables flavours to be extracted in the early stage of food and beverage processing, and held apart while other processing, often involving heating, is undertaken. The

flavour previously extracted is then returned to the product without the flavour loss normally associated with processing.

Following extensive research and development, including collaboration with local winemakers and with researchers at Charles Sturt University, A&G Engineering developed the spinning cone technology for use in the manufacture of complex food and beverage processing equipment. This activity was later hived off as a separate enterprise, Flavourtech, which was able to expand its output and become a significant regional exporter of capital equipment (FT Technologies, webpage).

Another example of innovation arising from problem solving at A&G Engineering was the solution devised when the firm faced the problem of their new stainless steel tanks overheating in the hot climate. Discussion with district winemakers resulted in the dimple plate concept, which resulted in far better temperature control. This involved putting a jacket on the outside of the tank by dimpling the plate, welding the jacket on, and circulating cool brine around the tank.

DeBortoli Wines also reported the development of innovative technology in response to dealing with a problem they faced. This enterprise was established at Bilbul near Griffith by Italian immigrants in 1928, and is now managed by the second and third generations of the founders' family. It is now one of Australia's largest wine producers with vineyards, wineries and other facilities in the Hunter, King and Yarra Valleys in addition to the original site at Bilbul (DeBortoli Wines, webpage).

The chief winemaker described how wineries had traditionally pre-gassed bottles with carbon dioxide because they needed an inert filling operation to prevent oxygen coming into contact with the wine. An additional requirement was to be able to fill bottles to different heights. This was because bottles going straight to the marketplace needed to be filled at a lower height than bottles being prepared for binning or aging. The latter needed to be filled higher to allow for a certain amount of evaporation and absorption by the cork over time. However, the firm faced the problem that modifying the fill height in the bottle caused a break in hygiene when filler tubes were replaced, resulting in the need for a re-sterilisation cycle. To overcome this problem they designed a machine that would evacuate the bottle similar to the process used in the brewing industry, then fill the bottle with an inert carbon dioxide or nitrogen mix, and then fill the bottle with wine. They found by experimentation that they could then adjust the fill height "by winding the machine up or down."

An interview with a senior executive of the Ricegrowers' Co-operative provided another example of problem solving leading to innovation. The Co-operative was established at Leeton in 1950 by a group of rice growers in the surrounding Murrumbidgee Irrigation Area to process and market the gradually expanding output of the area. It has grown to a very large organisation, operating a number of rice mills and other facilities throughout the rice-growing region of southern New South Wales and northern Victoria, as well as marketing most of the output in the domestic and international markets. The Co-operative faced the problem of cost-effective disposal of waste products from rice processing without generating environmental problems. Research into new technology by the firm's research and development division resulted in finding ways of converting the waste material into saleable products, including stockfeed and material for the nursery industry. These activities were eventually hived off as separate enterprises owned by the Co-operative, Coprice and Biocon.

Innovation through "Learning By Using and Doing"

There were also a number of examples of innovation arising from the closely related process of "learning by using and doing," one emerging at Celair-Malmet, a firm producing airconditioners and heaters, as well as hospital equipment.

The founder, Ted Celi, who had worked for the Ricegrowers' Co-operative in Leeton in engineering and electrical areas, decided to establish a business in 1972 after building an evaporative air conditioner for himself, and receiving orders for others. Later, the business was expanded to include the manufacture of heaters, and the hospital equipment manufacturer, Malmet, was purchased and added to the enterprise. In the early years of Celair-Malmet, each new model of air conditioner incorporated new ideas in content and manufacturing processes as staff learnt from their experience with previous models. Later, following the purchase of the hospital equipment manufacturer, Malmet, the same approach was used to upgrade appliances to meet new health standards.

Similarly, at the food-processing firm, Allgold Foods, much of the innovation was based on the experience previously gained by the founders in working as engineers at the Ricegrowers' Co-operative. They were able to adapt the processes of rice milling to the milling of other grains, making modifications to machinery as staff gained experience operating the plant, and as they sought to improve the quality of their products to meet clients' specifications.

At Precision Parts, there was an example of the process Kaldor (1972, 184) referred to as "repeated application of particular engineering principles to secure improvements in design." The founder, formerly an engineer at the RAAF Base near Wagga Wagga, set up an engineering partnership in the city after retiring from the RAAF in 1976, specialising in the manufacture of automotive parts, particularly harmonic balancers (Precision Parts, webpage).

The manager described the process of design improvement through "repeated application" as follows.

You start developing your own product, and there is a progression as the business grows. First, you have to start drawing things, and then you have to follow through with proper drawings and proper computer-based programs. Then all of a sudden, the fitter and turner turns into an engineer.

It was through processes such as these that Precision Parts was able to gradually increase its output, achieve economies of scale, and become competitive enough to enter the export market. The resulting increase in demand for its products in overseas markets has allowed the firm to further expand its operations.

The Path-Dependent Nature of Innovation

A key characteristic of innovation that emerged from the interviews is its path dependent and incremental nature as described in cumulative causation theory. Although not limited to the wineries among the cases studied, they often showed clear evidence of path dependency and incremental growth. For example Westend Estate Wines, established on the outskirts of Griffith in 1945 by immigrants from Italy, and taken over in 1974 by the founders' son, has taken an innovative approach in expanding its local and regional market by building a high quality retail outlet and function centre on the site of its vineyard and winery. Building on its sixty-year history, it has moved from sales at the door of the winery, initially a corrugated iron shed, through many gradual improvements, to the purpose-built high quality facility of today (Westend Estate Wines, webpage).

Similarly, DeBortoli Wines expanded its original cellar-door outlet by purchasing existing wineries in tourism-oriented regions including the Hunter, King and Yarra Valleys, and establishing other attractions such as function centres and restaurants at the newly-purchased wineries (see webpage for photographs). An innovation that allowed the firm to expand into international markets was the decision some years ago to enter the export market by selling wine in bulk to exporters who sold it under their own labels. Recognising the disadvantage of not establishing its own brand

name, the firm withdrew from this arrangement and later entered the export market under its own name (Bamberry, 2004).

Precision Parts was able to move into exporting as a result of having established a close relationship with the national automotive parts retailer, Repco, producing vehicle parts for the Australian market. In the period 1994 to 1999, the firm dramatically expanded its product range to supply Repco, and also achieved economies of scale through increasing its output for a larger market. It then sought to pursue export markets, sending a representative to the United States in September 1998 to evaluate the market for its products. As a result of that visit, the firm began selling automotive parts to an American firm, where the parts were initially sold under the latter's own brand. Later, Precision Parts was able to expand its export market and sell parts under its own brand.

The Cumulative Impact of Innovation

It also emerged from the interviews that many of the processes associated with innovation described above had generated a cumulative effect on the firms involved. The increasing specialisation at Precision Parts described above, resulting in the use of more advanced equipment and the subsequent need to upgrade the skills of workers, or employ new categories of skilled staff, are examples of this. The cumulative effect was also apparent on the firm's markets, the innovations enabling the firm to improve its economies of scale and move from operating in a small domestic market to a larger, more competitive international one. A similar cumulative effect was apparent at Celair-Malmet, where the firm was able to expand its domestic market to a level enabling it to take over the Adelaide-based company, Bonair-Vulcan, as well as move into export markets such as South Africa.

In the case of DeBortoli Wines, the cumulative effect of the firm's growth has allowed it to undertake an $84 million program to increase its crushing capacity by 80 percent, adding 65,000 tonnes per year to its existing production capacity of 85,000 tonnes. Sales in 2008 increased by $30 million over the previous year to $186.5 million (Daily Advertiser, 29 May, 2009). It has also been able to install and build a new high-speed bottling line, extra warehousing, increased wine storage, as well as undertake a number of environmental measures. New state-of-the art three million litre storage tanks have been added to the numerous existing million litre stainless steel storage tanks. By increasing its scale of operations, the firm was able to generate sufficient profits to undertake environmental measures to manage problems associated with odour emissions, groundwater and water storage, and deal with the impact of noise and dust (DeBortoli Wines, webpage).

Similarly the cumulative effect of innovation can be seen in the rapid growth of Casella Wines. Established by Italian immigrants who bought a farm near Griffith in 1965 and who established a winery in 1969, the firm, is now managed by the second and third generations of the family. After operating on a relatively small scale for many years, the firm decided to make a concerted effort to expand into the export market, particularly in the United States, by producing its Yellowtail brand especially for that market, and by introducing it there before selling it in the domestic market. Its major success in the US market necessitated the replacement of bottling lines, which were only a few years old, with three new bottling lines with a combined output of over 30,000 bottles per hour, with the intention of adding two more lines to give the winery a bottling capacity of over 65,000 bottles per hour. The cumulative growth of the firm also allowed it to install five new presses, three centrifuges and over 60 million litres of storage capacity, making the winery capable of crushing 120,000 tonnes of grapes during a vintage. Export sales worldwide grew from 500,000 cases in 2001 to almost 11 million cases (132 million bottles) in 2006/7, with 8.5 million cases being exported

to the United States in 2008 (Casella Wines, webpage; Daily Advertiser, 29 May, 2009).

The economies of scale gained from the large-scale production at Casella Wines has allowed the firm to respond to drought conditions in the region in recent years (the average annual rainfall of the area is 390mm, but in 2007 this dropped to 148mm), and improve its ability to cope with future droughts and the increasing cost of water. It has built the largest waste water treatment scheme of its type in Australia. Operating from the end of 2007, all waste water from the winery is now recycled, the $5 million scheme having the capacity to recycle 400 million litres of water per annum. This has allowed the firm to use an average of 2.5 litres of water for every litre of wine produced, compared with the industry average of approximately 3.5 litres per litre of wine. The estimated annual costs of about $150,000 to $200,000 to treat the wastewater is equivalent to 38 to 50 cents per kilolitre, which is cost-effective with the increasing cost of water, as well as being environmentally sound (Casella Wines, webpage).

Innovation through Collaboration

Collaboration with clients or between sections within an enterprise was found to be a significant influence on innovation. An example of this, both external and internal to the firm, was Yoogali Engineering at Griffith. This enterprise was established by an Italian migrant who had initially worked for an engineering firm in Griffith before establishing his own general engineering business in 1974, repairing and manufacturing equipment for the district agricultural industry, as well as for firms servicing that industry. Through collaboration with a client, the firm developed a better way to make pallets for the local horticultural industry, eventually resulting in the invention of a pallet-making machine. Other examples of inventions resulting from collaboration with clients included the development of an orange grader, an onion washer and a lettuce harvester.

In the latter case, the client "had a rough idea in his head," and after explaining this to staff, the design work was undertaken by the firm. This was followed up with the production of the equipment by the manufacturing section. Collaboration with the client ensured the equipment met his needs, as well as meeting requirements associated with engineering design, manufacturing practicalities and cost considerations (see Yoogali Engineering webpage).

At Parle Foods, a food-processing firm at Griffith, there was an example of internal collaboration between engineering and production staff. This firm grew out of a family farm, going into manufacturing in 1990 when it began processing the gherkins it produced. It later diversified into processing other fruit and vegetables that were counter-seasonal to gherkins, allowing for better utilisation of the company's resources, and reducing the risk associated with concentrating on a single product (Riverina Regional Development Board News 2000, 1). The firm produced much of its equipment in-house, having established a large engineering workshop for this purpose. The firm bought machinery and equipment from factories that were closing down, then re-located and re-built it to meet their particular needs. The manager commented that although the technology was not particularly complex, the innovations allowed the firm to process products more cheaply, giving it an advantage over its competitors.

At Allgold Foods, collaboration occurred with external contactors. The manager commented that much of the innovation adopted by the firm occurred as a result of suggestions that came from external contractors who had been called in to solve particular problems that had emerged. The contractors had frequently worked in other food-processing establishments, had come across similar problems, and had developed solutions to the problems. As he pointed out, "as long as you are not cutting in on something that they have developed and branded, they are quite willing to share it with you."

An example of collaboration with the local wine industry was the introduction of stainless steel equipment by A&G Engineering in the Riverina Region. A director of the firm reported that winemakers had commented that there was a need to replace the concrete tanks that were being used as they were labour intensive, difficult to clean and maintain, and were dangerous. Stainless steel was starting to be used, so A&G Engineering investigated its potential and began to make stainless steel vats and other equipment. One of the founders of the firm, Ron Potter had earlier invented and developed the Potter Fermenter in collaboration with winemakers in the region. Two of the managers of smaller wineries in the Griffith district Baratto Wines and Piromint Wines, referred to collaboration with colleagues in the industry as a source of advice and information in solving specific problems they had encountered in their day-to-day operations. They had established networks with other producers through membership and meetings of the Griffith Wine Producers Association, and commented on the willingness of other members, particularly larger producers with more specialised staff, to share their knowledge and expertise.

Innovation through Specialisation

Examples were mentioned above of how innovations arising from specialisation resulted in A&G Engineering being able to hive off the spinning cone technology at Flavourtech and allow it to develop into a significant separate exporting enterprise. The labour force was also specialised, and the hiving off of these workers enabled them to be employed more productively. The new enterprise also needed investment to expand, it needed to focus on the export market, and it needed specialised research and development. Flavourtech was established in its own premises adjacent to A&G Engineering in Griffith, with its own management, but with close links to A&G through some common membership of their boards. In recent years there has been further specialisation with Flavourtech becoming one branch of the broader enterprise now known as FT Technologies. Other branches of the enterprise include FT Industrial Pty Limited which purchased the Centritherm evaporator from a Swedish company in 2001, and Flavourtech Research, which undertakes research projects and manages the Group's intellectual property (FT Technologies, webpage).

Another case of hiving off as a result of innovation mentioned above was at the Ricegrowers' Co-operative. Rice processing results in the accumulation of a large quantity of waste rice hulls that are difficult to dispose of in an environmentally safe way. Following research, two commercial uses were found for the rice hulls, one as the basis for insulation material, and another as compost for the horticultural industry. The Co-operative set up a separate enterprise under the name Biocon at Griffith in 1979 to develop this business opportunity, but retained ownership. A similar arrangement was made with another division named Coprice, which produces stockfeed from rice by-products.

Another firm that had started to hive off some specialised activities was Celair-Malmet. The main objective was to allow the parent firm to concentrate on core activities, such as the assembly of finished products. The largest of these operations was the powder coating of the range of products made by the firm. Celair-Malmet decided to contract out this operation to Riverina Powder Coaters (RPC), a business established across the road from the factory. An advantage of this for Celair-Malmet was that because RPC was servicing other customers, it was able to stock a wider range of colours than was possible when Celair-Malmet did its own painting. This meant that Celair-Malmet could offer its customers a greater choice of colours, giving it a competitive advantage.

Innovation and Location

The findings of the research showed clear links between innovation and geographic location. This was particularly noticeable in the links between the wineries and the engineering industry in the Griffith area. Interaction and collaboration been the wineries and A & G Engineering, and later Flavourtech, resulted in a number of innovations for the wine industry. In addition, this has contributed to the development of a small industry cluster in the engineering and metal fabrication sectors, with the hiving off of Flavourtech and the R & D division of A & G Engineering, together with the development of the separate enterprise to manage the venture purchased from overseas. The innovative work undertaken at Yoogali Engineering in collaboration with the horticultural industry has also helped to strengthen this industry cluster.

Geographic factors were also found to be significant in the Leeton area where the pool of specialised labour at the Ricegrowers' Co-operative led to developments in the manufacture of airconditioners, heaters and hospital equipment, as well as developments in food processing and in the processing of new products based on by-products of the rice industry. These activities resulted in the establishment of new enterprises, all located within close proximity of the parent firms, with strong linkages in the supply chain, involved with producing inputs, using outputs, or in the supply of capital goods.

CONCLUSION

The findings of the empirical research reported in this chapter showed that the influences on innovation described in the literature on cumulative causation theory were evident in regional manufacturing enterprises in the Riverina Region of New South Wales. The processes of problem solving similar to those described by Argyrous (1995, 110), and evident at A & G Engineering and DeBortoli Wines, were shown to lead to innovations such as the spinning cone technology, the dimple-plating of wine tanks for cooling purposes, and new approaches to bottling wine that overcame the need for a re-sterilisation cycle. Innovation was also reported as emerging from the process of learning by using and doing in the upgrading and improvement of the products, such as air-conditioners and hospital equipment at Celair-Malmat, automotive parts at Precision Parts, and grain processing methods at Allgold Foods. This was similar to the process described by Kaldor (1972, 184) as learning resulting from "repeated application of particular engineering principles," and by Ricoy (1988, 732) as "the accretion of experience."

The incremental, path-dependent nature of innovation as suggested by Setterfield (1997, 368) and O'Hara (2008, 376) was evident at wineries such as West End, DeBortoli and Casella Wines, where innovations in processing allowed the firms to expand output in generating economies of scale to enter national and international markets, and to improve environmental standards. Furthermore, it was shown that new inventions such as the spinning cone technology at A & G Engineering grew out of processes and equipment designed to solve earlier problems, later having major cumulative impacts on the establishment of new enterprises linked to the parent firm. These are examples of the processes initially described by writers such as Myrdal (1968) who drew attention to the circular and cumulative impact of primary changes in society, and later by writers such as Dosi(1988) and Argyrous (1995) who focused more narrowly on the cumulative nature of in-house technological innovation in industry.

The role of workplace collaboration in promoting innovation suggested in cumulative causation theory was evident in the collaboration between staff and clients at Yoogali Engineering in the design of new equipment and capital goods for the local horticultural industry. Similarly, there were examples of collaboration between local winemakers and engineering staff at A & G Engineering in the development of new capital goods and stainless steel equipment for the wine industry, and at Celair-Malmet and Allgold Foods where collaboration with external contractors resulted in innovative approaches to solving problems. This evidence reflects the observation of cumulative causation writers such as Brusco (1989, 260) who referred to collaborative relationships as being "full of reciprocal stimulation," while Cook and Morgan (1998, 9) commented on "the associational capacity of the firm." Attention has also been drawn to innovations emerging from collaboration having the capacity to generate economies of scale at the regional level, which in turn have cumulative effects (Argyrous and Bamberry, 2009).

The interviews revealed examples of innovation resulting in increased specialisation leading to the hiving off of specialised divisions as new enterprises, including the hiving off of the spinning cone technology at A & G Engineering to Flavourtech, the establishment of Biocon & Coprice as offshoots of the Ricegrowers' Co-operative, and the development of component suppliers linked to Celair-Malmet. These cases reflect the nature of specialisation as described by one of the earliest exponents of cumulative causation, Young (1928, 531), who drew attention to the hiving-off process leading to economies of scale gained through the use of specialised equipment, and later linked more specifically to innovation by Toner (2000, 28).

The establishment of new enterprises in close proximity to their parent firms, together with the development of linkages and networks amongst other firms interviewed, provided examples of the significant role played by geographic proximity in generating industry clusters which support the diffusion of innovation through shared knowledge generated by pools of specialised labour, by local industry associations, and by education and training institutions. Numerous writers in the cumulative causation tradition have drawn attention to this phenomenon, in earlier years by pioneers such as Myrdal (1957) and Kaldor (1970), who saw the cumulative effect of industry clusters generating competitive advantage for certain geographic locations, and later observed by other writers including Porter (1996), Martin (1999), Toner (2000) and Bamberry (2006 a&b).

The findings of the research described in this chapter have implications for the development of innovation theory, showing that the use of key elements of cumulative causation theory provides a means of explaining how innovation occurs, as well as its impact on regional manufacturing. Another characteristic of the theory, that of the reciprocal relationships between cause and effects, was found to be relevant in explaining not only how innovations are generated, but also their cumulative impact on industry, as suggested by a number of writers (Argyrous, 1996; O'Hara, 2008; Berger, 2008). The theory is also useful in showing the need to go beyond the economic factors associated with innovation, and to include social ones as described by earlier writers such as Myrdal (1968) and Kapp (1961). The findings also support the argument by Malerba et al (1999) that history-friendly models of economic development are needed to explain innovation. In addition, the factors identified suggest areas for implementation of public policy that could help stimulate innovation in industry with long-term cumulative impacts on economic development. Further in-depth research into the operation of cumulative causations factors in a wider range of enterprises is likely to provide further useful insights into the nature and influence of innovation.

REFERENCES

A & G Engineering. (n.d.). *A & G Engineering*. Retrieved from www.agengineering.com.au

Argyrous, G. (1993). Emerging exporters: An evaluation. *Journal of Australian Political Economy, 32*, 106–126.

Argyrous, G. (1995). Economic evolution and cumulative causation. In Argyrous, G., & Stilwell, F. (Eds.), *Economics as a Social Science: Readings in Political Economy*. Sydney, Australia: Pluto Press.

Argyrous, G. (2000). The high road and the low road to international trade: Emerging exporters revisited. *Journal of Australian Political Economy, 45*, 46–67.

Argyrous, G., & Bamberry, G. (2009). Cumulative causation and industrial development: The regional stage. In Berger, S. (Ed.), *The Foundations of Non-Equilibrium Economics: The Principle of Circular and Cumulative Causation*. London: Routledge.

Argyrous, G., & Sethi, R. (1996). The theory of evolution and the evolution of theory: Veblen's methodology in contemporary perspective. *Cambridge Journal of Economics, 20*, 475–495.

Bamberry, G. (2006a). The influence of technology on regional development: Case studies from the Riverina Region. *Australasian Journal of Regional Studies, 12*(2), 173–190.

Bamberry, G. (2006b). The significance of linkages for regional manufacturers: A case study of the Riverina Region of New South Wales. In *Proceedings of the Third International Conference on Contemporary Business*, Leura. Edited by P.K. Basu and G. O'Neill. Charles Sturt University, Bathurst, Australia.

Bamberry, G., & Wickramasekera, R. (1999). *Manufacturing in the Riverina: A report for the Riverina Regional Development Board*. Wagga Wagga, Australia: Charles Sturt University.

Beer, A., Bolam, A., & Maud, A. (1994). Beyond the capitals: Urban growth in regional Australia. Canberra, Austraila: Commonwealth Department of Housing and Regional Development.

Beer, A., Maud, A., & Pritchard, W. (2003). *Developing Australia's regions: Theory and practice.* Sydney, Australia: University of New South Wales Press.

Berger, S. (2008). Circular cumulative causation (CCC) a la Myrdal and Kapp – Political Institutionalism for minimizing social costs. *Journal of Economic Issues, 42*(2), 357–365.

Berger, S., & Elsner, W. (2007). European contributions to evolutionary institutional economics: The cases of cumulative circular causation (CCC) and open systems approach (OSA): Some methodological and policy implications. *Journal of Economic Issues, 41*(2), 529–537.

Brusco, S. (1989). A policy for industrial districts. In Goodman, E., & Bamford, J. (Eds.), *Small firms and industrial districts in Italy.* London: Routledge.

Casella Wines. (n.d.). Retrieved from www.casellawines.com.au De Bortoli Wines (n.d.). Retrieved from www.debortoli.com.au

De Ridder, J. (1986). Cumulative causation versus comparative advantage. *Journal of Australian Political Economy,* (20), 44-48.

Dosi, G. (1988). Sources, procedures and microeconomic effects of innovation. *Journal of Economic Literature, 26,* 1120–1171.

Feldman, M. P. (2001). The entrepreneurial event revisited: Firm foundation in a regional context. *Industrial and Corporate Change,* 861–891. doi:10.1093/icc/10.4.861

Hirschman, A. (1959). Investment policies and 'dualism' in underdeveloped countries. *The American Economic Review, 47,* 550–570.

Kaldor, N. (1966). Causes of the slow rate of economic growth in the United Kingdom. In *Further Essays on Economic Theory.* New York: Holmes & Meyer.

Kaldor, N. (1970). The case for regional policies. In *Further Essays on Economic Theory.* New York: Holmes & Meyer.

Kaldor, N. (1972). Advanced technology in a strategy of development. In *Further Essays on Applied Economics.* New York: Holmes & Meyer.

Kapp, K. W. (1961). *Towards a science of man in society: A positive approach to the integration of social knowledge.* The Hague, The Netherlands: Martinus Nijhoff.

Kenny, M., & Burgh, U. (1999). Technology, entrepreneurship and path dependence: Industrial clustering in Silicon Valley and Route 128. *Industrial and Corporate Change, 8*(3), 67–103. doi:10.1093/icc/8.1.67

Kerlinger, F. N., & Lee, H. B. (2000). *Foundations of behavioral research* (4th ed.). Florence, KY: Wadsworth.

Lewis, G. (1994). *An illustrative history of the Riverina rice industry.* Leeton, New South Whales: Ricegrowers' Co-operative Limited.

Lowe, J., & Miller, P. (2001). Business clustering: Panacea or placebo for regional Australia. In Rodgers, M.F. & Collins, Y.M.J. (eds.), 2001 The Future of Australia's Country Towns. Melbourne, Australia: La Trobe University, Centre for Sustainable Regional Communities.

Malerba, F., Nelson, R., Orsenigo, L., & Winter, S. (1999). History-friendly models of industry evolution: The computer industry. *Industrial and Corporate Change, 8*(1), 3–40. doi:10.1093/icc/8.1.3

Marceau, J., Manly, K., & Sicklen, D. (1997). *The high road and the low road? Alternatives for Australia's future.* Sydney, Australia: Australian Business Foundation.

Martin, R. (1999). The New 'geographical turn' in economics: Some critical reflections. *Cambridge Journal of Economics, 23,* 65–91. doi:10.1093/cje/23.1.65

Matthews, J. (2002). Clusters of innovative firms: Absorptive capacity in larger networks. In *Proceedings of the Sixteenth ANZAM Conference.* Melbourne, Australia: La Trobe University.

McKinsey & Company. (1993). Emerging exporters: Report for the Australian Manufacturing Council. Sydney, Australia.

Myrdal, G. (1944). *An American dilemma: The Negro problem and modern democracy.* New York: Pantheon.

Myrdal, G. (1957). *Economic theory and underdeveloped regions.* London: Duckworth.

Myrdal, G. (1968). *Asian drama: An inquiry into the poverty of nations.* New York: Pantheon.

O'Connor, K., Stimson, R., & Daly, M. (2001). *Australia's changing economic geography: A society dividing.* Melbourne, Australia: Oxford University Press.

O'Hara, P. A. (2008). Principal of circular and cumulative causation: Fusing Myrdalian and Kaldorian growth and development dynamics. *Journal of Economic Issues, 42*(2), 375–387.

Owen, L. (1993). *Business growth and export development: Issues for firms in rural areas.* Armidale, Australia: The Rural Development Centre.

Pasinetti, L. (1981). *Structural change and economic growth.* Cambridge, UK: Cambridge University Press.

Patton, M. (1990). *Qualitative evaluation and research methods.* Newbury Park, CA: Sage.

Penmara Wines. (n.d.). Retrieved from www.penmarawines.com.au

Porter, M. (1996). Competitive advantage, agglomeration economics, and regional policy. *International Regional Science Review, 19*(1-2), 85–94.

Porter, M. (1998). Clusters and the new economics of competition. *Harvard Business Review,* (Nov-Dec): 77–93.

Precision Parts. (n.d.). Retrieved from www.precisionparts.com.au

Pressman, S., & Holt, R. P. (2008). Nicholas Kaldor and cumulative causation: Public policy implications. *Journal of Economic Issues, 42*(2), 367–373.

Ricoy, C. (1988). Cumulative causation. In Eatwell, J., Milgate, M., & Newman, P. (Eds.), *The new Palgrave: A dictionary of economics.* London: Macmillan.

Roberts, B. (2000). Facilitating industry cluster development. *Regional Policy and Practice, 9*(1), 36–45.

Rosenberg, N. (1976). *Perspectives on technology.* Cambridge, UK: Cambridge University Press. doi:10.1017/CBO9780511561313

Setterfield, M. (1997). History vs equilibrium and the theory of economic growth. *Cambridge Journal of Economics, 21,* 365–378.

Storper, M., & Scott, A. J. (Eds.). (1992). *Pathways to industrialization and regional development.* London: Routledge.

Swann, G. N. P., Prevezer, M., & Stout, D. (1998). *The dynamics of industrial clustering: International comparisons in computing and biotechnology.* Oxford, UK: Oxford University Press.

Sweeney, G. (1987). *Innovation, entrepreneurs and regional development.* London: Frances Pinter.

Targetti, F. (1992). *Nicholas Kaldor: The economics and politics of capitalism as a dynamic system.* Oxford, UK: Oxford University Press.

Taylor, S. J., & Bogdan, R. (1984). *Introduction to qualitative research methods: The search for meaning.* New York: Wiley.

Technologies, F. T. (n.d.). Retrieved from www.ft-tech.net.au

Thirlwall, A. (1987). *Nicholas Kaldor.* Sussex, UK: Wheatsheaf Books.

Ticehurst, G. W., & s, A. J. (2000). *Business research methods: A managerial approach.* Frenchs Forest, Australia: Longman.

Toner, P. (1998). *Main currents in the theory of circular and cumulative causation: The dynamics of growth and development.* New York: St Martin's Press.

Toner, P. (2000). Manufacturing industry in the Australian economy: Its roles and significance. *Journal of Australian Political Economy, 45,* 18–45.

Vassilakis, S. (1987). Learning by doing. In Eatwell, J., Milgate, M., & Newman, P. (Eds.), *The new Palgrave: A dictionary of economics.* London: Macmillan.

Veblen, T. (1898). Why is economics not an evolutionary science? *The Quarterly Journal of Economics, 12,* 373–397. doi:10.2307/1882952

Westend Estate Wines. (n.d.). Retrieved from www.westendestate.com.au

Wickham, M., & Hanson, D. (2002). Industrial clustering in regional Australia: The role of chance, entrepreneurs and government in the Tasmanian light ships industry. In *Proceedings of the Sixteenth ANZAM Conference.* Melbourne, Australia: La Trobe University.

Wickramasekera, R., & Bamberry, G. (2001). Australian wineries: Factors perceived to enhance or inhibit export market expansion. In Gray, S. J., McCaughey, S. L., & Purcell, W. R. (Eds.), *Asia Pacific Issues in International Business.* Cheltenham, UK: Edward Elgar.

Wickramasekera, R., & Bamberry, G. (2003a). An overview of a successful export industry from regional Australia. *International Journal of Wine Marketing, 15*(3), 15–27. doi:10.1108/eb008760

Wickramasekera, R., & Bamberry, G. (2003b). Exploration of born globals/international new ventures: Some evidence from the Australian wine industry. *Australasian Journal of Regional Studies, 9*(2), 207–219.

Yoogali Engineering. (n.d.). Retrieved from www.yoogaliengineering.com.au

Young, A. (1928). Increasing returns and economic progress. *The Economic Journal, 38*(152), 527–542. doi:10.2307/2224097

KEY TERMS AND DEFINITIONS

Circular And Cumulative Causation: A theory that has been developed to explain economic and social change where an initial change can have an incremental effect, either for the better or the worse, creating a 'virtuous' or 'vicious' cycle of growth or decline, and where the initial direction of the change tends to be self re-inforcing unless some major trigger occurs (or is implemented by policy-makers) to reverse the direction of the change. It draws attention to the influence of both social and economic factors, and points to their interaction in mutually dependent ways.

Economies of Scale: Occur where a firm produces a sufficiently large output of goods or services to allow for reduced unit costs of production, often through the efficient use of expensive capital equipment, or through the efficient use of specialised labour. Specialised divisions of a firm are often hived off as separate enterprises to achieve economies of scale by providing goods and services to a wider group of firms.

Industry Clusters: Groups or agglomerations of related industries in a particular location (e.g. the computer industry in Silicon Valley in the US), often occurring as a result of the availability of inputs such as primary resources, components, pools of specialised labour, or enterprises using a firm's outputs.

Innovation: Has been described as "a very complicated process emerging from the learning activities of human beings and the application of this learning activity to production." It includes not only new inventions, but also other activities such as re-organising old methods of production, making better use of materials, improving the quality of products, applying new methods of production, producing new products, finding new resources and discovering new sources of energy (Pasinetti 1981, 67).

Linkages: Describe supply-chain relationships between enterprises where the outputs of one firm (e.g. components) are the inputs for another firm. Linkages often develop from the hiving off of a specialised division of a firm, which in turn helps to create industry clusters in certain locations.

Path Dependency: In innovation is used to describe incremental change where complex developments are possible only after less complex innovations have been discovered and put into practice over a period of time. These developments often occur as part of the process of learning by using and doing in the workplace.

Specialisation: Occurs where an enterprise or one of its divisions focuses on a relatively narrow area, becoming expert in that field by gaining knowledge and experience over time, and building up a pool of labour with high levels of expertise. From time to time, specialised divisions of firms are 'hived off' as new enterprises, usually located close to the 'parent' firm, for which the new enterprise continues to supply goods and services.

Chapter 2
Lowering the Center of Gravity around Enterprise IT

Amy C. Hutchins
IBM Corporation, USA

Brian D. Goodman
IBM Corporation, USA

John W. Rooney
IBM Corporation, USA

ABSTRACT

In this chapter, we look at three key reasons why corporate development projects fail and how a technology and innovation management program can change a company's approach to information technology. First, we briefly provide context to typical IT management issues, covering business-as-usual management with the role it plays as part of supporting the enterprise and the issues that arise because of it. We then review three common issues – solutions that are dead on arrival, dead by committee and dead by adoption. An introduction to IBM's Technology Adoption Program describes one such innovation management discipline demonstrating through three brief case studies how to mitigate the common plagues of development projects. While the issues with technology and innovation management are obviously wide and varied, this chapter focuses on the need for a formal initiative to manage innovation. Similarly, fully understanding the workings of a program such as TAP is of considerable scope. The benefit to the reader is our focus on driving the decision making around technology to the users – the community – as a core part of making decisions.

INTRODUCTION

Enterprise IT is most commonly managed by one or more Chief Information Officer serving the needs of the business through unit representatives and committees. Formal processes exist to help develop

initiatives, determine budget needs and to release funding. This environment supports traditional solution development, but inhibits innovation. The CIO ends up spending time on relationship management, where business unit representatives are the customers. Moreover, this tends to force the utility tasks (infrastructure management, power, network etc) to be at the center of the CIO's responsibilities,

DOI: 10.4018/978-1-61520-643-8.ch002

with development projects managed by process and committee.

A survey on software project success and failure shows that around 50% of failures are due to scheduling and budget reasons. 27% failed because of customer dissatisfaction. (Cutter Consortium, 2005) Traditional solution development is a necessary part of delivering technology to the enterprise, however, if normal solutions face these odds, how do the riskier emerging technology and innovation activities make it through?

The next generation CIO realizes that treating operations as a utility, possibly outsourcing it, allows him/her to focus on delivering major IT transformation for their constituents and creating innovation programs leading future development. It is not enough to manage IT through a one-size-fits-all process. Additionally, simply sponsoring innovation initiatives fails to deliver an alternative management process to achieve faster, cost effective and valuable development.

Early in 2005, the CIO's Technology and Innovation Team realized the need for the creation of a new discipline, the Technology Adoption Program (TAP). By understanding where the team struggled in the past, the group came to this realization as they are uniquely positioned to institute change. The primary goal is to accelerate invention and innovation in the company, shortening the distance from creator to services, assets, offerings and IBM product. TAP is an innovation management program that is founded on lowering the center of gravity, driving the power of IT decision making into the hands of early adopters and innovators, radically shifting how technology is identified, developed, evaluated and transitioned.

BUSINESS AS USUAL

The job of the Chief Information Officer (CIO) is complex. Consistently under pressure to reduce the costs associated with the delivery of Information Technology (IT) services, CIOs are being asked to deliver strategic value for the enterprises they serve. Many organizations are looking to their teams to provide the foundation to fuel business growth in the coming years. In this environment, senior IT executives are challenged to find business methods and processes that allow them to effectively manage their investments while still meeting their growth objectives. By necessity, they must place their primary focus on a model of delivering a company's information on a technology infrastructure that is efficient; keeping an eye on stability of their systems, reliability of their information and cost-effectiveness of the delivery. Once they have squeezed the last drops of efficiency out of the system, reduced costs to near minimum, and implemented IT as a service utility to their organization, these same senior IT executives turn to drive flexibility into their organizations.

DELIVERING IT IN A LARGE ENTERPRISE

The rationales for rigorous processes within the enterprise IT function are evident. In order to contribute to their enterprise objectives, it is necessary that the IT and business strategies are well aligned (Alter, 2005). To achieve this alignment, the organization needs a strong IT governance program in place that controls both investment and project execution. In larger organizations with multiple business units executing on business strategies, IT governance requires the CIO Office to act as a coordinating function to ensure that the utility services and investments they provide, deliver maximum benefit for the enterprise as a whole. The pipeline begins with a set of processes to prioritize investment and spending from a portfolio of potential initiatives. Depending upon the discipline employed by the organization, each proposed initiative is supported by the creation of business cases with estimates of project duration, cost, savings, productivity benefits and risk. Some have even gone so far as to include classic methods for financial portfolio management (Henig, 2004) into this process as a way to determine risk and select alternatives. At each successive stage of the prioritization process, IT and business executives express their support for specific investment alternatives until a final list is determined. These decisions are reviewed with the organizations finance team and senior executives to create a final IT budget for the coming year. As described in an abstract manner, such a process seems sound and delivers a high-degree of predictability, but there are potential pitfalls which are discussed later in this chapter.

Following the prioritization efforts, the governance system focuses on execution of the project deliverables. This process is typically designed as a series of phases that projects are taken through, with regular checkpoints to assess progress and determine if the project will continue. These checkpoints are reviewed in a team-based environment, to ensure support from across the organization through representation from both the business strategy and IT teams. While the checkpoints are very much project focused, assessing status and achievement of key milestones, they often also control the release of funds for continuation of the effort.

Within IBM, the governing processes are a part of BTMS, the Business Transformation Management System (Radjou, 2005). BTMS provides a management structure and activities that support business planning, solution development, and operations management. BTMS is used worldwide by the IBM IT organization and throughout the enterprise for projects supporting IBM internal solutions; in fact, its use is codified as a corporate standard. The governance model and core processes defined by BTMS have resulted in better IT and business strategy alignment, a reduction in project cycle times and cost reductions for IT projects.

Even with a successful governance program such as BTMS, there are always opportunities for improvement. The BTMS process is continually

being improved to support IBM business objectives. This might involve reducing the required process steps for smaller projects of a short duration, or adding additional rigor for larger initiatives. However, the IT organization also requires methods and processes that provide flexibility to address other perceived and observed limitations of their rigorous governance models. For instance, the long planning and prioritization cycles associated with these processes, effectively using a funnel to reduce choices, limits the ability to rapidly apply technology to critical business efforts. Additionally, while close alignment is imperative to valuable IT delivery, shifting business strategies introduce challenges to effective allocation and application of funding. Lastly, months of planning, coupled with time for development, testing and deployment, results in long horizons to deliver IT solutions into the hands of employees.

In this chapter, we describe a new method IBM has put in place as a means to provide flexibility alongside our corporate IT governance structure. The Technology Adoption Program (TAP), takes the approach to quickly put new and emerging technologies in the hands of employees. It provides an environment for users to collaborate directly with the technology owner(s) to evolve a solution's potential deployment and a framework for assessing the value of the technology to seed its business case.

THE DELIVERY OF TECHNOLOGY SUFFERS FROM A VARIETY OF ISSUES

The shortcomings from the previous section can be thought of as the three "Fs" characterizing the current model of technology management: funnel, funding and future delivery. Each of these drives pressures that inhibit the ability for a project to reach success.

The classic funnel (See Figure 1) is used in a variety of ways (U. of Cambridge, 2006; Cooper

Figure 1. Project management funnel approach, breadth first

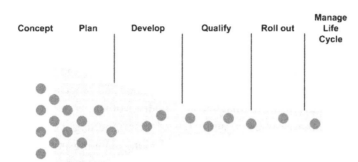

et al., 2004), often to communicate the increase of focus over time, or helping to choose and prioritize investments. It aligns well with IT's traditional waterfall development process (See Figure 2), where the schedules are well defined for a set of serial activities that flow start to finish: idea to production. Unfortunately, while ideal in its concept, the waterfall development process often fails to achieve desired results (Malveau et al., 2001). This encourages important IT investment commitments to hesitate, waiting to deploy mature IT products to realize expected value. Despite any maturity measures, and IT investments' risk can be buffered management teams squeezing the efforts, killing off projects as they develop. (Fenn, 2005) Some characteristics of risk include the more obvious budget or schedule overruns, to the more subtle issues of falling out of favor or offering relatively less value than initially projected. Projects do not get a chance to mature; their delivery date generally exceeds one year from the idea's conception, as a results of most enterprises funding cycles. For projects that continue, despite any apparent potential for failure, there are two major causes: the "Mum effect" and the "Deaf effect" where people who are in the position to highlight the problem fail to act and continue supporting the project (Robey et al., 2001). In short, Projects die from management discretion (as seen in the funnel model in Figure 1) and lack of action (Robey et al, 2001).

It is almost impossible to predict the availability of the funding that is committed to a given project. Any business is familiar with the shifting and reducing IT budgets, challenging teams to do what they can with less – overlooking how the investment supported a specific idea, which may disproportionably reduce the level of value contributed by a given initiative.

Finally, this model supports and conforms to IT delivery at some point in the far-reaching future. Equipped from the beginning with the right budget, right resources (often ideal case scenario) and executive support, projects will achieve a product delivery at that forecasted point in the future. Yet, changing budgets are rarely appropriately calculated into a successful delivery, resources are often not ideal, and executives know what they want, but rely on others to deliver the vision (Smith, 2002; Glass, 1997). The product invariably delivers short of what is required to achieve the initial vision (Smith, 2002; Robey et al, 2001). Balancing these three issues can easily persuade one to believe that the delivery of any project is doomed.

All of the three "Fs" have corresponding ideas contributing to the demise of technology projects: death upon arrival, death by committee and death by adoption. While successful delivery of IT can be disintermediated by a variety of forces, these three are central to understanding the change required to lower the center of gravity and manage in high-tech environments.

Figure 2. Basic waterfall process

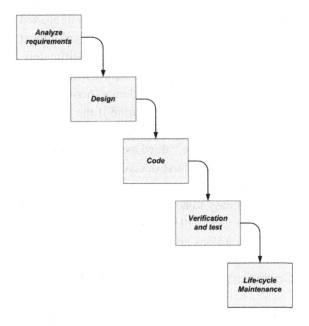

Death upon Arrival

Death upon arrival is when a project is successfully shepherded from paper to product and either falls short of delivering on the desired value, or worse, fails to deliver any value. This failure could be felt in several ways. That is, an IT solution's technical specifications are correct, yet its execution – the delivery to employees – challenged its adoption and ability to demonstrate the vision behind its investment. While the burden is not entirely felt by those executing, very often, project owners change requirements and modify design, fundamentally shifting the goal while the waterfall flows (Smith, 2002; Tamai et al., 1993). Only the highest potential projects are given another chance to recover under the now overweight deliverable in the hopes to improve and offer the value initially expected. Each of the three "Fs" make death upon arrival the first choice in why a project is abandoned or even continued in vain to achieve some level of finality.

Death by Committee

Funding is an aspect of IT management where its unpredictability can disrupt the projects' success at varying magnitudes. Project managers need a certain amount of money to run the projects they identify as being critical to help the business. Yet, people fail to freeze requirements and funding. Their funding is often challenged in-flight by a committee – an advisory board or senior executive – unilaterally changing what is going to be accomplished. (Smith, 2002) In the context of constrained resources, sometimes many "cheaper" activities that deliver less value become more strategic than squeezing fewer "expensive" efforts mid-stream. The committee is often referred to as an investment review board where senior leaders debate IT projects' strengths and weaknesses to help balance the investment portfolio. Each leader plays a tug of war with the funding, balancing fiscal responsibility with and strategic risk to help grow the business. Death by committee potentially increases as projects get more expensive and the timelines lengthen, introducing change requests, which trigger an increase risk of defects. (Javed et al., 2004) Projects fail because of the unnatural shift of removing resource while still expecting some value is better than no value.

Death by Adoption

Isolated from the process of building the technology offerings, death by adoption occurs when the target user community expresses dissatisfaction with the IT solution, refusing to adopt it into their working behavior. (Fenn, 2005) This situation often arises when the targeted audience for the solution is neglected or barely engaged until the delivery of the solution, wherein the users revolt by rejecting the IT solution. (Smith, 2002) This could cause death upon arrival, but in most cases, these solutions are mandated, required to be used. As such, death by adoption ignores the mandate, and kills the project due to user atrophy (See

Figure 3). At first glance, the conclusion suggests performing more user centered design (UCD) activities to really *understand* the target users' needs to deliver the right IT solution. Certainly, UCD can offer a solution its the best hope in landing on target, but a solution that addresses the problems of today, might actually be the inhibitor by the time it is delivered. No amount of UCD can guarantee adoption. Delivering IT solutions that do not address needs of future business actually complicates the environment, offering one more tool for users to assimilate. (Dresner, 2006) Death by adoption, or, lack of adoption, occurs when the effort necessary to attract users of an IT solution outweighs the value of the IT solution; that is, when no one uses the IT solution created to solve a problem.

INTERNAL TECHNOLOGY ADOPTION CAN ACCELERATE INNOVATION

Beginning in 2005, IBM's CIO made the commitment to encourage and enable the company to innovate for growth. As such, the corporate entity did not necessarily change their planning processes – it was augmented with a program called TAP, the Technology Adoption Program, established to manage technical development, deployment and diffusion across the company. Ultimately, TAP offers IBM employees the ability to use technology early, talk about their experience, and through the program, determine if the company should further invest in it. To do so, there were principles that were valued as critical to the new program's success. First, decisions will be made by the community. Second, support will be provided to make it easy to access new IT solutions. And finally, the team will focus on helping to promote these IT solutions and quantify their adoption.

Community-Based Decision Making

As IT continues to evolve alongside the Internet's growing collaborative capabilities, people have the tools to sound a more powerful voice in a shared (public) space (Sunstein, 2004). For instance, the consumer attack against Apple's ipod irreplaceable battery by Casey and Van Neistat was not only able to get their opinion out to fellow consumers; news stations also highlighted the story as humorous and effective. Interestingly, after such a public display of dissatisfaction, Apple released a

Figure 3. Slide from Gartner's emerging trends, 2010-2015, (Fenn 2005)

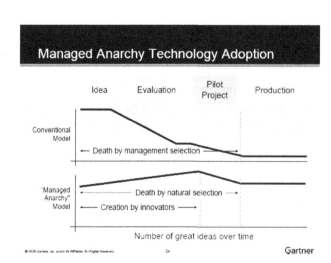

battery replacement program. This highlights how vocal people can be monumentally persuasive – they can overturn decisions, propose new things, and challenge the status quo. Empowering these people, along with their larger communities, not only helps to easily gauge how business can be improved for customers, but also helps to foster an adaptable and flexible work environment and culture. Allowing the communities, the consumers of your business, make the decisions of how to pursue new offerings relieves management teams of the complex world of research, analysis and experience (Brody et al., 1998). Furthermore, thinking back to IBM's BTMS, intricate processes are created to help large organizations determine how prioritize and invest in technology. Allowing communities to make the decision removes the complexity and mental models built into these organizations that have grown averse to change (Beinhocker, 2006). With this approach, those that want change ask for it, demand it, require it, and experience it.

Centralizing the Community

For an enterprise as large as IBM to support community-oriented influence, it is critical to centralize the resources to establish and cultivate the group. Naturally, as with any community development, it is important to have a common passion or goal that brings people together. That is, without an understanding of the community's purpose and expectations of its members, the organizational bond becomes a short-term interest and not a sustained program (Bernal, 2001). Yet this community is more than an interest group, discussing recent topics and keeping each other aware of upcoming events. This community of Early Adopters rallies around making change inside IBM – change to accelerate innovation – embracing it by working with any early version of all technologies. To do so, the community needs (1) access to early technologies, (2) ability to collaborate about them, (3) awareness of activities within the community, and (4) executive support

to allow the community to be influential. These needs are not something that can be provided from a single business unit – their focus is on meeting their profit targets and keeping expenses down. At the corporate, enterprise-wide level, specific advantages are afforded when these resources are available. The strategic view of the effort remains company-wide, where benefits can be realized.

Realized benefits include a common hosting infrastructure for early pilot programs – which also points to a centralized funding model; a balanced approach to making decisions on new technologies – assessing both technical advances and easy adoption of the technology; and a single place to look for what is new and what is available within the company – enabling everyone to know both the technologies and who is using them. Yet one benefit that is not as easily identified includes the ability to create and foster a culture around innovation. As business leaders rally their employees to become innovation leaders, (Tchong, 2005) these leaders must provide a culture within their company that empowers employees to brainstorm ideas, try new things, and make decisions on how new things can provide business value. Creating an enterprise-wide community that is empowered with the ability to try new technology, provide feedback from experiences and become the proving ground from which new technologies mature into a production-ready state, is a step in the direction of creating cultural change. In fact, creating such a community often disrupts normal processes currently in place and potentially challenges many groups' authority within the company. Such a dramatic swing requires a structured approach to how the community's feedback is aggregated, assessed and communicated for effective decision making.

Internal Value Framework

IBM's Technology Adoption Program (TAP) was created to provide such structure to making cultural change. Interestingly, this organization is not so much aimed at creating work breakdown structures for all projects deemed "innovative."

Ironically, this structure was created with the need to be flexible, responsive, dynamic and ever changing – much like TAP itself. With this as inspiration, the TAP Value Framework was born. Combining best practices from participatory design with rapid application development principles, the Value Framework sought to capture end users' feedback in an open, public arena so that development teams can respond to questions asked, requests made and comments posed.

The Value Framework is used for all technologies in TAP, allowing a basic comparison across the portfolio to understand each project's competitive stance, in terms of value. As a framework, it is a set of definitions used for assessments. The Value categories in this Framework are specific to IBM's culture, standards, requirements and strategy. The Value Framework is applied to a technology in three separate phases, over a timeframe longer than 6 months, by a business analyst on the TAP team who quantifies the feedback to help drive decisions on how the technology should (or should not) mature. These phases are (1) Setting Expectations, (2) Assessing Early Adoption and (3) Calculating Value.

The first phase, Setting Expectations, introduces a new technology to the TAP Community. Here, a those who access the technology first use a twenty question scorecard to quickly rank their experience in terms of value (including how easy is it to adopt, number of potential users, and if there is a competitive technology), and as well as in terms of change (such as impact to current enterprise architecture, affect to business processes, and funding needed to deploy). Individual scorecards are grouped, and a number is calculated to derive the mean value and mean change. This is made available to all, providing the first baseline for future users to quickly gauge the benefit that can be realized, and the barriers to realizing the potential benefit.

Assessing Early Adoption, the second phase, is less structured. Here, the TAP team provides tools and capabilities allowing Early Adopters to voice their feedback in an open environment, using web based collaboration tools: forums, blogs, wikis and polling to name a few. Early adopter usage of these tools is monitored by the TAP team, tracking who is using them and how often specific technologies are mentioned. Project owners, also called innovators, are encouraged to ask questions in the forum – finding out more about problems faced and issues encountered along which features and capabilities were valuable and important. This feedback time allows for innovators to learn from early adopters how their project is adding value (or what needs to be changed to be considered valuable), enabling direct feedback to channel into project iterations, potentially evolving the initial technology into a more mature, valuable one: a potential "innovation."

Finally, Calculating Value, is done by TAP's Business Analyst. This calculation categorizes the feedback gathered in the second phase into types of information, applying weights to the variables, summing them together for a value ranking. Meaning, the feedback created during the Early Adoption phase is interpreted, scored and ranked to quantify the amount of value for a given technology. This ranking drives decisions – deciding if a project is a potential innovation, and is given resources to mature; if it needs further development, identifying what areas need work; or if the project did not add value for users, and should no longer receive development resources. With this decision, a project graduates from TAP, transitioning into its next lifecycle phase.

Case examples below: Dogear, Sametime 7.5 and MyHelp1.0, show how the Technology Adoption Program has delivered business results. These results are not your typical cost avoidance or saved; they show how innovation cannot be managed by today's formal processes and governing bodies. Instead, by lowering the center of gravity, enterprise IT can learn how to manage innovation, which is the driver of growth.

DOGEAR: FIGHTING DEATH BY PROCESS

Early in 2005, an IBM Research team in Massachusetts created an enterprise social bookmarking service called Dogear, named after the idea of "dog-earing" pages of a book in hopes to easily find that spot in the future (Millen et al., 2006). Social bookmarking services enable users to create, share and tag URLs with friends and strangers alike. Del.icio.us, an early social bookmarking service was created in 2003 and has had continued success as a Yahoo acquisition in 2005 (Lomax, 2005). Dogear's inspiration began with the question of if enterprises could benefit as greatly from social bookmarking as Internet users did with Del.icio.us (Millen et al., 2006). As the team began to develop their solution, IBM's Technology Adoption Program was just getting off the ground – Dogear was its first customer.

Davila, Epstein and Shelton (2006) articulate seven rules of innovation, where number five is "neutralize organizational antibodies." Death by process is an example of where organizational antibodies win, preventing innovation from evolving rapidly. An IT technology like Dogear is a prime candidate for staying in the research and development cycle forever. While social bookmarking technology has web 2.0 buzz, it has typical challenges any software faces: Who is the customer and why would want it? What is the associated business value? How does this fit into the existing software portfolio? Is it economical to fund such a system in a large enterprise? But it also has the added challenges any early technology would face: Can people understand what it does? Is this stable? What is its version plan?

The typical development and deployment cycle of a large enterprise can be anywhere from six to nine months often being built one year and deployed the next. Dogear was an experiment that began in the research laboratory that, with the help of the Technology Adoption Program, avoided death by process, found its future in IBM product, and integrated into the IBM.

The Chicken and Egg

Large companies see research and development as their way to invest in hopeful ideas. Transitioning those ideas to product is challenging and therein gives rise to the chicken and the egg. The traditional job of IT for a company is to deliver a solution supporting their users –employees – as they run the business. Meaning, IT needs to have an obvious value and impact in order to garner investment. However, technology that is early in its development often fails to have a substantial, rewarding business case warranting aggressive investment for deployment.

Dogear is basically a spin-off of an established concept of social book marking, which successfully attracted a core dedicated set of users; yet it failed to show obvious company-wide impact. Early success was measured by mentions in the company's internal blogging system (Millen, et al., 2006). More specifically, in a company of over 300,000 employees (IBM, 2006), nearly 1000 can be considered active users. One third of one percent of IBM had adopted Dogear into their working routine. In the absence of an innovation management program, this success was beginning to be quickly overlooked as neither game changing or extraordinary. With less than one percent of the user population leveraging a "shared memory" web site, how could any investment be justified? What possible value could it deliver to the business? And more importantly, without further investment, how would the company know if and how this technology could influence and/or grow its business?

Have Business Will Follow

Assume that the Dogear experiment had a greater adoption rate and an obvious business value. The solution would then be prioritized for funding. Assume again that relative to the other IT investments, social bookmarking is seen as more important to other potential investments. Funding for the given year is decided the previous year. The solution would begin in earnest in 2007 where the Research prototype would be transitioned to a production development team. In the case of IBM, this would be IBM Global Services. Dogear would undergo a full architecture and design review, at least one additional development cycle, weeks of testing, and, finally, deployment for the company's employees to adopt. The process would likely take six to nine months and be deployed mid-to late 2007 if there were no issues. An interesting thought considering that, "major vendors obsolete their own products every 6 to 18 months." (Malveau et al., 2001) The cost to deliver and host such a solution would be significant. And, statistically, the risks of failure are great (Johnson, 1995). How does innovation survive the traditional process?

Innovation is Special

Traditional processes fail to support innovation. This is not to say those processes are ineffective, they are often very effective, just not at supporting risky, out of profile solutions, early in their life and unknown in their value. IBM's Technology Adoption Program offers support for innovation in several ways. For Dogear, this began with hosting, moving the experiment out of the Massachusetts Research lab and into a highly available hosting environment, getting the daily hosting responsibility out of the hands of the innovator. Shortly after, the Dogear and TAP team created a project Offering page on the corporate intranet, as part of TAP, to help communicate the technology and encourage more users. Providing such support enables the Innovators – the Dogear team – to focus on iterating on their product.

Such support encourages frequent iterations on IT solutions. Rapid enhancements and continual improvements that meet current needs in

the context of future issues point to how death by process necessitates the need to have an innovation management process separate from one that governs how mature technology is deployed into the enterprise.

SAMETIME 7.5: FIGHTING DEATH ON ARRIVAL

As early as 1999, IBM's innovation labs began creating derivations of their enterprise instant messaging product, Lotus Sametime. Innovators explored integration with other IBM products (Tannenbaum et al., 2006) and the use of publish/subscribe messaging as a means for unique collaborations (IBM alphaWorks, 2003). A quick look at recent Sametime 7.5 introductory material reveals the influence of this work (IBM, 2006). Quite literally, IBM Community Tools (IBM alphaWorks, 2003) is the foundation of IBM Lotus Sametime 7.5, a feat that fought death on arrival.

With software vendors releasing products every six, twelve and eighteen months (Malveau et al., 2001), the time it takes from innovation to product is precious. Software developed using the waterfall method is inappropriate in many circumstances (Malveau et al., 2001), making it difficult to get to market with a solution that addresses a customer's business needs. It has been suggested that ease of use and value of traditional project management methods have given rise to counter-reactions such as Agile software development (Hansen, 2006). Agile methods mitigate risk through iteration (Wikipedia, 2006). The more software releases, the more feedback, the better the end product matches the desires of the customer. Death on arrival can occur for a variety of reasons. Yet it is most closely related to the fact that most software ships late, over budget and failing to meet the needs of end users (Smith, 2002). One answer to fighting death on arrival is to institute a cultural change to the typical software development process – iterate more often and engage users in participatory development.

The following section illustrates IBM's cultural change in developing the Sametime 7.5 product faster and with higher user satisfaction. An interview with Konrad Lagarde, the development manager for Sametime 7.5 acts as the primary source for this section. His background managing IBM's WebAhead innovation team transitioned when IBM/Lotus decided to make IBM Community Tools application a product.

Managing Technology

One major role at IBM's CIO office is to enable employees with technology to help them be effective in their jobs. Technology management is often thought of as "rolling out" a solution. Piloting is a typical model for beginning the rollout, but it presumes the solution will be accepted by the end users – the customers, very often employees. Furthermore, IBM's CIO office prefers IBM software over other products, with the goal to showcase IBM's use of its own technology.

"The only way [deployed solutions] could be changed were by the internal team upgrading to a different version." (K. Lagarde, personal interview, August 14, 2006) This mentality inhibited the fundamental need to provide employees with the best technology. Sametime 7.5 was created by merging the best of two messaging clients that were in a long-term pilot mode, NotesBuddy and IBM Community Tools, into Lotus Sametime technology.

The Sametime 7.5 development team not only had an existing product base to leverage along with some emerging technology, but there were existing early adopters, committed users of innovation projects that have matured over several years. The missing ingredient was managing the early adoption alongside a the typical software development process.

Throwing Caution to the Wind

In the course of six months, the Sametime 7.5 development team released nine alphas and four betas. This business result was clear: leveraging the collective intelligence of the early adopter community, the software development cycle had dramatically shortened and returned a more usable product.

It was difficult – painful – to the team to receive such negative feedback so early. 1000 people in a week for the alpha1 was bigger than we thought. A lot of developers were not paying attention initially, to the bugs that were found in the alpha 1, 2, releases. Alpha 3 and 4 is when we hit 5K people, and the development team was starting to see the impact of their work – and starting to fix the bugs and really pay attention to things. 2100 bugs in bugzilla was nearly unmanageable! (K. Lagarde, personal interview, August 14, 2006)

The typical software development milestone, prior to TAP, was one beta per year. Any feedback received from that beta period could not be incorporated to the final product because of the tightly managed development cycle. Meaning, this beta was really a preview. The product team could get feedback, but not change what the customer was receiving in the product release.

There was a lot of churn for the team, and a lot of stress, but we saw a reality in how the product was really improving. We could validate things directly with our customer. Which is incredible. They could vent, they could be honest, and could receive builds to show [that] what they were saying was being addressed – real time, on demand and immediately. (K. Lagarde, personal interview, August 14, 2006)

In 2005 and 2006, the Technology Adoption Program's early adopter community was almost entirely comprised of IBM employees. Their ongoing participation with users and the product drastically reduced the risk of Sametime 7.5's deployment into IBM's IT environment. In fact, when the release candidate build was packaged, the software was actively being used by 20,000 early adopters. The typical concerns of the product group, "is it really ready?" began to subside. "Good software is not designed by committee; but it is validated by a community." (K. Lagarde, personal interview, August 14, 2006) At the time of this writing, nearly 50,000 early adopters have switched from the supported Sametime 3.1 client to the new Sametime 7.5 product.

Who Gets to Define High Quality?

One of the roles early adopters play is that of the tester. A traditional testing cycle is executed based on well-defined use case scenarios, written early in the process. If the user is able to successfully accomplish a scripted use case then the software passes. If there is an issue, the software is reworked to ensure the use case is supported. Yet designing by use case fails in two ways. First, use case scenarios must know how a user will actually use the product – but is it possible to know the many ways to use the product? Second, use cases can often be successfully executed – but are the pre-defined use case scenarios comprehensive? As part of the Sametime 7.5 development, Lotus had a team in China focused on traditional testing – executing scripts as development progressed for each written use case.

We have 23 testers in China who run through test scripts. However, the big bugs that came back were from the TAP community rather than the test scripts – we couldn't think about all the scripts. The scripts were written long before we even entered TAP. [In the future,] I would not put the focus on these scripts ... for usability feedback. Instead, I would use them for technical design and inner workings. (K. Lagarde, personal interview, August 14, 2006)

The only important impression is that of the customer; in software's case: the end user. TAP early adopters are these customers, providing consistent feedback to enable the development team to focus on their high value issues while still maintaining the product's overall performance and usability. Here, early adopters highlight issues in a holistic sense, not through a scenario driven script. In the past, the customer was the first adopter, sharing the pain of collaborating around software. In the case of Sametime 7.5 and TAP, IBM was able to more aggressively participate with 200 other companies using the beta, easing the pains of early adoption, and in the end, releasing a product that delivers on the desired user experience.

Making Change Stick

Leveraging the Technology Adoption Program to help fight death on arrival was new for the Lotus brand. While the Sametime 7.5 development team leveraged many of TAP's services, the culture change it supported drove two notable outcomes. First, IBM released a pre-mature product in its IT environment, not following its typical processes, to be its own important customer. TAP early adopters joined the front line in collaborative solution development, struggling with imperfect software and identifying all found imperfections. Their participation resulted in quickly shipping a better product. Second, the typical approaches to software testing are transformed. Development teams can be reallocated to focus on improving the product while early adopters iteratively validate and test. Leveraging TAP to help accelerate the transformation of innovation to product has instigated a change in the formal software development process – TAP is now a required part of development.

Business as usual would have left Sametime 7.5 with the risks associated with most software projects (Johnson, 1995). Death on arrival was avoided through a more dynamic engagement with early adopters, where the development team received feedback in the earliest stages.

MY HELP V1.0: FIGHTING DEATH BY ADOPTION

Lowering the center of gravity is about driving decisions as low in the hierarchy as possible, to the point at which the decisions are most informed and honest. This grassroots approach engages the people to create their own work environment. Fighting death by adoption is much different from death upon arrival or death by process. Users, especially in a corporate environment, use what they can access. In some companies, this access is very restricted. But the popularity in open source and shareware has introduced an unmanageable combination of platforms that suit the user, not the company. So, despite the desire to control the desktop – the philosophy shifts to define the workplace where users are the ultimate judge, asking "will I adopt what you are providing me?"

In the summer of 2004, IBM's CIO office sponsored an Extreme Blue project focusing on understanding and creating a prototype of how a client side component could help users solve their own problems. Extreme Blue is IBM's premier internship program that brings top students from the best technical and business universities together to focus on a real business problem. Teams are made up of one business and three technical students, assigned to either a senior technical mentor or a senior business mentor. In less than three months, one project culminated on a self-help client prototype demonstrating the key capabilities that would have the most impact if deployed to the company. This client was so appealing it was funded in 2005 as a major initiative to provide employees with better self-help and increased productivity.

The self-help client was an innovation project that was transitioned to the typical waterfall development project. The 2005 project was called

MyHelp v1.0 and to accelerate their waterfall timeline, they used the Technology Adoption Program. It was the first technology to graduate from TAP and provided the validation that the process works, despite unexpected results. This MyHelp case study illustrates what happens when a project is fighting death by adoption.

Forced Adoption, Business as Usual

The MyHelp team was positioned from the start to be a challenging IT project. The good news is that it was funded. The bad news was that there was a lot of excitement created with the Extreme Blue prototype and expectations were unusually high. The schedule appeared long – the prototype from the summer was done in a month or two, so how can a full services team take longer? The effort involved in the translation from the rapid prototype into a reliable IT solution was not clearly understood by most. With all the pressures, the MyHelp team saw TAP as a way to run a faster, cheaper waterfall project. The mind set was that this would about forced adoption.

I remember our first meetings talking through the plan where the project manager said that the transition would simply be that it gets automatically installed on every employee's laptop whether they like it or not. (A. Chow, personal communication, June 6, 2005)

Who is the Real Customer?

As MyHelp finished its first alpha release on TAP, a couple hundred users signed up to try it. Because of the great success of the prototype, there were many eyes on MyHelp's introduction, awaiting what it would deliver and what people thought of it. The feedback from the TAP early adopters was honest and frequent, some of it good, but plenty of it critical. TAP hosted feedback on the main project page so users could experience live contribution to the offering. However, issues communicating what could work in early alphas trumped what users expected would work. In fact, technical capabilities were basic and the resources required seemed daunting – larger than some of IBM's major applications. The MyHelp development team had the initial knee jerk reaction: take the feedback down, it provides a negative message and is slowing adoption. There ended up being around thirteen thousand early adopters.

Early adopters were identifying defects in the software and providing commentary on its value. The general conclusion was that it should not be released until there was more capability; however, this conclusion did not align with the traditional software development processes. The controversy was introduced: to delay the release until more features are implemented, or, to continue as planned. The MyHelp team delayed the early release of the two feature solution for the more useful solution a couple months later. Unfortunately, the feedback did not change. With the introduction of the additional features, the solution was still finding resistance among early adopters. The software was released, but had been affected in many major ways. First, more defects were found earlier in the development cycles. Defects included user experience issues, not just sightings of unexpected behavior after a button press. Second, the application re-instated an exit menu, so users could easily quit the solution. Third, the MyHelp team was forced to see who the customer really is, not the CIO office contracting the development, but the end users who would have to adopt the solution.

Fighting for Adoption

... one third of all corporate development projects are canceled. Five out of six projects are considered unsuccessful and unable to deliver desired features. Even average projects have schedule and budget overruns nearly double the original project estimates. (Malveau el al. 2001)

MyHelp is a great example of why many enterprise IT solutions suffer: failing to deliver value for end users. They mandate users to adopt the offering, instead of engaging users in the development process. MyHelp is on its third trip through the TAP process, learning what it takes to make collaborative development an open activity. MyHelp fought adoption and users revolted. People influenced the project, changed the attitudes of the prototypical service providers and became a core part of their new development process. This cultural change was great at an individual level, but the release of software could not be affected. Therein is one of the most critical balancing acts: the need to deliver on solutions to improve the overall goals of the company and the need to engage and reflect change brought on by early adopters quickly and frequently. The MyHelp team's first time through the TAP program required executive level support to change their idea of success. It was no longer making a milestone or a date; it was trying to satisfy employees. The less they listened the louder the early adopters buzzed. The Technology Adoption Program was able to provide the framework, and in some cases the therapy, to enable the MyHelp team to drastically decrease deployment time, increase alpha and beta releases, and focused the quality of the end product on features users required.

CONCLUSION

TAP is not the answer to all technical deployments – some IT efforts require the rigor of committee reviews, voting and prioritization when balancing a tight budget with the need to support a massive corporation such as IBM. However, TAP has enabled easy, early visibility to emerging technologies, and added the benefit of knowing if it is easily adopted by users. For decision-makers concerned with maintaining leading-edge technology strategies, such a program enables the flexibility of offering emerging technology with the maturity of making decisions about which ones can move into a production environment and out of a pilot one. By doing so, technology deployments are early, into the hands of users disgruntled about status quo – anxious for the latest and greatest. These users bond together around this desire to try new things, into a community that encourages ownership, engaging a passion that crosses organizational silos hierarchies. They speak to value gained from new things, wanting others to gain similar value – a benefit beyond ROI, as the returns are not necessarily predictable and easily quantifiable. Such value and return is innovation – a way of doing something differently. IBM's Technology Adoption Program offers a new way of measuring value, first by moving early into a technology's lifecycle and second by measuring adoption, shifting how technology is managed in such a large enterprise. Here, technology management, found within the CIO function, moves from utility manager to innovation enabler by doing something different: lowering the center of gravity for innovation management.

REFERENCES

Alter, A. (2005). CIOs Shift: Focus is On Revenue, Not on Saving Money. *CIO Insight.* Retrieved November 27, 2006 from http://www.cioinsight.com/article2/0,1397,1875251,00.asp

Beinhocker, E. (2006). The Adaptable Corporation. *The McKinsey Quarterly, 2*, 77–87.

Bernal, V. (2001). Building Online Communities. *Benton.* Retrieved October 1, 2006 from http://www.benton.org/publibrary/practice/community/assumptions.html

Brody, P., & Ehrlich, D. (1998). Can Big Companies Become Successful Venture Capitalists. *The McKinsey Quarterly, 2*, 50–63.

Cooper, J., Greenberg, D., & Zuk, J. (2004). Reshaping the funnel: Making innovation more profitable for high-tech manufacturers. *IBM Institute for Business Value.* Retrieved November 11, 2006, from http://www.ibm.com/industries/aerodefense/doc/content/bin/ibv_funnel_1.pdf

Cutter Consortium. (2005). *Press Release: Software Project Success and Failure.* Retrieved August 24, 2005, from http://www.cutter.com/press/050824.html

Davila, T., Epstein, M., & Shelton, R. (2005). *Making Innovation Work: how to Manage It, Measure It, and Profit from it.* Philadelphia: Wharton School Publishing.

Dean, D., & Dvorak, R. (1995). Do it, then fix it: The power of prototypes. *The McKinsey Quarterly, 4*, 50–61.

Dresner, H. (2006). Business Intelligence: Standardization and Consolidation of Tools. *Hyperion.* Retrieved November 11, 2006, from http://www.hyperion.com/company/overview/thought_leadership/exec_perspectives/BI_Tools.cfm

Fenn, J. (2005). Emerging Trends, 2010-2015. *Gartner.* Retrieved November 11, 2006, from http://www.gartner.com/teleconferences/attributes/attr_135627_115.pdf

Glass, R. L. (1997, June). Software runaways - some surprising findings. *SIGMIS Database, 28*(3), 16–19. doi:10.1145/272657.272687

Hansen, K. (2006, July). - Augst). Project Visualization for Software. *IEEE Software, 23*(4), 84–92. doi:10.1109/MS.2006.111

Henig, P. (2004). Thinking Out Loud: Dr. Harry M. Markowitz: When Harry Met Alfred. *CIO Insight.* Retrieved November 27, 2006, from http://www.cioinsight.com/article2/0,1397,1609468,00.asp

IBM. (2006). Extreme Blue. *IBM Corporation.* Retrieved November 21, 2006, from http://www.ibm.com/extremeblue/

IBM. (2006). Introducing IBM Lotus Sametime 7.5. *IBM Corporation*. Retrieved November 21, 2006, from ftp://ftp.software.ibm.com/software/lotus/lotusweb/product/sametime/Sametime_7.5_Detailed_View.pdf

IBM alphaWorks. (2003). IBM Community Tools. *IBM Corporation*. Retrieved November 21, 2006, from http://www.alphaworks.ibm.com/tech/ict

Javed, T., Maqsood, M. E., & Durrani, Q. S. (2004, May). A study to investigate the impact of requirements instability on software defects. *SIGSOFT Software. Engineering Notes, 29*(3), 1–7. doi:10.1145/986710.986727

Johnson, J. (1995, July). Creating Chaos, *American Programmer*.

Kanellos, M. (2004). IBM Heeds message to integrate IM, email, *News.com*. Retrieved November 21, 2006, from http://news.com.com/2102-1012_3-5165991.html?tag=st.util.print

Kirsner, S. (2000, April). Faster Company, *Fast Company, 43*, 162. Retrieved November 21, 2006, from http://www.fastcompany.com/online/34/ibm.html

Lomax, A. (2005). Yahoo!'s Delicious Deal, *The Motley Fool*. Retrieved on April 10, 2009, from http://www.fool.com/investing/general/2005/12/12/yahoos-delicious-deal.aspx

Malveau, R., & Mowbray, T. (2001). *Software Process Background. Software Architect Bootcamp*. Upper Saddle River, NJ: Prentice Hall.

Malveau, R., & Mowbray, T. (2001). *Doing Software Wrong. Software Architect Bootcamp*. Upper Saddle River, NJ: Prentice Hall.

Martin, J. (2006). Why Sametime 7.5 Was Created, *solutions-daily.com*. Retrieved November 21, 2006, from http://lotus.solutions-daily.com/mediafiles/ibm_lagarde.m4a

Millen, D. R., Feinberg, J., & Kerr, B. (2006). Dogear: Social bookmarking in the enterprise. In *Proceedings of the SIGCHI Conference on Human Factors in Computing Systems* (Montréal, Canada, April 22 - 27, 2006). R. Grinter, T. Rodden, P. Aoki, E. Cutrell, R. Jeffries, and G. Olson, Eds. CHI '06. New York: ACM.

Neistat, C., & Neistat, V. (2004). *Info about iPod's Dirty Secret*. Retrieved November 21, 2006, from http://www.ipodsdirtysecret.com/message.html

Radjou, N. (2005, March). IBM Transforms its Supply Chain to Drive Growth, *Forrester*.

Robey, D., & Keil, M. (2001). Blowing the whistle on troubled software projects. *Communications of the ACM, 44*(4), 87–93. doi:10.1145/367211.367274

Smith, J. (2002). The 40 root causes of troubled IT projects. *Engineering Management Journal, 12*(5), 238–242. doi:10.1049/em:20020506

Sunstein, C. R. (2004). Democracy and Filtering. *Communications of the ACM, 47*(12), 57–59. doi:10.1145/1035134.1035166

Tamai, T., & Itou, A. (1993). Requirements and design change in large-scale software development: analysis from the viewpoint of process backtracking. In *Proceedings of the 15th international Conference on Software Engineering*. Los Alamitos, CA: IEEE Computer Society Press. Presented at the International Conference on Software Engineering (May 17-21, 1993), Baltimore, MD.

Tannenbaum, A., Swearingen, C., Cook, J., Bardon, D., & Dong, J. (2006). NotesBuddy: A unified experience for messaging, *IBM Corporation*. Retrieved November 21, 2006, from http://www.ibm.com/easy/page/1979

Tchong, M. (2005). The Culture of Innovation, *Fast Company*. Retrieved November 13, 2006, from http://www.fastcompany.com/resources/innovation/tchong/101804.html

University of Cambridge. (2006). The Development Funnel, *Institute for Manufacturing Centre for Economic Policy*. Retrieved November 11, 2006, http://www.ifm.eng.cam.ac.uk/dstools/paradigm/innova.html

Weiss, A. (2005). The power of collective intelligence. *netWorker*, *9*(3), 16–23. doi:10.1145/1086762.1086763

Wikipedia (n.d.). *Agile Software Development*. Retrieved November 21, 2006, from http://en.wikipedia.org/wiki/Agile_software_development

KEY TERMS AND DEFINITONS

Adoption: The act of accepting with approval, transferring from one to another

Collaboration: The process of working together to achieve a common goal

Community: A group of people who agree on and align around common goals, interests despite their individual responsibilities, roles or positions

Early Adopters: Individuals that invest in new technologies when they first become available in an attempt to gain a competitive advantage despite the higher risk entailed that that involved in a more cautious approach

Emerging Technology: Significant technological developments that broach new territory in some significant way in their field

Feedback: The critical assessment on a newly produced product, technology, information or service

Innovation: Introduction of something that addresses a need in a previously unmet way

IT Governance: A system in which all stakeholders, including the company's board, internal customers, finance departments, have the necessary input into deciding the overall architecture of its company's IT applications portfolio

Software Development Process: Determining the requirements for a new computer-based function, and creating, and/or modifying one or more programs that performs that function in a systematic way

User Experience: Creation of the architecture and interaction models that impact a user's perception of a device or system

Chapter 3
Are the Pre–Diffusion Phases Shortening?

J.R. Ortt
Delft University of Technology, The Netherlands

ABSTRACT

This chapter focuses on the pre-diffusion phases for high-tech products. These phases last from the first time a technology is mastered and demonstrated up to the start of the large-scale production and diffusion of products based on that technology. The purpose of this chapter is to underline the managerial relevance of the pre-diffusion phases. Two questions will be answered in particular: (1) How long do these pre-diffusion phases last for high-tech products? (2) Have these phases shortened or not over the last 150 years? Fifty-three cases of high-tech products, invented between 1837 and 1998, are investigated. The pre-diffusion phases are shown to last 16 years on average, but their length varies considerably per case. No proof for the shortening of these phases over time is found. The resources devoted to research and development in different fields of expertise may have increased but the length of the pre-diffusion phases has not shortened accordingly.

INTRODUCTION

Central to this chapter is the question whether the length of the pre-diffusion phases, *i.e.* the phases preceding large-scale production and diffusion, has shortened or not over the last 150 years for high-tech products. In this chapter we define high-tech products as products, materials or components based on breakthrough technologies and representing an

advance that is so significant that attainable price/performance ratios are altered dramatically or that entirely new kinds of applications are enabled (Tushman & Anderson, 1986). Examples of high-tech products that, at the time of their invention, shifted price/performance ratios include dynamite, in comparison to nitro-glycerin, and strong fibers like Kevlar, in comparison to contemporary fibers. Examples of high-tech products that enabled entirely new applications at the time of their invention include radar, laser and communication appliances

DOI: 10.4018/978-1-61520-643-8.ch003

like telegraphy and television. We define the pre-diffusion phases as the period between the invention of the technology and the start of the large-scale production and diffusion of products, materials or components on the basis of this technology.

Scientific Relevance

In diffusion research, Rogers (2005) noticed an almost complete lack of attention to the pre-diffusion period. By ignoring this period, mainstream diffusion research seems to imply that large-scale diffusion starts directly after the market introduction of a new high-tech product. Large-scale diffusion is often represented by an S-shaped diffusion curve and that seems to imply that the diffusion process is quite predictable. In practice, that is hardly the case. Easingwood and Lunn (1992), for example, found different far more erratic patterns of diffusion for various telecommunication products and services. Rogers indicates that more attention should be devoted to the phases prior to the large-scale diffusion (the S-shaped pattern). Scientists outside the diffusion discipline indicate that these pre-diffusion phases usually last long (Agarwal & Bayus, 2002; Mansfield, 1968; Utterback & Brown, 1972). It is unknown, however, whether the length of these phases have changed or not in the course of time. In contrast, developments in the length of the product life cycle, *i.e.* the time period *after* these pre-diffusion phases, have evoked a lively debate. We want to extend this discussion to the pre-diffusion phases.

Scientific Focus

Scientists from different disciplines have investigated factors that explain the speed of diffusion. Institutional economists, for example, focus on the institutions such as the laws enabling appropriation or organizations facilitating knowledge exchange in industries (*e.g.* North, 1990; Wil-liamson, 1996). Diffusion researchers focus on characteristics of customers and their perception of the innovation to explain the diffusion (Rogers, 2005). In strategic management the characteristics of the market environment or the strategies and capabilities of the main companies that supply the innovation are used to explain the start of diffusion processes (for an overview of schools in strategic management see for example Teece and Pisano (1994)). Apparently, although the focus depends a bit on the discipline involved, variables explaining the start and the speed of diffusion processes seem to belong to a couple of categories such as: (1) the characteristics of the innovation; (2) the characteristics of the organizations that introduce the innovation; (3) the characteristics of the customers adopting the innovation or (4) the wider market environment in which diffusion processes occur. Ortt & Delgoshaie (2008) made a similar categorization of factors affecting the length of the adaptation phase, after they studied 18 cases of high-tech products.

Some authors also specifically investigate factors determining the process *prior to* diffusion of innovations. Nerkar and Shane (2007) for example focus on determinants that determine the commercialization of inventions from academia. In the entrepreneurship literature many of the factors determining the success of entrepreneurial activities prior to large-scale diffusion are investigated (*e.g.* Bekkers, R., Gilsing, V., and van der Steen, M., 2006; Di Gregerio and Shane, 2003; Dowling and Helm 2006; Shane, 2004). We also focus on these pre-diffusion phases but rather than explaining the length of these phases using a selection of the variables from the four categories, we focus on the question whether the length has changed over time. This focus on time requires that we randomize over (or control for) the other categories of variables. That is the reason why we deliberately selected a heterogeneous set of high-tech products developed by completely different types of organizations in different industries and with different types of customers.

Managerial Relevance of Investigating the Length of the Pre-Diffusion Phases

The length of the pre-diffusion phases is extremely important from a management perspective. In general, during the pre-diffusion phases the costs of developing and marketing high-tech products outweigh the income by far. In many cases, the invention is no more than a demonstration of a rudimentary technological principle. After the invention, the technology has to be improved in terms of reliability and performance, a product has to be developed, production and marketing have to be organized before the (first) market introduction, and so on. Usually before large-scale production and diffusion starts, an erratic exploration process can be witnessed in which subsequent product variants are introduced in different market segments. In the pre-diffusion phases, the companies commercializing the new-high tech product, usually have to invest and explore without making substantial profits. The average length of these phases illustrates the amount of investment and the endurance that is required, the variation in the length of these phases illustrates the uncertainty and the risk involved in commercializing new high-tech products.

The uncertainty and risk for companies that are involved in the commercialization of high-tech products can be estimated in more detail using a selection of references. Developing and subsequently commercializing high-tech products can be very rewarding but is also a risky endeavour for companies. On the one hand, there are potential high gains like achieving a competitive advantage that can contribute significantly to a firm's growth and profitability (Booz-Allen & Hamilton, 1982; Kleinschmidt & Cooper, 1991; Veryzer, 1998). Breakthrough technologies have been the source of new product categories, new markets and new industries (Abernathy & Clark, 1985; Christensen, 1997; Henderson & Clark, 1990; Olleros, 1986; Tushman & Rosenkopf, 1992). The history of the American company Raytheon, for example, is intimately connected with the radar, Xerox with the photocopying machine and The Bell Company with the fax and the transistor.

On the other hand, it is remarkable how many companies involved in the development of high-tech products lose out before their product is applied on a large-scale (Olleros, 1986; Pech, 2003). Projects dedicated to high-tech products are risky, expensive, and usually take several years to produce results (Leifer *et al.*, 2000). Technical, market and organisational uncertainties associated with these projects are much higher than with projects aimed at incremental improvement (Burgelman & Sayles, 1986; Moriarty & Kosnik, 1989). Two different types of risks have to be combined to assess the real risk that pioneers experience: (1) the risk that high-tech products on the basis of a breakthrough technology fail in the market; (2) the risk that the pioneer fails and vanishes before their product becomes a success in the market. The first risk has been estimated by Crawford (1977, 1979, 1987) for new products in general. He concludes on the basis of several studies that the failure rate is consistently around 35%. This failure rate is probably higher for high-tech products. The second risk was estimated by Tellis and Golder (1996) who use a historical analysis approach and focus on products that are known to be successful. They show that 47% of the pioneers that are first to introduce such a product in the market, fail and vanish. Examples of pioneering companies that vanished include Chux (disposable diapers), MITS (personal computers) and the Stanley Brothers (automobiles) (Tellis and Golder, 1996). Olleros (1996) refers to this phenomenon as the "burnout of the pioneers". These findings imply that the risk for pioneering companies is much higher than the risk for companies introducing incrementally new products. The findings also imply that the so-called pre-diffusion phases occupy a central role in this risk.

Research Questions and Contents of the Chapter

It would be highly relevant to see whether the length of the pre-diffusion phases has changed or not over the last 150 years. A significant shortening of these phases over the past 150 years would indicate that we are starting to master the market and technology uncertainty of high-tech products during these phases. Researching the length of these phases is also scientifically relevant because it complements the current focus on the product life cycles. The research questions in this chapter are:

1. How long do the pre-diffusion phases (the period from invention to large-scale production and diffusion) last for high-tech products?
2. Has the length of these phases changed (shortened) over the last 150 years?

Before answering the two research questions, the next section will describe a general pattern of development and diffusion of high-tech products. This pattern is based on the notion that the well-known S-shaped diffusion curve, often found to represent the product life cycle, is preceded in practice by so-called pre-diffusion phases. This section will also summarize the discussion about whether or not the length of the product life cycle has changed over time. The next sections cover the methodology, results, conclusions and discussion, respectively.

PREVIOUS WORK ON THE PATTERN OF DEVELOPMENT AND DIFFUSION

A General Pattern of Development and Diffusion of High-Tech Products

The diffusion of high-tech products shows a remarkably similar S-shaped pattern for many cases. The diffusion of many (tele)communication appliances, for example, also follows this pattern (Miles, 1988; Rogers, 1986; Williams, Rice & Rogers, 1988). This similarity seems to imply that the prediction of market results is relatively straightforward and the risks are relatively limited. There are at least two reasons why this S-shaped pattern does not reflect the actual pattern and the accompanying risks experienced by pioneering companies. Firstly, the S-shaped pattern shows the summed sales of a specific type of product from all the companies, and not the increase/decrease in sales per company. The pioneering companies have to attain or defend a market share vis-à-vis an increasing number of competitors that enter the market later. Secondly, empirical results show that the process of development and diffusion begins much earlier (Ortt & Schoormans, 2004) and that the S-curve is only the last phase of a longer, difficult to predict process. The invention, *i.e.* the demonstration of the technological principle, is often made decades before the start of the large-scale diffusion. The first market introduction also commonly takes place years before the start of large-scale production and diffusion of a high-tech product in a mass market. The process preceding the large-scale diffusion is much more erratic and therefore more risky than the S-shaped pattern.

Ortt and Schoormans (2004) propose a model with different phases to describe the entire process of development and diffusion of high-tech products. They distinguish three phases: the innovation phase, the adaptation phase and the stabilization phase. Our pre-diffusion phases refer to the innovation and adaptation phase (see Figure 1). We will describe these two pre-diffusion phases in a bit more detail. The innovation phase comprises the period from the invention of a technology up to the first market introduction of a product incorporating the technology. The second phase, referred to as the adaptation phase, begins after the (first) market introduction of a new high-tech product and ends with the large-scale production and diffusion of this product. After the first introduction, instead of a smooth S-curve, in practice

Figure 1. Phases in the pattern of development and diffusion of high-tech products

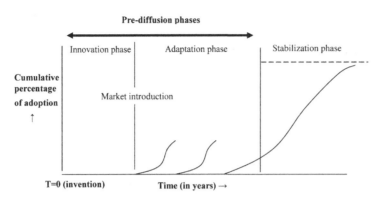

an erratic process of diffusion may occur (Clark, 1985). The diffusion is often characterized by periodic introduction, decline and re-introduction of multiple products in multiple small-scale applications (Carey & Moss, 1985). Together the innovation and adaptation phase form the pre-diffusion phases. The third phase, referred to as the stabilization phase, begins with the large-scale production and diffusion of a high-tech product and ends when that type of product is substituted completely. In this phase, the diffusion of a product mostly resembles an S-curve. A graph showing the phases is given in Figure 1.

Description of the Milestones in the Pattern

Tushman and Rosenkopf (1992) describe a technology cycle similar to our pattern. The first stage of the cycle, which they call variation, starts with a technological discontinuity (*i.e.* a discontinuity in terms of price/performance) that emerges either through scientific advance or through a unique combination of existing technologies. In the next stage, referred to as the era of ferment, parallel processes of substitution, competition and ongoing technical change unfold. In the third stage, the selection stage, a dominant design emerges. Anderson and Tushman (1990) define a dominant design as "a single configuration or a narrow range of configurations that accounted

for over 50% of new product sales or new process installations and maintained a 50% market share for at least 4 years" (p. 620). Finally, an era of incremental change sets in, where the dominant design essentially remains the same. The description of the cycle from Tushman and Rosenkopf is elaborated in two ways in this chapter: (1) explicit milestones are distinguished to define the phases; (2) the time-period of the pre-diffusion phases are assessed. The milestone are described below, the time-period is the topic of the remainder of the paper.

The invention is considered to be the first demonstration of the working principle of the new high-tech product. Materials are sometimes discovered in nature. Discovery, however, does not mean that the technology is understood and mastered (*i.e.* can be reproduced and used). So the discovery of Aspirin is much earlier than the invention of the process to produce a synthetic version of this medicine. Similarly, the material aluminum is discovered in nature long before mankind started to master its process of production. We consider the latter moment as the invention. *The Invention of a new high-tech product is defined to be the first time a technology, i.e. the technical principle of a new high-tech product, is demonstrated and mastered.*

The market introduction of a technological product is part of an array of subsequent activities. In the course of time a product is developed, maybe produced on a small scale for testing and for pilot projects, produced for actual use, maybe put in stock, then sold or transferred to the users in some way or another and finally it is used in practice or implemented in the daily practice of the users. In some cases products are not sold, for example if a government institute develops a new weapon that is used by the military forces, in these cases the introduction is the moment that the innovation can be transferred to the users. *The introduction date is defined to be the date at which the product is available for sales or can be transferred to users.*

Large-scale production and diffusion is an important milestone because it separates the pre-diffusion phases from the standard diffusion process represented by the S-shaped diffusion curve. On the other hand it is also a difficult milestone to define and assess in practice. Are the small-scale attempts to introduce the first high-tech product representing the start of the diffusion process or do they precede this process? In the latter case, it is important to define a milestone that distinguishes the pre-diffusion phases from the diffusion phase. *Large-scale production and diffusion is defined using 3 elements:*

- *A standard product is required that can be reproduced multiple times (or standard product modules that can be combined in many different ways but are based on the same standard platform);*
- *A (large-scale) production unit with dedicated production lines (industrial production of a standard product);*
- *(Large-scale) diffusion of the product.*

The next paragraph will summarize research that focused on the length of the stabilization phase. This phase is often referred to as the *product life cycle.*

Research on the Length of the Product Life Cycle

"The product life cycle represents the unit sales for some product, extending from the time it is first placed on the market until it is removed. (…) The product life cycle is often depicted as a bell-shaped curve with four phases: introduction, growth, maturity and decline." (Rink & Swan, 1979, p.219-220). Whether the length of the product life cycle has changed or not, evoked a lively debate. It is generally assumed that product life cycles shorten (Alsop, 1986; Rabino & Wright, 1993; Steffens, 1994) but the evidence is scant (Van den Bulte, 2000).

In practice one can distinguish three categories of sources referring to the length of the product life cycle. First, in the business press it is widely claimed that product life cycles shorten (See for example: Alsop, 1986; Hof, 1992 and 1995; Climento, 1993; Steffens, 1994; Verity, 1992). These articles refer to separate cases and present anecdotal evidence at best. These articles simply reflect a widely held idea. Second, in the scientific literature many articles mention the shortening of the product life cycle as a starting point that is neither researched nor questioned. These articles discuss the implications of the assumed shortening of the product life cycles, for example in innovation management (Dickson *et al.*, 1995; Sherman *et al.*, 2000). Third, a limited number of articles actually empirically investigate the length of product life cycle for a larger set of cases.

This third category of articles that more closely investigate the length of product life cycles will be discussed in more detail. In doing so, the focus will be on the computer and the home appliance industries. In the personal computer industry product life times are not shrinking (Bayus, 1998). Bayus distinguishes different levels of product markets in the computer industry among which a "brand model" (*e.g.* the IBM PC XT), a "product model" (286 CPU chip) a "product technology" (16-bit CPU), and a "product form" (desktop personal computer). He shows that the life time of brand models has decreased but the life time of product forms, product technologies and product models have not. Bayus' results imply that the pace of changes on the more fundamental level of the product and its technology have essentially remained the same whereas the more superficial changes in the marketing mix of these high-tech products have speeded up significantly.

In the home appliance industry diffusion rates are investigated also (Bayus, 1992; Van de Bulte, 2000). Van de Bulte investigates diffusion speed for 31 household durables over a period of 74 years. An increase in diffusion speed is found, but can be fully explained by three variables: 1) demographic change; 2) increased spending power; and 3) the changing nature of products. These results imply that diffusion rates have increased because the markets for the products have increased in size (variable 1 and 2) and the number of incrementally new products have increased (variable 3), but that does not necessarily imply that the length of the entire product life cycles on the more fundamental level of the product has decreased. Similar findings are reported by other authors and for other industries (For an overview see Bayus, 1994).

We conclude that the length of the product life cycle has evoked a lively debate. The actual data, upon closer inspection, seem to imply that the cycles do not shorten. The product cycle refers to the stabilization phase in Figure 1. Figure 1 displays three phases in the entire pattern of development and diffusion of high-tech products, the stabilization phase is the last of these phases. Apparently we can see a lack of research regarding the length of the early or pre-diffusion phases in this pattern. Bayus (1992) recognized this scientific need to look at early phases when he stated that research should not focus on the entire cycle but upon separate parts of it.

METHODOLOGY

Data Gathering

To answer the research questions, the year of invention and the year in which the large-scale production (and diffusion) started are needed.

Information about inventions can usually be found in articles and books or by contacting companies. The beginning of the large-scale production and diffusion of a high-tech product is sometimes more difficult to assess. This will be illustrated by the case of Dyneema. Dyneema is an ultra strong fiber. Already in 1982 a pilot plant was producing Dyneema, small portions were sold for testing. The large-scale production started in 1990, with the opening of a real production plant. The difference between a pilot and large-scale production plant is sometimes a matter of degree and requires close observation of company data. In most cases, however, the opening of a dedicated production plant is traceable.

The data on the year of invention and large-scale production and diffusion is gathered by team members. A high-tech product is thoroughly investigated. Every activity related to the product is placed in a time-table. This table starts with the beginning of the research or the activities that led to the invention and continues till the end of the life cycle or till now when this cycle is still continuing. The data are cross-checked by multiple sources and reviewed by experts.

We selected a large and heterogeneous set of high-tech products both in terms of the time of invention and the type of products (see Table 1). In Table 1 five periods are distinguished for the time of invention, the first invention taken into account is the telegraph (1837), the last invention is the Bluetooth communication standard (1998). In Table 1, six types of products are distinguished like "materials and alloys" and "medical equipment and medicines". An alphabetic list of the high-tech products is provided in Table 2 in the Appendix.

Table 1. Cases of high-tech products in various periods and various categories

↓Type of product	Time of invention→					
	< 1901	1901-1925	1926- 1950	1951- 1975	> 1975	Total
Materials or alloys	PVC	Bakelite Cellophane	Nylon	Dyneema Kevlar Memory Metal Astroturf		8
Medical equipment and medicines	Aspirin Hearing aid X-ray		Antibiotics Contraceptive pill	CT-scanner MRI		7
Communication and navigational systems and components	Telegraphy Fax	Mob telephony Radar Sonar	Television	Fiber opt com GPS Internet	SMS Bluetooth Browser	12
Electronic/optical appliances and components	Magnetic recording	Air-conditioning	Microwave oven Photocopier Transistor Electron micro-scope	Digital camera DVD Laser Optical disc Plasma display VCR		12
Automotive systems and components	Turbocharger	Aircraft Helicopter	ABS Jet-engine	Airbag Cruise control Wankel-engine		8
Diverse	Ballpoint Dynamite		Nuclear-energy bomb	Barcodes Nuclear-energy plant	DNA finger-printing	6
Total	10	8	11	20	4	53

Assessing the Length of the Pre-Diffusion Phases as a Function of the Time of Invention

The length of the period is related to the year of invention in the following regression equation:

$Y = C_0 + C_1 X$

Y = Length of early phases (in years)

C_0 = Constant

C_1 = Slope of regression line (C1 is negative when the lengths of the phases decrease)

X = Date of invention (in years)

Four issues have to be dealt with before the relationship between the lengths of the pre-diffusion phases and the time of invention can be assessed properly. In short these issues are:

1. **Heteroscedasticity.**

Scatterplots show that the variance of the data around the regression line changes with the time of invention. The high-tech products based on more recent inventions show less variance, the older products show more variance.

2. **Outliers in data.**

The dataset shows two outliers in the data: PVC (100 years) and the fax (97 years). These outliers may have an impact on the results because their invention date is early on (1838 and 1851 for PVC and the fax respectively) and their early phases are quite long. We removed these outliers.

3. **Selection of cases.**

Cases of breakthrough technologies are selected for our dataset *only* when the early phases are completed. In practice that means that the potential length of the early phases is restricted for cases that are invented recently. A technology that is invented in 1998 (Bluetooth) can only show early phases of less than eight years before 2006. The complete dataset may reveal a relationship between the length of the early phases and the date of invention that is simply the result of our way of selecting cases. In order to compensate for this effect we selected cases by restricting the length of the early phases of the cases to 40 years and by restricting the invention date before 1966; 36 cases satisfy these criteria.

4.   **Industry differences.**

Technologies from different industries may have early phases with different lengths. In order to remove the industry effect and focus on the effect of invention date, the cases will be standardized within industries.

After selecting the cases with a maximum length of 40 years for the time between invention and large-scale production/diffusion, the outliers are removed and the heteroscedasticity disappeared, so issue 1, 2 and 3 are tackled. In order to compensate for an effect of the type of industry (issue 4), the data is standardized within industries.

RESULTS

On average, the pre-diffusion phases (from the invention up to the start of large-scale production and diffusion) cover about one and a half decade (16.29 years for 51 cases after the outliers are removed). A full description of the data can be found in Table 2 at the end of the chapter. On average, these phases are remarkably long, this length stresses the importance of studying theses phases. The length of the pre-diffusion phases

varies considerably. The length of these phases of mobile telephony and the turbocharger, for example, took more than five decades, whereas the same phases only took one year in the case of DVD and dynamite.

Regression Equation

(Length) $= C_0 + C_1$ (year of invention)
Value -15.093 0.008
t-value -1.548 1.548
sign (.131) (.131)
$R^2 = 0.066$
F (sign) = 2.397 (.131)

The results show that C_1 is small, positive and insignificant. Or, to put it differently, no relationship can be found between the time of the invention and the length of the period from invention to large-scale production.

CONCLUSION AND DISCUSSION

The length of the period from invention to large-scale production is assessed for 51 high-tech products in this chapter. Analyzing this length leads to the following results: (1) on average the period lasts about one and a half decade; (2) the variance in the lengths of this period is large for individual products; (3) the length of the period does not decrease significantly over the last 150 years. We will provide a discussion and managerial implications for each of these results.

The Length of the Early Phases

In total the period from invention up to the large-scale production on average lasts 16 years. Similar findings are reported by other authors. It is claimed that the average time from invention to the start of the commercial development process is about ten to fifteen years (Mansfield, 1968). From the start of this process up to the market introduction, again, a couple of years elapses. It is estimated that, on average, this takes an additional five to eight years (Utterback & Brown, 1972). So, according to these authors the period from invention to the first market introduction comprises 15-23 years, a finding that is in accordance with our finding of 16 years. Longer periods are also reported: an average period of 28 years between invention and commercialization for thirty breakthrough innovations from diverse industries (Agarwal & Bayus, 2002).

The managerial implications of these findings are large. The length of this period implies that a strong and enduring commitment is required on behalf of companies that invent and subsequently want to commercialize breakthrough technologies on a large-scale (Lynn *et al.*, 1996). These phases generally require investments rather than generate income. Different strategies can be adopted to cope with the length of these phases.

The Variation in the Length of the Early Phases

The length of the early phases for individual high-tech products can deviate considerably from the average value. In some cases, like dynamite, this period almost disappears because large-scale production and diffusion emerges about one year after the invention. In other cases, like mobile telephony and the turbocharger, these phases last more than five decades.

The variation in length implies large levels of uncertainty and has considerable managerial implications. Without additional information it is uncertain how long the early phases will last for individual cases. These implications become apparent once it is understood that the period before and after large-scale production require completely different strategies. Consider production strategies, for example. Before large-scale production, different product forms are developed and produced on a small scale for various customer segments. This situation requires a small-scale and highly flexible production facility. A small-scale production unit is especially important because it enables a quick learning process and it limits the required investment and thereby reduces the financial risk. Large-scale production, however, is aimed at economies of scale. A large-scale production unit is especially important in markets with large network effects. In these markets, the first entrant may quickly reap the benefits of the network effects and thereby attain a leadership position that is hard to fight by competitors. The wrong type of production facility may entail large losses. An example of this loss is provided by the company that after the invention of the transistor built large-scale production facilities to produce germanium transistors. At the time the production facilities were ready to produce, silicon-based transistors were developed that rendered the germanium-based transistors obsolete.

Do the Early Phases Decrease in the Course of Time?

Our results imply that the length of the period from invention to large-scale production and diffusion does not shorten significantly.

In a discussion of these results a couple of remarks are important. Firstly, although 51 cases constitute a relatively large sample compared to similar studies, it should be noted that the size of the sample in combination with the large variation in the length of these phases may make detection of a significant decrease of these phases difficult. We think that this effect has no effect in our data because the length of the early phases shows a tendency to increase rather than decrease. It is unlikely that a larger sample will lead to a decrease of these phases.

Secondly, the analyses focus on the relationship between the length of the early phases and the time of invention of breakthrough technologies. Apparently, many more variables will have an impact on the length of these phases. The characteristics of the technology, the resources and characteristics of the companies involved in the commercialization of the technology and, finally, the characteristics of the market in which the technology is introduced may have an impact on the length of these phases. In the analyses potential variables representing the characteristics of the companies and the markets are left out. This may be one of the reasons why heteroscedasticity is found in the regression analyses (Harnett, 1982). The omission of these variables can have an effect on the results of the analyses once these variables are not randomized across the sample of technologies but co-vary with the time. Future research is required to explain the lengths of these phases using other variables and then compensate for the effect of these variables and assess the effect of time on the length of these phases again.

Thirdly, changes in the length of the early phases after the 1970s cannot be assessed using our procedure.

Final Considerations

Contrary to our expectations the time from invention to large-scale production and diffusion of high-tech products has *not* shortened. How can this be explained?

A first explanation is that technological progress does speed up, even for individual trajectories, but that the decrease in the length of the early phases has occurred after the 1970s (we considered breakthrough technologies that are invented before 1966). Several developments can be mentioned that may have significantly shortened these phases after the 1970s (Thomke, 2003). It is shown that the increased possibilities to simulate the performance of product variants have shortened the lengths of development processes. Furthermore, computer-aided design and subsequently computer-aided manufacturing may have increased the speed of the entire process from invention up to the start of large-scale production. However, these developments occurred much later than the 1970s.

Another explanation is that our expectation is primarily fuelled by the day-to-day observation that technological progress is speeding up. This observation is based on a perspective that supersedes individual technological disciplines. Both on the supply and the demand-side of the market developments stimulate this progress. A significant increase in research and development spending after the Second World War can be witnessed and, as a result, more technological product innovations are introduced. The spending power of consumers has increased considerably after the Second World War in the Western World, a trend that may have increased the diffusion of high-tech products (Van den Bulte, 2000). The increased allocation of resources to research and development in many different disciplines and in many parallel trajectories and the increased speed of diffusion, however, seem to obscure the fact that individual patterns of developing and diffusing high-tech products do not shorten at all. This explanation would be in accordance with the finding that product life cycles do not shorten significantly once the level of the product category rather than the level of product variants, is closely observed (Bayus, 1998).

REFERENCES

Abernathy, W. J., & Clark, K. B. (1985). Innovation: Mapping the winds of creative destruction. *Research Policy*, *14*(1), 3–22. doi:10.1016/0048-7333(85)90021-6

Agarwal, R., & Bayus, B. L. (2002). The Market Evolution and Sales Takeoff of Product Innovations. *Management Science*, *48*(8), 1024–1041. doi:10.1287/mnsc.48.8.1024.167

Alsop, R. (1986, July 10). Companies get on fast track to roll hot new brands. *Wall Street Journal*.

Bayus, B. L. (1992). Have Diffusion Rates Been Accelerating Over Time? *Marketing Letters, 3*(3), 215–226. doi:10.1007/BF00994130

Bayus, B. L. (1994). Are Product Life Cycles Really Getting Shorter? *Journal of Product Innovation Management, 11,* 300–308. doi:10.1016/0737-6782(94)90085-X

Bayus, B. L. (1998). An Analysis of Product Lifetimes in a Technologically Dynamic Industry. *Management Science, 44*(6), 763–775. doi:10.1287/mnsc.44.6.763

Bekkers, R., Gilsing, V., & van der Steen, M. (2006). Determining factors of IP-based spin-offs. *The Journal of Technology Transfer, 31,* 545–566. doi:10.1007/s10961-006-9058-z

Booz, A. (1982). *New Product Management for the 1980s. New York: Booz.* Hamilton: Allen and Hamilton, Inc.

Burgelman, R., & Sayles, L. R. (1986). *Inside corporate innovation.* New York: The Free Press.

Carey, J., & Moss, M. L. (1985). The Diffusion of Telecommunication Technologies. *Telecommunications Policy, 6,* 145–158. doi:10.1016/0308-5961(85)90038-2

Christensen, C. M. (1997). *The Innovator's Dilemma.* Boston: Harvard Business School Press.

Clark, K. B. (1985). The Interaction of Design Hierarchies and Market Concepts in Technological Evolution. *Research Policy, 14,* 235–251. doi:10.1016/0048-7333(85)90007-1

Climento, A. (1993). Excellence in Electronics. *The McKinsey Quarterly, 3,* 29–40.

Crawford, C. M. (1977). Marketing Research and the New Product Failure Rate. *Journal of Marketing,* (April): 51–61. doi:10.2307/1250634

Crawford, C. M. (1979). New Product Failure Rates - Facts and Fallacies. *Research Management,* (September): 9–13.

Crawford, C. M. (1987). New Product Failure Rates: A Reprise. *Research Management,* (July-August): 20–24.

Di Gregerio, D., & Shane, S. A. (2003). Why some universities generate more start-ups than others? *Research Policy, 32,* 209–227. doi:10.1016/S0048-7333(02)00097-5

Dickson, P., Schneier, W., Lawrence, P., & Hytry, R. (1995). Managing Design in Small High-Growth Companies. *Journal of Product Innovation Management, 12*(5), 406–414. doi:10.1016/0737-6782(95)00056-9

Dowling, M., & Helm, R. (2006). Product development success through cooperation: A study of entrepreneurial firms. *Technovation, 26*(4), 483–488. doi:10.1016/j.technovation.2005.06.015

Easingwood, C. J., & Lunn, S. O. (1992). Diffusion Paths in A High-Tech Environment: Clusters and Commonalities. *R & D Management, 1,* 69–80. doi:10.1111/j.1467-9310.1992.tb00789.x

Harnett, D. L. (1982). *Statistical Methods* (3rd ed.). Reading, MA: Addison Wesley.

Henderson, R. M., & Clark, K. B. (1990). Architectural Innovation. *Administrative Science Quarterly, 35*(March), 9–30. doi:10.2307/2393549

Hof, R. (1992, June 1). Inside Intel: It's moving at Double-Time to head off competitors. *Business Week,* 86-94.

Hof, R. (1995, February 20). Intel: Far beyond the Pentium. *Business Week,* 88-90.

Kleinschmidt, E. J., & Cooper, R. G. (1991). The Impact of Product Innovativeness on Performance. *Journal of Product Innovation Management, 8,* 240–251. doi:10.1016/0737-6782(91)90046-2

Leifer, R., McDermott, C. M., O'Connor, G. C., Peters, L. S., Rice, M. P., & Veryzer, R. W. (2000). *Radical Innovation: How Mature Companies Can Outsmart Upstarts.* Boston: Harvard Business School Press.

Lynn, G. S., Morone, J. G., & Paulson, A. S. (1996). Marketing and Discontinuous Innovation: The Probe and Learn Process. *California Management Review, 38*(3), 8–37.

Mansfield, E. (1968). *Industrial Research and Technological Innovation; An Econometric Analysis*. London: Longmans, Green & Co.

Miles, I. (1988). *Home Informatics. Information technology and the transformation of everyday life*. London: Pinter.

Moriarty, R. T., & Kosnik, T. J. (1989). High-tech marketing: concepts, continuity, and change. *Sloan Management Review, 7*, 7–17.

Nerkar, A., & Shane, S. (2007). Determinants of invention commercialization: an empirical examination of academically sourced inventions. *Strategic Management Journal, 28*(11), 1155–1166. doi:10.1002/smj.643

North, D. C. (1990). *Institutions, institutional change and economic performances*. Cambridge, UK: Cambridge University Press.

Olleros, F. (1986). Emerging Industries and the Burnout of Pioneers. *Journal of Product Innovation Management, 1*, 5–18. doi:10.1016/0737-6782(86)90039-1

Ortt, J. R., & Delgoshaie, N. (2008, April 6-10). Why does it take so long before the diffusion of new high-tech products takes off? In *Proceedings of IAMOT (International Association for Management of Technology) conference*, Dubai, UAE

Ortt, J. R., & Schoormans, J. P. L. (2004). The Pattern of Development and Diffusion of Breakthrough Communication Technologies. *European Journal of Innovation Management, 7*(4), 292–302. doi:10.1108/14601060410565047

Pech, R. J. (2003). Memetics and innovation: profit through balanced meme management. *European Journal of Innovation Management, 6*(2), 111–117. doi:10.1108/14601060310475264

Rabino, S., & Wright, R. (1993). Accelerated Product Introductions and Emerging Managerial Accounting Perspectives: Implications for Marketing Managers in the Technology Sector. *Journal of Product Innovation Management, 10*(2), 126–135. doi:10.1016/0737-6782(93)90004-A

Rink, D. R., & Swan, J. E. (1979). Product Life Cycle Research: A Literature Review. *Journal of Business Research*, 219–242. doi:10.1016/0148-2963(79)90030-4

Rogers, E. M. (1986). *Communication Technology. The New Media in Society*. New York: The Free Press.

Rogers, E. M. (2005). *Diffusion of Innovations. New York: The Free Press.Shane, S. A. (2004). Academic Entrepreneurship*. Cheltenham, UK: Edward Elgar Publishers.

Sherman, J. D., Souder, W. E., & Jenssen, S. A. (2000). Differential Effects of the Primary Forms of Cross Functional Integration on Product Development Cycle Time. *Journal of Product Innovation Management, 17*(4), 257–267. doi:10.1016/S0737-6782(00)00046-1

Steffens, J. (1994). *New Games: Strategic Competition in the PC Revolution*. New York: Pergamon Press.

Teece, D. J., & Pisano, G. (1994). Dynamic capabilities and strategic management. *Industrial and Corporate Change, 3*, 537–556. doi:10.1093/icc/3.3.537-a

Tellis, G. J., & Golder, P. N. (1996). First to Market, First to Fail? Real Causes of Enduring Market Leadership. *Sloan Management Review*, (Winter): 65–75.

Thomke, S. H. (2003). *Experimentation Matters. Unlocking the Potential of New Technologies for innovation*. Boston: Harvard Business School Press.

Tushman, M. L., & Anderson, P. (1986). Technological Discontinuities and Organizational Environments. *Administrative Science Quarterly, 31,* 439–465. doi:10.2307/2392832

Tushman, M. L., & Rosenkopf, L. (1992). Organizational Determinants of Technological Change. Towards a Sociology of Technological Evolution. *Research in Organizational Behavior, 14,* 311–347.

Utterback, J. M., & Brown, J. W. (1972). Monitoring for Technological Opportunities. *Business Horizons, 15*(October), 5–15. doi:10.1016/0007-6813(72)90042-0

Van den Bulte, C. (2000). New Product Diffusion Acceleration: Measurement and Analysis. *Marketing Science, 19*(4), 366–380. doi:10.1287/mksc.19.4.366.11795

Verity, J. (1992, November 23). Deconstructing the Computer Industry. *Business Week,* 90-100.

Veryzer, R. W. (1998). Key Factors Affecting Customer Evaluation of Discontinuous New Products. *Journal of Product Innovation Management, 15,* 136–150. doi:10.1016/S0737-6782(97)00075-1

Williams, F., Rice, R. E., & Rogers, E. M. (1988). *Research Methods and the New Media.* New York: The Free Press.

Williamson, O. E. (1996). *The Mechanisms of Governance.* New York: Oxford University Press.

KEY TERMS AND DEIFINITIONS

Adaptation Phase: Begins after the (first) market introduction of a new high-tech product and ends with the start of the large-scale production and diffusion of this product.

High-Tech Products: products, materials or components based on breakthrough technologies and representing an advance that is so significant that attainable price/performance ratios are altered dramatically or entirely new kinds of applications are enabled (Tushman & Anderson, 1986).

Innovation Phase: Comprises the period from the invention of a technology up to the (first) market introduction of a new high-tech product based on that technology.

Invention: the first time a technology, *i.e.* the technical principle of a new high-tech product, is demonstrated and mastered.

Large-Scale Production and Diffusion: is defined using 3 elements: A standard product is required that can be reproduced multiple times (or standard product modules that can be combined in many different ways but are based on the same standard product platform); A (large-scale) production unit with dedicated production lines (industrial production of a standard product); and (Large-scale) diffusion of the product.

Market Introduction: the first time that a product is available for sales or can be transferred to users *(also referred to as introduction date or introduction)*

Pattern of Development and Diffusion of High-Tech Products: The pattern from the invention of a technology up to the complete substitution of a type of product based on that technology. The general pattern comprises three phases, an innovation, adaptation and stabilization phase. In the case of specific high-tech products one or more of the phases may not appear.

Pre-Diffusion Phases: The period between the invention of a technology and the start of large-scale production and diffusion of products based on that technology. In general, the pre-diffusion phases refer to both the innovation and the adaptation phase but in the case of specific high-tech products one of these phases may not appear.

Product Life Cycle: The time period after the pre-diffusion phases, *i.e.* the time-interval from the start of large-scale production and diffusion of a high-tech product until the complete substitution of that product. The product life cycle coincides with the stabilization phase in the pattern of development and diffusion for high-tech products.

That seems in contrast with other definitions of the product life cycle: *extending from the time it is first placed on the market until it is removed* (Rink & Swan, 1979). The latter definition implies that the product life cycle comprises both the adaptation and the stabilization phase. The so-called bell-shaped product life cycle, however, is typically a curve representing the sales of a standard product from the time of large-scale production and diffusion on. The adaptation phase is a more erratic phase in which different product variants and or customer segments are explored before the "standard" product emerges.

Stabilization Phase: Begins with the large-scale production and diffusion of a high-tech product and ends when that type of product is substituted completely.

APPENDIX

Table 2. high-tech products with year of invention, mass production and the length of the pre-diffusion phases

Cases	Invention	Large-scale production	Pre-diffusion phases
ABS	1936	1978	42
Air conditioning	1902	1915	13
Airbag	1953	1988	35
Aircraft	1903	1914	11
Antibiotics	1928	1943	15
Aspirin	1853	1900	47
Astroturf	1964	1966	2
Bakelite	1907	1911	4
Ballpoint	1888	1945	57
Barcodes	1952	1974	22
Bluetooth	1998	2000	2
Browser	1990	1994	4
Cellophane	1908	1912	4
Contraceptive pill	1927	1962	35
Cruise control	1954	1958	4
CT-scanner	1967	1974	7
Digital camera	1970	1980	10
DNA fingerprinting	1984	1994	10
DVD	1995	1996	1
Dynamite	1866	1867	1
Dyneema	1964	1990	26
Electron microscope	1931	1939	8
Fax	1851	1948	97
Fiber optic comm	1966	1983	17
GPS	1958	1979	21
Hearing aid	1892	1899	7
Helicopter	1922	1942	20
Jet-engine	1937	1943	6
Kevlar	1965	1973	8
Laser	1960	1980	20
Magnetic recording	1898	1933	35
Memory metal	1961	1972	11
Microwave-oven	1946	1955	9
Mobile telephony	1924	1983	59

continued on the following page

Table 2. continued

Cases	Invention	Large-scale production	Pre-diffusion phases
MRI	1973	1983	10
Nuclear bomb	1945	1947	2
Nuclear power plant	1951	1957	6
Nylon	1934	1940	6
Optical disc	1962	1982	20
Photocopier	1938	1960	22
Plasma display	1964	2000	36
PVC	1838	1938	100
Radar	1904	1939	35
SMS	1992	1999	7
Sonar	1915	1917	2
Telegraphy	1837	1844	7
Television	1927	1946	19
Transistor	1947	1953	6
Turbo charger	1872	1923	51
VCR	1951	1957	6
Wankel-Engine	1957	1964	7
X-ray	1895	1896	1
Av length pre-diffusion (st dev)			**19.4 (21.8)**

Chapter 4
Links between Innovation, Change and Learning in Chinese Companies

Wei Sun
Estonian Business School, Estonia

Ruth Alas
Estonian Business School, Estonia

ABSTRACT

This chapter is an attempt to explore the links between the types of innovation, the types of organizational change and levels of learning based on a study of 160 Chinese organizations. The authors provide the classification of innovation, organizational change and learning as the theoretical framework. On the basis of survey results, the authors find out there are close connections between the three aspects: innovation type, change type and learning type. There is a direct link between the types of innovation and learning in lower level. However, in the companies which experienced administrative innovation and ancillary innovation, the rate of occurrence of triple-loop learning is almost the same. Moreover, there is not necessarily corresponding relation between the types of innovation and change. Despite the fact that the highest level of innovation is accompanied by the deepest change, the lowest level of innovation may not be necessarily accompanied by the lower level change, i.e. the deepest scope of change may take place even if the lowest level of innovation happens in a Chinese organization.

INTRODUCTION

Innovation is defined as the general organizational processes and procedures for generating, considering, and acting on novel and useful insights leading to significant organizational improvements in terms of improved or new business products, services, or internal processes (Wikipedia, 2006). In the organizational context, Innovation is generally understood as the introduction of a new thing or method. Innovation is the embodiment, combination, or synthesis of knowledge in original, relevant, valued new products, processes, or services (Luecke & Katz, 2003).Organizational change designates a fundamental and radical reorientation in the way the organization operates (McNamara, 2001). In the process of innovation and change, learning occurs.

DOI: 10.4018/978-1-61520-643-8.ch004

This paper is an attempt to explore the links between the types of innovation, the types of organizational change and levels of learning based on a study of 160 Chinese organizations.

China's development has attracted more and more attention from around the world. Dramatic changes taking place in the past two decades in China has also become a focus of study for different researchers. This study on the connections between types of innovation, organizational change and learning in Chinese organizations will contribute to innovation and change management and will be useful to Chinese managers who attempt to implement innovation or changes in their organizations.

LITERATURE REVIEW

Innovation in Organization

The primary criterion for survival and growth of an individual or organization is fitness for future. Fitness for future is primary a function of the development of skills and capabilities related to improving performance and managing change. Innovation and creativity are the driving force behind change, adaptation and evolution. Human creativity is the source of the new possibilities and hope of dreams, action and accomplishment. It is also a source of uncertainty and insecurity.

A convenient definition of innovation from an organizational perspective is given by Luecke and Katz (2003), who wrote: *Innovation is generally understood as the successful introduction of a new thing or method. Innovation is the embodiment, combination, or synthesis of knowledge in original, relevant, valued new products, processes, or services.* Innovation typically involves creativity, but is not identical to it: innovation involves acting on the creative ideas to make some specific and tangible difference in the domain in which the innovation occurs (Amabile et al, 1996). For innovation to occur, something more than the gen-

eration of a creative idea or insight is required: the insight must be ***put into action*** to make a genuine difference, resulting for example in new or altered business processes within the organization, or changes in the products and services provided.

A further characterization of innovation is as an organizational or management process. For example, Davila et al (2006), write: *Innovation, like many business functions, is a management process that requires specific tools, rules, and discipline.* From this point of view, the emphasis is moved from the introduction of specific novel and useful ideas to the general organizational processes and procedures for generating, considering, and acting on such insights leading to significant organizational improvements in terms of improved or new business products, services, or internal processes.

Types of Innovation

Normally innovation could be divided into three classifications: technical innovation, administrative innovation, and ancillary innovation. Technical innovation occur within the primary work activity of the organization, administrative innovations occur within the social system and are concerned with the organization of work and the relationships between organizational members (Damanpour & Evan, 1984). Ancillary innovation spans organizational-environment boundaries and go beyond the primary work functions of the organization (Damanpour, 1990).

There is also classification which distinguishes innovations as programmed or non-programmed; instrumental or ultimate; and according to radicalness (Zaltman et al, 1973). Programmed innovations are scheduled in advance, non-programmed are slack, distress and proactive innovations (King Anderson, 2002). Ultimate innovation is introduced as an end in itself, instrumental innovation is a mean to facilitate the adoption of a further innovation. Radicalness involves novelty and riskiness (Zaltman et al, 1973).

In this chapter the author mainly deals with the first classification: technical innovation, administrative innovation, and ancillary innovation.

Types of Change

The organizational change could be also divided into three types: developmental, transitional and transformational.

Ackerman (1984) has developed a model describing three types of organizational change: (1) developmental change, (2) transitional change, and (3) transformational change. Developmental change improves what already exists through the improvement of skills, methods, or conditions. Transitional change replaces current ways of doing things with something new over a controlled period of time. Transformational change means the emergence of a new state, unknown until it takes shape, out of the remains of the chaotic death of the old state.

The model created by Burke and Litwin (1992) helps to make a distinction between transformational and transactional changes. Transformational factors deal with areas that require different employee behavior as the consequence of external and internal environmental pressures. Transactional factors deal with psychological and organizational variables that predict and control the motivational and performance outcomes of the climate of the work group. Transactional change could be compared with transitional in Ackerman's terminology.

In content research most theorists divide change into two types according to scope: change taking place within the given system and change aiming to modify the system itself.

The most popular terms for this classification are first order change and second order change. First order change provides a method for managing stability. It helps one to manage current strategy more effectively and efficiently (Bartunek, 1993). This type of change proceeds via a sequential step-by-step assessment, guided by a specific objective, making systematic and rational evaluations of an organization and its environment. A first order change cannot produce transformation because it lacks the creativity to discover new strategic ideas (Hurst, 1986). Second order change calls for innovation in order to lead the change. It searches for agreement about what the end result should be and then considers how an organization could be changed to meet these new expectations. Second order change is difficult to carry out because information gathering in an organization will tend to reify the rules, culture, strategy and core processes that make up its current paradigm (Nutt & Backoff, 1997).

In this paper the author adopts the first classification of types of change: developmental, transitional and transformational.

Organizational Learning

The ability to adapt to change is enhanced through learning, both at individual and organizational levels (Garvin, 1993; Senge, 1997). The concept of a learning organization, which has gained popularity among practitioners since 1990 through Senge's book, "The Fifth Discipline", about the art and practice of the learning organization, has been developed to increase an organization's ability to adapt to change. Learning, both institutional and individual, and the ensuing corporate changes are seen as a prerequisite for the success and survival of organizations irrespective of their size and sector. A learning organization is good at creating new solutions and good at sharing knowledge with other members who may need it (Sugarman, 2001). It is the antithesis of the traditional bureaucratic organization (Driver, 2002).

Organizational learning has been generally defined as a vital process by which organizations adapt to change in their social, political, or economic settings (Rosenstiel & Koch, 2001). One critical issue in the literature dealing with the learning organization is the relationship between *individual and organizational learning*. According to Senge (1997), organizations learn only through learning individuals. But individual learning does not guarantee organizational learning. Organizational learning emphasizes a socially constructed process, which proceeds through sharing interpretations of events and through reflection on these interpretations (Mahler, 1997). Organizational learning is unique to an institution (Probst & Büchel, 1997) and differences occur as a result of differences in company history, culture, size, and age (DiBella & Nevis, 1998).

There are barriers to learning as there is resistance to change. These barriers exist due to the fundamental, conflicting ways in which individuals have been trained to think and act and include organizational barriers to discovering and using solutions to organizational problems (DiBella & Nevis, 1998). According to Salaman and Butler (1999), resistance to learning may stem from the culture and structure of the organization. The past organizational experiences of the members of the organization enable or hinder the 'learning process' equally. However, this is not easy to establish as it relates to what we may understand and interpret learning to be. If learning implies a 'change in behavior and mind set', resistance may be the outcome of as well as the barrier to learning.

Argyris (1990) identified skilled incompetence, organizational defensive routines and 'fancy footwork' as mechanisms and ways by which organizations and their people stick to the familiar and avoid uncertain and perceived threats. Here organizational memory and thus the internal stock of routines constitute the barriers to unlearning, which is *per se* a form of or the outcome of learning (also Hedberg, 1981). Nyström and Starbuck (1984) connect organizational learning with the unlearning of past methods and Senge (1997) stresses the unlearning of the old before the learning of the new.

Developing organizational learning requires the ability to work together as a team (Senge, 1997). Learning does not take place solely in the minds of individuals but rather stems from the

participation of individuals in social activities (Gherardi & Nicolini, 2001). In order to understand the relationship between institutionalization and organizational learning, the social construction of cultural systems appear to be central. Also, it has been stated, that creating lasting organizational change is inextricably linked with culture change (Manring, 2003).

Types of Learning

Learning can be grouped as single-loop, double-loop and triple-loop. Argyris and Schön (1978) differentiate single-loop learning and double-loop learning. Bateson (1973) defines four levels of learning: zero, single- and double-loop and deutero-learning. In case of zero-learning members fail to take corrective actions.

Single-loop learning means correcting the behavior, adding to the knowledge base, firm-specific competencies or routines without altering the nature of the activities (Maula, 1999). In single-loop learning individuals or groups make simple adaptive responses to environmental changes. But they adjust their behavior relative to fixed goals, norms, and assumptions. Plans are changed in the light of events, but basic assumptions remain the same. Members are helped to develop learning agendas and career paths to fit existing jobs and structures (Snell & Chak, 1998).

Double-loop learning means testing the assumptions and changing the governing values (Maula, 1999). In double-loop learning members are changing their views of their roles, of the business or of the business environment. Goals, norms, and assumptions are open to change, mental maps are transforming to generate new meanings and actions. Governing values may change on reflection in the light of them. Shared models are developed to represent dynamics of system and to help decision-makers. "Groupthink" is avoided by arranging many opportunities for members to be exposed to and to appreciate other business

Table 1. Connections between change, learning and innovation

Type of change	Development	Transition	Transformation	Ackerman 1984
Type of Learning	Single-loop	Double-loop	Triple-loop	Argyris, Schön 1978
Result	Change in action	Change in goals	Change in basic assumptions and thinking	Probst, Büshler 1997
Type of Innovation	Technical	Administrative	Ancillary	Damanpour,1984, 1990
Process	Preparation → Change → Evaluation	Preparation → Mobilization → Change → Evaluation	Crash → Creative process → Preparation → Mobilization → Change → Evaluation	

cultures and ways of thinking. Devil's advocacy and unusual ideas are valued and essential to performance breakthroughs. Flexible working patterns and reward schemes are designed for varied cases (Snell & Chak, 1998).

Triple-loop learning entails members developing new processes or methodologies for moving from paradigm-shifts to paradigm invention. Ongoing attempts are made to increase the openness of channels representing the full diversity of all stakeholder opinion, and to create policies which represent a critically reasoned response to issues raised. Assumptions behind all "information" and built into models of what is going on, are constantly reappraised in the light of users' experience. Assumptions about the rights of seniors and subordinates and internal customers and suppliers are questioned, and various means of improving open communication and mutual goal-setting explored. Structures remain flexible to allow initiative. (Snell & Chak, 1998).

Deutero-learning involves learning how to learn and is used for highest level of organizational learning. (Cummings & Worley, 1997).

Connections between Change, Learning and Innovation

There are links between types of change, learning and innovation as the following table illustrates.

METHODOLOGY

The research is based on interviews conducted with 160 managers from different organizations covering different industries.

The survey was carried out in 160 companies in several big cities in northern part of China: Beijing, Tianjin, Jinan and Zibo. Structured interviews were conducted with top managers or middle managers from different companies to acquire about change in their organizations. The questions in the interview were adopted from the survey conducted in Estonian organizations in 2001. The companies involved represented various industries and sectors, ranging from manufacturing and technology, banking and insurance organizations, to those in energy and education industries.

Among 160 companies, in 39.4% of companies, the top manager or CEO answered the questions. In 40% of the organizations, deputy directors or vice general manager were interviewed. The rest of the respondents are working as middle managers in different functional departments, of which 5% and 3.8% were respectively specialized in HR and marketing. The others were responsible for other departments, such as finance (3.1%), sales (2.5%), project management (2.5%), assistance (2.5%) and customer service (1.3%). All interviewees have experienced the recent organizational change in their organizations, and have been directly involved in strategy formulation and implementation.

Most questions were open-ended, however, in some cases closed-ended questions were used, for example, in order to figure out the factors which had changed in the process of changes. The interviews were first analyzed individually to identify issues relating to organizational change and then compared and summarized.

RESULTS AND DISCUSSION

Research Findings

On the basis of survey results, the authors find out the types of change, innovation and learning occurring in the sample companies and the links between them.

First of all, regarding the types of change, a fairly large percentage of companies underwent transformational change, deepest by scope while only 5% of companies witnessed developmental change. Only 5% of the changes were developmental changes. Meanwhile, 41.3% of the changes were transitional and 53.7% were transformational.

According to the survey, only 5% of the changes in Chinese organizations were developmental changes, which normally took place in one department. The examples can be the introduction of new software into the technological department or adjusting new systems within one department. Meanwhile, 41% of the changes were transitional and 54% were transformational in Chinese companies. As Chinese economy is still on the way towards transferring to market economy from planning economy, half of the organizations in the survey experienced dramatic changes in ownership transforming or business state transforming. For example, some state-owned enterprises experienced the transforming to a private limited company; some small state-owned enterprises were merged into a large-scale one, or some enterprises

were acquired by private owners or foreign investors. Even some governmental agencies under the planning economy system were transformed to independently-run companies or affiliates of local authorities.

Another fact should be taken into consideration, i.e. Chinese companies, especially some big production plants, were quite old with a long history of several decades or even longer. The author compared the companies founded before and after the economic reform (1978). The results revealed that more changes took place in the companies which were founded before 1978, normally state-owned or collective enterprises. In 90% of the companies, established before the drastic economic reform began, strategy changed. In 80% of these companies leadership were changed. Along with the national economic reform, government realized the urgency to change the previously centralized decision-making to more democratic leadership style in state-owned enterprises and made efforts to create a suitable environment for the cultivation of new leadership. In 78% of older companies mission, system and management practice were changed. Even organizational culture, normally regarded as an element hard to change, changed in 74% of the enterprises founded before 1978. This is mainly associated with the change of the whole system and management style. Under the planning economy their job was life-long and regarded as "iron rice bowl". Under the new system where the salary was distributed on the basis of the quality of work and competition system, employees were more initiated to be dedicated to their job.

In younger companies less change took place compared to the situation in older companies; however, the changes were still significant. Faced with the market economy and the enterprise reform, companies founded after 1978 were also active in implementing change. 77% of companies changed strategy, although the percentage is less than that of older companies, which indicated that great efforts had been made to adjust to the market economy and survive in the fiercer competition after the accession to WTO. Accompanying changes in transformational factors, all transactional factors had been changed in the organizations established after 1978, of which task requirements were changed in 69% of companies, larger than 62% of older companies. It can be seen that under the new price-driven market economy, younger companies were aware of the great importance to implement change in order to survive, keep competitive advantage and make more profits.

Secondly, in terms of types of innovation, according to the results, in almost half of the organizations administrative innovation took place while an almost equal number - a quarter, of the companies experienced technical and ancillary innovation respectively.

In 23.1% companies technical innovation occurred where the primary tasks of the organization changed, e.g. the company launched new products onto the market, adjusted their product range or created a new department inside the company.

For example, the general manager of a training company explained the process to establish a department in charge of the administrative work. The new department was parallel to language training department, overseas study department and accounting department. The vice general manager was appointed as the temporary manager of the new department.

Administrative innovations happened in 46.9% of organizations. The examples included the HR reform inside the company, the changes in the system and the structure, the change of employees' roles at work and the implementation of a new policy.

For example, the manager of one logistics company said that the top management group decided to change the managing system inside the company. The power of the headquarter was decentralized. The managers in sub-branches of the company were given more rights and freedom to make decisions, e.g. they could recruit employees and arrange daily administrative work by themselves. In this way the managers in lower level were motivated at work.

30.0% organizations underwent ancillary innovation, which went beyond the basic task of the organization. The most typical examples were privatization of State-Owned Enterprises, merging or acquisition between enterprises.

For example, a state-owned energy factory called Mingshui Energy located in northern part of China was privatized and merged into a large-scale private fertilizer production limited group called Dahua Group. First the Energy plant was liquidated. Then under the supervision of National Capital Bureau, National Development and Reform Bureau and National Economy Planning Committee, Mingshui Energy was successfully transferred to a sub-company of Dahua Group. Dahua Group made decisions on the change in finance and personnel arrangement in the previous individual company.

Thirdly, in terms of the types of learning, in 28.8% of companies single-loop learning took place. 45% and 26.3% of companies respectively experienced double-loop and triple-loop learning.

The following were some examples to give more vivid picture of the level of learning in Chinese organizations.

Firstly, an example of the single-loop learning was described. The top leader in a comprehensive hospital described a change and the situation in organizational learning as follows: The Eye Department in the hospital was separate from the headquarter and a new Eye Professional Hospital was built on the basis of the personnel and resources in the previous Eye Department. The staff in the hospital accepted the changes easily and believed this was beneficial to both old and new hospitals and the society. The staff in Eye Department made great efforts to improve their professional knowledge and skills during the period when the new hospital was established. The other staff supported them at work, meanwhile the top management group provided aid to them, e.g. organized training program for professional doctors and took managers for new hospital to visit famous Eye Hospital in order to equip them with updated managing competencies.However, the nature and daily routine of the hospital didn't alter.

Secondly, in almost half of the Chinese companies covered in the interview, second level of learning took place. The author selected an example of double-loop learning from the interview results. A big construction company in Jinan experienced a change in the managing system and the learning could be labeled as double-loop learning. After the company became listed in Hong Kong stock exchange market, the factory head and communist party secretary system were replaced by board committee, which was more democratic-oriented style. The power of head was decentralized and the management group became more democratic, e.g. they started more attention to employees' inner emotional needs.

Thirdly, about one quarter of Chinese organizations experienced highest level of learning. For example, a state-owned plant in a conservative city in northern China was acquired by a foreign company. The employees in the beginning were quite upset about the change. They were worried about their future in the plant. They were definitely not familiar with the new management system and daily work routine. They were also worried about their job responsibilities and the pay. However, they were ready to learn. They were happy to attend training seminars on the skills improvement. They started to understand that relationships now are not prior to work performance. They gradually accepted the deal-focused corporate culture at work although sometimes they were unhappy to be recorded as being late even if they were just 1 minute late, which previously was ignored. It was hard time for them to abandon their mindset, which was rooted in very hierarchical and relationship-focused Chinese culture. However, they were ready to learn and made efforts to adapt to totally new environment.

Discussion on the Links

The findings revealed there are close connections between the three aspects: innovation type, change type and learning type.

In the companies undergoing the technical innovation, three quarters of them experienced transitional change while 16% and 8% respectively saw developmental and transformational change. The process of changes in the companies undergoing the technical innovation involved preparation, implementation of change and evaluation of change. However, more attention was paid to preparation, e.g. communication and education with the employees. The evaluation was rather ignored. However, in Chinese organizations, people got accustomed to technical innovation after a period even if not so much work was done to consolidate the results of changes. Moreover, with regards to the link between technical innovation and single-loop learning, there is a corresponding link between these two factors. In the companies where technical innovation took place, the level of learning remained at the first level - single-loop at a rate of 100%.People in these organizations simply adapted their behaviors or improved their knowledge, however, the primary rules and functions of company didn't change at all.

In the companies which experienced administrative innovation, developmental change rarely took place whereas mostly triple-loop learning took place. In companies where administrative innovation occurs, only 1.3% underwent developmental changes. 46.7% and 52.0% companies experienced transitional changes and transformational changes, the deepest by scope. Therefore, the change process in these companies was more complex than that in those companies witnessing technical innovation. The preparation wais definitely needed. Mobilization was added before the implementation of changes as the good approaches of educating the employees of the importance of changes and encouraging them to participate in the changes could help make the process smoother and more effective. In these companies undergoing administrative innovation, the learning level was quite high. In 88% of these companies triple-loop learning occurred while double-loop learning occurred in 12% of them. In Chinese organizations the biggest obstacle to change and innovation was inertia in people's thinking. Due to the profound influence of socialism political regime and the centrally-planned economy regime, people tended to stick to what they believe and resist new ideas. Therefore, in these companies the third level learning already happened, where people reassessed the previous information and thoughts.

Considering the companies where the deepest innovation - ancillary innovation happened, about 90% of them experienced the deepest change – transformational and the deepest level of learning - triple-loop. As ancillary innovation spans the social system and involves more parties in society, the process of changes took longer time and required more efforts. In the beginning, the companies created plans for change and then according to plan thorough preparations were carried out, e.g. before the privatization of a SOE, the financial data were checked and election program of new leader group were organized. Anyway, preparation was a significant step in the whole process. Then detailed and organized work was done to empower and mobilize employees. Following the implementation, the consolidation helped to assess the results and improve the shortcomings. The change results were institutionalized. In companies where ancillary innovation happened, the level of learning was approximately the same as that in companies undergoing administrative innovation. In 88% of the companies where ancillary innovation happened, very high level learning - triple-loop learning occurred while double-loop learning occurred in 12% of them. These companies witnessed drastic changes, e.g. the ownership changed, so people's mentality and learning habits also changed. The basic rules and assumptions were changed and completely new processes of thinking and behaving were also developed.

CONCLUSION

To sum up, there are certain connections between the types of types of change, innovation and learning in Chinese organizations.

There is a direct link between the types of innovation and learning in lower level, i.e. in companies with lowest level of innovation, the lowest level of learning occurred. However, in the companies which experienced administrative innovation and ancillary innovation, the rate of occurrence of triple-loop learning is almost the same, achieving 88%. This phenomenon can be explained by Chinese people's persistence to old thinking. Even administrative innovation requires the facilitation of highest level of learning.

However, there is no necessarily corresponding relation between the types of innovation and change. The highest level of innovation is always accompanied by deepest change, nevertheless, the lowest level of innovation may not be necessarily accompanied by lower level change, and i.e. deepest scope of change may take place even if lowest level of innovation happens in a Chinese organization.

The findings imply that in Chinese organizations the managers should be aware of the following points. One point is that in order to facilitate innovation, changes should be implemented more thoroughly and especially more attention should be paid to institutionalization in the process of changes. Another significant point is that since innovation and changes in Chinese organizations require very high level of learning, managers should learn to equip themselves with skills to facilitate employees' learning and overcome the inertia in people's thinking style.

ACKNOWLEDGMENT

Research was supported by ETF grant 7537.

REFERENCES

Ackerman, L. S. (1986). Development, Transition or Transformation: The Question of Change in Organizations. *Organizational Development Practitioner, December*, 1-8.

Amabile, T. M., Conti, R., Coon, H., Lazenby, J., & Herron, M. (1996). Assessing the work environment for creativity. *Academy of Management Journal*, *39*, 1154. doi:10.2307/256995

Argyris, C. (1990). *Overcoming Organizational Defences: Facilitating Organizational Learning*. Boston: Allyn & Bacon.

Argyris, C., & Schön, D. (1978). *Organizational Learning: A Theory-in-Action Perspective*. Reading, MA: Addison-Wesley.

Bartunek, J. M. (1993). The Multiple Cognitions and Conflicts Associated with Second Order Organizational Change. In Murnighan, J. K. (Ed.), *Social Psychology in Organizations: Advances in Theory and Research*. Upper Saddle River, NJ: Prentice Hall.

Bateson, G. (1973). *Steps to Ecology of Mind*. London: Palladin.

Burke, W., & Litwin, G. (1992). A Casual Model of Organisational Performance and Change. *Journal of Management*, *18*, 523–545. doi:10.1177/014920639201800306

Cummings, T. G., & Worley, C. G. (1997). *Organization Development and Change* (6th ed.). South-Western College Publishing.

Damanpour, F. (1990). Innovation effectiveness, adoption and organizational performance. In West, M. A., & Farr, J. L. (Eds.), *Innovation and Creativity at work: Psychological and Organizational Strategies*. Chichester, UK: Wiley.

Damanpour, F., & Evan, W. M. (1984). Organizational innovation and performance: The problem of 'organizational lag'. *Administrative Science Quarterly*, *29*, 392–409. doi:10.2307/2393031

Davila, T., Epstein, M. J., & Shelton, R. (2006). *Making Innovation Work: How to Manage It, Measure It, and Profit from It*. Upper Saddle River, NJ: Wharton School Publishing.

DiBella, A. J., & Nevis, E. C. (1998). *How Organizations Learn. An Integreted Strategy for Building Learning Capability*. San Francisco: Jossey-Bass Publishers.

Driver, M. (2002). The learning organization: Foucauldian gloom or utopian sunshine? *Human Relations*, *55*(1), 33–53. doi:10.1177/0018726702055001605

Ghererdi, S., & Nicolini, D. (2001). The Sociological Foundation of Organizational learning. In Dierkes, M., Antal, A. B., Child, J., & Nonaka, I. (Eds.), *Organizational Learning and Knowledge*. Oxford, UK: Oxford University Press.

Hedberg, B. (1981). IIow Organisations Learn and Unlearn. In Nystrom, P. C., & Starbuck, W. H. (eds.), Handbook of Organisational Design. London

Hurst, D. K. (1986). 'Why Strategic Management is Bankrupt'. *Organizational Dynamics, Spring*, 5-27. Garvin, D. A., (1993). Building a Learning Organization. *Harvard Business Review*, (July-August): 78–91.

King, N., & Anderson, N. (2002). *Managing innovation and change: A critical guide for organizations*. Tampa, FL: Thomson.

Luecke, R., & Katz, R. (2003). *Managing Creativity and Innovation*. Boston: Harvard Business School Press.

Mahler, J. (1997). Influences of Organizational Culture on Learning in Public Agencies. *Journal of Public Administration: Research and Theory*, *7*(4), 519–541.

Manring, S. L. (2003). How do you create lasting organizational change? You must first slay Grendel's mother. In Woodman, R. W., & Pasmore, W. A. (Eds.), Research in Organizational Change and Development, 14, 195-224. Greenwich, UK: JAI Press.

Maula, M. (1999). *Multinational Companies As Learning and Evolving Systems: A Multiple-case Study of Knowledge-Intensive Service Companies. An application of Autopoiesis Theory*. Helsinki, Finland: Helsinki School of Economics and Business Administration.

McNamara, C. (n.d.). *Basic Context for Organizational Change*. Free Management Library. Retrieved Janurary 14, 2007, from h ttp://www.managementhelp.org/mgmnt/orgchnge.htm

Nutt, P. C., & Backoff, R. W. (1997). Crafting Vision. *Journal of Management Inquiry*, 6(4), 308–329. doi:10.1177/105649269764007

Nyström, P. C., & Starbuck, W. H. (1984). To Avoid Organizational Crises, Unlearn. *Organizational Dynamics*, (Spring): 53–65. doi:10.1016/0090-2616(84)90011-1

Probst, G., & Bücher, B. (1997). *Organizaional Learning. The Competitive Advantage of the Future*. Upper Saddle River, NJ: Prentice Hall.

Rosenstiel, L., & Koch, S. (2001). Change in Socioeconomic values as a trigger of Organisational learning. In Dierkes, M., Antal, A. B., Child, J., & Nonaka, I. (Eds.), *Organisational Learning and Knowledge*. Oxford, UK: Oxford University Press.

Salaman, G., & Butler, J. (1999). Why Managers Won't Learn. In Mabey, C., & Iles, P. (eds.), Managing Learning, 34-42, International Thompson Business Press.

Senge, P. M. (1997). *The Fifth Distcipline. The Art and Practice of the Learning Organisation*. Century Business.

Snell, R., & Chak, A. M.-Ky. (1998). The Learning Organization: Learning and Empowerment for whom? *Management Learning*, 29(3), 337–364. doi:10.1177/1350507698293005

Sugarman, B. (2001). A leaning-based approach to organizational change: Some results and Guidelines. *Organizational Dynamics*, 30(1), 62–67. doi:10.1016/S0090-2616(01)00041-9

Wikipedia. (n.d.). *Innovation*. Retrieved December 13, 2006, from www.en.wikipedia.org/wiki/Innovation

Zaltman, G., Duncan, R., & Holbek, J. (1973). *Innovation and Organizations*. New York: Wiley.

Chapter 5
What Makes Companies to be More Innovative and Profitable?

Ana Pérez-Luño
Pablo de Olavide University, Spain

Ramón Valle-Cabrera
Pablo de Olavide University, Spain

Johan Wiklund
Syracuse University, USA

ABSTRACT

The aims of this chapter are the following. First, we delimitate the innovation and imitation concepts. Secondly, using structural equation modeling method, we empirically test the impact of two dimensions of market and entrepreneurial orientations, respectively, on the decision to be more or less innovative. Thirdly, we relate this decision with the company's performance. Based on a survey of 304 companies, our empirical results support, on one hand, the view that proactivity is the most important determinant of the decision of weather to innovate or imitate. On the other hand, we find that the company's performance is not conditioned by the decision of innovating or imitating, but is rather determined by the company's proactivity and focus on customers.

INTRODUCTION

This chapter covers a review of the literature about the definition of "innovation" and "imitation" and some of their antecedents and performance consequences. In this sense, it is interesting to highlight that there is a wealth of studies that claim to demonstrate the positive effect of innovations on company's competitiveness. However, the management literature has forgotten that imitation is an organizational behavior that can also generate sustainable competitive advantages and, apart from very recent exceptions (Lieberman and Asaba, 2006; Zhou, 2006), imitation has only been analyzed from the point of view of a company that wishes to avoid being imitated (Barney, 1991) or of a company that may wish to encourage others to imitate it (McEvily et al., 2000). This situation, together with the lack of consensus on the conceptual delimitation of the terms "innovation" and "imitation", has led us to raise several research questions, such as: What are the differences between innovating and imitating?

DOI: 10.4018/978-1-61520-643-8.ch005

What factors determinate the firm's decision towards imitating or innovating? With the answers to these questions we contribute to the literature giving a clear conceptualization for the terms innovation and imitation. Our second contribution is empirically demonstrating that the different dispositions toward proactivity, risk taking, customers focus and competitors focus have a great impact on the decision to innovate or to imitate; and on the firms' performance. This analysis is conducted using environment dynamism, sophistication and firm size as control variables.

Build on the Resources Based View and the Contingency Theory, obtaining answers to these questions is the aim of this chapter.

In so doing, we make the following contributions to the literature. First, previous studies that have used models aimed at explaining variance in innovation have confounded imitation and innovation. That is, they have collectively estimated the extent to which firms innovate and imitate. For example, a common approach is to explain variance in new product releases, without considering that new products can be the result of innovation or imitation (Damanpour, 1991; Damanpour and Wischnevsky, 2006; Knight, 1967; Li and Atuahene-Gima, 2001). Instead, we explicitly address whether new market offers are the results of innovation or imitation and what drives this behavior.

Second, although the insight that firms can emphasize innovation or imitation is not new, we address it from a new vantage point. Previous research on innovation and imitation has only examined if one or the other is more profitable (Adner and Zemsky, 2006; Hodgson and Knudsen, 2006; Lieberman and Asaba, 2006; Lieberman and Montgomery, 1988; Lieberman and Montgomery, 1998; Pepall, 1997; Pérez-Luño et al., 2007; Trott and Hoecht, 2007; VanderWerf and Mahon, 1997; Zhou, 2006), and how companies avoid or encourage imitation (Barney, 1991; Conner, 1995; Kogut and Zander, 1993; MacMillan et al., 1985; Mansfield et al., 1981; Massa and Testa, 2004; McEvily et al., 2000; Rivkin, 2001).

In contrast, our study builds on the notion that firms can combine imitation and innovation and that the choice between the two is a matter of degree rather than a binary choice between two pure types of firms (innovators and imitators). We therefore explore the internal conditions that entice firms to emphasize imitation over innovation or vice versa and how this proclivity leads to a higher or lower performance.

The paper proceeds as follows. Firstly, after a bibliographic review of different conceptualizations utilized for the term innovation, we delimit the concepts of innovation and imitation. Secondly, we identify the factors that influence the firms' decision to innovate or to imitate. Thirdly, we empirically text how proactivity, risk taking, customers focus and competitors focus (dimensions usually analyzed as components of entrepreneurial and market orientation, respectively) influence the firm's to imitate or to innovate. Fourthly, we empirically analyze how this decision mediates the relation between these four factors and the company's performance.

DELIMITATION OF THE TERMS INNOVATION AND IMITATION

The review of the literature demonstrates that the results in the field of innovation have been inconclusive, inconsistent and characterized by limited explanatory power (Zmud, 1982; Wolfe, 1994; Becheikh et al., 2005; Damanpour and Wischnevsky, 2006). One possible explanation for the lack of similarity in the conclusions of researchers is the diverse range concepts, contexts, characteristics, types, stages, etc. used by different authors to study innovation. As a consequence, the current state of the organizational innovation literature offers little guidance to those interested in this concept (Wolfe, 1994; Damanpour and Wischnevsky, 2006).

Because of the different value judgments attached to the term, there are many problems in establishing a complete and tight definition of innovation. The only feature common to all the definitions is that innovation implies novelty (Schumpeter, 1961; Damanpour, 1991; Grossman and Helpman, 1991; Mahmood and Rufin, 2005). The way we see it, definitions of innovations differ along (at least) three important dimensions. The first dimension relates to whether or not the definition of innovation entails success for the innovating organization. Understanding by success, the achievement of the first sale (Nerkar and Shane, 2007). That is, for innovation, in contrast to the mere invention, the idea must be put into practice and be launched to the market (Damanpour, 1991; Schumpeter, 1961). The second aspect is referred to the subject of novelty. Is innovation linked to creating something that is "new to the world", or does it suffice to generate something that is new to the innovating organization only? The third differentiated dimension relates to the antecedents of innovation. Is innovation based on the combination of knowledge that gives rise to internally generated ideas, or can a firm innovate if it does not modify the knowledge and ideas of other firms at all? These questions have risen from an in-depth review of the literature in which we have found that while some authors consider that innovations should be new to the world (Grossman and Helpman, 1991; Mahmood and Rufin, 2005), be success in terms of being able to reach the market and result in a positive benefit (Grossman and Helpman, 1991; Knight, 1967; Schumpeter, 1961), and should be internally generated (Grossman and Helpman, 1991; Knight, 1967; Pérez-Luño et al., 2007; Subramaniam and Youndt, 2005), others do not mention any of these considerations.

In our case, we consider that, for innovation, in contrast to mere invention, the idea must be put into practice and reach the market (Damanpour, 1991; Schumpeter, 1961). That is, innovation entails success. Also, we understand that they will have to be new to the world and internally generated to be considered real innovations (Grossman and

Helpman, 1991; Mahmood and Rufin, 2005). In contrast, as we are going to explain next, if they are not new to the world or internally generated, they will be considered imitations.

There does seem to be a consensus in the literature that to imitate is to copy (Grossman and Helpman, 1991; Lieberman and Asaba, 2006; Mahmood and Rufin, 2005; Mansfieldet al., 1981; Zhou, 2006), although this statement does not clarify what is understood or implied by this copying activity or behaviour. Taking into account the three dimensions outlined to define innovation. We consider that imitation will also entail success. That is, for an imitation to be counted, the company that acquires external knowledge should be able to apply it and launch a product that reaches the market. However, we find that the other two dimensions used to delimitate the innovation concept, can be also used to differentiate it from imitations. That is to say, imitations will not be novel to the world and will not be based on internal generated knowledge (given that they are based on a copied knowledge). These assumptions lead us to understand that internal generation of knowledge and novelty operate jointly. The reason is that external ideas (not changed inside the firm), will also give rise to products that are already known in the market. If those external ideas are changed inside the firm, then, we would not be talking about external ideas, but rather we would be talking about the combination of external knowledge with internally developed knowledge, and then, the output could be new to the world. Lastly, we would not find internal ideas that give rise to known for the world products, because, as Schumpeter (1961) proposed, "the probability of two or more companies simultaneously developing the same innovation is so small, that it could be ignored". Therefore, we equally will not take this possibility into account here.

Some authors combine the three dimensions that we have identified to define innovations (success, novelty, and internal generation of the idea) and give a complete definition of what imitation implies. For example, Grossman and Helpman (1991) and Mahmood and Rufin (2005) argue that innovation is a form of technological development that not only expands a firm's existing knowledge set but also the existing world knowledge set, whereas they define imitation as the form of technological development that expands only the firm's existing knowledge set, and not the existing world knowledge set.

The most notable aspect of these author's innovation and imitation definitions is the statement that innovation expands the world's knowledge through its internal creation, while imitation only expands the firm's knowledge by the adoption of knowledge that already exists elsewhere. These statements show the two key elements that differentiate innovations from imitations. First, only those who expand the existing knowledge set, innovators, will launch real novel products into the market, while imitators will only expand their internal knowledge, launching products that are already served in the market. The second key factor that differentiates the two concepts is idea generation. Only the company that innovates actually generates the idea, whereas the others (the imitators) apply knowledge that already exists (Mahmood and Rufin, 2005). In imitation, the search for knowledge and its implementation is sufficient, but for innovation to take place, the generation of ideas from new knowledge or from the novel combination of existing knowledge is required (Galunic and Rodan, 1998). Knowledge generation and novelty are clearly related. Only internally generated ideas could lead to the launch of novel products, while knowledge acquired externally (without any transformation or combination) could not result in a novel product. In other words, the generation of knowledge together with the novelty of the knowledge used in the launched product, are the dimensions that distinguish innovation from imitation.

Being able to differentiate innovations from imitations is important because, in our judgment, there are articles that speak of imitation when they

are referring to what we understand as incremental innovations or analyze innovations when they are explaining what we have defined as imitative behaviour (Pérez-Luño et al., 2007). As an example of the first case, Zhou (2006) speaks of "creative followers" to refer to companies that make incremental innovations based on the radical innovations of others. That is, those creative followers have combined the radical change in knowledge introduced by the radical innovator with some new knowledge to obtain an improvement in the technology, which in our view is considered an incremental innovation. Regarding authors who utilize the term innovation to refer to what we have defined as imitations, we would include all those who consider that innovation covers "the adoption of an idea that is only new for the organization adopting it" (Damanpour, 1991).

FACTORS DETERMINING THE DECISION TO INNOVATE

In this section we want to identify the factors that influence the firm's decision to innovate or to imitate. At it has been mentioned in the previous epigraph the innovator generate new ideas to obtain success. These statements lead us to consider the proactive behavior of the innovator and the risk taking necessary to undertake this expansion of knowledge. On the other hand, we are going to analyze how depending on the markets forces on which the company is focused, this company will be more oriented toward innovations or imitations.

In summary, these four factors condition the strategic orientation of a firm. Strategic orientations are social learning and selection mechanisms that aim to maintain coherence between the strategic intent and operational activities of management (Burns y Stalker, 1961; Mintzberg, 1973; Miller y Friesen, 1978). They create internal environments in which desired behaviours are encouraged and supported (Atuahene-Gima and Ko, 2001). The strategic management literature presents evidence that the strategic orientation followed by a company is a significant indicator its innovative activity and of the possibility of it gaining sustainable competitive advantages (Gatignon and Xuereb, 1997; Atuahene-Gima and Ko, 2001; George and Zahra, 2002; Hult et al., 2004). Therefore, in the following lines, we are going to analyze how proactivity, risk taking, customers and competitors focus impact on the innovative behaviour of companies.

Proactivity

Proactivity is considered one of the main dimensions of the entrepreneurial orientation (Miller, 1983; Lumpkin and Dess, 1996) and is refereed to companies oriented to action. A proactive attitude or stance is identified with technological leadership and with the desire to be first or a pioneer (Ansoff, 1965), whereas a reactive attitude or stance better describes those companies that are always the second or the imitator (Ansoff, 1965; Porter, 1980; Sharma and Vredenburg, 1998). Expanding knowledge on a worldwide scale needs a proactive attitude, whereas expanding it within an organization (imitation) can be symptom of a mere reaction to the changes that are taking place in the environment of an organization. These assumptions lead us to propose the following hypotheses:

H1: *The higher the levels of proactivity, the higher the disposition to innovate rather than to imitate.*

Risk Taking

The risk taking factor has been analyzed in the literature from several perspectives (Lumpkin and Dess, 1996; Wiseman and Bromiley, 1996) and it is considered one of the main dimensions of the Entrepreneurial Orientation (Miller, 1983; Lumpkin and Dess, 1996). The degree of risk incurred by the innovator is understood to be much greater than that accepted by the imitator.

This is because the innovator confronts a change in the knowledge existing at the global level, and has to be able to assume the commercial risk and the technological risk inherent in true innovation (Zhou, 2006). The case of the imitator is different in that imitation assumes only an expansion of internal or local knowledge of an idea that is already functioning in the market; hence, the technological risk is much less and the commercial risk should be lower when the market of the imitator is similar to that being successfully supplied by the innovator. These assumptions lead us to propose the following hypotheses:

H2: *The higher the levels of risk taking, the higher the disposition to innovate rather than to imitate.*

Customers' and Competitors' Focus

Customer and competitor focus include all the activities involved in acquiring information about the buyers and competitors, respectively, in the target market and disseminating it throughout the business (Narver and Slater, 1990).

Specifically, customer orientation is the sufficient understanding of one's target buyers to be able to create superior value for them continuously. Because a seller creates value for a buyer in two ways: by increasing benefits to the buyer in relation to the buyer's cost and by decreasing the buyer's costs in relation to the buyer's benefits (Narver and Slater, 1990), the seller will be looking for new products to satisfy its clients. That means that this focus will be related to continuous innovations. These lines lead us to propose the following hypotheses:

H3: *The higher the focus on customers, the higher the disposition to innovate rather than to imitate.*

Competitors focus means that a seller understands the short-term strengths and weaknesses and long term capabilities and strategies of the key current and potential competitors (Porter, 1980). This way of facing the market means that, in the company, salespeople will share competitor information and top managers will discuss competitors' strategies. These actions are accomplished with the aim of rapidly respond to competitor's strategies. This focus will be more related to copy what competitors bring out to satisfy customer's needs than to create new products. That is, with this orientations, companies will be much more focus on imitations than on innovations. These assumptions lead us to propose the following hypotheses:

H4: *The higher the focus on competitor, the higher the disposition to imitate rather than to innovate.*

RELATION BETWEEN THE DECISION TO INNOVATE AND PERFORMANCE

The review of the literature leads us to believe that innovation is the main source of competitive advantage (Barney, 1991). The development of an innovation is usually projected as a contribution to the performance of a company (Damanpour, 1991). Although there is a debate on the literature claming that both innovators and imitators can achieve profits with their strategies (Zhou, 2006), in this research, we propose that innovators will be more profitable than imitators. The reason is that we consider that the proactive focus on satisfying customers' needs and the risk assumed with this way of acting is rewarded with higher benefits. These assumptions lead us to propose our last hypotheses:

H5: *The higher the disposition to innovate rather than to imitate, the higher the performance will be.*

METHOD

Sample

In order to test the relations formulated, we have conducted a survey on 1.070 firms of the most technological developed manufacturer sectors (Survey of the National Statistical Institute of Spain, 2004). The population is divided as follow: NACE 24, Chemical; NACE 32, Radio TV and communication equipment; NACE 33, Medical, precision and optical instruments; NACE 34, Manufacture of motor vehicles, trailers and semi-trailers; and NACE 35, Manufacture of other transport equipment. At the moment, we have a response rate of close to 30% (304 answers). We drew the sample from the SABI Data Base, the most comprehensive data base on company information in Spain.

Measures

Overall, all constructs in the model with the exception of the organization size were measured using multi-item scales (using seven-point Likert format) for each or our constructs. In general, we used well-validated measures reported in previous researches. When an item had to be modified or developed, we used Churchill's (1979) multiple-step and multi-validation methods. Proactivity, Risk taking, dynamism and sophistication were measured using Covin and Slevin (1989) scales; while competitors and clients focus were measured using Narver and Slater (1990) scales. We measured performance with Deshpandé et al., (1993) items. The organisation size variable was determined by the number of employees in the firm. The values of this variable range from 10 to more than 5000 workers. Because of its wide dispersion, a Napierian logarithm of the number of workers in the firm has been used to estimate it, in order to avoid the scale effect that could be produced if we considered the original variable. Lastly, the scale to measure the decision

Table 1. Squared Correlation Matrix

	F1	**F2**	**F3**	**F4**	**F5**	**F6**	**F7**	**F8**	**F9**
F1	0.71								
F2	0.02*	0.52							
F3	0.23*	0.24*	0.79						
F4	0.01	0.04*	0.16*	0.68					
F5	0.05*	0.02*	0.03*	0.00	0.77				
F6	0.03*	0.04*	0.07*	0.02	0.42*	0.72			
F7	0.08*	0.00	0.01	0.01	0.01	0.01	1		
F8.	0.00	0.05*	0.01*	0.08*	0.00	0.00	0.00	0.44	
F9	0.00	0.12*	0.13*	0.13*	0.01	0.03*	0.06*	0.23*	0.52
Significant at P<00.05 (n=301); AVE is represented in the Principal Diagonal									

to innovating or imitating was developed by us following core conceptual attributes developed by prior research.

Reliability and Validity

We took several steps to ensure data validity and reliability. First, we pretested the survey with 25 interviews with R&D managers and asked them to closely review the survey. We then revised any potentially confusing items. Then, we sent the questionnaire to the R&D managers of all the companies of our sample. Multiple-item measures were used for most constructs to enhance content coverage. All of our multiple-item constructs achieved Cronbach alphas of 0.69 or higher, indicating strong internal consistency.

The hypotheses were tested using Structural equation modeling method. We followed the two stage procedure recommended by Anderson and Gerbing (1988). In the first stage the measurement model was estimated using confirmatory factor analysis (CFA) in order to test whether the constructs exhibited sufficient reliability and validity. The second stage identified the structural model that best fit the data and tested the hypothesized relationships between the constructs.

The purpose of CFA was to test the unidimensionality of multi-item constructs and to eliminate unreliable items. Items that loaded on multiple constructs and had too low item-to-construct loadings were deleted. To ensure discriminant validity, a series of CFA was conducted with covariance matrix as inputs (See Table 1).

As it is presented in Table 2, we conducted two structural models to test the hypothesized relationships between the constructs. In the first one, we presented all the possible equations and in Model 2, we only presented those equations that best fixed the data.

RESULTS

As we can see in the Model 2 of Table 2, only proactivity has a significant positive influence on the decision to innovate. This means that from the first four hypotheses, only H1 is supported. The significant control variables for the decision of innovating are both size and environmental sophistication. It is important to remark that size is negative, so the smaller the firm is, the higher will be its disposition to innovate.

Performance is not determined by the decision of innovating or imitating. Therefore, we do not find support for H5. This is quite interesting because it supports the arguments that claim that imitating could be as important as innovating for

Table 2 Estimated coefficients and model fit indices

Latent Factors			
Dependents	Independents	Coeff1[a] (t-value)	Coeff2[a] (t-value)
Innovation	Proactivity	0.307(5.258)	0.297 (5.350)
	Risk Taking	-0.048 (-0.748)	---------
	Market	0.043 (0.550)	---------
	Competitors	0.037 (0.480)	---------
	Size	-0.086 (-2.254)	-0.084 (-2.194)
	Dynamism	0.065 (1.335)	---------
	Sophistication	0.199 (2.706)	0.210 (2.810)
Performance	Innovation	-0.004 (-0.039)	---------
	Proactivity	0.396 (0.748)	0.383 (7.066)
	Risk Taking	-0.039 (-0.629)	---------
	Market	0.177 (2.017)	0.145 (2.221)
	Competitors	-0.034 (-0.417)	---------
	Size	0.190 (4.844)	0.189 (4.810)
	Dynamism	-0.086 (-1.823)	---------
	Sophistication	-0.232 (-3.317)	-0.254 (-3.485)
Overall fit index		Model 1	Model 2
χ^2 (df)		291.262	137.221
Satorra-Bentler χ^2		255.132	131.115
GFI		0.918	0.941
AGFI		0.890	0.916
CFI		0.968	0.976
Robust CFI		0.969	0.967
RMSEA (90% CI)		0.042 (0.0320.0.052)	0.046 (0.0310.0.059)
Robust RMSEA (90% CI)		0.034 (0.0220.0.044)	0.043 (0.0280.0.057)
[a] coeff1= Model 1 parameters; coeff2= model 2 parameters			

competitiveness (Zhou, 2006). Both proactivity and market focus have a positive and significant influence on performance. Taking into account the control variables, it is interesting to remark that both size and sophistication are significant for performance. That is, more sophisticated environments lead companies to imitate; and the higher the firm is, the higher will be its performance.

CONCLUSION

Although innovation has generated substantial attention in the literature, few studies have analyzed the determinants of the decision to conduct an internal knowledge creation rather than acquiring such knowledge from the market in the form of an imitation. Also, this scarce number of studies is mainly theoretical and we have not found any empirical work analyzing this decision. Furthermore, the few studies that analyze empirically weather to innovate or to imitate have not found any support for their assumptions (Zhou, 2006). This study seeks to fill this void examining the determinants of the decision to innovate including contingency across different dimensions of the environment measured as control variables.

Our first main contribution, consistent with the leader and follower literature, is that we find that the decision of innovating or imitating is not the determinant of the firm's performance. Rather, it is the company's proactivity which best determinate both the decision to innovate and the firm performance. It is very interesting to highlight that listening to customers' needs is the second most important factor when determining the organization's performance.

Our second main contribution comes from the analysis of the control variables. While dynamism does not have any effect on either the decision of innovate or imitate, environmental sophistication has a positive effect on the decision to innovate and a negative effect on performance. This could be explained by the following argumentation: while sophistication can motivate firms to innovate, its cost is so important that the final firm's performance can be decreased. Company's size has also a double influence. The smaller the firm is, the more is it desire to innovate. This is well understood if we take into account that some of the industries analyzed in this research, as for example the chemical, are characterized by being compound by many very small laboratories which a great capabilities to combine knowledge and give rise new knowledge or innovations. Again, its sign is the contrary for the dependent variable performance. This is because big firms have the resources and capabilities to absorb all the benefits of the innovation process.

Limitations and Further Research

It is important to highlight the importance of be proactive and to listen to the market to be successful. This statement could be useful for those firms that may not have the strength to innovate but are capable to act in a proactive way copying other firms' innovations when they detect an unsatisfied need. It would be interesting to empirically analyze in future researches if those who copy products from competitors from other countries or markets to satisfy their target market are more profitable that those that copy competitors that are already working in their target market.

We have analyzed firms from five different sectors. For future researches, it could be interesting control the effect of the different sectors. Together with this possibility of future line of research, we have to signal that due that we have only analyzed five sectors and that we have focused on the Spanish market, we cannot generalize the results.

Lastly, we have to mention that risk taking and competitor focus have not appeared to have a significant effect on either the decision to innovate and performance. Also, customer focus has not appeared important for the decision to innovate. These voids of results should be analyzed deeper.

ACKNOWLEDGMENT

Financial support from the Ministry of Science and Technology of Spain, Grant SEC2006-08416, is gratefully acknowledged

REFERENCES

Adner, R., & Zemsky, P. (2006). A demand-based perspective on sustainable competitive advantage. *Strategic Management Journal*, *27*(3), 215–239. doi:10.1002/smj.513

Anderson, J. C., & Gerbing, D. W. (1988). Structural equation modeling in practice: A review and recommended two-step approach. *Psychological Bulletin*, *103*(3), 411–423. doi:10.1037/0033-2909.103.3.411

Ansoff, H. I. (1965). *Corporate strategy.* New York: McGraw-Hill.

Atuahene-Gima, K., & Ko, A. (2001). An empirical investigation of the effect of market orientation and entrepreneurship orientation alignment on product innovation. *Organization Science, 12*(1), 54–74. doi:10.1287/orsc.12.1.54.10121

Barney, J. B. (1991). Firm resources and sustained competitive advantage. *Journal of Management, 17*(1), 99–120. doi:10.1177/014920639101700108

Becheikh, N., Landry, R., & Amara, N. (2005). Lessons from innovation empirical studies in the manufacturing sector: a systematic review of the literature from 1993-2003. *Technovation, 26*(5-6), 644–663. doi:10.1016/j.technovation.2005.06.016

Burns, T., & Stalker, G. M. (1961). *The management of innovation.* London: Tavistock Publication.

Churchill, G. A. (1979). A paradigm for Developing better measures of Marketing Constructs. *JMR, Journal of Marketing Research, 16*(1), 64–73. doi:10.2307/3150876

Conner, K. R. (1995). Obtaining strategic advantages from being imitated: when can encouraging "clones" pay? *Management Science, 41*(2), 209–225. doi:10.1287/mnsc.41.2.209

Covin, J. G., & Slevin, D. P. (1989). Strategic management of small firms in hostile and benign environments. *Strategic Management Journal, 10*(1), 75–87. doi:10.1002/smj.4250100107

Damanpour, F. (1991). Organizational innovation: a meta-analysis of effects of determinants and moderators. *Academy of Management Journal, 34*(3), 555–590. doi:10.2307/256406

Damanpour, F., & Wischnevsky, J. D. (2006). Research on innovation in organizations: Distinguishing innovation-generating from innovation-adopting organizations. *Journal of Engineering and Technology Management, 23*(1), 269–291. doi:10.1016/j.jengtecman.2006.08.002

Deshpandé, R., Farley, J. U., & Webster, F. E. (1993). Corporate culture, customer orientation and innovativeness in Japanese firms: a quadrad analysis. *JMR, Journal of Marketing Research, 57*(1), 23–37.

Galunic, C., & Rodan, S. (1998). Resource recombinations in the firm: Knowledge structures and the potential for Schumpeterian innovation. *Strategic Management Journal, 19*(12), 1193–1201. doi:10.1002/(SICI)1097-0266(1998120)19:12<1193::AID-SMJ5>3.0.CO;2-F

Gatignon, H., & Xuereb, J.-M. (1997). Strategic Orientation of the firm and new product performance. *JMR, Journal of Marketing Research, 34*(1), 77–90. doi:10.2307/3152066

George, G., & Zahra, S. A. (2002). *Being entrepreneurial and being market-driven: exploring the interaction effect of entrepreneurial and market orientation on firm performance.* Paper presented at the Babson College. Babson Park, MA.

Grossman, G. M., & Helpman, E. (1991). *Innovation and growth in the global economy.* Cambridge, MA: MIT Press.

Hodgson, G. M., & Knudsen, T. (2006). Balancing inertia, innovation, and imitation in complex environments. *Journal of Economic Issues, 40*(2), 287–295.

Hult, G. T. M., Hurley, R. F., & Knight, G. A. (2004). Innovativeness: its antecedents and impact on business performance. *Industrial Marketing Management, 33*(5), 429–442. doi:10.1016/j.indmarman.2003.08.015

Knight, K. E. (1967). A descriptive model of the intra-firm innovation process. *The Journal of Business*, 40(4), 478–496. doi:10.1086/295013

Kogut, B., & Zander, U. (1993). Knowledge of the firm and the evolutionary theory of the multinational corporation. *Journal of International Business Studies*, 24(4), 625–645. doi:10.1057/palgrave.jibs.8490248

Li, H., & Atuahene-Gima, K. (2001). Product innovation strategy and the performance of new technology ventures in China. *Academy of Management Journal*, 44(6), 1123–1134. doi:10.2307/3069392

Lieberman, M. B., & Asaba, S. (2006). Why do firms imitate each other? *Academy of Management Review*, 31(2), 366–385.

Lieberman, M. B., & Montgomery, D. B. (1988). First-mover advantages. *Strategic Management Journal*, 9(Summer), 41–58. doi:10.1002/smj.4250090706

Lieberman, M. B., & Montgomery, D. B. (1998). First-mover (dis)advantages: retrospective and link with the resource-based view. *Strategic Management Journal*, 19(12), 1111–1125. doi:10.1002/(SICI)1097-0266(1998120)19:12<1111::AID-SMJ21>3.0.CO;2-W

Lumpkin, G. T., & Dess, G. G. (1996). Classifying the entrepreneurial orientation construct and liking it to performance. *Academy of Management Review*, 21(1), 135–172. doi:10.2307/258632

MacMillan, I., McCaffery, M. L., & Van Wijk, G. (1985). Competitors' responses to easily imitated new products–exploring commercial banking product introductions. *Strategic Management Journal*, 6(1), 75–86. doi:10.1002/smj.4250060106

Mahmood, I. P., & Rufin, C. (2005). Government's dilemma: the role of government in imitation and innovation. *Academy of Management Review*, 30(2), 338–360.

Mansfield, E., Schwartz, M., & Wagner, S. (1981). Imitation costs and patents: an empirical study. *The Economic Journal*, 91(364), 907–918. doi:10.2307/2232499

Massa, S., & Testa, S. (2004). Innovation or imitation? Benchmarking: a knowledge-management process to innovate services. *Benchmarking*, 11(6), 610–620. doi:10.1108/14635770410566519

McEvily, S. K., Das, S., & McCabe, K. (2000). Avoiding competence substitution through knowledge sharing. *Academy of Management Review*, 25(2), 294–311. doi:10.2307/259015

Miller, D. (1983). The correlates of entrepreneurship in three types of firms. *Management Science*, 29(7), 770–791. doi:10.1287/mnsc.29.7.770

Miller, D., & Friesen, P. H. (1978). Archetypes of Strategy formulation. *Management Science*, 24(9), 921–933. doi:10.1287/mnsc.24.9.921

Mintzberg, H. (1973). Strategy-making in three modes. *California Management Review*, 16(2), 44–53.

Narver, J. C., & Slater, S. F. (1990). The effect of a market orientation on business profitability. *Journal of Marketing*, 54(4), 20–42. doi:10.2307/1251757

Nerkar, A., & Shane, S. (2007). Determinants of invention commercialization: an empirical examination of academically sourced inventions. *Strategic Management Journal*, 28(11), 1155–1166. doi:10.1002/smj.643

Pepall, L. (1997). Imitative competition and product innovation in a Duopoly Model. *Economica*, 64(254), 264–279.

Pérez-Luño, A., Valle Cabrera, R., & Wiklund, J. (2007). Innovation and imitation as sources of sustainable competitive advantage. *Management Research, 5*(2), 67–79. doi:10.2753/JMR1536-5433050201

Porter, M. E. (1980). *Competitive advantage. Techniques for analyzing industries.* New York: The Free Press.

Rivkin, J. W. (2001). Reproducing knowledge: replication without imitation at moderate complexity. *Organization Science, 12*(3), 274–293. doi:10.1287/orsc.12.3.274.10106

Schumpeter, J. A. (1934/1961). *The theory of economic development: an inquiry into profits, capital, credit, interest, and the business cycle.* New Brunswick, NJ: Transaction Publishers.

Sharma, S., & Vredenburg, H. (1998). Proactive corporate environmental strategy and the development of competitively valuable organizational capabilities. *Strategic Management Journal, 19*(8), 729–753. doi:10.1002/(SICI)1097-0266(199808)19:8<729::AID-SMJ967>3.0.CO;2-4

Subramaniam, M., & Youndt, M. A. (2005). The influence of intellectual capital on the types of innovative capabilities. *Academy of Management Journal, 48*(3), 450–463.

Trott, P., & Hoecht, A. (2007). Product counterfeiting, non-consensual acquisition of technology and new product development; An innovation perspective. *European Journal of Innovation Management, 10*(1), 126–143. doi:10.1108/14601060710720582

VanderWerf, P. A., & Mahon, J. F. (1997). Meta-analysis of the impact of research methods on findings of first-mover advantage. *Management Science, 43*(11), 1510–1519. doi:10.1287/mnsc.43.11.1510

Wiseman, R. M., & Bromiley, P. (1996). Toward a model of risk in declining organizations. An empirical examination of risk, performance and decline. *Organization Science, 7*(5), 524–543. doi:10.1287/orsc.7.5.524

Wolfe, R. A. (1994). Organizational innovation: review, critique and suggested research directions. *Journal of Management Studies, 31*(3), 405–431. doi:10.1111/j.1467-6486.1994.tb00624.x

Zhou, K. Z. (2006). Innovation, imitation, and new product performance: the case of China. *Industrial Marketing Management, 35,* 394–402. doi:10.1016/j.indmarman.2005.10.006

Zmud, R. W. (1982). Diffusion of modern software practices: influence of centralization and formalization. *Management Science, 28*(12), 1421–1431. doi:10.1287/mnsc.28.12.1421

Chapter 6
Usage of ICT Tools in New Product Development:
Creating User-Involvement

Kristina Risom Jespersen
Aarhus University, Denmark

Nuka Buck
Aarhus University, Denmark

ABSTRACT

Involvement of users in new product development is needed more than ever due to the technological and the social progression in recent years. Usage of ICT tools is one approach forwarded in literature discussing user-involvement. This chapter explores the antecedents of ICT usage in NPD. We utilize five groups of factors: innovative climate, strategic emphasis on ICT tools, ICT champions, competencies and performance expectations. To this end three case studies were conducted. The case findings demonstrate that the most significant antecedents for sustained user-involvement in NPD with ICT tools are strategic emphasis, competencies and the type of ICT champion.

INTRODUCTION

The commercial expansion of the Internet in the early 1990s changed the Western world from an industrial to an information society, characterized by the rapid development and the adoption of new information and communication technologies (ICTs). Information accessibility and creation continues to become faster and easier as new ICTs are developed at a rapid pace. Another aspect of the progress in ICT is the change from a focus on the presentation of information to content collaboration through posting, commenting, and writing on the Web. Users search for, read, and compose knowledge together irrespective of group affiliation, and they talk directly to each other. Thus, the information society has transformed into a knowledge society. The knowledge society represents a significant change in the power relationship of users and corporations. The traditional control companies had over information that users of their products could access has eroded.

ICT usage has drastically modified communication, sales and information methods, thus enabling companies to achieve strong competitive advantages in both production and product development (Bayo-

DOI: 10.4018/978-1-61520-643-8.ch006

Moriones & Lera-Lopez, 2007; Ozer, 2000). Greater usage of ICT in a particular product development effort will lead to greater market success of a given product when launched. Research finds that ICT usage impacts the commercial success of new products in a positive direction (Barczak, Sultan, & Hultink, 2007). Progress with ICTs has made users an independent dimension of company new product development (NPD). Users communicate across markets, share experiences, and refine products outside the control of companies. The "corporate playground" has evolved into a three-dimensional space (technology, markets, and users) that must be navigated when developing new products.

Research has put ICT tools forward as instruments for connecting with users. ICT is regarded as a platform for relationship building between company and product/service users. The increase in numbers of virtual communities and self-service technologies reinforces this notion (Andersen, 2005; Casalo, Flavian, & Guinaliu, 2008; McWilliam, 2000). Virtual environments are an effective way of building relationships with users and motivating both the company and its users to participate in collaborative NPD (Miles, Miles, & Snow, 2005; Sawheny, Verona, & Prandelli, 2005). The aim of this chapter is to extend this body of research by addressing ICT tool usage in NPD that aims at creating user-involvement. This is significant as the main principle of user-driven NPD is the incorporation of user information and knowledge into new product projects throughout the stages of the development process. User knowledge includes input, comments, and feedback generated through a continuous dialogue with users. The application of user input optimizes product technology and/or product design, and matches a new product to extended and/or latent user needs (Jespersen, 2008; Von Hippel, 2005). The literature on customer relationship management and relationship marketing stresses the relationship between company and customer as a pre-requisite for involvement. Producers can

only involve customers and establish a dialogue if they are connected to them (Andersen, 2005; Dwyer, Shur, & Oh, 1987; Morgan & Hunt, 1994).

The purpose of this chapter is to explore the antecedents of the ICT usage process in NPD. Specifically, we investigate the choice of ICT tool, the type of user-involvement created, and whether ICT tool implementation is accomplished. To this end, we have conducted a longitudinal case study of ICT usage in NPD in three Danish international operating companies. The presented study contributes to existing research on ICT adaptation and user-involvement with observations from actual applications of ICT tools in new product projects. The opportunities and challenges facing companies when pursuing user-involvement through ICT tool usage are provided for research and practice to gain from.

In the following, the process of user-involvement and ICT usage in NPD is conceptualized. After this the antecedents of ICT usage are discussed. The cases are then presented and findings are discussed. Finally, conclusions are reached an recommendations given.

ICT USAGE AND USER-INVOLVEMENT IN NPD

ICT tool usage in NPD is a two phase process that builds on the innovation diffusion process (Venkatesh, Morris, Davis, & Davis, 2003). First, a company has to apply a minimum of one ICT tool in a NPD project. Through the ICT tool application, users are involved in the NPD project and the company forms an experience of user-involvement and the ICT tool. Based on this, the second phase of the process can be one of two possible: the company either implements the ICT tool in their NPD process, or does not do so. This part of the chapter connects user-involvement and ICT tool in the NPD process.

The initiative to involve users in new product projects (interaction control) may be taken by us-

Figure 1. ICT tools and user-involvement

User-involvement

	Task	Social
Synchronized	3D prints	Group technologies
Not-synchronized	3D images Mobile technology	Web 2.0 applications On-line communities

ICT tools

ers (unsolicited) and/or by companies (solicited). The focus of this chapter lies on user-involvement initiated by the company. Company controlled user involvement can be undirected or directed (Brockhoff, 2003). The difference of the two is whether the company knows the responding users. Undirected user-involvement is often used as part of product marketing in form of contests either between users (e.g. write the best commercial) or between products (e.g. users vote for their favorite product among a given set of products from a manufactory). Directed user-involvement pertains to company processes such as new product development, and gives the company the benefit of personal contact to users through direct invitations. This gives more control over input quality, though users cannot be forced to reply to an invitation. When a company has invited users to collaborate in the NPD process, the interaction of user and company may be task oriented or socially oriented (Kaulio, 1998; Nambisan, 2002). Task involvement of users refers to a short-tem engagement of users on a specific NPD project in a given NPD stage. Social involvement of users refers to a long-term engagement of users by the company. The company invites users to be part of a relationship on NPD that exceeds specific projects and process stages.

ICT tools may shorten the distance between company and users thereby increasing and

strengthening user involvement and engagement in new product development. Many software products do allow companies to establish virtual customers (Dahan & Hauser, 2002). By combining various new technologies, companies can provide a range of online services to the customers that facilitate user-involvement in NPD (Nambisan, 2002). How ICT involves users in NPD pertains to the characteristics of ICT tools. These can be characterized as either synchronized or not-synchronized tools Figure 1 illustrates various ICT tools applicable to the NPD process with synchronized/not-synchronized characteristics and how these relate to task/social user-involvement.

Synchronized ICT tools build on group logic. With these tools user-input and dialogue are created by a group of users who collaborate and discussion given topics in the NPD process. Not-synchronized ICT tools are those with an input generated on individual basis by users and collected on a shared platform accessible to all. Most ICT tools can be used for task-involvement, but not all have the functionalities to generate social user-involvement. With this understanding of ICT usage in NPD, we proceed to the antecedents of the process.

ANTECENDENTS OF ICT USAGE IN NPD

Technological progress and the evolution of Internet technology have turned the use of ICT tools from a question of mere acceptance to an estimation of whether an organization is ready to apply ICT tools. The challenge is not to make companies use ICT in general, since they already do this. Rather, ICT develop rapidly, and many solutions and systems exist to create the dialogue platform necessary for user-involvement in NPD. A number of prerequisites are required to establish the readiness of companies for holistic information generating ICT tools. This part of the chapter discusses the antecedents of ICT usage in NPD.

Figure 2. Antecedents of ICT usage in NPD

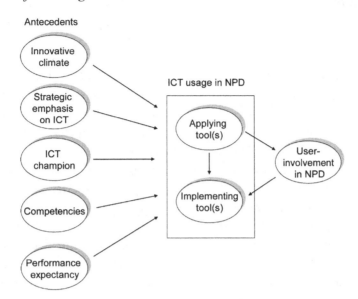

The chosen model, which is shown in figure 2, draws on concepts and insights from NPD and IT adaptation literatures such as those developed by (Barczak et al., 2007; Bayo-Moriones & Lera-Lopez, 2007; Sethi, Pant, & Sethi, 2003; Venkatesh et al., 2003). The right part of figure 2 depicts the ICT usage process.

Innovative Climate

An innovative climate is one that supports creativity, is not risk averse, is willing to try new things, and exemplifies open communication among employees. It is a culture that values the creation and sharing of knowledge as a key driver of NPD (Barczak et al., 2007). The innovative climate is shaped by a company's innovation orientation as it directs the organization's competencies in the domains of resource allocation, technology, markets, human resources, and operations (Siguaw, Simpson, & Enz, 2006). An innovation orientation comprises an organization's learning philosophy, strategic direction, and cross-functional collaboration.

Market orientation and learning in NPD are reported as significant to information acquisition in

the NPD stages and the performance of new products (Hills & Sarin, 2003; Matthyssens, Pauwels, & Vandenbempt, 2005). The NPD framework, NPD activities and performance of new products have been established as varying between prospectors and defenders (Dröge & Calantone, 1996; Slater & Mohr, 2006). Research has singled out a focus on technology as a factor that influences value creation, while market focus influences value appropriation (Mizik & Jacobson, 2003). NPD literature balances technology and market input to ensure NPD process practices (Moorman & Slotegraaf, 1999). Cross-functional teamwork and the collaboration between R&D and marketing have been investigated for their significance on product performance and use of information generated by NPD activities (Moenaert & Souder, 1996). Organizations with an innovative climate encourage and reward cooperation and knowledge sharing internally and externally across company boundaries. An innovative climate with these characteristics has been found to influence the usage of ICT tools in NPD positively (Hargadon, 2002; Sethi et al., 2003).

Strategic Emphasis on ICT Tools

Strategic emphasis is the focus and obligation of an organization to invest in ICT to increase user collaboration (Ritchie & Brindley 2005). Furthermore, a strategic emphasis on ICT is necessary for usage to overrule existing routines in NPD. A company's strategic focus determines the support of new ICT tools in NPD (Barczak et al., 2007). A strategic focus on differentiation through quality more likely encourages decision-makers to adopt ICT in NPD, rather than a low-cost competitive strategy (Bayo-Moriones & Lera-Lopez, 2007). The application of ICT tools in NPD is strategic as they change a company's relation to its users. Top management emphasis and support is therefore needed for a positive, permanent usage of these ICT tools in NPD.

ICT Champions

Research on innovation adoption and ICT implementation both suggest that the existence of an ICT champion has a positive influence on the usage of holistic ICT tools in the NPD process (Barczak et al., 2007; Markham & Griffin, 1998). The present focus is on champions at the project level as these will be involved in the interaction of users from end-to-end in the NPD process. Without a champion or multiple champions on a project, it is more unlikely that new ICT tools are tried and implemented.

The conventional profile of an ICT champion is an ICT expert. An ICT expert is a person in the NPD team who is knowledgeable about the technical operation of the ICT tool and can train the team in using it (Markham & Griffin, 1998). With the technological progression of the Internet we suggest two additional profiles of ICT champions that would influence the usage of new ICT tools in a positive way. Besides ICT experts, ICT champions may also be an ICT super-user or an ICT visionary. An ICT super-user is a person who uses the many Web 2.0 applications avail-able, such as blogs, wikis, chat rooms, podcasts, RSS feeds, social software and other online web services, or is experienced with platforms such as Second Life, Sims or 3-D visualization programs (Jespersen, 2008). The ICT champion profile of an ICT super-user is someone who is very knowledgeable about the portfolio of ICT tools available without having the technical insights of their construction. As an ICT champion, the ICT visionary differs from the previous two as this person is inexperienced with ICT. Regardless, the ICT visionary is a person who recognizes the potential of new tools when introduced to them, and will use his or her enthusiasm to promote the usage of a new ICT tool in the NPD process. The usage of ICT in NPD depends on the ICT champion profile and position in the NPD team. The ICT visionary is the weaker ICT champion compared to ICT experts and ICT super-users.

ICT Competencies

The competence of corporate ICT can be conceptualized as the degree to which an organization's infrastructure supports the use of ICTs. Due to the human capital held by the company, ICT competencies are found to vary between organizations. The qualifications and age of organizational members influence the adoption of ICT and the readiness to incorporate new ICTs into decision-processes such as NPD (Bayo-Moriones & Lera-Lopez, 2007). The younger and/or more educated the human capital, the more ready the organization is for new ICTs. This view of readiness follows the social and demographic diffusion and use of ICTs. Yet, though human capital is significant, it is also important that the organization has the internal competence to support the use and the maintenance of ICT. Without these the functionality of the ICT tool and its suitability to new or other NPD project can not be ensured. The scale of required set-up costs, including human capital and professional, technical advice, delays adoption (Ritchie & Brindley 2005).

Analytical Competencies

ICT tools increase the information flow into the NPD process. With ICT tools, the NPD team may ask questions in interview or survey form. The information flow can therefore be a short text, a story, and/or a string of numbers. To gain a high quality of information from users, it is important that the company posses the ability: i) to design good questions, ii) to choose the right dialogue method, and iii) to be able to analyze incoming information from users.

Information analytical competencies are the ability to extract meaning from these information flows and thereby make incoming user knowledge usable to the NPD team. Even if companies outsource this analytical task, they still need the internal capabilities to validate the quality. Resources are used on ICT and on maintaining user dialogue, but the benefit from user inputs is lacking because the organization does not have the ability to analyze the information input and generate valuable knowledge for the NPD process. In dialogue with a NPD team, users expect response to their inputs; the analytical ability must not block this expected feedback from the team (Jespersen, 2008).

An internal ability to handle information processing positively affects readiness for new ICTs in NPD. Without this ability, companies may view ICT and the dialogue with users as a non-leveraging investment.

Performance Expectancy

This antecedent of ICT usage and user-involvement in NPD pertains to faith. Performance expectancy is defined as the degree to which an NPD decision-maker believes that increased ICT usage and user-involvement in NPD will benefit product innovativeness and new product performance (Venkatesh et al., 2003). The performance expectancy construct within all user acceptance models (TAM, extrinsic motivation, innovation

diffusion theory among others) is the strongest predictor of intention and usage. It remains significant at all points of measurement both voluntary and mandatory settings (Venkatesh et al., 2003).

Performance expectations of ICT usage in NPD and user-involvement are linked. The ICT platform benefits listed by research is that companies i) become engaged with larger numbers of users; ii) experience increased speed in feedback from users; iii) experience a higher persistence of user involvement; iv) find that interactions can happen in real-time without a delay, and with a much higher frequency; v) enhance their capability to tap into the social situation in which user knowledge is created and vi) experience an increased flexibility in the relationship with users. (Maguire, Koh, & Huang, 2007). On this basis, the usage of holistic ICT tools is expected to increase NPD performance and effectiveness (Barczak et al., 2007; Sethi et al., 2003).

METHODOLOGY

The antecedents of ICT usage in NPD for the involvement of users is discussed on basis of three cases from companies which adapted one or more holistic ICT tools in a stage of their NPD process. Case analysis was chosen because empirical and analytical grounding of ICT usage in NPD is underdeveloped in NPD and ICT adaptation literature. For this purpose case analysis is a suitable research method. Our study builds on three different cases with various experience and competence levels of ICT and user-involvement. The three companies are a food producer, a potted plant farmer and a playground manufacturer. The empirical process consisted of four steps. First, the key NPD managers in each company were interviews to gain knowledge about antecedents of ICT usage. The interview guide was based on conceptualizations, questions and scales used by (Barczak et al., 2007; Bayo-Moriones & Lera-Lopez, 2007; Sethi et al., 2003; Venkatesh et al.,

2003). Second, the case companies were invited on a workshop where the ICT tools (see figure 1) were presented and demonstrated. Third, the companies chose one or more ICT tools to apply to a NPD project in their company. Each application period was observed and documented in detail. Fourth, the key NPD managers were interviewed once more after the ICT application period to follow up on user-involvement and ICT tool implementation. This interview guide was based on conceptualization, questions, and scales used by (Barczak et al., 2007; Bayo-Moriones & Lera-Lopez, 2007; Sethi et al., 2003; Venkatesh et al., 2003). All data was collected in 2008. In the following, the three case companies are presented with a description of the ICT usage antecedents. Hereafter follows a description of the ICT tool usage in NPD for each case.

CASES

Background

The food producer develops, produces and sells a range of processed meat products to the retail, fast food and food service sectors as well as the food industry in the Danish and international markets. The company operates on more than 130 markets. The Nordic region is the company's home market; other European countries are also important markets. The company is a well-known supplier to overseas markets, including USA and Asia. The company's roots date back to 1887 when the foundations for modern industrial food production were laid. Since then, the company has continued to adjust to market requirements through product adaptation and the development of new product categories. Over recent years, the company has turned its product development process into a more structured setting following theoretical guidelines to a larger extent. As part of this work, the company aims for larger user-involvement in NPD which is their reason for

joining our study. The food producer has an innovative climate, characterized by an incremental innovative strategy and a marketing focus. Market learning is generated through product tests and partly supported by cross-functional teamwork of NPD and marketing. The company experience with user-involvement in NPD may therefore be characterized as medium on the task dimension and low on the social dimension. The food producer holds no prior experiences with ICT tools in the NPD process. The food producer does not hold a strong innovative orientation and the innovative climate is 'low' following the earlier given definition of the concept in this chapter. This is not unexpected as the food industry in general is characterized by a primary focus on process innovations.

Though the food producer has little prior experience with ICT tools, the NPD manager may be characterized as ICT super-user champion who has enforced an increased strategic emphasis on ICT in NPD. The cross-functional teamwork with marketing and the restructuring of NPD revealed some analytical and ICT competencies in the company.

The potted plant farmer is a family owned company headed by the third generation. The company product portfolio includes potted plants and cuttings. The nursery is one of the world's leading breeders. Their users are horticultures and retailers including supermarket chains, market gardens, florists and end-users. The potted plant farmer is located in Denmark and exports to the entire European marked and parts of USA, Canada and Japan. The product development process of a potted plant takes three years from idea to production. It is a NPD process dominated by biotechnology. Technical issues such as the plants sustainability to temperature changes, flower size, leaf size and body richness are the main concerns through the concept, prototyping, production and launch stages. The potted plans farmer joined our study as they were unfamiliar with user-involvement on both dimensions (task and social) and had no ICT tool experience in NPD but wished to increase both in company NPD. The potted plant farmer has an innovative climate, characterized by a bio-technological focus and an incremental innovation strategy. Trend-spotting and surveillance of competitors are the foundation for market learning in the company where cross-functional teams work in the NPD process. Their innovative orientation holds a strong technical focus and within this, the innovative climate ranks as 'medium' following the earlier definition of the concept in this chapter.

The potted plant farmer has an enthusiastic NPD manager but not an ICT champion present in the company. Their inexperience with user-involvement and ICT may be explained partly by a lack of competence to apply ICT and to process input to usable NPD knowledge.

Within the market for playground activities, play and sports, the playground manufacturer is a global market leader. The company offers a wide range of playground equipment. The company was formed in 1970 where Tom Lindhardt Wils realized in what way his big, colorfully sculptures attracted children and created a great joy to children. With this starting point, he founded the company together with Hans Mogens Frederiksen. The company exports its products to the entire world. The main market is Europe, but secondary markets also include Asia/Pacific and Northern America. The company has a comprehensive assortment of products which are being sold without further adjustments. Furthermore, the playground manufacturer develops and produces products which have been adjusted or developed to suit specific customer requests. The company has recently begun a product development process where the idea is to ad technology to the more classic playground concept.

The NPD process of the playground manufacturer follows a Stage Gate Plan, with focus on deliveries. The five stages are conceptualization, design, technical design, implementation and availability. There is an intensified focus on the last stage because launch often relates to implementation functions. At this point, the company supports the customer in building and installing the playground. This focus is particularly present in relation to the new playgrounds where technology is involved. The company development of all products is categorized as playing tools where the child is the pivotal point. The playground manufacturer has traditionally involved different kinds of users in product testing. The company's user-involvement experience may therefore be characterized as high on the task dimension and low on the social dimension. A primary concern has been the ability of the product to further children's development and learning while securing their safety. For this reason the company is motivated to take user-involvement to a new level and therefore entered our study.

The playground manufacturer has an innovative climate that is at the same time conservative and proactive. Buyers order from a catalogue of products, but the company acts as an innovative market leader introducing new products to the market. The company's innovative strategy is therefore split in an incremental (80 percent) and a radical part (20 percent). Market learning in the company is based on qualitative exploration of markets and users. The ICT tool experience in NPD of the playground manufacturer is higher than for the food producer and the potted plant farmer. The company has used cultural probes, focus groups and questionnaires in the attempt to involve users. The result is lots of input but little success in implementing it into NPD. In the company cross-functional teams are not working structured on new products. The innovative climate and the innovative orientation of the company rank as 'high' according to the earlier definition of the concept in this chapter. Despite the high experience levels of user-involvement and ICT tool usage, the playground manufacturer revealed low competence levels of both ICT and information analysis as these had been outsourced and if not, then information still stood in its boxes waiting

Table 1. Antecedent levels and ICT tool application

	Food producer	Potted plant farmer	Playground manufacturer
Innovative climate	Low	Medium	High
Strategic emphasis on ICT tools	High	Low	Low
ICT tool champion	ICT super-user	No champion	ICT visionary
ICT competencies	Medium	Low	Low
Analytical competencies	Medium	Low	Low
Performance expectancy	High	Medium	High
ICT tool	Not-synchronized	Synchronized	Both
NPD stage	Idea/Concept	Concept	Prototyping

to be processed. Still, the NPD manager saw the potential of ICT tool and may be characterized as a visionary champion. Table 1 depicts the case companies' antecedent levels of ICT usage. The choice of ICT tool by each company is described in the following.

ICT Tool Application in Food Product Development

The food producer wished to increase their user-involvement in the idea and concept generation stages of the NPD process. The purpose was to collect the users' ideas, comments on concepts, identify interests and spot new trends. Rather than solemnly testing products, the company sought early input to the NPD process. The food producer had recently built a large panel of end-users based on personal invitations and screening criteria regarding consumer food behavior and demographic characteristics. The company would like to apply ICT tools to support them in building strong relations with the panel members and increase the interaction frequency with the panel. They were especially interested in creating a virtual platform for dialogue and knowledge exchange with users. The users included both end-users and company employees as both groups were seen as valuable resources by the NPD department. To honor this, a web-platform with an ICT tool based on group technology were chosen for the food product de-

velopment case. The basic idea of this ICT tool, Ideastormer, is that panel members can come up with ideas on invited topics or on their own initiative. This virtual platform is closed and entrance requires an invitation. The food producer's NPD department may oversee the creative work of the panel, ask specific questions, provoke with statements, refine ideas with own inputs, and related it all to consumer characteristics. Also, with the platform, the food producer can give feedback and demonstrate actions taken on specific ideas or clusters of ideas. The Ideastormer makes it possible for both the NPD team and the users to interact. As the ICT tool operates on a closed platform, the company can address the user-panel members through a campaign system. Thereby they ensure that not only the currently active users receive questions or challenges given on the platform.

ICT Tool Application in Potted Plant Development

From their end-users, the potted plant farmer wanted to get input about the physical attributes of plants such as flower size, plant size, color, plant dimensions, overall plant liking. For this purpose, a 3-D visualization technology was applied to the concept phase. This ICT tool was expected to be beneficial for the company as prototyping is a three-year process. Seven existing plants were manipulated in a 3-D computer program witch resulted in 21 computer manipulated plants. The 3-D visualization made it possible to present not yet bio-technically possible colors and flower combinations. The 3-D visualizations of manipulated plants were presented in an experimental setup in combination with a survey. The purpose was to collect impressions from the end-users, being able to compile those in the NPD process. Involvement of the users made it possible to pick up plant attributes that the users found attractive and thereby target prototyping with this input. The user inputs were collected at an open reception on company grounds.

ICT Tool Application in Playground Innovation

The playground manufacturer chose to apply ICT tools for tests of a new product entering the market. The ICT tools applied were a mix of mobile technologies and group technologies, named MBOARD, ZING and Pimp-the-concept version 2. The combination of these three ICT tools made it possible to test specific product attributes (MBOARD), then evaluate the prototype based on user experience with the product (ZING) and end with a visualization of the ideal concept (PIMP). The users involved were end-users; they represented different age groups of children and a group of teachers. The experiment took place at their school, where a playground was set up. The use of three different ICT tools made it possible for all children to give their comments in a controlled way where all had equal time to formulate an answer. The purpose was to collect comments from end-users about the playground before working further with it in the NPD process.

The first ICT tool applied in the session was MBOARD which is a mobile technology. The users were playing at the playground as usual for half an hour, and during the playing session the users send SMS text messages from labeled areas to specific numbers. After the playing session, the users went to a meeting room where they could see their SMS text messages at a big screen. In focus groups, the users discussed and elaborated on their comments from the playground session. The focus group followed up on the SMS text messages. Thereby the ICT tool provided information about product use, product options and how product fit with behavior.

The overall evaluation of the playground prototype was evaluated with the ICT tool ZING which is a group technology. This second ICT tool application took place in a meeting room with a big screen, and a wireless keyboard for each of the users. The moderator wrote questions and each of the participants anonymously wrote their comment which was added to the others comments and numbered continuously. The users commented on each other's comments and added other aspects to the questions from the moderator. The purpose of applying ZING as an ICT tool was to collect data from a group discussion with predefined questions about the product prototype.

The third applied ICT tool was PIMP. The purpose of applying this ICT tool was to enable a visual development of an ideal playground. The users were split up into two gender specific groups. At each of the screens, a blank white document with a picture of the playground in the middle was the starting point. The users were told to download pictures to visualize features and functions they image as part of their ideal playground. The users added pictures from Google pictures, and added short comments to the document.

RESULTS AND DISCUSSION

Case findings with regard to the influence of antecedents on ICT usage (application and implementation) and user-involvement in NPD is outlined in table 2. In each cell it is stated how the antecedent characteristics of the case companies influenced ICT application, user-involvement and ICT implementation respectively. These finding are elaborated on and discussed in the following.

Table 2. Research findings

Antecedents	ICT tool application		User-involvement		ICT tool implementation
	Synchronized	Not-synchronized	Task	Social	
Innovative climate	High	Low/ Medium/High	Medium/ High	Low	Low
Strategic emphasis on ICT tools	Low	Low/ High	Low	High	High
ICT tool champion	Visionary No champion	Visionary Super-user	Visionary No champion	Super-user	Super-user
Competencies	Low	Low/ Medium	Low	Medium	Medium
Performance expectations	High	Medium/ High	High/ medium	High	High

ICT adaptation literature suggests that an aggressive innovative focus is more likely to lead to ICT tool integration (Sethi et al., 2003). Studies on ICT usage in NPD find that innovative climates do not affect ICT usage (Barczak et al., 2007). Though these previous findings contradict each other, our case findings support both. First, a highly innovative climate leads to a choice of synchronized and non-synchronized ICT tools while a less innovative climate leads to a choice of non-synchronized tools. Hence, there is a difference of innovative climate, but not an either/or of ICT usage. Rather, what we see is a selective difference on ICT tools. Second, innovative climate does not act as a strong determinant of neither user-involvement nor ICT tool implementation. Antecedents like ICT champion, strategic emphasis and competencies are stronger drivers than innovative climate.

From the case findings it can be stated that the presence of an ICT champion influences ICT application and user-involvement. Innovation literature supports that champions get necessary things done to get products into the market ((Markham & Griffin, 1998). The existence of champions is important (Barczak et al., 2007). The case findings extend this notion by showing that the type of ICT champion matters for ICT tool application and user-involvement. An ICT visionary Champion creates enthusiasm for ICT tools and thus leads his or her company to the application of several ICT tools in NPD as in the playground manufacturer cases. The playground manufacturer chose a combination of synchronized and not-synchronized tools. Interestingly enough, an ICT super-user champion does not lead to a choice of several ICT tools, but rather a more selective choice. The food producer chose a web 2.0 application tool. In cases of web 2.0 applications the design can be outsourced, but the operation of the tool has to be handled by the organization which requires a solid amount of competencies. Contrary, the potted plant farmer with no champion chose 3D images which can be ordered from a supplier and require little competencies to operate afterwards. These findings are important as they support the significance of ICT champion presence and give insights as to the roles played in the ICT adoption process by different types of ICT champions.

Also significant from the cases is that user-involvement and ICT implementation created by ICT champions is contingent upon the NPD manager's competence level. The importance of ICT and information analytical competencies in user-involvement is stressed by the findings in the three cases. Though competencies do not affect choice of ICT tool(s), they do influence the out coming user-involvement and ICT implementation significantly. The playground manufacturer applied synchronized, social ICT tools in combination with not-synchronized, task ICT tools.

From the case observations it was found that the low competence level pulled user-involvement towards a task-oriented type irrespective of the overweight of ICT tools with social involvement functionalities. The low competence level (ICT and information analytical) stands as a barrier for user-involvement and ICT tool implementation in NPD. This is illustrated in the low-low quadrant in figure 3. Also, the findings show that a high competence level is not needed to accomplish ICT implementation. The ICT super-user champion opted for social user-involvement and secured ICT tool implementation. As noted by Jespersen in her research, some insights of what to do with the ICT and the user input is needed. Otherwise ICT adoption may most likely be regarded as a waste of time (Jespersen, 2008). This is illustrated in the high-medium quadrant in figure 3.

The importance of ICT as part of the company strategic profile is supported by research (Dubelaar, Sohal, & Savic, 2005; Mahmood, Hall, & Swanberg, 2001). The case findings not only concur with this notion, they extend it. Strategic emphasis is found to be for user-involvement and ICT tool implementation, but less influential on ICT tool application and as significant. Strategic emphasis influences the type of user-involvement aimed for through the chosen ICT tool. A high emphasis on ICT strategically leads to social user-involvement. The Food producer wanted to create long-term relations to users, whereas the potted plant farmer and the playground manufacturer focused on the task to be done in NPD.

CONCLUSION AND RECOMMENDATIONS

The case findings demonstrate that the antecedents of ICT usage are significant for the choice of ICT tool, for the type of user-involvement created, and for sustained ICT tool implementation in the NPD process. The most significant antecedents for sustained user-involvement in NPD with ICT

Figure 3. User-involvement determined by ICT champion and competence level

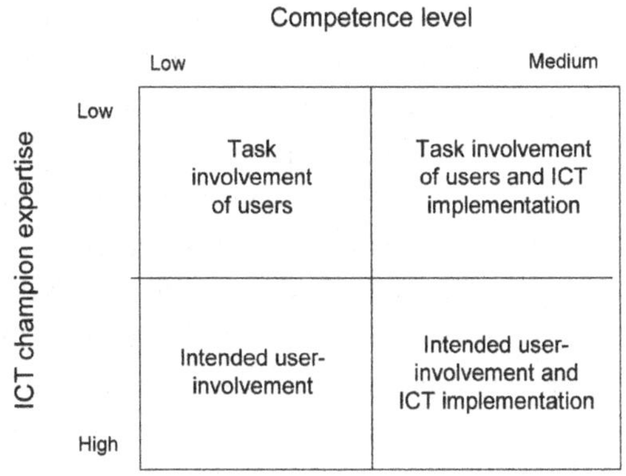

tools are strategic emphasis, competencies and the type of ICT champion. ICT tools have the potential to create user-involvement; whether they succeed depends on organizational competencies. The created user-involvement and the implementation of ICT tool in NPD is elaborated in the following.

User-involvement in NPD becomes task-oriented if there is a low strategic emphasis on ICT, a low level of competencies, and no ICT champion or an ICT visionary champion present in the organization. In these case companies the ICT tools become a digitalized version of existing data collection methods such as focus groups, interviews and questionnaires. Methodologies that are beneficial to NPD but not driving NPD towards user-driven NPD. This finding stresses the challenge of user-involvement in NPD (Jespersen, 2008). NPD managers have to ensure a competence level to handle the technological and social progress of users. Otherwise, resources, energy and creativity held by users will not be accessible to the company; leading the company to miss out on innovative opportunities (Jespersen, 2008).

The determinants of ICT implementation in NPD are high strategic emphasis, the presence of an ICT super-user champion, at least medium competencies (ICT and information analytical) and fulfillment of performance expectations. The food producer honored these four and is today seeking to implement more ICT tools; all web-based.

When the food producer had run Ideastormer for two weeks, users had already given input to line-extensions with high turnovers filling a niche market in catering. Users were rewarded for these inputs and the new products were scheduled for launch in 2009. This experience encouraged the continuation of ICT tool application, but also became an occasion to involve more creative and visionary applications of other ICT tools in NPD.

In case of the play ground manufacturer, the ICT visionary champion was positive as to the user input generated by the ICT tools; especially the digital compilation of data was found beneficial. The challenge in such a case as the playground manufacturer is that the enthusiasm was not anchored in the organization. In fact, despite the innovative climate of this organization, a decision was made to close NPD projects involving user-involvement through ICT tools. The organization found that the ICT tools were too resource demanding to be beneficial. This emphasizes the importance of strategic emphasis on ICT and organizational competencies to handle ICT and user-involvement.

For the potted plant farmer, the ICT application did not lead to user-involvement in NPD as the ability to see the benefits of user-involvement in NPD has large barriers to cross in the organization. Still, the experience with the ICT tool has initiated a discussion of the strategic issue of ICT and user-relations in the future potted plant market. This demonstrates that user-involvement demands a change of mindset in the organization that cannot be taken lightly (Hargadon, 2002; Jespersen, 2008).

These findings may provide useful guidelines for successful ICT usage in NPD that creates user-involvement in companies. The study holds three recommendations for managers. First, we recommend that organizations assess their strategic focus on ICT tools. In this process it is, as suggested earlier, central that user-involvement is established as an organizational purpose. Such a reflection would ensure full commitment to the task.

Second, we recommend that managers include information competence development in their work. This can be accomplished through formal individual education, but should be extended to the organizational level as part of the resource optimization of NPD. Through information competence enhancement, the appreciation of ICT-incorporated information sources would increase in NPD. This would allow decision-makers to secure the innovativeness of new products and a higher performance on markets as 'the needs of users' are transferred into the NPD process.

Third, it was interesting to find that ICT champions may not be technology experts to create user-involvement and sustain ICT tool implementation. We recommend that organizations pay careful attention to the type of ICT champion forwarding user-involvement in NPD through ICT tools to ensure the necessary organizational support of ICT usage in stages of the development process.

ACKNOWLEDGMENT

We would like to thank the project team members Lars Nielsen, Dan Skovgaard, Jan Lindegaard Christensen, and Lone Thuroee and the companies for their collaboration on this study.

REFERENCES

Andersen, P. H. (2005). Relationship marketing and brand involvement of professionals through web-enhanced brand communities: The case of Coloplast. *Industrial Marketing Management, 34,* 39–51. doi:10.1016/j.indmarman.2004.07.002

Barczak, G., Sultan, F., & Hultink, E. J. (2007). Determinants of IT usage and New Product Performance. *Journal of Product Innovation Management, 24,* 600–613. doi:10.1111/j.1540-5885.2007.00274.x

Bayo-Moriones, A., & Lera-Lopez, F. (2007). A firm-level analysis of determinants of ICT adoption in Spain. *Technovation, 27*, 325–366.

Brockhoff, K. (2003). Customers' perspectives of involvement in new product development. *International Journal of Technology Management, 26*(5), 464–481. doi:10.1504/IJTM.2003.003418

Casalo, L. V., Flavian, C., & Guinaliu, M. (2008). Promoting customer's participation in virtual brand communities: A new paradigm in branding strategy. *Journal of Marketing Communications, 14*(1), 19–36. doi:10.1080/13527260701535236

Dahan, E., & Hauser, J. R. (2002). The Virtual Customer. *Journal of Product Innovation Management, 19*, 332–353. doi:10.1016/S0737-6782(02)00151-0

Dröge, C., & Calantone, R. (1996). New product strategy, structure, and performance in two environments. *Industrial Marketing Management, 25*, 555–566. doi:10.1016/S0019-8501(96)00064-8

Dubelaar, C., Sohal, A., & Savic, V. (2005). Benefits, impediments, and critical success factors in B2C E-business adoption. *Technovation, 25*, 1251–1262. doi:10.1016/j.technovation.2004.08.004

Dwyer, F. R., Shur, P. H., & Oh, S. (1987). Developing buyer-seller relationships. *Journal of Marketing, 51*(April), 11–27. doi:10.2307/1251126

Hargadon, A. B. (2002). Brokering Knowledge: Linking learning and innovation. *Organizational Behavior, 24*, 41–85. doi:10.1016/S0191-3085(02)24003-4

Hills, S. B., & Sarin, S. (2003). From market driven to market driving: An alternate paradigm for marketing in high technology industries. *Journal of Marketing Theory and Practice*(summer), 13-24.

Jespersen, K. R. (2008). User-driven product development: Creating a user-involving culture (1 ed.). Denmark: Forlaget Samfundslitteratur.

Kaulio, M. A. (1998). Customer, consumer and user involvement in product development: A framework and a review of selected methods. *Total Quality Management, 9*(1), 141–149. doi:10.1080/0954412989333

Maguire, S., Koh, S. C. L., & Huang, C. (2007). identifying the range of customers listening tools: a logical pre-cursor to CRM? *Industrial Management & Data Systems, 107*(4), 567–586. doi:10.1108/02635570710740706

Mahmood, M. A., Hall, L., & Swanberg, D. L. (2001). Factors Affecting Information Technology Usage: Meta-analysis of Empirical Literature. *Journal of Organizational Computing and Electronic Commerce, 11*(2), 107–130. doi:10.1207/S15327744JOCE1102_02

Markham, S. K., & Griffin, A. (1998). The Breakfast of Champions: Associations between Champions and Product Development Environments, Practices and Performance. *Journal of Product Innovation Management, 15*, 436–454. doi:10.1016/S0737-6782(98)00010-1

Matthyssens, P., Pauwels, P., & Vandenbempt, K. (2005). Strategic flexibility, ridigity and barriers to the development of absorptive capacity in business markets: Themes and research perspectives. *Industrial Marketing Management, 34*, 547–554. doi:10.1016/j.indmarman.2005.03.004

McWilliam, G. (2000). Building stronger brands thorugh online communities. *Sloan Management Review*, (Spring): 43–54.

Miles, R. E., Miles, G., & Snow, C. C. (2005). *Collaborative Entrepreneurship: How Communities of Networked Firms Use Continuous Innovation to Create Economic WEalth*. Stanford, CA: Stanford University Press.

Mizik, N., & Jacobson, R. (2003). Trading off between value creation and value appropriation: the financial implications of shifts in strategic emphasis. *Journal of Marketing, 67*(January), 63–76. doi:10.1509/jmkg.67.1.63.18595

Moenaert, R. K., & Souder, W. E. (1996). Context and Antecedents of information utility at the R&D/Marketing interface. *Management Science, 42*(11), 1592–1610. doi:10.1287/mnsc.42.11.1592

Moorman, C., & Slotegraaf, R. J. (1999). The contingency value of complementary capabilities in product development. *JMR, Journal of Marketing Research, 36*(May), 239–257. doi:10.2307/3152096

Morgan, R. M., & Hunt, S. D. (1994). The commitment-trust theory of relationship marketing. *Journal of Marketing, 58*(July), 20–38. doi:10.2307/1252308

Nambisan, S. (2002). Designing virtual customer environments for new product development: Toward a theory. *Academy of Management Review, 28*(3), 392–413. doi:10.2307/4134386

Ozer, M. (2000). Information Technology and New Product Development: opportunities and pitfalls. *Industrial Marketing Management, 29,* 387–396. doi:10.1016/S0019-8501(99)00060-7

Sawheny, M., Verona, G., & Prandelli, E. (2005). Collaborating to create: The Internet as a platform for customer engagement in product innovation. *Journal of Interactive Marketing, 19*(4), 4–17. doi:10.1002/dir.20046

Sethi, R., Pant, S., & Sethi, A. (2003). Web-Based Product Development Systems Integration and New Product Outcomes: A conceptual framework. *Journal of Product Innovation Management, 20,* 37–56. doi:10.1111/1540-5885.201004

Siguaw, J. A., Simpson, P. M., & Enz, C. A. (2006). Conceptualizing Innovation Orientation: A framework for study and integration of innovation research. *Journal of Product Innovation Management, 23,* 556–574. doi:10.1111/j.1540-5885.2006.00224.x

Slater, S. F., & Mohr, J. J. (2006). Successful Development and Commercialization of Technological Innovation: Insights Based on Strategy Type. *Journal of Product Innovation Management, 23,* 26–33. doi:10.1111/j.1540-5885.2005.00178.x

Venkatesh, V., Morris, M. G., Davis, G. B., & Davis, F. D. (2003). User Acceptance of Information Technology: Toward a unified view. *MIS Quaterly, 27*(3), 425–478.

Von Hippel, E. (2005). *Democraticing Innovation.* Cambridge, MA: MIT Press.

KEY TERMS AND DEFINITIONS

ICT Champion: A person in the NPD team that ensures the use of ICT tools.

ICT Tools: Technology-based tools used for involving users in NPD.

Innovative Climate: The air of innovation in an organization.

NPD: New product development.

Strategic Emphasis: The focus on ICT in the organization and by management.

User-Involvement: The inclusion of users in the product development process.

Section 2
Innovation Capability and Performance

Chapter 7
Factors and Dimensions of National Innovative Capacity

Maria Manuela Santos Natário
Polytechnics Institute of Guarda, Portugal

João Pedro Almeida Couto
University of the Azores, Portugal

Maria Teresa Borges Tiago
University of the Azores, Portugal

Ascensão Maria Martins Braga
Polytechnics Institute of Guarda, Portugal

ABSTRACT

A country's national economic capacity depends on that country's institutional efficiency, its national culture, and its Innovation framework. This chapter reflects upon the factors that influence national innovative capacity, based on the European Innovation Scoreboard database. By using clusters analysis to verify how different countries are positioned in terms of patent registration indicators, we determine which factors distinguish their innovative capacity. The results point to the existence of four groups of countries, and the factors identified point to aspects related to the institutional efficiency, the societies' cultural values associated with the level of hierarchy or "power distance" and with aspects such as the level of population with tertiary education and the percentages of expenses with research and development applied by the companies.

INTRODUCTION

Innovation as a concept or as an application has gone through profound changes. We may consider Innovation in the more traditional sense of radical Innovation when it follows the introduction of new elements, according to the (Schumpeter, 1934) perspective, or incremental Innovation when it follows the adaptation, modification and improvements of products, the development of processes or services.

Innovation may not be linear or sequential process, with origins in applied research, with a well defined sequence of connexions, but rather a system of internal interactions, of feedback, and forward or backward linkages, between functions and actors in

DOI: 10.4018/978-1-61520-643-8.ch007

a network of cooperation and in which experience and knowledge are accumulated and reinforced. Therefore we consider the need to a have a more wide vision of the concept of Innovation.

During the 1970s and 1980s, the literature on the Innovation process started contesting the designated linear model, which assumes that technology is developed on the basis of scientific efforts and in which the research is followed by a progressive and sequential development.

Empirical studies have demonstrated that most Innovations reflect a process of feedback from the markets and the interaction between the production of knowledge and managerial initiative from the supply (Lundvall, 1999).

Thus, in opposition to the linear model of Innovation, we have noticed the rise of the systemic approach through the national, regional and local Innovation systems, published in several scientific papers (Braczyk, Cooke, & Heidenreich, 1998; Edquist, 1997; Edquist & Mckelvey, 2000; Guimarães, 1998; Lundvall, 1992; Lundvall, Patarapong, & Vang, 2006; Nelson, 1988, 1993, 2000; OCDE, 1997; Pavitt, 1999; Vang-Lauridsen & Chaminade, 2006) and Cross-Border Regional Innovation System (Trippl, 2006).

The objective of this paper is to reflect upon the factors that influence national innovative capacity. In this sense, and taking into consideration the data on 33 countries from the European Innovation Scoreboard Database, we analyze innovative capacity in terms of innovative output and patents registration, and identify the main factors which differentiate the countries' dynamics.

This paper presents the following framework. Section 2 consists of a literature review on innovative capacity, enhancing the importance of the Innovation systems. In section 3 we describe the hypotheses and the methodology. Section 4 contains the results and section 5 discusses these results and their implications, stressing the limitations of the paper and suggesting avenues for future research.

LITERATURE REVIEW

Innovative capacity has a decisive and crucial role in determining who is prospering in the global arena. Innovation is the base for the development of strategic advantages in companies, so necessary in the current context of global competitiveness (Porter, 1990). Thus innovative capacity enables countries to increase their productivity and attract investments, thereby sustaining continuous progress in the quality and standard of living.

(Suarez-Villa, 1990) introduced the concept of innovative capacity to measure a nation's level of invention and innovative potential. According to this author, measuring the innovative capacity may provide important knowledge about the dynamics of economic activity. Such knowledge may be used by policy-makers or academics for understanding the changes in the Innovation, technology and competitiveness.

At the national level, innovative capacity may provide comparisons about the evolution of inventive activity and its relationship with the main factors of invention, such as access to education and protection of intellectual property.

The concept of national innovative capacity was explained in the works of (Porter & Stern, 1999) Porter and Stern, (1999) and Stern, Porter and Furman (2001, 2002). Their main purpose was to measure the origin of the differences among countries regarding the innovative production, by analyzing the clusters of Innovation. For these authors, national innovative capacity is a country's capacity (as a political and economic entity) to produce and trade in a new flow of technologies, reflecting the fundamental determinations of the Innovation process, not only at the output level (Stern et al., 2001).

Several recent works have enriched this analysis. Each one enhances one or more determinants for the innovative capacity. In a managerial approach, Suarez-Villa, (2003) analyzed the relationship between the inter-organizational networks and innovative capacity, from which emerges a new type of organization: the "experimental firm." Henttonen, (2006) points out the role of internal and external Innovation networks in driving forward the firm's innovative capacity. Belderbos, Carree, and Lokshin, (2004) analyzed the impact of the Research and Development (R&D) in cooperation with the innovative performance of the firm at the level of employment creation and Innovation productivity, by considering the partners in the Community Innovation Survey II.

Riddel and Schwer, (2003), using the model proposed by Romer, 1(990) and operationalized by (Stern et al., 2002), cite the endogenous relation between employment growth and innovative capacity in United States of America.

Archibugi and Coco, (2005) then compared the methodologies used by worldwide organizations such as the World Economic Forum (WEF), the UN Development Program (UNPD), the UN Industrial Development Organization (UNIDO) and the RAND Corporation, to measure national technological capacity. The research of Pontikakis, McDonnell, and Geoghegan, (2005) and of Jaumotte, (2006), pointed out the functioning of the national Innovation systems, its performance, and the role of incentives to maintain and improve national innovative capacity.

(Hu & Mathews, 2005) extend and modify the Stern, Porter and Furman (2002) approach by applying it to five "latecomer" countries from East Asia, and especially to Taiwan. While the results are in broad agreement with the findings of Stern, Porter and Furman (2002), Hu and Mathews document some important differences for latecomer East Asian economies: fewer national factors matter, and there seems to be an important (though subtle) role for public R&D expenditure to act as a steering mechanism for the private sector, while university-based R&D (a basic research resource) does not show a significant effect over the past two decades. Hu and Mathews (2005) demonstrate that the public R&D funding in East Asia greatly strengthens the contribution of specialization in the high-tech industries—but this effect will only

be registered where a latecomer country is pursuing a targeted strategy of catch up, as is Taiwan. (Mathews & Hu, 2007) examine the efforts of Taiwan's academic Innovation through institutional and organizational reforms, and evaluate its impact in assisting Taiwan in moving beyond the phase of being a catch-up manufacturing fast follower to that of an Innovation-based technology developer.

The innovative capacity of a territory, nation or region, is grounded in its microeconomic environment and related to the number of scientists and engineers in the workforce, in the degree of protection of intellectual property and in the power of the clusters. This last reflects the concentrated location of the resources that harnesses the managerial competitiveness.

Innovation is also the solution to many of the world's social problems, such as the health care and the environmental quality. For Stern, Porter and Furman (2001) national innovative capacity lays on three vectors: (1) the endogenous growth based on the ideas of Romer (1990); (2) the theory of the industrial clusters based on the nation's competitive advantages developed by Porter (1990); and (3) the research developed in the national Innovation systems presented by Nelson, (1993). Its differences reflect the variations in economic geography (impact of the knowledge and spillovers of Innovation amongst closely situated companies) and in the Innovation's policies (the level of public support for basic research or protection of intellectual property).

Several authors (Porter & Stern, 1999; Stern et al., 2001; Stern et al., 2002) have highlighted the importance not only of the present competitiveness, but also the capacity of sustaining it in the future, considering the following aspects as determinants of the national innovative capacity: common facilities (public institutions, resources committed, policies that support Innovation); the conditions of nations' clusters (the environment for Innovation in the industrial clusters of a nation); and the quality of the relations amongst the previous categories (capacity to narrow the gap between research and the companies and the collective efforts that contribute to a whole set of specialized personnel and technology).

The innovative performance of economies results from the interaction among these three categories. The national innovative capacity is supported by the Innovation systems' approach, amongst others. This systemic Innovation approach has brought a new knowledge about the performance and the innovative and economic capacity of the countries. The concept of national Innovation system (NIS) has been stressed by several authors. Freeman, (1987b) originally defined NIS as the institutions' network in the private and public sectors which activities and interactions initiate, modify, and diffuse new technologies. Supported by this definition, he describes the Japanese National Innovation System in terms of four elements: the Ministry of International Trade and Industry, R&D companies, education and training and the industrial agglomerates.

The relevance of this theme has brought several contributions to the definition of the NIS (Asheim & Coenen, 2006; Braczyk et al., 1998; Edquist, 1997, 2005; Edquist & Mckelvey, 2000; Guimarães, 1998; Lundvall, 1992; Lundvall et al., 2006; Nelson, 1988, 1993, 2000; OCDE, 1997; Pavitt, 1999; Vang-Lauridsen, Coenen, Chaminade, & Asheim, 2007).

Common to most definitions is the concept of participation of the public and private institutions (Lundvall, 1992; Nelson, 1993; OCDE, 1997; Patel & Pavitt, 1994), whether individually or in networks in the creation of Innovation.

However, these different approaches are vague in the specification of the boundaries of the Innovation system. Therefore, Edquist (1997) includes in the system all the determinants of Innovation: the economic, social, political, organizational, institutional and other factors that influence the development, diffusion and use of Innovation, in addition to the relations among these factors (Edquist, 2001).

Guinet, (1999) conceptualized the Innovation system as a set of institutions which individually and jointly determine the countries' and the international community's capacity to respond efficaciously to the following challenges: making the economy more innovative and adjustable, ensuring the sustainability of the trajectories of development in the long run (economic, sociocultural, ecological and demographic), and dealing with the risks associated to the Innovation and empower the entrepreneurial structure. This is, therefore, an all-embracing definition.

Based on the ideas exposed by these authors (Chung, 1999; Edquist, 1997; Freeman, 1987a; Lundvall, 1992, 1998; Nelson, 1993) the Innovation system may be defined as a complex set of elements and actors (companies and institutions) of the territory, in a dynamic interaction, and organized to innovate in order to promote the competitiveness of a nation or region.

This system relies upon the organization and pattern of activities that contribute to innovative behaviour in the countries and that encourage its competitiveness, and in the identification of the institutions and actors which have a decisive role in promoting Innovation.

The Innovation systems approach encompasses a wide set of the Innovation determinants in the national, regional or sector-based context. Thus, the NIS includes the economic factors that influence Innovation, but also the institutional, organizational, social and political factors, to which Arocena and Sutz, (2000) add the cultural and Pontikakis et al., (2005) the motivational.

This is an interdisciplinary approach in which one of the central characteristics is the interdependency and interaction among the elements of the system. The Innovation system is by definition a set of interdependent activities (Solal, 1997), and Innovation is not just stipulated by the elements of the system but also by the relations amongst them (Edquist, 1997).

These complex relations are characterized by reciprocity, interactivity and feedback mechanisms and constitute the major advantage of the Innovation systems approach. Therefore, the efficient functioning of the Innovation system improves the national innovative capacity (Stern et al., 2002) and its competitive performance. The National Innovation Systems are today widely used within the structuralism/evolutionist field (Clark & Guy, 1998). These are presented as structural frameworks of technical-economical adaptations to the social environment to define trajectories and paradigms of Innovation, aim to model the interaction between the local environment, the knowledge and Innovation, and represent an attempt to turn the determinants of Innovation and knowledge endogenous (Hauknes, 1999).

In this way, national Innovation systems are seen as an instrument to induce economic growth, development (Arroyabe & Pena, 1999; Chung, 1999; Dosi, Freeman, Nelson, Silverberg, & Luc Soete, 1988; Edquist, 2001; Hauknes, 1999; Lundvall, 1998; Mothe & Paquet, 2000), and national competitiveness. The Innovation system is at the center of modern thought on Innovation and its relation with economic growth, competitiveness and employment (Edquist, 2001). Its objective is to enforce and sustain the national competitiveness, being one of the most important strategic factors to acquire competitive advantages.

However, this is not a new idea. Even the neoclassical theories of growth considered technological progress one of the main factors of growth. The new theories of growth combine other type of resources: tangible and non-tangible resources (namely knowledge) and consider the public character of knowledge.

The Innovation systems' perspective embraces a wider and more interdisciplinary approach to the theory of economic growth. The objective is to better understand the role of knowledge in economics and how its creation, distribution and use take place (including its spatial dimension).

HYPOTHESIS AND METHODOLOGY

Considering these theoretical foundations, we can consider the following dimensions or groups of factors as determinants of the territorial innovative capacity: institutional efficiency (based on the commitment and performance of the institutions), the national culture and the collective infrastructure (based upon human capital, in the Innovation's workers skills and in the technological intensity).

Thus, the national innovative performance is conditioned by the specific characteristics of each country on the basis of these three dimensions. In this paper, three hypotheses are proposed: the first is related to the influence of the institutional efficiency on innovative capacity, the second pertains to the role of national culture and the third refers to the influence of the Innovation's infrastructures in the promotion of innovative capacity.

Academic institutions are increasingly seen as influencers in the Innovation capacity in a triple perspective or mission: *tripla hélix* (Vang-Lauridsen et al., 2007) acting as a spiral of knowledge capitalization.

They produce and coordinate the available scientific and technological knowledge; they give superior graduation and skills for the industry, and through interaction with industry and the creation of incubators, directly contribute to the development of the region (Vang-Lauridsen et al., 2007).

Relying on the Innovation systems' approach of Lundvall (1992), Nelson (1993), Edquist (1997), Lundvall et al. (2006) and Asheim and Coenen (2006) and considering that the national Innovation system is defined as a complex set of actors (companies, and institutions), that whether in interaction or assembled, they are organized to foment Innovation (creation, diffusion and appropriateness) and promote competitiveness of this country, one can admit that the efficient functioning of these systems is associated with its *institutional efficiency*. In order to test this hypothesis, we considered as measurement variables the stability, efficiency, regulatory activity, rule of law, corruption and accountability as defined by Evans and Rauch, (1999). The first hypothesis is:

H1: *Institutional efficiency has a positive influence on innovative capacity.*

Another determinant of national innovative capacity is the national culture. This influences the relations, the constitution of Innovation and cooperation networks, the Innovation system, and therefore, the innovative capacity.

Porter (1990, 1998) and Dunning, (1998) reiterate the importance of the national elements in international localization and the importance of the clusters to promote competitive advantages. The conditions to innovate are not applied universally, but each nation must find its own characteristics in light of its own history, culture and values.

Thus, to measure the influence of the national culture upon the innovative capacity, the cultural dimensions of Hofstede, (1987) were taken in to consideration. The first of these dimensions is Power Distance, the capacity of a society to accept an asymmetrical distribution of power and which varies from country to country. The second dimension is Individualism, which may be apprehended as the importance that is given to the objectives and individual efforts as opposed to the objectives and collective efforts.

The third is Uncertainty Avoidance, which is the amount of uncertainty about future events that people of a certain national culture are willing to accept. The fourth is Masculinity, defined as the level of assertiveness which is promoted in the national culture. Taken together, these dimensions allow us to classify and distinguish national cultures. The definition of the second hypothesis rests upon a body of literature which includes papers by Hofstede (1987), Hofstede, (1987), Ronen and Shenkar, (1985), Kogut and Singh, (1988) and Schneider and Barsoux, (1997). Based on these theoretical foundations we define the second hypothesis in the following terms:

H2: *The National Culture has a positive influence on the Innovative Capacity.*

The Innovation's collective framework is the pillar of the innovative activity. The Innovation's framework is one of the determinants of national innovative capacity, according to several authors (Asheim & Coenen, 2006; Riddel & Schwer, 2003; Stern et al., 2001; Stern et al., 2002; Suarez-Villa, 1990, 1997).

The creation of new knowledge is fundamental to the existence of a set of available scientists and engineers; for diffusion to take place, what matters is the competence and talent of the workforce. In this sense, the Human Resources qualification is essential for the success or failure of a country's Innovation efforts (creation, diffusion and new knowledge).

Beyond that, the creation of new knowledge may be stimulated through the increase of public and managerial R&D and through the investment in information and communication technologies.

Therefore, to test this hypothesis as the following variables were considered: science and engineering (S&E) graduates (percentage of 20 – 29 year olds); Population with tertiary education (percentage of 25 – 64 year olds); Business expenditures on R&D (percentage of GDP) e ICT expenditures (percentages of GDP). The third hypothesis derives has the following configuration:

H3: *The Innovation's Framework has a positive influence on Innovative Capacity.*

The main data source used to evaluate the territorial innovative capacity was the European Innovation Scoreboard 2004 Database (Attachment 1) which contains data from 33 countries: Austria (AT), Belgium (BE), Germany (DE), Denmark (DK), Greece (EL), Spain (ES), Finland (FI), France (FR), Ireland (IE), Italy (IT), Luxembourg (LU), the Netherlands (NL), Portugal (PT), Sweden (SE), the United Kingdom (UK), Cyprus (CY), Czech Republic (CZ), Estonia (EE),

Table 1. ANOVA analysis

	Cluster		Error			
	Mean Square	df	Mean Square	df	F	Sig.
EPO high-tech patent applications (per million)	8032,4	3	158,4	29	50,7	0,000
USPTO high-tech patents granted (per million)	3881,7	3	48,0	29	80,9	0,000
EPO patent applications (per million population)	141777,5	3	1346,4	29	105,3	0,000
USPTO patents granted (per million population)	66330,6	3	375,5	29	176,6	0,000

Hungary (HU), Lithuania (LT), Latvia (LV), Malta (MT), Poland (PL), Slovenia (SI), Slovakia (SK), Bulgaria (BG), Romania (RO), Turkey (TR), Switzerland (CH), Iceland (IS), Norway (NO), the United States of America (US) and Japan (JP).

The methodology used for the analysis is based on the application of the multivariate statistic: clusters' analysis, in order to group the countries according to innovative capacity, and in terms of Innovation output. To verify the hypothesis we have applied multiple means comparison tests to distinguish the unique characteristics of each cluster.

RESULTS

The use of clusters analysis proved adequate and the variables used to classify the countries were all significant for the final solution estimated, as we can verify by the results of the ANOVA analysis in Table 1.

The application of the clusters' analysis identified four groups of countries with distinct patterns regarding its performance in terms of innovative capacity. Clusters 1 and 2 present an elevated innovative capacity (Table 2).

The first, with preponderance in terms of the European Patent Office (EPO) high-tech patent applications (per million population) and of EPO patent applications (per million population), groups five countries (DE, NL, FI, SE, CH). The second cluster presents the best results in terms of the United States Patent and Trademark Office (USPTO) high-tech patents granted (per million population) and USPTO patents granted (per million population) and consists of two countries (US and JP). The third cluster, with average values of patents registration per million habitants, presents an intermediate level of innovative capacity and consists of nine countries (BE, DK, FR, IE, LU, AT, UK, IS, NO). The fourth cluster with modest results in terms of patents (a relatively lower of patents registration per million habitants) shows

Table 2. Clusters' constitution

Final Cluster Centres	Cluster 1	Cluster 2	Cluster 3	Cluster 4
	(n=5)	(n=2)	(n=9)	(n=17)
EPO high-tech patent applications (per million)	78,0	44,4	28,9	1,7
USPTO high-tech patents granted (per million)	27,7	75,9	10,5	0,6
EPO patent applications (per million population)	332,5	160,6	150,9	13,6
USPTO patents granted (per million population)	151,6	287,7	66,0	4,1

Table 3. Mean differences among groups - institutional efficiency

Final Cluster Centres	Cluster 1 (n=5)	Cluster 2 (n=2)	Cluster 3 (n=9)	Cluster 4 (n=17)	Mean Differences
Stability	1,16	1,55	1,19	0,81	
Efficiency	1,88	1,90	1,83	0,66	1,2,3>4
Regulatory	1,72	1,55	1,54	0,95	1,2>4
Rule of Law	1,82	2,00	1,73	0,68	1,2,3>4
Corruption	2,10	2,10	1,82	0,51	1,2,3>4
Accountability	1,56	1,55	1,40	0,91	1,2>4

a low innovative capacity. This cluster consists of 17 countries (EL, ES, IT, PT, BG, CY, CZ, EE, HU, LT, LV, MT, PL, RO, SI, SK, TR) (Tables 2).

To interpret the relation between the explicative variables and the dependent variable of the innovative capacity we have tested the groups' mean differences regarding the variables considered in the hypothesis.

Regarding the importance of the institutional efficiency in the innovative capacity (Table 3), we may state that Cluster 4, with minor innovative capacity, evidences a lower institutional efficiency in most of the variables used to measure this item, with the exception of the stability indicator.

Considering the influence of the differences in the dimensions of the national culture on the innovative capacity, we observed a limited effect (Table 4). We have verified that the countries that constitute Cluster 4, by opposition to the ones of

Cluster 2, are the ones that reveal a national culture characterized by a higher power distance. This higher power distance, verified in the countries of Cluster 4, seems to have a negative influence on communication channels, leading to lower cooperation, to minor network relations and to less communication, which, in turn, limits the country's innovative capacity.

Regarding the collective infrastructures for Innovation, the differences among clusters are significant particularly at the levels of population with tertiary education and of business expenditures on R&D (percentage of GDP). The pattern is identical to the one already observed regarding the institutional efficiency and power distance, in which countries belonging to Cluster 4 show less spending in terms of R&D (percentage of GDP) and have a lower percentage of population with higher degree of education (Table 5).

Table 4. Mean differences among groups - national culture dimensions

Final Cluster Centres	Cluster 1 (n=5)	Cluster 2 (n=2)	Cluster 3 (n=9)	Cluster 4 (n=17)	Mean Differences
Power Distance	35,4	30,5	42,3	63,1	4>2
Individualism	74,4	64,5	71,4	47,9	
Uncertainty Avoidance	50,5	31,0	58,0	69,2	
Masculinity	34,6	28,0	60,4	63,8	

Table 5. Mean differences among groups – infrastructures of the innovation indicators

Final Cluster Centres	Cluster 1	Cluster 2	Cluster 3	Cluster 4	Mean
	(n=5)	(n=2)	(n=9)	(n=17)	Differences
S&E graduates *	10,5	6,5	11,7	6,8	
Population with tertiary education **	27,3	37,2	25,7	16,8	2>3,4
Business expenditures on R&D (% of GDP)	2,1	2,2	1,4	0,3	1,2,3>4
ICT expenditures (% of GDP)	7,0	6,2	6,1	7,6	
*(percentage of 20 – 29 years age class)					
**(percentage of 25 – 64 years age class)					

DISCUSSION AND CONCLUSION

The main differences in the level of innovative capacity are associated with the efficient functioning of the national Innovation systems which requires a combination of the economic framework and the different institutions of the countries, in the determination of the direction and of the ratios of the innovative activities, a strong national culture for Innovation and infrastructures supporting Innovation.

The results have enabled us to draw a profile of the countries' innovative capacity. Considering these profiles we can conclude that the conditions associated with the worst performance in terms of Innovation are related to a lower institutional efficiency in terms of Efficiency, Regulatory, Rule of Law, Corruption and Accountability; a national culture in which a high power distance is present and a less endowment infrastructure for Innovation in terms of population with tertiary education and business expenditures on R&D (percentage of GDP).

The practical implications of this study suggest in order to stimulate their innovative capacity, countries need a constant commitment to and the active involvement in their institutions and organizations.

However, this research presents some limitations to the comprehension of the micro mechanisms which create Innovation: the analysis of the influence of the cooperation networks upon the innovative capacity and a more detailed analysis of the effectiveness of the several national innovative strategies.

These limitations arise as a pathway for future research about this theme, and appear to be of great interest to the embodiment of indicators about the influence of the cooperation networks and about national innovative strategy.

REFERENCES

Archibugi, D., & Coco, A. (2005). Measuring Technological Capabilities at the Country Level: A Survey and Menu for Choice. *Research Policy*, *34*, 175–194. doi:10.1016/j.respol.2004.12.002

Arocena, R., & Sutz, J. (2000). Looking at National Systems of Innovation from the South. *Industry and Innovation*, *7*(1), 55–75. doi:10.1080/713670247

Arroyabe, J. C. F. D., & Pena, A. N. (1999, 30 August - 2 September). *Technological Cluster Integrated Model for SMEs*. Paper presented at the 3rd International Conference on Technology and Innovation Policy: Assessment, Commercialisation and Application of Science and Technology and Management of Knowledge, Texas, USA.

Asheim, B. T., & Coenen, L. (2006). Contextualising Regional Innovation Systems in a Globalising Learning Economy: On Knowledge Bases and Institutional Frameworks. *The Journal of Technology Transfer, 31*(1), 163–173. doi:10.1007/s10961-005-5028-0

Belderbos, R., Carree, M., & Lokshin, B. (2004). Cooperative R&D and Firm Performance. *Research Policy, 33*, 1472–1477. doi:10.1016/j.respol.2004.07.003

Braczyk, H.-J., Cooke, P., & Heidenreich, M. (Eds.). (1998). *Regional Innovation Systems: The Role of Governance in a Globalized World*. London: UCL Press.

Chung, S. (1999, 30 August – 2 September). *Regional Innovation Systems in Korea*. Paper presented at the 3rd International Conference on Technology and Innovation Policy: Assessment, Commercialization and Application of Science and Technology and Management of Knowledge, Texas, USA.

Clark, J., & Guy, K. (1998). Innovation and Competitiveness: a Review. *Technology Analysis and Strategic Management, 10*(3), 363–395. doi:10.1080/09537329808524322

Dosi, G., Freeman, C., Nelson, R., Silverberg, G., & Luc Soete. (1988). *Technical change and economic theory*. London: Pinter Publishers.

Dunning, J. (1998). Location and the Multinational Enterprise: A Neglected Factors? *Journal of International Business Studies, 25*(1), 39–73.

Edquist, C. (1997). *Systems of Innovation: Technologies, Institutions and Organizations*. London: Pinter Publisher.

Edquist, C. (2001). Innovation Policy - A Systemic Approach. In D. L. B.-A. Archibugi, (eds) (Ed.), The Globalizing Learning Economy (pp. 220-238). Oxford, UK: Oxford University Press.

Edquist, C. (2005). Systems of Innovation: Perspectives and Challenges. In J. Fagerberg, Mowery, D., and Nelson, R. (eds.). (Ed.), The Oxford Handbook of Innovation (pp. 181-208). Oxford, UK: Oxford University Press.

Edquist, C., & Mckelvey, M. (2000). *Systems of Innovation: Growth, Competitiveness and Employment (Vol. 1-2)*. Cheltenham, UK: Edward Elgar Publishing Limited.

Evans, P., & Rauch, J. (1999). Bureaucracy and growth: A cross-national analysis of the effects of "Weberian" state structures on economic growth. *American Sociological Review, 64*, 748–765. doi:10.2307/2657374

Freeman, C. (1987a). *Technology Policy and Economic Performance: Lessons from Japan*. London: Pinter Publisher.

Guimarães, R. (1998). *Política Industrial e Tecnológica e Sistemas de Inovação*. Oeiras, Portugal: Celta Editora.

Guinet, J. (1999). Libertar o Potencial de Inovação:o Papel do Governo. *Revista Economia & Prospectiva, 10*, 53–80.

Hauknes, J. (1999). *Innovation Systems and Capabilities*. Paper presented at the Paper prepared within the framework of the "TSER/RISE, Program, for the European Commission (DGXII) STEP Gruppen.

Henttonen, K. (2006, 15-17 March). *Innovation in Complex Networks - the State -of-the-Art and propositions for Further Research*. Paper presented at the The Innovation Pressure, International ProAct-Conference, Tampere, Finland.

Hofstede, G. (1987). *Culture and Organizations: Software of the Mind*. New York: McGraw-Hill.

Hu, M.-C., & Mathews, J. A. (2005). Innovative capacity in East Asia. *Research Policy, 34*(9), 1322–1349. doi:10.1016/j.respol.2005.04.009

Jaumotte, F. (2006). Maintaining Switzerland's Top Innovation Capacity. *OECD ECO/WKP, 15*(487).

Kogut, B., & Singh, H. (1988). The Effect of National Culture on the Choice of the Entry Mode. *Journal of International Business Studies, 19,* 411–432. doi:10.1057/palgrave.jibs.8490394

Lundvall, B.-Å. (1992). *National Systems of Innovation: Towards a Theory of Innovation and Interactive Learning.* London: Pinter Publishers.

Lundvall, B.-Å. (1998). Why Study National Systems and National Styles of Innovation. *Technology Analysis and Strategic Management, 10*(4), 407–421. doi:10.1080/09537329808524324

Lundvall, B.-Å. (1999). National Business Systems and National Systems of Innovation. *International Studies of Management & Organization, 29*(2), 60–77.

Lundvall, B.-Å., Patarapong, I., & Vang, J. (2006). *Asia's Innovation systems in transition.* Cheltenham, UK: Edward Elgar.

Mathews, J. A., & Hu, M.-C. (2007). Enhancing the Role of Universities in Building National Innovative Capacity in Asia: The Case of Taiwan. *World Development, 35*(6), 1005–1020. doi:10.1016/j.worlddev.2006.05.012

Mothe, J. D., & Paquet, G. (2000). *National Innovation Systems and Instituted Processes.* London: Pinter Publishers.

Nelson, R. (1988). Institutions Supporting Technical Change in the United States. In Dosi, G. E. A. (Ed.), *Technical Change and Economic Theory.* London: Pinter Publishers.

Nelson, R. (1993). *National Systems of Innovation: a Comparative Study.* Oxford, UK: Oxford University Press.

Nelson, R. (2000). National Systems of Innovation. In Acs, Z. J. E. (Ed.), *Regional Innovation, Knowledge and Global Change* (pp. 11–26). London, New York: Pinter Publisher.

OCDE. (1997). *National Innovation System.* Paris: OECD Publications.

Patel, P., & Pavitt, K. (1994). *Nature et Importance Économique des Systèmes Nationaux D'Innovations* (*Vol. 14*). Paris: OCDE.

Pavitt, K. (1999). *Technology, Management and Systems of Innovation.* Cheltenham, UK: Edward Elgar.

Pontikakis, D., McDonnell, T., & Geoghegan, W. (2005). *Conceptualising a National Innovation System: Actor, Roles and Incentives.* Unpublished manuscript.

Porter, M. E. (1990). *The Competitive Advantage of Nations.* New York: Free Press.

Porter, M. E., & Stern, S. (1999). *The New Challenge to America's Prosperity: Finding from the Innovation Index.* New York: Free Press.

Riddel, M., & Schwer, K. (2003). Regional Innovative Capacity with Endogenous Employment: Empirical Evidence from the U.S. *The Review of Regional Studies, 33*(1), 73–84.

Romer, P. (1990). Endogenous Technological Change. *The Journal of Political Economy, 98,* S71–S102. doi:10.1086/261725

Ronen, S., & Shenkar, O. (1985). Clustering Countries on Attitudinal Dimensions: A Review and Synthesis. *Academy of Management Review, 10*(3), 435. doi:10.2307/258126

Schneider, S., & Barsoux, J.-L. (1997). *Managing Across Cultures.* Upper Saddle River, NJ: Prentice Hall.

Schumpeter, J. (1934). *The Theory of Economic Development.* Cambridge, MA: Harvard University Press.

Solal, P. (1997). Système National d'Innovation, Division du Travail et Territoire: un Retour a F. List et H.C. Carey. *Revue d'Economie Régionale et Urbaine - RERU, 4*, 545-564.

Stern, S., Porter, M., & Furman, J. (2001). *The Determinants of National Innovative Capacity*. Paper presented at the MIT Industrial Performance Seminar. Cambridge, MA.

Stern, S., Porter, M. E., & Furman, J. L. (2002). The Determinants of National Innovative Capacity. *Research Policy, 31*, 899–993. doi:10.1016/S0048-7333(01)00152-4

Suarez-Villa, L. (1990). Invention, Inventive Learning and Innovative Capacity. *Behavioral Science, 35*(4), 290–310. doi:10.1002/bs.3830350404

Suarez-Villa, L. (1997). Innovative Capacity, Infrastructure and Regional Inversion: Is there a Long-term Dynamic? In Bertuglia, S. L. A. P. N. E. C. S. (Ed.), *Innovative Behaviour in Space and Time* (pp. 291–305). Berlin, Heidelberg, New York: Springer-Verlag.

Suarez-Villa, L. (2003). *Innovative Capacity, Networks and the rise of Experimental Firm: Implications for Regional Development and Policy*. Paper presented at the International Workshop on Modern Entrepreneurship, Regional Development and Policy: Dynamic and Evolutionary Perspectives.

Trippl, M. (2006). *Cross-Border Regional Innovation Systems*. Retrieved from http://epub.wu-wien.ac.at

Vang-Lauridsen, J., & Chaminade, C. (2006). *Globalization of Knowledge Production and Regional Innovation Policy: Supporting Specialized Hubs in Developing Countries*. Unpublished manuscript.

Vang-Lauridsen, J., Coenen, L., Chaminade, C., & Asheim, B. (2007). Universities, Regional Innovation Systems and the Bangalore Experience: Towards a Contextual and Evolutionary Perspective. Paper presented at the Managing Total Innovation and Open Innovation in the 21st Century. In *Proceedings of the 5Th international. Symposium on Management of Technology* (IS-MOT'07), Zhejiang, China.

APPENDIX

European Innovation Scoreboard Database

Data per country		Data per indicator	
Jump to:		**Jump to:**	
AT	Austria	E11	S&E graduates (‰ of 20 – 29 years age class)
BE	Belgium	E12	Population with tertiary education (% of 25 – 64 years age class)
DE	Germany	E13	Participation in life-long learning (% of 25 – 64 years age class)
DK	Denmark	E14	Employment in medium-high and high-tech manufacturing (% of total workforce)
EL	Greece	E15	Employment in high-tech services (% of total workforce)
ES	Spain	E21	Public R&D expenditures (% of GDP)
FI	Finland	E22	Business expenditures on R&D (% of GDP)
FR	France	E231	EPO high-tech patent applications (per million population)
IE	Ireland	E232	USPTO high-tech patents granted (per million population)
IT	Italy	E241	EPO patent applications (per million population)
LU	Luxembourg	E242	USPTO patents granted (per million population)
NL	Netherlands	E31	SMEs innovating in-house (% of all SMEs)
PT	Portugal	E32	SMEs involved in Innovation co-operation (% of all SMEs)
SE	Sweden	E33	Innovation expenditures (% of total turnover)
UK	United Kingdom	E34	SMEs using non-technological change (% of all SMEs)
EU15	EU15	E41	Share of high-tech venture capital investment
CY	Cyprus	E42	Share of early stage venture capital in GDP
CZ	Czech Republic	E431	Sales of 'new to market' products (% of total turnover)
EE	Estonia	E432	Sales of 'new to the firm but not new to the market' products (% of total turnover)
HU	Hungary	E44	Internet access (composite index)
LT	Lithuania	E44a	Level of internet access - % of enterprises who have Internet access
LV	Latvia	E44b	Level of Internet access - % of households who have Internet access at home
MT	Malta	E45	ICT expenditures (% of GDP)
PL	Poland	E46	Share of manufacturing value-added in high-tech sectors
SI	Slovania		
SK	Slovakia	FULL	Full database (all countries all indicators)
EU25	EU25		
BG	Bulgaria	Rank	Countries ordered by rank per indicator
RO	Romania		
TR	Turkey		
CH	Switzerland		
IS	Iceland		
NO	Norway		
US	United States		
JP	Japan		

Source: http://trendchart.cordis.lu/scoreboards/scoreboard2004/scoreboard_papers.cfm

Chapter 8

Entrepreneurship Competencies and Management Capabilities for Innovation and Sustainable Growth:
Empirical Study

Maktoba Omar
Edinburgh Napier University, UK

Michael Lewrick
Edinburgh Napier University, UK

ABSTRACT

The aim of this chapter is to challenge the context of entrepreneurship competences and management capabilities needed for innovation. We build our arguments in step with actual practice analyzing data from over 200 innovative companies which have been created under the formal requirements of a regional business plan competition during the last 10 years. This study explores the crucial capabilities to start an innovative business and discuss the capabilities have to be developed to sustain innovation and business growth. Therefore, it can be hypothesised that entrepreneurship and innovation education provided by Universities, Centres for Entrepreneurship and through coaching by Business Plan Competitions should focus on building awareness for the necessity of innovations and prepare inventors, entrepreneurs and students for not simply starting an enterprise but the change process in growing companies. The questions are not of whether or not to educate people about entrepreneurship and innovation but rather what are the context and the capabilities needed to sustain business and become an innovative and successful entrepreneur?

INTRODUCTION

The term innovation derived from the Latin term *innovare* (to make something new) and most defini-

tions about innovation highlight the exploration and exploitation of new knowledge. The first point to make is that innovation is not invention. Invention must be seen as the initial step *"in a long process to bringing a good idea to widespread and effective*

DOI: 10.4018/978-1-61520-643-8.ch008

use" (Ex., Tidd, et al, 2003:38). Innovations are the commercialization of inventions (idea-to-cash). Within this chapter innovation includes radical and incremental innovations in different typologies, which include orangisational change and non-technological characteristics of products, services and processes. This is in line with the OECD (2005:46) definition of innovation, which describes innovation *"as the implementation of a new or significantly improved product (good or service), or process, a new marketing method, or a new organisational method in business practices, workplace organisation or external relations"*.

However, the conception of innovation has evolved significantly in recent times. It appears that the complex theories of innovation can be explained by the increasing extent of social in-gredients in the explanation of innovativeness. Originally based on tangible forms of capital and the necessity of pull and technological push, innovation management is today integrated in a much larger system (Ex., Lewrick, 2007)

We have seen in the last 10 years the dot-com bubble bursting, a hype establishing Bio-technology companies and lately a run launching businesses in arena of web 2.0. It is mainstream to establish businesses norm in certain areas at a certain time, encouraged by VCs, Business Angels and media to make fast cash. How many dot-com's have survived? How many companies had the right talent on board to steer the company in turbulent times and the capabilities to undergo a continuous change process? Useem (2001) categorized for example the dot-com business founders as "opportuneurs" rather than entrepreneurs. The "opportuneurs" objectives are different, decoupling wealth from contribution, replacing risk taking with risk faking, and exploiting external resources instead of following inner vision.

More companies are incubators which found their origin within university infrastructures triggered by university business plan competitions and supplementary centres of entrepreneurship. Therefore entrepreneurial education must be two

folded: Firstly, it becomes of paramount importance to learn from the successful entrepreneurs and enterpriser, to develop this knowledge, transfer it into educational content and develop on this basis our society. Secondly, learners need to have contact to founders of companies which faced the challenges of starting and growing a business, which failed, changed or succeed with their vision.

Different capabilities are needed in different stages of business growths and Di Masi (Ex., 2006:1) highlights in this conjunction: "...the entrepreneurial characteristics required to launch a business successfully are often not those required for growth and even more frequently not those required to manage it once it grows to any size. The role of the entrepreneur needs to change with the business as it develops and grows, but all too often he or she is not able to make the transition". This is caused by two main facts, firstly growing organisations become more complex and not only the growing infrastructure has to be managed but also the awareness of the change and transition process. Secondly, the dynamic and competitive environment requires continuous adoption and innovation. Each growth stage poses its own challenges for the venture (Nieman and Pretorious, 2004).

Drucker (Ex., 1985, p. 32) points out innovation and entrepreneurship are interlinked. He explains and analyzes the challenges and opportunities of a new entrepreneurial economy. "Innovation is the specific tool of entrepreneurs, the means by which they exploit changes as an opportunity for a different business or service. It is capable of being presented as a discipline, capable of being learned, capable of being practiced".

Entrepreneurship and the definition of the entrepreneur are quite different depending on the premises of the discipline. The word entrepreneur originates from the French term entreprendre (to undertake), which is associated with to start a venture. Putting entrepreneurship in a historical sequence, six major views can be identified: (1) the "great person" school; (2) classical and neoclas-

Figure 1.

Views of the entrepreneur	Focus	Assumption	Behaviour and skills	Situation
"Great person" school	born with intuitive ability, traits and instincts	entrepreneurship is born and pre-given	intuition, vigour, energy, persistence, and self-esteem	start-up
Classical	innovation	entrepreneurship is doing rather than owning	innovation, creativity, and discovery	start-up and early growth
Psychological	unique values, attitudes, needs and characteristics	people behave in accordance with their values	personal values, risk taking, need for achievement	start-up
Sociological	family and environmental dynamics	early childhood influences or affects career decision	shared sources and networks	early growth and maturity
Management	planning, organizing, leading and controlling	entrepreneurs can be developed and trained	production planning, people organizing, capitalization and budgeting	early growth and maturity
Intra-preneurship	venture teams within organizations; development of independent units to create, market, and expand services	entrepreneurs effect change within organizations, lead to organizational building and become managers	alertness to opportunities, maximizing decisions	maturity and change

sical economics; (3) psychology; (4) sociology; (5) management; and (6) intrapreneurship (see Figure 1). Filion (1997:1) distincts and states that "the economists have associated entrepreneurs with innovation, whereas the behaviourists have concentrated on the creative and intuitive characteristics of entrepreneurs."

The critical change process from an entrepreneurial setting into a mature company seems to be one of the major challenges. Ardichvilia, et al (2003) recognised that the development process is a cyclical and iterative endeavour. As a company grows, entrepreneurs must learn to adapt to all changes in order to survive. Companies find it difficult to develop an appropriate strategy and it is necessary to identify different innovation styles in the stages of the growing company. Morris et al (1994) for example point out that start-up companies have to manage cash flows and profits, while mature companies focus more on the strategic outcomes. The competences that individuals require to start a new venture are different to the managerial approach needed in mature businesses (Watson, 2001 and Wickham, 2001).

Entrepreneurship has become offered as a course in many business schools and universities, even entire study paths have been emerged since the 1970s. It seems that entrepreneurship or the facets of being an entrepreneur can be taught as Drucker (1985) states that It's not magic, it's not mysterious, and it has nothing to do with the gens. It's a discipline. And, like any other discipline, it can be learned. Many other publications agree on the fact that entrepreneurship can be learned or at least that learners are somehow inspired by the "mystique" entrepreneurship to go this path. Such a research outcome does not provide any specific recommendation on the content of entrepreneurship education. Globally, it seems that countries try to establish an "enterprise and entrepreneurial culture" to keep-up with the challenges globalization brings (e.g. OECD, 2006). It seems that the public celebrates the business idols which become multi-million enterprisers over night by selling a well marketed business idea. The statistics of companies' survival rate however, show different pictures. Only a few companies are high-technology start-ups and even less companies have the capabilities to grow and sustain a business.

Failure Rates of New Ventures

A study from the U.S Small Business Administration (SBA) indicated that only 67 percent of all start-ups are successful after four years. The survey was conducted along 12,185 ventures in 2003 (USA Today, 2003). The study also revealed that businesses are most likely to succeed if they are equipped with more than $50,000 in capital, an owner with a university degree and running the business from home (Ex., Hopkins, 2003). Earlier studies in the 90s (Ex., Phillips, 1993) found that 76% of all firms survive at least two years, 47% survive at least four years, 38% survive at least 6 years, and 29% survive at least 8 years. However, out of 100 new businesses launched tomorrow, only 30 will still be alive in five years. Of those, 20% will be scraping by, 60% will be doing middling well, but only 20% will be spectacularly successful. In the 90s, a research by the Small Business and Special Surveys of Statistics Canada found that 56% of all Canadian firms started in 1990 and 1991 survived at least 2 years, and 39% survived at least 4 years. In Scotland, a study published by the *The Scotsman* (Ex., Lyons, 2003) newspaper show the high number of liquidations of businesses in various Scottish cities. Glasgow, for example peaked with nearly 60% of liquidations in the first quarter of 2003, compared to Edinburgh with 19% and Aberdeen and Dundee with 1%, a tremendously high failure rate. In the first three months of 2006, 4818 British companies collapsed. A research conducted by Experian (2006) highlight that the failure rate increased by 15.3%, making the highest rise since 1999. In Germany, the success rate of start- ups participating in regional and national business plan competition is 83% (Ex., Niefert, et. al., 2006). Over the last 20 years the success rate of new ventures in Germany has been 58%.

Entrepreneurship Competences and Management Capabilities

It seems that the likelihood of failure is fairly high, because companies often mismanage the venture process. For example, they are too risk adverse, their cultures are inappropriate, they fail to provide sufficient incentives, and they involve the wrong mangers.

To identify "what" should be taught in entrepreneurship education some views and opinions from various scholars are outlined in the following. It seems that entrepreneurship is different from general management (Ex., Gartner and Vesper, 1994). There is a need to focus on developing core skills needed to be a successful entrepreneur. Mostly these are skills associated with leadership, steering a product development process, exploring and exploiting innovations, etc. (Ex., McMullan and Long, 1987), but also capabilities to obtain resources for starting a venture (Ex., Vesper & McMullen, 1988; Zeithaml and Rice, 1987). Other areas to be included in any eductational programme are associated with entrepreneurship as career possibility (Ex., Donckels, 1991, Hills, 1988), and the protection of ideas and patents (Ex., Vesper and MacMullen, 1988). Views from McMullan and Long (1987) as well as Plashka and Welsch (1990) highlight the importance of the challenges in each stage of the venture process (Ex., Solomon, Duffy, and Tarabishy, 2002). Gibb (2002) argues that entrepreneurial education should deal with complexity and uncertainty and the education programmes should be embedded in globalisation frame to lecture the right context.

Beside class room learning a variety of paths are known in entrepreneurial education to provide a more practical educations. This might include computer simulations, virtual start-up competitions, real business plan competitions, entrepreneurial workshops, discussions and knowledge exchange with participating entrepreneurs, and work experience and internship in the start-up activities of a company.

Most educational programmes in Europe highlight the positive impacts of entrepreneurial behaviour to economic growth and the motivation of people to become entrepreneurs. Garvan and Cinneide (1994) recommend to focus on knowledge acquisition relevant to entrepreneurship, skills development and use of techniques, identification and stimulation of entrepreneurial drive and talent, risk evaluation and analytical techniques, the aspects of developing, enjoying and supporting a venture, development of attitudes to change, and encouragement for start-up and ventures creation. However, none of the elements can be associated to the capabilities needed to grow a business from a start-up phase to a more mature phase of business. The US and Europe encourage entrepreneurs to explore the venture process by developing a business plan (Ex., Gartner and Vesper, 1998; Hills and Morris, 1998). But Gibb (1996) states that the business plan might not be the adequate metaphor for the entrepreneurial act. He argues that the business plan is more a reflection of the attempt by the providers of banking, accounting, and commercial services to the entrepreneur and owner-manager to reduce the world and make sense of things in there terms.

From an ontological perspective it might be necessary to discuss the education approach by the context offered to students. Kyro (2000) posits the theory that the entrepreneurial paradigm must be fundamental to the postmodernist world. He suggests including emotions, values and interests rather than characterising the entrepreneur as a rational thinking decision taker. Other scholars like Chia (1996) argue that entrepreneurial education should stay away from analytical problem-solving and suggest characterising the entrepreneur as an "intellectual entrepreneur" or someone "crating of relationships between sets of ideas". In contrast Fiet (2001:101) deny the importance of theory in social science by arguing that: *"Entrepreneurship theory as a set of empirical generalizations about the world economy and how entrepreneurs should behave that allows for prediction of true outcomes"*

Methodology

The data used for the study reported in this chapter has been derived from two questionnaires which had the objective to obtain data from firms classified as start-up and mature companies. The questionnaires contained over 60 questions in domains related to the management capabilities, market and customer orientation, competitive environment, knowledge infrastructure and strategy, learning and diversification, the measurement of innovation and success as well as the use of different network types (business, personal, organisational). The degree of innovativeness is measured by the amount of (radical and incremental) innovation realised in a typical year in different innovation typologies (product, service, process, administrative, technical). The total amount of innovativeness was measured by the sum of incremental and radical innovations realised. All participating companies in the study have been established under same formal requirements of the Munich Business Plan Competition. Demographic questions have been added to obtain information related to business performance, company age, business sector, core competences, number of employees, and position of the respondent. 216 out of 530 companies completed the questionnaire data cleaning resulted in a further reduction of 45 responses yielding a response rate of 32%. The distribution by level of total innovativeness as measured by number of innovations per annum, by business type is displayed in Table 1.

No significant differences were found in the degree innovativeness across the different business sectors examined in this research. This suggests that at least in the high technology cluster region of Munich that the management of innovation is generic rather than industry specific.

No significant differences were found in the degree innovativeness across the different business sectors examined in this research. This suggests that at least in the high technology cluster region

Table 1.

	N	Percentage Total Innovativeness		
		< 10 innovations	10 - 30 innovations	3> 30 innovations
Health Care Sector	32	21.9%	56.3%	21.9%
Knowledge Services	31	29.0%	54.8%	16.1%
Manufacturing	43	41.9%	46.5%	11.6%
Traditional Services	53	28.3%	54.7%	17.0%
Energy Sector	12	16.7%	50.0%	33.3%

of Munich that the management of innovation is generic rather than industry specific.

To analyse the survey data factor analysis with varimax rotation was conducted on the 60 questions, and 12 factors were generated to provide insight of the importance of key capabilities for sustaining innovation and success. The variation in the factors was examined to determine if they are related to incremental, radical and total innovation. To do this multinomial logistic regression in SPSS 16.0 was used to determine the likelihood that a particular case belongs to the category of less than 10, between 10 and 30 and over 30 total innovations per annum. This categorisation was used to indicate companies who had a low, medium and high propensity to innovate.

The details of this is not reported here but are provided in Lewrick (2007a). This categorisation was used to indicate companies who had a low, medium and high propensity to innovate. In addition, the link of innovation to sales increase is explored to give justification to the assumption that innovation drives companies' performance (Ex., Lewrick, 2007). A strong association between sales and total innovativeness, significant at the P level of < 1% was found.

The actual change in these factors over the time perspective is examined to determine how core capabilities change and why it becomes important to educate and prepare entrepreneurs about the change. The difference of the main domains in the time perspective is examined and linked to the factors derived above.

Depicted in Figure 2 is how total innovativeness varies with the factors generated from over 60 statements. Some factors have a significant positive correlation to incremental innovations and or radical innovations, while other factors not show any significant relation to innovativeness, notably management ability, formal networks and key performance indicators. For most of the factors, scores are negative for the low propensity to innovate and the highest positive scores appear with the high propensity to innovate category.

This first exploration helps to define some important capabilities for growing companies to sustain innovation. From Figure 2 it becomes obvious that knowledge is paramount to generate a high amount of innovations. Innovativeness is triggered by a continuous process of upgrading current knowledge and skills for familiar products and technologies to sustain mainly incremental innovations. The growing companies must invest to enhance skills in exploiting mature technologies with the overall aim to improve productivity of current innovation operations. This is one of the most important capabilities which have to be developed with regard to the management of knowledge (Ex., Lewrick, 2007a). Further it seems to be mandatory to put strong emphasis on the constant improvement of the product development process even the company posses' already significant experience. In the process from a start-up phase to a mature phase of business the enterpriser has to create a culture where knowledge can be shared freely and build awareness for knowledge platforms.

Figure 2.

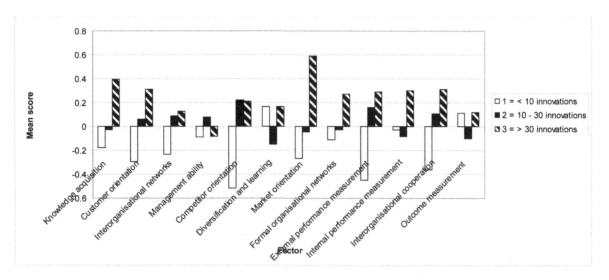

A strong correlation is also observed in the orientation towards the customer and innovation success. To sustain innovations it seems to be mandatory to constantly monitor and reinforce the understanding of the current and future customers and their needs. This improves the knowledge about emerging customers. It is important for a growing company to develop and utilise research techniques such as focus groups, surveys, and observation to gather customer information and to enrich customer intelligence. While competitor orientation has an insignificant impact on inno-vativeness it is different for market orientation. In some cases a strong competitor orientation has even a negative impact on radical innovations for mature companies (Ex., Lewrick, 2008). A strong market orientation allows reacting to changing customer preferences. This also includes the con-stant observation of actions of local and foreign competitors. This might support decision taking in markets and technologies which are highly unpredictable.

A strong impact on innovation and success is seen in the ability to build a strong interorganisa-tional network. The interorganisational network might be helpful to accelerate growth of the com-pany by establishing cooperative R&D agreements

with other companies. The interorganisational collaboration for the design and manufacture process has also been identified as important factor as well as an agreed and systematically planed introducing of new products or services to the market. These findings are very much in line with the desirability of the concept of open innovation as advanced by Chesbourgh (2003).

The measurement of innovations and business performance seems to be essential to sustain in-novations. Especially the internal performance measurement is essential to for generating high innovation output. The measurement of the out-comes of the innovation process is also important. Next, a summary of the actual change in the 11 domains which had a significant effect on inno-vation is presented. The comparison shows the different focus of companies in a start-up phase in comparison to a more mature phase of business in different performance levels. The performance levels are based on firms' current sales perfor-mance/increase per annum. Displayed in Figure 3 depicts arc the domains customer orientation, competitor orientation, and the market and competitive environment. It appears that market orientation is a fundamental element to sustain in-novations and business success. Successful firms

Figure 3.

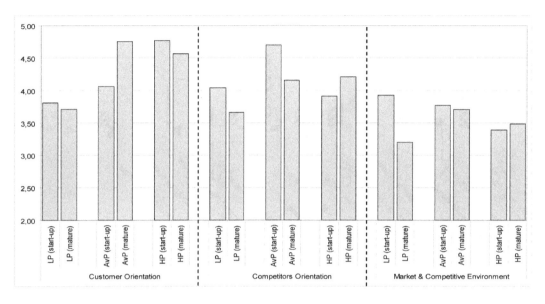

have in a high customer focus when starting the business while low performing firms tend to be more product centric.

The Competitor Orientation is in many cases very high in the start-up phase of companies. It seems that two success paths are possible depending on the innovation agenda of the company. Almost all start-ups tend to investigate the competitors carefully within the start-up activities. This might be caused by the necessity to compare the company's strategy with major competitors within the development activities of a solid business plan. Companies focusing more on radical innovations tend not to focus on competitor orientation in bringing innovation successfully into the market. They might co-develop there innovations with customers, using trend prediction methods or tapping into new undeveloped markets, following a blue ocean strategy.

The Market and Competitive Environment seems to be another trigger or driving force for innovations. Low performing companies might not be close enough to the market to experience the pressure of global competitors. It seems to be important for innovations to monitor the actions

of local, national and global competitors to know there market movements.

The exploration of diversification and learning, resources for innovation, and the management of knowledge are laid out in Figure 4. It seems that diversification and learning becomes essential to sustain long term strategy of innovation. Successful companies tend to put more emphasis on diversification and learning which results in higher innovation outputs. The low performing mature companies provide an excellent example of how an environment without continuous learning and exploring new business fields result in low innovation outputs.

Resources for innovations are important to sustain innovations and to increase companies' performance. High performing companies tend to have the capabilities to maintain resources at a high level. Perhaps average performing companies show that they are able to generate more resources in shorter time which will lead to higher innovation performance in the future. Losing the capability of generating resources in the transformation process from a start-up to a more mature phase of the business affects the innovativeness and leads

Figure 4.

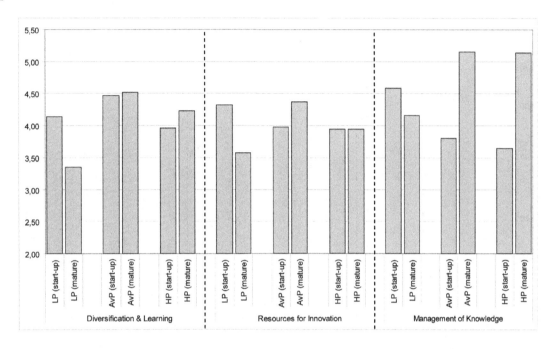

to a low likelihood of success. The management of knowledge becomes one of the key factors in converting ideas into innovations. Both, average performing and high performing companies demonstrate a strong focus on the management of knowledge and this is highly associated with innovation success. Start-ups companies without strong emphasis on sharing and acquiring knowledge tend to become low performing companies.

Figure 5 provides the change in management capabilities, organisational network and interorganisational network. The required management capabilities to grow the business and to sustain innovations show the importance of the background, education and experience of the management team (Ex., Lewrick, 2007b). It seems that successful companies are equipped with more experienced managers right from start in comparison to low performing companies which have less powerful management capacities within their organisations. While the successful companies expand and develop management capacity, low performing companies decrease their management capabilities.

The development of the organisational network depends on the growth of the company. Low performing companies increase only slowly and without impacting on the organisational network. In contrary high performing companies show a high increase in developing and expanding the organisational network in the change process from a start-up to a more mature phase of business. A similar pattern is seen in the interorganisational network. Average and high performing companies double their efforts in developing cooperative R&D, joint market strategies and in teaming-up with other companies in open innovation to jointly design and manufacture new products or utilise new technologies.

Finally, outlined in Figure 6 are the changes in conjunction to strategic focus versus the financial focus and the importance of the measurement of innovations and success. This indicates that almost all companies tend to become more financial and control driven after the change from start–up to mature. However, it seems that companies which are less financial driven become more successful in

Figure 5.

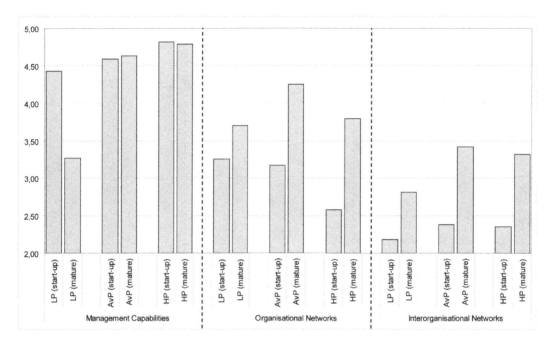

growing and becoming innovative. For measuring key performance outcomes mature companies it appears that mature companies have developed a strong process and have tools in place to measure innovation and performance.

From these findings it is possible to set an agenda for entrepreneurship and innovation education. In the following it is outlined how these capabilities might be transferred into a educational setting. It is hoped that this might help to structure and develop entrepreneurship and innovation educational curriculum in the future.

It is clear that in the context of innovation and entrepreneurship education there is a need for building awareness for the change process of new ventures in order to become successful mature companies. The pre-requisite is to see the management of innovations embedded in a larger complex system. However, Lewrick (2007a) shows that focusing on R&D in conjunction with the management of innovations does not lead towards a more open view of the triggers, supporters and drives for innovation and ultimately

success. The different typologies of innovation, e.g. product innovation, service innovation, process innovation should be discussed. Using for example the life-cycle of a company depict which kind of typology of innovation might be relevant at which level of the life-cycle of a venture will assist in understanding the typologies of innovation and their development. In addition, the external drivers might be added to show for example how the competitive environment forces companies to innovate. The results show that some capabilities which effect companies performance and innovation success. Teaching entrepreneurship and innovation must include ways of how to expand, develop and sustain these capabilities. Current entrepreneurial education programs focus too much on the capabilities of the entrepreneur and the immediacy of starting a business. This might be important but even more important is in our view is the capacity of the entrepreneur to go through a continuous development process which allows surviving and growing the business. Successful start-ups have in most cases an

Figure 6.

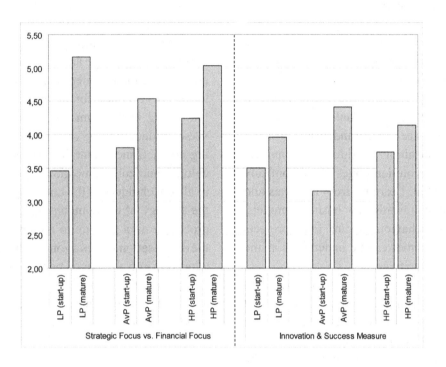

experienced management team with knowledge in a specific industry. The management team need also to general management skills gained in large or small firms by experiencing operational practice. Further, entrepreneurship and innovation education has to build awareness for the necessity of learning and diversification. Both elements are of paramount importance to bring a unique idea towards the market. In addition, it seems to be necessary to discuss and show the impact of radical verse incremental innovations. In many cases me-too products and services do not lead to business success. Markets are already occupied by established companies with a strong customer relationship. New entrants might be successful to participate actively in a regional setting but will not sustain the business on a national or global scale. It is also important to educate about the need for resources to develop and market ideas. Successful companies managed to have resources available from an early stage and they tend to continue generating resources on a high level. Companies starting with a low budget and

without the potential to tap into fresh money have problems to sustain innovations. Another important factor which needs to be considered for entrepreneurial and innovation education agendas are the development of social networks and the access and mobilisation of social capital embedded with in them. Recalling the earlier argument about the need for resources, a strong network including venture capitalist, business angels, and bankers might be very helpful to tap into fresh money. In many cases the personal networks to former peers helps to discuss ideas or provide entrance to potential customers and clients. The management of knowledge has been identified to be one of the major drivers for innovation and success. Entrepreneurial and Innovation education is also about education on the value of knowledge, knowledge sharing and dealing with all kinds of challenges of keeping and acquiring knowledge. Entrepreneurship and Innovation education need to provide learners with methods and tools to evaluate and secure the knowledge within the company.

After educating learners about the complexity of innovations and the capabilities needed it is the responsibility of educators to show the challenges starting a company and to show at the same time how change can be managed actively to promote business growth. Starting a new company is a risky endeavor but the real challenge is to grow the company and steer change and sustain business in the future. The ability to educate the founders in the different evolution stages of the company becomes essential. Learning from mistakes and taking decisions towards new business models, organisational behaviour and/or joint projects with other companies can be understood as the management capacity needed.

Further learners must be aware of the rising organisational requirements which are needed in a growing company because these elements influence the innovation performance and how this is to be managed. Again, investigation the life-cycle of a venture will help to identify major challenges and prepare learners how to keep-up with the change in the dynamic environments.

This might include discussion about actions needed in the first stage including the conception of a business idea, business plan writing, analysis of the competitive environment, building proto-types, co-developments with customers, or selling the service the first time to customers and how to identify market trends and obtain feedback from customers. Starting the business is already a big change from conceptualising the business idea because: resources are needed, price and business portfolio strategies have to be developed, social networks need development and attention, strategic partners might be necessary to bring ideas to market, high performing and operational employees are required. Further, the company has to develop measurement systems to control innovation initiatives and strategic direction. Reporting systems must be implemented and standardised processes are need to work efficient, however it is important to retain the spirit of creativity and

innovative within the organisation. In addition to all this sales structures and distribution strategies must be created and implemented. As the company becomes more mature and again more challenges are face the management team including efforts to get fresh money for innovation and growth, innovating in different typologies, creating diverse products and services, or improving existing products incrementally, creating a corporate cultures and communication the change process to all stakeholders of the company, rationalising the strategy of the company and so forth In the process from a start-up to a more mature phase the organisation leaves a zone without limitations (start-up) into a zone of control (mature). This change becomes crucial for survival and growth and thus the educational agenda must educate and build awareness for the change process.

DISCUSSION

Entrepreneurs and start-up companies play a vital role in the innovations that lead to breakthrough technological change and productivity growth. Growing companies are about change and the awareness of how the change is best managed. This must be integral part of entrepreneurial and innovation education and entrepreneurial education should not be allowed to focus solely on business start-up. Being taught how to write a comprehensive business plan might be essential but it seems even more important to teach how to sustain business success, raise companies' survival rate and educate students and entrepreneurs about the challenge of the transformation from a start-up phase to a more mature phase of business. Learning from successful companies is one path to generate best practice examples (Ex., Lewrick, 2007c), but it is also essential to show that a lack of core capabilities leads to failure or even bigger challenges in the future to survive and to sustain innovations. Entrepreneurship should be characterised as continues innovation and creativity – long term thinking and continuous change. It is not about quick exists, fast cash, investment and liquidity, and short term thinking.

CONCLUSION

The competences to start a business are different from the capabilities sustaining business success. The high failure rate of start-up companies give evidence for a lack of entrepreneurship competences and management capabilities sustaining business success. The research observed the capabilities managing and sustaining start-up business to conclude which competences are essential to start a business and sustain business success. The study argues that these capabilities are not taught to the right extend at universities and centres of entrepreneurship. A revised curriculum should be focus on preparing for the actual change while businesses grow. Examples of changes in capabilities are provided to present the requirements needed in entrepreneurship education. This includes for example the shift from competitor orientation towards market and customer orientation or the improved skills in sharing and developing knowledge. Moreover, growing companies need to establish processes and structures to operate on a larger scale. Supplementary research should be conducted from a practitioner's point of view with the aim to reflect the current path teaching entrepreneurship and innovations.

REFERENCES

Ardichvilia, A., Cardozob, R., & Rayc, S. (2003). A theory of entrepreneurial opportunity identification and development. *Journal of Business Venturing, 18*(1).

Bridge, S., O'Neill, K., & Cromie, S. (1998). *Understanding Enterprise, Entrepreneurship, and Small Businesses*. Manchester, UK: Manchester University Press.

Chesbrough, H. (2003). *Open Innovation: The New Imperative for Creating and Profiting from Technology*. Boston: Harvard Business School Press.

Chia, R. (1996). Teaching paradigm shifts in management education: university business schools and the entrepreneurial imagination. *Journal of Management Studies, 33*, 409–428. doi:10.1111/j.1467-6486.1996.tb00162.x

Di-Masi, P. (2006). *Defining Entrepreneurship*. Retrieved January 27, 2006, from http://www.gdrc.org/icm/micro/define-micro.html

Donckels, R. (1991). Education and entrepreneurship experiences from secondary and university education in Belgium. *Journal of Small Business and Entrepreneurship, 9*(1), 35–42.

Drucker, P. (1985/1999). *Innovation and entrepreneurship*. London: HarperBusiness Publishing.

Drucker, P. F. (1985). *Innovation and entrepreneurship*. New York: Harper & Row.

Experian (2006). *Failure rate of British Companies*. Retrieved April 15, 2006, from http://experian.de/download/2006/companyreport/pdf

Fiet, J. (2001). The pedagogical side of entrepreneurship theory. *Journal of Business Venturing, 16*(2), 101–117. doi:10.1016/S0883-9026(99)00042-7

Filion, L. (1997). From Entrepreneurship to Entreprenology, HEC University of Montreal Business School. Retrieved January 10, 2006, from http://www.usasbe.org/knowledge/proceedings/1997/P207Filion.PDF

Garavan, T., Cinnéide, B., & Fleming, P. (1997). *Entrepreneurship and Business Start-Ups in Ireland*. Dublin, Ireland: Oak Press.

Gartner, W., & Vesper, K. (1998). Experiments in entrepreneurship education: Success and failures. *Journal of Business Venturing, 9*(2), 179–187.

Gibb, A. (1996). Entrepreneurship and small business management: can we afford to neglect them in the twenty-first century business school? *British Journal of Management, 7*, 309–321. doi:10.1111/j.1467-8551.1996.tb00121.x

Gibb, A. (2002). In pursuit of a new enterprise and entrepreneurship paradigm for learning: creative destruction, new values, new ways of doing things and new combinations of knowledge. *International Journal of Management Reviews, 4*(4), 223–269.

Hills, G., & Morris, M. (1998). Entrepreneurship education: a concept model and review. In Scott, M., Rosa, P., & Klandt, H. (Eds.), *Educating Entrepreneurs in Wealth Creation* (pp. 38–58). Aldershot: Ashgate.

Hills, (1988). Variations in university entrepreneurship education: An empirical study of an evolving field. *Journal of Business Venturing, 3*(2), 109-122.

Hopkins, J. (2003, February 18). Study: New company failure rate not so high, *USA Today.*

Kyro, P. (2000). *Is there a pedagogical basis for entrepreneurship education?* Jyväskylä, Finland: Department of Economics, Jyväskylä University.

Lewrick, M. (2007a). *Changes in Innovation Styles: Comprehensive Study of the changes in innovation styles to identify the causes and effects of different influencing factors and capabilities to create a general innovation pattern.* Edinburgh, Scotland: Napier University Business School.

Lewrick, M. (2007b). The Innovators Social Network: A cross-sector exploration on the influence of social networks and social capital on innovation and success. *Journal of Technology Management Innovations, 2*(3), 38–48.

Lewrick, M. (2007c). *Learning from the successful companies in a regional entrepreneurial and innovation system.* Presented at the 2nd International Seminar on Regional Innovation Policies, Oct 2007, pp 26-46

Lewrick, M. (2008). *The Influence of Customers and Competitors on the Market Orientation and Innovators on Start-up and Mature Companies* (Working Paper, RP033/2008), Edinburgh, Scotland: Napier University

Lyons, W. (2003). Glasgow's failure rate hits 60%, *The Scotmans.* Retrieved June, 2003, from http://thescotsman.scotsman.com/business. cfm?id=516142003

McMullan, W., & Long, W. (1987). Entrepreneurship education in the nineties. *Journal of Business Venturing, 2*(3), 261–275. doi:10.1016/0883-9026(87)90013-9

Morris, M., Lewis, P., & Sexton, D. (1994). Reconceptualizing Entrepreneurship: An Input-Output Perspective. S.A.M. *Advanced Management Journal, 59*(1), 21–31.

Niefert, M., Metzger, G., Heger, D., & Licht, G. (2006). Hightech Gründungen in Deutschland: Trends und Entwicklungsperspektiven, Endbericht ZEW GmbH, Mannheim, Juni 2006 OECD and Eurostat (2005). Oslo Manual: The Measurement of Scientific and Technological Activities. Guidelines for Collecting and Interpreting Innovation Data, 3rd edition, Paris: OECD and Eurostat publication.

Nieman, G. (2003). Growth Strategies and Options. In Nieman, G., Hough, J., & Niewenhuizen, C. (Eds.), *Entrepreneurship: A South African Perspective.* Pretoria, South Africa: Van Schaik.

Phillips, B. (1993). The influence of industry and the location on small firms failure rates, in N.C. Churchill, et al. (Eds.), Frontieres of Entrepreneurship Research (pp. 286-301), Wellesley, MA: Babson College Plashka and Welsch (1990). Emerging structures in entrepreneurship education: Curricula designs and strategies. Entrepreneurship Theory and Practice, 28, 129-144.

Solomon, G. T., Duffy, S., & Tarabishy, A. (2002). The state of entrepreneurship education in the United States: A nationwide survey and analysis. *International Journal of Entrepreneurship Education, 1*(1), 65–86.

Tidd, J., Bessant, J., & Pavitt, K. (2003). *Managing innovation*. Chichester, UK: John Wiley and Sons.

Today, U. S. A. (2003). Retrieved June 10, 2008, from http://www.usatoday.com/educate/college/business/casestudies/20030521-entrepreneurs.pdf

Useem, J. (2001, May). The risk taker return. *Fortune Small Business*, 70-72.

Vesper, K., & McMullen, W. (1988). Entrepreneurship: Today courses, tomorrow degrees? *Entrepreneurship Theory and Practice, 13*(1), 7–13.

Watson, C. (2001). Small business versus entrepreneurship revisited. In Brockhaus, R. (Ed.), *Entrepreneurship education: a global view*. Burlington, UK: Ashgate.

Wickham, P. (2001). *Strategic Entrepreneurship: A decision-making approach to new venture creation and management* (2nd ed.). Upper Saddle River, NJ: Person Education.

Zeithaml, C., & Rice, G. (1987). Entrepreneurship/Small business education in American universities. *Journal of Small Business Management, 25*(1), 44–50.

Chapter 9
Building a Radical Innovation Mechanism at Large Firms

Chintan M. Shah
Delft University of Technology, The Netherlands

J. Roland Ortt
Delft University of Technology, The Netherlands

Victor Scholten
Delft University of Technology, The Netherlands

ABSTRACT

Large firms are generally good at managing incremental innovations, yet they often lack the capabilities that are conducive to developing and deploying radical innovations (RI). Even though many large firms recognise the importance of RI, most of them fail to establish a mechanism, that is, a well defined organisational structure, management processes and resource allocation system that facilitates a systematic and continual development of RI. Drawing on extant literature we build a research framework that explains the obstacles which large firms face with respect to developing radical innovations. We collect data among three large firms, namely Shell, Nokia and IBM, and identify the practices that these firms have developed and a radical innovation mechanism that they have established to circumvent the obstacles for tapping into RI. Following these practices we conclude with implications for managers that are building a RI mechanism for their firms.

INTRODUCTION TO INNOVATION

In this chapter we discuss how large companies can foster radical innovation. We will study three cases - Royal Dutch/Shell, Nokia and IBM, and compare their approaches to innovate radically. Radical innovation in large firms is an intriguing topic, both from a managerial and a scientific perspective, because these firms almost invariably tend to block this type of innovation although it is imperative for their long term survival. We start with defining radical innovation and then present the questions that we address in this chapter.

The classification of innovations into different types focuses attention to the outcomes of the innovation process (Kola-Nystrom, 2005; Damanpour, 1991). An innovation can be classified as a new product, process, service or market innovation

DOI: 10.4018/978-1-61520-643-8.ch009

among others. On a broader level though what remains the core is the *change* that the innovation brings along. This change can be an incremental or a radical one. For example, an incremental innovation in car engine development could be improving fuel efficiency through the use of variable fuel injection technology, while a radical innovation from the perspective of the automotive, energy and distribution industry would be to run the engine on an alternative fuel such as hydrogen or bio-fuel. Taking this perspective, innovations can be classified as 'incremental' and 'radical' (Leifer et al., 2000; Dewar and Dutton, 1986).

Incremental innovations are often targeted at existing customers by providing, for example, better performance levels than previous solutions could reach. This can take the form of either incremental year-by-year improvements or more random inclusions of technological advances (Christensen and Raynor, 2003). Succeeding in incremental innovation depends on how well a firm performs relative to its existing competitors and involves doing more of the same, but better, quicker or cheaper. There are winners and losers in this race, but the kind of players and the dynamics of the game are relatively predictable when compared to the radical innovations. The mechanisms that firms deploy to excel in incremental innovations include total quality management, Kaizen, knowledge management practices, streamlined processes, integrated product development, close customer interaction and traditional R&D, amongst others (Leifer et al., 2000).

The other side of the innovation coin is radical innovation (RI). Radical innovation can manifest in new businesses, markets, new technology paradigms, new product lines and may result in a fundamental change of the conventional business model (Morene, 1993; Leifer et al., 2000; O'Reilly III et al., 2004). Radical innovations frequently leverage advanced technology or a combination of known technologies as a basis for advantage (Kelley, 2005). They often result in product or value propositions which undermine the competences

and complementary assets on which existing competitors have built their success (Constantinos and Geroski, 2005), and disturb prevailing consumer habits and behaviours (Constantinos and Geroski, 2005) in a major way. Similarly, radical innovations are often characterized by undefined customer demands and uncertain market projections that require a substantial amount of time to prove their value (Ortt and Schoormans, 2004), making RI financially risky (Christensen and Raynor, 2003). It must be noted that the conventional R&D in large organisations is also cited as an instrument for radical innovations. Nonetheless such innovations are normally related to the mainstream line of businesses. We term such innovations as 'major innovation' (see Figure 1) instead of radical innovation. For example, a breakthrough technology developed by an internal R&D unit for enhanced oil recovery which can extract more oil than traditionally possible is a *major innovation*. Such innovations are important in order to keep the firm competitive. For example, 2-5% increase in oil recovery could potentially lead to millions in additional profit. But such innovations can hardly defend a company against external changes in environment or competitive landscape. For example, the ability to extract more oil although important may not defend an oil giant against the rising demand for energy from renewable sources which may gradually replace oil as a main source of energy. Likewise, a breakthrough technology which can reduce the thickness of a CD-player to a half can hardly defend a company from the advent of portable MP3 players by a competitor.

From a practical perspective, if radical innovation becomes successful they offer improvements in known performance features of five times or greater, an entirely new set of performance feature or a 30 percent or more reduction in costs (Leifer et al., 2000). Examples of successful radical innovations include CT or MRI scanners which brought an entirely new set of performance features when compared to two-dimensional medical imaging; PCs, which made mainframe

Figure 1. Technology – market matrix (adapted from Roberts and Berry, 1985)

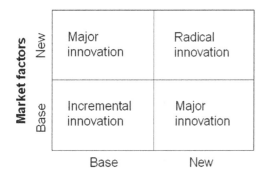

performance affordable for small businesses and consumer households; xerography, which brought major advances in photocopying technology. These radical innovations opened up new markets, significantly changed the competitive landscape and introduced new business models.

In studying how large firms can innovate radically, we will focus on the following questions:

1. Why do firms need a radical innovation mechanism?
2. Why do firms have difficulties with radical innovation?
3. How do firms organize for radical innovation?

By answering these questions we contribute to existing knowledge about the mechanisms that large firms can deploy to tap into radical innovation. The first two questions will be addressed in the following section by discussing relevant literature. The third question will be answered in the section 'RI mechanism in practice' using the results from case-studies at Shell, Nokia and IBM respectively. These results will lead to some general insights into RI mechanisms at large firms as described in the second to last section. The managerial implications will be discussed in the last section.

THE RADICAL INNOVATOIN IMPERATIVE

Various researchers have proposed establishing dedicated unit(s) within large firms in order to successfully incubate and develop RI projects (Chesbrough, 2003; Christensen and Raynor, 2003; Leifer et al., 2000; Shah et al., 2008). Most researchers agree that small firms are the usual source of RI, while large firms often fail to develop and deploy such innovations (Schumpeter, 1934; Sharma, 1999; Stringer, 2000; Christensen, 1997; Hill et al., 2003). This is especially the case for RI that are competence destroying and fulfill needs of customers outside the current customer base of these large companies (Christensen et al., 2004). Relatively unknown and small firms of the past like AT&T (Bell), Sony, Xerox (Haloid), Microsoft and Amazon have introduced radical innovations like telephony, transistor based radios, photocopying machines, the dos operating system and an online bookstore, when compared to large firms of their time - Western Union, RCA, Kodak, IBM and Barnes & Noble respectively.

Note that firms failing to invest in radical innovations may achieve a certain degree of success on a shorter term, but may limit their growth potential and put their long term survival at risk (Day, 1994; Leifer et al., 2000; Kelley, 2005). According to Tidd et al. (1997), 40% of the Fortune Top 500 companies in 1980 disappeared by the end of the 20th century, whilst of the 1970 list 60% have been acquired or gone under. Of the top 12 companies that made up the Dow Jones index in 1900 only one – GE – survives today. Even apparently robust giants like IBM, GM or Kodak can suddenly display worrying signs of mortality (Tidd et al., 1997). If true, such facts carry serious implications for large firms (Constantinos, 2006). A wise way to respond to the threats of radical innovations is to consider them as an opportunity and then find ways to exploit them. Hence, it is important that firms develop an appropriate *mechanism* for tapping into radical innovations.

WHY DO LARGE FIRMS NEED A RADICAL INNOVATION MECHANSISM?

The following three reasons justify the need for a distinct radical innovation mechanism within large firms. One, researchers largely agree that for long-term survival and growth, it is imperative that a firm taps both incremental and radical innovations (Dewar and Dutton, 1986; Drucker, 2002; O'Reilly III et al., 2004). Incremental innovations are essential to remain competitive with existing product-market combinations, whereas signaling for radical innovations may prevent the firm from missing out opportunities/ threats that destroy existing product-market combinations (Constantinos and Geroski, 2005; Leifer et al., 2000). Two, the inherent organizational and inter-organizational situations can inhibit the capacity of large firms to take actions in the favour of RI projects. The challenges of RI projects are different when compared to regular incremental innovation projects (Dougherty and Hardy, 1996; Leifer et al., 2000), and the ways to manage RI projects differ substantially from managing incremental innovations and existing businesses (Dougherty and Hardy, 1996; Kelley, 2005). The management of RI projects requires more room for pioneering activities and more room for failure. Important ingredients for the organizational mindset include an entrepreneurial orientation that is characterized by innovativeness, risk taking and proactiveness (Covin and Slevin, 1989). However, the middle management that is responsible for institutionalizing current competencies that sustain the efficiency of mainstream business is at the same time also expected to promote new competencies that allow for recognizing and implementing radical innovations. This duality may result in ambiguous managerial perceptions about the need for change and the need to remain with the current strategy (Floyd and Lane, 2000). A third reason for large firms to organize radical innovations is that these firms have vast resources, strong

network and commanding power to incubate and deploy RI (Sharma, 1999). If they establish the right organizational structure, working processes and resource allocation system, in other words if they design an appropriate RI mechanism, a continuous generation of radical innovations is possible. Before describing the RI mechanism deployed by a few leading firms, we will discuss the obstacles that large firms face which prevents them from innovating radically.

WHY DO LARGE FIRMS HAVE DIFFICULTIES WITH RADICAL INNOVATION?

Scholars have argued that large firms are often reluctant and slow in reacting to larger shifts in environmental changes (Sharma, 1999; Constantinos and Geroski, 2005). A number of researches observe that market demand shifts more rapidly than the strategy of large firms. The main obstacles for large firms to embrace radical innovations include: (1) inertial forces and complacency, (2) size of the opportunity, (3) differential economic incentives, (4) embeddedness in established networks, and (5) inappropriate metrics.

Forces of Inertia and Complacency

Hannan & Freeman (1984) argue that large firms are valued for their predictability and reliability. This predictability and reliability flows from the focus on the development of highly structured routines that produce efficiency and a reduction of costs (Hill and Rothaermel, 2003). Their internal resource allocation processes are designed to maximise the profitability of current operations. The drawback of such routines and processes is the difficultly in reallocating resources fast enough to capitalise on a new opportunity; normally anything that requires funding must wait until next fiscal planning. This makes managers to focus on their short-term challenges. Managers often ignore areas beyond their standard frame of reference and as a result, may fail to notice, analyse and respond with alacrity to the competitive threat posed by radical innovations. An attempt at organisational change through RI disturbs the system which is built upon predictability and reliability, hence creating a natural resistance.

Likewise, the managers at large firms are often busy with maintaining and growing the core. Given the limited time and resources, they seldom want to be disturbed by RI projects because their first natural priority is to put mainstream business in order and solve current challenges. In addition, it is often difficult to predict the long term potential of a radical technology (Stringer, 2000). Proving the potential of a risky radical innovation project gives them a feeling of high risk (Day and Schoemaker, 2000) as their career may be tied with the success of the project. Moreover, skills, mindset and capabilities of managers are tuned to effectively operate existing business. Past successes and experience often reinforces a certain way of problem solving (Day and Schoemaker, 2000), and anything radical is turned down by pointing at the risks and uncertainties. After all, the reward system for managerial behaviour facilitates the focus on existing businesses and its improvement.

Size of the Opportunity

Radical innovations usually represent uncertain, and at first, small-scale market opportunities which form a safe place for new entrants, but are unattractive for large organisations. Large firms demand large opportunities; vis-à-vis a new entrant or a small firm can only handle relatively smaller opportunities. The forces of inertia and complacency within large firms seem to convey the impression that the managers in large firms are short-sighted and conservative rather than being oriented towards the long-term company goals. Peters & Waterman (1982) in their famous book 'In search of excellence' investigated the practices of some of the best-run companies in the United

States. About a decade later the same companies turned out to be in bad shape. The common opinion to explain the demise of these previously successful companies was exactly this short-sightedness and conservatism. In contrast, Christensen (1997) explained how even the best managers, also when they know that radical innovation is imperative, experience obstacles when trying to promote RI projects within their organisation. A large company, when it is managed as a hierarchy, requires a large overhead. That overhead and the sheer size of the company in turn demand a minimum size for a new opportunity, which a RI project may not offer upfront though it may have strong future potential. Furthermore, Christensen et al. (2004) explain how small companies can build up a position in market segments that are too small for the incumbent to invest in. The new entrant searches for a niche that is often too small for the incumbent to feel challenged. Nonetheless, if the entrant can build a strong position and the niche market grows the incumbent may be challenged (Ortt et al., 2008). For example Chester Carlson, the inventor of xerography technology, was rejected by more than 20 companies including IBM, Kodak, RCA and GE citing xerography as relatively complicated and a risky development. IBM, based on findings from a consultancy firm, concluded that the market potential of xerography based products was no greater than 4000 units. Later Carlson himself continued developments and deployed this RI technology which the world now uses as a mainstream photocopying technology.

Differential Economic Incentives between New Entrants and Large Firms

Based on the assumption that large firms enjoy market power and monopoly rents owing to entry barriers, Henderson (1993) emphasises that large firms have an incentive to invest in incremental innovations that add to their established knowledge base, maintain entry barriers, and protect and enhance their existing rent stream. Under conditions of uncertainty, managerial rationale at large firms will be to invest more in their current business, while less in producing radical innovations than new entrants. They seek to maximise the returns from known products, know-how and assets, rather than devote resources to pioneering new technology with an uncertain payoff. This behaviour is often rooted in the cognitive experience of management which has a tendency to focus on their dominant logic. Managers prefer the known instead of the unknown since it is less risky and more predictable (Levinthal and March, 1993). A good example is the current situation of large oil companies. Many of these companies prefer to invest substantial resources in going to extreme water depths, politically insecure nations, and harsh offshore environment while deploying only limited or no resources to incubating and developing RI projects such as renewable energy sources.

New entrants, on the other hand, neither have to battle internal forces of inertia, nor do they have long-standing commitments to established business partners. These firms can focus on small, out-of-the-way market niches and grow with those niches, migrating up-market as their technology matures and its performance attributes improve (Christensen, 1997). New entrants also have the economic incentive to make investments in unproven technologies that have a high-risk, high return profile. Often the entire organisation can be built around a single breakthrough concept (Stringer, 2000).

Embeddedness in Established Networks

Every firm is embedded within a value network of suppliers, customers, investors, complementary product providers and communities to which the firm has made strategic commitments (Christensen, 1997; Christensen and Raynor, 2003; Sull, Tedlow, & Rosenbloom, 1997; Hill et al., 2003). Large firms pay attention to this established net-

work since their historic success has been based upon satisfying the demands of and cooperating with various partners in its value network. Their goal is then to strengthen the relationships with the existing network in order to build trust, improve communication and thereby make transactions more efficient and less expensive (Coleman, 1990). Although these strong networks are in favour of predictable behaviour and lowers opportunism and thus lowers risk, it may turn against the firm when facing disruptive events, such as the appearance of a radical innovation. In such cases, the strong network may produce fatal inflexibility and firms may be trapped in their network which prevents them from identifying and establishing new network relationships that are crucial for tapping into new technological and market developments (Gargiulo and Benassi, 2000; Burt, 1992). For example, a mobile phone company embedded in its value network will find it difficult to change its business model or offer radically different service such as voice over internet (VOIP).

Inappropriate Evaluation Metrics

Often large firms apply a same set of evaluation criteria to radical innovation as applied to regular projects, technologies or businesses. In such an evaluation, a RI project can hardly pass the criteria because they are often more risky and have unproven market potential. Even if a RI project may have good business potential, it will be only in the medium to long term and thereby making the investment financially unattractive. Concurrently, the business value of existing markets is assessed in terms of the current value of future income which, in turn, can be reasonably accurately assessed by forecasting the market size, future costs and price evolution. These markets behave as a kind of savings account. In contrast, radical innovations represent an option for future success, most of which will fail yet some of which represent the company's future viability.

Evaluation criteria in firms are not adapted to the option-type of activities, which can serve as future choices and potential for proprietary access to outcomes (McGrath et al., 2004). Too often, managers who intuitively believe in radical innovation or an emerging opportunity have to prove the business-potential based on hard data. Without putting initial efforts and resources to access the potential of an idea or concept it may be too difficult to arrive at hard financial data. Besides, if the managers decide to work on the development of a radical innovation they may put their career at risk. They are evaluated annually, while the potential value of RI project is normally difficult to access within a year. Also their bonuses will be thwarted. Bonuses or rewards are based on returns and returns from radical innovation normally come after several years.

These five main obstacles that impede large firms from developing and benefiting from radical innovations necessitate large firms to develop a RI mechanism. Using this RI mechanism, the large firms are more likely to counter the obstacles and thereby are more likely to benefit from incubating and developing RI projects.

RADICAL INNOVATION MECHANISM IN PRACTICE

Academia use various terms to represent the organisational structure developed by a firm to tap radical innovations. Whether titled as an exploratory unit (O'Reilly III et al., 2004), a new business development function (Constantinos and Geroski, 2005), a corporate venturing program (Chesbrough, 2003), an independent business unit (Christensen and Raynor, 2003) or a radical innovation hub (Leifer et al., 2000), these organisational entities share similar characteristics. They use techniques and processes which have been developed within the venture capital industry. These include the separation of radical innovation projects from mainstream business

operations, the stimulation and screening of RI projects and facilitating processes to nurture, assess, develop and fund such projects. It is these common features that cause authors to refer to such a mechanism generically and distinguish its activities from the management processes used to run the mainstream businesses. In this research the term 'radical innovation mechanism' is used for such a unit/ program.

Deployment of *RI mechanism* in essence enables a firm to develop and deploy radical innovations on a systematic and continuous basis with the help of an appropriate organisational structure, management processes and resource allocation system. The instruments deployed for a RI mechanism may include among others an incubation unit, a technology validation unit, an exploratory unit, a venture capital arm and/ or an emerging business development program.

We conducted a multiple case study research to investigate RI mechanisms in practice. We selected three large multinational companies - Royal Dutch/ Shell, Nokia and IBM. These companies were chosen for their well-established venturing program and their successful track record in managing RI mechanism. We found only a handful of companies which had their venturing program surviving for over 10 years. Out of these handful companies, we screened Shell, Nokia and IBM because of their positive response to participating in the research. The three companies operate in different industries and therefore there were industry specific differences among them. The amount of resources and time required from idea development to market deployment being an obvious difference, however, they also share substantial commonalities: including, simultaneously managing mainstream and RI activities, the process of RI development, and dealing with venturing risks and uncertainties, among others. Moreover on a broader level these firms have a similar motivation: to tap into radical innovations for strategic renewal and growth.

Information on these companies was collected from three sources - first, by studying the publicly available data including annual reports, press releases and other publications; second, from the study of confidential documents within the company; and third by conducting interviews. Three sets of questionnaires were prepared for the interviews. Each set based on the position held by the interviewee. For example, a senior manager who heads the venturing program was asked a different set of questions than the manager who actually managed a RI project. Multiple interviewees were taken to reduce the risk of undue influence that any individual interviewee may have on the case study. For Shell and IBM, interviews were conducted face-to-face, while for Nokia they were conducted over the phone. Interviews varied in length from one to two hours and at least four interviews per company were carried out. This approach satisfies the minimum level of data collection that is needed to develop reliable results from case-study research (Eisenhardt, 1989; McCutcheon and Meredith, 1993).

A comparison of the three large firms is made based on a multiple case study method. We investigated the following aspects of each large firm:

- The extent to which they were facing the obstacles that we found in literature.
- The organizational structure, decision making processes and resource allocation system to understand how the firm countered the obstacles and organized for radical innovations

Following the investigation of each firm individually, we analyzed for the three firms:

- Their common factors which might be the essential elixir for a successful radical innovation mechanism
- The similarities between the actual practices in these firms and the obstacles that we identified in literature, and
- The differences in practices for managing RI projects.

The following describes the RI mechanism deployed by Shell, Nokia and IBM.

A Bottom-Up Approach: Radical Innovation Mechanism at Shell

Royal Dutch/ Shell Plc ("Shell") applies a bottom-up approach to incubating and developing RI. Shell invites ideas/ projects from employees on all levels and from outside. Subsequently senior managers, in charge of a RI instrument, have the autonomy to judge and select the projects.

Two main RI instruments are deployed by Shell – GameChanger (GC) and Shell Technology Ventures (STV). GC is a team of managers with seed stage incubation funds to sponsor radical ideas to turn them into technically working proof-of-concepts. Ideas come from internal as well as external sources. Projects are evaluated with respect to predefined milestones. If an idea continues to pass the milestones, the funding increases from an average of $25,000 to $250,000. Many of the projects are handed over to internal Exploratory Research group or to Shell Technology Ventures when they reach a proof-of-concept phase. Ten percent of the exploratory research budget goes into GC activities, and over 30% of the exploratory research projects have their origin in GC. The 'swellable elastomers' technology developed by the GameChanger team is one such example. This technology dramatically improved the effectiveness of zonal isolation in oil wells, and offers an option to replace the traditional use of cement.

Shell Technology Ventures is a venture capital (VC) arm partially owned by Shell. It provides VC funds for technologies that are strategic to Shell in the medium and long term. STV also serves as a route for commercialising radical technologies that do not find home within Shell. This unit has developed over 25 new start-up companies which bring in strategic returns for Shell.

A Bottom-Up and Top-Down Approach: Radical Innovation Mechanism at Nokia

Nokia applies a combination of bottom-up and top-down approach to RI mechanism. While a part of RI projects are targeted at individual ideas coming from employees and from outside Nokia, the other part is aimed at opportunities that fall under the strategic domains identified by top management. Various RI instruments are deployed within Nokia under a broad umbrella of RI mechanism. Each instrument has a unique objective, either of opportunity recognition, incubation or venture capital activity.

Two instruments: Insight & Foresight team (I&F) and Innovation Acceleration Team pursue the task of 'opportunity recognition'. I&F is a Nokia version of scenario analysis. It looks at trends and disruptions happening outside the boundary of the company and brings pragmatic insights into the company. The Innovation Acceleration Team organises workshops and idea challenges to capture radical ideas.

Two instruments are active in incubating and validating ventures: the Nokia Venture Organisation (NVO) and Innovent. NVO incubates ventures internally. This unit screens ideas, develops proof-of-concept, does pilot tests, and designs business plans. The project is later transferred to a business unit for commercialisation if appropriate. Innovent provides an early stage VC fund for entrepreneurs based in the US.

To capitalise on mid and late stage external ventures, Nokia engages two VC arms: BlueRun Ventures and New Growth Business. While BlueRun provides mid-to-late stage VC funding, New Growth Business (NGB) offers late stage VC funds. Funds for these disparate instruments come directly from the Chief strategy officer. Approximately 1% of total sales income is invested in RI mechanism at Nokia. Through this mechanism,

Nokia is developing several radical innovations such as Mobile RFID kit, Mobile TV and Media Changer among others. The previously non existing business units 'Multimedia' and 'Enterprise solutions' were born out of the work done at NVO and other RI instruments.

A Top-Down Approach: Radical Innovation Mechanism at IBM

Tapping radical innovations at IBM mainly takes place through its Emerging Business Opportunity (EBO) program, while its venture capital arm: IBM Venture Capital Group (VCG) plays a unique role. The EBO program is in place to identify, incubate and deploy radical innovations, called 'EBO', in the form of new growth businesses. The IBM EBOs are selected by and managed under the supervision of the top management – a top-down approach to managing RI projects.

An opportunity is considered an EBO if it has a potential to generate over €1 billion in revenue within 3 to 5 years. EBOs are created around a radical technology, a new market or a new business model. Financial mechanisms are put in place to protect an EBO from the vulnerability of expense cuts in an effort to manage short-term unit profitability. Once the EBO has a proven business design and a clear ownership, the EBO is considered to be 'graduated' and is transferred to the sponsoring business unit (BU). Since its inception, IBM EBO has produced 5 multi-billion dollar businesses.

The IBM Venture Capital Group complements EBO management by helping to identify and refine EBO ideas, to identify external partners and to build an ecosystem that is necessary for the success of an EBO. It acts as a link between the EBO program and the VC community. The venture capital community, whose focus overlaps with an EBO, can serve as partners by offering complementary solutions.

ANALYSES OF RADICAL INNOVATION MECHANIMS

The case studies show that these companies have deployed different mechanisms to overcome the obstacles that large firms face when developing and deploying radical innovations. We identified five major obstacles in the earlier section. The following section describes the approach that Shell, Nokia and IBM have taken to overcome these obstacles. Table 1 gives an overview of our findings.

Inertial Forces and Complacency

All three firms have established separate units for identifying, validating and commercializing radical innovations. These units operate in semi-autonomous manner to explore and fund new opportunities. To a large extent, they operate independently from mainstream activities and thereby are not limited by the short-term interests of the mainstream business units. Managerial cognitive maps and resource competitions are detached from mainstream business units.

Size of the Opportunity

Shell applies small scale funding budgets through its Game Changer program. These budgets allow RI ideas to get started while the GameChanger team assesses its initial technology feasibility. Nokia uses two distinct units for identifying small size opportunities: Insight and Foresight (I&F) and Innovation Acceleration Team (IAT). In contrast to Shell and Nokia, IBM focuses on larger opportunities. IBM requires that opportunities must be able to grow up to €1 billion of cash flow in 3 to 5 years. An individual project falling within an EBO maybe larger or smaller; the projects combine together form a large EBO. In general we observed that the RI mechanism was customised to the vision of the senior management with respect to the size of the opportunity they want to invest in.

Differential Economic Incentives

Large firms have an incentive to make the mainstream businesses more efficient. This often involves a top-down approach. Economies of

Table 1. Attributes designed by large firms to circumvent radical innovation obstacles

Obstacle	Shell	Nokia	IBM
Inertial forces and complacency	Separate venturing units	Separate venturing units	Separate venturing units
Size of the opportunity	Small funding budgets by GameChanger *$25,000 - $ 250,000*	Small funding by Insight and Foresight (I&F) and Innovation Acceleration Team (IAT)	Focus on high growth opportunities: > € 1 billion in 3 to 5 years
Differential economic incentives	Bottom-up approach; Internal and external idea sources identified by GameChanger	Bottom-up and top-down approach; Workshops and idea challenges by I&F and IAT.	Top-down approach; Emerging Business Opportunities (EBO) program under top management supervision
Embeddedness in established networks	Shell Technology Ventures as corporate venture capital unit operating outside Shell	Two venture capital arms: BlueRun ventures and New Growth Business that operate outside Nokia	Venture capital group working closely with external partners and VC firms
Inappropriate metrics	Distinct units based on project goals; *GameChanger for identification and incubation; Shell Technology Ventures for commercializing*	Distinct units based on project goals; *I&F and IAT for identification; NVO and Innovent for incubation; BlueRun and NGB for commercializing*	Distinct units based on project goals; *EBO for identification and incubation; VCG for commercializing*

scale and outsourcing decisions that facilitate efficiency are decided upon by top management. On the contrary, new technology leads and emerging niche markets are often identified by operational management.

All three firms have initiated diverse programs to facilitate new business opportunities to emerge from the operational management. Shell and Nokia have delegated the scanning and screening authority for relatively small size investments with committees at the operational level; these investments naturally fall under broad technology domains identified by the senior management. IBM in contrast applies a different approach. Here the top management is closely involved in this decision making process.

Embeddedness in Established Networks

To develop connections beyond the established networks, all three firms have set up a corporate venture capital arm. These corporate VC arms are organized outside the main business units and are kept semi-autonomous for making operational decisions. They developed strong ties with a specific group of external venture capitalists to circumvent the established network and to create new ones. We also observed that each of the three firms developed loose linkages with expert firms that were developing radical innovation relevant for their industrial domain.

Inappropriate Evaluation Metrics

A remarkable finding we did was that each firm has distinct venturing unit(s) customised to meet for different goals. For the recognition of opportunities all three firms have institutionalised a dedicated unit that is aimed at this goal. When the opportunities are identified and recognised as strategically potential for the firm, they are trans-

ferred to another unit that aims at *validating* the opportunity. This validation unit in turn focuses at developing a prototype to assess the technical feasibility. The next stage is then exploring ways to commercialize the radical innovation which was, for all three firms, conducted in a separate unit in close collaboration with external venture capital firms or passed to an internal BU with relevant capabilities. This multi-unit approach to facilitate radical innovation allows for better assessment of specific metrics for each stage. In addition the metrics are more clearly visible for radical innovation managers and thereby help developing better incentives to meet these metrics.

MANAGERIAL IMPLICATIONS

By summarizing the relevant literature, this chapter explained that radical innovations are important for the long-term viability of large firms. Although these firms usually have the resources to develop and introduce RI they also inherit several obstacles for these types of innovations. We distinguished five of these obstacles:

- Forces of inertia and complacency in large firms;
- Minimum required size of new opportunities for large firms;
- Differential economic incentives of large and small firms;
- Embeddedness of large firms in established networks;
- Inappropriate metrics to assess the potential of radical innovation projects

On the basis of the case studies at Nokia, Shell and IBM, this chapter describes how these obstacles can be removed or circumvented. The findings can be summarized in the following points.

Radical Innovation Requires Distinct Organizational Unit(s)

When designing organizational unit(s) to foster radical innovations, the following attributes should be kept in mind:

1. The units should have leeway to enable agility. Markets and technology tend to change rapidly and the organizational units involved with RI projects should be able to react to the speed of the changing conditions.
2. If appropriate, create dedicated units for each phase of the RI project. As RI projects evolve, distinct types of units will be beneficial for subsequent stages. All the three case-study companies have both - an incubation and a corporate VC unit, for example.
3. For the specific identified domains, the organizational units should become an active member in networks of organizations outside the network of large firm.
4. Apply distinct metrics to evaluate the value of RI projects.

A Balance between Radical and Incremental Innovation is Required

Both radical and incremental innovations require significant investments and management effort. Both are important for the firm in different ways. For example, through incremental innovations Nokia is able to launch better products, which in turn sustains Nokia's competitive position. Through its radical innovation mechanism, Nokia is able to develop new products such as Mobile RFID kit, Mobile TV and Media Changer among others, which in turn helps creating new businesses for Nokia. Each of the case study firms invested between 1-10% of their resources to incubate and develop radical innovations systematically.

Different Type of Governance Model Needs to be Applied

In our case-studies we found that Nokia, IBM and Shell govern the radical innovation units and their proposals differently when compared to the mainstream units. Furthermore, each of the participating firms used a different approach and deployed a variety of instruments to incubate radical innovations, which was customised to the specific needs of their firm. For example, while Shell uses a bottom-up approach and deployed an incubation and corporate VC unit, IBM uses a top-down approach and deployed an emerging business program. It is important that a firm designs its customised approach to radical innovation mechanism and deploys instruments accordingly.

This chapter has provided insight into the obstacles that large firms face when trying to develop and exploit radical innovations. Based on the case studies of three large multinational firms we identified several major managerial interventions that allowed large firms to benefit from radical innovations and thereby improve their future competitive potential.

REFERENCES

Burt, R. S. (1992). *Structural Holes: The Social Structure of Competition*. Cambridge, MA: Harvard University Press.

Chesbrough, H. (2003). *Open Innovation: The New Imperative for Creating and Profiting from Technology*. Boston: Harvard Business School Press.

Christensen, C. M. (1997). *The innovator's dilemma*. Collins Business Essentials.

Christensen, C. M., Anthony, S. D., & Roth, E. A. (2004). *Seeing what's next. Using theories of innovation to predict industry change*. Boston: Harvard Business School Press.

Christensen, C. M., & Raynor, M. E. (2003). *The innovator's solution: creating and sustaining successful growth*. Boston: Harvard Business School Press.

Coleman, J. (1990). *Foundations of Social Theory*. Cambridge, MA: Harvard University Press.

Constantinos, M. (2006). Disruptive innovation: in need of better theory. *Journal of Product Innovation Management, 23*, 19–25. doi:10.1111/j.1540-5885.2005.00177.x

Constantinos, M., & Geroski, P. A. (2005). Fast Second: how smart companies bypass radical innovation to enter and dominate new markets. San Francisco: Jossey-Bass publication.

Covin, J. G., & Slevin, D. P. (1989). Strategic management of small firms in hostile and benign environments. *Strategic Management Journal, 10*, 75–87. doi:10.1002/smj.4250100107

Damanpour, F. (1991). A meta-analysis of effects of determinants and moderators. *Academy of Management Journal, 34*, 555–590. doi:10.2307/256406

Day, D. L. (1994). Raising radicals. *Organization Science, 5*, 148–172. doi:10.1287/orsc.5.2.148

Day, G., & Schoemaker, P. J. H. (2000). *Wharton on Managing Emerging Technologies*. New York: Wiley.

Dewar, R. D., & Dutton, J. E. (1986). The adoption of radical and incremental innovations: an empirical analysis. *Management Science, 32*, 1422–1433. doi:10.1287/mnsc.32.11.1422

Dougherty, D., & Hardy, C. (1996). Sustained product innovation in large, mature organizations. *Academy of Management Journal, 39*, 1120–1153. doi:10.2307/256994

Drucker, P. F. (2002). The discipline of innovation. *Harvard Business Review, 80*, 77–83.

Eisenhardt, K. (1989). Building theory from case study research. *Academy of Management Journal, 14*, 532–550. doi:10.2307/258557

Floyd, S. W., & Lane, P. J. (2000). Strategizing throughout the organization: Managing role conflict in strategic renewal'. *Academy of Management Review, 25*, 154–177. doi:10.2307/259268

Gargiulo, M., & Benassi, M. (2000). Trapped in your own net? Network cohesion, structural holes, and the adaptation of social capital. *Organization Science, 11*(2), 183–196. doi:10.1287/orsc.11.2.183.12514

Hannan, M. T., & Freeman, J. (1984). Structural inertia and organizational change. *American Sociological Review, 49*, 149–164. doi:10.2307/2095567

Henderson, R. M. (1993). Underinvestment and incompetence as responses to radical innovation. *The Rand Journal of Economics, 24*, 248–270. doi:10.2307/2555761

Hill, C. W. L., & Rothaermel, F. T. (2003). The performance of incumbent firms in the face of radical technological innovation. *Academy of Management Review, 28*, 257–274.

Kelley, D. (2005). *Corporate entrepreneurship and venturing*. New York: Springer.

Kola-Nystrom, S. M. (2005). In search of corporate renewal: how to benefit from corporate venturing? PhD dissertation, Lappeenrannan teknillinen yliopisto, Acta Universitatis.

Leifer, R., Rice, M., & Veryzer, R. (2000). *Radical innovation: how mature companies can outsmart up-starts*. Boston: Harvard Business School Press.

Levinthal, D. A., & March, J. G. (1993). The Myopia of Learning. *Strategic Management Journal, 14*, 95–112. doi:10.1002/smj.4250141009

McCutcheon, D., & Meredith, J. (1993). Conducting case study research. *Journal of Operations Management*, *11*, 239–256. doi:10.1016/0272-6963(93)90002-7

McGrath, R. G., Ferrier, W. J., & Mendelow, A. L. (2004). Real options as engines of choice and heterogeneity. *Academy of Management Review*, *29*, 86–101.

Morone, J. G. (1993). *Winning in high-tech markets: the role of general management*. Boston: Harvard Business School Press.

O'Reilly, C. A. III, & Tushman, M. L. (1986). *The ambidextrous organization*. Harvard Business Review.

Ortt, J. R., & Schoormans, J. P. L. (2004). The pattern of development and diffusion of breakthrough communication technologies. *European Journal of Innovation Management*, *7*(4), 292–302. doi:10.1108/14601060410565047

Ortt, J. R., Shah, C. M., & Zegveld, M. A. (2008). Commercialising breakthrough technologies: Scenarios and strategies. *Management of Technology Innovation and Value Creation*, *13*, 205–220.

Peters, T. J., & Waterman, R. H. Jr. (1982). *In Search of Excellence: Lessons from America's best - run companies*. New York: Harper.

Roberts, E. B., & Berry, C. A. (1985). Entering new businesses: Selecting strategies for success. *Sloan Management Review*, (Spring): 3–17.

Schumpeter, J. (1934). *The theory of economic development*. Boston: Harvard University Press.

Shah, C. M., Zegveld, M. A., & Roodhart, L. (2008). Designing ventures that work. *Research Technology Management*, *51*(2), 17–25.

Sharma, A. (1999). Central dilemmas of managing innovation in large firms. *California Management Review*, *41*, 146–164.

Stringer, R. (2000). How to manage radical innovation. *California Management Review*, *40*(4), 70–88.

Tidd, J., Bessant, J., Pavitt, K., Tidd, J., & Bessant, J. R. (1997). *Managing innovation: integrating techno-logical, market and organizational change*. New York: John Wiley & Sons.

KEY TERMS AND DEFINITIONS

Economic Incentive: Prioritisation of projects by the corporate management team based on their economic returns while making the investment decision

Established Network: Existing group of partners, suppliers and clients of a firm

Evaluation Metrics: Set of criteria used by a committee for evaluating/ screening a project or the project's milestone.

Forces of Inertia and Complacency: Cognitive mindset of managers which reinforces decision-making based on their earlier experiences, in turn supporting conventional low-risk projects while resisting support for new ventures which they perceive as having relatively high risk because of their newness and their personal lack of experience with that specific venture.

Incremental Innovation: Gradual improvements or random inclusions of technological advances for better performance of a product or a service than the previously available solution which is often targeted at existing group of customers.

Large Multinational Firm: In general terms, a firm employing more than 200 personnel, with over a million dollar in revenue and having at least one subsidiary in a country outside its home base can be a considered a large multinational firm.

Radical Innovation Mechanism: RI mechanism implies the organisational structure, management processes and resource allocation system deployed by firms to scan, screen, incubate, develop and deploy innovative ventures in a systematic and continual way. This often manifests in the form of a venturing program or dedicated organisational unit(s) which is semi-autonomous in its decision-making.

Radical Innovation: From a practical perspective, radical innovation can be defined as an improvement in known performance features of five times or greater, an entirely new set of performance feature or a 30 percent or more reduction in costs for a given solution (a product or service). Radical innovation can manifest in new businesses, markets, new technology paradigms, new product lines and may result in a fundamental change of the conventional business model.

Size of Opportunity: Evaluating a particular project based on the perceived return on investment and future growth potential.

Chapter 10
A Performance Evaluation Framework for Innovation

Stefan Cedergren
Mälardalen University, Sweden

Anders Wall
ABB Corporate Research, Sweden

Christer Norström
Mälardalen University, Sweden

ABSTRACT

This chapter presents a framework for a conceptual evaluation of the performance of industrial product innovation activities. The framework promotes a holistic view of performance by considering three categories of activities: Planning, Implementation, and Sales and Delivery. Successful performance evaluation comes from acknowledging the fact that there are different objectives for each of the three activity categories. Moreover, performance may be expressed as a function of the performance of the Planning, the Implementation, and the Sales and Delivery activities. In this chapter the results of research involving seven large companies in Sweden, with the objective of improving the understanding of what is required to be successful when developing complex industrial products, are presented. Key factors for success as well as some general conclusions are discussed.

INTRODUCTION

Sustainable growth is often argued to be one of the most elusive goals a company faces (Christensen & Raynor, 2003); a high performing innovation process is a key aspect for achieving sustainable growth. One important ingredient in a high performing product innovation process is to be able to evaluate performance and use this information to decide on

improvement actions (Davila, Epstein, & Shelton, 2006). Traditionally, performance improvements are achieved by focusing on and strengthening the processes that are easy to quantify in measurements e.g. the manufacturing process or the purchasing function. As a result there are plenty of performance measures related to, for example, the productivity of the operation process (Hill, 1993; Slack, Chambers, & Johnston, 2007). However, within innovation and product development there are no commonly accepted methods for evaluating performance,

DOI: 10.4018/978-1-61520-643-8.ch010

even though the total R&D spending in the 1000 largest companies in the world, in the year 2002, exceeded one quarter of a trillion dollars (Cooper, 2005). The stock market shows increasing interest in a firm's ability to be successful with innovation and product development, and measures such as the New Product Sales of Total Sales (Whitley, Parish, Dressler, & Nicholson, 1998) is one of the most commonly used measures for a company's product development process (Teresko, 2008). Still, being able to measure the outcome of the innovation process does not help an enterprise to improve or pinpoint where improvements need to be made in the process. Hence, it is important to differentiate between achieving high performance and performance evaluation. The ability to evaluate performance may influence performance, focus tends to be on what is evaluated, but it is only a first step in the quest for increased performance levels. An example which illustrates this point is when driving a car, there are several measures presented for the driver, e.g. a speed measurement showing current speed. However, a speed measurement does not imply that the car is able to travel at the speed the driver requires. On the other hand, it may assist the driver in understanding the car's capabilities; information that enables the driver to decide if a stronger engine is needed in order to reach the desired speed.

The difficult task of valuing promising ideas for new products in monetary terms has forced companies to view their spending on innovation and product development as a cost rather than an investment. Accounting rules require that investments in R&D are treated as a cost; even though the economic reality is that it is more of an investment (Hartmann, Myers, & Rosenbloom, 2006). This may explain why real time productivity measures related to innovation and product development are almost nonexistent. Research in the US reveals that only 52 percent of the total spending on product development is made on projects that are financially successful (Page, 1993). There are of course differences depending on market segment, type of product etc. Still, if a production site showed similar results it would not survive, at least not with the present management. Important to acknowledge is the fact that it is that 52 percent that will have to account for 100 percent of the R&D investment. An increase in the success rate of the product development process will therefore not only increase future revenues but also decrease the overall cost load, which directly affects a company's profit positively. An alternative is to increase the efficiency of the product development process and thereby be able to do more with less.

The research areas of performance evaluation, product development, and innovation are large and diverse. This research focuses on the development of complex industrial products, i.e. products that often include various technical capabilities like mechanics, electronics, and software. As a result these products are often developed in large organizations, often in a business-to-business context. Moreover, these products have long life-cycles and as a result the development activities are often incremental or evolutionary in their character rather than radical. The evolutionary character is the result of a technical complexity that has evolved over decades, by generations of engineers. This technical complexity also represents a large investment for an organization. An architecture or platform is therefore commonly used in these products, in order to decrease the time to market, share development cost, and increase the quality of the developed products.

In this research it is argued that in order to conceptually reason about performance in innovation and product development activities in large industrial companies, a holistic framework for performance evaluation is needed. In this chapter such a framework is presented starting by introducing our view on product innovation from the definitions of innovation and product development. With this in mind workshops, together with senior managers, with genuine experience in developing complex industrial systems within telecommunications, commercial vehicles, and automation, at seven large international companies, were held with the aim of identifying different aspects of what is needed to succeed with product development. A holistic view of product development enables the recognition of several different competences and understandings needed for the product innovation process to be successful. The proposed framework is then compared to other success factors in the product innovation literature in order to compare the results and verify the findings. However, a limitation with this research is that it has not been empirically tested. The chapter concludes with a discussion of performance and value creation in industrial product innovation and some general conclusions and recommendations.

Performance and Product Innovation

In the literature, several different ways of describing performance exist, but there is no commonly accepted definition or terminology. In this research performance is closely related to efficiency and effectiveness. In the Oxford dictionary efficiency is used to describe the ratio of the amount of energy going in to a system and the amount it produces (Wehmeier, Hornby, & McIntosh, 2005). It can also be used to mean the skillfulness in avoiding wasted time and effort. Effectiveness is more an interpretation of whether the produced result was intended or wanted. Neely et al. (2005) argue that effectiveness refers to the extent to which customer requirements are being met, while efficiency is a measure of how economically a firm's resources are being utilized, providing a given level of customer satisfaction. Sink and Tuttle (1989) describe effectiveness as doing the right things at the right time, with the right quality. Efficiency is similarly described as doing things right, often expressed as a ratio between resources expected to be consumed and resources actually consumed. However, this definition of efficiency seems to be more of an efficiency aspect of the planned activities and the predictability of the organization, not of the product development process. Moreover, Cordero (1990) defines efficiency evaluation as measuring resources to determine whether minimum amounts are used in the making of these outputs. Similarly, the same author defines effectiveness as measuring outputs to determine if they help accomplish objectives.

Similar to performance, innovation and product development are often discussed but seldom defined in the literature. The term "innovation" originates from the Latin word *nova* meaning new. Innovation is also related to the term invention that implies the creation of something new, but invention differs from innovation in the sense that it does not need to add value to something or someone, as an innovation does. An invention is more of finding a solution to a problem or an issue. Burgelman et al (2001) argue that an invention is the result of a creative idea or concept, while innovation is the process of turning the invention into a commercial success. Luecke (2003) defines innovation in a more abstract way as *"the embodiment, combination, or synthesis of knowledge in original, relevant, valued new products, processes or services."* Moreover, ideas and creativity are often mentioned as important ingredients of innovation. To be creative means to look at an issue in a novel way and an idea can be described as a recipe for dealing with an issue. Davila et al. (2006) make the relationship between business value and technology more explicit by categorizing innovation as incremental, semi-radical and radical depending on whether the innovation involves changes to the business model, the technology or both. With this in mind we define the term innovation as the implementation of a creative idea and a benefit from the result.

The product development process is also ambiguous in the sense of what is included in the process and what is not included. In this research an emphasis is put on taking a holistic view of product development by proposing an extension of the one argued for by Ulrich and Eppinger (2003).

Figure 1. Categorization of activities in product innovation

"*Product development is the set of activities beginning with the processes and tools used to perceive a market opportunity and ending in the production, sale, and delivery of a product fulfilling that market opportunity.*"

The proposed definition of the product development process implies it spans several different functions within a company, not just the R&D department. Product development is therefore a process that needs to integrate all functional areas at a company and not just the engineering department as is traditionally the case. In this research a product development project is to be considered successful if its output not only fulfils the needs and requirements of its customers, but also generates profit for its shareholders, and creates value for its stakeholders at large. It is interesting to note that innovation and product development are very similar. In this chapter we therefore use the term product innovation to describe the process of producing new, better, and more profitable products that meet the targeted customer's needs and requirements.

A FRAMEWORK FOR PERFORMANCE IN PRODUCT INNOVATION

The product innovation process must involve all of the functions in a company, in order to be successful. From a performance evaluation perspective on the product innovation process,

we argue in our research that the activities of the product innovation process may be divided into three different categories, which need to be addressed if the overall process is to be successful. The product innovation process is categorized into: *Planning activities* (what to develop), *Implementation activities* (product realization), and *Sales and Delivery activities* of the product to the customer, see Figure 1. All the three categories require unique specific competences and objectives to be prosperous; at the same time different criteria for performance evaluation are needed in the different categories.

This categorization of the product innovation process easily gives the wrong impression of a linear process i.e. first planning activities are conducted, and then the implementation activities followed by sales and delivery activities. Instead the proposed product innovation framework is to be viewed as a categorization of activities in order to be able to evaluate the activities accordingly. It is a very different task to evaluate a market environment analysis activity than to evaluate the task of software implementation. At the same time it is important to acknowledge the importance and how the different activity categories contribute to the overall performance of the product innovation process. From a value perspective the planning activities can be viewed as enabling value, implementation activities may then be interpreted as creating the value enabled in the planning activities, and sales and delivery activities are where the value is capitalized on in monetary terms.

Product Innovation Planning Activities

The product innovation planning activity category, i.e. deciding on the objectives for the product innovation activities, is definitely an important category of activities but often disregarded during performance evaluation. It is during the planning activities that the boundary for the overall success

Table 1. Important factors for what and why, and how and when to develop (without mutual ranking)

What and why		How and when	
Market Environment Analysis	Involves different aspects: technology, competitors, the customers' future business and processes, market knowledge etc.	Technology Roadmap	Develop the technology needed to support the product roadmaps.
Customer Needs and Wants	The ability to fully understand the customer needs and wants.	Metrics	Different metrics assisting the decision making.
Business Case	Clearly specify what kind of profit this product generates and why.	Organization	It should have clear responsibility, mandate, culture, competence and roles to support the planning.
Product Roadmaps	A clear plan of how the product will evolve in the future.	Ownership from Top Management	It is important that the CEO understands how the innovative product development process will generate future revenues and profit.
Risk Management	The ability to assess risks and to work actively with them.	Planning Competence	Understanding all the aspects: technical, market, economic, production, purchase etc. needs and addressing them.

and value creation from the product innovation investment is set. The overall objective of planning activities is to identify and decide how to transform customer needs and requirements into something that utilizes a company's resources in the best possible way i.e. generates the best possible future profit for the organization. There are two main question sets to answer during planning activities; the first set is *what and why* to develop something and the second is *how and when* to develop it. What and why are crucial, since they set the boundaries for both the technical and the economical value. When an enterprise has decided what to develop and why, the value creation is limited in some ways. However, this limitation is necessary in order to decide on the output.

Table 1 shows the result from our research, what managers in international high-tech industrial companies active in Sweden consider most important in the quest of answering *what and why* and *how and when* during the planning activity category:

The most important determinant of profitability is developing a unique, superior product with real value for the customer (Cooper, 1995; Luecke, 2003). It is through the planning activity category of the product innovation framework that this issue should be addressed and it is vital

for the whole company that it is performed successfully. The market environment analysis is the main activity that serves as the foundation for the information input to the company. It is important that the analysis covers all aspects for the intended customer and market segment e.g. technology, competitors, the customer's future business and process, market and more. The market environment analysis activity is important since the sources of innovation are typically found among users, manufacturers, suppliers and others (Hippel, 1988). On average 70 percent of the product cost is fixed after the specification and design process (Christensen & Raynor, 2003). The best way to handle this is to have front-loaded projects with adequate competence present when the important early decisions are made in the project (Morgan & Liker, 2006). Success comes from improving the understanding and cooperation between different departments in a company, especially between R&D and marketing (Griffin & Hauser, 1996). In contrast to *what and why*, the *how and when* questions are more focused on utilizing a company's resources in an optimal way with project execution as the most important variable. A key success factor for *how and when* is not to initiate implementation activities if key resources are unavailable. If a new development project is started in an already fully utilized organization it will only slow the other projects down (Seider, 2006). Many companies initiate project after project, believing performance is thus increased, without securing the key competence and resources first (Goldense & Power, 2005). Technology planning that will support and speed up the implementation activities is also an important success factor (Wheelright & Clark, 1992).

Product Innovation Implementation Activities

Product innovation implementation activities are all about the realization of the objectives decided on by the planning activities. The ultimate success for product innovation implementation is to create exactly what is specified, on time and to the specified quality. If key requirements cannot be met or the business case is jeopardized it is important to kill the project if necessary (Cooper, 2005), and focus scarce resources on other development activities. In our research it is concluded that the implementation activities include several different parts in order to enable high performance. Table 2 illustrates four main aspects, i.e. process, management, people, and technology, affecting the success of the product innovation implementation activities according to our research.

The product innovation implementation activities can be compared with a manufacturing process, since the best possible performance is to deliver what is specified and planned for by the product innovation planning activities. However, for that to be a good comparison an essential factor is that the *Technology* supports the project with pre-development and re-use. For product innovation implementation activities it is also vital that the *People* involved understand what is needed from them in order to create and realize the planning activities. In the implementation category the ultimate success is all about achieving the specified time-to-market with sufficient quality. In order for *Management* to make *People* motivated and

productive it is essential that the project members find their assignments professionally challenging, and leading to accomplishments, recognition, and professional growth (Kahn, 2005). For management during the implementation activities it is important to continuously update and communicate organizational goals and project objectives decided on during the planning activities. It is also important for management to illustrate the relationship and contribution of individual activities to the overall product development and business case (Kahn, 2005).

An illustrative metaphor to describe the product innovation implementation activity categories is to relate them to the systems needed for railway transportation. It may be possible to run a train with bad tracks but it will be a lot smoother ride, enabling a higher speed of the train, using maintained and well functioning tracks and it is the same thing with *Processes,* in the sense that they will disable or enable high performance of the product innovation activities. The train operator is responsible not just for the train running from A to B but also for meeting the timetable, similar to the responsibilities of *Management.* To be able to transport passengers the operator uses trains, which represents the *Technology* and it is important that the train is able to keep to the specified timetable. The train operator uses the signaling system to enable safe train rides and the possibility exists to run multiple trains, similar to handling multiple projects and the function of a performance measurement system. For the train operator to be successful skilled personnel are needed that understand the passengers' needs, in the same way skilled *People* are needed that understand *Customer* needs and requirements. Success for the train company depends on having the whole system working together, because when the train is moving in the right direction and the *Customers* are sitting comfortably in the railway car, they want to stay on the train and they will use the train again, since it fulfills their needs and expectations.

Table 2. Four main aspects of the implementation activities: Processes, Management, Technology, and People

Processes		Management	
Process Quality	The maturity of the processes	Professional Project Implementation	Important to have skilled project leaders for effective project execution.
Clear Development Process	In the sense that everyone in the organization understands and is able to execute the processes in use.	Multi-project/Portfolio management	The company must be able to handle multiple projects and maintain effective project execution.
Tools	Updated tools that support the innovative product development work the best way possible.	Risk Management	All risks must be identified and assessed.
Industrial Structure	Meaning that the right support systems are in place and can be used by the projects.	Handle Dependencies	Dependencies could involve business, resources, technical issues and project.
Clear Metrics	The use of metrics will improve the understanding the performance of the process.	Global and Local Development	Find the right setting for what should be developed where.
Requirement Management	A structured way of handling requirements.	Clear Objectives / Requirements	Management must be clear about what is expected from the people involved in the project.
		Supplier / Partners	The ability to handle suppliers and partners during the development.
People		Technology	
Feedback	Feedback to the people involved in the project to further develop their competence.	Technical Platform / Architecture	Makes it possible to share technology and thereby development cost between projects /applications.
Culture / Attitude	In the global world of today it is important to have all involved working together as a team.	Pre-development of Technology	Should support the implementation to improve time-to-market and quality.
Organization	Important that the organization evolves with the changes that occur in the firm and thereby support projects the best way possible.		
Resources	Important to have motivated and the right amount of resources available for the project.		
Competence	Involves securing a diverse and excellent competence in the company		
Incentives	Could be in the form of bonuses and other carrots.		

Product Innovation Sales and Delivery Activities

The third activity category of the proposed framework consists of the product innovation sales and delivery activities. It is during these activities an enterprise capitalizes on the value of its developed products since the activities in this category are directly related to the revenues and profits. This gives a clear indication of the success not just of product innovation sales and delivery, but also of the total product innovation performance. It

is important to acknowledge that the sales and delivery activities are not necessarily conducted when a new product is developed. Within the context of complex industrial products it is often the case that a tender process is carried out before the actual development project is conducted. A tender process may include not only sales activities but also planning activities. There may also be implementation activities if a demonstrator or similar needs to be developed in order to demonstrate the product or solution tendered. This chapter will not discuss product innovation sales and delivery activities further since there are already well established theories in the literature (e.g. Kotler, 1996; Slack et al., 2007), but this category is important for the completion of the holistic product innovation framework.

CRITICAL SUCCESS FACTORS IN THE PRODUCT INNOVATION LITERATURE

The research literature and industry best practices report a vast number of success factors that contribute to successful product innovation (Tang, Liu, Kellam, Otto, & Seering, 2005). The thought of having a limited amount of factors that positively affects the outcome and underlie excellent performance of the product innovation process is appealing for every manager. As a result there are vast amounts of research available within the area of success factors within product innovation (Ernst, 2002). Success factors are often identified either at the business unit level or at the product level; by comparing a successful business unit or product with a less successful one, success factors are identified.

Tang et al. (2005) identified a distinct set of success factors for product development: *Leadership, Organizational culture, Human resources, Information, Product strategy, Project execution, Product delivery, and Results*. Leadership involves key characteristics of the project manager, the power delegated, and whether there is a clear strategic direction for the development project. The organizational culture involves the extent to which management take advantage of the established values of the people to improve project output. Human resources involve management's actions to improve the skills and the work environment. Information is concerned with the treatment of information as a valuable asset, its quality, and whether it is systematically collected, shared, and analyzed. Product strategy includes the product planning processes and the extent to which they

promote readiness for implementation and product delivery. Project execution involves key issues of the product development process. Product delivery considers to what extent manufacturing, sales, service and support are considered; or whether the product is just "tossed over the wall" when developed. Results evaluate the project from multiple dimensions such as financial and market, customer satisfaction and loyalty, organizational effectiveness, product results, and benchmarking.

In a thorough review of critical success factors by Ernst (2002), the following categorization, as previously developed by Cooper and Kleinschmidt (2007), was adopted: *Sustomer integration, Organization, Culture, Role and commitment of senior management* and *Strategy*. Adams et al. (2006) present another review drawing on a wide body of the product innovation literature, and identified the following seven categories as important in the product innovation process: *Inputs management, Knowledge management, Innovation strategy, Organizational culture and structure, Portfolio management, Project management*, and *Commercialization*. Further, Bessant and Tid (2007) argue for the following success factors in product innovation: *Market knowledge, Clear product definition, Product advantage, Project organization, Top management support, Risk assessment, Proficiency in execution*, and *Project resources*. Product advantage involves product superiority in the eyes of the customer e.g., delivering unique benefits to the user and a high performance-to-cost ratio. Market knowledge, i.e. customer and user needs assessment and understanding, is critical. A clear product definition, defining target markets, clear concept definition and benefits to be delivered, must be assemble before the development activities begin. Holistic risk assessment including market-based, technological, manufacturing and design sources must be built into the business and feasibility studies. The use of cross-functional multidisciplinary teams carrying responsibilities is important within the *Project organization* from beginning to the end. *Project resources* include

Table 3. Illustrates how the categorization of success factors identified in this research, maps to the success factors identified in the literature

	(Tang et al., 2005)	(Ernst, 2002) / (Cooper & Kleinschmidt, 2007)	(Adams et al., 2006)	(Bessant & Tidd, 2007)
What	Product strategy	Customer integration, Strategy	Portfolio management Innovation strategy Commercialization	Market knowledge Clear product definition, Product advantage
Why	Product strategy	Strategy	Portfolio management Innovation strategy Commercialization	Market knowledge, Product advantage Clear product definition
How	Product strategy	Strategy		Market knowledge Clear product definition
When	Product strategy	Strategy	Portfolio management Commercialization	Market knowledge
Technology				
Management	Leadership, Organizational culture, Information, Human resources	Organization, Role and commitment of senior management Culture	Innovation strategy, Knowledge management, Project management, Organizational structure	Project organization, Top management support
Process	Project execution, Information, Product delivery Results	Product development process	Input management Knowledge management Project management	Risk assessment, Proficiency in execution
People	Information	Organization, Culture	Organizational culture Input management	Project resources, Proficiency in execution

financing, human skills, and material resources; the firm must possess the right skills to manage and develop the new product. *Proficiency in execution* includes all the activities of the product innovation process. *Top management support* is important through the complete product innovation process from concept to launch. Table 3 illustrates how the categorization of success factors identified in this research, presented in Tables 1-2, maps to the success factors identified in the literature presented above.

It is difficult to directly compare success factors in the literature with the ones identified in our research because they are defined at different level of abstractions. An example to illustrate this issue is strategy, as identified in Ernst (2002) and in Cooper and Kleinschmidt (2007) as an important success factor. In our framework this strategy is sorted into the *why*, *what*, *how*, and *when* categories. In this analytical validation of the

success factors identified in our research, the main objective is not to emphasize detailed variations but rather highlight major differences compared to the literature. With this in mind, an analysis of the mapping in Table 3 clearly indicates that the technology category is not explicitly addressed by any of the other studies found in the literature. This is an interesting finding that might be explained by the fact that they focus on a wider set of companies and products, while this research explicitly focuses on the development of complex industrial systems. In our context, technology is per definition one important aspect of product innovation performance. The technology category involves, for instance, platforms or product-line architectures that are used across a set of related products, making it possible to share and re-use technology and thereby share costs between different products and applications. Pre-development of technology, as support for the product innovation implementation activities, is another factor that will affect important aspects such as time-to-market and quality of the developed product. Moreover, the technological infrastructure, e.g. a system's architecture, can have both positive and negative effects on an enterprise's product innovation performance. The architecture may exhibit different levels of quality attributes such as evolvability, flexibility, and testability which have an effect on performance when evolving a long-lived system. Christensen (2003) has conducted a thorough study within the disk drive industry, highlighting the importance of this issue. Both the rate of a technology's performance improvement and the rate at which the technology is adopted by the market have repeatedly been shown to conform to an s-shaped curve (Schilling, 2006). The ability to assess when the currently used technology reaches the end of such an s-curve, and hence is in need of, for example, improving inner qualities in the architecture, would clearly be beneficial especially for the efficiency dimension of product innovation performance.

The *how* and *when* questions in the product innovation planning are less emphasized compared to the questions of *what* and *why* in Table 3. The aspect *when* is important since it is a common phenomenon to overload the product innovation portfolio in the search for higher efficiency. However, such an overload often results in an increased product innovation project lead time. From a product innovation manager perspective the success of the overall portfolio is of more importance than the performance of an individual product innovation project. Studies focusing on the success of an individual product innovation project, is likely to miss out on the importance of the *when* perspective of the product innovation portfolio performance. During the product innovation implementation activities it is *management* that is highlighted as the most important success factor; this result is in line with all the studies included in Table 3.

PERFORMANCE OF PRODUCT INNOVATION

As stressed earlier, all the three categories of the product innovation framework are important, but it is also essential to separate and acknowledge what is important for being successful within each category individually from a performance perspective. Especially the differences between planning and implementation activities must be acknowledged before it can be supported and cultivated, in order to create sustainable success. A high performing product innovation process may only be established through efficiency and effectiveness in each of the three categories. As a consequence failing with one of the activities may lead to a decrease in the performance of the overall product innovation process. Hence, it is important for an organization to be able to identify and reflect on their weakest activities and focus future improvements accordingly. Conceptually, the performance of the product innovation process can be expressed as a function according to:

$$\eta_{PI} = \eta(\eta_P, \eta_I, \eta_{S\&D})$$

The proposed function expresses performance (η) of the product innovation process as a relation between the performance of the planning, the implementation, and the sales and delivery activities. Performance of the planning activities is a balancing act between what the enterprise may handle to develop from a technical perspective, and how the product will generate future revenues. This is a difficult task and there are no easy solutions since the decisions made during planning activities may take several years until the result can be measured in practice. However, the first step is to make sure that the implementation activities create the value that has been enabled during the planning activities. In the sales and delivery activities the value enabled and created is capitalized on by generating revenues to the organization.

An illustrative example of performance in the three different categories is the automotive industry, especially in the US, an industry regarded as one of the most high performing product development industries. High product innovation performance has been achieved through strong technical platforms and architectures for the different products in order to share development cost, but also to enable distributed development e.g. among the many suppliers. In that sense focus has been on the efficiency and the effectiveness of particularly the implementation activities, i.e. what is normally perceived as product innovation performance. This together with a strong focus on the sales and delivery activities has made the automotive industry prosperous. This strategy have proven to be successful up on till now when the market is turning and the need for smaller, more fuel efficient cars is rapidly increasing. Changing from a large SUV with a strong engine to a smaller more fuel-efficient car may be an easy change for the customers, but since the automotive industry has focused on incremental updates to a cost and quality optimized platform this is a more difficult step to take. A study by Booz Allan Hamilton reveals that most new products, from automobiles to washing machines, are over-engineered as a result of not communicating and managing the customer needs properly (Koehler & Weissbarth, 2004). What the automotive industry needs to do is to focus more on the efficiency and effectiveness of the planning activities, e.g. by enabling a more flexible platform for developing their future cars. The changing needs of the customer require technical platforms and architectures supporting flexibility, along with a performance evaluation framework extending the scope of performance to include flexibility and not just quality and cost. Moreover, there is a need to extend the perception of performance in order to achieve high planning efficiency and effectiveness, and this cannot be achieved only by focusing on the implementation activities. By extending the view of performance an important first step is taken.

SUMMARY AND CONCLUSION

Peter Drucker made the following famous observation: "*Because the purpose of business is to create a customer, the business enterprise has two and only two basic functions: marketing and innovation. Marketing and innovation produce results; all the rest are costs.*" (Drucker, 1985). Today, when top management is surveyed in the US, their priorities in order are: finance, sales, production, management, legal, and people. Missing from the list are marketing and innovation (Trout, 2006). With this in mind, this chapter has presented a holistic performance evaluation framework. Since product innovation is a complicated process it is essential to adopt a holistic framework to be able to understand the different aspects needed, because the product innovation process can never be stronger than its weakest parts. The product innovation process is divided into planning, implementation, and sales and delivery activities. High performance is the result of having efficiency and effectiveness in all the activities in each of the three categories. Moreover, important factors for the planning and implementation activities have been presented as identified through workshops and case studies within seven companies developing complex industrial products.

It is also concluded that improving the weakest activities gives the best increase in the total product innovation performance. The product innovation framework should be viewed as a conceptual tool to reason about performance and for improving an organization's ability to successfully develop and bring new profitable products to the market. In our opinion a competitive advantage arises when an organization understands its strengths and weaknesses in the product innovation framework. It is therefore interesting to compare our product innovation framework with the work of core competence and capability; if it is managed well it provides customer benefits in the form of new products, it is difficult for competitors to imitate since every organization is unique and it will be leveraged into all new products and thereby markets (Prahalad & Hamel, 1990). Core competence and capabilities constitute a competitive advantage for an enterprise; they have been built up over time and cannot be easily imitated (Leonard-Barton, 1995). If a company manages to turn its activities in the product innovation framework into core competence and capabilities it will have the product innovation process as a competitive advantage. If this is achieved it may transform sustainable growth from an elusive goal to a natural fact.

There are two fundamental principles when creating core competence and capability; the competence must steer the power structure in a company and the core competence strategy must be chosen by the CEO (Coyne, Hall, & Clifford, 1997). The first part is supported by the product innovation framework but it must also be managed by senior management in that way. Also as we have pointed out in Table 2 support and understanding from top management including the CEO is a crucial success factor. One possible approach for handling this may be to adopt an evolutionary approach involving implementation and coordinating dozens of organizational efforts. This method is fruitful in the sense that it will deliver payoffs along the way even if there is only partial success (Coyne et al., 1997). Furthermore, it is important to acknowledge that even if a firm initially is successful with its product innovation process the work is not over. Working with the product innovation framework should be characterized by small continuous improvement steps and is not something that is solved over night; it must always be a natural part of a company's focus.

REFERENCES

Adams, R., Bessant, J., & Phelps, R. (2006). Innovation management measurement: A review. *International Journal of Management Reviews, 8*(1), 21–47. doi:10.1111/j.1468-2370.2006.00119.x

Bessant, J., & Tidd, J. (2007). *Innovation and entrepreneurship*. Chichester, UK: John Wiley & Sons Ltd.

Burgelman, R. A., Maidique, M. A., & Wheelwright, S. C. (2001). *Strategic Management of technology and innovation* (3rd ed.). New York: McGraw-Hill/Irwin.

Christensen, C. M. (2003). *The Innovator's Dilemma: The Revolutionary Book that Will Change the Way You Do Business*. New York: Collins.

Christensen, C. M., & Raynor, M. E. (2003). *Innovator's Solution: Creating and sustaining successful growth*. Boston: Harvard Business School Press.

Cooper, R. G. (1995). Developing new products on time, in time. *Research Technology Management, 38*(5), 49–58.

Cooper, R. G. (2005). Product leadership: Pathway to profitable innovation (2 ed.). New York: Basic Books.

Cooper, R. G., & Kleinschmidt, E. J. (2007). Winning business in product development: The critical success factors. *Research Technology Management, 50*(3), 52–66.

Cordero, R. (1990). The Measurement of Innovation Performance in the Firm: An Overview. *Research Policy, 19*(2), 185–193. doi:10.1016/0048-7333(90)90048-B

Coyne, K. P., Hall, S. J. D., & Clifford, P. G. (1997). Is your core competence a mirage? *The McKinsey Quarterly*, 1.

Davila, T., Epstein, M. J., & Shelton, R. (2006). *Making innovation work - How to manage it, measure it and profit from it*. Upper Saddle River, NJ: Wharton School Publishing.

Drucker, P. F. (1985). *Innovation and entrepreneurship*. New York: Harper and Row.

Ernst, H. (2002). Success Factors of New Product Development: A Review of the Empirical Literature. *International Journal of Management Reviews, 4*(1), 1–40. doi:10.1111/1468-2370.00075

Goldense, B. L., & Power, J. R. (2005). Developmental Overload. *Mechanical Engineering (New York, N.Y.), 127*(3), 13A–13A.

Griffin, A., & Hauser, J. R. (1996). Integrating R&D and Marketing: A Review and Analysis of the Literature. *Journal of Product Innovation Management, 13*(3), 191–215.

Hartmann, G. C., Myers, M. B., & Rosenbloom, R. S. (2006). Planning your Firm's R&D Investment. *Research Technology Management, 49*(2), 25–36.

Hill, T. (1993). *Manufacturing strategy: The strategic management of the manufacturing function* (2nd ed.). London: Macmillan.

Hippel, E. v. (1988). *Sources of innovation.* New York: Oxford University Press.

Kahn, K. B. (2005). The PDMA handbook of new product development (2 ed.). Hoboken, NJ: John Wiley & Sons.

Koehler, C., & Weissbarth, R. (2004, 070704). The Art of Underengineering. *Strategy+Business Magazine.*

Kotler, P. (1996). *Marketing management: Analysis, planning, implementation and control* (9th ed.). Englewood Cliffs, NJ: Prentice Hall.

Leonard-Barton, D. (1995). *Wellsprings of knowledge: Build and sustaining the sources of innovation.* Boston: Harvard Business School Press.

Luecke, R. (2003). Managing creativity and innovation. Boston: Harvard Business School Press.Morgan, J. M., & Liker, J. K. (2006). The Toyota Product Development System: Integrating People, Process And Technology (1 ed.) Florence, KY:Productivity Press.

Neely, A., Gregory, M., & Platts, K. (2005). Performance measurement system design: A literature review and research agenda. *International Journal of Operations & Production Management, 25*(12), 1228–1263. doi:10.1108/01443570510633639

Page, A. L. (1993). Assessing new product development practices and performance: Establishing crucial norms. *Journal of Product Innovation Management, 10*(4), 273–290. doi:10.1016/0737-6782(93)90071-W

Prahalad, C. K., & Hamel, G. (1990). The Core Competence of the Corporation. *Harvard Business Review, 68*(3), 79–92.

Schilling, M. A. (2006). Strategic management of technical innovation (2 ed.). New York: McGraw-Hill.

Seider, R. (2006). Optimizing Project Portfolios. *Research Technology Management, 49*(5), 43–48.

Sink, D. S., & Tuttle, T. C. (1989). *Planning and Measurement in your Organisation of the Future.* Norcross, GA: Industrial Engineering and Management Press.

Slack, N., Chambers, S., & Johnston, R. (2007). Operations Management (5 ed.): Pearson Education Limited.

Tang, V., Liu, B., Kellam, B. A., Otto, K. N., & Seering, W. P. (2005). *Enabling factors in successful product development.* Paper presented at the International conference on engineering design.

Teresko, J. (2008). Metrics Matter. *Leaders in manufactoring* Retrieved November, 2008, from http://www.industryweek.com/ReadArticle.aspx?ArticleID=16116

Trout, J. (2006). *Tales from the marketing wars – Peter Drucker on marketing.* Retrieved December 1, 2007, from http://www.forbes.com/columnists/2006/06/30/jack-trout-on-marketing-cx_jt_0703drucker.html

Ulrich, K. T., & Eppinger, S. D. (2003). Product design and development (3 ed.). New York: McGraw-Hill Education.

Wehmeier, S., Hornby, A. S., & McIntosh, C. (Eds.). (2005). *Oxford Advanced Learner's Dictionary of Current English* (*Vol. 7*). New York: Oxford University Press.

Wheelright, S. C., & Clark, K. B. (1992). *Revolutionizing product development: Quantum leaps in speed, efficiency, and quality*. New York: Free Press.

Whitley, R., Parish, T., Dressler, R., & Nicholson, G. (1998). Evaluating R&D performance using the new sales ratio. *Research Technology Management, 41*(5), 20–22.

KEY TERMS AND DEFINITIONS

Complex Industrial Products: Products that include various technical capabilities like mechanics, electronics, and software that are developed in large organizations, often in a business-to-business context.

Core Competence: Constitute a competitive advantage for an enterprise that have been built up over time and cannot be easily imitated.

Effectiveness: Refers to the extent to which customer requirements are being met, whether the produced result was intended or wanted.

Efficiency: Refers to how economically a firm's resources are being utilized, providing a given level of customer satisfaction.

Implementation Activities: All activities related to the realization of the objectives decided on in the planning activities.

Performance: Efficiency and effectiveness.

Planning Activities: All activities related to deciding on the why, what, how and when something is to be developed.

Product Innovation: Refers to the process of producing new, better, and more profitable products that meet the targeted customer's needs and requirements.

Section 3
Social Aspects of Innovation

Chapter 11
The Impact of Labour Flexibility and HRM on Innovation

Haibo Zhou
Erasmus University Rotterdam, The Netherlands

Ronald Dekker
Delft University of Technology, The Netherlands & ReflecT at Tilburg University, The Netherlands

Alfred Kleinknecht
Delft University of Technology, The Netherlands

ABSTRACT

We investigate the impact of labour relations (including use of flexible labour and certain HRM practices) on a firm's innovative output. Using firm-level data for the Netherlands, we find that active HRM practices such as job rotation, performance pay, high qualification levels of personnel, as well as making use of employees with long-term temporary contracts contribute positively to innovative output, the latter being measured by the log of new product sales per employee. Furthermore, firms that retain high levels of highly qualified personnel are more likely to introduce products that are new to the market (other than only 'new to the firm'). Our findings contribute to the growing literature on determinants of innovative performance.

INTRODUCTION

It tends to be generally recognized that firms need to be innovative in order to sustain their competitive advantage (e.g. Brown and Eisenhardt, 1997; Cohen and Levinthal, 1990; Leonard-Barton, 1995; McGrath, 2001; Tsai, 2001). Innovation can be regarded as a business process which creates unique and perceptive ideas that are being pushed towards commercial success (e.g. Verloop, 2004).

With the increasing availability of firm-level data such as through the European Community Innovation Survey (CIS) exercise by the European Commission, econometric studies of determinants of innovative behaviour are growing in recent years. This literature focuses on determinants of innovation such as market structure, firm size, (regional and international) knowledge spillovers, R&D collaboration, conditions for appropriation of innovation benefits, and others. By lack of good data on firm level labour relations within the CIS questionnaire, there are only sparse studies on the latter. This is

DOI: 10.4018/978-1-61520-643-8.ch011

regrettable, as labour relations can be expected to have a significant impact on innovation, among others through their influence on knowledge processes (see e.g. David 1997, Trott 1998)

The role of personnel for enhancing creativity and innovation is also recognized by Amabile et al. (1996). An OECD (1997) study indicates that the key of the innovative process is the flow of technology and information among people, enterprises and institutions. Individuals are the carriers of knowledge. Among others, knowledge diffusion can take place via mobile personnel. Furthermore, literature on the impact of labour relations on innovation suggests that active Human Resource Management (HRM) policies might be rewarding for a firm's innovation and productivity growth (e.g. Kleinknecht et al., 2006; Verburg 2005). As empirical evidence is still sparse, we investigate the nexus between labour relations and innovative output by conducting an empirical study among firms in the Netherlands.

LABOUR RELATIONS IN THE NETHERLANDS

Among enterprises in the Netherlands, we find a fairly wide spectrum of different types of labour relations and HRM practices. One end of the spectrum covers typically 'Rhineland' enterprises with internal labour markets that offer their personnel good wages, fair protection against dismissal, and long-term commitments. The other end of the spectrum includes enterprises that follow Anglo-Saxon practices; the latter employ lots of labour on fixed-term contracts, labour hired temporarily from temporary work agencies or freelance workers, i.e. self employed entrepreneurs that have no personnel.

There is a strand of literature that suggests that 'Rhineland' practices are more conducive to labour productivity growth (e.g. Buchele and Christiansen, 1999 for evidence from macro data; Kleinknecht et al., 2006 for evidence from firm-level data). The rationale is that a longer-term commitment between the firm and its employees may function as an investment into 'social capital'; i.e. into loyalty, trust and commitment. The latter will diminish the probability of opportunistic behaviour such as the stealing of a firm's properties or leaking to competitors of crucial trade secrets or new technological knowledge. Moreover, one can argue that, in a Schumpeter II innovation model, the quality of a firm's products and/or its efficient process performance crucially depends on the long-run historical accumulation of (incremental) technological knowledge. Much of this knowledge is 'tacit'. Other than publicly documented and codified knowledge, tacit knowledge is defined as 'un-codified', ill-documented and idiosyncratic; tacit knowledge is based on personal experience (e.g. Polanyi, 1966). The continuous and long-run accumulation of knowledge, and of 'tacit' knowledge in particular, is favoured by continuity in personnel, i.e. by keeping people in the firm for longer time periods. A longer stay with the same employer will also enhance a firm's readiness to invest in education and training.

Against this one can argue that 'Anglo-Saxon' practices might be favourable to a firm's innovation potential. With higher rates of labour turnover, firms have a high inflow of fresh people with new ideas, skills and networks. Moreover, less productive people can be more easily replaced by more productive ones, and the threat of firing might prevent shirking. Easier hiring and firing could also help to keep wages low and allow for a more flexible re-allocation of labour. Moreover, it has been argued that innovation might be difficult to implement among (long) tenured employees due to their lack of openness to new products and processes (e.g. Ichniowski and Shaw, 1995). From this viewpoint, one could argue that some flexibility of labour is needed for innovation, especially for radical innovation.

Labour Flexibility and Innovative Output

Flexibility of labour can be categorized into three types, i.e. numerical flexibility, functional flexibility and wage flexibility (e.g. Beatson, 1995; Michie and Sheehan, 2003). In the following, we focus on numerical and functional flexibility. Numerical flexibility is defined as the ability of firms to change the volume of personnel by making use of fixed-term employment contracts, labour hired temporarily, either directly or through temporary work agencies or freelance workers. Numerical flexibility relates to the possibility of responding quickly to changes in demand by easy hiring or firing of personnel through the external labour market. Functional flexibility is the ability of firms to re-allocate labour in their internal labour market, relying on training that allows personnel carrying out a wider range of tasks (e.g. Beatson, 1995; Michie and Sheehan, 2003). Indicators of numerical flexibility are percentages of people on temporary contract, labour hired from temporary work agencies, freelance workers or general labour turnover (i.e. percentages of people that join or leave the firm). An indicator of functional flexibility is the internal labour turnover, i.e. percentages of people that change function or department within the firm.

Ichniowski and Shaw (1995) show that long tenured employees may be conservative to outdated products and processes; it may be difficult for them to accept changes and it may require more money and time for them to adapt to a significant change. Innovation will be difficult to implement with them. Therefore, to a certain extent, external labour turnover is needed by firms; it can stimulate innovation, especially radical innovation.

A high external labour turnover, however, may harm the firms' stability and the continuity of learning. High frequency of hiring and firing of people will de-motivate employees and diminish trust, loyalty and commitment to their firms. As a consequence, productivity gains will be lower.

High external labour turnover will make it difficult for firms to store innovative knowledge, in particular of 'tacit' knowledge that is attached to individuals. At the same time, firms will hesitate to make investments in manpower training. Coutrot (2003) investigated the relationship between innovation and job stability with the data from the REPONSE ("Industrial relations and firm negotiations") surveys. Although his hypothesis was that there would be a negative correlation between the intensity of innovation and labour turnover, his econometric analysis does not confirm this. Based on earlier studies (e.g. Coutrot, 2003; Ichniowski and Shaw, 1995), one could argue that external labour turnover has a positive effect on innovative output, becoming negative beyond some optimal point.

Internal labour turnover is measured by percentages of employees that are reassigned and rehired inside the firm during a year. Internal labour turnover can reduce hiring and training costs, improve employee morale and motivation, and reduce the effect of uncertainty. Internal labour turnover also gives chances to employees to develop their career inside a firm. Often, internal labour turnover concerns employees in higher positions, i.e. mainly core employees. They typically have higher levels of knowledge and/or experience. By retaining them, firms can sustain their competitive position and ensure the success of their innovation projects. Furthermore, communication barriers between different departments can be reduced by reassigning and reallocating labour inside the firm. It will decrease the number of misunderstandings in future cooperation on innovation projects and increase knowledge sharing and transfer between different departments, thereby stimulating the process of generating organizational knowledge which is favourable for incremental innovation. We therefore expect internal labour turnover to have a positive impact on innovative output.

Human Resource Management Practices and Innovative Output

The aim of human resource management (HRM) is to create and enhance the competitive advantages of firms by recognizing the human resources inside firms (e.g. Verburg and Den Hartog, 2005). Bratton and Gold (2003) define that "human resource management is a strategic approach to managing employment relations which emphasizes that leveraging people's capabilities is critical to achieving sustainable competitive advantage, this being achieved through a distinctive set of integrated employment policies, programmes and practices" (p. 3). The process of HRM embraces three phases: entry, performance and exit of employees while HRM practices play crucial roles in the whole process (e.g. David, 1997).

For innovative firms, hiring knowledgeable and creative people who can bring ideas and skills into the firm will directly affect innovative performance. A mistake in a hiring decision will not only cause more expenditure on recruitment processes but also slow down innovation projects due to a lack of qualified people. Recruitment and selection requirements such as education and experience are important for finding the right people for the right position. In general, firms would like to hire highly educated or more experienced people because they have the capability to independently learn new knowledge and skills. Compared to low educated or less experienced employees, they can quickly adapt to a changing environment. Therefore, we suggest that a higher number of highly qualified employees with the appropriate educational background and sufficient experience will contribute positively to innovative output.

Performance management concentrates on evaluating, motivating and developing employees' capabilities and performance in order to improve the effectiveness and efficiency of firms. Appraisal, reward and career development systems are main activities of performance management (e.g. Verburg and Den Hartog, 2005). The reward system can be made up with both financial and non-financial incentives. The financial reward system includes competitive wage, financial compensation for hard working, rewards for learning new skills, knowledge and contributing innovative and creative ideas. The non-financial reward system includes employee care facilities such as child-care and health centres, opportunities abroad and work mobility. A competitive reward system is defined by horizontal comparison with other firms and has been argued that it can stimulate employees' performance and organizational learning processes. Laurens & Foss (2003) investigate the interrelation between complementarities of HRM practices and innovative performance. Using data from a Danish survey of 1900 business firms, they found that reward systems such as variable pay systems and internal mobility practices will motivate skilled employees to contribute and share their knowledge. Eventually this will be conducive to innovative performance. Similarly, we suggest that incentives within the competitive reward system such as job rotation and performance pay will have a positive effect on innovative performance.

DATA AND VARIABLES

In this study, we use firm-level data collected by the *Organisation for Strategic Labour Market Research* (*OSA*) in the Netherlands. OSA is sampling all organizations in The Netherlands that employ personnel, with a minimum of five people. Organizations that have taken part in the survey in previous years are again approached for the next survey. Data collection is done by a combination of face-to-face interviews and a written questionnaire to be filled in by a manager and returned by mail. For this chapter, we use data from the 2001 survey, which contains information on the period 1998-2000 for 1482 commercial establishments, covering all manufacturing and commercial service sectors.

Dependent Variables

For a test of the impact of flexible labour and HRM practices on innovative output, the OSA database offers a wide range of interesting indicators. The respondents were asked to subdivide their present product range into three types of product in the OSA Survey:

1. Products that remained *largely unchanged* during the past two years;
2. Products that were *incrementally improved* during the past two years; and
3. Products that were *radically changed* or introduced *entirely new* during the past two years.

Subsequently, firms are asked to report the share of these three types of product in their last year's total sales. That is the definition of innovative output in this chapter. This definition is also relevant for companies with a small number of products in their portfolio, because the definition is based on the turnover share, not on the number of products.

As dependent variables, we use:

- The log of sales per employee from products 'new to the firm' (introduced during the past 3 years) in year 2000 and
- A categorical variable measuring to what extent new products are 'new to the *market*'.
  ◦ Hardly new to the market
  ◦ Partially new to the market
  ◦ Completely new to the market

To construct the log of new product sales per employee, we add up categories (2) and (3), i.e. incremental and radical innovations. One should note that the new product sales according to definition (2) and (3) need to be novel in that they include new technological knowledge or, at least, they should be based on novel (and creative) combinations of existing technological knowledge. The products under (2) and (3) can include products that are new to the *firm* (already known in the market) or products that are first in the *market*. In a subsequent question, firms are asked to grade the newness of their present products on a 3-point scale, ranging from 1 'hardly new to the market' to 3 'completely new to the market'.

Independent Variables

Explaining a firm's score on the log of 'new product sales per employee' and the newness of these products, we use a number of labour relations indicators. The latter include shares of flexible labour and specific HRM practices as independent variables, besides a number of control variables. Descriptive information on these variables is presented in Table 1.

Indicators of flexible labour include proxies for external flexibility (percentages of workers on temporary contracts) and internal labour flexibility. HRM practices include proxies for recruitment and selection practices measured by the educational level of the workforce (percentage of workers with higher education). Furthermore we include two dummy variables as proxies for a competitive reward system: job rotation and performance pay. In principle, we expect the six independent variables in the table to have a positive impact on volumes of sales of innovative products as well as the degree of innovativeness, although the impact of temporary contracts might be ambiguous. On the one hand, short-term commitments might undermine loyalty of workers and the continuity in knowledge accumulation. On the other hand, lots of highly educated people are, notably in their first job, hired on a temporary basis, often with a perspective of tenure. Moreover, specialist technical and commercial consultants can often be hired on a temporary basis. We make a distinction between short-term and long-term temporary hiring, the division line being 9 months of contract. We would expect that

Table 1. Description of variables

Variable name	Variable description	Mean
Dependent variable (Innovative output)		
Innovation productivity	Log of new product sales per employee	3.93
Innovativeness	Was the new product new for the market, partially new for the market or hardly new for the market?	1.82
Independent variable (Labour flexibility)		
High external flexibility	Share of workers on temporary contract*short-term contracts (<9 months are more important); cross dummy	0.86
Low external flexibility	Share of workers on temporary contract*longer-term contracts (>9 months are more important); cross dummy	1.58
Internal flexibility	Percentages of workers that changed their function and/or department within the firm	2.85
Independent variable (HRM practices)		
Highly qualified personnel	Percentages of workers with university or higher professional education degrees	13.33
Performance pay	Dummy: Firm has systems of performance pay (e.g. profit sharing arrangements)	0.48
Job rotation	Dummy: Firm employs job rotation systems	0.69
Control variables		
IT infrastructure	Dummy: Firm uses internet or will have internet access within two years	0.91
Communication technology	Dummy: Organization introduced new logistic or ICT processes in the last 2 years	0.19
R&D intensity	Percentage share of turnover spent on Research & Development	2.18
Small size firm	Dummy: number of employees is between 5 and 49	0.58
Medium size firm	Dummy: number of employees is between 50 and 249	0.27
Large size firm	Dummy: number of employees is 250 and 499	0.07
Industry average new product sales	Average of logs of new product sales per employee in a firm's sector of principal activity	3.91

notably when hired on a longer-run basis, such people may positively add to innovative output, even if hired only temporarily.

Control Variables

Our three most important control variables include:

1. A firm's R&D intensity. Of course, if there is more R&D input, we expect there to be more innovative output.
2. Firm size. Small firms have advantages such as little bureaucracy, short communication lines, or dedicated management by the owner.

The literature also reports, however, typical shortcomings of the innovation process in small firms: A strong dependence on the owner as a key person; or a chronic lack of financial and other resources (e.g. technological knowledge; see Tidd et al., 2006). In smaller firms, the innovation process often is a zero/one decision: failure of a single project can mean the end of the firm, while success can mean exceptional growth. Larger firms also have the advantage that they can maintain larger portfolios of risky projects, thus diminishing their innovative risks by means of diversification.

3. Industry average of new product sales: A firm's score on the dependent variable (log of new product sales per employee) crucially depends on the typical length of the product life cycle in a firm's sector of principal activity. Obviously, sectors with typically short product life cycles (such as food or fashion) will have higher rates of new product introductions (and higher sales of new products) than sectors with long life cycles such as aircraft production. The dependent variable can therefore not be compared across sectors, unless we correct for life cycle differences. As life cycle data are not easily collected in postal surveys, we use, as a substitute, the log of average new products sales in a firm's sector of principal activity. Besides correcting for typical differences in product life cycles between sectors, this variable can also pick up other unobserved specifics of sector. Not surprisingly, inclusion of this variable made sector dummies insignificant. Besides, we also include dummies for a firm's focus on information and communication technologies which is an indication of high technological opportunities.

METHODOLOGY

The Tobit model is suitable for analysing the relationship between a dependent variable y_i and a vector of independent variables x_i, where the domain of the dependent variable is restricted between a lower (left-censoring) and an upper (right-censoring) bound (e.g. Tobin, 1958). The model suggests a linear dependence of a latent variable on x_i via a parameter (vector) β. The disturbance terms, u_i, follow a normal distribution to capture random influences on this relationship. In this chapter we use a version of the Tobit model with only a lower bound, the observable variable y_i is defined to be equal to the latent variable whenever the latent variable is above zero and zero other-

wise. In order to have a consistent estimator for the parameter β, a maximum likelihood estimator has been suggested (e.g. Amemiya, 1973). The mathematical representation of a simple Tobit model is as follows:

$$y_i = \begin{cases} y_i^* & if \; y_i^* > 0 \\ 0 & if \; y_i^* \leq 0 \end{cases}$$

Where y_i^* is a latent variable

$$y_i^* = \beta x_i + u_i, u_i \sim (0, \sigma^2)$$

We use a Tobit procedure (e.g. Maddala, 1985) in this chapter to correct for the specific non-normality of the distribution of our dependent variable (log of 'new product sales per employee'). This non-normality stems from the relatively large number of firms that have zero new product sales. These are the left-censored observations in the Tobit output. Our empirical tobit model is formulated as follows:

Model 1:
$$y_1 = \alpha + \beta_1 LF + \beta_2 HR + \beta_3 Con + \varepsilon_i$$

Where y_1 denotes the log of 'new product sales per employee'; 'LF' includes variables of external flexibility measured by percentages of temporary workers and internal flexibility measured by percentage of employees changing function/department within firms; 'HR' are variables of HRM practices including percentage of highly qualified personnel, dummies for job rotation and performance pay; 'Con' represents control variables. The disturbance term ε_i follows a normal distribution.

We apply an *Ordered Logistic* Model for analysis of determinants of the degree of innovativeness. It can be regarded as an extension of the logistic regression model for dichotomous dependent variables. It is also referred to as ordered logit and ordered-response model (e.g. Maddala, 1983). The econometric logic behind this model is a linear relationship between a latent continuous variable y_i^* ($i=1,...,n$) and the independent variables Xi, $y_i^* = \beta X_i' + \varepsilon_i$, where the disturbance term ε_i follows a logistic distribution with fixed variance at $\pi^2/3$ with zero means. We use the observed variable y_i to estimate the parameter β of equation explaining latent y_i^*. Corresponding to each observed variable y_i ($y_i = 1,...,$ J), the latent variable y_i^* can be divided by some unobserved threshold $\alpha_1,...,\alpha_{J-1}$. It can be illustrated as $ln(\Theta_j) = \alpha_j - \beta X$ and $\Theta_j = prob(y_i \leq j)/prob(y_i > j)$, ($j=1,...,$ J-1). The results of the Ordered Logistic Model can be interpreted by 'log-odds ratios'. Given a positive coefficient and holding constant all other variables, an increase in a particular variable raises the likelihood of moving to a higher engagement level comparing to the present level (e.g. Van der Zwan, 2008). Our Ordered Logistic Model is formulated as follows:

Model 2:

$$\ln\left(\frac{\Pr(Y_1 = j)}{\Pr(Y_1 = j-1)}\right) = \alpha + \beta_1 LF + \beta_2 HR + \beta_3 Con + \varepsilon_i$$

(j=2 or 3)

where Y_1 denotes the degree of innovativeness measured by 3-point Likert-type scale; 'LF' includes variables of external flexibility measured by percentages of temporary workers and internal flexibility measured by percentages of employees changing function or department within the firm; 'HR' covers HRM practices, including percentage of highly qualified personnel, dummies for job rotation and performance pay; 'Con' represents control variables.

RESULTS

Our regression estimates are summarized in Table 2. In the Tobit Model (Model 1), we explain the log of new product sales (per employee) achieved by firms that have such sales. In other words, our interpretation is strictly confined to the group of innovating firms among the respondents to the OSA survey. It is no surprise that R&D intensity has a positive impact on innovative output, which is significant at a 5% level. Processes related to a firm's innovativeness such as the introduction of new logistic or ICT processes are, as expected, positively (at a 5% significant level) related to innovative productivity. Not surprisingly, we find that an individual firm's innovative output depends on the average output of its sector of principal activity (at a 5% significant level). Inclusion of the latter variable implies that our model explains a (positive or negative) deviation of an individual firm's new product sales from its sector average. As to firm size, we have to conclude that the typical advantages or disadvantages of a firm being small or big seem to cancel out each other: there is no difference in sales of innovative products across size classes.

Furthermore, we can conclude that most of our variables on flexible labour and on HRM practices behave as expected. High shares of highly qualified personnel enhance innovative productivity, although this is only significant at a 10% level. The same holds for job rotation. Moreover, performance pay (including profit sharing arrangements) is positively related to innovative productivity (at a 5% significant level). This reflects the practice that firms give financial incentives to qualified people in order to keep them in the firm, rather than letting them leave and take along their (tacit) knowledge to competitors. To our surprise, however, a high rate of internal ('functional') flexibility does not seem to contribute to innovative output. In related estimates, we found that high internal flexibility did contribute to overall sales growth, notably among innovating firms (e.g. Kleinknecht et al. 2006). As to people on temporary contracts, it is interesting to note that higher shares of people with longer contracts (> 9 months) have a weakly significant positive impact on innovative

Table 2. Summary of estimates

Dependent variable	Model 1 (Log) sales per employee of products new to the firm		Model 2 Probability of having products new to the market (other than new to the firm)	
Variables for flexible labour:	Coefficients	t-values	Odds ratio	t-values
High external flexibility	0.100	1.39	0.005	0.45
Low external flexibility	0.091*	1.73*	0.005	0.83
Internal flexibility	-0.017	-0.24	0.002	0.30
HRM practices variables:				
Highly qualified personnel	0.042*	1.89*	0.004**	1.96**
Performance pay	2.500**	2.58**	0.114	0.87
Job rotation	1.703(*)	1.61(*)	-0.000	0.00
Control variables:				
IT infrastructure	6.631**	3.32**	0.077	0.28
Communication technology	3.847**	3.18**	0.257*	1.73*
R&D intensity	0.311**	3.46**	0.025**	2.57**
Small firm	0.475	0.23	-0.443**	-2.13**
Medium-sized firm	0.169	0.08	-0.390*	-1.76*
Large firm	1.707	0.62	-0.147	-0.51
Industry average new product sales	2.168**	4.08**	0.022	-0.25
Constant term	-22.401**	-5.98**		
/cut1			-0.830	
/cut2			1.760	
	335 uncensored observations, 565 censored observations LR chi2(13) = 93.04 (Pr > χ² =0.0000) Log likelihood = -1623.9698 Pseudo R² = 0.0278		1014 observations; LR chi2(13) = 26.17 (Pr > χ² =0.0161) Log likelihood= -979.3277 Pseudo R² = 0.0132	

(*) Coefficient just fails to be significant at 10% level
* = significant at 10% level
** = significant at 5% level

productivity (at a 10% significant level), while higher shares of people on shorter contracts do not contribute significantly. In an alternative version of our estimate (not documented here) we found that high rates of temporary contracts (without distinction by contract length) had a significant positive impact on innovative performance. This gives some support to the above-quoted argument by Ichniowski and Shaw (1995).

Results from the Ordered Logistic Model (Model 2) show that high shares of 'highly quali-fied personnel' have a positive impact on the degree of innovativeness (significant at 5% level). Neither flexible labour nor reward systems influence the degree of innovativeness. It is no surprise again that R&D intensity is also positively related to a higher degree of innovativeness (at a 5% significant level). Furthermore, introducing new logistic or ICT processes has a weak positive impact on the degree of innovativeness (at 10% level). Seemingly, communication technology (new logistic or ICT processes) or IT infrastructure (internet access) contribute to the efficiency of innovation processes. High shares of new product sales (new to the firm) at the sector level have no significant impact on the probability of introducing products new to the market. However, firm size seems to matter. The smaller the firm, the less likely are innovations 'new to the market'.

CONCLUSION AND IMPLICATIONS

We examined the impact of labour relations on innovative output, distinguishing two sorts of innovative output: (1) Innovative productivity: measured by the logs of new product sales per employee (i.e. products new to the firm, other than new to the sector) and (2) Innovativeness: measured by the probability that new products are new to the market (and not only new to the firm). Our labour relations indicators differ in their contribution to the two different dimensions of innovative output. The only robust indicator is highly qualified personnel which has a positive impact on both sales of innovative products as well as on the probability that new products will be 'new to the market'. This underlines the role of human capital to the innovative process. Highly educated employees allow for high learning capabilities, high absorptive capacity, and high analytical and problem-solving abilities, which tend to be individualized and tacitly embedded.

Further, we find strong indications that active HRM practices, including job rotation and performance pay do contribute positively to sales of innovative products, while the impact of flexibility remains ambiguous. We should add that the model estimated in Table 2 is fairly robust to small model changes (e.g. replacing our size class dummies by a continuous variable). We also experimented with quadratic terms, finding only little evidence of non-linear relationships. An important qualification of our findings is that we use cross-sectional data only. This did not allow introducing time lags between our exogenous and endogenous variables. This implies that one should be extremely cautious with causal inferences. Future research should include the use of longitudinal data which will, however, lead to a substantial loss of observations due to panel attrition.

While some of our findings are in favour of the view that 'Rhineland' practices may support innovative performance, the evidence is not clear-cut. On the one hand, we find that systems of job rotation and performance pay contribute positively to innovative output; on the other hand, and against our expectation, high rates of internal flexibility do not. Intuitively one would expect that innovative activities are related to high rates of people changing their function or department within the firm. It is therefore puzzling that we do not find a positive coefficient for internal flexibility. Moreover, our estimates give indications that high shares of temporary employees seem to contribute positively to new product sales, while the same variable contributed negatively to the growth of labour productivity in a recent study using the same database (e.g. Kleinknecht et al. 2006). As a qualification, one should remind that our models in table 2 are estimated on one cross-sectional wave of the OSA database only. Future research should exploit the longitudinal character of the OSA database. Despite these qualifications, it is reassuring that our model in table 2 is fairly robust to changes in model specifications. Nevertheless, our result indicate that a firm is able to stimulate its innovative output by means of making use of employees on long-term temporary contract or implement competitive reward systems inside firms.

REFERENCES

Amabile, T. M., Conti, R., Coon, H., Lazenby, J., & Herron, M. (1996). Assessing the work environment for creativity. *Academy of Management Journal, 39*, 1154–1184. doi:10.2307/256995

Amemiya, T. (1973). Regression analysis when the dependent variable is truncated normal. *Econometrica, 41*(6), 997–1016. doi:10.2307/1914031

Audretsch, D., & Thurik, R. (2004). A model of entrepreneurial economy. *International Journal of entrepreneurship. Education, 2*(2), 143–166.

Beatson, M. (1995). Labour market flexibility. In *Research Series (No. 48)*. Sheffield: Employment Department.

Brown, S. L., & Eisenhardt, K. (1998). *Competing on the edge: strategy as structured chaos*. Boston, MA: Harvard Business School Press.

Buchele, R., & Christiansen, J. (1999). Employment and productivity growth in Europe and North America: The impact of labour market institutions. *International Review of Applied Economics, 13*(3), 313–332. doi:10.1080/026921799101571

Cohen, W. M., & Levintal, D. A. (1990). Absorptive capacity: A new perspective on learning and innovation. *Administrative Science Quarterly, 35*, 128–152. doi:10.2307/2393553

Coutrot, T. (2003). Innovation and job stability. In *Working Paper*. Paris: Centre D'Etudes Prospectives et D'Informations Internationales.

Ichniowski, C., & Shaw, K. (1995). Old dogs and new tricks; determinants of the adoption of productivity-enhancing work practices, Brookings Papers: Microeconomics, pp. 1-55.

Kleinknecht, A., Oostendorp, R. M., Pradhan, M. P., & Naastepad, C. W. M. (2006). Flexible labour, firm performance and the Dutch job creation miracle. *International Review of Applied Economics, 20*(2), 171–187. doi:10.1080/02692170600581102

Laursen, K., & Foss, N. J. (2003). New Human Resource Management Practices, Complementarities, and the Impact on Innovative performance. *Cambridge Journal of Economics, 27*(2), 243–263. doi:10.1093/cje/27.2.243

Leonard-Barton, D. (1995). *Wellsprings of knowledge: Building and sustaining the sources of innovation*. Boston, MA: Harvard Business School Press.

Maddala, G. S. (1983). *Limited-Dependent and Qualitative Variables in Econometrics*. Cambridge, UK: Cambridge University Press.

McGrath, R. G. (2001). Exploratory learning, innovative capacity and managerial oversight. *Academy of Management Journal, 44*, 118–131. doi:10.2307/3069340

Michie, J., & Sheehan, M. (2003). Labour market deregulation, 'flexibility' and innovation. *Cambridge Journal of Economics, 27*, 123–148. doi:10.1093/cje/27.1.123

Polanyi, M. (1966). *The tacit dimension*. London: Routledge.

Tidd, J., Bessant, J. R., & Pavitt, K. (2006). *Managing Innovation*. Chichester, UK: Wiley.

Tobin, J. (1958). Estimation for relationships with limited dependent variables. *Econometrica, 26*(1), 24–36. doi:10.2307/1907382

Trott, P. (1998). *Innovation management and new product development*. London: Financial Times.

Tsai, W. (2001). Knowledge transfer in intra-organizational networks: Effects of network position and absorptive capacity on business unit innovation and performance. *Academy of Management Journal, 44*, 996–1004. doi:10.2307/3069443

Van de Zwan, P., Thurik, A. R., & Grilo, I. (2008). (forthcoming). The entrepreneurial ladder and its determinants. *Applied Economics*.

Verburg, R. M., & Hartog, D. (2005). Human Resource Management for advanced technology. In Verburg, R. M., Ortt, J. R., & Dicke, W. M. (Eds.), *Managing Technology and Innovation* (pp. 43–46). London: Routledge.

Verloop, J. (2004). *Insight the Innovation: Managing innovation by understanding the laws of innovation*. Amsterdam: Elsevier Science.

KEY TERMS AND DEFINITIONS

(Degree of) Innovativeness: A categorical variable measuring to what extent new products are 'new to the market'.

Functional Flexibility: The ability of firms to re-allocate labour in their internal labour market, relying on training that allows personnel carrying out a wider range of tasks.

HRM Practices: Human resource management is a strategic approach to managing employment relations which emphasizes that leveraging people's capabilities is critical to achieving sustainable competitive advantage, this being achieved through a distinctive set of integrated employment policies, programmes and practices.

Innovative Output: A two dimensional measure including innovative productivity and the degree of innovativeness.

Innovative Productivity: The log of new product sales (new to the firm) per employee.

Labour Flexibility: A combined measure of flexibility at firm level including numerical flexibility, functional flexibility and wage flexibility.

Numerical Flexibility: The ability of firms to change the volume of personnel by making use of fixed-term employment contracts, labour hired temporarily, either directly or through temporary work agencies or freelance workers.

Performance Management: A HRM practice concentrating on evaluating, motivating and developing employees' capabilities and performance in order to improve the effectiveness and efficiency of firms.

Recruitment and Selection: A HRM practice aim at hiring the right people for the right position based on observable characteristics such as education and experience.

Chapter 12

Harnessing Knowledge for Innovation in Social Enterprises:
An Intellectual Capital Perspective

Eric Kong
University of Southern Queensland, Australia

ABSTRACT

Very little research has investigated the role of intellectual capital (IC) in innovation processes in social enterprises. After reviewing the literature, the central argument in this research study is that IC assists social enterprises to harness knowledge that leads to innovation for the pursuit of social and commercial activities. Thus the study contributes to the literature by theoretically arguing that IC can be utilized in innovation processes in social enterprises. An IC conceptual framework is proposed which helps social entrepreneurs to visualize IC and its components in their organizations. Finally, the framework's implications for the development of effective innovation-based strategies in social enterprises are discussed.

INTRODUCTION

Social enterprises are not purely commercial and yet, they are not purely philanthropic (Borzaga & Defourny, 2001; Dees, 1998). They "enact hybrid nonprofit and for-profit activities" (Dart, 2004: 415) all "under one roof" (Fowler, 2000: 645). Social enterprises accomplish their social missions through the development of innovative ventures or by reorganizing existing activities to improve operational efficiency (Pomerantz, 2003; Weerawardena & Sullivan-Mort, 2006; Zappala,

DOI: 10.4018/978-1-61520-643-8.ch012

2001). Thus they represent a step forward of the concept of traditional nonprofit organizations in achieving social needs (Manfredi, 2005). Indeed, social enterprises often challenge the status quo and our conventional thinking about what is feasible to alleviate social problems and to improve general public well being (Seelos & Mair, 2005).

Although social enterprises involve adopting innovative business approaches for dealing with complex social problems, their primary objective is to create social value for the community that they serve for (Pomerantz, 2003; Thompson & Doherty, 2006). Economic value creation through commercial revenues and business activities is often perceived as a strategic means that allows the organizations to achieve sustainability and self-sufficiency, generate income to support their mission, and carry out mission-related functions expeditiously (Seelos & Mair, 2005; Young, 2001). Social enterprises that reply on for-profit strategic management techniques for strategic decisions may find themselves uneasy to reconcile commercial objectives for organizational survival and social mission to meet client needs. This is because for-profit strategic management methods that emphasize profit maximization are arguably compromising the principle of investing in human and social concerns in mission-driven nonprofit organizations (Alexander, 2000; Chetkovich & Frumkin, 2003; Eisenberg, 1997; Kong, 2008; Mulhare, 1999; Weisbrod, 1998). Social enterprises must be managed strategically through innovative approaches, with the social dimension being central. Thus these organizations require a strategic management method that enhances their ability to pursue social missions, improves their efficiency and effectiveness, and, at the same time, maximizes their capability to constantly generate innovative ideas for sustainable ventures in the competitive environment.

Based on a review of the literature, this study argues that intellectual capital (IC) can be utilized as a valid strategic management framework in the innovation process in social enterprises for the pursuit of social and commercial objectives. IC refers to the collective knowledge that is embedded in the personnel, organizational routines and network relationships of an organization (Bontis, 2002). IC is therefore applicable to any organization regardless of whether it is profit oriented or not (Kong, 2008; Kong & Thomson, 2006). Social enterprises are likely able to create value for long-term success if they implement strategies that responds to market opportunities and environmental dynamics by exploiting and exploring their IC resources.

The original contribution of the research study is threefold. First, little systematic research has examined the application of the IC concept as a strategic management conceptual framework in innovation processes in social enterprises. Therefore the study contributes to fill this gap in the strategic management literature. Second, suggestions on how the IC concept can be utilized effectively in the unique context of social entrepreneurship are presented. Finally, an IC conceptual framework is proposed which assists social entrepreneurs to conceptually visualize how the utilization of IC resources for growth and enhanced performance can be maximized.

The chapter is organized as follows. Firstly, a review of the emergence of social enterprises and the need for a valid strategic management method in innovation processes in the organizations are provided. This is followed by a brief overview of the IC literature and its implications in the context of social entrepreneurship. Then this leads to a discussion of an IC conceptual framework and strategic advantage in social enterprises' innovation strategy development. Finally, a discussion of how the framework can be used effectively in the innovation process to advance strategic advantage in social enterprises is presented.

SOCIAL ENTERPRISES AND STRATEGIC MANAGEMENT METHODS

Social entrepreneurship is an emerging area of investigation within the entrepreneurship and not-for-profit marketing literatures (Hitt, Ireland, Camp, & Sexton, 2001; Weerawardena & Sullivan-Mort, 2006). The emergence of social enterprise can be linked to resource constraints in the nonprofit sector (Dees, 1998; Gray, Healy, & Crofts, 2003). Traditional nonprofit organizations are now facing challenges stemming from diminishing fiscal supports in the form of public funds and donations (Alexander, 1999; Craig, Taylor, & Parkes, 2004; Eisenberg, 1997). In addition, growing competition for service delivery with for-profit organizations (Kong, 2008; Ramia & Carney, 2003), declining volunteer support (Jamison, 2003; Lyons, 1999; Lyons, 2001; Lyons & Fabiansson, 1998) and losing commitment from nonprofit employees (Eisenberg, 1997, 2000; Kim & Lee, 2007) are adding significant strategic pressures to the organizations. Traditional nonprofit organizations increasingly seek alternative financial sources such as fees or service charges and other essentially commercial forms of income to generate more self-finance for their operations (Fowler, 2000; Liebschutz, 1992; Salamon, 1986, 1996, 1999; Weisbrod, 1997). An example of the alternative financial sources can be found in the Salvation Army. The organization's Store Division has shops in different areas which generate income for the broader social purpose. However, traditional nonprofit organizations remain restricted from using trade as a means to raise capital, making them heavily dependent on donations and grants for achieving their social missions (Mason, Kirkbride, & Bryde, 2007).

The study of corporate social responsibility in more recent times has seen some strategic partnerships between business corporations and traditional nonprofit organizations (See e.g. Husted & Allen, 2007; Lee, 2008; Lichtenstein, Drumwright, & Braig, 2004; Matten & Moon, 2008; Porter & Kramer, 2006). It is, however, important to note that social problems require more than just spare cash but commitment to resolving social problems and continuous financial support (Jamali & Keshishian, 2009; Kanter, 1999), particularly in times of global economic crisis. Indeed, traditional nonprofit organizations are already facing sharply lower corporate charitable contributions as many corporations are struggling with financial difficulties themselves (Brock, 2008). Corporate social responsibility does not seem to be able to provide all solutions to the nonprofit sector.

Social enterprises have emerged as a strategic response to many of the mentioned challenges that traditional nonprofit organizations are facing today (Dart, 2004; Frances, 2008; Sullivan-Mort, Weer-

awardena, & Carnegie, 2003; Thompson, 2002; Weerawardena & Sullivan-Mort, 2006). Unlike their nonprofit counterpart, social enterprises are not restricted to use innovative business approaches in trading of products and services (Spear, 2001). Therefore the organizations are more flexible than traditional nonprofit organizations in terms of raising capital through commercial revenues and business activities. More importantly, social enterprises can gradually become self-financing through organic growth, making the organizations less dependent on donations and grants (Mason et al., 2007). In contrast to for-profit organizations in which profits are often distributed to their owners and shareholders, economic value creation in social enterprises is perceived as a by-product which allows the organizations to achieve sustainability and self-sufficiency (Fowler, 2000; Seelos & Mair, 2005). The production surplus of social enterprises is reinvested in the development of organizational activities that ensures viability in tackling social problems or to be used for the benefit of people other than those who control the organizations (Defourny, 2001). Adapted from Gees' (1998) *Social Enterprise Spectrum*, Figure 1 clearly distinguishes social enterprises from traditional nonprofit organizations and business corporations.

Social enterprises are neither traditional nonprofit organizations nor business corporations (Borzaga & Defourny, 2001; Dees, 1998). They represent a hybrid form of organizations that involve taking business-like, innovative approaches to deliver public services (Dart, 2004; Fowler, 2000) and characterize an alternative for resourcing new services, particularly service innovations that do not fit neatly within government funding guidelines (Gray et al., 2003). Thompson and Doherty (2006) have concluded that organizations that fall neatly into the category of social enterprises conform to several criteria. These include: having a social purpose, using assets and wealth to create benefit to its community, pursuing social purpose with (or at

Figure 1. The social enterprise spectrum. (Adapted from (Dees, 1998, p.60))

		Purely philanthropic	Social enterprises	Purely commercial
Motives		Appeal to good will	Mixed motives	Appeal to self-interest
Methods		Mission driven	Mission and market driven	Market driven
Goals		Social value	Social and economic value	Economic value
Key stakeholders	**Beneficiaries**	Pay nothing	Subsidized rates, or mix of full payers and those who pay nothing	Market-rate prices
	Capital	Donations and grants	Below-market capital, or mix of donations and market-rate capital	Market-rate capital
	Workforces	Volunteers	Below-market wages, or mix of volunteers and fully paid staff	Market-rate compensation
	Suppliers	Make in-kind donations	Special discounts, or mix of in-kind and full-price donations	Market-rate prices

least in part) trade in a market place, being seen as accountable to both its members and a wider community, involving members or employees in decision making and/or governance, being nonprofit-distributing to its shareholders and owners, and having either a double- or triple-bottom line paradigm (Thompson & Doherty, 2006). A notable example of this form of enterprises is the Grameen Bank. The Grameen Bank was founded by Muhammad Yunus, an economics professor, in Bangladesh in 1976. The Bank aims to improve the condition of its clientele by extending unsecured loans to the poorest villagers, primarily economically and socially impoverished women, who would not normally qualify as customers of established banks. Not only that the Bank has a unique philosophy towards its clientele, but also it has adopted an innovative group-based credit approach utilizing peer-pressure within groups to ensure that borrowers eventually repay their loans and develop good credit standing (Seelos & Mair, 2005). Today the Grameen Bank is so profitable that it can fund many other social projects.

Despite the ongoing development of strategic management research in the for-profit and non-profit fields over the last few decades (Backman, Grossman, & Rangan, 2000; Goold, 1997; Hoskisson, Hitt, Wan, & Yiu, 1999; Stone, Bigelow, & Crittenden, 1999), the attention to strategic management in social enterprises has been rela-

tively under-researched. There is more literature pointing to the critical role of innovation in social enterprises (See e.g. Borins, 2000; Sullivan-Mort et al., 2003; Waddock & Post, 1991; Weerawardena & Sullivan-Mort, 2006). There is, however, relatively little written on what adapted strategic management methods are most appropriate in innovation processes in social enterprises for the pursuit of social and commercial activities. As a major part of a social entrepreneur's responsibility is to consider the effect of strategy on a social mission rather than simply on financial performance, for-profit strategic management concepts that embrace profit motivated attitudes are likely less effective in the organizations. In the case of Grameen Bank, it would be extremely difficult to improve the condition of economically and socially impoverished women had financial results been seen as the only focus to the Bank. The success of Grameen Bank suggests that social enterprises should not depend on for-profit strategic management methods for strategic decisions. The need for an applicable strategic management method that enables social enterprises to seize marketing opportunities in the competitive environment and develop strategic directions that respond to social needs simultaneously is increasingly pressing.

Many scholars have explicitly highlighted that knowledge is the only strategic resource that leads to strategic advantage in organizations (e.g.,

Ambrosini & Bowman, 2001; Massingham, 2008; Mouritsen & Larsen, 2005; Probst, Buchel, & Raub, 1998; St. Leon, 2002; Zack, 2005). Within the context of social entrepreneurship, strategic advantage can be interpreted as the ability to utilize dynamic and unique resources for strategic renewal in the competitive environment and develop strategic directions that create new opportunities and shape the organizations' future environment. Marr and Roos (2005) argue that organizations often perform more efficiently and effectively if they understand what knowledge they possess and how to configure their intellectual resources to create organizational value. McCann III and Buckner (2004) also argue that it is essential to gain a better conceptual and operational appreciation of what it means to strategically manage knowledge in organizations. Marr and Roos, and McCann III and Buckner's comments are also applicable to social enterprises. Thus, accumulated, applied and shared knowledge likely enables social enterprises to gain strategic advantage. One form of conceptualizing knowledge in innovation-based strategy development processes in social enterprises is through the lens of intellectual capital (IC).

INTELLECTUAL CAPITAL (IC) AND ITS COMPONENTS

The Concept of Intellectual Capital (IC)

Irving Fisher's capital theory at least partly constituted the founding base of intellectual capital (IC). Fisher (1906: 52, his italics) outlined that "[a] *stock of wealth* existing at an *instant* of time is called *capital*. A *flow of services* through a *period* of time is called *income*". Thus, according to Fisher, as long as a stock, including knowledge, gives rise to income, it can be called *capital*. The *stock* in the concept of IC are intellectual resources; in other words, to realize the specific monetary value of intellectual resources in an organization

(Boedker, Guthrie, & Cuganesan, 2005). The *flow*, on the other hand, is about identifying the intellectual resources that can be utilized to add value to the organization (Boedker et al., 2005). Accordingly, the stock of IC is used to help realizing the historical monetary value of IC generated by the organization, and the flow of IC is related to the understanding and managing of the organization's capacity to enhance organizational performance now and in the future (Boedker et al., 2005). Accordingly, any intellectual resource that can contribute to value added for the organization can be categorized as IC (Kong, 2008; Massingham, 2008; Stewart, 1997; Sullivan, 1998).

Edvinsson and Malone (1997: 44) describe IC as "the possession of knowledge, applied experience, organizational technology, customer relationships and professional skills that provide … a competitive edge in the market". Youndt, Subramaniam, and Snell (2004: 337) define IC as "the sum of all knowledge an organization is able to leverage in the process of conducting business to gain competitive advantage". It is widely accepted that IC is associated with an organization's innovative performance (Anand, Gardner, & Morris, 2007; Leiponen, 2008; McAdam, 2000; Nelson & McCann, 2008; Spencer, 2003; Subramaniam & Youndt, 2005; Tsai, 2001; Wu, Chang, & Chen, 2008). IC promotes the creativity possessed by all organizational members, indirectly accounting for an organization's future financial prospects (Mouritsen, 1998; Roos, Roos, Dragonetti, & Edvinsson, 1997). This is because IC is concerned with the control and alignment of human and non-human knowledge flow across organizational levels in order to create value for organizations (Choo & Bontis, 2002; Petty & Guthrie, 2000). This conceptualization stresses the internally generated, historically forged efficiencies that have a long term horizon through the knowledge, skills, talents and know-how of individuals in organizations (Bukh, Johansen, & Mouritsen, 2002; Kong, 2003b, 2008; Mouritsen, Larsen, & Bukh, 2005). Organizations are often able to create value for long-term success if they implement strategies that respond to market opportunities by exploiting and exploring their IC resources (Marr & Roos, 2005).

Following the work of a number of scholars in the field, IC is generally taken to encompass three primary interrelated components: human capital, relational capital and structural capital (Bontis, 1996, 1998; Dzinkowski, 2000; Kong, 2008; Roos et al., 1997; Saint-Onge, 1996; Stewart, 1997). In other words, IC is the intelligence that can be found in human beings (or human capital), network relationships (or relational capital), and organizational routines (or structural capital) in organizations (Bontis, 2002).

Human Capital

Human capital includes various human resource elements, including attitude, competencies, experience and skills, and, perhaps most importantly, the innovativeness and talents of people (Bontis, 2002; Choo & Bontis, 2002; Fletcher, Guthrie, Steane, Roos, & Pike, 2003; Guerrero, 2003; Roos & Jacobsen, 1999; Roos et al., 1997). Human capital is important to organizations as it assists organizations to innovatively respond to environmental changes by sensing the need for changes, developing innovative strategies to meet the changes and efficiently implementing the strategies for complex and dynamic environments (Wright, McMahan, & McWilliams, 1994). A higher level of human capital is often associated with more innovative ideas, greater productivity and higher incomes or compensation (Wilson & Larson, 2002). In other words, human capital is a source of innovation and strategic renewal (Bontis, 2002; Bontis, Keow, & Richardson, 2000; Webster, 2000).

Relational Capital

Relational capital represents an organization's relations with its external stakeholders and the perceptions that they hold about the organization, as well as the exchange of knowledge between the organization and its external stakeholders (Bontis, 1998, 2002; Fletcher et al., 2003; Grasenick & Low, 2004; Marr & Roos, 2005). Relational capital incorporates: the loyalty of valuable customers; the mutual trust and commitment given by key suppliers and clients; the reliability and reliance partnership from alliance or contractual partners; and the reputation and relationships that an organization has developed over time in its surrounding community (Knight, 1999; Marr & Roos, 2005).

All organizational relationships involve knowledge exchange and these relationships can be considered as organizational knowledge assets (Schiuma, Lerro, & Carlucci, 2005). An exchange of knowledge between an organization and its external stakeholders likely enhances the organization's ability to generate more innovative ideas. This is because when existing knowledge is articulated and challenged, new knowledge may be developed. In other words, relational capital is capable of harnessing knowledge that leads to innovation in organizations.

Structural Capital

The third component of IC is structural capital. As opposed to human capital which can be lost easily due to organizational members' departure, structural capital is the pool of knowledge that remains in an organization at the end of the day after individuals within the organization have left (Grasenick & Low, 2004; Mouritsen & Koleva, 2004; Roos et al., 1997). Structural capital refers to the learning and knowledge that are enacted in day-to-day activities. It includes all of the non-human storehouses of knowledge in organizations, such as databases, process manuals, strategies, routines, organizational culture, publications, and copyrights which creates value for organizations, thus adding to their material value (Bontis et al., 2000; Guthrie, Petty, & Ricceri, 2006; Ordóñez de Pablos, 2004). Structural capital is important to organizations as it deals with the mechanisms and structures of the organizations which, when complemented by individual innovative behavior, can assist individuals in their quest for optimum organizational innovation.

Defining the three IC components separately does not suggest that the components are completely separated constructs. Rather, the single concept of IC is a multi-dimensional construct and the three IC components are inter-dependent (Subramaniam & Youndt, 2005; Youndt et al., 2004). As Knight (1999: 24) argues:

... as investments are made in human capital, more competent and capable people develop better structural capital for an organization. Improved human capital and structural capital go on to create more productive external [relational] capital through the delivery of better products and services to high-value customers ... a virtuous cycle begins its upward spiral into further organizational value and growth.

Thus, IC is designed to be synergetic. It becomes meaningless to attempt to assess the value of the constituent parts of IC by simply adding them together (Peppard & Rylander, 2001). That is why it is essential to gain a better conceptual and operational appreciation of what it means to strategically manage knowledge in organizations (McCann III & Buckner, 2004). Kong (2008) argues that the characteristics of IC offer more than just competitive advantage to organizations. In fact, the combination, utilization, interaction, alignment, and balancing of the three types of IC, along with knowledge flow between the three components, provide strategic advantage with the best possible value to organizations. The significance of interactions between the three types of IC is evidenced in the arguments of Nonaka and Takeuchi:

[An] organization supports creative individuals or provides contexts for them to create knowledge. Organizational knowledge creation, therefore, should be understood as a process that "organizationally" amplifies the knowledge created by individuals and crystallizes it as a part of the knowledge network of the organization. This process takes place within an expanding "community of interaction" which crosses intra- and inter-organizational levels and boundaries (1995: 59).

THE IMPORTANCE OF INTELLECTUAL CAPITAL IN SOCIAL ENTERPRISES

The Concept of Intellectual Capital (IC) in Social Enterprises

IC is a robust concept capable of cross-sectoral application, which makes it particularly applicable to social enterprises as the organizations often involve both nonprofit and for-profit activities at the same time. Social enterprises' primary objective focuses on investing in people rather than profit; and that objective is in line with the characteristics of IC, which focus on qualitative, non-financial intellectual resources for future strategic prospects. Roos (1998) argues that although IC may superficially be concerned with competitive advantage in organizations, it has a deeper purpose.

The deeper purpose of an IC approach is to change people's behavior, not least through changing the corporate language. The concept of IC brings with it a whole set of new values about what is good and what is bad management, what is the right and the wrong things [sic] to do in corporations [emphasis added] (Roos, 1998: 151).

Values embedded in IC are essential to social enterprises particularly in the dynamic environment that the organizations are operating in. An

IC approach forces social entrepreneurs to rethink their mission and social *raison d'être* in the innovation strategy development process. This is because IC relates to questions about identity, such as "who you are, and what you want to be" (Mouritsen et al., 2005: 12) and thus, IC is not merely an objective in relation to intellectual resources, but an identity crafted around ability and knowledge of what an organization can and should do (Mouritsen et al., 2005; Roos et al., 1997). In other words, IC helps social enterprises to reinforce their social *raison d'être* by placing social dimension at the center of their innovation-based strategies. This is extremely important to social enterprises as social dimension should always be the *raison d'être* of the organizations' existence no matter what innovative business approaches social entrepreneurs have decided to adopt.

IC assists social enterprises to utilize their existing resources and generate new resources effectively in the knowledge-based economy. Thus IC is capable to facilitate innovation in social enterprises by shifting the organizations' strategic focus to intellectual resources including knowledge, skills and experience. This is particularly important to social enterprises as the success of the organizations lies with their ability to facilitate innovative approaches to achieve social missions (Fowler, 2000).

The essential role of IC in innovation strategy development processes is not merely about formulating strategies for resource allocation; for example sharing knowledge and expertise among existing paid employees and volunteers. It is also for resource acquisition such as sustaining a positive image to draw funding from potential donors and to attract potential new employees and volunteers. Marr and Roos (2005) argue that organizations that have a better understanding of how their intellectual resources interact are more able to create value for long-term success. Their perspective on organizations implies that a better understanding of the interrelationships among the three types of IC will also assist social

entrepreneurs to develop innovative strategies that create value for their organizations in the future. If social entrepreneurs are provided with accurate and timely information of what capability their organizations hold and lack, they are able to formulate and implement innovative strategies that best fit their circumstances.

On the contrary, failing to account for IC may lead to a misallocation of intellectual resources and run the risk of making poorly informed decisions, which lead to high employee turnover, inadequate training and development, inexperienced top management teams, and inability to turn data into information in social enterprises.

Human Capital in Social Enterprises

Human capital is important to social enterprises. Wallis and Dollery (2005: 488) argue that nonprofit organizations' "performance depends most crucially on the quality of leadership exercised at the top by their presidents, CEOs, or executive directors". Hambrick, Finkelstein, and Mooney (2005) also echo this, arguing that top executives often rely on their personal experiences or internalize the knowledge and skills through other leaders' actions to make strategic decisions. Whether it is personal experiences or internalization, the concept of leadership reflects the professional knowledge, skills and experience that leaders embraced. This is in line with Finkelstein and Hambrick's (1996) argument that leadership is a unique resource that represents the professional knowledge and skills of individuals (such as CEOs or senior executives), groups (such as top management teams) or other governance bodies (such as board of directors) in organizations. This connects with research in the area which finds that unique knowledge created by entrepreneurs, especially through their idiosyncratic information gathering behaviors, might be used to attract others such as employees or volunteers to become involved in their effort, to build more effective organizations, and to attract financial capital for future development (Nanus

& Dobbs, 1999; Wallis & Dollery, 2005; West III & Noel, 2009). Thus social entrepreneurs' leadership skills play a significant role in strategy development processes in social enterprises. But more importantly, social entrepreneurs recognize the importance of innovation and seize market opportunities on a continuous basis in social enterprises. Roper and Cheney (2005) argue that social entrepreneurs' ability to offer "[a] balance between the open and democratic generation of ideas and the discerning of genuinely good and feasible ones is crucial" because "[t]oo much openness risks impracticality; too linear and controlled a process can mean a loss of potentiality". Accordingly, human capital is significant to social enterprises since social entrepreneurs' leadership skills and decisions have considerable influence on strategic choices, organizational designs, and ultimately, organizational performance.

Also, social enterprises often deal with social problems that require face-to-face interactions. For instance, the Hong Kong Federation of Handicapped Youth (HKFHY) Flower Shop, a self-help charitable organization adopting a self-financed mode, aims to provide floral arrangement training and job opportunities for people with disabilities. Their objective is to assist people with disabilities to re-integrate into the society. The organization's day-to-day operations involve substantial interpersonal skills and tacit knowledge between non-executive members and people from outside the organization. Since the ability of social enterprises to achieve their objectives depends heavily on the competency of their non-executive organizational members, those social enterprises that have the strongest base of skilled and experienced non-executive members are in the best position to raise the largest sums of funding (Hudson, 1999). In short, social enterprises rely heavily on human capital to achieve their social objectives.

Relational Capital in Social Enterprises

External relationships are crucial to social enterprises since the organizations are operating in a dynamic environment that has multiple groups of external stakeholders (Kristoffersen & Singh, 2004; Mason et al., 2007). Stakeholders are people or organizations that have a real, assumed, or imagined stake in an organization, the organization's performance and its sustainability (Anheier, 2005). Thus, external stakeholders in social enterprises include, but not limited to, government agencies, traditional nonprofit organizations, business corporations, potential employees and volunteers, and customers and end-users. Social enterprises often rely on volunteer support, alliance partnerships and public trust for legitimacy (Alexander, 1998; Balser & McClusky, 2005; Luke & Verreynne, 2006). Researchers such as Hamori (2003) and Martin, Beaumont, Doig, and Pate (2005) also argue that prospective employees and volunteers are more willing to join nonprofit organizations with a strong community reputation. Accordingly, social enterprises can gain strategic advantage if they are able to nurture or enhance the knowledge that their external stakeholders hold about their organizations.

As environmental turbulence in the form of social and economic change generates unintended consequences, single organizations can be weak or unprepared (Mulroy, 2003; Selsky & Parker, 2005). Organizational relationships often involve knowledge exchange (Schiuma et al., 2005). Social enterprises may benefit from collaboration with other stakeholders (Huxham & Vangen, 2005) such as government agencies and business corporations. Such benefits may include sharing resources and risks, increasing efficiency, enhancing co-ordinations, facilitating mutual learning and nurturing expertise from working collaboratively with other stakeholders. Relational capital is deemed to be critical to social enterprises as it helps to create value by connecting an organization with its external stakeholders (Knight, 1999; Ordóñez de Pablos, 2004). Most importantly, relational capital acts as a catalyst for innovation within social enterprises. This is because a frequent exchange of knowledge between a social enterprise and its external stakeholders helps to articulate and challenge existing knowledge for new knowledge creation in innovation processes.

On the contrary, if external relationships are not managed effectively, social enterprises may end up losing valuable external resources such as volunteers and donations as well as their legitimacy (Alexander, 1998; Ospina, Diaz, & O'Sullivan, 2002).

Structural Capital in Social Enterprises

Structural capital is the supportive infrastructure for innovation in the strategy development in organizations. This is because structural capital helps to amplify the values arising from human capital and relational capital and thus multiply the overall IC (Edvinsson, 1997; Mouritsen & Koleva, 2004). Human capital is much more volatile in nature (Edvinsson, 1997). Individuals take their talent, skills, tacit knowledge, creativity and innovation with them when they leave an organization (Bontis et al., 2000; Grasenick & Low, 2004; Massingham, 2008; Roos et al., 1997). A loss of organizational memory due to individuals' departure may be a threat to the organization. On the other hand, relational capital is external to the organizations and thus it is difficult to manage, codify and control (Bontis, 1998, 1999, 2002; Knight, 1999). Unlike human and relational capital, structural capital can be owned and traded by an organization (Edvinsson, 1997). This is because some of the intellectual assets may be legally protected and become intellectual property rights which are legitimately owned by the organization (Fletcher et al., 2003). Thus, structural capital represents the only knowledge stock that remains in organizations at all times (Grasenick

& Low, 2004; Mouritsen & Koleva, 2004; Roos et al., 1997). In other words, structural capital assists social enterprises to create organizational value that facilitate organizational learning and knowledge creation that leads to innovation for the pursuit of social and commercial activities simultaneously.

In short, the three IC components assist to create value for social enterprises by balancing the utilization and usage of the existing and unborn intellectual resources. This becomes important to social enterprises in particular in today's highly competitive dynamic environment.

AN IC CONCEPTUAL FRAMEWORK

West III and Noel (2009: 1) argue that "[a] new venture's strategy—and thus its performance—is based upon the knowledge the firm has about its market, its opportunity in that market, and its appropriate conduct to take advantage of that opportunity". An IC conceptual framework is proposed on the basis of a review of the existing literature. The IC conceptual framework, along with knowledge flow between the three components and with the external conditions in the environment, helps social entrepreneurs to visualize conceptually where they might put their attention and resources, and provides them broad guidelines on how to seek to maximize the utilization of resources for growth and enhanced performance. The framework also provides a guideline in innovation processes in social enterprises. The framework is shown in Figure 2.

As can be seen in Figure 2, the three types of capital frequently interact with each other and that interactions between the three IC components create value for social enterprises. Value creation allows social enterprises to gain strategic advantage in the dynamic environment; that is to harness knowledge that leads to innovation for the pursuit of social and commercial activities. For instance, a social entrepreneur verbally presents innovative

Figure 2. An IC conceptual framework of harnessing knowledge in social enterprises

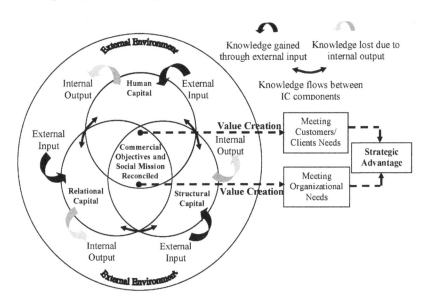

ideas to potential customers and clients. This human communication allows knowledge about the social enterprise to be developed in the mind of the potential customers, which may lead to mutual trust between the social enterprise and the customers. Over time the mutual trust and commitment given by the customers likely enhances reputation and relationships that the organization has with its surrounding community. In other words, knowledge is transferred from human capital to relational capital. When the social entrepreneur makes use of the knowledge about the potential customers' needs in the innovation process to develop new products or services, knowledge is transferred from relational capital to structural capital. When the new products or services are publicly advertised online for the general public, the knowledge of the new product or service (as well as the knowledge of the social enterprise) constitutes a form of knowledge transfer; that is from structural capital to relational capital. Table 1 provides more examples of value creation through interactions in between the three IC components.

The input of new knowledge ("external input" in Figure 2) from external sources, whether they

are tacit or explicit in nature, constitutes external knowledge flows which are important in innovation processes within organizations (Rigby & Zook, 2002). Examples of new external knowledge flows in social enterprises may include newly recruited employees and volunteers who bring in extra skills and experience, an input of novel management concepts from profit-seeking and public sector organizations which lead to renewed policies and work procedures, or newly established relationships with external new stakeholders due to recently explored service areas.

Martin de Holan and Phillips (2004) argue that whenever an organization generates new knowledge, it will likely generate outdated or unwanted knowledge simultaneously. Managers must become skilled at learning new knowledge as well as forgetting unwanted knowledge as managing outdated knowledge can be very costly (Martin, 2000; Martin de Holan & Phillips, 2004; Sirmon, Hitt, & Ireland, 2007). Accordingly, successful social enterprises should divest themselves of outdated or unwanted knowledge, which applies to the three types of capital. Accordingly, organizations that embrace higher levels

Table 1. Examples of harnessing knowledge through the interaction of IC components in social enterprises

Knowledge transfers from Human Capital to Relational Capital	Knowledge transfers from Relational Capital to Structural Capital	Knowledge transfers from Structural Capital to Human Capital
Social enterprise staff members present research papers on behalf of their organization at international seminars/conferences Social enterprise staff members are encouraged to rotate jobs in order to meet customers/suppliers	Profiles of clients/ customers/donors are inputted into system databases Customers/Clients/Donors fill in organizational surveys/questionnaires	Newly recruited social enterprise staff members familiarize internal organizational policies/manuals Existing social enterprise staff members analyze customer profiles in order to understand customer/client needs
Knowledge transfers from Relational Capital to Human Capital	Knowledge transfers from Structural Capital to Relational Capital	Knowledge transfers from Human Capital to Structural Capital
Social enterprise staff members conduct face-to-face survey to clients/customers 24-hour online enquiry available to customers/the general public	Social enterprise makes organizational information publicly available in their organizational website Organizational publications/newsletters are sent to customers/clients/ donors	Senior management formulates organizational strategic plans Social enterprise staff members prepare training manuals for newly recruited employees or volunteers

of absorptive capacity can manage knowledge flows more efficiently, and stimulate innovative outcomes (Escribano, Fosfuri, & Tribó, 2009). The IC conceptual framework visualizes how outdated or unwanted knowledge is eliminated through an "internal output". From a strategic point of view, internal knowledge may be lost intentionally and unintentionally (Kong, 2003a). Some of the examples of intentional reduction of knowledge include throwing out an outdated user manual, terminating an alliance with a partner or reinventing a new organizational image. Voluntary employee turnover (not lay-off), however, is an example of loss of knowledge unintentionally.

In the IC conceptual framework, value is generated through the interactions of the three primary IC components, along with the knowledge flow and the "external inputs" and "internal outputs" of knowledge. Accordingly, the management of IC is not only about knowledge creation, but also knowledge lost (Caddy, Guthrie, & Petty, 2001). Social enterprises need to be able to remove outdated and unwanted knowledge, plan for the acquisition of knowledge or assess areas of knowledge weaknesses. This would provide social entrepreneurs with an up-to-date understanding of intellectual resources which would facilitate a better decision-making process.

The IC conceptual framework also highlights the importance of external environment to social enterprises. External environment is crucial to social enterprises' ability to function (Giffords & Dina, 2004). In this study external environment refers to any factor or trend that is external to social enterprises but which has direct or indirect impact on the organizations' day-to-day operations and strategies. Social enterprises might have direct or indirect influence over some of their external environment. For instance, social enterprises may be able to enhance their public image through their public relations activities. However, more often the organizations have no or very little power to prevent and control external factors. This environment includes current global financial crisis, change of technology such as online payment through internet, malicious events such as the 9/11 attack on the United States in 2001, and natural disasters such as the Asian tsunami in 2004.

External environment conditions might be perceived as opportunities as well as threats to organizations (Weihrich, 1982). In the context of social enterprises, external environment might instantly increase the demand for charitable activities which puts immense pressures on organizational resources or they might create opportunities for social enterprises to enhance efficiency. Although the influence of the external environment in social enterprises may not be readily seen frequently, its impact to the organizations can be profound. Sull (2005) argues that major opportunities and threats often emerge sporadically and thus, what executives do during the lulls in external developments often matters more than the dramatic actions taken during times of crisis. Accordingly, whether social enterprises are capable of capturing the opportunities (or eliminating the threats) will depend strongly on the capabilities of the organizations to innovate new ideas that produce new products or services and/or seize market opportunities. Sull (2005) puts forth that leaders must probe the future and remain alert to anomalies that signal potential threats or opportunities during the lulls. Thus, when an opportunity or threat emerges, their organizations will be in the best position to face the challenges from the threat or concentrate resources to seize the opportunity. The emphasis of external environment in the IC conceptual framework allows social entrepreneurs to fully recognize the capabilities of their organizations for future challenges.

STRATEGIC IMPLICATIONS

The proposed IC conceptual framework provides several strategic implications to social enterprises. Firstly, the framework helps social enterprises to maintain a dynamic and flexible strategy. Strategic change is a fact of life, it is unrealistic to believe that social entrepreneurs can plan everything and the intellectual resources that their organizations embrace will always be sufficient to face future challenges. Thus an effective strategic management framework must be able to reveal the mysterious mechanisms that lead to the formulation of strategy and to its evolution over time (Hafsi & Thomas, 2005). The IC conceptual framework suggested in this study emphasizes the stocks and flows of knowledge within and outside the organizations in order to maximize value creation.

External new knowledge comes into individual IC component one at a time or simultaneously. The knowledge flows from one IC component to the others before it is transformed into strategic advantage to social enterprises; that is to harness knowledge that leads to innovation for the pursuit of social and commercial activities. Acs, Braunerhjelm, Audretsch, and Carlsson (2009) argue that knowledge created endogenously leads to a development of new knowledge, which allows entrepreneurs to identify and exploit opportunities. Accordingly, the framework realistically offers not only the opportunity for social enterprises to focus on peripheral vision and broad strategic direction, but also to maintain flexibility when changes of strategies are needed. In other words, the framework helps to unveil the inner workings of the black box that guides strategy formulation and its development over time.

Secondly, the IC conceptual framework enables social enterprises to priorities strategic resources. Even though strategic decisions by definition are important, some are of more importance than others (Cray, Mallory, Butler, Hickson, & Wilson, 1991). Since IC is a dynamic concept (Bontis, Dragonetti, Jacobsen, & Roos, 1999), the IC level may increase as well as decrease during any given period of time. For instance, the overall IC level of an organization may decrease significantly when the organization's members depart from the organization, taking with them their knowledge and skills, the organization loses a contract with strategic partner, representing an end of a relationship with the partner, and the organization loses a customer database due to a major system failure. This can be a significant challenge to the organization when it attempts to leverage IC. The strategic development and management of IC, which stresses the balancing of the three types of IC components, forces social entrepreneurs to constantly re-think, re-design, re-organize and review the intellectual resources in their organizations' strategies for value creation (Klein, 1998). Thus the framework enables social entrepreneurs to have a complete and up-to-date picture of what capabilities their organizations embrace or lack of. With the updated organizational capabilities in mind, social entrepreneurs are able to prioritize and refocus their organizational resources towards their strategic objectives.

Thirdly, the core value is placed at the center of the model. Nørreklit (2000) asserts that if a model is to be effective in an organization, the model must be rooted in the language of the organization's people and communicated to all parts of the organization. This draws another important point, that if a model is to apply in social enterprises, it must be kept simple and easy to use or disseminate through the whole organization. Bontis et al. (1999) argue that IC is flexible and easy to understand because it represents the collection of intellectual resources and their flows. This enables members in social enterprises to direct their energy towards the same organizational goals. As argued by Letts, Ryan and Grossman (1999), having the mission and values truly shared is the biggest challenge in nonprofit organizations. This IC conceptual framework therefore helps to achieve a strategic alignment between organizational strategy and value creation in social enterprises.

Finally, the framework emphasizes the importance of external knowledge input and the significance of internal knowledge divestment. This helps to create a learning culture within social enterprises by realizing the value of acquiring new external knowledge and retaining useful internal knowledge. One could also argue that by creating a culture that assesses their status on a regular basis and is willing to divest itself of outdated knowledge is more willing to accept change. This implies a greater flexibility within the organization to adapt to crisis or new opportunities. As a result, this learning culture will enable them to better deal with new challenges.

This research study takes an initial step to propose an IC conceptual framework which helps social entrepreneurs to visualize the importance of knowledge as a strategic resource in social enterprises. The framework also explains how strategic advantage can be obtained through the utilization of knowledge in the organizations. As put forth by this research study, IC redirects social entrepreneurs' attention to qualitative intellectual resources rather than quantitative performance measurement; and value creation instead of financial management. Thus, IC aids social enterprises to refocus their objectives on social questions. In other words, IC helps social enterprises to harness knowledge that leads to innovation for the pursuit of social and commercial objectives.

CONCLUSION

Knowledge is power and that power has not diminished throughout the ages. The importance of knowledge cannot be understated and is recognized as a key factor in the success of organizations in the knowledge-based economy. This contention has been recognized by researchers in the for-profit environment but too little research has been conducted out in the context of social enterprises. For this reason, the study has taken an exploratory step applying IC as a strategy development concept in innovation processes in social enterprises. The IC conceptual framework that has been proposed in this study offers social entrepreneurs a clear and more holistic understanding of the role of IC and the interrelationships between the three IC components. Through the IC components, social entrepreneurs are able to better conceptualize the strategic significance of their organization's intellectual resources and knowledge management activities. As IC embraces a comprehensive viewpoint of both internal and external aspects of intellectual resources that are embedded in the personnel, organizational routines and network relationships, the IC conceptual framework provides social entrepreneurs a better understanding of the internal and external issues in their organizations. The IC conceptual framework suggested in this study represents a significant addition to our understanding of IC and its components within the context of social enterprises. Further research involving specific methodologies needs to be carried out to empirically test the findings in the study.

REFERENCES

Acs, Z. J., Braunerhjelm, P., Audretsch, D. B., & Carlsson, B. (2009). The knowledge spillover theory of entrepreneurship. *Small Business Economics*, *32*(1), 15–30. doi:10.1007/s11187-008-9157-3

Alexander, J. (1999). The impact of devolution on nonprofits: A multiphase study of social service organizations. *Nonprofit Management & Leadership*, *10*(1), 57–70. doi:10.1002/nml.10105

Alexander, J. (2000). Adaptive strategies of nonprofit human service organizations in an era of devolution and new public management. *Nonprofit Management & Leadership*, *10*(3), 287–303. doi:10.1002/nml.10305

Alexander, V. D. (1998). Environmental constraints and organizational strategies: Complexity, conflict, and coping in the nonprofit sector. In Powell, W. W., & Clemens, E. S. (Eds.), *Private action and the public good* (pp. 272–290). New Haven, CT: Yale University Press.

Ambrosini, V., & Bowman, C. (2001). Tacit knowledge: Some suggestions for operationalization. *Journal of Management Studies*, *38*(6), 811–829. doi:10.1111/1467-6486.00260

Anand, N., Gardner, H. K., & Morris, T. (2007). Knowledge-based innovation: Emergence and embedding of new practice areas in management consulting firms. *Academy of Management Journal*, *50*(2), 406–428.

Anheier, H. K. (2005). *Nonprofit organizations: Theory, management, policy*. London: Routledge.

Backman, E. V., Grossman, A., & Rangan, V. K. (2000). Introduction. *Nonprofit and Voluntary Sector Quarterly*, *29*(Supplement), 2–8. doi:10.1177/0899764000773746319

Balser, D., & McClusky, J. (2005). Managing stakeholder relationships and nonprofit organization effectiveness. *Nonprofit Management & Leadership*, *15*(3), 295–315. doi:10.1002/nml.70

Boedker, C., Guthrie, J., & Cuganesan, S. (2005). An integrated framework for visualizing intellectual capital. *Journal of Intellectual Capital*, *6*(4), 510–527. doi:10.1108/14691930510628799

Bontis, N. (1996). There's price on your head: Managing intellectual capital strategically. *Business Quarterly*, *60*(4), 40–47.

Bontis, N. (1998). Intellectual capital: An exploratory study that develops measures and models. *Management Decision*, *36*(2), 63–76. doi:10.1108/00251749810204142

Bontis, N. (1999). Managing organizational knowledge by diagnosing intellectual capital: Framing and advancing the state of the field. *International Journal of Technology Management*, *18*(5-8), 433–462. doi:10.1504/IJTM.1999.002780

Bontis, N. (2002). Managing organizational knowledge by diagnosing intellectual capital: Framing and advancing the state of the field. In Choo, C. W., & Bontis, N. (Eds.), *The strategic management of intellectual capital and organizational knowledge* (pp. 621–642). Oxford, UK: Oxford University Press.

Bontis, N., Dragonetti, N. C., Jacobsen, K., & Roos, G. (1999). The knowledge toolbox: A review of the tools available to measure and manage intangible resources. *European Management Journal*, *17*(4), 391–402. doi:10.1016/S0263-2373(99)00019-5

Bontis, N., Keow, W. C. C., & Richardson, S. (2000). Intellectual capital and business performance in Malaysian industries. *Journal of Intellectual Capital*, *1*(1), 85–100. doi:10.1108/14691930010324188

Borins, S. (2000). Loose cannons and rule breakers, or enterprising leaders? Some evidence about innovative public managers. *Public Administration Review*, *60*(6), 498–507. doi:10.1111/0033-3352.00113

Borzaga, C., & Defourny, J. (2001). Conclusions: Social enterprises in Europe - A diversity of initiatives and prospects. In Borzaga, C., & Defourny, J. (Eds.), *The emergence of social enterprise*. London: Routledge.

Brock, C. (2008). *Financial crisis hits charities.* Retrieved January 5, 2008, from http://www.mortgageloan.com/financial-crisis-hits-charities-2621

Bukh, P. N., Johansen, M. R., & Mouritsen, J. (2002). Multiple integrated performance management systems: IC and BSC in a software company. *Singapore Management Review*, *24*(3), 21–33.

Caddy, I., Guthrie, J., & Petty, R. (2001). Managing orphan knowledge: Current Australasian best practice. *Journal of Intellectual Capital*, *2*(4), 384–397. doi:10.1108/14691930110409679

Chetkovich, C., & Frumkin, P. (2003). Balancing margin and mission nonprofit competition in charitable versus fee-based programs. *Administration & Society*, *35*(5), 564–596. doi:10.1177/0095399703256162

Choo, C. W., & Bontis, N. (Eds.). (2002). *The strategic management of intellectual capital and organizational knowledge*. Oxford, UK: Oxford University Press.

Craig, G., Taylor, M., & Parkes, T. (2004). Protest or partnership? The voluntary and community sectors in the policy process. *Social Policy and Administration*, *38*(3), 221–239. doi:10.1111/j.1467-9515.2004.00387.x

Cray, D., Mallory, G. R., Butler, R. J., Hickson, D. J., & Wilson, D. C. (1991). Explaining decision processes. *Journal of Management Studies*, *28*(3), 227–251. doi:10.1111/j.1467-6486.1991.tb00946.x

Dart, R. (2004). The legitimacy of social enterprise. *Nonprofit Management & Leadership*, *14*(4), 411–424. doi:10.1002/nml.43

Dees, J. G. (1998). Enterprising nonprofits. *Harvard Business Review*, *76*(1), 55–69.

Defourny, J. (2001). Introduction: From third sector to social enterprise. In Borzaga, C., & Defourny, J. (Eds.), *The emergence of social enterprise*. London: Routledge.

Dzinkowski, R. (2000). The measurement and management of intellectual capital: An introduction. *Management Accounting*, *78*(2), 32–36.

Edvinsson, L. (1997). Developing intellectual capital Skandia. *Long Range Planning*, *30*(3), 366–373. doi:10.1016/S0024-6301(97)90248-X

Edvinsson, L., & Malone, M. S. (1997). *Intellectual Capital - The proven way to establish your company's real value by measuring its hidden brainpower*. New York: HarperBusiness.

Eisenberg, P. (1997). A crisis in the nonprofit sector. *National Civic Review*, *86*(4), 331–341. doi:10.1002/ncr.4100860409

Eisenberg, P. (2000). The nonprofit sector in a changing world. *Nonprofit and Voluntary Sector Quarterly*, *29*(2), 325–330. doi:10.1177/0899764000292007

Escribano, A., Fosfuri, A., & Tribó, J. A. (2009). Managing external knowledge flows: The moderating role of absorptive capacity. *Research Policy*, *38*(1), 96–105. doi:10.1016/j.respol.2008.10.022

Finkelstein, S., & Hambrick, D. (1996). *Strategic leadership: Top executives and their effects on organizations*. Minneapolis, St. Paul: West Publisher.

Fisher, I. (1906). *The nature of capital and income*. New York: Reprints of Economic Classics, Augustus M. Kelley Publisher. Reprinted in 1965

Fletcher, A., Guthrie, J., Steane, P., Roos, G., & Pike, S. (2003). Mapping stakeholder perceptions for a third sector organization. *Journal of Intellectual Capital*, *4*(4), 505–527. doi:10.1108/14691930310504536

Fowler, A. (2000). NGDOs as a moment in history: Beyond aid to social entrepreneurship or civic innovation? *Third World Quarterly*, *21*(4), 637–654. doi:10.1080/713701063

Frances, N. (2008). *The end of charity: Time for social enterprise*. Crows, New South Wales: Allen and Unwin.

Giffords, E. D., & Dina, R. P. (2004). Strategic planning in nonprofit organizations: Continuous quality performance improvement - A case study. *International Journal of Organization Theory and Behavior*, *7*(1), 66–80.

Goold, M. (1997). Institutional advantage: A way into strategic management in not-for-profit organizations. *Long Range Planning*, *30*(2), 291–293. doi:10.1016/S0024-6301(96)00001-5

Grasenick, K., & Low, J. (2004). Shaken, not stirred: Defining and connecting indicators for the measurement and valuation of intangibles. *Journal of Intellectual Capital*, *5*(2), 268–281. doi:10.1108/14691930410533696

Gray, M., Healy, K., & Crofts, P. (2003). Social enterprise: Is it the business of social work? *Australian Social Work*, *56*(2), 141–154. doi:10.1046/j.0312-407X.2003.00060.x

Guerrero, I. (2003). How do firms measure their intellectual capital? Defining an empirical model based on firm practices. *International Journal of Management and Decision Making*, *4*(2/3), 178–193. doi:10.1504/IJMDM.2003.003503

Guthrie, J., Petty, R., & Ricceri, F. (2006). The voluntary reporting of intellectual capital: Comparing evidence from Hong Kong and Australia. *Journal of Intellectual Capital*, *7*(2), 254–271. doi:10.1108/14691930610661890

Hafsi, T., & Thomas, H. (2005). The field of strategy: In search of a walking stick. *European Management Journal*, *23*(5), 507–519. doi:10.1016/j.emj.2005.09.006

Hambrick, D. C., Finkelstein, S., & Mooney, A. C. (2005). Executive job demands: New insights for explaining strategic decisions and leader behaviors. *Academy of Management Review*, *30*(3), 472–491.

Hamori, M. (2003). The impact of reputation capital on the career paths of departing employees. *Journal of Intellectual Capital*, *4*(3), 304–315. doi:10.1108/14691930310487770

Hitt, M. A., Ireland, R. D., Camp, S. M., & Sexton, D. L. (2001). Strategic entrepreneurship: Entrepreneurial strategies for wealth creation. *Strategic Management Journal*, *22*(6/7), 479–491. doi:10.1002/smj.196

Hoskisson, R. E., Hitt, M. A., Wan, W. P., & Yiu, D. (1999). Theory and research in strategic management: Swings of a pendulum. *Journal of Management*, *25*(3), 417–456. doi:10.1177/014920639902500307

Hudson, M. (1999). *Managing without profit: The art of managing third-sector organizations* (2nd ed.). London: Penguin.

Husted, B. W., & Allen, D. B. (2007). Strategic corporate social responsibility and value creation among large firms lessons from the Spanish experience. *Long Range Planning, 40*(6), 594–610. doi:10.1016/j.lrp.2007.07.001

Huxham, C., & Vangen, S. (2005). *Managing to collaborate: The theory and practice of collaborative advantage*. London: Routledge.

Jamali, D., & Keshishian, T. (2009). Uneasy alliances: Lessons learned from partnerships between businesses and NGOs in the context of CSR. *Journal of Business Ethics, 84*(2), 277–295. doi:10.1007/s10551-008-9708-1

Jamison, I. B. (2003). Turnover and retention among volunteers in human service agencies. *Review of Public Personnel Administration, 23*(2), 114–132. doi:10.1177/0734371X03023002003

Kanter, R. M. (1999). From spare change to real change: The social sector as beta site for business innovation. *Harvard Business Review, 77*(3), 122–132.

Kim, S. E., & Lee, J. W. (2007). Is mission attachment an effective management tool for employee retention? An empirical analysis of a nonprofit human services agency. *Review of Public Personnel Administration, 27*(3), 227–248. doi:10.1177/0734371X06295791

Klein, D. A. (Ed.). (1998). *The strategic management of intellectual capital*. Boston: Butterworth-Heinemann.

Knight, D. J. (1999). Performance measures for increasing intellectual capital. *Planning Review, 27*(2), 22–27.

Kong, E. 2003a. *Human capital as a key component of intellectual capital in nonprofit organizations*. Paper presented at the Conference on Challenging the Frontiers in Global Business and Technology (GBATA): Implementation of Changes in Values, Strategy and Policy, Governance and Knowledge Management (GKM), Budapest, Hungary.

Kong, E. (2003b). Using intellectual capital as a strategic tool for nonprofit organizations. *International Journal of Knowledge. Culture and Change Management, 3*(1), 467–474.

Kong, E. (2008). The development of strategic management in the nonprofit context: Intellectual capital in social service nonprofit organizations. *International Journal of Management Reviews, 10*(3), 281–299. doi:10.1111/j.1468-2370.2007.00224.x

Kong, E., & Thomson, S. B. (2006). Intellectual capital and strategic human resource management in social service nonprofit organizations in Australia. *International Journal of Human Resources Development and Management, 6*(2-4), 213–231.

Kristoffersen, L., & Singh, S. (2004). Successful application of a customer relationship management program in a nonprofit organization. *Journal of Marketing Theory and Practice, 12*(2), 28–42.

Lee, M.-D. P. (2008). A review of the theories of corporate social responsibility: Its evolutionary path and the road ahead. *International Journal of Management Reviews, 10*(1), 53–73. doi:10.1111/j.1468-2370.2007.00226.x

Leiponen, A. (2008). Control of intellectual assets in client relationships: Implications for innovation. *Strategic Management Journal, 29*(13), 1371–1394. doi:10.1002/smj.715

Letts, C. W., Ryan, W. P., & Grossman, A. (1999). *High performance nonprofit organizations - Managing upstream for greater impact*. New York: John Wiley and Sons, Inc.

Lichtenstein, D. R., Drumwright, M. E., & Braig, B. M. (2004). The effect of corporate social responsibility on customer donations to corporate-supported nonprofits. *Journal of Marketing, 68*(4), 16–32. doi:10.1509/jmkg.68.4.16.42726

Liebschutz, S. F. (1992). Coping by nonprofit organizations during the Reagan years. *Nonprofit Management & Leadership, 2*(4), 363–380. doi:10.1002/nml.4130020405

Luke, B., & Verreynne, M.-L. (2006). Social enterprise in the public sector. MetService: Thinking beyond the weather. *International Journal of Social Economics, 33*(5/6), 432–445. doi:10.1108/03068290610660698

Lyons, M. (1999). Service industries: Special article - Australia's nonprofit sector, Year Book Australia: 536-551. Canberra: Australian Bureau of Statistics (ABS).

Lyons, M. (2001). *Third sector: The contribution of nonprofit and co-operative enterprises in Australia.* St. Leonards, New South Wales: Allen and Unwin.

Lyons, M., & Fabiansson, C. (1998). Is volunteering declining in Australia? *Australian Journal on Volunteering, 3*(2), 15–21.

Manfredi, F. (2005). Social responsibility in the concept of the social enterprise as a cognitive system. *International Journal of Public Administration, 28*(9/10), 835–848. doi:10.1081/PAD-200067371

Marr, B., & Roos, G. (2005). A strategy perspective on intellectual capital. In Marr, B. (Ed.), *Perspectives on intellectual capital: Multi-disciplinary insights into management, measurement, and reporting.* Amsterdam: Elsevier Butterworth-Heinemann.

Martin, B. (2000). Knowledge-based organizations: Emerging trends in local government in Australia. *Journal of Knowledge Management Practice, 2.*

Martin, G., Beaumont, P., Doig, R., & Pate, J. (2005). Branding: A new performance discourse for HR? *European Management Journal, 23*(1), 76–88. doi:10.1016/j.emj.2004.12.011

Martin de Holan, P., & Phillips, N. (2004). Organizational forgetting as strategy. *Strategic Organization, 2*(4), 423–433. doi:10.1177/1476127004047620

Mason, C., Kirkbride, J., & Bryde, D. (2007). From stakeholders to institutions: The changing face of social enterprise governance theory. *Management Decision, 45*(2), 284–301. doi:10.1108/00251740710727296

Massingham, P. (2008). Measuring the impact of knowledge loss: More than ripples on a pond? *Management Learning, 39*(5), 541–560. doi:10.1177/1350507608096040

Matten, D., & Moon, J. (2008). "Implicit" and "Explicit" CSR: A conceptual framework for a comparative understanding of corporate social responsibility. *Academy of Management Review, 33*(2), 404–424.

McAdam, R. (2000). Knowledge management as a catalyst for innovation within organizations: A qualitative study. *Journal of Knowledge and Process Management, 7*(4), 233–241. doi:10.1002/1099-1441(200010/12)7:4<233::AID-KPM94>3.0.CO;2-F

McCann, J. E. III, & Buckner, M. (2004). Strategically integrating knowledge management initiatives. *Journal of Knowledge Management, 8*(1), 47–63. doi:10.1108/13673270410523907

Mouritsen, J. (1998). Driving growth: Economic value added versus intellectual capital. *Management Accounting Research, 9*(4), 461–482. doi:10.1006/mare.1998.0090

Mouritsen, J., & Koleva, G. (2004). The actorhood of organizational capital. *International Journal of Learning and Intellectual Capital, 1*(2), 177–189. doi:10.1504/IJLIC.2004.005070

Mouritsen, J., & Larsen, H. T. (2005). The 2nd wave of knowledge management: The management control of knowledge resources through intellectual capital information. *Management Accounting Research, 16*(3), 371–394. doi:10.1016/j.mar.2005.06.006

Mouritsen, J., Larsen, H. T., & Bukh, P. N. (2005). Dealing with the knowledge economy: Intellectual capital versus balanced scorecard. *Journal of Intellectual Capital, 6*(1), 8–27. doi:10.1108/14691930510574636

Mulhare, E. M. (1999). Mindful of the future: Strategic planning ideology and the culture of nonprofit management. *Human Organization, 58*(3), 323–330.

Mulroy, E. A. (2003). Community as a factor in implementing inter-organizational partnerships: Issues, constraints and adaptations. *Nonprofit Management & Leadership, 14*(1), 47–66. doi:10.1002/nml.20

Nanus, B., & Dobbs, S. M. (1999). *Leaders who make a difference: Essential strategies for meeting the nonprofit challenge.* San Francisco: Jossey-Bass Publishers.

Nelson, K., & McCann, J. E. (2008). Developing intellectual capital and innovativeness through knowledge management. *International Journal of Learning and Intellectual Capital, 5*(2), 106–122. doi:10.1504/IJLIC.2008.020147

Nonaka, I., & Takeuchi, H. (1995). *The knowledge-creating company: How Japanese companies create the dynamics of innovation.* New York: Oxford University Press.

Nørreklit, H. (2000). The balance on the balanced scorecard: A critical analysis of some of its assumptions. *Management Accounting Research, 11*(1), 65–88. doi:10.1006/mare.1999.0121

Ordóñez de Pablos, P. (2004). The importance of relational capital in service industry: The case of the Spanish banking sector. *International Journal of Learning and Intellectual Capital, 1*(4), 431–440. doi:10.1504/IJLIC.2004.005993

Ospina, S., Diaz, W., & O'Sullivan, J. F. (2002). Negotiating accountability: Managerial lessons from identity-based nonprofit organizations. *Nonprofit and Voluntary Sector Quarterly, 31*(1), 5–31. doi:10.1177/0899764002311001

Peppard, J., & Rylander, A. (2001). Using an intellectual capital perspective to design and implement a growth strategy: The case of APiON. *European Management Journal, 19*(5), 510–525. doi:10.1016/S0263-2373(01)00065-2

Petty, R., & Guthrie, J. (2000). Intellectual capital literature review. Measurement, reporting and management. *Journal of Intellectual Capital, 1*(2), 155–176. doi:10.1108/14691930010348731

Pomerantz, M. (2003). The business of social entrepreneurship in a 'down economy'. In Business, 25(2), 25-28.

Porter, M. E., & Kramer, M. R. (2006). Strategy and society: The link between competitive advantage and corporate social responsibility. *Harvard Business Review, 84*(12), 78–92.

Probst, G., Buchel, B., & Raub, S. (1998). Knowledge as a strategic resource. In von Krogh, G., Roos, J., & Kleine, D. (Eds.), *Knowing in firms* (pp. 241–252). London: Sage.

Ramia, G., & Carney, T. (2003). New public management, the job network and nonprofit strategy. *Australian Journal of Labor Economics, 6*(2), 249–271.

Rigby, D., & Zook, C. (2002). Open-market innovation. *Harvard Business Review, 80*(10), 80–89.

Roos, G., & Jacobsen, K. (1999). Management in a complex stakeholder organization. *Monash Mt. Eliza Business Review, 2*(1), 83–93.

Roos, J. (1998). Exploring the concept of intellectual capital (IC). *Long Range Planning, 31*(1), 150–153. doi:10.1016/S0024-6301(97)87431-6

Roos, J., Roos, G., Dragonetti, N. C., & Edvinsson, L. (1997). *Intellectual capital: Navigating the new business landscape.* London: Macmillan Press Limited.

Roper, J., & Cheney, G. (2005). Leadership, learning and human resource management: The meanings of social entrepreneurship today. *Corporate Governance, 5*(3), 95–104. doi:10.1108/14720700510604733

Saint-Onge, H. (1996). Tacit knowledge: The key to the strategic alignment of intellectual capital. *Strategy and Leadership, 24*(2), 10–14. doi:10.1108/eb054547

Salamon, L. M. (1986). Government and the voluntary sector in an era of retrenchment. *Journal of Public Policy, 6*(1), 1–20. doi:10.1017/S0143814X00003834

Salamon, L. M. (1996). The crisis of the nonprofit sector and the challenge of renewal. *National Civic Review, 85*(4), 3–15. doi:10.1002/ncr.4100850403

Salamon, L. M. (1999). The nonprofit sector at a crossroads: The case of America. *Voluntas: International Journal of Voluntary and Nonprofit Organizations, 10*(1), 5–23. doi:10.1023/A:1021435602742

Schiuma, G., Lerro, A., & Carlucci, D. (2005). An interfirm perspective on intellectual capital. In Marr, B. (Ed.), *Perspectives on intellectual capital: Multi-disciplinary insights into management, measurement, and reporting* (pp. 155–169). Amsterdam: Elsevier Butterworth-Heinemann.

Seelos, C., & Mair, J. (2005). Social entrepreneurship: Creating new business models to serve the poor. *Business Horizons, 48*(3), 241–246. doi:10.1016/j.bushor.2004.11.006

Selsky, J. W., & Parker, B. (2005). Cross-sector partnerships to address social issues: Challenges to theory and practice. *Journal of Management, 31*(6), 849–873. doi:10.1177/0149206305279601

Sirmon, D. G., Hitt, M. A., & Ireland, R. D. (2007). Managing firm resources in dynamic environments to create value: Looking inside the black box. *Academy of Management Review, 32*(1), 273–292.

Spear, R. (2001). United Kingdom: A wide range of social enterprises. In Borzaga, C., Defourny, J., Adam, S., & Callaghan, J. (Eds.), *The emergence of social enterprise.* London: Routledge.

Spencer, J. W. (2003). Firms' knowledge-sharing strategies in the global innovation system: Empirical evidence from the flat panel display industry. *Strategic Management Journal, 24*(3), 217–233. doi:10.1002/smj.290

St. Leon, M. V. (2002). Intellectual capital: Managerial perceptions of organizational knowledge resources. *Journal of Intellectual Capital, 3*(2), 149–166. doi:10.1108/14691930210424743

Stewart, T. A. (1997). *Intellectual capital: The new wealth of organizations.* New York: Currency Doubleday.

Stone, M. M., Bigelow, B., & Crittenden, W. E. (1999). Research on strategic management in nonprofit organizations: Synthesis, analysis, and future directions. *Administration & Society, 31*(3), 378–423. doi:10.1177/00953999922019184

Subramaniam, M., & Youndt, M. A. (2005). The influence of intellectual capital on the types of innovative capabilities. *Academy of Management Journal, 48*(3), 450–463.

Sull, D. N. (2005). Strategy as active waiting. *Harvard Business Review, 83*(9), 120–129.

Sullivan, P. H. (Ed.). (1998). *Profiting from intellectual capital: Extracting value from innovation.* New York: John Wiley and Sons, Inc.

Sullivan-Mort, G., Weerawardena, J., & Carnegie, K. (2003). Social entrepreneurship: Towards conceptualization. *International Journal of Nonprofit and Voluntary Sector Marketing, 8*(1), 76–88. doi:10.1002/nvsm.202

Thompson, J., & Doherty, B. (2006). The diverse world of social enterprise: A collection of social enterprise stories. *International Journal of Social Economics, 33*(5/6), 361–375. doi:10.1108/03068290610660643

Thompson, J. L. (2002). The world of the social entrepreneur. *International Journal of Public Sector Management, 15*(5), 412–431. doi:10.1108/09513550210435746

Tsai, W. (2001). Knowledge transfer in intra-organizational networks: Effects of network position and absorptive capacity on business unit innovation and performance. *Academy of Management Journal, 44*(5), 996–1004. doi:10.2307/3069443

Waddock, S., & Post, J. E. (1991). Social entrepreneurs and catalytic change. *Public Administration Review, 51*(5), 393–401. doi:10.2307/976408

Wallis, J., & Dollery, B. (2005). Leadership and economic theories of nonprofit organizations. *Review of Policy Research, 22*(4), 483–499. doi:10.1111/j.1541-1338.2005.00151.x

Webster, E. (2000). The growth of enterprise intangible investment in Australia. *Information Economics and Policy, 12*(1), 1–25. doi:10.1016/S0167-6245(99)00024-4

Weerawardena, J., & Sullivan-Mort, G. (2006). Investigating social entrepreneurship: A multidimensional model. *Journal of World Business, 41*(1), 21–35. doi:10.1016/j.jwb.2005.09.001

Weihrich, H. (1982). The TOWS matrix: A tool for situational analysis. *Long Range Planning, 15*(2), 54–66. doi:10.1016/0024-6301(82)90120-0

Weisbrod, B. A. (1997). The future of the nonprofit sector: Its entwining with private enterprise and government. *Journal of Policy Analysis and Management, 16*(4), 541–555. doi:10.1002/(SICI)1520-6688(199723)16:4<541::AID-PAM2>3.0.CO;2-G

Weisbrod, B. A. (Ed.). (1998). *To profit or not to profit: The commercial transformation of the nonprofit sector.* Cambridge, UK: Cambridge University Press. doi:10.1017/CBO9780511625947

West, P. III, & Noel, T. W. (2009). The impact of knowledge resources on new venture performance. *Journal of Small Business Management, 47*(1), 1–22. doi:10.1111/j.1540-627X.2008.00259.x

Wilson, M. I., & Larson, R. S. (2002). Nonprofit management students: Who they are and why they enrol? *Nonprofit and Voluntary Sector Quarterly, 31*(2), 259–270. doi:10.1177/08964002031002005

Wright, P. M., McMahan, G. C., & McWilliams, A. (1994). Human resources and sustained competitive advantage: A resource-based perspective. *International Journal of Human Resource Management, 5*(2), 301–326.

Wu, W.-Y., Chang, M.-L., & Chen, C.-W. (2008). Promoting innovation through the accumulation of intellectual capital, social capital, and entrepreneurial orientation. *R & D Management, 38*(3), 265–277. doi:10.1111/j.1467-9310.2008.00512.x

Youndt, M. A., Subramaniam, M., & Snell, S. A. (2004). Intellectual capital profiles: An examination of investments and returns. *Journal of Management Studies, 41*(2), 335–361. doi:10.1111/j.1467-6486.2004.00435.x

Young, D. R. (2001). Organizational identity in nonprofit organizations: Strategic and structural implications. *Nonprofit Management & Leadership, 12*(2), 139–157. doi:10.1002/nml.12202

Zack, M. H. (2005). The strategic advantage of knowledge and learning. *International Journal of Learning and Intellectual Capital, 2*(1), 1–20. doi:10.1504/IJLIC.2005.006803

Zappala, G. (2001). From 'Charity' to 'Social Enterprise': Managing volunteers in public-serving nonprofits. *Australian Journal on Volunteering, 6*(1), 41–49.

Chapter 13
Factors Predicting the Innovation Climate

Ülle Übius
Estonian Business School, Estonia

Ruth Alas
Estonian Business School, Estonia

ABSTRACT

The purpose of this chapter is to investigate how such factors as corporate social responsibility, individual and organizational level factors predict the innovation climate. The survey was conducted in Estonian, Chinese, Japanese, Russian and Slovakian electric-electronic machine, retail store and machine-building enterprises. Linear regression analysis was done in order to analyze connections between the innovation climate, corporate social responsibility, individual and organizational level factors. The total number of respondents was 4632. The results of an empirical study show that both facets of corporate social responsibility - the firm performance concerning social issues and the firm respects the interests of agents, individual and organizational level factors predict the innovation climate, but it differs according to different countries. The 5 models developed explain how corporate social responsibility, individual and organizational level factors predict the innovation climate in Estonian, Chinese, Japanese, Russian and Slovakian electric-electronic machine, retail store and machine-building enterprises.

INTRODUCTION

Today, pioneering enterprises integrate social entrepreneurship into their core activities by actively channelling their research-and-development capabilities in the direction of socially innovative products and services (Schwab, 2008). Research has called for organisations to be more entrepreneurial, flexible, adaptive and innovative to effectively meet

the changing demands of today's environment (Orchard, 1998; Parker and Bradley, 2000; Valle, 1999).

The main aim of the study is to find connections between corporate social responsibility, individual, organisational level factors and innovation climate.

A standardised corporate social responsibility, job satisfaction, meaning of work, attitude toward the firm, powerfulness of firm in competition against rivals, behaviour of management and policy of firm questionnaires were developed by the Denki Ringo research group (Ishikawa et al, 2006). Based on the

DOI: 10.4018/978-1-61520-643-8.ch013

Innovation climate Questionnaire by Ekvall *et al.* (1983), the authors developed an Innovation Climate Scale.

The linear regression analysis was used in order to find statistically relevant connections between corporate social responsibility, individual, organisational level factors and innovation climate.

The main research question is: Do corporate social responsibility, individual and organisational level factors predict innovation climate?

This study, therefore, investigates how corporate social responsibility, individual and organisational level factors predict innovation climate. Data is collected from empirical studies in Estonian, Chinese, Japanese, Russian and Slovakian electric-electronic machine, retail store and machine-building enterprises. Results are discussed.

The following section will explore the theoretical framework of the study by presenting an overview of the literature on this topic. This will be followed by a brief discussion of the relationship between the innovation climate and corporate social responsibility, individual and organisational level factors. Then the empirical study will be presented followed by the results and some concluding remarks.

THEORETICAL FRAMEWORK

The Innovation Climate

In this study, we examine the innovation climate. In particular we examine how the degree to which an organisation offers its employees support and encouragement to take initiative and explore innovative approaches can influence the degree of actual innovation in that organisation (Martins and Terblanche, 2003; Mumford and Gustafson, 1988).

Many authors (Van de Ven, 1986; Amabile, 1988; Smith, 2000; Unsworth and Parker, 2003) have found that individual innovation helps to attain organisational success. Employee innovative behaviour depends greatly on their interaction with others in the workplace (Anderson et al., 2004; Zhou and Shalley, 2003). According to Damanpour and Schneider (2006), the climate for innovation is a direct result of the top managers' personal and positional characteristics.

Previous studies treat innovative behaviour among employees as a one-dimensional construct that encompasses both idea generation and application behaviour (Scott and Bruce, 1994; Janssen, 2000). This implies that differences in the relevant leader behaviour between the two phases remain invisible, which is why recent work recommends keeping these phases of the innovation process separate (Mumford and Licuanan, 2004). Innovation theorists often describe the innovation process as being composed of two main phases: initiation and implementation (Zaltman et al., 1973; Axtell et al., 2000).

The Schumpeterian definition (Shumpeter, 1934) of innovation states that the commercialization of all new combinations is based upon the application of any of the following: new materials and components, the introduction of new processes, the opening of new markets and the introduction of new organisational forms. Only when a change in technology is involved is it termed an "invention", but as soon as the business world becomes involved, it becomes an "innovation" (Janszen, 2000).

Innovation involves the creation of a new product, service or process. "New" products can be viewed in terms of their degree of newness, ranging from a totally new, or discontinuous, innovation to a product involving simple line extensions or minor adaptations/adjustments that are of an evolutionary or incremental nature (Brentani, 2001).

According to Buckler and Zien (1996) innovation is the purpose of the whole organisation – a broad activity. In this kind of culture, new ideas come forward into an atmosphere of enthusiastic support and a desire to contribute to them, even though everyone knows that the majority of these ideas will not make it to market. Innovative companies are on the lookout to continually refresh this climate, because it can be undermined.

Thinking "outside the box" is certainly a major characteristic of an innovative environment. It is essential to become somewhat comfortable with the idea that at times the "unreasonable" solution is exactly what's called for (Buckler and Zien, 1996).

Corporate Social Responsibility (CSR)

Different organisations have formed different definitions of CSR, although there is considerable common ground between them. Today, corporate leaders face a dynamic and challenging task in attempting to apply societal standards of ethics to responsible business practice (Morimoto et al., 2005). Nowadays, corporate social responsibility is an integral part of the business vocabulary and is regarded as a crucially important management issue (Cornelius et al., 2008; Humphreys and Brown, 2008).

Hillman and Keim (2001) suggest that when assessing the returns on CSR, it is critical to discriminate between stakeholder management CSR and social CSR. This is consistent with Baron's (2001) distinction between altruistic and strategic CSR. More specifically, the authors concluded that while stakeholder-oriented CSR is positively correlated with financial performance, social CSR is not.

The tendency to invest in companies that practice and report CSR is increasing (Sleeper et al., 2006). Corporate social responsibility forces organisations to reposition their strategies from being profit-driven to organisations that consider their influence on social and environmental aspects (Quaak et al., 2007).

The Firm's Performance in Regard to Social Issues

Sethi (1975) stated that while social obligation is proscriptive by nature, social responsibility is prescriptive. Jones (1980) stated that corporate social responsibility is the notion that corporations have an obligation to constituent groups in society other than stockholders and beyond that which is prescribed by law and union contract. Epstein (1987) provided a definition of CSR in his quest to relate social responsibility, responsiveness and business ethics.

According to Frederick (1960) social responsibility in the final analysis implies a public posture toward society's economic and human resources and a willingness to see that those resources are used for broad social ends and not simply for the narrowly circumscribed interests of private persons and firms. The proper social responsibility of business is to tame the dragon – to turn a social problem into an economic opportunity and economic benefit, into productive capacity, into human competence, into well-paid jobs and into wealth (Drucker, 1984).

In the 1990s, the concept of the corporate social performance stream emerged (Wood, 1991). Carroll's (1999) CSR model identifies four components: economic, legal, ethical and voluntary (discretionary). The economic aspect is concerned with the economic performance of the company, while the other three categories – legal, ethical and discretionary – address the societal aspects of CSR.

Waddock and Graves (1997) found a positive relationship between a firm's social performance and its financial performance, whereas Wright and Ferris (1997) found a negative relationship. Orlitzky et al. (2003) claim that there is strong empirical evidence supporting the existence of a positive link between social and financial performance.

Marcel van Marrewijk (2003) has narrowed down the concept of corporate social responsibility so that it covers three dimensions of corporate action: economic, social and environmental management. Garriga and Mele´ (2004) grouped theories of corporate social responsibility into four groups: instrumental, political, integral and ethical.

The Firm's Respect for the Interests of Agents

Stakeholder Theory, popularized by Freeman (1984; 1994), essentially argues that a company's relationships with stakeholders (and treatment of the natural environment) is central to understanding how it operates and adds value as a business. Freeman (1994) argues that stakeholder language has been widely adopted in practice and is being integrated into concepts of corporate responsibility/citizenship by scholars who recognize that it is through a company's decisions, actions and impacts on stakeholders and the natural environment that its corporate responsibility/citizenship is manifested.

Corporate social responsibility is a concept whereby companies fulfil accountability to their stakeholders by integrating social and environmental concerns in their business operations (Tanimoto, Suzuki, 2005). Companies will necessarily have to take into account cultural differences when defining their CSR policies and communicating to stakeholders in different countries (Bird and Smucker, 2007).

Individual Factors

Job Satisfaction

Locke's Range of Affect Theory (1976) states that satisfaction is determined by a discrepancy between what one wants in a job and what one has in a job.

According to Judge's (2001) Core Self-evaluations Model there are four Core Self-evaluations that determine one's disposition towards job satisfaction: self-esteem, general self-efficacy, locus of control and neuroticism.

Herzberg's (1968) two-factor theory explains satisfaction in the workplace. This theory states that different factors – motivation and hygiene factors drive satisfaction and dissatisfaction. Motivating factors are facets of the job that bring along job satisfaction and make people want to perform, for example, recognition and achieve-

ment in work. Hygiene factors include facets of the working environment such as company policies, a pay and other working conditions.

Hackman and Oldham's (1976) Job Characteristics Model is used to study how job characteristics impact on job satisfaction. Hackman and Oldham (1975) suggested that jobs differ in the extent to which they involve five core dimensions: skill variety, task identity, task significance, autonomy and task feedback. They suggest that if jobs are designed in a way that increases the presence of these core characteristics, three critical psychological states can occur in employees: experienced meaningfulness of work, experienced responsibility for work outcomes and the knowledge of the results of work activities. When these critical psychological states are experienced, work motivation and job satisfaction will be high.

Silverthorne (2004) found that organisational culture plays an important role in the level of job satisfaction and commitment in an organisation.

Lund (2003) examined the impact of types of organisational culture on job satisfaction according to Cameron and Freeman's (1991) model of organisational cultures comprising clan, adhocracy, hierarchy and market. The results indicate that job satisfaction levels varied across corporate cultural typology. Job satisfaction was positively related to clan and adhocracy cultures and negatively related to market and hierarchy cultures.

Meaning of Work

Dewey (1939) saw goodness as the outcome of "valuation", a continuous balancing of personal or cultural value, which he called "ends in view." An end in view was said to be an objective potentially adopted, which may be refined or rejected based on its consistency with other objectives or as a means to objectives already held.

According to Seel (2000), organisational culture is the emergent result of continuing negotiations about values, meanings and proprieties between the members of that organisation and with its environment. According to Stevens (1991), effective strategy implementation depends on the extent to which resultant changes conform to existing knowledge structures used by members of the organisation to make sense of and give meaning to their work. Such cognitive paradigms form the culture construct of the organisation.

Attitudes toward the Firm

Organisational commitment is a work-related attitude and it means the employee's psychological attachment to the organisation. According to Meyer and Allen's (1991) three-component model of commitment, prior research indicated that there are three "mind sets" which can characterize an employee's commitment to the organisation: affective commitment is defined as the employee's positive emotional attachment to the organisation; continuance commitment is where the individual commits to the organisation because he/she perceives high costs of losing organisational membership, including economic costs and social costs that would be incurred; normative commitment is where the individual commits to and remains with an organisation because of feelings of obligation.

Organisational culture is important because shared beliefs and norms affect employee perceptions, behaviours and emotional responses to the workplace. For example, culture has been found to influence organisational climate and provider attitudes including work attitudes (Aarons and Sawitzky, 2006; Carmazzi and Aarons, 2003; Glisson and Hemmelgarn, 1998; Glisson and James, 2002), as well as employee behaviours that contribute to the success or failure of an organisation (Ashkanasy, Wilderom, and Peterson, 2000).

Organisational Factors

The Behaviour of the Management

Behavioural management theory addresses the human dimension of work. Behavioural theorists believe that a better understanding of human behaviour at work through such aspects as motivation, expectations and group dynamics, improves productivity. The theorists of this school view employees as individuals, resources and assets to be developed and worked with.

McGregor's (1957) idea was his belief that managers who hold either set of assumptions can create self-fulfilling prophecies — that through their behaviour, these managers create situations where subordinates act in ways that confirm the manager's original expectations.

According to Schein (2004), organisational cultures are created by leaders and one of the most decisive functions of leadership may well be the creation, management and – if and when necessary – the destruction of culture.

According to Kanne-Urrabazo (2006), many managers do not deny the importance of organisational culture in employee satisfaction, few fail to realize the direct impact they have in shaping it. It is crucial that managers at all levels are aware of their roles and responsibilities in upholding positive workplace environments that can increase employee satisfaction.

Company Policy

Ansoff's (1957) matrix is one of the most well-known frameworks for deciding upon growth strategies. Strategic options relating to which products or services an organisation may offer in which markets are critical to the success of companies. The Ansoff matrix is a useful, though not an exhaustive, framework for an organisation's objective setting process and marketing audits. According to Porter (1980), strategy is the choice of an attractive industry and good positioning within this industry (Porter, 1985).

According to Cronqvist, Low and Nilsson (2007) and consistent with predictions from economic theories of corporate culture, the effect of corporate culture in company policies is long-term and stronger for internally grown business units and older firms. Their evidence is also consistent with firms preserving their cultures by selecting management teams that fit their cultures. Their evidence showed that a firm's corporate culture matters in its policy choices and performance.

The Powerfulness of the Firm in Competition with Rivals

Porter (2008) has grouped competition and competitive strategy into three categories: core concepts, location as a competitive advantage and competitive solutions to societal problems.

According to Cameron and Quinn (1999), the major distinguishing feature in successful companies – their most important competitive advantage and the most powerful factor they all highlight as a key ingredient in their success – is their organisational culture. Barney (1986) states that three attributes that a firm's culture must have to generate sustained competitive advantage are isolated. Previous findings suggest that the cultures of some firms have these attributes; thus, these cultures are a source of such advantage.

Connections between the Innovation Climate and CSR

According to Asongu (2007), the key to success in using any type of innovation to a company's advantage from the CSR perspective is to communicate with local municipal authorities, the press and most importantly, the general public that stands to benefit from such initiatives. Asongu (2007) states that companies that have sustainable policies tend to be technological leaders, as they seek imaginative new methods to reduce pollution and increase efficiency. In many cases, these companies are able to come out with new, innovative products that out-pace most of their competitors.

According to Phills *et al.* (2008) many social innovations involve the creation of new business models that can meet the needs of underserved populations more efficiently, effectively, and if not

profitably, at least sustainably. Many innovations tackle social problems or meet social needs, but the distribution of financial and social value is only tilted toward society as a whole as a result of social innovations.

Connections between the Innovation Climate and Individual Factors

The Innovation Climate and Job Satisfaction

According to Shipton et al (2004) aggregate job satisfaction was a significant predictor of subsequent organisational innovation, even after controlling for prior organisational innovation and profitability. Moreover the data indicated that the relationship between aggregate job satisfaction and innovation in production technology/ processes (but not product innovation) is moderated by organisational job variety, harmonization and contingent pay.

Research also shows that job satisfaction is significantly associated with measures of discretionary behaviours classed as "Organisational citizenship": helping, loyalty, compliance and innovation (Podsakoff et al., 2000).

The Innovation Climate and Meaningful Work

According to Judge (1997) Rand units are more innovative when the firm emphasizes personalized, intrinsic rewards (those that were related to the work and elicited feelings of accomplishment, such as peer and supervisor recognition, meaningful work opportunities) as opposed to extrinsic (bonuses, stock options).

The Innovation Climate and Attitude toward the Firm

According to Jones (1995) consultants and academics are urged to highlight the need to tackle core attitudes at the head of organisations as the key prerequisite of radical culture change, high learning and innovation, and long-term competitiveness.

According to García-Goñi (2007) perception of innovation is different for managers and front-line employees in public health institutions. While front-line employees' attitude depends mostly on the overall performance of the institution, managers feel more involved and motivated, and their behaviour depends more on individual and organisational innovative profiles.

Connections between the Innovation Climate and Organizational Level Factors

The Innovation Climate and Powerfulness of Firm in Competition against Rivals

Several common themes emerge repeatedly across studies to suggest that the link between innovation activities and competitive advantage rests primarily on four factors. One, innovations that are hard to imitate are more likely to lead to sustainable competitive advantage (Clark, 1987; Porter, 1985). Two, innovations that accurately reflect market realities are more likely to lead to sustainable competitive advantage (Deming, 1983; Porter, 1985). Three, innovations that enable a firm to exploit the timing characteristics of the relevant industry are more likely to lead to sustainable competitive advantage (Betz, 1987; Kanter, 1983). Fourth, innovations that rely on capabilities and technologies that are readily accessible to the firm are more likely to lead to sustainable competitive advantage (Ansoff, 1988; Miller, 1990).

The Innovation Climate and Behaviour of Management

According to Ortts and Smits (2006) four general consequences of the trends in innovation management are: 1) the end of the linear model; 2) the rise of the systems approach; 3) the inherent uncertainty and need for learning; 4) innovation becomes more entrepreneurial. The significant progress in innovation management has been obtained, but the failure rate has remained the same because of the changing conditions.

Brown et al. (2004) unfold the subjectivity of innovation management, and the essential role that sub-cultures and innovation process outcome criteria play in the innovation journey.

According to Birkinshaw (2006) management innovation tends to be diffuse and gradual. It typically follows four stages. The first stage is some type of dissatisfaction with the status quo, such as a crisis or strategic threat. That stage is followed by inspiration from other sources. The third stage is the invention of the management innovation itself. While most innovators identified a precipitating event that preceded the innovation, such as a challenge from a boss or a new assignment, few recalled a distinct "eureka moment" when the innovation occurred. The fourth stage is validation, both internally and through external sources such as academics, consultants, media organisations or industry associations.

The Innovation Climate and Policy of Firm

According to Teece (1981) public policy aimed at promoting innovation must focus not only on Rand, but also on complementary assets, as well as the underlying infrastructure.

According to Nguyen (2007) the impact of innovation policy on firms' innovative performance is one of the major issues to be dealt with in society in constant evolution and with strong competitiveness.

Based on the Relevant Literature We Developed the Following General Propositions

P1. Two facets of corporate social responsibility - the firm performance concerning social issues and the firm respects the interests of agents predict the innovation climate.

P2. Individual level factors - job satisfaction, meaning of work and attitude toward the firm predict the innovation climate.

P3. Organisational level factors - powerfulness of firm in competition against rivals, behaviour of management and policy of firm predict the innovation climate.

EMPIRICAL STUDY

In order to find connections between corporate social responsibility, individual and organisational level factors and the innovation climate in Estonian, Chinese, Japanese, Russian and Slovakian enterprises, an empirical study was conducted in 2007-2008. The research was done in Estonian enterprises with 623 respondents, in Chinese enterprises with 1150 respondents, in Japan enterprises with 1570 respondents, in Slovakian enterprises with 605 respondents and in Russian enterprises with 684 respondents. The companies were selected in a non-random manner, as the organisation registers do not have a solid basis for random sampling because only a fraction of the registered enterprises are active in Estonian, Chinese, Japanese, Russian and Slovakian. The total number of respondents was 4632.

Methodology

A standardised corporate social responsibility, job satisfaction, meaning of work, attitude toward the firm, powerfulness of firm in competition against rivals, behaviour of management and policy of firm questionnaires were developed by the Denki Ringo research group (Ishikawa et al, 2006) and translated from English into Estonian, Chinese, Japanese, Russian and Slovakian. The questions in the survey addressed 2 facets of corporate social responsibility – the firm's performance concerning social issues (11 items) and the firm's respect for the interests of agents (8 items), job satisfaction (16 items), meaning of work (6 items), attitude toward the firm (6 items), powerfulness of firm in competition against rivals (10 items), behaviour of management (6 items) and policy of firm (10 items). The questionnaire was administered in Estonian, Chinese, Czech, German, Finnish, Slovakian and Japanese electrical-electronic machine, retail and machine-building enterprises. The authors conducted the survey in the Estonian enterprises themselves by making contact with a member of the board and getting permission to conduct the study. After that the questionnaire was sent by e-mail to the respondents in each enterprise, and the answers were also sent back by e-mail. Then the answers from the Chinese, Japanese, German, Finnish and Slovakian respondents were collected by their Japanese co-partner and coordinator of the study.

The authors then developed an innovation climate scale based on the Innovation climate Questionnaire prepared by Ekvall *et al*. (1983). Items to measure the innovation climate were selected. The internal consistency, or Cronbach Alpha coefficient was 0.70. The final version of the questionnaire for measuring innovation consisted of 14 items.

The linear regression analysis was used in order to find statistically relevant connections between the two facets of corporate social responsibility, individual and organisational factors and the innovation climate.

The main research question is: Do corporate social responsibility, individual and organisational level factors predict the innovation climate?

RESULTS

Connections between Corporate Social Responsibility, Individual and Organizational Level Factors and the Innovation Climate

Our main purpose was to evaluate how corporate social responsibility, individual and organizational level factors predict the innovation climate. The authors used Linear Regression analysis. In the analysis corporate social responsibility, individual and organizational level factors were taken as an independent variables and the innovation climate as a dependent variable. We calculated a standardised regression coefficient Beta, which enabled us to know how strongly corporate social responsibility, individual level factors - job satisfaction, meaning of work and attitude toward the firm and organizational level factors - powerfulness of firm in competition against rivals, behaviour of management and policy of firm predict the innovation climate. Analysis was applied separately for 2 facets of corporate social responsibility, for 3 individual level factors, for 3 organizational level factors and for 1 innovation climate factor.

There are similarities and differences concerning the connections between corporate social responsibility, individual level factors - job satisfaction, meaning of work, attitude toward the firm, organizational level factors - powerfulness of firm in competition against rivals, behaviour of management, policy of firm and the innovation climate.

From this study 1 facet of corporate social responsibility - the firm performance concerning social issues predict innovation in 4 countries. Facet of corporate social responsibility - the firm respects the interests of agents, individual level factors - job satisfaction, meaning of work and attitude toward the firm and organizational level factors - powerfulness of firm in competition against rivals, behaviour of management and policy of firm predict the innovation climate differently in different countries (Table 1, 2, 3).

According to the linear regression analysis results in Table 1, both facets of corporate social responsibility predict the innovation climate in Estonian enterprises (R^2=.418, $F(2.620)$=223.00, $p<.000$) and also in Slovakian enterprises (R^2=.213, $F(2.400)$=54.159, $p<.000$). One facet

Table 1. How do 2 facets of corporate social responsibility - the firm performance concerning social issues and the firm respects the interests of agents predict the innovation climate (according to standardised regression coefficient Beta)

		B	Beta	t	Sig.
INNOVATION					
ESTONIA					
N=623, R^2=.418, F(2.620)=223.00,p<.000	FPSI	.653	.576	18.329	**.000***
	FRIA	.399	.189	6.009	**.000***
CHINA					
N=1150, R^2=.009, F(2.1134)=5.4592,p<.000	FPSI	.225	.095	2.524	**.011***
	FRIA	.011	.003	0.090	.928
JAPAN					
N=1570, R^2=.067, F(2.1526)=55.480,p<.000	FPSI	-.468	-.227	-6.281	**.000***
	FRIA	-.121	-.042	-1.165	.243
SLOVAKIA					
N=605, R^2=.213, F(2.400)=54.159, p<.000	FPSI	.459	.368	7.412	**.000***
	FRIA	.182	.157	3.171	**.001***

Notes. * - coefficient statistically significant, p<0,01

FPSI – The firm performance concerning social issues

FRIA – The firm respects the interests of agents

Table 2. How do individual level factors - job satisfaction, meaning of work and attitude toward the firm predict the innovation climate (according to standardised regression coefficient Beta)

		B	Beta	t	Sig.
INNOVATION					
ESTONIA					
N=623, R²=.497, F(6.616)=101.71, p<.000	Job satisfaction	-.035	-.054	-1.205	.228
	Meaning of work	-.089	-.060	-1.749	.080
	Attitude toward the firm	.608	.292	6.216	**.000***
CHINA					
N=1150, R²=.034, F(6.1118)=497.69, p<.000	Job satisfaction	.077	.039	1.147	.251
	Meaning of work	.030	.022	0.772	.440
	Attitude toward the firm	.058	.013	0.398	.690
JAPAN					
N=1570, R²=.018, F(6.1495)=4.6457, p<.000	Job satisfaction	.094	.090	3.333	**.000***
	Meaning of work	.093	.062	2.422	**.015***
	Attitude toward the firm	.135	.034	1.242	.214
SLOVAKIA					
N=605, R²=.265, F(6.396)=23.846, p<.000	Job satisfaction	-.003	-.003	-0.072	.942
	Meaning of work	.086	.082	1.743	.082
	Attitude toward the firm	.250	.206	3.537	**.000***
RUSSIA					
N=684, R²=.226, F(5.678)=39.786, p<.000	Job satisfaction	.046	.041	1.109	.267
	Meaning of work	.213	.222	6.224	**.000***
	Attitude toward the firm	.260	.181	4.275	**.000***

Notes. * - coefficient statistically significant, p<0,01

of corporate social responsibility – the firm performance concerning social issues predict the innovation climate in Chinese enterprises (R²=.009, F(2.1134)=5.4592, p<.000) and in Japanese enterprises (R²=.067, F(2.1526)=55.480, p<.000). The determinant coefficients R² are calculated for the regression model including both facets of corporate social responsibility as independent variables.

According to the linear regression analysis results in Table 2, two individual level factors – job satisfaction and meaning of work predict the innovation climate in Japanese enterprises (R²=.018, F(6.1495)=4.6457, p<.000). Two individual level factors – meaning of work and attitude toward the firm predict the innovation climate in Russian enterprises (R²=.226, F(5.678)=39.786, p<.000). One individual level factor – attitude toward the firm predicts the innovation climate in Estonian enterprises (R²=.497, F(6.616)=101.71, p<.000) and in Slovakian enterprises (R²=.265, F(6.396)=23.846, p<.000). The determinant coefficients R² are calculated for the regression model including all three individual level factors as independent variables.

Table 3. How do organizational level factors - powerfulness of firm in competition against rivals, behaviour of management and policy of firm predict the innovation climate (according to standardised regression coefficient Beta)

		B	Beta	T	Sig.
INNOVATION					
ESTONIA					
N=623, R²=.497, F(6.616)=101.71, p<.000	Powerfulness of firm in competition against rivals	.109	.078	1.582	.114
	Behaviour of management	.024	.014	0.268	.788
	Policy of firm	.428	.471	11.806	**.000***
CHINA					
N=1150, R²=.034, F(6.1118)=497.69, p<.000	Powerfulness of firm in competition against rivals	.145	.054	1.441	.149
	Behaviour of management	-.089	-.021	-0.534	.593
	Policy of firm	.278	.147	4.548	**.000***
JAPAN					
N=1570, R²=.018, F(6.1495)=4.6457, p<.000	Powerfulness of firm in competition against rivals	-.175	.074	-2.335	**.019***
	Behaviour of management	.197	.058	1.772	.076
	Policy of firm	-.062	-.026	-0.924	.355
SLOVAKIA					
N=605, R²=.265, F(6.396)=23.846, p<.000	Powerfulness of firm in competition against rivals	.033	.034	0.701	.483
	Behaviour of management	.245	.211	3.846	**.000***
	Policy of firm	.249	.164	3.446	**.000***
RUSSIA					
N=684, R²=.226, F(5.678)=39.786, p<.000	Behaviour of management	.220	.150	3.364	**.000***
	Policy of firm	.154	.113	2.881	**.004***

Notes. * - coefficient statistically significant, p<0,01

According to the linear regression analysis results in Table 3, two organizational level factors – behaviour of management and policy of firm predict the innovation climate in Slovakian enterprises (R²=.265, F(6.396)=23.846, p<.000) and in Russian enterprises (R²=.226, F(5.678)39.786, p<.000). One organizational level factor – policy of firm predict the innovation climate in Estonian enterprises (R²=.497, F(6.616)=101.71, p<.000) and in Chinese enterprises (R²=.034, F(6.1118)=497.69, p<.000). One organizational level factor – powerfulness of firm in competition against rivals predict the innovation climate in Japan (R²=.018, F(6.1495)=4.6457, p<.000). The determinant coefficients R^2 are calculated for the regression model including all three organizational level factors as independent variables.

CONCLUSION

National culture where organization is operating influences how corporate social responsibility, individual and organizational level factors predict the innovation climate. In different countries concepts of corporate social responsibility, job satisfaction, meaning of work, attitude toward the firm, powerfulness of firm in competition against rivals, behaviour of management, policy of firm and innovation are understood and applied differently in organisations.

There are similarities and differences concerning the connections between corporate social responsibility, individual level factors - job satisfaction and meaning of work, organisational level factors - attitude toward the firm, powerfulness of firm in competition against rivals, behaviour of management, policy of firm and the innovation climate in different countries.

From this study 1 facet of corporate social responsibility - the firm performance concerning social issues predict the innovation innovation climate in all 4 countries. Facet of corporate social responsibility - the firm respects the interests of agents, individual level factors - job satisfaction, meaning of work and attitude toward the firm and organizational level factors - powerfulness of firm in competition against rivals, behaviour of management and policy of firm predict the innovation climate differently in different countries (Table 1, 2, 3).

The propositions discussed at the beginning of the paper will now be re-evaluated.

P1 postulated that two facets of corporate social responsibility - the firm performance concerning social issues and the firm respects the interests of agents predict the innovation climate. In Estonian, Chinese, Japanese and Slovakian enterprises

facet of corporate social responsibility - the firm performance concerning social issues predicts the innovation climate. In Estonian and Slovakian enterprises facet of corporate social responsibility - the firm respects the interests of agents predicts the innovation climate.

P2 which postulated that individual level factors - job satisfaction, meaning of work and attitude toward the firm predict innovation. In Japanese enterprises job satisfaction predicts the innovation climate. In Japanese and Russian enterprises meaning of work predicts the innovation climate. In Slovakian, Russian and Estonian enterprises attitude toward the firm predicts the innovation climate.

P3 postulated that organisational level factors - powerfulness of firm in competition against rivals, behaviour of management and policy of firm predict the innovation climate.

In Slovakian and Russian enterprises behaviour of management and policy of firm predict the innovation climate. In Estonian and Chinese enterprises policy of firm predicts the innovation climate. In Japanese enterprises powerfulness of firm in competition against rivals predicts the innovation climate.

Our findings are consistent with following studies.

According to Borger and Kruglianskas (2006) there are many evidences of a strong relationship between the adoption of a CSR strategy by the firm and an effective environmental and innovative performance.

According to Zhu (2006) innovation assimilation is influenced by contextual factors and the effects may vary across different stages and in different environments.

According to Falck and Heblich (2007) due to globalization, companies are now less constrained by society's basic order than they have been in the past. Because different countries have different laws and standards, there are more ways to get away with less than ideal behavior in the quest for greater profits. Offers an understanding of CSR that could be the answer and contends that practicing CSR is not altruistic do-gooding, but rather a way for both companies and society to prosper. This is especially true when CSR is conceived as a long-range plan of action.

Summarizing the above, there are similarities and differences concerning the connections between corporate social responsibility, individual level factors, organisational level factors and the innovation climate in different countries.

From this study 1 facet of corporate social responsibility - the firm performance concerning social issues predicts the innovation climate in all 4 countries. Facet of corporate social responsibility - the firm respects the interests of agents, individual level factors - job satisfaction, meaning of work and attitude toward the firm and organizational level factors - powerfulness of firm in competition against rivals, behaviour of management and policy of firm predict the innovation climate differently in different countries.

Implications for Managers

The innovation climate is a complex entity. Facets of corporate social responsibility – firm performance concerning social issues and the firm respects the interests of agents, individual level factors - job satisfaction, meaning of work and attitude toward the firm and organizational level factors - powerfulness of firm in competition against rivals, behaviour of management and policy of firm predict the innovation climate, but it differs according to different countries

Limitations of Study

There are also limitations in this study connected with its general framework. The authors have focused only on certain factors – corporate social responsibility, individual and organizational level factors that influence the innovation climate, but there could be other factors influencing the innovation climate. The author explored concrete

connections between a limited number of factors and the other influences have been left for future research. Organizational culture and ethical values in business could be studied and analyzed concerning the innovation climate.

This research was done in Estonian, Chinese, Japanese, Slovakian and Russian retail store, information-software production, electronic and machine-building enterprises.

Further Research Proposal

The concept of the innovation climate could be studied in more detail by using the models developed in this research. Concepts the innovation climate and corporate social responsibility are understood and valued differently in different countries and in different organizations. Other factors that influence the innovation climate should be find out.

ACKNOWLEDGMENT

Research was supported by ETF grant 7537.

REFERENCES

Aarons, G. A., & Sawitzky, A. C. (2006). Organisational culture and climate and mental health provider attitudes toward evidence-based practice. *Psychological Services, 3*(1), 61–72. doi:10.1037/1541-1559.3.1.61

Amabile, T. M. (1988). A model of creativity and innovation in organisation. In Shaw, B. M., & Cummings, L. L. (Eds.), *Research in Organisational Behaviour, 10, 123-67.*

Anderson, N. R., de Dreu, C. K. W., & Nijstad, B. A. (2004). The routinization of innovation research: a constructively critical review of the state-of-the-science. *Journal of Organizational Behavior, 25*(2), 147–174. doi:10.1002/job.236

Ansoff, I. H. (1957). Strategies for diversification. *Harvard Business Review*, *35*(2), 113–124.

Ashkanasy, N. M., Wilderom, C. P. M., & Peterson, M. F. (2000). *Handbook of Organisational culture and climate*. Thousand Oaks, CA: Sage.

Asongu, J. J. (2007). Innovation as an Argument for Corporate social responsibility. *Journal of Business and Public Policy*, *1*(3), 1–21.

Axtell, C. M., Holman, D. J., Unsworth, K. L., Wall, T. D., Waterson, P. E., & Harrington, E. (2000). Shopfloor innovation: facilitating the suggestions and implementation of ideas. *Journal of Occupational and Organizational Psychology*, *73*, 265–285. doi:10.1348/096317900167029

Baron, D. P. (2001). Private politics, corporate social responsibility and integrated strategy. *Journal of Economics & Management Strategy*, *10*(1), 7–45. doi:10.1162/105864001300122548

Betz, F. (1987). *Managing technology: Competing through new ventures, innovation, and corporate research*. Englewood Cliffs, NJ: Prentice Hall.

Bird, F., & Smucker, J. (2007). The Social Responsibilities of International Business Firms in Developing Areas. *Journal of Business Ethics*, *73*, 1–9. doi:10.1007/s10551-006-9192-4

Birkinshaw, J., & Mol, M. (2006). How Management Innovation Happens. *Management of Technology and Innovation*, *47*(4), 81–88.

Borger, F. G., & Kruglianskas, I. (2006). Corporate social responsibility and environmental and technological innovation performance: case studies of Brazilian companies. *International Journal of Technology. Policy and Management*, *6*(4), 399–412.

Brentani, U. (2001). Innovative versus incremental new business services: Different keys for achieving success. *Journal of Product Innovation Management*, *18*(3), 169–187. doi:10.1016/S0737-6782(01)00071-6

Brown, C. J., & Frame, P. (2004). Subjectivity in innovation management. *International Journal of Innovation and Learning*, *1*(4), 351–363. doi:10.1504/IJIL.2004.005496

Buckler, S. A., & Zien, K. A. (1996). From Experience: The Spirituality of Innovation: Learning from stories. *Journal of Product Innovation Management*, *13*(5), 391–405. doi:10.1016/0737-6782(96)00056-2

Cameron, K. S., & Quinn, R. E. (1999). *Diagnosing and Changing Organisational Culture: Based on the Competing Values Framework*. Reading, MA: Addison Wesley Longman.

Carmazzi, A., & Aarons, G. A. (2003). Organisational culture and attitudes toward adoption of evidence-based practice. Paper presented at the NASMHPD Research Institute's 2003 Conference on State Mental Health Agency Services Research, Program Evaluation, and Policy, Baltimore, MD.

Carroll, A. B. (1999). Corporate social responsibility: Evolution of a definitional construct. *Business & Society*, *38*(3), 268–295. doi:10.1177/000765039903800303

Clark, K. (1987). Investment in new technology and competitive advantage. In Teece, D. J. (Ed.), *The competitive challenge* (pp. 59–82). Grand Rapids, MI: Harper & Row.

Cohen, W. M., Levin, R. C., & Mowery, D. C. (1987). Firm size and r&d intensity: A reexamination. *The Journal of Industrial Economics*, *35*(4), 543–565. doi:10.2307/2098587

Cornelius, N., Todres, M., Janjuha-Jivraj, S., Woods, A., & Wallace, J. (2008). Corporate social responsibility and the Social Enterprise. *Journal of Business Ethics*, *81*, 355–370. doi:10.1007/s10551-007-9500-7

Cronqvist, H., Low, A., & Nilsson, M. (2007). Does Corporate Culture Matter for Firm Policies? *A Research Report From Swedish Institute For Financial Research, 48*(2), 1-60. Damanpour, F., & Schneider, M. (2006). Phases of the adoption of innovation in organisations: Effects of environment, organisation and top managers. *British Journal of Management, 17*, 215–236.

Deming, W. E. (1986). *Out of the crisis*. Cambridge, MA: MIT Center for Advanced Engineering Study.

Dewey, J. (1939). *Theory of Valuation*. Chicago, IL: University of Chicago Press.

Drucker, P. F. (1984). The new meaning of corporate social responsibility. *California Management Review, 26*, 53–63.

Ekvall, G., & Avrvonen, J. Waldenström-Lindblad's, I. (1983). Creative Organisational climate: Construction and validation of a measuring instrument. Report 2. Stockholm: FA rådet, The Swedish Council for Management and Organisational Behaviour.

Epstein, E. M. (1987). The corporate social policy process: Beyond business ethics, corporate social responsibility and corporate social responsiveness. *California Management Review, 29*, 99–114.

Falck, O., & Heblich, S. (2007). *Corporate social responsibility: Doing Well by Doing Good*. Business Horizons.

Frederick, W. C. (1960). The growing concern over business responsibility. *California Management Review, 2*, 54–61.

Freeman, R. E. (1984). *Strategic Management: A Stakeholder Approach*. Boston: Pitman.

Freeman, R. E. (1994). The Politics of Stakeholder Theory: Some Future Directions. *Business Ethics Quarterly, 4*, 409–422. doi:10.2307/3857340

Garriga, E., & Melé, D. (2004). *Corporate social responsibility Theories: Mapping the* Territory. *Journal of Business Ethics, 53*(1-2), 51–71. doi:10.1023/B:BUSI.0000039399.90587.34

Glisson, C., & Hemmelgarn, A. (1998). The effects of Organisational climate and interOrganisational coordination on the quality and outcomes of children's service systems. *Child Abuse & Neglect, 22*(5), 401–421. doi:10.1016/S0145-2134(98)00005-2

Glisson, C., & James, L. R. (2002). The cross-level effects of culture and climate in human service teams. *Journal of Organizational Behavior, 23*, 767–794. doi:10.1002/job.162

Hackman, R. J., & Oldham, G. R. (1975). Development of the Job Diagnostic Survey. *The Journal of Applied Psychology, 60*(2), 159–170. doi:10.1037/h0076546

Herzberg, F. (1968). One more time: how do you motivate employees? *Harvard Business Review, 46*(1), 53–62.

Hillman, A., & Keim, G. (2001). Shareholder value, stakeholder management, and social issues: what's the bottom line? *Strategic Management Journal, 22*(2), 125–139. doi:10.1002/1097-0266(200101)22:2<125::AID-SMJ150>3.0.CO;2-H

Humphreys, M., & Brown, A. D. (2008). An Analysis of Corporate social responsibility at Credit Line: A Narrative Approach. *Journal of Business Ethics, 80*, 403–418. doi:10.1007/s10551-007-9426-0

Ishikawa, A., Mako, C., & Warhurst, C. (2006). *Work and Employee Representation: Workers, Firms and Unions. Part 3*. Tokyo, Japan: Chuo University Press.

Janssen, O. (2000). Job demands, perceptions of effort-reward fairness and innovative work behaviour. *Journal of Occupational and Organizational Psychology*, *73*, 287–302. doi:10.1348/096317900167038

Janszen, F. (2000). *The Age of Innovation: making business creativity a competence, not a coincidence*. London: Prentice-Hall.

Jones, T. M. (1980). Corporate social responsibility revisited, redefined. *California Management Review*, 59–67.

Judge, T. A., Thoresen, C. J., Bono, J. E., & Patton, G. K. (2001). The job satisfaction-job performance relationship: A qualitative and quantitative review. *Psychological Bulletin*, *127*(3), 376–407. doi:10.1037/0033-2909.127.3.376

Kanne-Urrabazo, C. (2006). Management's role in shaping Organisational culture. *Journal of Nursing Management*, *14*(3), 188–194. doi:10.1111/j.1365-2934.2006.00590.x

Kanter, R. M. (1983). *The change masters*. New York: Simon & Schuster.

Locke, E. A. (1976). The nature and causes of job satisfaction. In Dunnette, M. D. (Ed.), *Handbook of Industrial and Organisational Psychology* (pp. 1297–1349). Chicago: Rand McNally.

Lund, D. B. (2003). Organisational culture and job satisfaction. *Journal of Business and Industrial Marketing*, *18*(3), 219–236. doi:10.1108/08858620310473313

Martins, E. C., & Terblanche, F. (2003). Building organisational culture that stimulates creativity and innovation. *European Journal of Innovation Management*, *6*(1), 64–74. doi:10.1108/14601060310456337

McGregor, D. (1957). An uneasy look at performance appraisal. *Harvard Business Review*, *35*(May/June), 89–94.

Meyer, J. P., & Allen, N. J. (1991). A three-component conceptualization of Organisational commitment. *Human Resource Management Review*, *1*, 61–89. doi:10.1016/1053-4822(91)90011-Z

Miller, D. (1990). *The icarus paradox: How exceptional companies bring about their own downfall*. New York: Harper-Collins.

Morimoto, R., Ash, J., & Hope, C. (2005). Corporate social responsibility Audit: From Theory to Practice. *Journal of Business Ethics*, *63*, 315–325. doi:10.1007/s10551-005-0274-5

Mumford, M. D., & Gustafson, S. B. (1988). Creativity syndrome: Integration, application, and innovation. *Psychological Bulletin*, *103*, 27–43. doi:10.1037/0033-2909.103.1.27

Mumford, M. D., & Licuanan, B. (2004). Leading for innovation: conclusions, issues and directions. *The Leadership Quarterly*, *15*(1), 163–171. doi:10.1016/j.leaqua.2003.12.010

Nguyen, T. T. U. (2007). *Impact of public support on firms' innovation performance Evidence from Luxemburg's firms*. International Network for Studies in Technology, Environment, Alternatives, Development CEPS/INSTEAD – Luxembourg.

Orchard, L. (1998). Managerialism, economic rationalism and public sector reform in Australia: Connections, divergences, alternatives. *Australian Journal of Public Administration*, *57*(1), 19–32. doi:10.1111/j.1467-8500.1998.tb01361.x

Orlitzky, M., Schmidt, F., & Rynes, S. (2003). Corporate social and financial performance: a meta-analysis. *Organization Studies*, *24*(3), 403–441. doi:10.1177/0170840603024003910

Ortt, J. R., & Smits, R. (2006). Innovation management: different approaches to cope with the same trends. *International Journal of Technology Management*, *34*, 296–318. doi:10.1504/IJTM.2006.009461

Parker, R., & Bradley, L. (2000). Organisational culture in the public sector: Evidence from six organisations. *International Journal of Public Sector Management, 13*(2), 125–141. doi:10.1108/09513550010338773

Phills, J. A., Jr., Deiglmeier, K., & Miller, D. T. (2008). Rediscovering Social Innovation. Stanford, Leland Stanford Jr. University: Social Innovation Review.

Podsakoff, P. M., Mackenzie, S. B., Paine, J. B., & Bachrach, D. G. (2000). Organizational citizenship behaviors: A critical review of the theoretical and empirical literature and suggestions for future research. *Journal of Management, 26,* 513–563. doi:10.1177/014920630002600307

Porter, M. E. (1980). *Competitive strategy: techniques for analyzing industries and competitors.* New York: Free Press.

Porter, M. E. (1985). *Competitive advantage: creating and sustaining superior performance.* New York: Free Press.

Porter, M. E. (2008). *On Competition.* Boston: Harvard Business School Press.

Quaak, L., Aalbers, T., & Goedee, J. (2007). Transparency of corporate social responsibility in Dutch Breweries. *Journal of Business Ethics, 76,* 293–308. doi:10.1007/s10551-006-9282-3

Schein, E. H. (2004). *Organisational Culture and Leadership.* New York: John Wiley and Sons.

Schumpeter, J. (1911). "*Theorie der wirtschaftlichen Entwicklung* (transl. *The Theory of Economic Development: An inquiry into profits, capital, credit, interest and the business cycle*) Leipzig, Verlag von Duncker and Humblot. Internet translation Retrieved from http://findarticles.com/p/articles/mi_m0254/is_2_61/ai_86469065/pg_24

Schwab, K. (2008). Global Corporate Citizenship. *Foreign Affairs (Council on Foreign Relations), 87*(1), 107–118.

Scott, S. G., & Bruce, R. A. (1994). Determinants of innovative behaviour: a path model of individual innovation in the workplace. *Academy of Management Journal, 38,* 1442–1465.

Seel, R. (2005). Culture and Complexity: New Insights on Organisational Change. *Organisations and People, 7*(2), 2–9.

Shipton, H., West, M. A., Parkes, C., & Dawson, J. F. (2004). *Aggregate job satisfaction, HRM and organizational innovation.* Birmingham, UK: Aston Business School, Aston University.

Silverthorne, C. (2004). The impact of Organisational culture and person-organisation fit on Organisational commitment and job satisfaction in Taiwan. *Leadership and Organization Development Journal, 25*(7), 592–599. doi:10.1108/01437730410561477

Sleeper, B. J., Schneider, K. C., Weber, P. S., & Weber, J. E. (2006). Scale and Study of Students Attitudes Toward Business Education's Role in Addressing Social Issues. *Journal of Business Ethics, 68*(4), 381–391. doi:10.1007/s10551-006-9000-1

Smith, G. P. (2002). *The new leader: bringing creativity and innovation to the workplace, Chart Your Course.* Georgia: Conyers.

Stevens, J. E. (1999). *An Organisational Culture Perspective of Strategic Leadership and Organisational Change: Shaping the Future of the Army.* Study project.

Tanimoto, K., & Suzuki, K. (2005). *Corporate social responsibility in Japan: Analyzing the participation companies in global reporting initiative.* Working Paper 208.

Unsworth, K., & Parker, S. (2003). Proactivity and innovation: Promoting a new workforce for the new workplace. In Holman, D., Wall, T., Clegg, C., Sparrow, P., & Howard, A. (Eds.), *The New Workplace: A Guide to the Human Impact of Modern Working Practices*. West Sussex, UK: Wiley.

Valle, M. (1999). Crisis, culture and charisma: The new leader's work in public organisations. *Public Personnel Management, 28*(2), 245–257.

Van de Ven, & Andrew H. (1986). Central Problems in the Management of Innovation. *Management Science, 32*(5), 590–607. doi:10.1287/mnsc.32.5.590

van Marrewijk, M. (2003). Concepts and definitions of CSR and Corporate Sustainability: Between Agency and Communication. *Journal of Business Ethics, 44*(2/3), 95–105. doi:10.1023/A:1023331212247

Waddock, S., & Graves, S. (1997). The corporate social performance - financial performance link. *Strategic Management Journal, 18*(4), 303–319. doi:10.1002/(SICI)1097-0266(199704)18:4<303::AID-SMJ869>3.0.CO;2-G

Wood, D. J. (1991). Social Issues in Management: Theory and Research in Corporate Social Performance. *Journal of Management, 17*(2), 383–406. doi:10.1177/014920639101700206

Wright, P., & Ferris, S. (1997). Agency conflict and corporate strategy: the effect of divestment on corporate value. *Strategic Management Journal, 18*(1), 77–83. doi:10.1002/(SICI)1097-0266(199701)18:1<77::AID-SMJ810>3.0.CO;2-R

Zaltman, G., Duncan, R., & Holbek, J. (1973). *Innovations and Organisations*. New York: Wiley.

Zhou, J., & Shalley, C. E. (2003). Research on employee creativity: a critical review and proposal for future research directions. In Martocchio, J. J., & Ferris, G. R. (Eds.), *Research in Personel and Human Resource Managemen*. Oxford, UK: Elsevier.

Zhu, K., Kraemer, K. L., & Xu, S. (2006). *The Process of Innovation Assimilation by Firms in Different Countries: A Technology Diffusion Perspective on E-Business*. Management.

KEY TERMS AND DEFINITIONS

Attitudes Toward The Firm: Employees mentality in the firm.

Behaviour of Management: Leaders/managers actions.

Corporate Social Responsibility: CSR business would monitor and ensure their adherence to law, ethical standards and international norms. Business takes responsibility for the impact of their activities on the environment, consumers, employees, communities, stakeholders and all other members of the public sphere.

Innovation Climate: The degree of support and encouragement an organization provides its employees to take initiative and explore innovative approaches.

Job Satisfaction: Describes how content an individual is with his or her job.

Meaning of Work: Working makes sense.

Policy of Firm: Firms strategies and guidelines.

Powerfulness of Firm in Competition Against Rivals: Firms competitiveness.

APPENDIX A

Figure 1. How corporate social responsibility, individual and organizational level factors predict the innovation climate in Estonian enterprises

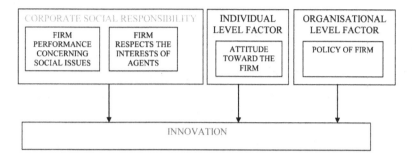

Figure 2. How corporate social responsibility and organizational level factor predict the innovation climate in Chinese enterprises

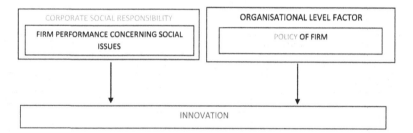

Figure 3. How corporate social responsibility, individual and organizational level factors predict the innovation climate in Japanese enterprises

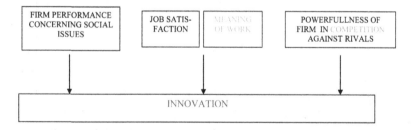

Figure 4. How corporate social responsibility, individual and organizational level factors predict the innovation climate in Slovakian enterprises

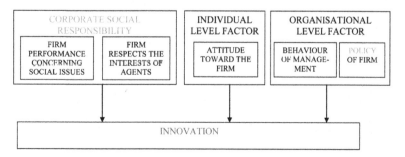

Figure 5. How corporate social responsibility, individual and organizational level factors predict the innovation climate in Russian enterprises

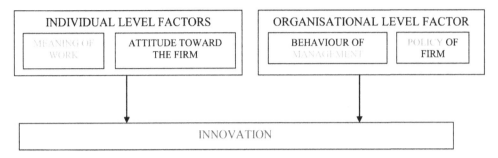

APPENDIX B

Questionnaires about Individual Level Factors

Table 4. Job satisfaction

Are you satisfied with the following working conditions?	Dissatisfied		More or less		Satisfied
a. Self-actualization of your ability at work	1	2	3	4	5
b. Range of your competence at work	1	2	3	4	5
c. Labour conditions (e.g. lighting, heating, noise)	1	2	3	4	5
d. Trust between workers and management	1	2	3	4	5
e. Work load	1	2	3	4	5
f. Length of working time	1	2	3	4	5
g. Payments and bonuses	1	2	3	4	5
h. Competence of management	1	2	3	4	5
i. Promotion opportunities	1	2	3	4	5
j. Training and retraining	1	2	3	4	5
k. Security of employment	1	2	3	4	5
l. Equal opportunities for men and women	1	2	3	4	5
m. Welfare provisions in the firm	1	2	3	4	5
n. Interaction with your boss	1	2	3	4	5
o. Interaction with your colleagues	1	2	3	4	5
p. Access to information about the organisation	1	2	3	4	5

Table 5. Meaning of work

What do you think about the meaning of work?	Entirely disagree		More or less		Completely agree
a. Work gives you status and prestige	1	2	3	4	5
b. Work provides you with income that is needed	1	2	3	4	5
c. Work keeps you absorbed and excited	1	2	3	4	5
d. Work provides you with social contact with other people	1	2	3	4	5
e. Work is a way for you to serve society	1	2	3	4	5
f. Work is in itself interesting	1	2	3	4	5

Table 6. Attitudes toward the firm

What do you think of your attitudes toward the firm?	disagree		Unsure		agree
a. I always have ideas that can be approved by management	1	2	3	4	5
b. I would like to take part in the company's decision-making, because I think my opinion is important	1	2	3	4	5
c. I could take a managerial position if the situation demanded it	1	2	3	4	5
d. I am ready to take risks if it is approved	1	2	3	4	5
e. It is normal to sacrifice something for the organisation's sake	1	2	3	4	5
f. Sometimes I feel like a screw in a large machine	1	2	3	4	5

APPENDIX C

Questionnaires about Organisational Level Factors

Table 7. The powerfulness of the firm in competition with rivals

How powerful do you think your firm is in competition with rivals concerning different aspects raised below?	Completely powerless		Unsure		Powerful enough
a. Image of the firm	1	2	3	4	5
b. Quality of products and service	1	2	3	4	5
c. Cost	1	2	3	4	5
d. Brand	1	2	3	4	5
e. Technology	1	2	3	4	5
f. Marketing	1	2	3	4	5
g. Scale merit	1	2	3	4	5
h. Aftercare service	1	2	3	4	5
i. Quality of human resources	1	2	3	4	5
j. Capability of Top management	1	2	3	4	5

Table 8. The behaviour of the management

As for the behaviour of management, do you agree with the following views?	disagree		Unsure		Agree
a. If the management promised something, than it will do what it promised	1	2	3	4	5
b. The management is sure that it controls the activity of all departments	1	2	3	4	5
c. The leaders of the organisation have long-term goals	1	2	3	4	5
d. The management sets clear goals for the workers	1	2	3	4	5
e. The leaders and managers follow the principles they set for the organisation	1	2	3	4	5
f. There is a clear set of principles that are followed by the organisation in its activities	1	2	3	4	5

Table 9. Company policy

How do you perceive the policy of your firm?	disagree		unsure		agree
a. The management tends to be behind the times when reacting to a changing market	1	2	3	4	5
b. We always try to overcome our rivals	1	2	3	4	5
c. If the market demands it, our organisation can quickly restructure	1	2	3	4	5
d. The goals of organisation are clearly set at all Organisational levels	1	2	3	4	5
e. In some situations instructions and regulations are obstacles to effective work	1	2	3	4	5
f. It is possible to be a good manager even without knowing the answers to all the subordinates' questions	1	2	3	4	5
g. In some cases one worker is under two managers	1	2	3	4	5
h. Every process at work is governed in detail by instructions and rules	1	2	3	4	5
i. The order of the organisation is not rigidly structured hierarchically	1	2	3	4	5
j. Employee qualifications is considered to be a very important source of competitive advantage	1	2	3	4	5
k. Resources including human resources are not allocated properly nor integrated totally	1	2	3	4	5
l. Reward for success does not go to the department although everyone made an effort	1	2	3	4	5
m. We realize our input to society and feel our importance	1	2	3	4	5

APPENDIX D

Questionnaire about Two Facets of Corporate Social Responsibility: The Firm's Performance Concerning Social Issues and the Firm's Respect for the Interests of Agents

Table 10. Firm's performance concerning social issues

To what extent does your firm make an effort to perform for the following issues?	not at all		more or less		very actively
a. Compliance with the laws for business activities	1	2	3	4	5
b. Compliance with the laws for worker protection	1	2	3	4	5
c. Care and service for consumers	1	2	3	4	5
d. Environmental protection	1	2	3	4	5
e. Trustworthy relations with customers	1	2	3	4	5
f. Safety and Security of products and services	1	2	3	4	5
g. Realization of the best quality of products and services	1	2	3	4	5
h. Aftercare for users	1	2	3	4	5
i. Transparency of company information for society	1	2	3	4	5
j. Contribution to science and culture	1	2	3	4	5
k. Public activities for the local community	1	2	3	4	5

Table 11. Firm's respect for the interests of agents

How much does your firm respect the interests of the following agents?	not at all		more or less		very actively
a. Customers	1	2	3	4	5
b. Subsidiaries, subcontracted firms	1	2	3	4	5
c. Consumers	1	2	3	4	5
d. Stock holders	1	2	3	4	5
e. Employees	1	2	3	4	5
f. Trade union	1	2	3	4	5
g. Public administration	1	2	3	4	5
h. Local community	1	2	3	4	5

APPENDIX E

Questionnaire about the Innovation Climate

Table 12. The innovation climate

a. How do you think you are valued properly at your work?	1.Not at all	2.Less valued	3.Unsure	4.Rather valued	5.Greatly valued
b. What do you feel toward the firm you are working for?	1. I don't care for the firm	2. I feel almost nothing towards the firm	3. Unsure	4. I would apply as much effort, as will be rewarded by the firm	5. I would put maximum effort toward the firm's success
c. Over the last five years have you attended courses or seminars organized by the firm inside or outside?	1. Yes, I have	2. No, I haven't	3. It doesn't happen in our firm		
How do you perceive the situations at your workplace?	disagree		unsure		agree
d. The rules of the firm are occasionally disobeyed when an employee thinks it would be in the interests of the firm	1	2	3	4	5
g. Our organisation relies more on horizontal control and coordination, rather than strict hierarchy	1	2	3	4	5
h. The most capable persons commit to decisions to solve an urgent problem	1	2	3	4	5
i. Fresh creative ideas are actualized on time	1	2	3	4	5
j. The current vision creates stimuli for workers	1	2	3	4	5
k. The company realizes a clear mission that gives meaning and sense to work	1	2	3	4	5
l. If the department is short handed, the department's leader may hire temporary workers by himself	disagree		unsure		agree
m. Our organisation cares even about temporary workers	1	2	3	4	5
n. We can all clearly imagine the future of our organisation	1	2	3	4	5
o. Failure is considered a stimulus to learning and development	1	2	3	4	5
p. All the employees should be aware of the important role of their firm in society	1	2	3	4	5

Chapter 14
Advancing the Potential of Diversity for Innovation

Nancy D. Erbe
California State University - Dominguez Hills, USA

ABSTRACT

This chapter introduces a collaborative conflict resolution model with a focus on cultural diversity and innovation. Its practices are research based, presented with explanatory theories, and uniquely suited to the multicultural teams of the global market. The chapter presents the optimal criteria for multicultural process identified in evaluative research conducted in four parts of the world: the Balkans, Cameroon, Nepal and Ukraine. It aims to demonstrate the correlations between collaborative conflict process at its best and innovation within diverse teams and organizations.

INTRODUCTION

This chapter introduces the connections between contemporary conflict talents and optimal facilitation of multicultural groups. It begins with scholarly links between cultural diversity and ingenuity along with resultant challenges. The chapter then shows how conflict skills can create and sustain the cooperative conditions promoted by scholars for nurturing innovation. Research evaluating ideal multicultural process will be shared. The author hopes that understanding these specifics will encourage business to adopt best practices in their pursuit

of innovation. Ultimately, business will also recognize and embrace the rich assets of multicultural employees, teams and approaches. Daniel Goleman describes this as schooling in emotional intelligence (Goleman, 1995). He believes that competitive advantage requires cooperative training in the social skills described here. Exemplary collaboration is necessary to fully leverage business, particularly intellectual, assets.

For readers unfamiliar with contemporary business scholarship, this article exemplifies the growing academic use of qualitative research for in-depth exploration of the real world complexities and nuances faced by business today. One popular example of qualitative methods is the business

DOI: 10.4018/978-1-61520-643-8.ch014

case study. Laurence Lynn of the University of Chicago is one of many respected proponents acknowledging that, in the face of complex problems, like the relationship between diversity and innovation, there is no one right or best answer (Lynn, 1999). In response, business case analysis must necessarily draw upon the entire body of behavioral and social science and make use of it in myriad ways. "The reasoning process is more experiential and associative, involving pattern recognition and intuition, than it is logical.... or scientific reasoning (Lynn, 1999)." This does not mean that traditional quanitative statistical analysis is not also valued in business scholarship as demonstrated by this book's varied studies. In fact, ideally the qualitative research presented in this chapter will be used to inform and shape rich longitudinal studies designed to identify the variables that can be replicated in business to produce optimal innovation. Without preliminary qualitative exploration, like that presented in this chapter, however, academic research risks being overly simplistic (Lewicki, Barry & Saunders, 2007). "Several important qualitative...activities inform most, if not all, quanitative projects (Druckman, 2005)."

Thirty years ago the author started facilitating cross ethnic groups. This work evolved into mediating and advising cross-functional problem-solving, teambuilding, labor-management disputes and complex processes involving many perspectives. As one example, the author led cross ethnic dialogue with different professions from the Balkans during their war. She has worked with about seventy different countries and myriad cultures and business functions: engineering, science, service, and human resources—to name a few. Organizations have requested her assistance with escalating crisis involving actual and potential violence. At times, management-labor relationships are so broken that communication and information have essentially stopped. Without the qualitative evaluative research presented in this chapter, no research study could have even

begun to imagine the reasons and perceived reasons for such problems. Qualitative surveys and observations were necessary to begin exploring nuances that might have been missed or masked by premature attempts at quantification (Druckman, 2005).

Even if the qualitative data presented here is used to create more informed behavioral categories for future research, though, business cannot rely on traditional academic research alone. Because of the complex and dynamic problems contemporary global businesses constantly face, unfortunately more often than not without the benefit of relevant academic research, it must somehow learn to conduct its own applied research on an on-going basis (Bordens and Abbott, 1999). For example, in the field of negotiation, much research has studied Japanese and American behavior, leaving much of the rest of world cultures a negotiation mystery (Lewicki, Barry & Saunders, 2007). Applied research, aspiring to investigate real world problems as they arise, must somehow fill this enormous academic gap. Thus this chapter also aspires to guide and shape applied research and guide actual business success with designing structures that create pioneering innovation. The author's work mirrors the shifting realities of the contemporary workplace. More and more workers are being asked to work as part of cross functional teams that include various cultures. Their ability to effectively cooperate with each other in performing tasks is key to business success. In this chapter the author hopes to share the best of her experience and insight, along with research based knowledge, so that business can act proactively rather than reactively. The proactive path avoids the enormous costs inherent in conflict and loss from failure to maximize the potential of diverse teams. The author will share her proven practices for structuring groups in ways that effectively stimulate the synergy of difference. They generate creative passion while avoiding the many pitfalls that predictably arise. She will describe step by step capacity building in the exact structure that the majority of her clients and students from around the world embrace with great enthusiasm.

DIVERSITY'S POTENTIAL FOR INNOVATION

Diversity is often linked to heightened creativity whether finding new answers to questions, developing new perspective, or solving problems with fresh solutions (Fink, 2003). One contemporary expert, who has studied companies effectively fostering innovation, states that "innovation communities recognize that diversity is important for growth and development" (Dundon, 2008). Other experts go so far as saying that "diversity fuels innovation" (Skarzynski and Gibson, 2008). Still others posit that the greater an organization's diversity, the better its chance for launching innovation (Snyder and Duarte, 2008). At the very least, enough diverse ideas must be available to combine them into novel and varied patterns.

Broadly defined, the diversity promoted as enhancing creativity includes not only ethnic and gender difference but also expertise, life experience, perspective and function. In the contemporary workplace, more and more employees are what Peter Drucker calls knowledge workers, like computer programmers, who must work as part of cross functional teams. While multicultural diversity will be stressed here, all difference, whether in style, background, profession, philosophy or ability, has potential to spark innovation. History abounds with examples of creative partnerships and teams where disparate members complement and stimulate each other.

The reasons for this resonance between variety and creativity will be elaborated throughout this chapter. To begin, diversity's potential for conflict, ironically, when facilitated skillfully, creates the conditions linked with innovation. By its very nature, difference creates the disequilibrium and new questions that many believe must be present to spark innovation: "original thinking….(or) something never created before" (Tubbs, 1995). Wonderfully, conflict can also create motivation. It is possible that a group facing escalating tensions and struggling with difference will be fueled to greater heights of innovation in its attempts to move forward. In light of what scholars have learned about creative process, it is likely in fact that the best of innovators and innovation will emerge from struggling with frustration and discomfort (Deutsch, 1973). Brilliant "a ha" insight is reported after periods of concentrated effort focused on more familiar territory; followed by apparent impasse resulting in shifting perspective.

CHALLENGES INHERENT IN BOTH DIVERSE COMMUNITIES AND CREATIVE PROBLEM-SOLVING

So why is the world not seeing more innovation as a natural result of its growing multicultural communities, within and outside of business? Instead, "creative thinking and reasoning, while vitally important to effective groups and teams, is hard to find in the real world" (Johnson and Johnson, 2000). More visible is the innovation of Japanese companies, who at the management level can be about as homogeneous as can be imagined. Yet, taking the auto industry as one prominent example, Japanese managers have been remarkably successful in launching popularly received innovation. In contrast, a creative endeavor like the recent election of Barack Obama in the United States, where people from a wide range of life experiences; economic and ethnic groups aligned to create an event and movement truly new—one that had never occurred before, is remarkably difficult to find. The reason is likely the need, rarely met, for skillful collaboration effectively embracing the conflict and challenge predictably arising in the face of difference (Triandis, 2003). Research indicates that cross cultural negotiations yields poorer outcomes than negotiations within one's own cultural group or between similar cultures (Lewicki, Barry and Saunders, 2007).

To bring something new into existence, explore new opportunities, and change, those concerned must be sufficiently motivated (Deutsch, 1973). Different perspectives, or ways of viewing a problem or situation, are inherently present with diverse cultures. Conflict itself can generate requisite motivation. Ethnic difference alone, however, has been found to dramatically threaten core identity. In fact, ethnic violence represents the greatest challenge with contemporary war (Erbe, 2004). This may sound overly dramatic until one considers the following explanation. "Identity [is] defined as an abiding sense of selfhood that is the core of what makes life predictable to an individual…To have no ability to anticipate events is essentially to experience terror…Events which threaten to invalidate the core sense of identity will elicit defensive responses aimed at avoiding psychic and/or physical annihilation" (Erbe, 2003).

At the very least, research demonstrates that those threatened by ethnic difference may exhibit defensive response. They attempt to "defend" their identity and create a sense of security by cognitively minimizing and otherwise distorting the very difference which is needed to stimulate innovation.

Alternatively, communications theory—the theories of coordinated management of meaning and confrontation episodes as two instances—describes how difference can easily lead to destructive rather than creative understanding. Coordinated management of meaning focuses on the rules and expectations that individuals bring to any communication. It explains how when individuals share understandings and expectations they are likely to interpret cues of communication in similar ways. When, however, they come from cultures with different communication norms and practices, they risk violating each other's expectations, offending and otherwise (often unknowingly) inciting conflict.

The day to day routine of the contemporary workplace provides numerous examples of how difference alone easily leads to misunderstanding. Many employees understand little, if anything, of cultures, functions and perspectives other than their own. They can easily construe innocent difference as intentionally disrespectful and even hostile. Seemingly simple communication practices like interruption, timing and eye contact can catalyze long standing conflict with costly ramifications for business organizations. Even in the author's conflict resolution classrooms, it is challenging for students to understand, for example, that interruption and direct eye contact communicate passion and genuine interest to some. Others feel deep offense and irritation. Working with engineers at one of the United States' most successful and global technical corporations, the author encountered much suspicion, frustration and impatience when attempting to explain that a group of Japanese managers needed substantial time to confer with each other. The Japanese tradition of consensus building had nothing to do with the American engineers. Yet these engineers felt disrespected. On the other hand, many cultures around the world feel disrespected when American employees insist on business, or task focus, first and foremost. Such Americans are seen as insensitive to business relationships.

INTENTIONAL PERSPECTIVE TAKING FACILITATES INNOVATIVE PROCESS

Research of closed minded individuals demonstrates that they are more likely to act with the defensive responses described above, frequently rejecting information that is potentially threatening to their perspective. Such rigidity counters the flexibility needed for creativity. At the very least, information gathering suffers. At worst, destructive conflict is incited. Furthermore, participants will not likely be aware that they are limiting themselves to a narrow perspective and blocking construction of complex ideas. To most observers, they will simply appear to be disagreeing with each other, showing yielding, dominating or compromising.

Researchers examining creativity promote the opposite —that different perspectives and information are actively sought. Multicultural teams tasked with innovation must somehow respond to difference with openness and curiosity rather than closed defensiveness. They must initiate the practice that William Gordon termed compressed conflict—to force themselves to perceive an object or concept from two or more frames of reference; in short, perspective-taking. This is similar to a creative negotiation process. Researcher Rackham found that the best negotiators listened actively to ensure understanding, while less effective were more likely to argue. Those intent on innovation must be encouraged to engage in dialogue and even controversy with each other regarding their ideas, opinions, assumptions, experience and perspective.

Some experts say that creativity requires conflict (Deutsch and Coleman, 2000). To create top quality innovation, those involved must not only be open and curious about new ideas but actively work to maximize diverse possibilities and sustain vigorous critique of those options—not to destroy or discard, but to further create.

Somehow innovators must find ways to avoid or effectively address the hesitation, judgment and doubt that often arise when truly fresh ideas emerge. Otherwise, innovative efforts will be inhibited and possibly defeated. In response to these challenges, this chapter advocates schooling in the best of collaboration. In the author's experience, skilled collaboration is proving itself as an effective facilitator of innovation with multicultural teams. Perspective taking is just one example of its helpful approach and tools. While collaboration does not ensure innovation, team members trained to skillfully cooperate are better equipped to avoid defensive and destruc-

tive reactions. At the very least, they will share a commitment to active exploration rather than mere judgment and reaction. Bringing diverse people together to work on a common goal can start to break down deeply held stereotypes and other negative reaction. Varied research projects, including Prisoner's Dilemma, mixed motive and "generous tit for tat" mathematical research, demonstrate that maximizing gains to self interest occurs with strategic cooperation (Bevir, 2007). In other words, even if team members do not create stunning innovation, their collaborative abilities will likely benefit the business bottom line through enhanced and even custom designed responsiveness to long term institutional priorities.

The author would like to share an observation from her experience guiding diverse multicultural teams. It is possible that her students, who chose to study conflict resolution, and her clients, who hire a conflict consultant, demonstrate, through these choices, a capacity to embrace complexity, unpredictability, and ambiguity. Occasionally, though, the author has worked with individuals who appear to lack such capacity. These individuals are threatened by open dialogue and difference. They often seek one "right" answer rather than creative construction of multiple models and possibilities. Business may need to begin its innovation process by doing some type of psychological assessment. This would determine if employees are capable of embracing complexity and uncertainty; most importantly, of taking the risk and initiative of imagining what has not existed before. Employees who are smug or simply satisfied with the status quo, who are generally passive, perhaps lacking in confidence and waiting for someone else's lead, or who generally focus on conforming and pleasing, will not be well suited to innovation. Some level of confidence, tolerance for ambiguity and frustration, and dissatisfaction with, or at least the ability to question, the status quo is requisite.

The following section will introduce right and left brain research and discuss how both are necessary for the highest quality innovation. Not all employees are suited for both. It may be that a business decides to ask its more open minded free thinkers to create ideas and its more conservative and judgmental employees to critique ideas. During Barack Obama's election, scientists studying the neurobiology of politics at the University of California, Los Angeles and New York University reported that liberals tolerate ambiguity and conflict better than conservatives because of how their brains work. Conservatives tend to block what they perceive to be "distracting" information. Frank Sulloway, a researcher at the University of California Berkeley's Institute of Personality and Social Research, says that based on the results of this study, he believes liberals should be expected to more readily accept new ideas (Gellene, 2008).

INNOVATION'S REQUISITE AND DISPARATE FUNCTIONS

Readers are likely familiar with what is called the "left" or rational brain and the "right" or intuitive brain. The first describes logical analysis, either/or thinking with one right answer requiring evidence and comparison against standards of performance, like what is found in science and law. The second is less systematic. It may involve flashes of unexplained insight, emotional reactions, subjective use of imagination, and artistic expression---all that business case studies attempt to stimulate as they are necessary for innovation. The best of innovation in business, however, must also be scrutinized by the left brain at some point.

The collaborative dispute resolution attitudes and skills promoted throughout this chapter require both the left and right brains and guide their optimal use. First participants are led in creating a safe and supportive environment encouraging and validating the right brain's subjective unique expression without judgment or critique. In-depth understanding is the goal. The step by step process asks for myriad alternatives before engaging the left brain in its rigorous evaluation.

In looking at diversity's relationship with innovation, a natural and fascinating question is whether different business functions and cultures exhibit different strengths in relationship to the right and left brains. Years ago, for example, the Massachusetts Institute of Technology compared Indian and American mathematicians and found that the Indian professionals often solved mathematical equations quickly in a flash of apparent intuition and use of the right brain. Americans, in contrast, were more likely to solve the same problems step by step through the application of equations. Does this mean that certain cultures are more left brained and others right brained? It appears that professional functions express a dominant preference and skill. Engineers are predictably logical and pragmatic while designers more nonverbally oriented with graphic descriptions. For the purposes of this chapter, what matters most is the appreciation that difference enhances creative process and is more likely to lead to true innovation.

SAFETY, UNDERSTANDING AND ACCEPTANCE ARE LIKELY PRECURSORS TO THE EMERGENCE OF UNTESTED IDEAS

It is inherently contradictory to pressure employees into independent thinking as part of conforming to company culture. Business aspiring to nourish innovation must find a way to effectively embrace this dilemma. Scholar Goleman has found that business nurturing the best of innovation hire and sustain employee self initiative. The rewards can be rich. Visionary initiative regularly creates unexpected opportunities. Business leaders who can operate flexibly, with access to people and networks that can be mobilized quickly, mirror the behavior of star employees.

In the author's experience, facilitative mediation often builds the employee confidence needed to exercise the enterprising self initiative described above. Furthermore, it is a popular process with unique capacity to bridge difference. Mediation, as described throughout this chapter, guides creative problem-solving's step by step process and intimately addresses the common obstacles to innovation encountered in diverse teams and organizations.

In interviewing experts around the world, the author quickly learned that prohibitive difference goes far beyond the vast ethnic differences involved with transnational business. Some of the greatest challenges global practitioners face include finding ways to effectively transcend professional and functional differences such as conflicting philosophies and goals. To begin, many, if not most, business employees are not schooled in the assumptions and approaches of collaboration. Instead, they come to a collective process prepared to promote their function's perspective rather than listen to the others present. One of the global experts interviewed by this chapter's author, for example, mentioned that scientists and engineers too often see their mandate and achievement as exclusive rather than shared and collective (Erbe, 2006). They are prepared to compete rather than cooperate—at least when asked to work with non-engineers and scientists. Scholar Naomi Roht-Arriza describes a similar dilemma. She sees difference in professional vocabulary, biases, mandates and goals as inhibiting development projects world wide (Roht-Arriza, 2004). At their worst, perspectives are myopic and approaches rigid—destined to incite conflict, defensive reaction and distance rather than productive relations.

Fortunately, as mentioned above and described throughout this chapter, facilitative mediation has inherent capacity to bridge difference, without asking any of the players to change their approach. It creatively builds through the very difference that would otherwise block innovation. It begins to do this by asking all participants to start their creative process focusing on perspective taking, or getting to know and understand all

present. Perspective taking describes the popular "walking in another's shoes," or attempting to see through another's eyes and experience. "(O)ne encourages the other to communicate. One allows free expression, seeks understanding and avoids value judgments that stifle. One shows desire and capacity to listen without anticipating, interfering…warping meanings into preconceived interpretations. Assumptions and prejudgments are minimized" (Johannesen, 1996). In the global evaluation mentioned earlier, such perspective taking was one of the most lauded cross cultural practices, particularly in Cameroon and throughout the Balkans. Many students of conflict process, as well as participants, see facilitative mediation as naturally promoting cultural understanding through emphasis on storytelling. Hearing others humanizes them. In the process elaborated here, participants normally report increased appreciation for each other and corresponding growth in positive climate

Participants are further coached in consciously suspending judgment and thus avoiding reactive blocks. In studying groups, scholar Gibb found defensive communication and climate in response to criticism, judgment, other evaluation and even "cold silence" and non-response. Not surprisingly, he concluded that such groups wasted more time with ego protecting discussions and accomplished less than more supportive groups. Consequently, a conscious commitment to suspending judgment is the first step to creating a climate where innovation can flourish.

In the author's advanced classes, suspending judgment has been the most popular choice in naming helpful behaviors. (Erbe, 2003). It has been three times more popular than any other behavior. Likewise, in the evaluative survey of multicultural group process mentioned earlier, positive climate was listed as the second most important requirement for an effective experience (Erbe, 2004). Respect was the most popular way of describing this positivism. Other words used included support, serious interest and concentration, concern, trust, a cooperative attitude, empathy, humane and "good spirit." Psychologist Carl Rogers used the term unconditional regard. After a lifetime of research, he named unconditional regard as instrumental to growth. When suspension of judgment is consistently ensured, group members feel free to test out ideas without fear of stigma. Conversely, the worst members of cross cultural process are evaluated as lacking deep understanding (Erbe, 2004). They are criticized for failing to suspend judgment and otherwise demonstrating insensitivity to others.

Students' second recommendation is to show a true desire to understand culture in its depth and encouragement to share uniqueness. One of their comments follows. "If something confuses you, there is nothing wrong with asking!...You might not understand most things that are done in a certain culture but the other person will appreciate [your willingness] to try to understand. All it takes is a little bit of enthusiasm. Being enthusiastic about the differences and the wonder of another's culture is a wonderful thing. The feelings will be reciprocated." Related recommendations include giving sufficient time and patience to speakers whose first language is not English. Also advised is noticing nonverbal feedback regarding group members' discomfort and responding to ensure comfort.

Suspension of judgment is promoted above for encouraging group members to speak freely and thus allow innovation to emerge. It also plays a vital role in guiding the open mindedness necessary to fully understand another's perspective. "A party gives recognition...when: He realizes that he feels secure enough to stop thinking exclusively about his own situation and to focus to some degree on...the other...He consciously lets go of his own viewpoint and tries to see things through the other's perspective (Bush and Folger, 1994)."

Related to open mindedness are the flexibility and willingness to change one's perspective with new information. Research shows that the opposite, or misunderstanding, results from closed minds filled with prejudice, judgment and pre-

conceived assumptions (Erbe, 2004). All cognitive bias precludes actual experience with and an opportunity to get to know another. By chosing to defend what is familiar rather than focusing on learning what is new, less true information is received.

Of course, if open minded and flexible perspective taking of differences was easy it would occur more readily. The author would like to share some of her proven practices for building a positive climate where group members feel comfortable and safe with beginning to explore their difference. Surprising but true, in the face of prospective ethnic tension, members of multicultural groups appreciate and request an easy going spirit including fun, play and humor. If group members can find a way to enjoy each other while exploring difference, this spirit will likely further enhance creativity and innovation. Some call play the midwife of creativity. It encourages imagination, hopefully reduces inhibitions and other mental constraints, and at the very least, assists innovators in relaxing with each other.

The author provides multicultural groups with a few structured activities to begin creating a friendly, fun and low risk environment. In one, over one hundred statements describe various cultural approaches to communication and decision making. Group members are asked to pick or create multiple statements describing their own approaches, as well as a few statements which describe the opposite of their style. Participants then mingle, introduce their cultural preferences and attempt to rid themselves of all statements not describing their approach. The point of this game is to become acquainted with differences in a fun spirited activity and start to identify commonalities within the group. Group members usually build light hearted rapport and comfort with each other and discover that difference can be quite stimulating. Once surviving open acknowledgment and articulation of difference, confidence grows. Participants normally start to see the intriguing and creative potential found within difference.

If nothing else, by beginning time together with elucidation of difference, the resultant knowledge benefits later creative exploration.

In another popular exercise, participants are encouraged to use visual, descriptive, poetic, and even musical, metaphor to introduce their cultural perspective. This activity actively embraces the creative expression and exploration found with innovation. If participants limit themselves to rational analysis and thought alone, they will often simply revisit what has already been discovered rather than ask and see something rare and unique. Fortunately, "(p)eople are story-making creatures who long used symbols and images to convey meaning and identity" (LeBaron, 2005).

The most innovative, productive and successful employees appear to be found within organizations consistently exhibiting a strong regard for employees. Harvard political scientist Putnam has developed the concept of social capital to describe the difference observed between effective and ineffective organizational governance (Reuben, 2005). Strong social capital describes public trust of institutions and resultant connection, cooperation (reciprocity) and civic virtue. In contrast, less effective governance correlates with distrust, unhealthy competition and alienation.

Researchers of organizational behavior have carried this study of social capital into the workplace. Their research documents the value of management behavior like responsiveness, or listening to and implementing employee ideas, investment in priority common interests, and investment in the employee interests that matter most to them. Other studies show that institutions can retain employees through listening to and implementing employee ideas as well as investing in their interests. Such a contemporary workplace is posited as a collaborative partnering between employees and employers. Both are stakeholders "sharing strengths for mutual gain" as long as their individual interests are served. Loyalty and job security become irrelevant if counter to self-interest. As a result, employers are more attuned to employee's authentic needs.

Only a minimal or surface level of social capital can be mandated in the workplace. Civic virtues like respect and cooperation must be inspired and nurtured rather than forced (Cohen, 2001). Even if organizational policy commands polite behavior, such policy would be difficult to enforce. Assuming organizational stakeholders are successfully intimidated, the resultant social capital will likely fall far short of that encouraged by reciprocal respect. Thus, as with legal influence, organizational influence is at its best when it mediates rather than dictates social capital.

Until a business creates strong social capital, however, it must somehow create an environment where employees feel safe and secure in expressing themselves freely. One scholar describes the requisite state as relaxed but alert. Achieving this ease can be particularly challenging in times of economic insecurity and frequent employment turnover. Compounding these natural stresses, in an organizational survey conducted last year, the greatest reported challenge was confronting historically abusive working environments—the sad but true opposite of the social capital described above. (Note: For readers needing to tackle abusive dynamics as a prerequisite to building social capital and conditions where innovation flourishes, the author advises reading her book listed in references and the articles written on ombuds practice).

One way that business can begin building its social capital in order to attract and retain stellar innovators is to create an organizational ombuds office responsible for responding to employee concerns. The very best ombuds have a reputation for compassion and support—exactly what is needed to create the environment promoted here. The term "Organizational Ombudsman" was first used by Mary Rowe of the Massachusetts Institute of Technology in the mid-1980's. Rowe defined the term as: "... a confidential and informal information resource, communications channel, complaint-handler and dispute resolver, and a person who helps an organization work for change" (Rowe, 1995). In recent years, transnational corporations have been one of the main places where organizational ombuds can be found (Erbe and Sebok, 2008). In onesurvey, organizational ombuds indicated that their second most popular role was training employees in the collaborative skills described throughout this chapter.

Another small step towards creating the safety needed for innovation to flourish is to give working teams the authority to create their own process parameters. Their purpose is ensuring that all participants feel comfortable and respected with open expression of ideas and opinions. Team members may decide, for example, to agree to confidentiality—that creative ideas will not be linked with team member names until management has demonstrated unequivocal buy-in. Such ground rules, or negotiated understandings, can respect and include all personal and cultural norms equally. Thus they create a solid multicultural foundation that helps everyone feel comfortable.

OPTIMAL MULTICULTURAL PROCESS IS INCLUSIVE WITH EQUAL PARTICIPATION BUILT ON COMMON GROUND

Once group members begin to know each other through low risk activities like those described earlier, they often recognize similarities, or common ground, as well as difference. These commonalities offer a resilient platform for multicultural process since they are pre-existing and will endure beyond the group process (Lowy & Littlejohn, 2006). Researcher Rackham, mentioned earlier, found that the best of negotiators zealously search for common ground. It is even more important that multicultural innovators be guided and encouraged to continually recognize and explicitly express what they share and how they resonate to prepare them to handle difference.

Hearing their commonality validated over and over again inspires confidence in the group. Publicly recognizing common ground can also shift the group members' perceptual frame of reference from separate individuals to a collective unity.

One of the author's students specifically found that her group's task performance was enhanced by first taking the time to discover common connection (Davis, 2001). She believes that relationship building and mutual support must begin before facing collective challenge. Once group members effectively built alliance so that they trusted each other, she found less defensiveness and improved communication and understanding. Group members were able to openly share complaints and critique with each other. In her words, everyone seemed to contribute ideas and accept critiques without ego.

This inclusive democratic approach to process strongly promotes creativity. No one is asked to conform to another's norm or change their uniqueness in any way. No opinion is discounted or ignored. Instead, difference is already seen, from the very beginning of working together, as richly enhancing the group experience.

Researchers Sternberg and Williams found that the most effective corporate groups emulate this democratic process. Innate intelligence and talent do not matter as much as equal participation of team members—that no one dominates and no one refuses to participate. Sternberg and Williams' findings match the author's global evaluation of multicultural groups. Respondents described the best cross cultural experience as including all voices and encouraging active and serious participation. If a business has the organizational ombuds office introduced earlier, it might consider asking the ombuds to facilitate an impartial process that balances power and participation so that all levels of employees feel safe and encouraged. Some ombuds describe this as multipartiality: commitment to the best interests of all.

An alternative meeting forum available when higher and lower status employees are asked to be part of an innovation team and lower status employees do not feel safe is anonymous computer mediated discussion. Research has found that computers create a democratic environment where all feel comfortable with participation and open expression. The downside of this approach, though, is that participants report less satisfaction with its impersonal approach.

SKILLED LISTENING "MINES FOR GOLD"

Once an innovation team feels safe with each other and its dynamics mirror those described above, the discovery process can begin. The cross cultural model promoted here organizes a structured step by step process, with myriad tools, beginning with careful listening, or what one scholar calls the deep capacity to understand unarticulated needs (Skarzynski and Gibson, 2008). Active listening is taught at several levels, including the deeper level of meaning. Interest analysis, which at its best discerns unarticulated needs, became quite popular in the dispute resolution world when Roger Fisher and William Ury of the Harvard Negotiation Project promoted interest based bargaining (Fisher and Ury, 1991). In depth identification of the interests and needs underlying a particular problem, challenge, conflict or decision is promoted as the basis for stimulating generation of creative ideas.

Related to interest identification is another skill emphasized by creativity and innovation scholars: validation, or the ability to leverage assets—process, business and industry, appreciate individual contributions, and celebrate successes (Kennedy and Barker, 2008). Assets include all employee and organizational strengths, talents and interests (Barge, 2001). Careful listening alone can provide the most potent of validation. "Gratitude at being heard transcends all cultures...This recognition leads to empowerment "(Author's student).

In accord with principles of behavioral reinforcement, students of conflict resolution are taught to consciously stress the positive meaning and need underlying any message no matter how destructive or inappropriate it may initially sound. Through reframing "toxic" language, they mine for implicit veins of gold and bring them forward, while leaving disrespectful and hostile material behind. They also learn the power of not reacting with reciprocity to perceived criticism and misunderstanding.

In talking to students, the author has found that the practice of frequent and conscious validation of all group members, through reframing and other practice, is fundamental to their feeling of safety and trust with each other (Erbe and Smith, 2008). In contrast, the normal human being often emphasizes his or her point of view while minimizing or ignoring others' contribution. Such ethnocentrism deadens both multicultural rapport and innovative risk-taking.

To prevent impasse, students of cooperative group work are also taught concrete ways to express themselves assertively rather than aggressively. As one example, they learn to use "I statements" rather than "you statements." By taking responsibility for their own opinions and ideas, they are less likely to be heard as criticizing or attacking another group member.

Another skill involved with careful listening and linked with creativity and innovation is the ability to pose a good, challenging, and astutely insightful question. "The word *question* is derived from the Latin *quaerere* (to seek), which is the same root as the word for *quest*. A creative life is a continued quest, and good questions are useful guides. We have found that the most useful questions are open ended: they allow a fresh, unanticipated answer to emerge" (Goleman, 1992). In Rackham's research, the most skillful negotiators asked two to three times more questions than the less successful. Students of conflict process are taught to frame collaborative questions to stimulate as many creative ideas as possible. They do this through explicitly incorporating the articulated and unarticulated interests they have identified in a particular context. For example, if the group is attempting to generate ideas for making General Motors cars more environmentally friendly and popular with a new generation of customers, they would frame this sentence as an open ended question, asking how can General Motors make its cars more environmentally compatible and popular with its youngest consumers?

Creativity researcher Gruber posits that "having a novel point of view is the main thing." The skilled perspective taking introduced earlier, when paired with stellar listening that combines active paraphrasing, validation, reframing and excellent questioning, fully allows and encourages novel points of view. All involved with a particular project generously attend to deeply understanding, recognizing and encouraging each and every point of view. Collaborative process expects that diverse stakeholders will define what is desired in highly subjective ways. Perspectives are consciously mined and reframed in search of creative ideas.

SKILLED TEAMS ARE THE PROVEN INNOVATION LEADERS

After custom framing of collaborative questions to stimulate ideas, team members then use common brainstorming and visioning processes to create actual ideas. Once again, it is critically important that they suspend judgment and proceed with open minds. They must delay critique of ideas until several are created. The author of brainstorming, Osborn, proposed these guidelines: 1) suspend judgment, 2) the more unique the idea, the better, 3) go for quantity and speed (to circumvent judgment), 4) have fun, and 5) build off of each other's ideas. His emphasis on quantity is validated by Rackham's research which found that the best negotiators considered at least twice as many ideas as lesser negotiators. Once again, the right questions can stimulate brainstorming, asking how about…? what if…? has anyone considered…? and has anyone heard what they did…? Some

practical recommendations for creating ideas include, once again, noting and building from areas of commonality, starting "easy," and validating the ideas given.

Creativity researcher Gruber, like collaborative conflict process, stresses the importance of imagination in discovering, constructing or inventing alternatives. This is where all struggles inherent in cooperative group work bear fruit. Research shows that teams generate more alternatives than individual innovators, suggesting the power of collective imagination.

Contextual safety is still important. Alternatives that pose minimal threat are the most likely to go forward. The advent of computer assisted groups is particularly interesting when studying generation of alternatives, especially unique ideas. Studies have found that the anonymity provided in computer facilitated group discussions can increase the number and uniqueness of ideas. Despite the lack of anonymity and resultant risk, however, team participants still report higher satisfaction in face-to-face meetings. Apparently, team members' social needs are more important to them than promised safety. Yet, since generation of innovative ideas may occur more often with anonymous computer mediated discussion, a combination of face to face and computer discussions might prove optimal.

At the very least, structured collaborative process insists on generation and evaluation of multiple alternatives, countering the human tendency to quickly accept the first plausible alternative available—even when relatively unsatisfactory. To a certain degree, structured cooperative process asks for the in-depth prolonged engagement linked with the most creative and highest quality innovations.

At some point in a creative process, innovators must be "forced" to synthesize their ideas, or somehow integrate divergent pieces and perspectives into a holistic progression. The collaborative process described here does this, insisting that participants do their utmost to reach agreement after rigorous evaluation of their ideas. Once again, cooperative teams show enhanced ability to do such evaluation and creation, being open to each other's ideas and suggestions and thus profiting from the differences present in their groups. Being able to embrace group members' scrutiny deepens analysis.

CONCLUSION

As described throughout this chapter, when collaborative group work is effective, the creative process is enriched. This is particularly so with multicultural teams. More ideas result. Additional resources are present and offered. Social support encourages creative synergy that maximizes use of the talents and skills present. To arrive at this optimal place, however, many skills are required, including communication, perspective taking, validation and trust building. Even more important, control of egocentrism is required. Somehow open mindedness and curiosity must be created and nurtured.

In working with several companies in crisis over the last decade, the author is struck by the disconnect and distance between innovation rhetoric and realities. Scholars urge organizations to find the new question while diverse workforces keep many new questions to themselves. The newness being sought is often already present. The global workplace is rich in the variables needed for innovation. Is business, in truth, actually afraid to let the fresh idea emerge?

As the author's students and clients risk intimacy, they quickly feel enthusiasm and intrigue. They face their fear and become authentically curious about learning more. Difference is not difficult when approached with an open mind. When commonalities resonate and differences are validated, all feel welcome, accepted and valued. Such relationship building lays the foundation for candid dialogue and critique. Collaborative conflict process provides structure that sustains

engagement enough to mine the riches of the global world.

Those who have studied creativity and innovation find that the aforedescribed level of optimism is a requisite variable. Without the confidence that employees can face uncertainty and frustration, innovation is unlikely to happen. Disagreement, misunderstanding, and even impasse are often reported before novel perspective.

Group facilitators are hired to observe team dynamics and make suggestions to improve process. Innovation teams, however, can be trained to observe and evaluate themselves. This is called reflective practice, developing the habit of self and other observation (witnessing), evaluating the impact and success of various behaviors, and attempting on-going improvement (Oetzel & Ting-Toomey, 2006). In effect, team members are asked to persist in continually innovating their own process, striving for optimal relationships and results.

The organizational ombuds introduced earlier are optimally experts in generating alternatives and facilitating others' exploration of alternatives. The most seasoned ombuds are purportedly experts in all the collaborative skills described in this chapter, including mediation. They can serve as resourceful models and teachers for all of a business' constituencies. The most important skills include reframing and persuading others to one's perspective in ways that strengthen rather than jeopardize relationships. Developing some ombuds' uncanny intuitive radar to sense the unspoken may ignite the innovative insight.

Businesses that commit to employee mastery of the above skills can look forward to becoming bold pioneers. They may even become known for having the capacity to dare what others cannot. These cooperative skills, while foundational for encouraging innovation, are also the best of conflict resolution and prepare business to harness their assets proactively in ways that will only enhance reputation and competitive edge.

REFERENCES

Barge, K. (2001). Integrating theory, research and practice in select conflict contexts: creating healthy communities through affirmative conflict communication (pp. 92-93). *Conflict Resolution Quarterly, 19*(1), 89–101.

Bevir, M. (2007). *Encyclopedia of governance.* Thousand Oaks, CA: Sage.

Bordens, K., & Abbott, B. (1999). *Research design and methods.* Mountain View, CA: Mayfield Publishing.

Bush & Folger. (1994). *The promise of mediation.* San Francisco: Jossey Bass.

Cohen, J. (2001). When people are the means: negotiating with respect. *The Georgetown Journal of Legal Ethics, 14*, 739–802.

Deutsch, M. (1973). *The resolution of conflict: constructive and destructive processes.* New Haven, CT: Yale University Press.

Deutsch, M., & Coleman, P. (2000). *The handbook of conflict resolution: theory and practice.* San Francisco, CA: Jossey-Bass.

Druckman, D. (2005). *Doing research: methods of inquiry for conflict analysis.* Thousand Oaks, CA: Sage.

Dundon, E. (2002). *The seeds of innovation: cultivating the synergy that fosters new ideas.* New York: AMACOM.

Erbe, N. (2003) Holding these truths: empowerment and recognition in action (interactive case study curriculum for multicultural dispute resolution. Berkeley, CA: Berkeley Public Policy Press.

Erbe, N. (2004). The global popularity and promise of facilitative adr. *Temple International and Comparative Law Journal, 18*(2), 345–371.

Erbe, N. (2006). Appreciating mediation's global role in promoting good governance. *Harvard Negotiation Law Review, 11*, 370–419.

Erbe, N., & Sebok, T. (2008). Shared global interest in skillfully applying ioa standards of practice. *Journal of the International Ombudsman, 1*, 28–38.

Erbe, N., & Smith, R. (2008, October). *Falling in Love With Teaching and Learning: Proven Activities for Engaging Diverse Students in Collaborative Learning.* Paper presented at the annual meeting of the International Society for Teaching and Learning, Las Vegas, Nevada.

Fink, D. (2003). *Creating significant learning experiences.* San Francisco: Jossey-Bass.

Fisher, R., & Ury, W. (1991). *Getting to yes: negotiating agreement without giving in.* New York: Penguin Books.

Gellene, D. (2008, September 10). Study finds left-wing brain, right-wing brain. *Los Angeles Times.*

Goleman, D. (1997). *Emotional intelligence.* New York: Bantam.

Johannesen, R. (1996). Ethics in human communication (pp. 67-68). Prospect Heights, Il: Waveland Press.

KEY TERMS AND DEIFINITIONS

Collaboration: Working with; willing cooperation.

Commonality: Shared interest, need or any other feature/ attribute.

Diversity: A variety; the state of being varied; including myriad distinct things or people.

Mediation: Any force, outside of a conflict, that assists with that conflict; a structured problem solving process.

Multicultural: Relating to or constituting many cultural or ethnic groups, traditions and approaches.

Perspective Taking: Understanding another's frame of reference or way of viewing things, as well as the underlying experience and personality.

Reframing: In conflict process, changing a description to emphasize the essential content or meaning productively or positively.

Chapter 15
Managing Corporate Social Responsibility as an Innovation in China

Maria Lai-Ling Lam
Malone University, USA

ABSTRACT

Many foreign multinational enterprises (MNEs) focus on legal compliance and charity in their corporate social responsibility (CSR) programs in China. The strategic approach of CSR requires many innovations that are new to the organizations adopting them. The key barriers for the strategic approach of CSR are the apathy attitude of many executives toward CSR and the shortcomings of the institutional framework in China. This chapter describes a few innovative CSR initiatives being utilized within an industrial association and within partnerships between local non-government organizations. It also explores institutional incentives for managing the process by using the social movement theory. It may inspire foreign MNEs to improve the CSR practices of their affiliated companies and their suppliers in China through a few social innovations. Corporations also learn how to engage in social change through their CSR programs in China.

INTRODUCTION

In China, corporate social responsibility (CSR) has been initiated by the government with the purpose of creating a "harmonious" society. The Chinese government is interested in establishing competitive business environments, promoting social cohesion, and fostering collective responsibility for the betterment of society through the CSR programs of

foreign multinational enterprises (MNEs) (Ho, 2005; van Rooij, 2006; Aguilera, Rupp, Williams, and Ganapathi, 2007; Financial Times, 2008). MNEs are expected to be very effective vehicles to improve CSR practices of their affiliated companies and suppliers in China (OECD, 2000; Murdoch & Gould, 2004; Tateisi, 2004; World Business Council for Sustainable Development, 2005; Asia Monitor Resource Center, 2006; China Finance Economic Company, 2006; Welford, 2006; APEC Human Resources Development Working Group Capacity

DOI: 10.4018/978-1-61520-643-8.ch015

Building Network, 2007; China Entrepreneurs Survey System, 2007).

However, the author found nine foreign MNEs in China focused primarily on economic responsibility and the society and legal compliance in their CSR programs (Lam, 2007). These nine Chinese subsidiaries were mainly in the "compliance stage"—'adopt a policy-based compliance approach as a cost of doing business' (Zadek, 2004). These Chinese subsidiaries must learn how to move beyond their "compliance stage" if they would like to engage in social changes through their CSR programs in China. They must be innovative when they initiate to move beyond their "compliance stage" and learn to treat CSR as their core business decisions and strategies in China in which there are neither strong and well-enforced governmental regulations nor strong private independent organizations to monitor the behavior of foreign MNEs (Daft, 1978; Damanpour, 1991; Lyon, 2004; Zadek, 2004; Mirvis and Googins, 2006). What institutional incentives can be used to enable foreign MNEs to embed and integrate societal issues in their core management processes and business strategies respectively? Are there any innovative CSR initiatives in China? What values, attitudes, perceptions, competences and patterns of behavior of Chinese executives need to have when their corporations develop their CSR programs are strategic, well-integrated with their existing business operations?

This chapter is concerned with the development of corporate social responsibility (CSR) in the Chinese subsidiaries from the "compliance stage" to "managerial or strategic stage." The development involves many organization innovations when CSR programs are strategically managed in the pursuit of competitive advantages in China. It builds upon the author's ongoing studies with Chinese expatriates concerning the United States and China business negotiations (Lam, 2000; 2003; 2004; 2005) and the transfer of CSR from foreign MNEs to Chinese subsidiaries (Lam, 2007; 2008; 2009a). It is based on an extensive

literature review, three years' field work in China, Japan, and U.S., and personal reflections. Thirty Chinese and Japanese executives who are involved in the CSR practices in China and Japan between 2006 and 2008 were interviewed. Nineteen foreign MNEs: seven Japanese companies, seven American companies, two German companies, one American-China joint venture, one Belgium, and one Canadian company were studied. Data gathered from the interviews were compared to the corporate social responsibility reports, literature reviews, and interviews of researchers and consultants. The author talked with more than fifty Chinese executives and fifty graduate students about their expectations for foreign multinational enterprises in various cities in China including Chongqing, Dalian, Qingtao, Zhejiang, Nanjing, Shanghai, Beijing and Hong Kong. They represented the normative beliefs about CSR adopted by foreign MNEs.

The chapter is organized as follows: The first section reviews the literature about the strategic approach of CSR and discusses why the approach is innovative to many foreign MNEs in China. The second section describes the findings about the development of CSR in China and the internal and external barriers of adopting strategic approach of CSR in China. The third section describes a few innovative CSR initiatives. The fourth section explores institutional incentives for managing CSR as an innovation in China by using the social movement theory. The fifth section discusses the implications to foreign enterprises in China.

LITERATURE REVIEW

Corporate social responsibility (CSR) is defined as any corporate action that "benefit society beyond the requirements of the law and the direct interest of shareholders." (McWilliams and Siegel, 2001). Corporations are expected not only to fulfill economic and legal responsibilities but also ethical and philanthropic responsibilities (Carroll,

1991). Corporate social responsibility is regarded as the commitment of the corporations to "contribute to the sustained economic development by working with employees, their families, the local community, and the entire society in order to improve life quality (The World Business Council for Sustainable Development's definition of corporate social responsibility, 2005). The author (Lam, 2007) found that the Chinese executives' interpretations of CSR were much narrower than the above definitions of CSR. Quazi and O'Brien (2000:36) classified these Chinese executives' view point as "classical view of CSR" –"there is no provision to look beyond a narrow view of profit maximization as it is seen to generate a net cost to the company without any real benefit flowing from an activity."

Based on this "classical view of CSR", many leading MNEs are found to practice less corporate social responsible actions in developing countries even though they are legally mandated by their global supply chain partners (Abdul-Gafaru, 2006; Philipp, 2006; Rondineli, 2006). Many foreign MNEs only gain their legitimacy and reduce their risks by fulfilling minimum legal requirements in developing countries (Murdoch & Gould, 2004). Many foreign MNEs tend to increase their emphasis on the developed countries' CSR principles and to decrease their emphasis on the Chinese CSR principles when they are faced with more pressure from their consumers and investors in developed countries (Schepers, 2006). Some foreign MNEs appear to pay only lip service to environmental and labor welfare within their CSR programs and do not appear to be committed to monitoring the behavior of their suppliers in China. The tensions between the companies' social compliance auditing programs and their buying behavior in China can create false reports (Harney, 2008:205). Some companies set up a few "five star" factories to impress auditors while many products are being produced in other extremely poor environments. Many CSR programs and international codes are criticized as being marketing devices to mask the

problem of environmental degradation and social injustice in China (Sum & Ngai, 2005; Yu, 2006).

Some scholars propose that corporations will tend to start from a "compliance stage" and then move toward more strategic and innovative orientations to CSR (Zadek, 2004; Mirvis and Googins, 2006). Organizations must learn how to "embed the societal issues in their core management processes" in their "managerial stage" and gradually "integrate the societal issues into their core business strategies" in their "strategic stage" before they can "promote broad industry participation in corporate responsibility" in their "civil stage" (Zadek, 2004). It will be an innovative practice when these Chinese subsidiaries move from the elementary stage of corporate citizenship (i.e., focus primarily only on economic responsibility to the society and legal compliance) to the advanced stage of corporate citizenship (i.e., focus on stakeholder management, sustainability, and a change of game) according to the normative stage of corporate citizenship development by Mirvis and Googins (2006).

The process of the development of CSR from the "compliance stage" to "managerial stage" and "strategic stage" in China will include many innovations which are novel "devices, systems, policies, programs, products, or services" (Damanpour, 1991:556) and "new to the organization adopting them" (Daft, 1978:197). The development of CSR in China requires an organization culture that supports corporate responsibility in the daily operations. The organization culture includes rewards and recognition, learning and managing change, awareness and involvement, questioning culture and flexibility underpinned by mutual respect (Lyon, 2004).

During the process of development of CSR in China, companies must focus on the social impacts of their core activities in their value chain analysis and use CSR practices as their core competitive strategies (Porter and Kramer, 2002). They must maintain its relationships "with the broad matrix of society where there are net benefits flowing from socially responsible action in the long run, as well as in the short term" (Quazi and O'Brien 2000:36). They must develop strategic approach of CSR such that the cost of the CSR programs will be paid off (Burke and Logsdon, 1996). Strategic approach of CSR means to strategically manage the visibility, appropriability, voluntarism, centrality, and proactivity dimensions of CSR programs. Visibility means to increase the customers' and stakeholders' awareness of product with CSR value added. Appropriability means to manage stakeholder relationships to add values to the company. Voluntarism means to participate in social actions are beyond the requirements of the law. Centrality is to create product or service innovations that are linked to social issues. Proactivity is to capture market opportunities through anticipating social changes. Managers need to understand how to pursue value creation through CSR and develop strategic CSR in their business by focusing on different strategic dimensions of CSR programs (Husted and Allen, 2007). When CSR activities are integrated with existing business operations (i.e., corporate responsibility integration) and develop new business models for solving social and environmental problems (i.e., corporate responsibility innovation), CSR will be valuable to corporations and will not be diminished when the external economic situation is poor. CSR programs that emphasize corporate responsibility integration and corporate responsibility innovation will be treated as assets to many corporations (Kourula and Halme, 2008).

In summary, when foreign MNEs develop their CSR from "compliance stage" to "managerial" or "strategic stage" in China, their CSR programs will be strategic, well-integrated with existing business operations, valuable, and accountable to wide-range of stakeholders in China. Their Chinese executives will change from the "classical view to CSR" to the "modern view of CSR." Their corporations will learn how to embed the key societal issues in China in their daily operations through being engaged in various systems, policies, structures, and stakeholders. Their learning process includes experimentation and innovation in their corporate development of CSR in China. The strategic approach of CSR creating positive economic and social outcomes to corporations will be new to corporations that have treated CSR mainly as philanthropy or cost only. Corporate responsibility integration and innovation will be a new paradigm for many Chinese subsidiaries which are in the legal compliance stage in China.

According to the social movement theory, organization actors will initiate some innovative changes in the market when they perceive that they can actualize their available political opportunities, organization capacities, and group resources for collective actions. They will prioritize the external demands and deal with the power and politics within the organization and its relation to the environment (McAdam and Scott, 2005; McAdam, McCarthy and Zald, 1996). Thus, a group of companies with similar interests and a shared identity can easily actualize positive political opportunities and mobilize their group members to make social change through their CSR practices (Davis and Thompson, 2004). Thus, political opportunities, mobilizing structures and framing process are the three broad set of actors in analyzing the emergency and development of social movement (McAdam, McCarthy and Zald, 1996). The early innovators of CSR will change the rules of game in the market. They communicate their CSR practices to small and medium sized supply chain partners through high level of collaboration between MNEs' subsidiaries and supply chain partners in China (Wood and Kaufman, 2007). The followers may conform to similar CSR practices according to institutional theory (DiMaggio and Powell, 1983).

FINDINGS ABOUT THE DEVELOPMENT OF CSR IN CHINA

In this study, many interviewees tended to view corporate social responsibility (CSR) as charity, legal compliance, internal employee conduct, technical and operational efficiency of environmental activities, and public relationships. Internal employee conduct means to adhere to sound financial accounting principles, not to misuse funds designated for business purposes, and not to accept certain gifts or pay bribes. CSR programs were easily treated as political means for improving relationships with the local government. The executives, who were responsible for the CSR programs, were eager to get recognition from the Chinese government when they implemented some CSR programs. One interviewee admitted that the good relationships with the Chinese government led them to get many corporate citizenship awards. CSR was treated as an investment in the embedded party-state relationships rather than a strategic tool. Two interviewees confessed that their companies still searched for the CSR strategies even though their companies have published many CSR reports and received several CSR awards in China.

In general, many interviewees' interpretation of corporate social responsibility (CSR) was mainly related to the performance required by their corporations. They were described as "transactional leaders" who were primarily interested in "corporate *self*-interest" by van Tulder & van der Zwart (2006). They perceived that corporate social responsibilities should be implemented by designated departments or high-ranking leaders in their corporations. They could not see the possibility of inviting many stakeholders to respond to local demands as their responsibility and could not see responding to local demands as an important competitive strategy. Their narrow perspective of CSR was partly related to the economic development of China and strong internal control of Chinese subsidiaries by the MNEs. They were expected by their respective MNEs to maximize economic return and efficiency in China.

In the study, the major internal barriers of adopting strategic approach of CSR are the attitude and company culture toward CSR. Chinese executives

in foreign MNEs are largely ill-informed about the strategic approach of CSR or "modern view of CSR", how it works and what benefits can be derived from the implementation of broad stakeholders' management in the CSR programs. Many executives at functional areas tend to have apathy attitude towards CSR. The CSR practices are not integrated with the existing managerial decision making process. Many valuable insights and new shared understandings about the CSR programs among members of Chinese subsidiaries are not explored as new learning of MNEs due to the hierarchical structure of organizations (Crossan, Lane, and White, 1999).

Other barriers are the shortcomings of the institutional framework in China and the uncertainty about economic returns by adopting new approach of CSR. As the Chinese market is very price-competitive, many customers are not willing to pay premium prices for products or services with CSR components and companies would put themselves in a disadvantaged position according to the comment of one executive who works very hard to persuade her internal colleagues to accept the strategic approach of CSR. When the Chinese government has much control upon the local stakeholders, companies tend to use their CSR programs to please the Chinese government without incorporating CSR seriously in their core business and strategic plans. Many foreign MNEs do not like to have much cooperation with local non-government organizations and can easily rely on the local government to protect their economic interests and to discard many negative criticism from the local non-government organizations (Lam, 2009b). Thus, foreign MNEs do not face much pressure from the Chinese non-government organizations in their CSR programs. They tend to focus on reporting CSR activities rather than managing relationships with Chinese environmental NGOs even though they fulfill international environmental standards such as ISO 14001 and the Global Reporting Initiative Sustainability Reporting Guidelines (Lam, 2009c). There is no central governance structure to manage the activities of multinational enterprises in China (Zerk, 2006). Several executives told the researcher the companies wanted to do good to increase their share price in the U.S. market. Their companies can fulfill the requirements of international reports without describing their work in China in details. Companies that are small and are not so visible in the international market will not like to invest in CSR programs in China as CSR programs are very expensive to their companies (interviewees' data).

INNOVATIVE CSR INNITIATIVES

From the fieldwork, the author found a few foreign MNEs initiated some innovative CSR initiatives through the development of industry codes of conduct, industrial associations and partnerships with selected non-government organizations. These innovative CSR initiatives represent new business models for solving social and environmental problems. They are valuable to these corporations and will inspire other companies to know how to manage appropriability (i.e., add value through managing stakeholder relationships), voluntarism (i.e., participate in social actions beyond the requirements of the law), and centrality (i.e., create product or service innovations that are linked to social issues) in their CSR strategies (Burke and Logsdon, 1996; Husted and Allen, 2007).

Electronic Industry Codes of Conduct

Company A[1] initiated the development of electronic industry codes of conduct (EICC) and collaborated with members to adopt the codes. Company A seriously implemented the codes and developed their Chinese subsidiaries to have capacity to monitor the safety and development of their Chinese suppliers in the process of the development of CSR in China. Company A also developed the codes through their existing global

leadership network and partners in their current organization culture. The EICC also collaborated with other groups in the electronic sector and welcomed inputs from many stakeholders including non-government organizations. Thus, Company A could use its leverage upon existing resources and the linkage with existing international partners to foster the learning process of Chinese subsidiaries in the process of developing EICC and applying its EICC to its Chinese suppliers. In return, Company A's Chinese subsidiaries earned trust from their Chinese suppliers through their dedicated process to help their Chinese suppliers to understand the rationale behind the EICC and to participate in the global production network. The learning of Chinese subsidiaries could enable Company A to know how to mobilize their members to "collaborate to help ensure safe conditions, worker rights and environmental responsibility in the global electronics supply chain" (ECIC objective). As a result, their companies' Chinese executives experienced growth and learning through frequent communication with external partners in their industrial districts while they implemented the codes of conduct (Vaill, 2007). They learn good practices from their customers, suppliers, and professional bodies in their industry districts when there are close physical proximity to other members, linkage among various cliques, stable personal relationship, cooperative interactions, norms and rules to govern informal knowledge trading, and process-based trust embedded in social ties.

The Chinese workers in the electronic industry in general are better educated than those in the toy industry or garment industry. They can learn good practices from ECIC and improve their working conditions by themselves. Company A not only passes its knowledge of corporate social responsibility to its Chinese subsidiaries through its existing organization structure and culture, but also enables its subsidiaries to teach other Chinese suppliers about its corporate social responsibility programs. Through the practices of new norms, standards, and values in the ECIC, Company A's Chinese subsidiaries can develop strong internal culture and become better corporate citizens in China. Thus, the development of the industrial codes of conduct enables the company's Chinese executives to experience stable and cooperative relationships with external partners and non-government organizations in their industry districts.

An Association of Foreign Enterprises

An association of foreign enterprises has assisted the Chinese government during the past five years in drafting the new regulations for controlling certain polluting substances by providing comprehensive corporate data and sharing their companies' research on environmental issues. The five-year process of consultation and relationship building between the association and the Chinese government improved the enforceability and the acceptance of the new regulations (an interviewee). In return, these foreign MNEs can comply with the new regulations and also set up industry norms. The association is independent of the Chinese government and is highly self-regulated for the interests of their members. Chinese government officials are not held accountable to a particular company when they consult with the entire association. The association can mobilize their members to share their environmental data and information with the government. The members can represent their interest in government policy making and draft the environmental regulations. They also set up higher industry standards and norms. They not only implement efficient environmental programs in their operation systems but also invest in new equipment and human resources to fulfill higher environmental standards that are drafted through long-term collaboration work between the industry association and the government. Their companies can also set up realistic corporate social responsibility programs that correspond to the new regulations and the need of the local

and the central government. This is an example of a long-term politicized collaboration with the Chinese government and the industrial association in the area of environmental welfare in China.

The industry association is regarded as an non-government organization pursuing interest for their own members (van Tulder and Zwart, 2006). Many foreign MNEs in the association present environmental and labor welfare as an important sustainable strategy in their corporate social responsibility or environmental reports (The American Chamber of Commerce People's Republic of China, 2006; Japanese Foundation Beijing Office, 2008). Their reports show their legal compliance concerning the local environment, present helpful environmental information, and illustrate how their companies integrate their environmental commitment and financial bottom lines. Through the association, foreign MNEs can fashion common interests and common identities among collective actors for better environmental regulations. These foreign MNEs are encouraged to experiment some corporate practices that improve environmental welfare and pass their insights to the Chinese government through the association. Their learning among members are fostered through the association.

Partnership with Local Selected Non-Government Organizations

One foreign MNE developed a partnership with a local non-government organization (NGO) in the area of labor issues. The local NGO provided basic education which the company did not provide in headquarters and in subsidiaries in other countries. The company invested U.S. $2 for each worker's training per year. Through a series of programs, ten thousand factory workers were facilitated to develop a sense of belonging in the factories, dormitories, and the cities which they first encountered in their adult lives. Many line workers were between 17 to 20 years of age and had migrated from rural areas. These immigrant workers were restricted around the factory as they seldom got permanent residence in the cities in which they worked according to the government regulations. In general, factories were built in some new industrial areas where there are not many public facilities and entertainment for residents. The company provided public health, education, social security for the workers in the community. Social issues were part of the company's core business decision. In return, the company took up many genuine governmental responsibilities and fostered "harmonious society" that is heavily advocated by the Chinese government. The company transferred its experience to its Chinese suppliers and improved the suppliers' labor conditions through shared codes of conduct and numerous education and training in China. Thus, the partnership increased the capacity and learning of the Chinese subsidiaries, Chinese suppliers, and the headquarter. The program was primarily initiated by the moral consciousness of the leaders in the company and the external pressure from an international non-government organization about the labor conditions of its factories in China. The leaders took the criticism from the non-government organization seriously and explored possible alternatives to improve the turn-over rate of labors in China through their CSR programs. When the company succeeded in solving its labor problems in China, it transferred its experience to its Chinese suppliers as they encountered similar problems in China.

The above innovative CSR initiatives share some common characteristics. A few leaders from the foreign MNEs are committed to develop long term perspectives to manage the social and environmental issues in their daily practices with a wide range of stakeholders. They are willing to develop and nurture a few NGOs as long-term partners. The leaders have a passion for the environmental or labor welfare. The leaders initiate the CSR programs and develop trusting relationships with selected NGOs. The above innovative CSR practices can increase the participants' awareness of the strategic approach of CSR. These participants can be employees and external stakeholders such as suppliers. The participants also learn how to manage relationships with multiple stakeholders to add values to their corporations through CSR programs.

From the interviews, Chinese and Japanese executives who were involved in the innovative CSR practices always told the author about their learning from NGOs and labors whom they seldom had face to face interactions. One Japanese executive had to convince her headquarter to recognize the Chinese labor as part of the company's labor. She told the author many of her colleagues in Japan did not consider labor outside Japan as their colleagues even though these labor generate more than 50% of the corporate revenue. Her involvement in the strategic CSR practices enabled her to be an opinion leader in her headquarters and professional meetings about the improvement of labor conditions in China. Her practices might lead her Chinese subsidiaries to go beyond the existing economic and legal requirements. Thus, the above innovative CSR practices may change the prevailing perceptions of executives about CSR in China when these executives can see how innovative CSR practices can increase their companies' sustainable competitive advantage.

INSTITUTIONAL INCENTIVES FOR MANAGING CORPORATE SOCIAL RESPONSIBILITY AS AN INNOVATION IN CHINA

The institutional incentives will be derived from the interactions among political opportunities, mobilizing structure, and the framing strategies of foreign MNEs in the process of the development of CSR from the "compliance stage" to "managerial" and "strategic stage" in China. The conditions for foreign MNEs to initiate and adopt the innovative CSR practices are discussed as follows:

Positive Political Opportunities

Several foreign MNEs in the above innovative CSR initiatives mobilize their group members to have better social and environmental welfare in China through their industry codes of conduct and an industry association. They actualize the positive political opportunities available in China. These opportunities are: several CSR committees and Chinese CSR codes initiated by the Chinese government for national stability and "harmonious society", the increasing attention of key shareholders and international media upon China business and elite Chinese institutions upon CSR issues, and more Chinese entrepreneurs expect leading foreign MNEs to exemplify good practices in the industry, and there are more discussions on "social responsibility of Chinese MBA education" and conferences about social responsibility of corporations in China. Foreign MNEs can easily gain social and political capital by being key members in the Chinese CSR committees and maintain their dominate positions in the global production and marketing networks by fulfilling the higher standards of CSR initiated by the Chinese government. Through actualizing the positive political opportunities, foreign MNEs will develop product or service innovations that are closely related to the social issues that the Chinese government care.

Capacity of Mobilizing Structure

In the above innovative CSR initiatives, a few foreign MNEs mobilize their Chinese suppliers to follow CSR practices through higher level of collaboration between their companies and their suppliers in their industry network. There are frequent communication and shared identities among the members in a network of industry. These early adopters of innovative CSR initiative are those foreign MNEs being classified as global corporate citizens according to the definition of Logsdon and Wood (2005). These corporations are oriented to pursue their universal values through systematic implementation and accountability process in their subsidiaries (Logsdon and Wood, 2005). These organizations are capable to pass their environmental innovation in China when they have already experimented these innovations in their home countries and the values of environmental innovation are easily accepted by their expatriates from the headquarters.

When these few corporations initiate the adoption of environmental innovation through their CSR programs in China, they can request many small and medium Chinese enterprises in the supply chain network to adopt the practices through close communication (Wood and Kaufman, 2007). Some develop self-regulatory mechanism with other companies by fulfilling the environmental and social standards initiated by the international corporate responsibility organizations and international codes of conduct through their industry codes of conduct and their industrial association. These foreign multinational enterprises exert their influence upon their Chinese enterprises through their supply chain networks or industry codes of conduct. These few corporations recommend the Chinese government to adopt new environmental regulations or higher labor standards because these innovative CSR initiatives fulfill Roger's (2005) five attributes of innovation including relative advantage, compatibility, complexity, trialability, and observability. The small and medium enterprises use their network to learn these innovative CSR initiatives from these few early adopters (Halia, 2007). Corporations adopt innovative CSR initiatives because the return is higher than the cost, the innovation can be easily integrated with existing system, the employees are well-trained and have high-communication abilities, there are benchmarking similar companies implementing an environmental and labor innovation, and when the innovation is visible. In return, these innovative CSR initiatives foster the communication networks with various constituents in China and their Chinese subsidiaries are more responsive to local needs in China.

The Chinese executives who are responsible for CSR programs in China are like middle managers who are working as boundary spanners between their own organizations and external organizations. These Chinese executives' innovative abilities are confirmed by the unified view of working, learning, and innovating proposed by Brown and Duguid (1991). They can be innovative agents by accessing internal and external knowledge through their social capital. Many develop significant innovation and learning in their informal communities-of-practice in which they work, their insights can enable foreign MNEs to develop strategic approach of CSR and innovative CSR programs. However, they are frustrated as their voices are not heard by their headquarters. Foreign MNEs need to know how to motivate these executives to bring innovative practices to the corporations through their organizational incentives. Their organization culture should be proactive to CSR and respect the voices of their CSR managers when the companies want to develop from compliance stage to managerial and strategic stage of CSR in China. Thus, companies need to pass the values that drive the commitment to the strategic approach of CSR to the Chinese subsidiaries and their Chinese suppliers through some investments. These investments are personal transfer between their headquarters and their Chinese subsidiaries, low turnover of expatriates in the Chinese subsidiaries, shared visions and goals about CSR practices, accommodation of local Chinese culture and concerns of local staff, increased trust between Chinese employees and employers in the intracorporate networks (Inkpen and Tsang, 2005). Thus, the innovative CSR practices are integrated with the existing knowledge from the headquarters and be more responsive to the local needs when many unique experiences of CSR practices in China are acknowledged.

Framing Strategy

In the above innovative CSR initiatives, it is important for organization actors to choose framing strategies that can fashion common interests and common identities among collective actors for better corporate citizenship in China. The few foreign MNEs initiate higher environmental and social standards in their corporations. They use the standards as contributions to the members in their own industry and their suppliers. They also can use their contributions to national idea "harmonious society" to earn trust from their external stakeholders. When there is increasing trust between these foreign MNEs and their external stakeholders in China, they can leverage on these resources and invite these external stakeholders to hold them to be accountable to these higher standards.

IMPLICATIONS FOR FOREIGN MULTINATIONAL ENTERPRISES

Foreign multinational enterprises (MNEs) need to develop their CSR from the present "compliance stage" to "managerial stage" and "strategic stage" in China through adequate investment in their Chinese employees and organization culture. They must change their employees' "classical view of CSR" to "modern view of CSR" through internal change and stable and cooperative relationships with external stakeholders. They can prioritize the resources to actualize positive political opportunities provided by the "Guidelines on Corporate Social Responsibility" issued by the Chinese government. They can mobilize the members who share similar identities or interests with them, establish new rules of interacting with the government or other stakeholders, and increasingly contribute to an institutionalization of industry norms and regulations. In return, their innovative CSR initiatives can enable their own Chinese subsidiaries to move beyond the present economic and legal compliance stage in the corporate citizenship development by managing dynamic and complex relationships among foreign MNEs and governments or other stakeholders. As a consequence, much learning from stable and cooperative relationships with partners affect their internal organization culture and promote new learning among Chinese executives. When Chinese subsidiaries of foreign MNEs exemplify or communicate strategic CSR approaches to their partners in China, they can articulate the concept of social responsibility that responds to the needs of their headquarters and the local Chinese communities through frequent and honest communications among the members in a network of industry. They must continue to learn how to pursue value creation through strategic CSR programs. When foreign MNEs are committed to develop their CSR to be strategic, well-integrated with existing business operations, valuable, and accountable to wide-range of stakeholders in China, they will adopt many innovations that inspire their partners in China.

ACKNOWLEDGMENT

The author thanks Dr. Peter Vaill, Dr. Georgia L. Eshelman, Dr. Martha Cook, Lewis Lam, Alice Lam, Gretchen Sudar, Kaoru Hidaka, Stephen Frost, and many corporate executives for their helpful support.

REFERENCES

Abdul-Gafaru, A. (2006). Are multinational corporations compatible with sustainable development? The experience of developing countries. Paper presented at the *MESD 2006 International Research Colloquium*. Atlanta, GA.

Aguilera, R., Rupp, D., Williams, C., & Ganapathi, J. (2007). Putting the "S" back in corporate social responsibility: A multilevel theory of social change in organizations. *Academy of Management Review*, *32*(3), 836–863.

APEC Human Resources Development Working Group Capacity Building Network (2007). *Corporate Social Responsibility in the Global Supply Chain: An APEC case book*. Singapore: APEC Secretariat.

Asia Monitor Resource Centre. (2006). Retrieved August 14, from http://www.amrc.org.hk

Brown, J., & Duguid, P. (1991). Organization learning and communities-of-practice: Toward a unified view of working, learning, and innovation. *Organization Science*, *2*(1), 40–57. doi:10.1287/orsc.2.1.40

Burke, L., & Logsdon, J. (1996). How corporate social responsibility pays off. *Long Range Planning*, *29*, 495–502. doi:10.1016/0024-6301(96)00041-6

Carroll, A. (1991). The pyramid of corporate social responsibility: Toward the moral management of organizational stakeholders. *Business Horizons*, *34*, 39–48. doi:10.1016/0007-6813(91)90005-G

China Entrepreneurs Survey System. (2007). *Report on Chinese Entrepreneurs Growth and Evolution*. Beijing, China: China Machine Press. (in Chinese)

China Finance Economic Company. (2006). CSR report in China (in Chinese) The annual report of the Chinese Institute of Business Administration, 2005-2006, Beijing, China.

Christmann, P., & Taylor, G. (2001). Globalization and the environment: Determinants of firm self-regulation in China. *Journal of International Business Studies*, *32*(3), 439–458. doi:10.1057/palgrave.jibs.8490976

Crossan, M., Lane, H., & White, R. (1999). An organizational learning framework: From intuition to institution. *Academy of Management Review, 24*(3), 522–537. doi:10.2307/259140

Daft, R. L. (1978). A Dual-core model of organizational innovation. *Academy of Management Journal, 21*(2), 193–210. doi:10.2307/255754

Damanpour, F. (1991). Organization innovation: A meta analysis of effects of determinants and moderators. *Academy of Management Journal, 34*, 555–590. doi:10.2307/256406

Davis, G. F., & Thompson, T. A. (1994). A social movement perspective on corporate control. *Administrative Science Quarterly, 39*, 141–173. doi:10.2307/2393497

DiMaggio, P. J., & Powell, W. W. (1983). The iron cage revisited: Institutional isomorphism and collective rationality in organizational fields. *American Sociological Review, 48*, 147–160. doi:10.2307/2095101

Halila, F. (2006). Networks as a means of supporting the adoption of organizational innovations in SMEs: The case of environmental management systems (EMSs) based on ISO 14001. *Corporate Social Responsibility and Environmental Management, 14*, 167–181. doi:10.1002/csr.127

Harney, A. (2008). *The China Price*. New York: The Penguin Press.

Ho, P. (2005). Greening industries in newly industrializing countries: Asian-style leapfrogging? *Int. J. Environmental and Sustainable Development, 4*(3), 209–226. doi:10.1504/IJESD.2005.007738

Husted, B., & Allen, D. (2006). Corporate social responsibility in the multinational enterprise: Strategic and institutional approaches. *Academy of International Business Studies, 12*, 838–849. doi:10.1057/palgrave.jibs.8400227

Husted, B., & Allen, D. (2007). Strategic corporate social responsibility and value creation through large firms: Lessons from the Spanish experience. *Long Range Planning, 40*, 594–610. doi:10.1016/j.lrp.2007.07.001

Inkpen, A., & Tsang, E. (2005). Social capital, networks, and knowledge transfer. *Academy of Management Review, 30*(1), 146–165.

Japanese Foundation Beijing Office (2008). *Corporate Social Responsibility: Philanthropic Activities by Japanese Companies in South China* (in Japanese)

Kostova, T., & Roth, K. (2002). Adoption of an organizational practice by subsidiaries of multinational corporations: Institutions and relational effects. *Academy of Management Journal, 45*(1), 215–233. doi:10.2307/3069293

Kostova, T., & Zaheer, S. (1999). Organizational legitimacy under conditions of complexity: The case of the multinational enterprise. *Academy of Management Review, 24*(1), 64–81. doi:10.2307/259037

Kourula, A., & Halme, M. (2008). Types of corporate social responsibility and engagement with NGOs: an exploration of business and societal outcomes. *Corporate Governance, 8*(2), 557–570. doi:10.1108/14720700810899275

Lam, M. L. L. (2000). *Working with Chinese expatriates in business negotiations: Portraits, issues, and applications*. Westport, UK: Quorum Books.

Lam, M. L. L. (2003). Chinese executives' perceptions of United States-Chinese negotiating styles and relationships. In *Proceedings of the 2003 Marketing Management Association Conference*. Chicago.

Lam, M. L. L. (2004). Hong Kong Chinese executives' perceptions of United States-Chinese negotiating styles and relationships. In *Proceedings of the 38th Academy of Marketing Conference*. University of Gloucestershire, Cheltenham, Gloucestershire, U.K.

Lam, M. L. L. (2005). Trust building: Some of the American and Chinese business negotiators' cross-cultural challenges. In *Proceedings of the Academy of International Business Northeast Annual Conference*. Cleveland, OH.

Lam, M. L. L. (2007). A study of the transfer of corporate social responsibility from well-established foreign multinational enterprises to Chinese subsidiaries. In Hooker, J., Hulpke, J., & Madsen, P. (Eds.), *Controversies in international corporate responsibility. International Corporate Responsibility Series* (*Vol. 3*, pp. 343–363). Pittsburgh, PA: Carneige Mellon University.

Lam, M. L. L. (2008). *Proceedings of Academy of Innovation and Entrepreneurship 2008, Tsinghua University*. Beijing, China: Being Innovative by Doing Good.

Lam, M. L. L. (2009a). Beyond Credibility of Doing Business in China: Strategies for Improving Corporate Citizenship of Foreign Multinational Enterprises in China. *Journal of Business Ethics*, *86*(1).

Lam, M. L. L. (2009b) Non-government organizations as the salt and light in the Corporate Social Responsibility movement in China. In *Proceedings of the 2008 Christian Business Faculty Association Annual Conference*. Indianapolis, IN.

Lam, M. L. L. (2009c) Sustainable development and corporate social responsibility of multinational enterprises in China. In Ivanaj and McIntyre (Eds.), Multinational Enterprises and the Challenge of Sustainable Development. Cheltenham, UK and Northampton, MA: Edward Elgar.

Logsdon, J., & Wood, D. (2005). Global business citizenship and voluntary codes of ethical conduct. *Journal of Business Ethics*, *59*, 55–67. doi:10.1007/s10551-005-3411-2

Lyon, D. (2004). How can you help organizations change to meet the corporate responsibility agenda? *Corporate Social Responsibility and Environmental Management*, *11*, 133–139. doi:10.1002/csr.60

McAdam, D., McCarthy, J. D., & Zald, M. N. (1996). Introduction: Opportunities, mobilizing structures, and framing process—toward a synthetic, comparative perspective on social movements. In McAdam, D., McCarthy, J. D., & Zald, M. (Eds.), *Comparative Perspectives on Social Movements* (pp. 1–22). New York: Cambridge University Press.

McAdam, D., & Scott, W. R. (2005). Organizations and movements. In, Gerald F. Davis, Doug McAdam, W. Richard Scott, and Mayer N. Zald (Eds.), Social movements and organization theory (pp xviii). New York: Cambridge University Press.

McWilliams, A., & Siegel, D. (2001). Corporate social responsibility: A theory of the firm perspective. *Academy of Management Review*, *26*(1), 117–127. doi:10.2307/259398

Mirvis, P., & Googins, B. (2006). Stage of corporate citizenship. *California Management Review*, *48*(2), 104–126.

Murdoch, H., & Gould, D. (2004). *Corporate social responsibility in China: Mapping the environment. A study commission by the Global Alliance for Communities and Workers*. Baltimore: GA Publication Series.

OECD. (2000). *OECD Guidelines for Multinational Enterprises: 2000 Review*. Retrieved September 15, 2008, from http://www.oecd.org

Philipp, B. (2006). Multinationals' sustainable supply chains and influence exertion upon suppliers in the U.S. and outside the U.S.: A comparative approach. Paper presented at the *MESD 2006 International Research Colloquium*. Atlanta, GA.

Quazi, A. M., & O'Brien, D. (2000). *An empirical test of a cross-national model of corporate social responsibility. Journal of Business Ethics, 2533-51*. The Netherlands: Kluwer Academic Publishers.

Rogers, E. M. (1983). *Diffusion of innovations* (4th ed.). New York: Free Press.

Rondinelli, D. (2006). Globalization of sustainable development? Principles and practices in transnational corporations. Paper presented at the *MESD 2006 International Research Colloquium*. Atlanta, GA.

Schepers, D. (2006). The impact of NGO network conflict on the corporate social responsibility strategies of multinational corporations. *Business & Society, 45*(3), 282–299. doi:10.1177/0007650306289386

Sum, N. L., & Ngai, P. (2005). Globalization and paradoxes of ethical transnational production: Code of conduct in a Chinese workplace. *Competitive & Change, 9*(2), 181–200. doi:10.1179/102452905X45427

Tateisi, N. (2004). *Corporate social responsibility leads to sustainable economic growth in China— Observations from the leader of the CBCC Dialogue mission on CSR in the People's Republic of China*. Retrieved September 8, 2006, from http://www.keidanren.or.jp/CBCC/english/report/2004

The American Chamber of Commerce People's Republic of China (2006).*Corporate Social Responsibility Initiatives of AmCham-China Member Companies: Partnering for Progress.*

Times, F. (2008, October 9). China explores new ways to tackle its environmental challenges. *Financial Times (North American Edition)*, 4.

Vaill, P. (2007). Organizational epistemology: Interpersonal relations in organizations and the emergence of wisdom. In Kessler E. and Bailey J. (eds.), The Handbook of Managerial and Organizational Wisdom (327-355). Thousand Oaks, CA: Sage Publications.

van Rooij, B. (2006). Implementation of Chinese environmental law: Regular enforcement and political campaigns. *Development and Change, 37*(1), 57–74. doi:10.1111/j.0012-155X.2006.00469.x

van Tulder, R., & van der Zwart, A. (2006). *International business-society management*. Oxford, UK: Routledge.

Welford, R. (2006). New guidelines for Chinese CSR. *CSR Asia Weekly, 2*(35). Retrieved September 4, 2006, from http://www.csr-asia.com/upload/csrasiaweeklyvol2week35.pdf

White, A. Paper from the Business Roundtable (2000). *Corporate social responsibility in China: Practices by U.S. companies.*

Wood, C. H., & Kaufman, A. (2007). The communication of corporate social responsibility (CSR) through the supply chain: an SME perspective. In Gerald I. Susman (ed.), Small and Medium-Sized Enterprises and the Global Economy, 140-153. Cheltenham, UK and Northampton, MA: Edward Elgar.

World Business Council for Sustainable Development. (2005). *Perspective: Corporate responsibility and business success in China*. Retrieved August 14, 2006 from http://www.wbcsd.org

Yu, X. M. (2006*). Putting corporate codes of conduct regarding labor standards in a global-national-local context: A case study of Reebok's athletic footwear supplier factory in China.* Unpublished dissertation, The Hong Kong University of Science and Technology.

Zadek, S. (2004, December). The path to corporate responsibility. *Harvard Business Review*, 125–132.

KEY TERMS AND DEFINITIONS

Corporate Social Responsibility: The commitment of the corporations to benefit society beyond the requirements of the law and the direct interest of shareholders.

Strategic Development of Corporate Social Responsibility: To strategically manage the visibility, appropriability, voluntarism, centrality, and proactivity dimensions of corporate social responsibility programs.

Corporate Social Responsibility Integration: When corporate social responsibilities are integrated with existing business operations.

Corporate Social Responsibility Innovation: To develop new business models for solving social and environmental problems in the corporate social responsibility programs.

Local Non-Government Organizations in China: According to the present Chinese legal and administrative system, only non-profit organizations registered at the Ministry of Civil affairs are recognized as NGOs (*feizhengu zhushi*). There are three types registered NGOs—social organization (*shetuan*), foundations (*jijinhui*), and private non-profit enterprises (*minban feiqiye danwi*).

ENDNOTE

[1] An unreal name was used to disguise the identity of the company.

Section 4
Innovative Systems

Chapter 16
Study of SME Innovation in two Queensland Industries

David Thorpe
University of Southern Queensland, Australia

Steven Goh
University of Southern Queensland, Australia

ABSTRACT

This chapter describes research in innovation in smaller SME firms in Southern Queensland, Australia. The industries selected for this study were micro manufacturing in the Darling Downs Region and domestic building constructions in South East Queensland. Results of this research and its implications for innovation in the SME industry sector are discussed. While the firms studied, and the research methodology used, were quite different in each case, it was found that there were common factors that aided and inhibited innovation in each industry. These factors have implications for SME firms in other industries. Suggestions are made in the chapter with respect to the ongoing facilitation of innovation in such firms.

BACKGROUND

Australian businesses have increasingly investing in innovation in the last few years. According to the Australian Bureau of Statistics (2006), just over a third (34%) of Australian businesses undertook some type of innovation during the two years to December 2005. This was up four percentage points from the two years ended December 2003. By type of innovation, 'implementing new or significantly improved organizational/managerial processes' (25%) had the highest result. Approximately 22%

of businesses reported 'implementing new or significantly improved operational processes' and 19% of businesses reported 'introducing new or significantly improved goods or services'. Over 7% of innovating business reported introducing new-to-the-world goods or services.

From the 2005 figures, the proportion of innovating businesses increased with business size. This is most noticeable in the difference between innovating businesses that employ 5-19 persons (28.4%) and the results for businesses that employ 20-99 persons and 100 or more persons (46.6% and 51.5% respectively). This pattern is followed for each type of innovation with the exception of

DOI: 10.4018/978-1-61520-643-8.ch016

businesses that employ 20-99 persons which recorded the highest proportion of businesses that introduced new goods or services. More than 58% of innovating businesses reported cost as a barrier to innovation. Lack of skilled staff was reported as a barrier to undertaking innovation by 27% of innovating businesses. Profit-related drivers were reported as a key reason for all types of innovation by 94% of innovating businesses.

During 2006/07, over one-third (37%) of Australian businesses reported undertaking some form of innovation. Across the three statuses of innovation, larger businesses were more likely to have undertaken innovative activity than smaller businesses. This scenario is consistent with that observed in the 2005 survey. The proportion of businesses that were innovation-active was greater for each successive employment size range, from 31% for businesses with 0-4 persons employed to more than double this proportion for businesses with 200 or more persons employed (66%). (In considering these results, populations for each of the employment size groups should be taken into account. For example, for businesses with 200 or more persons employed, an innovation-active rate of 66% represents approximately 2,000 businesses, whereas an innovation-active rate of 31% for businesses with 0-4 employees represents approximately 136,000 businesses.) Over 25% of businesses claimed that a lack of skilled staff significantly hampered their ability to innovate. More than three-quarters (76%) of innovative-active businesses claimed that the most common driver of innovation was profit-related (Australian Bureau of Statistics, 2008).

These statistics above provides a background to which this chapter examines the innovation process in Small and Medium Enterprises (SME) within two Queensland industries. All except two of the firms discussed in this chapter employed less than 20 employees, typically placing them in the smaller group of SME firms.

INTRODUCTION

Much of the academic research undertaken on innovation is based on large organizations. Some of the factors that influence the performance of this process include organizational culture, government policies and support mechanism, structural framework, investment communities, intellectual property protection, financial stability, research-industry relationships, the organization's financial profile and stability, economic and corporate environment. However, there is increasing evidence to show that the most innovative and fast growth enterprises are from the Small-to-Medium Enterprise (SME) sector, such as small manufacturers who are operating with flexibility and innovation in niche markets within a very competitive global market place.

There is also increasingly improved structural support for these small enterprises from governments at all levels. However, such programs are often unable to flow down to the micro-manufacturers (less than yearly AUD 2 Million turnover per year), and access to relevant field officers for assistance are often very difficult especially within regional areas.

This poses an interesting scenario where it is often very difficult for these SMEs to access the available financial and non-financial assistance for their innovation activities. Because they are dependent on cash flow from existing operations as their innovation funding source (Featherstone, 2008), the incentives for SMEs to invest in innovation are diminished.

It is noted that business failure in SMEs is a comparatively rare phenomenon. Only around 2 per cent of SME businesses cease operations each year because the owners, while solvent, are unable to secure a sufficient return. And less than 0.5 per cent of businesses cease operations each year due to insolvency - down significantly from the rate applying in the early 1990s. Unfortunately, common misperceptions about the level of business failure and the chances of survival may lead some entrepreneurs to overestimate the risk of failure, thus reducing their willingness to innovate (Commonwealth of Australia, 2000).

The construction industry, which is one of the two industries discussed in this chapter, is not considered highly innovative with respect to other industries, including comparable sectors such as manufacturing and transport. For example, the OECD, in its 1998 *Science, Technology and Industry (STI) Outlook*, observed that the global construction industry has failed to achieve productivity improvement rates comparable to those of more mature manufacturing industries (such as textiles, steel and automobile manufacture). In Australia, the Australian Bureau of Statistics (ABS) has found that over the period 2001-2003 the construction industry, at 30.7 per cent, had one of the lowest proportions of innovating businesses (Australian Bureau of Statistics, 2005a). This result was comparable to the mining industry, yet well behind many other industries such as manufacturing, electricity, gas and water supply, and communications (45 per cent or more of firms innovating). The 2006-7 survey by the ABS found that the proportion of innovative-active construction firms had subsequently decreased to 27 per cent (Australian Bureau of Statistics, 2008)

It has been reported that many of the small businesses (almost half) in Australia today started in the past six years and in the past decade they have provided four out of five of all the new jobs created. Small businesses employ around 40% of the workforce, and are responsible for generating around a quarter of our gross domestic product (GDP) (ABC Radio, 2008). It may be argued that good ideas that have been generated by SMEs have a low probability of developing into commercial successes although there may be more opportunities for innovation. Given the propensity of SMEs to create jobs, this is an important challenge for Australia if it was to be successful in developing a comparative advantage globally as the "clever country". Thus, it has been noted that even a small increase in innovation intensity in SMEs would

have significant flow-on effect given the sector provides a significant employment and economic activity (Featherstone, 2008). This conclusion applies to both the manufacturing and construction sectors, which is noted as contributing, across the various OECD countries, 6.0 per cent to gross value added (a measure of the contribution made to GDP) in 1995, and 5.4 per cent to gross value added in 1999 (OECD, 2004)

Innovation in SMEs is often poorly understood, in that it is often a disordered, unpredictable process that is hard for SMEs to manage effectively. Innovation effort can also see attention diverted from the core business and operations. Relative risks are higher because there are fewer margins for errors in SME. The ability to experiment with different options has great merit in larger companies with surplus cash flow, stronger balance sheets and excess staff, but it is not suited for SMEs. A further reported issue in innovation in the SME sector is that there is too much discussion about innovation and not enough action (Featherstone, 2008). SMEs want more practical, cost effective ways to maintain or increase their innovation intensity.

There is evidence to date that governments are acting to enhance the innovation intensity in SMEs. For example, government agencies in Australia at the state and federal levels have always been trying to improve the innovation outcomes from industry, and in recent cases, in the SME sector. The establishment of the "Enterprise Connect" federal program in Australia, for example, is designed to provide small and medium enterprises with access to practical advice and mentoring. It has been reported that, according to Senator Kim Carr (Douglas, 2008), 10 Enterprise Connect centers to be opened around Australia will provide businesses with confidential mentoring and support, to gain access to a range of government and non-government services including business planning, prototype development, grant applications and advice regarding human resources. This program is based on similar programs which have proved successful in Ireland and the United Kingdom.

This chapter describes research projects in two significant smaller components of the SME sector – micro-manufacturing and smaller domestic building construction firms. While each project used a different methodology, both projects investigated the innovation process within representative firms of their particular sector. They also considered the mechanism for transfer of knowledge from researchers (such as universities) to the SME sector. The micro-manufacturing research project, in particular, investigated the innovation process in the SME sector within a university-industry collaboration (working jointly or cooperatively) context.

OVERVIEW OF THE INNOVATION PROCESS

Innovation Adoption and Development

An innovation may be described as "an idea, practice, or object that is perceived as new by an individual or other unit of adoption" (Rogers, 2003, p. 12). Rogers outlines the innovation development process as consisting of the steps of recognition of a problem or need, research, development, commercialization, diffusion and adoption, and consequences, i.e., changes that occur in an individual or social system as a result of adoption or rejection of an innovation. He also divides adopters of innovations into five ideal types, each of which is defined by specific characteristics such as the subject's ability to take risks, the subject's resources, and the subject's position within the overarching social system. The five types are innovators, early adopters, the early majority, the late majority, and laggards.

Knowledge and its organization and dissemination within the firm are significant factors with regard to innovation (Egbu, 2004). Such knowledge may be created within the firm rather than externally to it. Thus, the knowledge creation process can be considered as a continuous process through which one overcomes the individual boundaries and constraints imposed by information and past learning by acquiring a new context, a new view of the world, and new knowledge (Nonaka *et al.*, 2006).

Firms need to continuously innovate, adapt and improve on existing technologies, in order to exist, compete and grow. The better organizations are leveraged to the evolutionary nature of technology, the better their performance will be. This is supported by Moncrief & Cravens (1999) where technology is changing markets and buyer's preference, and organizations that are market driven and leverage technologies, can provide better market growth and performance.

There is also a need to develop a systematic approach to review an organization's ability not just to innovate but to create value through innovation. It is important not to view innovation in isolation but as an integral part of any business strategy. There are inherent hindrances to the adoption of technological innovation such as corporate culture, organizational composition, and its structure. In addition, the effective benefits, market and profit performance that technological innovation delivers tend to be hard to measure and are often underestimated, and therefore create a disincentive to invest in innovation.

Technological change is one of the significant influences on business enterprises, which companies both dying and emerging from every evolutionary technological innovation. Hill and Rothaermel (2003) provide a theoretical platform in that technology discontinuity does affect the performance of the incumbent firm, but that some firms some adapt and improve their performance, and some get ahead of the change and exploit the new technology and experience sustained performance. Macher & Richman (2004) have complemented this theory that firms tend to restructure and develop new strategies in pursuing a new technology in response to "discontinued" technologies. They have also found that certain organizational strategies are more appropriate for particular stages of the innovation life cycle. There is a common theme emerging that firms need to continuously innovate, adapt and improve on existing technologies, in order to it to exist, compete and grow.

Dillon, Lee & Matheson (2005) propose that technology and research and development (R&D) are insufficient to create value and wealth when used in isolation, and that current business practices fail to support the activities crucial to value innovation. There is a need to develop a systematic approach to review an organization's ability not just to innovate but to create value through innovation. Orr & Sohal (1999) have complemented this theory by using a German example of innovation by successfully managed technology transfer from home country to overseas productions, which delivered superior quality and competitive advantage, and indirectly provided an entry and presence in the respective market. They also demonstrated that managing the innovation process is not only about creating new ideas and gadgets, but also that it forms part of a holistic business strategy to enable the firm to ensure its sustainability as a business enterprise.

Finally, it is important not to view innovation in isolation but as an integral part of any business strategy, which may take into account other factors proposed in Zhuang (1995); where the composition of an organization in terms of gender, age, industry type, and management level can influence its ability to devise and implement business strategies that focus on innovation. This theme is further supported by Roberts & Amit (2003) in proposing the view that innovative activity that is differentiated from industry norms tends to deliver superior performance, in which the successful firm has focused on a point of differentiation as its competitive advantage.

Innovation Development and Adoption in the Construction Industry

The residential construction sector is recognized as a particularly important component of the construction industry (Miller *et al.*, 2004). In Australia, for example, the residential building sector, over the financial years 1997-98 to 2002-03, accounted for, on average, 43.3 per cent of the value of work undertaken, i.e., a total of AUD28.1 billion per year (Australian Bureau of Statistics, 2005b). In view of this, a one per cent gain in productivity in this sector has the potential to add about AUD280 million to the economy on an annual basis.

Given the importance of the residential building sector, and its potential to contribute significant improvements to national economies through innovation, it is important, as highlighted above, to develop an improved understanding of the innovation process. To achieve this goal, research was undertaken, with the aid of sponsorship from Australia's Cooperative Research Centre (CRC) for Construction Innovation[1], into assessing innovation development and adoption in a sample of 20 firms in the residential construction industry of South-East Queensland, Australia. The research was undertaken by means of a semi-structured interview process.

BARRIERS AND ENABLERS OF INNOVATION

While organizational knowledge and its use are important in the innovation process, and factors like those related to profit can be important drivers for firms to innovate, there are also a number of barriers and enablers (both within and external to the firm) that have the potential to impede or aid the innovation process in construction firms. A number of these barriers and enablers are discussed below.

Barriers to Innovation

There are inherent hindrances to the adoption of technological innovation such as corporate culture, organizational composition, and firm structure (Zhuang, 1995).

In the construction industry, Gyampoh-Vidogah & Moreton (2002) note that the industry has always been a collaborative business environment. However, the corporate or collaborative information technology framework is lacking as the result of the culture that dictates each individual function maintains total independence in all respects including information. In addition, the effective benefits, market and profit performance that technological innovation delivers tend to be hard to measure and often underestimated, and therefore create a disincentive to invest in innovation. This view is supported for that particular industry through the identification by Hampson & Brandon (2004) of a number of barriers preventing the Australian construction industry from taking more responsibility for leading and investing in research and innovation. Such barriers include the cyclical nature of the industry, a lack of client and industry leadership, a limited history of business deliverables from researchers, the self-interest of many participants, an inability of the industry to foresee the tide of competition, insufficient trust between industry and researchers with respect to sharing vital information, and lack of a long-term funding basis for a national R&D centre.

Similar barriers were observed by Koivu & Mantalya (2000) in the European construction sector, which they stated had not been very successful in adopting new technology and processes. Some of the issues in that sector included fragmentation, low potential for added value because of a price and project-based focus, fluctuation of demand with time, slow process or project improvement cycles, a relative inability to manage the innovation process, lack of educated personnel, limitations to risk taking, a conservative culture,

and a relatively significant level of government oversight and control.

The culture of the firms themselves can be the source of additional barriers to innovation. Acar *et al.* (2005) found, for example, that organizational culture was a factor in implementing information and communications technology (ICT) in construction firms. The importance of these barriers to innovation is also noted by Egbu (2004), who observed that, if the construction industry is to benefit from innovation, it should change from an adversarial and blame culture to a sharing one. Further, a study by Manley *et al.* (2005) of 383 Australian construction firms found that key obstacles to innovation included high costs of developing innovations and insufficient time.

Finally, Zhu (2004) has demonstrated that where the impact of ICT as a tool for e-commerce, profit performance and its value is underestimated,, there may not be enough financial justification to invest in ICT, which in turn may not reap the full benefit of e-commerce.

Enablers of Innovation

The study of the Australian construction industry by Manley *et al.* (2005) found that the determinants of innovation outcomes in that particular industry included business strategies, innovation drivers and obstacles, and the number of sources of ideas. In addition, the same researchers found that key drivers of innovation were efficiency, productivity improvements and customer needs, and that stand-out innovators a) developed innovations with higher degrees of novelty, b) adopted a higher number of advanced practices, and c) invested in research and development. Approximately one-third of the respondents maintained a culture that supported innovation.

Dulaimi *et al.* (2003) found that an innovative proposal can be successfully implemented if effort is put into carrying the innovation through, if favorable results can be expected and there is high managerial commitment. Ling (2003) similarly concluded that the extent to which an innovation would prove beneficial is closely correlated to the level of interest of project team members, the working environment, the formation of task groups, and the capabilities of the people involved.

Successful innovation requires support from senior management. Egbu (2004), for example, found that any meaningful innovation strategy must have unequivocal support from the top, be communicated to and accepted by the organization's rank and file, and sit naturally within the organization's overall strategy. Similarly, Sexton & Barrett (2003) found that owners of small firms have the power to ensure rapid decision-making while the type of innovation and the different organizational factors brought into play largely depend on the firm's operating environment.

It is concluded that the barriers to innovation are related to industry culture (of both the industry and the firm), cost, client factors, and the issues in adopting new technology, while enablers of innovation include commitment to innovation, firm characteristics, commitment of firm management, and organizational strategy.

University and Industry Collaboration in Innovation

University-industry collaboration has always been a mechanism for innovation. MacPherson (1998) examined the academic-industry linkages and small firm innovation in the scientific instruments sector, and found data from a sample of 204 SMEs in the New York State region that suggest that the university can play a helpful role in SME innovation. Knowledge spillovers from the academic sector were shown to be geographically localized. A key finding is that the intensity of academic-SME interaction varies inversely with the time-distance that separates firms from major campuses; and innovation rates are higher among SMEs that enjoy close proximity to academic resources.

Freel (2000) expanded linkage collaboration further by examining external linkages and product innovation in small manufacturing firms. Based on a sample of 228 small West Midlands manufacturers in the UK, this study found that innovators are making greater use of external linkages, of a certain type and in a particular direction (predominately in vertical value chain linkages). It is observed that the data suggested the importance of interpersonal dynamics, attitude and expectations in facilitating successful collaboration.

In the construction industry, Hampson & Brandon (2004) have noted that commitment to collaborative research and innovation is required, with genuine mutual consultation with industry being essential for research and development to make a difference. They have also commented that it is important for researchers to engage with SMEs (94 per cent of firms in the Australian construction industry employ fewer than five people).

These studies indicate that, on the whole, successful innovation can be considerably aided by the involvement of universities, other research institutions, and business coaching approaches.

STUDY OF A MICRO MANUFACTURER

Overview

The first study discussed in this chapter is the exploration and reflection of the innovation experience of a regional micro-manufacturer through embedment of one of the authors in a particular firm, in an analogy to an anthropological study. The case study involved learning and discovering the obstacles and barriers for innovation, seeking and proposing ways to reduce them, and improving the overall innovation process within micro-manufacturers in regional areas.

During the experience, the researcher embedded within the firm provided advice and analysis, and at times, physical labor on the process transformation for the micro-manufacturing firm via process improvements, semi-automation, and systemization of the business operation, and in the process initiated preliminary study into the innovation process in regional micro-manufacturing sector.

The approach to the overall case study is separated into three different components:

- Study of the Business & Working Owner
- Study of the Manufacturing Processes
- Study of the innovation Process

The intention in this chapter is to focus on the innovation experiences to gain an understanding of the influencing factors that affect it.

Background of the Firm

The firm was founded and owned by an individual based at the regional township of Pittsworth (located 50 km south-west from Toowoomba in Queensland, Australia). The operation started off as a commercial flower growing business focusing on organic and medicinal herbs. Now, it specializes in and manufactures a range of high-quality organic/pure "chemical-free" soap & shampoo and skin care products. The business has been in operation for about 10 years. Along with a good domestic distribution, it also exports to New Zealand, the United Kingdom and Asia. The products that it manufactures are varied and include:

- Soap-based products (over 200)
- Hair care products
- Skin care products
- Natural "Bush" products
- Medicinal based products
- Miscellaneous products (e.g. Hemp).

Research Findings

The findings from the overall study were categorized into 3 segments:

- Study of the business and working owner
- Study of the manufacturing processes
- Study of the innovation process.

Business and Working Owner

Following a SWOT (strengths, weaknesses, opportunities, threats) analysis, it was observed that there is a comparative advantage in the firm's niche high-quality product specializations, and its willingness to innovate and its perceived intellectual properties (owner's knowledge on soap making). Though the broad range of products was seen as a strength (to the customers), without systems, manufacturing a wide range of products can be a difficult logistic exercise. This was observed during operations. It may also present a case for market confusion for the consumer with the wide choices. The SWOT analysis also provided some evidence to show that the attributes of the owner is the most important factor that influence innovation in the micro-manufacturer.

It was observed the weaknesses are many, and presented a challenge for the process transformation task. Interestingly, many of the perceived weaknesses are related to the owner's personal attributes and an intrinsic tie to the business and the manufacturing processes. This can be solved by leveraging the working owner from the operation (to work on the business not in the business), and instilling systems and good practices within the operations. However, time and money (the lack of it) are the major source of weaknesses. This finding is consistent with other research into barriers to innovation, as discussed previously in this chapter. Addressing this lack of money needs external sources of support such as government agencies (subsidies and innovation grants) or larger enterprises (that form a vertical supply chain).

It was observed that a number of opportunities could be taken without incurring large capital cost or expenses. Most of the recommendations for the process transformation derived from this observation. One aspect is to focus on decreasing manufacturing cost, both in overheads and unit costs; the other aspect is to specifically target major distribution channels, and consolidate product range to address this wholesale market.

It was observed that the perceived threats were related to macro-environmental factors such as raw material price increases, increased global competition, increased labor costs etc, and this is well supported by the literature. However, one interesting view is tied to the owner's personal attributes, as discussed previously.

The SWOT analysis provided an initial understanding of the business to progress to the process transformation stages. Specific areas from the findings; such as the decreasing manufacturing costs, product consolidation, installing systems and procedure and less reliance on the working owner for day-to-day operations; were addressed. However, the findings also indicated that one of the biggest hurdles for the business is the lack of time and capital, and presented a challenge to the transformation tasks and achieving innovation objectives.

The Manufacturing Processes

The study of the manufacturing processes encompassed an initial familiarization of the basic soap making processes, categorization of the firm's soap manufacturing line, and then engagement in the process transformation, resulting in key findings and recommendations.

The most common type of soap making is known as the "Cold Process." This process has been adopted by the firm as the process used in the manufacturing of its main line of soaps. It is made by combining fatty acids and sodium hydroxide (lye) together. Fatty acids can be almost any oil – from beef tallow to olive oil to hemp oil. In simple terms, this process combines a proportion of lye (sodium hydroxide) and water with fatty acids, resulting in a chemical reaction called "saponification." During saponification, the oils and lye mix and becomes soap.

One competitive advantage the firm has over other commercial soap manufacturers are in its superior ingredients. They contain organic herb, oil, distilled water, real fruits, vegetable, rice/nut oils, jojoba & macadamia wax, vegetable glycerin. The firm does not use any sodium laurel sulphate, propylene glycol, parabens, or peanut oil; as is common in ingredients in commercial soaps.

The soap manufacturing line is composed of an "L" shape configuration, encompassing the following processes:

- Mixing of lye and fatty acids
- Luxury Bars Making
- Fun Soaps Making
- Soap Cutting / Slicing
- Saponication/Drying
- Packaging
- Storage

These manufacturing elements were analyzed with data collected (through work study) with the view to improve the manufacturing operation to decrease manufacturing costs and increase production output.

Process transformation was mainly achieved through analyzing the processes with data collected through video recording of the individual manufacturing elements, and applying work study principles to evaluate and seek increased productivity and improvements in output quality and quantity.

It was determined that the manufacturing costs and units cost are comparatively high as the result of high labor utilization. The solution desired was to decrease the direct manufacturing cost by optimizing factory layout and introduce semi-automation into some processes. The project initially targeted to increase the production rate of Luxury bars from 800 to 3000 bars in an eight hour day with minimal investment needed.

The findings from the process transformation were to to:

- Improve workstations layouts
- Decrease manual handling in the manufacturing
- Semi-automate manufacturing processes
- Decrease transfer between workstations
- Reposition and increase storage space.

It was also determined during the discussion and analysis that there were inadequate distribution channels and poor marketing strategies, mainly attributed to the time limitation from the demand of being a full-time working owner. The solution desired was to identify and successfully recruit two major and two minor distribution channels to establish sales consistency and volume. As part of the process, it was also envisaged that there would be consolidation of selected products into a "high-volume" product range to assist in forming a suitable "high-volume" wholesale marketing strategy.

In general terms, it was observed that there are three critical deficiencies within the firm which commonly are endemic within the SME sector in Australia, and all of which impact on innovative capacity of the firm. These were:

- Lack of planning and organization
- Lack of systems and procedures (or lack the training of personnel)
- Lack of expert input into structures and technologies.

There were two separate complementary recommendations, one aimed at the process transformation and the other into improving the distribution channel. As at the time of writing this paper, part of the first stage, layout optimization, had been implemented, with consequent work flow improvements.

The Innovation Process in the Firm

The study of the innovation process in this particular firm involved the identification of factors influencing the innovation process. These are listed below, where they are categorized as internal and external factors.

Internal Factors:

- Lack of time and money
- Inadequate external support
- Lack of systematic Approach
- Lack of planning & monitoring
- Adhoc approach.

External Factors:

- External support is crucial and provides an avenue for innovation
- Government agencies have the grants/funds for innovation but lack suitable delivery for regional enterprises: need to restructure for regional SME
- There is opportunity for universities to exploit: provide education, advice and structured innovation (similar to business coaching services)
- Customers and Suppliers can be a good source of innovation
- Employees and Owners need innovation training
- Larger enterprises can act as a conduit for vertical supply chain innovation (act as innovation host and pseudo-financier).

It can be argued that the major hurdle for the successful innovation hinges on the specific owner's attributes and ability to systematically plan, implement and monitor the business environment and its operations. It is also acknowledged (as previously discussed) that the major hurdle is the lack of capital and time to reinvest into innovation, even though SMEs are perceived as the organizations most responsive and agile to innovation opportunities. This then points to the abilities of government agencies to support such SMEs through targeted financial and facilitation support, collectively with universities (who have the knowledge base and resources to advice). An addition to this is the ability of larger enterprises to form vertical supply chain clusters involving the hosting of SMEs' innovation activities.

There is opportunity in this area for academic-industry collaboration, whereby university resources can be provided for a government-subsidized fee to enhance SMEs in their planning, establish systems, and provide innovation advice. In some ways, there is adequate anecdotal evidence to suggest that the business coaching industry that has been established to fill this gap has gained popular demand from the SME sector.

STUDY OF SMALL RESIDENTIAL BUILDERS

Method

The study of innovation in the domestic building sector was undertaken through contacting 100 small residential builders operating in the South-East of the Australian state of Queensland. This sample of builders was obtained through selecting fifth firm, in alphabetical order, in publicly available lists of selected residential property builders in this region. In order that the study considered smaller builders, the study sample was limited to builders constructing houses up to AUD 750,000 in value. This value was considered a reasonable upper limit for the type of small builders interviewed for this particular study.

In order to obtain reasonably detailed information about the behavior of the firms in the study, a qualitative methodology incorporating a semi-structured interview process was adopted. The objective of the interview questions was to explore the extent of innovation in the firms selected; provide an understanding of how they developed or adopted innovations; qualitatively assess the value of innovations to the firm; and assess their readiness to adapt to changes in their working environment.

Since there was considerable activity in the residential building industry in the study area during the time of data collection, representatives of only 20 of the 100 contacted firms were able to be interviewed. It was therefore decided to use these 20 firms as the study sample. A semi-structured questionnaire that aimed to obtain useful information, but which also had to meet the tight time-frames of the interviewees, was developed as the research instrument. The interviews, which took about 45 minutes each, took place in September and October 2006.

The firms in the study constituted small independent domestic building firms, seven of which had four or fewer permanent staff, and only two over nineteen permanent staff. All firms were principal contractors with little or no interaction with the other firms in the sample. Of the firms, eighteen undertook new construction, and two were primarily engaged in maintenance or renovation. Eleven of the firms undertook design as well as construction.

All firms worked with private clients undertaking private sector residential work in which small projects, such as private dwellings, predominated. In addition to working for private clients, four of the firms also worked for government clients. About three of the firms also undertook larger projects such as construction of apartment blocks and commercial buildings.

Innovation in the Sample Firms

The research found 50 examples of innovations, or "something new" (Rogers, 2003), in the 20 firms surveyed, ranging from one to five innovations per firm. This was a good result given the relatively poor reputation of the industry for innovation. Examples of such innovations, which illustrate the variety of innovations used, include the following:

• Use of new engineered products (e.g. LVL - laminated veneer lumber - I-beams).

- Polyethylene pipe for internal water supplies (as opposed to copper).
- Use of new structural products (primarily in insulation).
- Use of polystyrene blocks as substitutes for other materials such as fiber cement boards. These blocks were insulating and did not emit dust (an important issue in occupational health and safety) when cut.
- Adoption of new building materials that improve (energy) efficiency
- A "Greensmart" design and construction process.
- Use of a web-based system that enabled customers to track building plans and follow construction.
- The use of electronic estimating packages.
- A custom-designed mobile toolbox for use in a mental health maintenance environment.

The innovations could mainly be classed as either product or process innovations (21 in each category), as defined by the third edition of the Oslo Manual (OECD, 2005). The remainder of the innovations could be classed as were organizational (three), product and process (two), product and marketing (one) and process and marketing (two).

Very few of the innovations were completely new to the construction industry. However, all were new to each particular firm.

Participants in the study were asked to nominate one particular innovation for further discussion, giving the reason for developing or adopting the innovation, the process of developing or adopting the innovation, implementation issues, and the results achieved from using the innovation.

With respect to the reason for developing or adopting the innovation, the predominant answer was improvement of productivity in the firm (selected by 9 firms), followed by the need to meet requirements of the client and improvement efficiency of the firm (each elected by 7 firms). One firm advised that the innovation had been developed in response to legislative requirements.

Other reasons for developing the innovation included a commitment to leadership in the industry, customer service, sustainability, safety, or desire to achieve good practice.

Results of Using Innovations

With respect to the result of using the innovation selected for further study, all firms in the survey reported that they had gained increased knowledge to their advantage. There was also a positive response by clients and firms with which the builders dealt with respect to the innovation. Twelve of the firms reported a positive effect on profitability as a result of using this innovation, with none reporting a decrease in profitability. In addition, 11 of the firms reported reduced risk as a result of using it. Examples of such risk reduction included improved safety, improved time and cost estimates, less fatigue in tradesmen, less theft, reduction in long-term maintenance needs and reduced stress levels in management and staff. Factors assisting this risk reduction included improved safety through lighter and safer materials, improved handling practices and improved systems and documentation.

All firms interviewed reported that they gained increased knowledge to their advantage as a result of using the innovation. However, only 10 of the 20 firms interviewed reported that the innovation provided them with a competitive advantage. This outcome is likely to be related to the difficulty of measuring any competitive advantage, and to perceptions by builders about what constituted a competitive advantage rather than to whether such an advantage was actually achieved. Other firms reported improved productivity and positive client responses.

Seven of the firms reported that they were required to make changes to their business as a result of adopting or using the selected innovation. The main change identified was in human resources management, such as staff training and development, changes in employment arrangements, and employing different staff. Marketing was also considered an area that required change. This minimal impact on business operations, combined with the view of all firms that they would use the innovation again, indicates that the firms tended to view their innovations positively.

One of the results from the study of the domestic building firms was that participating firms tended to develop their innovations through a) identifying a need or business objective; b) developing or obtain knowledge of an innovation to meet the need or objective; c) deciding whether to use the innovation; d) trialing and testing it; and e) undertaking a pilot implementation of it. Once the pilot implementation proved satisfactory, the firm would move to full implementation of it and further refine and improve it. This process is similar to Rogers's (2003) innovation development process, i.e., recognition of a problem or need, research, development, commercialization, diffusion, adoption, and consequences; which indicates that the process followed by the builders interviewed in this study was consistent with the results of previous studies in the field of innovation development and adoption.

The firms in the study also listed at least one factor that aided the innovation process. The main categories into which these factors could be grouped were ease of use, commitment, personal desire for the innovation's success, and customer acceptance. Other factors that aided the innovation process included the importance to the firm of the innovation, improving the firm's reputation, ease of implementation, and staff acceptance of the innovation.

Of the selected innovations (one per builder) nominated by each builder for further discussion, those in 16 firms (80 per cent of the sample) originated within the firm. An external information source contributed to the development and adaptation of innovations in 12 of the 20 firms in the research. The main such source of external information in these cases was trade literature. Other sources of information included industry training seminars, supplier representatives, design

professionals, adaptation from another industry, and sub-contractors. Only one of the firms directly used a researcher to assist with the innovation process.

These results possibly reflect the difficulty in disseminating innovation in a loosely coupled industry (Dubois & Gadde, 2002). They are supported by the findings of Manley et al. (2005), who noted that in-house staff members were the primary source of innovation ideas and that research institutions ranked in twelfth place as a source of such ideas. They would also tend to support the research discussed in the section on barriers and enablers of innovation, and in the micro-manufacturer cases study, that in small firms the owner is an important driver and facilitator of innovation.

Implementation of Innovations

Only eight of the 20 firms reported that they had experienced difficulties in implementing the nominated innovation. This good result might be attributable to the fact that many of the innovations were developed within firms, and thus were driven by the owner or senior management.

Where difficulties were experienced in the implementation process, the most common issues were human resource related, such as unwillingness to depart from entrenched ways of doing things, and technical problems such as the failure of the first attempt at innovation. Other implementation issues included time and cost, a need to meet customer requirements, and legislative impediments.

DISCUSSION

Results from the Research

One of the important results from the research into residential builders was that although it is contended by a number of researchers that larger firms have more capacity to innovate than smaller ones (Arias-Aranda *et al.*, 2001; Gopalakrishnan & Santoro, 2001), there was considerable innovation in the firms in the study. The research described in this chapter also indicates that the small size of the firms studied is likely to enhance their ability to develop, test and implement innovations. This is consistent with the findings of Sexton & Barrett (2003) previously discussed in this chapter.

Eighteen of the 20 firms interviewed identified themselves as either innovators or early adopters of innovations in the classification system developed by Rogers (2003). The desire to meet changes in the business environment with a high level of rapidity also indicates that smaller building firms may be prepared to take risks in the expectation of receiving gain in the long term, in spite of the financial issues involved.

The research into these builders also indicates how information about innovation flows to firms. The participating builders advised that sources of knowledge for innovations not personally developed by the firm included journals and magazines, advertisements, industry association events, sales representatives, and design professionals. As was previously observed, only one of these firms reported directly receiving information from a researcher.

The sources of information are valuable to the firms, who tend to form a loosely-coupled group of organizations (Dubois & Gadde, 2002), linked to other firms, sub-contractors and their knowledge sources. This loose network allows them to exchange information, or obtain information from industry associations, design professionals, material and equipment suppliers, their operating environment, clients, subcontractors, and other builders. At the same time, direct communication with researchers and development of trust between the industry and researchers would be highly desirable.

The study into the micro-manufacturer indicated that there were roles for government agen-

cies, universities and other education providers in assisting the SME sector. Thus, for government agencies and relevant policy development, implications included the following:

- The desirability of developing a "One-Stop-Shop" for SME support.
- Improvement of accessibility of field officers to regional areas.
- Provision of financial support for advisory/coaching services.
- Provision of financial support for education and training.
- Facilitation of establishment of vertical supply chain clusters.
- Provision of financial incentives for larger enterprises to host innovation activities with SMEs in the form of innovation clusters.

Universities and education providers could:

- Exploit opportunities in the "business coaching" market.
- Develop targeted educational/training products for SME in the form of short customized courses.
- Established technical advisory, process auditing and mentoring consultancies in collaboration with government agencies.
- Be hosts for SMEs' innovation activities supported by relevant government funding to form clustered applied research and SME "nurturing" centers.

Regional Knowledge Diffusion Model

Both studies indicate that there are some common elements, with respect to the innovation process, in the SME firms researched for this study. While such firms can be quite innovative in their own right, and in fact their small size can in fact be an advantage with respect to being able to quickly adopt innovations, it is clear that little use is being directly made of the knowledge and skills of universities and researchers to assist the innovation. A suggested model of this process for smaller regional firms has therefore been developed to demonstrate the dependency of the business to the owner, and the need to rely on systematic planning and organization. Such a process will require changes in the owner's behavior and sufficient education/training, along with relevant advisory and financial support needed to improve the probability of a successful innovation experience. The model is termed a "Regional Knowledge Diffusion" (RKD) model, and is illustrated in Figure 1.

CONCLUSION

SMEs are an important sector of the Australian economy. While not all have good success rates in innovation, especially within regional areas, they are generally receptive to opportunities to innovate and adopt new technologies to lift business growth. The innovation processes in SMEs are not easily understood and not well researched within the literature. Existing support for these processes is also not particularly suited to SMEs. The lack of time, capital and new technology knowledge may be seen as hurdle in innovation, particularly for regional SMEs. In addition, the strategy and organization that is the result of working owners being highly focused on their businesses also need to be addressed.

Figure 1. Suggested model for innovation experience in small regional firms: regional knowledge diffusion (RKD)

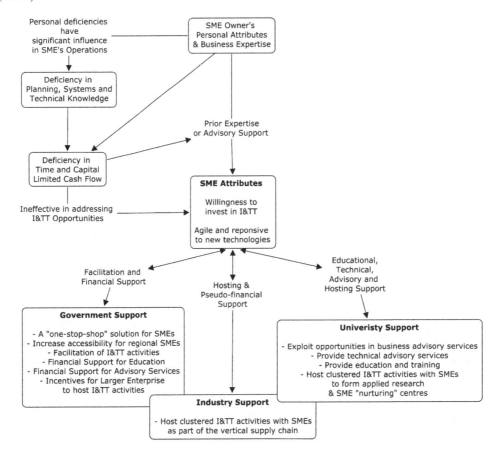

At the same time, the study of 20 domestic building firms has shown that small firms can be quite innovative in their own right, particularly with respect to the development and adoption of new or improved products and processes. Such innovation is driven by improved productivity and efficiency within the firm, as is meeting perceived client requirements. Personal goals and values (e.g., those of the firm's management, often the firm's owners) were also important drivers of the innovations reported. The innovations developed and pursued ultimately benefited the firm and, in particular, resulted in a positive perception of the firm by both clients and competing firms. At the same time, there was an ill-defined benefit with respect to profitability, although the firms generally indicated that they would continue to use their key innovations.

One of the important aspects in the innovation process is the transfer of research knowledge within the industry. It would appear in both studies that research knowledge is largely being received indirectly by firms through indirect sources such as industry associations and design professionals. As is considered beneficial for the results of research to be more directly accessible to the firms, and for the firms to receive direct input from universities and other research organizations, it is recommended that researchers develop closer links with the industry representatives who undertake the intermediary's role, and that universities should take a stronger role in collaborating with the firms. To this end, the Regional Knowledge Diffusion model has been developed as a result of this research.

To conclude, future research should aim at extending this research to a larger group of SME organizations, across a range of industries in a range of geographical locations in Australia and elsewhere, in order to evaluate the extent of and commitment of this sector to innovation at a wider level, and to better understand how this industry sector might benefit form closer links with universities and researchers.

REFERENCES

Acar, E., Kocak, I., Sey, Y., & Arditi, D. (2005). Use of information and Communication technologies by small and medium-sized enterprises (SMEs) in building construction. *Construction Management and Economics*, *23*, 713–722. doi:10.1080/01446190500127112

Agnihothri, S., Sivasubramaniam, N., & Simmons, D. (2002). Leveraging technology to improve field service. *International Journal of Service Industry Management*, *13*(1), 47–68. doi:10.1108/09564230210421155

Arias-Aranda, D., Beatriz Minguela-Rata, B., & Rodríguez-Duarte, A. (2001). Innovation and firm size: an empirical study for Spanish engineering consulting companies. *European Journal of Innovation Management*, *4*(3), 133–142. doi:10.1108/EUM0000000005671

Australian Bureau of Statistics. (2005a). *2005 Year Book Australia*. Canberra, Australia: Australian Government.

Australian Bureau of Statistics. (2005b). *Innovation in Australian Business 2003, cat. no. 8158.0*. Canberra, Australia: Australian Government.

Australian Bureau of Statistics. (2006). *Innovation in Australian Business 2005, cat. no. 8158.0*. Canberra, Australia: Australian Government.

Australian Bureau of Statistics. (2008). *Innovation in Australian Business 2006-2007, cat no. 8158.0*. Retrieved April 27, 2009, from http://www.abs.gov.au/AUSSTATS/abs@.nsf/Latestproducts/8158.0Contents2006-07?opendocument&tabname=Summary&prodno=8158.0&issue=2006-07&num=&view=

Commonwealth of Australia. (2000). *Business Failure and Change: An Australian Perspective. Staff research paper 2000/12/20*. Canberra, Australia: Australian Productivity Commission.

Dillon, T., Lee, R., & Matheson, D. (2005, March-April). Value Innovation: Passport to wealth creation. *Research Technology Management*, 22-37.

Douglas, J. V. (2008, August 28-October 1). Small Business Help. *Business Review Weekly,*, 22.

Dubois, A., & Gadde, L.-E. (2002). The construction industry as a loosely coupled system: implications for productivity and innovation. *Construction Management and Economics, 20*, 621–631. doi:10.1080/01446190210163543

Dulaimi, M. F., Ling, F. Y. Y., & Bajracharya, A. (2003). Organizational motivation and inter-organizational interaction in construction innovation in Singapore. *Construction Management and Economics, 21*(3), 307–318. doi:10.1080/0144619032000056144

Egbu, C. O. (2004). Managing knowledge and intellectual capital for improved organizational innovations in the construction industry: an examination of critical success factors. *Engineering, Construction, and Architectural Management, 11*(5), 301–315. doi:10.1108/09699980410558494

Featherstone, T (2008, September 4-10). Ideas Wanted. *Business Review Weekly*, 58.

Freel, M. (2000). External linkages and product innovation in small manufacturing firms. *Entrepreneurship & Regional Development, 12*, 245–266. doi:10.1080/089856200413482

Gopalakrishnan, S., & Santoro, M. D. (2001). Do size and slack matter? Exploring the multidimensions of organizational innovation. In *Proceedings, Portland International Conference on Management of Engineering and Technology 2001*. Portland, OR.

Gyampoh-Vidogah, R., & Moreton, R. (2002). Implementing information management in construction: establishing problems, concepts and practice. *Construction Innovation, 3*, 157–173.

Hampson, K. D., & Brandon, P. (2004). [*A Vision for Australia's Property and Construction Industry*. Brisbane, Australia: CRC for Construction Innovation, Brisbane.]. *Construction (Arlington)*, 2020.

Hanna, V., & Walsh, K. (2002). Small networks: a successful approach to Innovation. *R & D Management, 32*(3), 201–207. doi:10.1111/1467-9310.00253

Hill, G., & Rothaermel, F. (2003). The performance of incumbent firms in the face of radical technological innovation. *Academy of Management Review, 28*(2), 257–274.

Koivu, T., & Mantyla, K. (2000). Innovation management in the Finnish construction industry. In *Proceedings of the International Conference: Technology Watch and Innovation in the Construction Industry*, (pp. 147-152), Brussels, Belgium.

Ling, F. Y. Y. (2003). Managing the implementation of construction innovations. *Construction Management and Economics, 21*(6), 635–649. doi:10.1080/0144619032000123725

Love, P., Irani, Z., & Edwards, D. (2004). Industry-centric benchmarking of information technology benefits, costs and risks for small-to-medium sized enterprises in construction. *Automation in Construction, 13*(4), 507–524. doi:10.1016/j.autcon.2004.02.002

Macher, J., & Richman, B. (2004). Organisational Responses to Discontinuous Innovation: A case study approach. *International Journal of Innovation Management, 8*(1), 87–114. doi:10.1142/S1363919604000939

MacPherson, A. D. (1998). Academic-industry linkages and small firm innovation: evidence from the scientific instrumentations sector. *Entrepreneurship & Regional Development, 10*, 261–275. doi:10.1080/08985629800000015

Majdalani, Z., Ajam, M., & Mezher, T. (2006). Sustainability in the construction industry: a Lebanese case study. *Construction Innovation*, *6*(1), 33–46.

Manley, K., Allan, D., Blayse, A., Coillet, M., Hardie, M., & Hough, R. (2005). *BRITE Innovation Survey*. Brisbane, Australia: CRC for Construction Innovation.

Miller, C. J. M., Packham, G. A., Pickernell, D. G., & McGovern, M. (2004). Building for the future: the potential importance of the construction industry in Welsh economic development policy. *Construction Management and Economics*, *22*(5), 533–540. doi:10.1080/0144619031001649128

Moncrief, W., & Cravens, D. (1999). Technology and the changing marketing world. *Marketing Intelligence & Planning*, *17*(7), 329–332. doi:10.1108/02634509910301142

Nonaka, I., von Krogh, G., & Voelpel, S. (2006). Organizational knowledge creation theory: evolutionary paths and future advances. *Organization Studies*, *27*(8), 1179–1208. doi:10.1177/0170840606066312

OECD. (1998). Science, Technology and Industry Outlook. Paris: Organization for Economic Co-operation and Development.

OECD. (2004). Science, Technology and Industry Outlook. Paris: Organization for Economic Co-operation and Development.

OECD. (2005). Oslo Manual – Guidelines for Collecting and Interpreting Innovation Data" (3rd ed.), Paris: Organization for Economic Co-operation and Development/European Commission Eurostat.

Orr, S., & Sohal, A. (1999). Technology and global manufacturing: some German experience. *Management Decision*, *37*(4), 356–363. doi:10.1108/00251749910269401

Radio, A. B. C. (2008). *From S to M: Small to Medium Businesses in Australia, Lifelong Learning*. Retrieved June 24, 2008, from http://www.abc.net.au/rn/learning/lifelong/features/smallbiz

Roberts, P., & Amit, R. (2003). The dynamics of innovative activity and competitive advantage: The case of Australian Retail Banking, 1981 to 1995. *Organization Science*, *14*(2), 107–122. doi:10.1287/orsc.14.2.107.14990

Rogers, E. M. (2003). *Diffusion of Innovations* (5th ed.). New York: Free Press.

Sexton, M., & Barrett, P. (2003). Appropriate innovation in small construction firms. *Construction Management and Economics*, *27*(6), 623–633. doi:10.1080/0144619032000134156

Tushman, M., & O'Reilly, C. (1997). *Winning Through Innovation: A Practical Guide to Leading Organizational Change and Renewal*. Boston: Harvard Business Press.

Zhu, K. (2004). The Complementarity of Information Technology Infrastructure and E-Commerce Capacity: A Resource based Assessment of Their Business Value. *Journal of Management Information Systems*, *21*(2), 167–202.

Zhuang, L. (1995). Bridging the gap between technology and business strategy: a pilot study on the innovation process. *Management Decision*, *33*(8), 13–21. doi:10.1108/00251749510093897

KEY TERMS AND DEFINITIONS

Fiber Cement Board: A composite material made of sand, cement and cellulose fibers. In appearance fiber cement cladding most often consists of overlapping horizontal boards, imitating wooden cladding, clap-board and imitation shingles. Fiber cement siding is also manufactured in a sheet form and is used not only as cladding but is also commonly used as a soffit / eave lining and as a tile underlay on decks and in bathrooms. Fiber cement cladding is not only used as an exterior cladding, it can also be utilized as a substitute for timber fascias and barge boards in high fire areas.

Glycerin: A chemical compound also commonly called glycerol or glycerine. It is a colorless, odorless, viscous liquid that is widely used in pharmaceutical formulations. It is commonly derived in soap products. Glycerol is sweet-tasting and of low toxicity.

"GreenSmart" Design and Construction Process: *GreenSmart* is a voluntary practical approach to building that focuses on educating builders, designers, product manufacturers and consumers about the benefits of environmentally responsible housing. It is an industry-driven initiative that aims to encourage a mainstream application of its principles to today's housing. As a voluntary initiative, it provides appropriate market recognition for environmental endeavors in the residential construction industry.

Hemp: The common name for plants of the entire genus Cannabis, although the term is often used to refer only to Cannabis strains cultivated for industrial (non-drug) use. Industrial hemp has many uses, including paper, textiles, biodegradable plastics, construction, health food, and fuel, with modest commercial success. The commercial success of hemp food products has grown considerably.

insulation: Building insulation refers broadly to any object in a building used as insulation for any purpose. Whilst the majority of insulation in buildings is for thermal purposes, the term also applies to acoustic insulation, fire insulation, and impact insulation (e.g. for vibrations caused by industrial applications). Often an insulation material will be chosen for its ability to perform several of these functions at once.

jojoba: (Simmondsia chinensis): A shrub native to the Sonoran and Mojave deserts of Arizona, California, and Mexico. It is the sole species of the family Simmondsiaceae, placed in the core

Caryophyllales. It is also known as goat nut, deer nut, pignut, wild hazel, quinine nut, coffee-berry, and gray box bush. Jojoba is grown commercially for its oil, a liquid wax ester, expressed from the seed.

Laminated Veneer Lumber: (LVL): An engineered wood product that uses multiple layers of thin wood assembled with adhesives. It offers several advantages over typical milled lumber: it is stronger, straighter, and more uniform. It is much less likely than conventional lumber to warp, twist, bow, or shrink due to its composite nature. Made in a factory under controlled specifications, LVL products allow users to reduce the onsite labor. They are typically used for headers, beams, rimboard, and edge-forming material

Lye (Sodium Hydroxide): (NaOH), also known as caustic soda, is a caustic metallic base. Sodium hydroxide forms a strong alkaline solution when dissolved in a solvent such as water. However, only the hydroxide ion is basic. It is used in many industries, mostly as a strong chemical base in the manufacture of pulp and paper, textiles, drinking water, soaps and detergents and as a drain cleaner. Sodium hydroxide is a common base in chemical laboratories.

Macadamia: A genus of nine species of flowering plants in the family Proteaceae, with a disjunct distribution native to eastern Australia, New Caledonia and Sulawesi in Indonesia. They are small to large evergreen trees growing to 2–12 m tall. The fruit is a very hard woody globose follicle with a pointed apex, containing one or two seeds. The seeds are often consumed and used in confectionary, and its oil are often used in skin care products.

Parabens: A group of chemicals widely used as preservatives in the cosmetic and pharmaceutical industries. Parabens are effective preservatives in many types of formulas. These compounds, and their salts, are used primarily for their bactericidal and fungicidal properties. They can be found in shampoos, commercial moisturizers, shaving gels, personal lubricants, topical pharmaceuticals, spray tanning solution and toothpaste. They are also used as food additives.

Polyethylene: A thermoplastic commodity heavily used in consumer products (notably the plastic shopping bag). Over 60 million tons of the material is produced worldwide every year. Polyethylene is a polymer consisting of long chains of the monomer ethylene. Polyethylene is created through polymerization of ethene.

Polystyrene: A thermoplastic substance, which is in solid state at room temperature, but flows if heated above its glass transition temperature for manufacture, and becoming solid again when cooling off. Pure solid polystyrene is a colorless, hard plastic with limited flexibility. It can be cast into molds with fine detail. Polystyrene can be transparent or can be made to take on various colors. Solid polystyrene is used, for example, in disposable cutlery, plastic models, CD and DVD cases, and smoke detector housings. Products made from foamed polystyrene are nearly ubiquitous, for example packing materials, insulation, and foam drink cups.

Propylene Glycol: An organic compound, usually a faintly sweet, and colorless clear viscous liquid that is hygroscopic and miscible with water, acetone, and chloroform. It is used as a solvent in many pharmaceuticals, including oral, injectable and topical formulations. It is also used as a moisturizer in medicines, cosmetics, food, toothpaste, mouth wash, and tobacco products

Queensland: A state of Australia which occupies the north-eastern section of the mainland continent. It is bordered by the Northern Territory to the west, South Australia to the south-west and New South Wales to the south. To the east, Queensland is bordered by the Coral Sea and Pacific Ocean. The state is Australia's second largest by area, following Western Australia, and the country's third most populous after New South Wales and Victoria.

Saponification: The hydrolysis of an ester under basic conditions to form an alcohol and the salt of a carboxylic acid. Saponification is commonly used to refer to the reaction of a metallic alkali (base) with a fat or oil to form soap. Saponifiable substances are those that can be converted into soap

Sodium Laurel Sulfate: (SLS) or sodium dodecyl sulfate: An anionic surfactant used in many cleaning and hygiene products. The molecule has a tail of 12 carbon atoms, attached to a sulfate group, giving the molecule the amphiphilic properties required of a detergent. SLS is a highly effective surfactant used in any task requiring the removal of oily stains and residues. As such the compound is found in high concentrations in industrial products including engine degreasers, floor cleaners, and car wash soaps.

ENDNOTES

[1]   The research into small building firms was partially funded by the Cooperative Research Centre (CRC) for Construction Innovation, which commenced operations in July 2001 and was based at Queensland University of Technology's Gardens Point campus in Brisbane, Australia. The CRC was the result of an AUD14 million Commonwealth grant through the CRC Program and is complemented by AUD50 million of cash and in-kind support from partner organizations.

[2]   Acknowledgement is given to the Emerald Group Publishing Limited, publishers of *Construction Innovation* journal, for permission to publish material in the section of this chapter discussing innovation in small residential builders. This particular material was first published in the following article over which Emerald have copyright ownership: Thorpe D, D Ryan, N and Charles, M (2009), Innovation and small residential builders: an Australian study. *Construction Innovation*, 9(2), 184-200.

Chapter 17
Innovation System Linkages in Indian Hydrocarbon Sector

Prashant Dhodapkar
Oil India Limited, India

Anup Gogoi
Oil India Limited, India

Agadh Medhi
Oil India Limited, India

ABSTRACT

With the liberalization of Indian hydrocarbon sector, the various organizations that comprise this sector face the challenge of becoming globally competitive. This chapter elaborates the concept of innovation system, that is, the formal or informal linkages between the policy makers, industry, academic and research institutions, etc. and its relevance for organizational effectiveness. Using creative and visual thinking tools, authors explore the reasons for the fragmentation of innovation system of Oil India Limited (OIL), a national oil company operating mainly in the northeast India. This fragmentation is evident from several issues such as stagnating oil production, technological obsolescence, continued impact of natural calamities and conflicts in the region and prolonged dependence on central government funding. The authors suggest a high impact solution consisting of policy-making directed at promoting entrepreneurship, strengthening the innovation system through improved stakeholder communication and prioritizing the science and technology investments to address the regional problems.

BACKGROUND: INDIAN ECONOMY IN THE POST INDEPENDENCE PERIOD

Historically speaking, Indian economy has been the largest in the world, constituting about 20-30% of the global economy before the British ruled India. Under the British rule, the indigenous manufacturing base was decimated and the artisans were forced to lives of destitution. The global position of the Indian economy declined sharply. Some of the positive contributions of the British regime were the establishment of railways, roadways and postal system, educational system and institutions, etc. In the post-independence era, the Indian government adopted a socialist model and industrialization received a high priority. Also, it strived for supremacy

DOI: 10.4018/978-1-61520-643-8.ch017

in nuclear and space technologies. Protectionist measures were considered necessary to take care of the weaker sections of the society (Roy, 2007) and licenses were required for starting most of the businesses. The government wrested control of the hydrocarbon exploration, production and refining sector; considering these areas as too vital for national growth to be left in the control of private or multinational players.

Some of the notable achievements of the government in the post independence period were the 'green revolution', which transformed India from a country with frequent food shortages to one having surplus food. The expertise of India in nuclear energy and space technology has been considered to be on par with global standards.

With the increase in population and growth of economy, however, several constraints became obvious. The infrastructure was found to be inadequate and aging. The energy shortages were becoming acute and the promise of self-sufficiency in fossil fuels was becoming a distant dream. The licensing policy and protectionism was encouraging complacency and inhibiting competitive spirit of the businesses. While the urban landscapes provided contrasting images of slums alongside modern structures, the rural areas suffered due to migration to cities, outdated practices of agriculture, inadequate healthcare, etc.

The Liberalization Imperative

The balance of payment and fuel crisis in the 1990s forced the government of India to abandon the policy of protectionism. Policies for liberalizing the economy in order to integrate it with the global economy were taken up. It became apparent that the protectionist measures were stifling the growth and competitiveness of businesses. The most notable initiatives that formed the liberalization process were the capital market and hydrocarbon sector reforms, selective disinvestment from public sector enterprises, etc.

Another shift in the macroeconomic scene in recent years has been the emergence of India as the IT superpower and global destination for outsourcing. Economic growth picked up in the post-liberalization period, and one of the major factors contributing for the economic growth has been the emergence of a large middle class with disposable income and propensity for consumption. This has made India as one of the most important economies in the world after USA and China.

Liberalization, as it is being learnt in the wake of recent economic crises, brings in mixed results. Indian investors and businesses are exposed to volatility and uncertainties in a manner they had never imagined before. The stock market crash in the aftermath of economic crisis resulted in a standoff between government and businesses, with each side expecting other to do something about the situation.

Even with crises such as the prevailing one, the liberalization process will not be abandoned. Rather, these should serve to make the economy a 'learning' one. Some of the major concerns at this juncture are the underperforming agricultural sector and the relatively lower contribution of science and technology (S&T) to the economic growth process. Indeed, if the perception strengthens that economic growth or crises are the result of external factors, it will lead to the mindset that the circumstances are beyond one's control.

Post Liberalization Scenario in Hydrocarbon Sector

The liberalization of hydrocarbon sector (Atmanand, 2000) was necessitated due to the rising demand for fuels accompanying the economic growth and the stagnation in indigenous output of crude oil. The liberalization package of government of India, therefore, consisted of opening up the exploration, production and refining activities to private players, dismantling the administered price mechanism, offering a level playing field to national oil companies (NOCs) as well as private players. Financial incentives were offered for exploring in deep offshore areas, where the risks and rewards are perceived to be very high. The practice of offering exploration blocks to national oil companies on nomination basis was discontinued and private or multinational companies can hold up to 100% stake in exploration blocks and need not involve the stake of NOCs. Several rounds of bidding for exploration blocks have been carried out under the new exploration licensing policy (NELP).

The refining and petrochemical sector has seen a major change with the emergence of strong private players. This has resulted not only in self sufficiency in refining, but an exportable surplus of refined products. The legacy of socialist policies continues with respect to the pricing policies of petroleum products, and the refining companies have to shoulder considerable burden of subsidy on kerosene and diesel. This caused lot of financial trouble to the refiners in the recent period when the crude oil prices were very high. The scenario is not as good on the front of crude oil production. New hydrocarbon finds are either smaller in size or accompanied by decline from older oilfields. Many hydrocarbon finds by private companies such as Cairn Energy India Limited (CEIL) and Reliance Energy India Limited (REIL) are yet to gain commercial status. The natural gas market in India is still in the emerging stage, although some commercial level exploitation in the form of petrochemicals production is established.

The demand for liquid fossil fuels continues to be high, and the NOCs have been encouraged to explore for oil overseas to strengthen the efforts for national self-sufficiency. The NOCs have also acquired stakes in hydrocarbon value chain and Oil and Natural Gas Corporation Limited (ONGCL) is now a vertically integrated company with presence in all the regions of India and several countries abroad. It is the biggest company in India and figures in the list of 'Fortune 500' companies. The production of Oil India Limited (OIL) is limited

mostly to northeastern state of Assam, with some stake as a joint venture partner in Arunachal Pradesh and gas production from Rajasthan. OIL is also pursuing stakes in in-country and overseas exploration blocks, as well as in hydrocarbon value chain. The distinction in upstream and downstream is therefore getting blurred, especially since national companies (ONGCL, OIL, Indian Oil Corporation, Gas Authority of India Limited, Bharat Petroleum Corporation Limited, Hindustan Petroleum Corporation Limited, etc.) are forming consortiums for exploration within and outside the country. This is considered as a significant strategy to counter stiff competition for exploration blocks, especially in exploration 'hotspots' such as Africa.

The impact of private sector and multinational companies' participation in exploration and production of hydrocarbons has been mixed. Companies such as CEIL, REIL, Gujarat State Petroleum Corporation, British Gas, Hindustan Oil Exploration Corporation, Shell have been successful in many exploration ventures and demonstrated technology capabilities and helped in establishing critical infrastructure. On the other hand, these companies depend heavily on NOCs for sourcing experienced manpower. The bulk of the crude oil production still comes from NOCs, and some of the non-NOCs' contribution of production comes from blocks which were discovered and developed by NOCs.

Implications of Liberalized Regime for NOCs

The liberalization of hydrocarbon sector has meant more competition for the NOCs. This has only compounded the problems of upstream hydrocarbon companies. There are many uncertainties in the business of finding and producing hydrocarbons: the price of crude oil, a commodity which is actively traded worldwide, is subjected to supply and demand changes and as such is very volatile. Various factors such as new finds of reserves, decline in old reserves, disruptions in supply due to wars or bad weather, technological changes, regulations, economic and social factors, etc. affect the demand and supply and hence the price. In the new liberalized scenario, the challenges for upstream companies have increased: Study of complex geological settings that form the underground reserves, negotiating in a competitive environment, carrying out operations in difficult or unknown terrains, establishing and producing oil in complex technical and environmental settings, etc. Most of the exploration methods cannot directly detect presence of hydrocarbons before the drilling of oil wells is actually completed. Typically, oil companies drill many wells before presence or absence of hydrocarbons can be established. Indeed, it is like a costly gamble.

The prevailing prices of crude oil dictate the level of exploration activity. However, even experts have failed to correctly predict the crude oil prices. The rising trend in crude oil prices is not necessarily good for exploration companies. Firstly consumption declines and investments become risky. Oilfield services, supplies and expertise also become costly proportionately. Developing economies suffer due to balance of payment situation. The decline in oil prices lead to reduced income from sales. Thus the profitability of oil companies is very uncertain due to fluctuating oil prices.

HOW TO TACKLE THE CHALLENGES?

The long term future of hydrocarbon industry continues to be debated due to the complexities of issues such as the non-renewable nature of hydrocarbons, the uneven geographical distribution and the conflicts arising out of it, the global warming effects associated with the usage of fossil fuels, etc. Even though the reasons for moving away from fossil fuels are well understood, there

is a reluctance to do so because many economies depend on the revenues from fossil fuels and there are hardly any alternatives to fossil fuels in transportation sector.

The biggest question in the minds of policy makers is: What is the future of Hydrocarbons? As per the "Peak oil theory" (Deffeys, 2001), made famous by the influential think-tank Club of Rome, the world should have seen an irreversible decline in crude oil production sometime around 2005. The level of consumption cannot be supported by the diminishing reserves of crude oil, and all the major reservoirs have already been discovered. As per another theory that supports the "technology view" (Holditch, 2007) the hydrocarbon resources base can be represented by a pyramid, with the easy-to-produce resources at the apex of the pyramid and the most difficult at the base of the pyramid. With the advancements in technology, even the more difficult resources can be exploited, the decline in existing reservoirs minimized and hence the amount of resources is virtually inexhaustible. This theory can be supported by the fact that resources which were considered of very poor quality, e.g., heavy oil, shale oil, hydrocarbons in low permeability reservoirs or deepwater offshore, coal bed methane, etc. are being exploited with the advancements in technology. Technologies for extraction of hydrocarbons from coal, shale, biomass and waste, etc. continue to be developed and hence the resource base continues to be widened.

A growing number of experts now favor a move towards exploitation of renewable energy sources. This is also a valid view since the environment may not be able to sustain the level of consumption of developed and developing countries. With increased focus on complex reservoirs and low quality reserves, the dependence on hydrocarbons will not be ecologically or economically sustainable.

All these mean that the nature of hydrocarbon industry will continue to change. The organizations comprising hydrocarbon industry have to develop a long term vision. In the immediate context, there will be demands on technology and competencies.

Role of Technological Capability

The foregoing discussions bring out the urgent need for the hydrocarbon organizations to become technologically competitive. The nature of hydrocarbon industry has not changed very much over the years. Broadly, the upstream hydrocarbon industry comprises of national oil companies, major multinationals, independent companies, service companies, companies that provide engineering and process support and consultants, etc. New technologies, embodied in new knowledge, equipment or skills, are mostly developed by service companies in-house or acquired through licenses. Technological developments are generally slow in hydrocarbon sector due to long lead times, uncertainty regarding viability of investments, etc. Many oil companies also have in-house research and development infrastructure for technology absorption. Creativity and innovations, however, take a back seat in the hierarchical decision making that characterize the national oil companies.

Internal Restructuring for Competitiveness

The restructuring efforts of hydrocarbon upstream companies, ONGCL and OIL, have focused on efficient organizational structures and better decision making and/or autonomy. Globally, multidisciplinary teams are a norm in E&P operations and hence ONGCL has restructured from a conglomeration of regional business units to a more flat structure comprising of subsurface and surface divisions.

OIL is also undergoing a process of organizational change. Its core activities of exploration, drilling, production and transportation of hydrocarbons are being restructured as per the multidisciplinary team concept and an organiza-

tion vision has been co-created. This vision has six component statements that emphasize fastest growth and profitability, knowledge enhancement and teamwork, core organizational values and stakeholder orientation, etc. Rather than focusing on profits (which could change as per market conditions), the organization intends to make learning as its core competence. Addressing technological obsolescence and becoming a global operator are high priority goals. The company has implemented enterprise resource planning software to streamline its non-core activities, and its change programs are being implemented through specially trained and oriented "Breakthrough Performance" coaches.

EXTERNAL ORIENTATION: COMPETITION AND COLLABORATION

Internal restructuring alone cannot guarantee the superior performance of organizations in a global economy where the rules of competition and market are changing rapidly. Instead of generating profits only, organizations are expected to ensure sustainability and social wellbeing. Rather than controlling a larger part of the environment beyond their boundary, organizations can ensure their own progress through collaboration with stakeholders and recognizing that social capital is as important as other tangible and intangible assets. Whereas the restructuring efforts normally focus on supply chain management, quality management, downsizing or rightsizing; the new paradigms emphasize interdependence.

A NEW PERSPECTIVE: INNOVATION SYSTEM

Since 1990s, a perspective that is becoming increasingly important is the 'innovation system' (National innovation systems, 1997). As per this concept, the linkages between the different institutions, public or private, determine the innovative performance of the firms and hence the competitiveness of a region. The linkages refer to the exchange of knowledge or resources between the different institutions, whether in a formal or informal way. Innovation systems are broadly classified as national and regional (sub-national and trans-national).

The concept of innovation system is new as well as evolving, and therefore needs some elaboration. The definition implies some kind of synergy between institutions in a region. This synergy exists because of some pre-defined objectives and complementarities between the institutions. Superficially, institutions in a region may be related to each other as suppliers and buyers, competitors, research or technology providers and technology end-users, etc. However, without any formal or informal understanding and stated objectives between such actors, synergy cannot emerge. On some occasions, the competitiveness of a region has been the result of cooperation between firms, without any formal agreements.

The competitiveness of a region may be transient as in the case of a new enterprise where the linkages between suppliers, venture capitalists, entrepreneurs and policy makers are emerging. In a mature industrial area, obsolescence of existing technology or inability of the enterprise to absorb new technology is a sign of fragmented innovation system. As per the "growth pole" theory, concentration of capital and resources takes place in a region due to the relative advantage with respect to some resource. Other theories of differential growth point out the abilities of certain urban regions to attract capital, knowledge, human resource; which leads to higher growth in that area. Thus, growth of a region leads to development inequality, as economic migration from other regions takes place. Other theories, such as the 'five forces model' of Porter, explain the superior performance of a region or firm.

From the foregoing discussion it is clear that unequal development is common, and indeed this has been observed even in the case of very developed countries and regions (Knowles & Wareing, 2007). It may be possible to achieve the profitability of the firm through short term measures, but this will not address the systemic causes of problems. Organizations such as OECD and UNIDO are attempting to address economic growth and competitiveness through regional initiatives for 'wiring up' national innovation systems.

In a regional setting, the entities such as universities are typically the 'knowledge producers' and the industries are 'knowledge consumers'. Together with the venture capitalists and the policy makers, these knowledge producers and consumers form the 'innovation ecosystem'. The linkages in the innovation system determine the knowledge, wealth creation and growth of the region. These linkages can be of various forms: industry-institution or public-private partnerships, joint research projects, science or technology incubators or parks, innovation clusters, knowledge sharing and creating activities such as fairs, workshops and conferences, etc. and result in complex synergistic effects.

Micro-economic and macro-economic studies and theories may be able to explain the reasons for performance of a firm (on the basis of its structure, technology, leadership, motivation, values etc.) or region (on the basis of available resources, policies, infrastructure, GDP, intellectual property, etc) but do not necessarily offer solutions to problems. In fact, the micro-economic or macro-economic theories do not take into consideration the interdependencies in the system. The innovation system perspective offers a method for addressing the problem of chronic underperformance of a region. Though the dynamics of innovation system is very complex, we offer a simple framework for understanding a particular innovation system. This framework is depicted in figure 1.

As per the framework, the innovation system is characterized by the complementary resources as identified by the actors and the shared objectives

Figure 1. Framework for understanding innovation system linkages

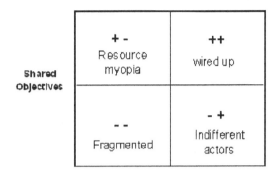

(such as promoting S&T activities or entrepreneurship, informing policy makers, mutual learning, etc). Ideally, the entities in the innovation system will have shared objectives and also identify complementary resources such as knowledge and skills. In such a case, the innovation system actors will be willing to work for the regional development and the innovation system may be said to be 'wired up'.

The Hydrocarbon Industry and Its Innovation System

The national innovation system of the hydrocarbon industry (comprising of the 2 upstream national oil companies, several private exploration companies and joint ventures, 17 public sector and 1 private refining company, petrochemical and other downstream companies etc) is rather complex. The overall functioning of the industry is regulated by the Ministry of Petroleum and Natural Gas and its related organizations (The organization, n.d.). The Petroleum and Natural Gas regulatory Board provides regulatory framework in the form of policies, rules, acts and notifications. The Petroleum Planning and Analysis Cell (replacing the erstwhile Oil Coordination Committee) oversees the hydrocarbon pricing issues. The Directorate General of Hydrocarbons oversees the status of exploration licenses granted to various companies

and the production sharing contracts, the work programs for new areas offered for exploration, etc and also the status of blocks offered for exploitation of coal bed methane. The Oil Industry Development Board administers the common fund of the participating companies that is made available for projects of national importance. The Oil Industry Safety Directorate and the Petroleum Conservation Research Association provide the safety and conservation awareness support and measures. ONGC Videsh Limited is the overseas arm of ONGCL. The Petroleum Federation of India provides technical support to the industry by organizing conferences and disseminating relevant information.

The Ministry and its organizations work in close cooperation with other bodies and ministries such as the Planning Commission, Finance, Human Resources Development, Science and Technology, etc. The high profile Planning Commission provides the long term projections, policies and allocations for the entire economy including the energy sector. The state and central governments collect revenues from the industry in the form of royalty, cess, duties and taxes and formulate the environmental guidelines through central and state pollution control boards.

The S&T organization of India consists of Ministry of S&T at the apex and the various departments, autonomous institutes, and in-house R&D institutes comprising the infrastructure. The broad S&T policy, formulated in 1983, emphasizes poverty alleviation and social well being, capability building in key areas, technology absorption, making optimum utilization of the S&T infrastructure, etc. India has shown an impressive growth in knowledge sector and it is the main component of economy today, in comparison to agriculture or manufacturing. India's human resource is very good, and ranks 4th in the world, ahead of many developed countries (Indian manufacturing industry, 2005).

The innovation ecosystem of the hydrocarbon industry, however, presents several challenges.

The industry has been traditionally a profit making one, thanks to the continued demand for petroleum and the hitherto regulated environment provided by the "administered price mechanism". However, under the progressively deregulated scenario, the profitability of the companies will be determined by their ability to confront uncertainties. The refining sector was under tremendous pressure in the recently concluded phase of high crude oil prices, since it was not able to pass on the price burden to consumers. With dropping of oil prices, there is some relief for the country on the balance of payment front, but the upstream oil companies will be under pressure to maintain their profitability.

Increasing thrust is given to technological capability building and talent management by the upstream hydrocarbon companies, ONGCL and OIL. Overall, the technological capability in the hydrocarbon sector can be considered as intermediate one. In the period immediately following the economic liberalization, great emphasis was given on indigenization of mature technologies which were critical for the operations. As a result of such efforts, organizations such as Engineers India Limited, Bharat Heavy Electrical Limited; and research institutes such as Indian Institute of Petroleum and Council of Scientific and Industrial Research have supplemented the in-house R&D efforts of the hydrocarbon companies. Unfortunately, although India is well positioned with respect to the S&T manpower and infrastructure, there is a general shortage of S&T programs specifically for the industry. The industries have to rely on in-house R&D, and on outsourcing to global service companies for the latest technologies. The fragmentation of innovation system is in fact a common problem to the India economy.

With regard to the manpower sourcing, the industry suffers from the "tragedy of commons" in a labor surplus economy (Workforce sustainability and talent management, 2006). The global hydrocarbon exploration and production companies have, from time to time, sourced skilled manpower requirements from the national oil

companies. Manpower attrition in large numbers has been a common phenomenon during high oil price regimes. There is dearth of educational institutes offering courses especially for hydrocarbon industry, although the number of general engineering and science graduates is quite high. Training and retaining talent therefore remains a priority area for hydrocarbon industry.

ONGCL AND OIL: CONTRASTING PROFILES

OIL and ONGCL share some of the challenges in hydrocarbon exploration and production, especially on the front of growth and competitiveness. However, ONGCL and OIL have very contrasting profiles. ONGCL is a conglomerate of global presence and has achieved integration in hydrocarbon value chain. It has exploration as well as producing assets overseas, apart from the majority stake in domestic hydrocarbon production. It has several R&D institutes that give it an advantage in developing and absorbing key technologies. It also has formed a consortium with the Steel giant Arcelor-Mittal for securing stakes in global hydrocarbon infrastructure.

In comparison to ONGCL, OIL has limited presence at the national level. It has reached a production plateau of around 3 million tons per annum for several decades. It is aggressively pursuing opportunities in hydrocarbon sector in India and abroad. One of the main issues for achieving breakthrough performance is technology innovation on a sustained basis. There are several barriers for enhancing technology absorption capability, some of which are cultural in nature and have been discussed in an earlier work (Dhodapkar, et al., 2006).

The greatest challenge for OIL in the coming years will be to fight extreme marginalization in the overall hydrocarbon scenario. The relatively new entrants in the hydrocarbon exploration and production business, namely, Reliance Energy India Limited, Cairn Energy India Limited and Gujarat

State Petroleum Corporation Limited; have been reasonably successful in their exploration ventures in the country. The crude oil production of OIL is concentrated in the northeastern region with gas production from Rajasthan. The oil production and refining facilities in the region are land locked and hence there is mutual dependence between OIL the refineries in this region. Any event with a potential to cause disruption or non-sustenance of refineries could also adversely affect OIL. A change in OIL's fortunes, on the contrary, may not make a huge impact at the national level, since there is an exportable refining capacity.

The northeast India has enough potential in conventional as well as unconventional hydrocarbons and energy. Apart from OIL, ONGCL has oil producing assets. Active exploration in many of the sedimentary basins is on. Monetization of stranded gas, coal liquefaction or gasification, shale oil, etc. is a less conventional opportunity in the hydrocarbon sector. The region also has hydroelectric potential which has not yet been fully tapped.

There are several challenges to be surmounted if the region has to emerge as a major energy hub. The primary energy consumption in the region is very low, as it is underdeveloped. Years of social and political unrest has made this region very unattractive for investment. For OIL, it is very important to understand and integrate the innovation system for its own survival and growth.

In following sections, we discuss the subnational regional innovation system of OIL.

SUB-NATIONAL REGIONAL INNOVATION SYSTEM: INDIA'S NORTHEAST REGION

The northeastern region of India consists of the states of Assam, Nagaland, Arunachal Pradesh, Meghalaya, Mizoram, Tripura, Manipur (the seven sisters) and Sikkim is often included in the region. Apart from geographical proximity, these states share historical ties since it was an integrated region prior to India's independence. The region has various ethnic groups and cultural diversity that makes it different from the other regions of the country. Unfortunately, these states share a very narrow strip of land with India's mainland. The diverse physiographical features of this region include mountains, hills, alluvial flood plains of the mighty Brahmaputra river, lakes and wetlands, etc.

The northeastern region holds lot of charm due to the various tribes and their culture and cuisine. The region's biodiversity consists of primates, cats, elephants, rhinos, many species of orchids, birds, etc. The region receives very heavy rainfall, about 3 to 10 m annually. Northeastern India accounts for a substantial amount of tea and rice production and forest cover in the country. The coal deposits amount to about 980 million tones, mainly in Assam and Meghalaya. The region accounts for 45% of India's onshore crude oil production (with OIL producing 3.5 million tonnes per annum and ONGCL 1.4 million tonnes per annum. In addition to crude oil, the region has natural gas as well as oil shales and hydroelectric potential. As per the latest perceptions, the northeast has very high potential for tourism, telecommunications, IT and IT enabled services.

The region has a reasonable educational infrastructure, with about 500 colleges, 12 universities, 10 colleges providing BE/ BTech or ME/ MTech degrees approved by the All India Council of Technical Education (AICTE), 18 polytechnic colleges, and Indian Institute of Technology at Guwahati. The major research infrastructure consists of the Regional Research Institute at Jorhat, in-house research and development facilities of OIL and ONGCL and the biotechnology research facilities with various universities. The literacy rates of northeastern states are very high (65 to 70%) and compare favorably with national average.

The northeastern region is seismically the most active region in the world (zone V) and 19th and 20th centuries witnessed some very devastating earthquakes. The river Brahmaputra, with its shallow channels and wide banks, causes havoc due to floods year-after-year, earning it the sobriquet of 'the river of tears'. The hilly regions of Nagaland and Manipur are prone to landslides, causing disruptions in road movements and supplies. The air, rail and road links within the region and with the mainland are very limited. Once an integrated and thriving region, years of isolation after the independence has caused the region to fall back on development. The primary energy consumption is very low. The agricultural methods are very basic and inefficiencies in power supplies are common.

Years of underdevelopment has resulted in sense of alienation. There was insurgency in the region following the reorganization of the erstwhile integrated Assam state, and unrest in some form or other has continued till date. The various insurgents have demanded separation from mainland India, or at least greater autonomy, on the basis of alleged exploitation of the regional resources by 'imperial India'. The regional problems have been compounded by the influx of people from other states and countries. These immigrants have become part of the economy as unskilled labor in brick kilns, coal mines and other menial tasks. The political controversies over the disputed citizenship of such polulation have added to the woes of this region. Illicit drugs, unemployment and extortions have further affected the progress of this region.

The government of India has tried to address the development agenda for the region through liberal funding and various schemes and initiatives (Transforming the northeast, 1997). In 1972, North East Council (NEC) came into existence specifically for the development of northeast India. Also, Ministry for Development of Northeast Region (MDoNER) has been functioning for sometime. Presently, the NEC is chaired by Minister, DoNER with other members, secretaries, advisors, etc. The North East Development Federation of India, a consortium of banks, was formed with the objective of funding enterprises in the region for achieving growth. The central government

provides the bulk of the state outlays, upto 90%, with only 10% as loan and the remaining as grant. After 1990s, realizing that the development in the region was inadequate; it was decided to allocate 10% of the national budget for northeast India. Sensing the difficulties in disbursing the funds, a scheme known as 'Non-relapsable Central Pool of Resources' was announced. In recent years, the Prime Minister of India has released funds for several northeastern states as "special package for northeast" (Prime Minister package for north east states, n.d.). The central government is considering another initiative with the state governments of northeast region, namely the "Look East Policy" wherein the infrastructure development in the region will also consider the possibility of forging ties with neighboring countries such as Bangladesh, Myanmar, Thailand, and China by re-establishing old trade links and waterways.

Presently, a few development projects with international aid are underway. One such project for assessment and development of natural resources, managing of river erosion and environment; is funded by the World Bank. Another project with the funding of Asian Development Bank envisages urban development in 5 cities of northeast India and poverty reduction. The International Fund for Agriculture and Development was a special scheme with NEC collaboration that started in 1998 and concluded in 2006. The focus of the scheme was strengthening the regional communities, including self help groups, and capacity building for rural poverty alleviation and providing sustainable livelihood. The project was reported to be quite successful and plans are underway to replicate the model.

Overall, the decades of efforts have yielded inadequate results. The reports of Planning Commission in respect of northeast region highlight the slow progress in terms of infrastructure, basic amenities and healthcare, etc. Even though the importance of exploiting the natural advantages and addressing the development bottlenecks are well understood, the major hurdle in implementing the development agenda seem to be the inadequate scientific studies on various issues. For example, although the devastation in the form of floods and erosion caused by river Brahmaputra is a common occurrence, the scientific information on channel morphology at various places is lacking due to the sheer magnitude of the task. Even basic demography and economic indicators are not available for some of the states.

The sustainable development of the northeast region, therefore, will be achieved through bottom-up initiatives from the innovation system actors. Such initiatives will raise the profile of S&T in addressing the regional problems (Using foresight to improve the science-policy relationship, 2006), promote mutual learning and trust and inform the policy makers on priority areas. Without initiatives for building social capital and wiring up the innovation system, the impact of precious funds will continue to remain diluted. Such initiatives can be taken up after understanding the regional issues in systemic perspective. This has been attempted in the following section.

SYSTEMIC UNDERSTANDING THROUGH CAUSAL LOOP DIAGRAM (CLD)

As per the concept of innovation system, the organizations (such as OIL) do not operate in isolation but have a complex socio-technical system which affects how it can create or absorb innovations. Persisting organizational problems such as underperformance, stagnation or technological obsolescence indicate that the innovation system is fragmented. As a first step in integrating or 'wiring up' the innovation system, the interdependencies of the various events and variables needs to be understood in the form of a cause-and-effect relationship. It must be emphasized that the cause-and-effect relationships in a system are not linear, but form complex feedback loops. Thus there is an element of interdependency in the system, and

intervention strategies must consider the system as a whole rather than the sum of parts.

The interdependencies in any socio-technical system can be better appreciated with the help of systems theory (Senge, 2006) and visual thinking tools such as causal loop diagrams or stock-and-flow diagrams.

We have depicted the fragmentation of the innovation system in northeastern region with the help of causal loop diagram (figure 2) consisting of several sub-loops. Unlike a linear system, there is no definite beginning or end point in the system. For the purpose of discussion, we can start with an important variable such as regional growth (shown simply as 'growth' in the diagram). The lack of growth leads to unemployment, which in turn leads to unrest in the region and creates an unfavorable investment climate. Ultimately, this completes a vicious cycle by inhibiting the regional growth.

Prolonged stagnation leads to the community in the region becoming demanding towards the businesses or industries of the region. Such demands may be of somewhat legitimate nature, say requests for investment in healthcare or public facilities; or could be in the form of extortions. Repeated requests of such nature increase the standoff between the business/industries and the community, resulting in an environment characterized by low social capital.

The low social capital and the perception of regional backwardness results in a situation wherein the state and central governments concentrate on welfare measures such as relief and rehabilitation (in the events of natural calamities) or providing basic amenities (primary education or healthcare) and infrastructure to improve the situation. Capacity building activities, however, suffer due to inadequate managerial expertise and other geopolitical difficulties. Indicators such as delayed projects, insufficient utilization of funds become prominent and result in dilution of policy focus from innovation based activities. Due to the continued dependence on funding without

Figure 2. Casual loop diagram for the innovation system in northeast India

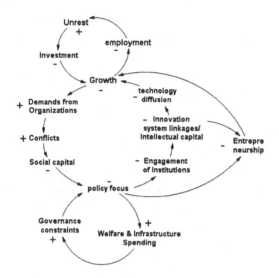

any means to make the investments effective, governance becomes difficult and another vicious cycle results.

Thus the region continues to suffer from fragmentation of innovation system in the form of low industry-academia interaction or generation of intellectual property (scientific or technical publications, patents, etc.). Diffusion of technical innovations is slow and entrepreneurship is a rare quality. The regional growth, therefore, continues to suffer.

The above 'picture' of the region can be considered to be valid since the various events recur and form a pattern and are amenable to study through observation or reports. The causal loop diagram helps to explain the reasons for the regional problems and issues. Some of the innovation system actors might argue that the picture offered by the CLD is too negative, in real life situation many initiatives exist for solving the regional problems. This can be a real problem, and agencies responsible for the region can become very defensive, inhibiting or paralyzing the capability building process.

The CLD can be used to facilitate communication between the regional stakeholders.

Especially, it can be used to open up discussion on some key issues: What are the reasons for chronic underdevelopment in the region? Why is the generous and prolonged funding by various agencies not yielding the desired outcome? What could be the actions that will be beneficial for the region? Indeed, if the regional agencies share the perceptions about the regional problems, it could pave the way for development of lasting solutions.

The most powerful use of CLD lies in identifying one (or at the most two) actions that could have a high positive impact on the regional innovation and growth. This is because a lot of energy and resources can be wasted in trying to address too many issues at a time. A careful look at the CLD suggests that the key to regional innovation lies in formulation of appropriate policies. The focus of the policy should be on strengthening of networks in the innovation system in order to enhance the profile of science and technology. This will help in several ways: 1. Focus on S&T development will increase the regional intellectual capital and ultimately in technopreneurship. 2. The S&T solutions to address regional disasters and calamities will result in lower dependence on relief and rehabilitation funding and thus conserve resources and ultimately enhance the quality of life in the region. 3. The capability of innovation system actors to address the various issues will lead to enhanced social capital. Thus, the various vicious loops in the CLD will turn into virtuous ones.

Another creative communication method, namely, force field analysis, helps us to understand that the prevailing situation in a region is a result of equilibrium between two sets of opposing forces, one acting in positive direction to try and improve it; whereas there is an opposing force trying to worsen the situation. The situation has been depicted in the accompanying figure 3. The positive forces could be the development policies of the government, entrepreneurship qualities in the people of the region, the intellectual property generated by the researchers and the industries, the natural resources of the region, etc. The nega-

Figure 3. Force field analysis for the innovation system in northeast India

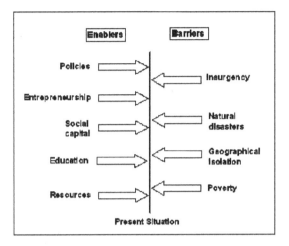

tive forces could be the natural and man made disturbances (earthquakes, floods and coastal erosion, landslides; acts of insurgency, problems arising out of migration from neighboring countries and other states such as Bangladesh, Nepal, Bihar and UP, etc) and inadequate utilization of developmental funds, lack of trust in the political environment, etc.

It is worth noting that the positive and negative forces need not be equal in number. We need not estimate the magnitude of these forces in any way. To use the tool effectively, we need to list the positive and negative influences as exhaustively as possible. To improve the situation the positive forces have to be reinforced and the impact of negative ones minimized.

What makes it so difficult to identify the high leverage actions such as effective policy making? The various stakeholders such as government, institutions and businesses often adopt reactive measures to address the regional issues. Government is quick to announce relief and rehabilitation measures in the event of disasters, to avoid political backlash. Industries are often engaged in 'imitative' innovation, purchasing modern technology embodied in equipment and machinery from outside the region or country.

Political exploitation of problems and issues is a common occurrence. A long term effect of these factors is a decline in the technology absorption capacity in the region. The Planning Commission has noted in its reports that the funds provided for the region have not yielded the desired results (Report on evaluation study of the growth centres scheme, n.d.). Senge (2006) has described such situations in the form of archetypes of systemic causal loop diagrams. For example, the situation in northeastern part of India can be described as an archetype called "shifting the burden to intervener". The symptoms of problems are relieved by short term measures such as help from external agency, in the case of northeast region, the central government. Fundamental solutions require time for deploying, and are therefore overlooked. In the long run, undesirable side effects appear, urgency to remedy the situation increases and the inclination or capability to effect fundamental, radical changes diminishes.

Importance of 'Wiring up' Innovation System in Northeast Region

The implications of the foregoing discussion are obvious. In absence of fundamental interventions, the central and other development funds will continue to be wasted. This may not be agreeable to all actors in the innovation system, especially the state governments who have been the chief beneficiaries of the funds. We argue that there are several reasons for inefficient utilization of funds: the inadequate absorptive capacity in the region, and the inherent inefficiency of government machinery in distributing and utilizing funds. Most of the funds, for example, could be taken up by expenses towards the salaries and administrative activities, rather than core development activities. Moreover, the objectives of the government are often too broad to make an impact on specific issues. Lack of progress can result in a mindset of helplessness in achieving any positive change.

PRELIMINARY STEPS IN STRENGTHENING THE INNOVATION SYSTEM LINKAGES

Often the high leverage actionable areas for regional problems cannot be identified in a straightforward manner. For example, it is not easy to state that enhancing entrepreneurship or employment generation will lead to reduction in insurgency. The factors that lead to deepening of insurgency related issues are often not perceived or shared by all agencies and hence are not amenable to systemic analysis. Various researchers are studying the inter-relationship between factors such as entrepreneurship development, strong multi-level governance, social cohesion and regional development. As non-military initiatives, the importance of educating the public (Fotion, et. al., 2008) and networking and communicating with the stakeholders cannot be overemphasized.

A Review of Visions and Perspective Plans

It can be argued that the initiatives of the government are thorough and short term measures as well long term plans and visions are often in place. The government carries out its development agenda through the Planning Commission's 5-year plans. The plan components are designed by very high level committees with the Prime Minister as the highest authority and the other functionaries include ministers, members, sectoral experts, etc. Additionally, the perspective plans such as Vision 2020 provide the details of long term trends and the actions that will be needed on vital issues such as energy security.

What could be the possible shortcomings of the plans that lead to slow or inadequate development? Definitely there is no lack of funds or political will. From the trends in innovation system studies, however, following points emerge as the weaknesses of the perspective plans. Firstly, these are mostly 'experts only' initiatives that rarely involve larger stakeholders. Innovation system and foresight experts often point out the importance of tapping distributed knowledge, since an individual is unlikely to possess all the solutions to problems in an era of uncertainty. Secondly, these studies rely on trends and extrapolation. Thus scope for diversions from the trends, hence the opportunities and threats, are missed out. The perspective plans are too broad; they do not focus on areas that could be vital for national or regional competitiveness. Again, one may be missing some opportunities or ignoring potential threats.

It can be concluded that the various studies done at the central government level are definitely effective in identifying the areas of concern, such as entrepreneurship, but the policy focus and program delivery has some serious weaknesses. This is not to criticize the government (we do that too often), but to introspect as businesses and stakeholder, and explore exciting opportunities that lie in networking and joint action.

WHAT HAS BEEN DONE ELSEWHERE?

Unequal development is a common phenomenon. In fact, development of a region or urban area always leads to some kind of development inequality since the resources from other regions get diverted to the developing region. Experts study unequal development from different perspectives: to see why certain regions are doing better than others, and trying to replicate the model elsewhere. On the other hand, the chronically depressed or problem regions are studied for intervention opportunities and policies. Therefore, the literature is full of positive and negative case studies.

Economic prosperity and wellbeing is a common goal of all interventions or studies, though there are regional flavors. What makes the case of northeast India regional innovation system very unique is the dimension of the problems. One cannot have a very broad, generalized solution for the region, at the same time it is very important to identify focus areas so that some impact can be achieved that can boost the confidence of stakeholders to achieve change.

Examples from other regions are important during discussions with stakeholders, and need to be studied in details. Some of the parallels to the case of northeast India are the Rhine-Neckar-Triangle region in Germany (Stahl, 2007), the SME cluster in northern Italy, (Humphrey & Schmitz, 1995) etc. UNIDO is taking up regional initiatives for economic integration through foresight activities in Central and East European countries and the newly independent states from the erstwhile USSR. The rationale for these initiatives is very clear: the young nations could lapse into serious economic crises unless priority areas and suitable policies are identified. This is a lesson for many of the separatist groups and leaders in the Indian subcontinent, one cannot demand independence, and interdependence is the key to progress and growth.

Use of Technology Foresight for Wiring up Innovation System

Fragmentation of innovation system is the most notable feature of the sub-national regional innovation system of northeastern India and the host national innovation system. On one hand, the nation ranks high in human resource index, ahead of many developed countries. But the research, technology development and innovation (RTDI) efforts are not as spectacular. The education system has been criticized as 'factories' for producing graduates, without accompanying accrual of intellectual property that can be exploited. Technology absoption capacity at the regional or sectoral level tends to be low. This is clearly manifested in the slow growth of agricultural sector where the technology in use is at basic level. Besides workforce development at organizational, regional and national level, enhancing the profile of S&T

in dealing with regional problems will remain a high priority objective.

Technology foresight (UNIDO technology foresight manual, 2005 and Experience and ideas for developing foresight, 2004) is a long range planning tool that involves anticipatory intelligence, participation of stakeholders and building networks, vision and action. When carried out at the regional level, foresight has the potential to identify areas of uncertainty and impact for the region. In a typical bottom up approach, the innovation system actors identify areas for joint action and inform policy makers on issues relevant to them. Thus it is a more proactive approach and there could be many tangible as well intangible benefits for the participants. It is a very attractive option for wiring up the innovation system in northeast India.

From the voluminous literature available on the foresight initiatives, it is clear that lot of groundwork needs to be done prior to initiating the foresight activity in a regional setting. We have already made some progress in identifying the key issues in hydrocarbon sector and the regional innovation system in northeast India. A broad picture of the policies and programs for the region and their shortcomings has been identified.

The challenge in the near future will be to identify actors and institutions that can play a major role in achieving the success of interventions such as foresight. The scoping for the foresight initiative will be far from straightforward. Apart from involving the Management of OIL, which might play the role of initiator, the involvement and sponsorship of MDoNER will be very crucial. The steering committee will be a mix of experts from disciplines such as social and natural sciences, universities and research institutes, etc. To effectively interact with the stakeholders, the Strength, weaknesses, opportunities and threats (SWOT) framework is a very useful tool. This tool conveys a lot of information about the internal environment and external threats to the system.

A tentative SWOT analysis for northeast region is depicted in figure 4.

There are several steps involved in the foresight exercise, namely (1) preforesight: identifying the major problem areas and collecting information, identification of key persons for expert panel and carry out the scoping, (2) Carry out the foresight exercise that will result in formulation of key policies and recommendations, (3) implementation and follow-up action, as well as dissemination of the information about the foresight to larger stakeholders.

The concept of learning regions is becoming increasingly important. In most of the innovation system interventions, the outcomes such as networking of stakeholders and mutual learning are very important. In fact, a sustainable change can be achieved if the actors in the region collaborate, learn from each other and tackle regional problems effectively.

Though the foresight exercise can be initiated by an organization that feels the need for change, the objective of the exercise has to be relevant for the region. In the case of northeast India, the objective can be capability building in a single sector, such as energy or biotechnology. On the other hand, informing the policy makers can emerge as the most key impact area. Industrial innovation also can be achieved through clustering activities. Again, the options can be very diverse: from cluster of SMEs to supplier dominated energy clusters.

Communication and Dissemination Strategies: Content, Reach and Interaction

As has been discussed, strengthening the regional innovation system can be done in various ways. Whatever may be the nature of initiatives, one thing is common to all of them: communication. After all, innovation system is about linkages and 'wiring up' calls for mobilizing support and action, exploring issues, legitimizing initiatives, ensuring commitment and informing priorities. While at the commencement of the initiative the focus is on sharing earlier work and building up expectations, at the conclusion of the initiative the reports, policies and other outcomes have to be monitored and communicated periodically. A sound strategy for communication and dissemination is, therefore, a must.

There is a risk of communicating too little or too much, both can be damaging for the credibility of the actors. For example, it may appear unimportant to inform laypersons regarding a foresight exercise. However, all development efforts affect the people (the ultimate stakeholders) and their support and interest is crucial. Even if laypersons cannot be expected to actively participate in the linkages, their concerns and expectations can provide vital insights for the policy makers and efforts must be made to understand the same. Researchers, industry chiefs, academicians and

Figure 4. SWOT analysis for northeast India

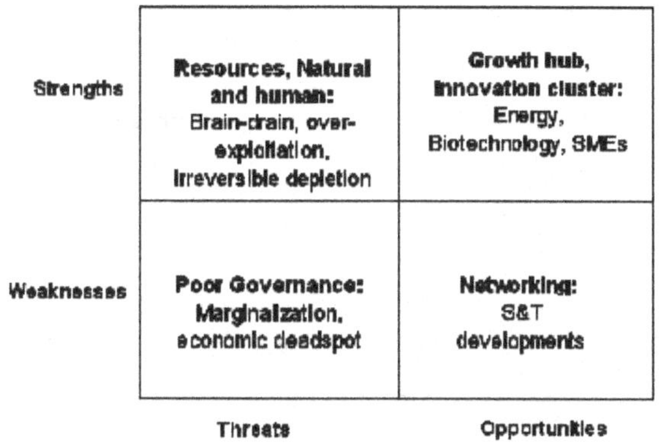

key decision makers must not only be aware about what was done earlier, but must achieve mutual learning and understand priority areas.

We therefore, propose a simple framework that summarizes the communication and dissemination strategy to be adopted for a given innovation system initiative. The framework has three elements: Content, reach and interaction. 'Content' basically describes how much of information is to be communicated to a stakeholder. 'Reach' refers to the extent of stakeholder spectrum that is to be targeted for information sharing; that is, whether particular information is to be shared with selected or limited group such as researchers only; or to be shared with civil society at large. Interaction is also desired in the innovation system, it may range from minimal or passive (e.g. providing reports without eliciting response) to use of very interactive tools such as response through SMS messages, interviews (personal or through mass media), forum, websites, etc.

The accompanying figures 5a and 5b depict this framework, with the three elements forming axes of a coordinate system. Here we have illustrated two cases, in the first case the content is relatively high (reports and publications), the reach and interaction is limited (informing experts group). In the second case, high reach has been achieved (use of mass media) but the content and interaction is limited (people responding in 'yes' or 'no' or similar short answers to queries). Of course, a large number of combinations can be achieved as per the requirement.

CONCLUSION

The competitiveness of hydrocarbon sector is very important for the Indian economy. However, this sector experiences periodic shocks in the form of oil price volatility. Sustained technological innovation could lead to the growth of hydrocarbon sector. However, a fragmented innovation system is a major barrier for achieving technological innovation and diffusion. Using systemic and creative thinking tools, we have discussed the various aspects of the fragmentation of regional innovation system of northeast India and explained how this inhibits the performance and capability building in organizations such as Oil India Limited. The reactive orientation of the stakeholders in the region leads to inadequate capability building, which strengthens the perception that the region is backward and causes various conflicts as well as perpetual dependence on central government funding. Funds are often poorly utilized, and this leads to a vicious cycle.

The situation can be reversed if an initiative with potential for causing high positive impact in the region can be identified by the stakehold-

Figure 5. (a) Communication and dissemination strategy example: high content, limited reach and interaction. (b) Communication and dissemination strategy example: wider reach, limited content and interaction

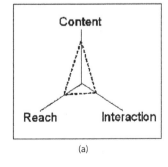 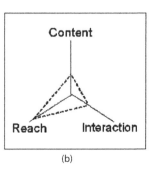

ers in the region. In particular, a participative policy-making for promoting S&T developments in the region is highly desirable. The enhanced profile of S&T in the region will help in several ways: minimizing effect of calamities and disasters, increasing wealth and well being through higher entrepreneurial activities, and achieving organizational growth through higher level of intellectual capital.

A regional technology foresight exercise is a very effective way of bringing together and engaging the regional stakeholders. The visual and creative thinking tools help the stakeholders to perceive the regional situation accurately and help them in identifying their individual and collective roles in the regional development. The various barriers to an effective foresight exercise are expected to be overcome through the creative and visual thinking tools presented in this chapter. Communication and dissemination strategies are also important to inform and engage the stakeholders in an innovation system and for managing a foresight properly. A framework comprising of three elements (namely, content, reach and interaction) has been presented in this chapter for formulating communication and dissemination strategies at various stages of the foresight exercise.

ACKNOWLEDGMENT

The views expressed herein are the personal views of the authors and do not necessarily reflect those of the Management of Oil India Limited.

Mr. Prashant Dhodapkar would like to acknowledge the benefit of personal discussions that he had with the organizers of the UNIDO training program on "Technology Foresight for Organizers", in November 2008.

REFERENCES

Atmanand. (2000). *Growth and deregulation of Indian oil industry (post reform analysis)*. New Delhi: Excel Books.

Deffeyes, K. S. (2001). *Hubbert's peak: The impending world oil shortage*. Princeton, NJ: Princeton University Press.

Dhodapkar, P. K., Gogoi, A. K., Kalita, P. K., & Medhi, A. (2006). *Technology innovation requirements in an upstream hydrocarbon company*. Retrieved November 21, 2008, from http://www. iamot.org/conference/index.php/ocs/10/paper/ viewFile/1750/794

Experience and ideas for developing foresight. (2004). *Experience and ideas for developing foresight in a regional innovation strategy context*. Retrieved September 21, 2008, from ftp://ftp. cordis.europa.eu/pub/foresight/docs/blueprint-for-ris.pdf

Fotion, N., Kashnikov, B., & Lekea, J. K. (2008). *Terrorism: the new world order*. New Delhi, India: Viva-Continuum.

Holditch, S. A. (2007). Tight gas reservoirs. In Warner Jr., H. R. & Lake, L. W. (Eds.), Petroleum engineering handbook vol. VI: Emerging and peripheral technologies (pp 297-351). Richardson, TX: Society of Petroleum Engineers.

Humphrey, J., & Schmitz, H. (1995). *Principles for promoting clusters and networks of SMEs*. Retrieved September 17, 2008, from http:// www.unido.org/fileadmin/media/documents/pdf/ SME_Cluster/Humphrey.pdf

Indian manufacturing industry. (2005). *Indian manufacturing industry: Technology status and prospects*. Retrieved October 12, 2008, from http:// www.unido.org/fileadmin/import/81586_IndManuf1Rep131005.pdf

Knowles, A., & Wareing, J. (2007). *Economic and social geography*. New Delhi, India: Rupa & Co.

National innovation systems. (1997). *National innovation systems*. Retrieved August 14, 2008, from www.oecd.org/dataoecd/35/56/2101733.pdf

Organization. (n.d.). *The organization*. Retrieved 09 August, 2008, from http://petroleum.nic.in/affpsus.htm and http://petroleum.nic.in/affothe.htm

Prime Minister package for north east states. (n.d.). *Prime Minister package for north east states*. Retrieved September 03, 2008, from http://www.mdoner.gov.in/index2.asp?sid=225

Report on evaluation study of the growth centres scheme. (n.d.). *Report on evaluation study of the growth centres scheme*. Retrieved May 21, 2008, from http://planningcommission.nic.in/reports/peoreport/peoevalu/peo_cgs.pdf

Roy, S. (2007). *Macroeconomic policy environment: An analytical guide for managers*. New Delhi, India: Tata-McGraw Hill.

Senge, P. M. (2006). *The fifth discipline: The art & practice of learning organizations*. London: Random House.

Stahl, T. (2007). The Rhine-Neckar-Triangle regional development partnership. In Ennals, R., Gustavsen, B., & Nyhan, B. (Eds.), *Learning together for local innovation: Promoting learning regions*. Luxembourg: Cedefop.

Transforming the northeast. (1997). *Transforming the northeast: Tackling Backlogs in Basic Minimum Services and infrastructural needs*. Retrieved November 28, 2008, from http://planningcommission.nic.in/reports/genrep/ne_exe.pdf

UNIDO technology foresight manual. (2005). *UNIDO technology foresight manual vol. 1: Organization and methods*. Retrieved August 22, 2006, from https://www.unido.org/foresight/registration/dokums_raw/volume1_unido_tf_manual.pdf

UNIDO technology foresight manual. (2005). *UNIDO technology foresight manual vol. 2: Technology foresight in action*. Retrieved August 22, 2006, from https://www.unido.org/foresight/registration/dokums_raw/volume2_unido_tf_manual.pdf

Using foresight to improve the science-policy relationship. (2006). *Using foresight to improve the science-policy relationship*. Retrieved August 07, 2008, from http://ec.europa.eu/research/foresight/pdf/21967.pdf

Workforce sustainability and talent management. (2006). *Workforce sustainability and talent management in the Indian oil and gas upstream industry*. Retrieved April 03, 2008, from http://petrofed.winwinhosting.net/upload/manpower-study2006.pdf

KEY TERMS AND DEFINITIONS

Hydrocarbon(s): Also known as fossil fuels. Linear or branched organic compounds of carbon and hydrogen naturally occurring as crude oil or natural gas under the earth's surface at different depths. Useful as fuels after a process of refining.

Hydrocarbon Industry: An industry comprising of public and private organizations engaged in the exploration, production, transportation and refining of crude oil and utilization of natural gas, and also organizations from allied services.

Innovation System: Formal or informal linkages between the industry, academic and research institutions and financial organizations that lead to innovative performance of a region or nation.

Liberalization: The process of deregulating a sector of economy or industry and exposing it to market forces, in order to make it more competitive.

Protectionist Policies: Government policies that are aimed at retaining control over economy, sector(s) or industries.

Regional Growth: The superior performance of the one or more economic sectors (agriculture, industry or services) in a region, that leads to wealth creation.

Visual Thinking Tools: Tools that make creative use of graphics for facilitating understanding and communication on a subject of interest.

Chapter 18
Nanotechnology Innovation Systems:
A Regional Comparison

Nazrul Islam
Cardiff University, UK

ABSTRACT

The general aim of this chapter is to provide a systematic comparison of nanotechnology innovation systems (NanoSI) at the national level in Europe and Japan. In particular, the characteristics of the national NanoSI that relate to the evolving structure and dynamics of the systems, demand and push factors for driving nanotechnology innovation are investigated, as well as other framework conditions shaped by government policies. In this chapter, a deductive research approach has been adopted rather than an inductive one, a research hypothesis has been put forward and supported by qualitative data analysis. Having carried out a detailed analysis on the primary data, relevant attributes of nanotechnology innovation infrastructure have been identified and similarities and disparities between European and Japanese NanoSI have been explored. The author addresses strengths and weaknesses, major drivers and barriers to a detailed understanding and smooth functioning of NanoSI.

INTRODUCTION

The 'nanotechnology' concept first captured the world's attention when the Nobel Prize winner Richard Feynman advocated the possibility of widespread nanotechnology research by delivering his famous speech, "There's Plenty of Room at the Bottom" just half a century ago. The emerging nanotechnology field comprises one of the fastest-growing research and development (R&D) areas in the world (National Science and Technology Council, 2006). Developed countries, as well as many developing countries, have prioritized nanotechnology as a core scientific and technological research agenda since the early 2000s. R&D activities in nanotechnology have been strengthened worldwide recently to provide a foundation for technological advancement, since governments of many countries have invested aggressively in the relevant research through academic funds and subsidies for private

DOI: 10.4018/978-1-61520-643-8.ch018

companies (Roco, 2005). Nanotechnology is attracting ever larger private and public investments in many parts of the world, for example, the Unites States, Japan, and the European Union have about the same annual government investment for nanotechnology R&D – approximately $1 billion US. Corporations are thus directing their R&D activities towards the exploration of nanotechnology opportunities for sustainable economic development and for the comfort and safety of the people.

Like biotechnology, nanotechnology exists strategically on the borders between disciplines, including physics, chemistry, materials science, biology, medicine, engineering, and information and communication technology. Nanotechnology conforms to a pattern of science-based innovation, which represents a multi-disciplinary field of research and development, since it requires multi-disciplined networked research (Meyer and Persson, 1998; Roco and Bainbridge, 2002; Islam and Miyazaki, 2009), education and the improvement of human skills performance. It also requires input from, amongst others, chemists, physicists, materials scientists through to biologists, engineers and pharmacologists. Therefore, it has been of importance to explore how nanotechnology has evolved through different scientific disciplines and technology domains. The main objective of this chapter is to explore the attributes that are likely to enable an overall understanding of nanotechnology innovation infrastructures in the case of Europe and Japan. The chapter's aim includes identifying critical factors and identifying effective nanotechnology innovation systems (NanoSI) that increases the awareness of nanotechnology from an innovation system perspective. This chapter also seeks to understand the basic strategies of nanotechnology research management and technology development, and attempts to exhibit a forward-looking approach in characterizing nanotechnology innovation trajectories between the regions.

Advancing the understanding of innovation systems requires a methodology, which makes it possible to investigate these systems in depth as well as to make comparisons across borders. This study adopts a qualitative research methodology which includes primary data analysis. A series of face-to-face interviews were carried out with representatives (e.g. scientists, practitioners, researchers) from the universities, public research institutes, government organizations and funding agencies in Europe (e.g. UK, Germany, France, Italy, and Switzerland) and in Japan (e.g. Tokyo, Tsukuba, Osaka, Hiroshima, Kyushu, and Tohoku). A core team of scientists and researchers from ten European institutes and eight Japanese institutes conceptualized and conducted the interview survey and analyzed the results. These qualitative data have provided a key understanding of R&D management, the roles of government bodies and the activities of funding organizations that have helped to shape nanotechnology innovation infrastructures.

Foresight studies predict that nanotechnology will be all around us in 10-15 years and it looks like developing in a series of overlapping S curves of technology maturity. As an emerging field, nanotechnology is too diverse to be treated as one industry or to be thought of as one technology. It is necessary to consider various kinds of technology (e.g. materials, sensors, pharmaceuticals) and the different parts of the industry (e.g. information & communication, biotech, design and construction, manufacturing) individually for an effective innovation process of nanotechnology to take place. Davies and Gann (2003) suggested that nanotechnology is currently in the stage of the innovation cycle just prior to the beginning of commercialization where the technology breaks out of its original locus of R&D and is adopted by industrial sectors. At this stage, innovations have to be linked to achieve full potential benefits. Nevertheless, several questions arise, for example, which technology sectors will be the potential early carrier industries and who will begin to articulate their demands for nanotechnology? And how will the interaction between academia and industry develop? Hypotheses on the key innovation dynamics of nanotechnology have been few up to now and the two mentioned here vary in their argument: Darby and Zucker (2003) proposed that the main engine of nanotechnology development will be start-ups founded by scientists, with alliances between start-ups and large incumbents, close ties between academia, start-ups, and available venture capital as the critical factors. Mangematin *et al* (2006) on the other hand, proposed that large firms and start-ups from the previous generation of general-purpose technologies (e.g. biotechnology) are playing a key role in the development of nanotechnology. The technology does not develop from scratch but represent a second wave dominated by convergence mechanisms.

These earlier studies inform us comprehensively on the long-term time perspective of the technology, its possible impacts and key actors in the development of the technology. However, they inform us little on the evolution of the nanotechnological field and the patterns of its innovation infrastructures. Further studies on nanotechnology will provide novel insights into this technology innovation dynamic. The author argues that for knowledge to flow in NanoSI, the actors need to co-create nano-knowledge. This study develops the hypothesis "*Nanotechnology can be imagined as a hybrid and spiral process of innovation, which neither forces scientific and technological convergence nor integration, rather it co-creates nano-knowledge and bridges divergent disciplines and technology domains, bringing different experts to work together due to its nano dimension*". Since nanotechnology offers a significant opportunity to use nano-instruments for exploring new nano-materials (e.g. carbon nanotubes, fullerenes)[1], which are seamlessly applicable to a wide range of technologies or industries, there is a need to understand the sectors of nanotechnology through which it fuses and how this co-evolution affects the whole spectrum of its innovation infrastructures.

FRAMEWORK OF THE NANOTECHNOLOGY INNOVATION SYSTEMS

Exponential research growth, pronounced market potential and international initiatives in nanotechnology are pushing ahead the construction of the nanotechnology innovation systems (NanoSI). The NanoSI is currently at an early stage of development, mostly centred on nano-research and the creation of nano-knowledge. Although several application sectors have already been identified for nanotechnology, some uncertainty still exists regarding regulation, standards, critical mass of expertise, specific market and business needs. Commercialization of nanotechnology is facing new experimentation and is hampered in some cases due to the lack of linkages between industry and academia as well as the low levels of knowledge in production and marketing. It is important to understand the development of nano-knowledge and the diffusion of nano-information around nanotechnology from a systems point of view. Designing an innovation strategy related to nanotechnology thus requires a cohesive understanding of any description of the innovation system. No single theory or approach can explain nanotechnology's system dynamics and thus the overall concepts relating to NanoSI are drawn by reviewing a number of theories from different angles and then integrating them to establish the conceptual framework of this study. Theories and studies of innovation cycles argue that some changes in technology have so pervasive an impact on the economy that they will entail a techno-economic paradigm change (Dosi, 1982; Freeman and Perez, 1988; Nelson and Winter, 1982; Perez, 2000). Nanotechnology is widely considered as being such a general-purpose technology (Bresnahan and Trajtenberg, 1995; Helpman, 1998), affecting a variety of industries in the economy. Through nanotechnology, breakthrough inventions may create the basis for entirely new industries and a techno-economic paradigm change entails a disruption or renewal of many existing industries. Such a major industrial transition is likely to take 20-30 years since nanotech development appears analogous to that of two other major general-purpose technologies, biotechnology and ICT, 25-30 years ago (Freeman and Louca, 2001). In addition, Wonglimpiyarat (2005) proposes that nanotechnology is entering the sixth Kondratieff wave through nano-engineering and manufacturing, and is likely to bring revolutions in the research and technology arenas[2]. It is reasonable to say that the bottom-up manufacturing approach is a key to creating a nanotechnology paradigm (Ikezawa, 2001). This, however, raises the question of whether one can expect a new type of technical change with nanotechnology evolution?

The characterizing features of nanotechnology make it challenging to analyse the determinants of its innovation as they are involved in a variety of scientific disciplines and technology domains. At present, the nanotechnological system still focuses on research and the method of accumulation of knowledge, with high levels of uncertainty regarding regulations and markets, difficulties in identifying standards and a lack of critical mass of expertise or trade organizations. This obviously creates a possible opportunity to attract new participants to the system, to change standards and market rules, to generate confidence and support for the technology as well as to generate guidelines. In this context, the innovation system (SI) approach (Carlsson and Stankiewicz, 1991; Edquist, 1997; Freeman, 1987; Lundvall, 1992; Malerba, 2002; Nelson, 1993) seems adequate as a suitable analytical tool which can also identify obstacles or bottlenecks to the formation of a well-functioning SI. An innovation system requires some unit of study or dimension of analysis to delineate its boundaries (Metcalfe, 1997; Carlsson et al., 2002). Analysis may focus on the spatial (e.g., national, regional or geopolitical units), the sectoral (e.g. manufacturing, agriculture, or any subsector), the technological (e.g., information and communications technology, biotechnology,

or other distinct technology sets). Further, analysis may focus on a temporal dimension by studying how relationships among agents change over time as a result of knowledge transfers, feedback mechanisms, institutional learning, decision rules, adaptive behavior, and organizational transformation (Nelson and Winter, 1982). In short, a diversity of analytical dimensions falls within the SI approach. The conceptual framework of NanoSI does not center on exclusively national, technological or sectoral aspects, since things are a little unusual in the case of nanotechnology as it is not really a specific technology or product group, nor is there any defined group of scientific disciplines and/or technology domains behind its development. Drawing on the SI approach and considering additional elements to fill the gaps and to adapt the approaches to the specificities of nano-knowledge creation, diffusion and use, the author defines a comprehensive framework showing the major elements of NanoSI, within which the relevant institutions and organisations are embedded to shape NanoSI which will provide an overall picture of the structure and mechanisms of nano-knowledge flows among the actors. Figure 1 illustrates an overview of the NanoSI framework.

As a technology, nanotechnology seems to be an emerging and disrupting field, a type of cross-disciplinarity that has an impact on various industrial processes or technologies as no boundaries exist at the nano-scale. Therefore, *systems of innovation related to nanotechnology (NanoSI) can be thought of as a complex system consisting of different science & engineering disciplines and technology domains operating at nano-scale; comprised by a set of actors engaged in the development, diffusion and utilization of the technology; setting up linkages among multiple interacting actors that particularly focus on a nanotech domain (e.g. nanomaterials, nanoelectronics, bionanotechnology, and nano-manufacturing & tools) having collaborations and exchange mechanisms.* NanoSI may also be considered as a dynamic process, which changes

Figure 1. Nanotechnology innovation system framework

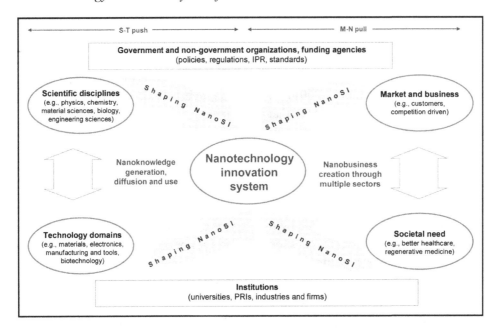

patterns over time, involving multiple interacting and co-operating actors. It is almost impossible for Individual organizations to possess all the knowledge necessary for the whole process of innovation. As a result, they need to combine scientific, engineering and operational knowledge from different sources. The core institutions for generating nano-knowledge are universities and public research institutes, where scientific disciplines such as chemistry, physics, materials sciences and biology are extensively involved as curiosity drivers. The basic scientific disciplines connect to different types of technology domains. For example, within the electronics domain, demand for increased performance through smaller components has paved the way for the nano-scale. The driver in the materials domain has been the search for new properties in materials. In recent times, performance demands on new materials have also come from the biotechnology domain through the development of regenerative medicine and drug delivery. Similarly, companies complement their activities by interacting with each other and help the evolution of the technology. The way

the scientific disciplines and technology domains interact is through technology fusion with each other at the common platform of nano-scale, since no disciplinary boundary exists at this scale. It should be noted that nanotechnology evolution is not one directional, rather different technology domains and scientific disciplines act in shaping the technology. The shaping pattern of nanotechnology is not the same as the other technologies such as biotechnology and information & communication technology, where relevant fields are responsible for the exploration of the technologies. Equally important are organizations such as government agencies and departments, patent offices, regulatory bodies, and private-public funding organizations that support the smooth functioning of NanoSI. The proposed framework of NanoSI is comprised of Science-Technology (S-T) push and Market-Need (M-N) pull. NanoSI is currently driven by S-T push that helps in the generation and use of nano-knowledge, finding possible applications and raising awareness among passive actors. In the future, NanoSI will be driven by M-N pull which will incorporate customer demand, product competition, raise societal need (e.g., better healthcare) and help pull nano-knowledge for its own demand. The M-N pull side, at the moment, lacks the knowledge necessary to absorb nanotechnology, while the S-T push side finds difficulty interacting with existing markets and business for possible applications. Since nanotechnology is currently in its embryonic stage of commercialization, the present study chooses to focus on nano-scientific and technological infrastructures, skipping the market and demand structures.

NANOTECHNOLOGY INNOVATION INFRASTRUCTURES – THE CASE OF EUROPE

In this chapter, the author investigates both the nature of nano-knowledge conflation in NanoSI and the consequences for the actors that are engaged in the co-creation, transformation and utilization of relevant knowledge. To map such a NanoSI system a breadth of understanding as to the existence of, and prospects for, nanotechnology within two regional innovation infrastructures is required. For this, a core team of scientists and researchers from European and Japanese institutions conceptualized and conducted the interview survey and analyzed the results. Each of them focused on a particular nanotechnology discipline and domain. Care was taken to provide the right mix of experts in relation to their background, professional position and size of the group. Experts were asked to fill in a questionnaire containing four categories in order to frame this investigation. The four categories were 1) nanotechnology research system, 2) nanotechnology research conflation, 3) nanotechnology transfer and industry relations and 4) NanoSI at the national level. Interviews were held and site observation data collated as transcriptions and observation notes that were then analyzed with respect to identifying nanotechnology innovation infrastructures. The results

are summarized in Table 1 and Table 2, which list almost all categories and factors related to innovation infrastructures cited by 20 percent or more of the interviewees.

Nanotechnology Research System

It appears from the analysis done that the research interest in nanotechnology has been driven by the researchers' own experience in their previous fields of practice. Researchers tend neither to select the nanotechnology field nor diversify into it, rather nanotechnology research has undergone a natural sort of development in an evolutionary way. In most cases, researchers' interest lies in nanotechnology research projects that are generously funded by local and federal government and industry. Nanotechnology research was initiated by government projects, and a strong collaboration between companies and universities both locally and internationally. The case of European scientists shows that nanotechnology draws people of different disciplines towards a hybrid platform that is a mix of multiple fields, primarily because of the merits of utilizing nano-tools. In this sense, an expert in the field needs knowledge of another discipline to work at the nano scale and make cross-links among researchers, which helps them to move into what is, in effect, a multi-disciplinary system. Some experts believe that nowadays it is impossible to do research in the nanotechnology area without there being a strong connection between science and technical disciplines[3]. This technology has appeared purely because of the scientific opportunities presented by working with existing expertise from different fields. The main sales point is that it affects many technology sectors and divergent disciplines due to need to understand the nano-scale properties and functions of materials and to explore their potential applications. The impact between disciplines is also quite pronounced in that it can initiate the beginning of addressing a new system for practitioners (e.g. biological system for physicists and engineers;

Table 1. Factors explaining the nanotechnology research system in the case of Europe (percentage of interviewees believing this factor to have been important)

Reason of Research Interest on Nanotech	i) Experience with own research in nano-scale system	100
	ii) Interest of government and industry	80
	iii) Scientific opportunity	25
Research Specialty and Type	Nanotech research practices in traditional scientific fields e.g., chemistry, physics, material science, biology and instrumentation	100
	Research type:	
	i) Top-down approach	100
	ii) Hybrid system of Bottom-up and Top-down approach	65
	ii) Bottom-up approach	35
Research Mode	i) National Projects	100
	ii) Collaboration with companies and universities	90
	iii) In-house projects	45
Trend of Nanotech Research	i) Scientific disciplines are co-creating nano-knowledge since it is an interface of all divergent disciplinary areas	90
	ii) Making a bridge between expertise from different background to work together	65
	iii) Exploring a new system for all scientific and engineering disciplines to grasp scientific opportunity	35
Factors Driving Nanotech Research	i) Trend of re-labeling research	90
	ii) New nanomaterials discovered with novel properties and new applications	70
	iii) Instruments or techniques to control the functionality and manipulate materials at nanometer scale	55
Nanotech Research Transfer	Transferred to industry by direct contract with small and big companies or in-house efforts	80
	Bottlenecks:	
	i) Lack of nanotech knowledge in industry	55
	ii) Lack of financial support	45

Table 2. Factors explaining NanoSI in the case of Europe (percentage of interviewees believing this factor to have been important)

Nanotech Innovation Type	Innovation is driven by	
	i) Science push	100
	ii) Technology push	55
	iii) Demand or market pull	35
Role of Government	i) Drives nanotech R&D by giving funds	90
	ii) Supporting new infrastructures for nanotech (e.g. interdisciplinary research centres)	45
	iii) Should strictly monitor the excellence of research	35
European Nanotech R&D Strength	i) European nanotech research system is in higher level than the US and Japan in terms of basic research, not in terms of exploitation	90
	Bottleneck:	
	i) Less big companies are involved and lack of interest by big companies	35
Nanotech R&D Management	Research and development is managed by	
	i) Good research facilities (e.g. IRCs), although some lack of exploitation	100
	ii) Rapid development of instruments for observing and manipulating materials at nano-scale exploring a wide variety of nanotech applications	90
Nanotech R&D Style or Practices	i) Multi-disciplinary type by interacting with all disciplines' expertise	100
	ii) Enable R&D practice to move from specific discipline to multi-disciplines	90
	iii) Nanotechnology is an evolutionary development	55
Uniqueness of Nanotech	i) Nano dimension or size	100
	ii) New nanomaterials (e.g. CNTs, Fullerenes) with lot of applications	75
Safety and Risks by Nanotech	Safety and risk is as usual	100

chemistry for biologists, material scientists and engineers). Therefore, it would be a very real and useful reflection of the existing reality to begin purposely bridging disciplines by coming together and taking elements from each of them. In short, it can be argued that nanotechnology offers a new way to approach science, and focuses on establishing a new route to do science in this decade.

Basic research conducted in scientific disciplines has coined itself 'nano' recently, although nano-scale research has been around for at least a few decades. Through a top-down material processing approach, practitioners realized new phenomena, new applications and novel properties of matter due to nano-instruments, which had not been explored or understood before. However, nanotechnology is a field which receives a great deal of public and private funds for research these days and researchers are doing very interesting work within this emerging field. For example, Dr. Karl-Heinz Haas, spokesman for nanotechnology from the Fraunhofer Institute, says that nano-scale research existed previously, but under a different name, e.g., around 50 years ago it was called colloid processing and 20-25 years ago it was called sol-gel processing. In the same way, "thin films" has been categorized as a nanotechnology area although it has existed for 20-30 years. An important factor in the case of Europe is the trend of the re-labeling of research, to pull funding for nano-research both from government and industry sources. Some basic factors for re-labeling research are identified as:

- To attract more public and private funding for continuing nanotechnology research
- The scope of using new nanomaterials such as carbon nanotube which is revolutionizing research activity in different scientific fields for examining and studying the material and applying it as devices, sensors, and other multi-purpose applications due to its novel and significantly improved properties and functions

- The rapid development of nano-instruments pushes researchers and practitioners to become involved in nanotechnology research, enabling them to control and manipulate structures and materials' properties.

Nanotechnology Research Conflation

Nanotechnology can be regarded as a hybrid field of science & engineering, since it is an interface of scientific fields when operating at the nano-scale. Scientists and researchers from Europe have argued that nanotechnology holds great promise to create a new platform in terms of both scientific collaboration and opportunities to interact with colleagues across disciplines. This field is simply 'jellying' among different research fields, as Professor Kostas Kostarelos from University of London puts it. Due to having new material such as CNTs, a physicist (who has no knowledge of its biological, physical or chemical properties) has to interact with biologists, material scientists, and chemists in order to develop an understanding of its versatile properties and find its applications in different sectors[4]. In this sense, it is necessary to stimulate interaction between multi-disciplinary people who need capabilities and knowledge of different disciplinary topics. In other words, in order to make a contribution in nanotechnology, material scientists need knowledge of e.g., chemistry, physics and biology. Even inside a discipline, several branches are fusing into nanotechnology research. Several examples of evidences of this exist in Europe, e.g.

- In searching for answers to biological questions, biophysics and cell biology are conflated towards nanotechnology research
- Gene therapy and generated medicine are conflated into nanotechnology research
- Chemistry and electronics are fused into chemtronics.

In other cases, each scientific discipline is fused into nanotechnology research in the sense that one group of physicists is working on atomic physics while another group is working on quantum computing. This trend started to happen gradually 10-15 years ago[5]. Scientists from Europe recommended that researchers from general disciplines (e.g. physicists, chemists and biologists) should train themselves to nurture human resources facing the complexity of nanotechnology evolution in terms of a critical mass of expertise.

The data obtained from the interview survey show that people from different research fields have a tendency to work for inter-disciplinary research centers that appear to become an excellent nanotechnology research cluster, whether real or virtual. Real inter-disciplinary conflation is, in a sense, when people from different expertise backgrounds contribute in part by their physical presence (e.g. centers have chemists to synthesize materials; physicists to carry out instrumental experiments; biologists to do the biological assay; computer scientists to calculate or design structures and explain their function; and engineers to maintain the instruments). Within an interdisciplinary research centre (IRC) every researcher is assigned projects, discusses or interprets on a scientific level about the systems, shares with others with their expertise, and thus contributes to nanotechnology research evolution and accelerates technology fusion. Therefore, the key to achieving this is to make a bridge between different branches of scientific knowledge in the nano-scale and to develop interaction among all practitioners. Virtual inter-discipline is when people with different expertise from different scientific & engineering departments and institutions contribute in part by their virtual presence. For example, IRC Bionanotechnology at Oxford: where researchers from several disciplines are working and collaborating with each other within the institution, as well as several working groups from different locations, collaborating with each other virtually through IRCs. On the other hand, the IRC Nanoscience Center at Cambridge operates as a real and a virtual centre, sharing knowledge and facilities with a number of university departments and national laboratories across Europe and Asian countries. People can access common equipment, and run facilities where they have specially planned multi-disciplinary projects. Representatives of the departments are, for example, engineers, physicists, chemists and material scientists who are creating an interdisciplinary environment to do nanotechnology research. This trend in the working environment develops gradually by fusing different scientific disciplines, as biochemistry and biophysics evolved earlier. Therefore, to survive the race of nanotechnology, people must change their academic and business attitude, culture and behavior in this respect of working together in a technology platform of nano-scale[6]. If this is not done, it will decrease the development speed of nanotechnology in general. Nanotechnology thus must be defined not as a traditional field of science & technology, but as a real hybrid field.

Nanotechnology Transfer and Relations to Industry

Industry relations are not easy in the case of nanotechnology as the field is so diverse and it may not be sensible to think of it as one technology. However, it appears that the bulk of nanotech research output has been transferred to industry in several ways. This transfer can be thought of as either

- Direct contract or agreement with industry, e.g. *collaboration*: industry projects both local and international; *investment*: industry driven research by using grants and exchanging researchers between university, industry and national labs
- Through patent licensing, e.g., license contract

Some bottlenecks have been identified in transferring and collaborating research with industry. Scientists and researchers are still finding it problematical to apply nanotechnology research output. Part of the reason for this is that industry itself does not understand the opportunities of nanotechnology. Universities face difficulties explaining to industry that opportunities exist, as nanotechnology is a novel production technique which could replace traditional techniques. In truth, the sharing of knowledge is sometimes difficult due to the lack of nano-knowledge in industry. In this regard, European researchers recommended that academia should communicate directly with industry to let those operating within it know what the opportunities and needs of society are in respect of nanotechnology, and how they can engage with such a new multidisciplinary field. Therefore, instead of convincing industry, it is a question of getting information to them related to nanotechnology.

The big companies (e.g. multinationals) are theoretically supposed to be very knowledgeable, but actually this has been seen to not be the case. Large companies need to find out what is actually feasible in the labs, what can be done using nanotechnology and how it might impact on their businesses. On the other hand, start-ups do not have sufficient resources to think laterally, although their thinking about technology transfer is often 10 years ahead and sometimes they are closer to the market. The critical mass of expertise in industry has appeared as one of the bottlenecks. In response to this, universities could play a significant role in overcoming this barrier between industries, as universities have the necessary expertise in nanotechnology. In addition, academics should begin to develop relationship with industry, for taking up the technologies and not only the techniques.

NanoSI: The Case of Europe

The author will now goes on to analyze the nature of the actors within this emerging NanoSI through which nano-knowledge is being explored and commercially exploited. Nanotechnology appears very much to be a new science and technology push, as much work done by researchers has originated from the fundamental science disciplines. Since the potential of nanotechnology has required co-operation and links between scientific, engineering and commercial fields, it is logical for academic institutions to act as initiating as active actors in the emergence of NanoSI. There are definitely some markets that need to be pull driven by industry and firms who will act as passive actors. However, industry has come up with the 'nano' term to label or sell their products. Academic research from various scientific fields is also re-labeling to attract and pull funding from both private and public sources. The role of government and funding agencies is very important, persistence in giving research grants or funding at a constant level is essential for the smooth functioning of NanoSI. However, governments' role is to support public research and to assess the quality and excellence of research. Scientists from Europe believe that local and federal government should support small companies, since it would be very difficult for them to survive without such support. Many small companies spinning out from universities do not survive, although they have something quite new to exploit. New firms, including universities whose engagement with nanotechnology allowed them to closely follow relevant developments, often act as entrepreneurs in bringing novel developments to the market. Therefore, government should look at the ways to make it easier to overcome the gap identified in the analysis. In addition, any government has to continue to support its own country or region, and they should be much more receptive to new opportunities arising out of nanotechnology.

As elaborated in the previous section, nanotechnology research output from universities and public research institutions have been transferred to industry through patent licensing and by direct contract with small and big companies and in-house efforts in some cases. In Europe, small and start up companies have a much greater interest in involvement in nanotechnology than big companies do. The main bottlenecks have been identified for nanotechnology innovation: industries' limited ability to understand nanotechnology opportunities, lack of culture to uptake new technologies other than the techniques involved and the lack of financial support of small companies. Therefore, from the community of nanotechnology scientists and researchers in Europe, several suggestions were made to government bodies:

- To establish a new infrastructure or platform for nanotechnology research with access for all organizations (e.g. more centralized infrastructures)
- By being persistent and keeping funding at a constant level
- To support small companies that have something new to explore and exploit in nanotechnology, and to provide tax breaks for them
- To promote strict monitoring of the quality and excellence of research

NanoSI has been identified as an evolutionary development from micro technology, which comes up mainly in the semiconductor and electronics sectors. However, nanotechnology is dispersed through all technology sectors as an evolutionary possibility, except the biotechnology sector where nanotechnology could really revolutionize the whole spectrum of pharmaceutical and drug discovery processes by changing the whole paradigm of high throughput screening[7]. In terms of R&D strength, nanotechnology scientists and researchers believe that Europe is much stronger than the US and Japan in terms of basic research, but less effective in exploitation, since the spectrum of nanotechnology is narrower in this region.

NANOTECHNOLOGY INNOVATION INFRASTRUCTURES: THE CASE OF JAPAN

To further compare and refine the understanding of such innovation systems, the author has applied the concept of NanoSI to empirical studies of actors (e.g. universities, public research institutes, government bodies, funding organizations) working on nanotechnology in Japan. By summarizing the face-to-face interviews with the actors, a detailed analysis has been made to explore major attributes relevant to the nature of Japanese innovation infrastructures. The results are summarized in Table 3 and Table 4, which list almost all categories and factors cited by 20 percent or more of the interviewees.

Nanotechnology Research System

Similarly to the case of Europe, the main reason behind taking up nanotechnology research in Japan has been the researchers' previous own experiences in nano-scale systems in different scientific fields. The research grants from the government and industry projects in parallel have pushed researchers in different disciplines into the nanotechnology area. In particular, many academics from various scientific disciplines conduct nanotechnology research driven by curiosity to explore new functions and potential applications of matter. Although nano-scale research has been conducted for several decades, it expanded its boundaries once nano-instruments made more versatile usage possible. Japanese scientists believe that nanotechnology has the ability to drive research in multiple disciplines, as no subject boundary exists between disciplines (physics, chemistry, material science, engineering and biology) and the classical laws of science do

Table 3. Factors explaining the nanotechnology research system in the case of Japan (percentage of interviewees believing this factor to have been important)

Reason of Research Interest on Nanotech	i) Experience with own research at nano-scale systems	100
	ii) Interest of government and industry	85
	iii) Curiosity of exploring new things	60
Research Specialty and Type	Nanotech research practices in traditional scientific fields e.g., chemistry, physics, material science, biology and instrumentation	100
	Research type:	
	i) Top-down approach	100
	ii) Hybrid system of Bottom-up and Top-down approach	70
	iii) Bottom-up approach	30
Research Mode	i) National projects	85
	ii) Collaboration with industry and universities	85
Trend of Nanotech Research	i) Touches almost all scientific fields in creating scientific advantages	100
	ii) Drives research in multi-disciplines as nano dimension requires several traditional fields	70
	iii) Nanotech research spreads as a reality after adoption of nano-instruments	70
Factors Driving Nanotech Research	i) Scope to utilize nano-instruments in every discipline	70
	ii) Curiosity to explore new things and new applications of materials	70
	iii) Good government funding	70
	iv) Trend of re-labeling research topic	30
Nanotech Research Transfer	i) Research output is close to commercialization	60
	ii) Research output is transferred to industry by direct contract with companies and patent licensing	40
	Bottlenecks:	
	i) Bureaucracy and improper distribution of funding	60
	ii) Lack of communication across industry, university and government	40

Table 4. Factors explaining NanoSI in the case of Japan (percentage of interviewees believing this factor to have been important)

Nanotech Innovation Type	Nanotech innovation is driven by science and technology push, demand pull is emerging	100
Role of Government	i) Provide funding, should more systematic in allocation	100
	ii) Motivate nanotech researchers by establishing infrastructure or initiative	85
	iii) Should identify more nanotech application areas	30
Japanese Nanotech R&D Strength	i) Japan is strong in semiconductors, surface technology and electronic devices (i.e. top-down)	60
	ii) Japan is competing recently with the US and EU in basic research	60
Nanotech R&D Management	R&D is managed by	
	i) Sharing nano-instruments and national nanotech infrastructures	60
	ii) Productivity of researchers and their hard credential	30
	Bottlenecks:	
	i) Missing or not enough collaboration inside and outside of the institutions	60
	ii) Lack of researchers (critical mass of expertise)	40
Nanotech R&D Style or Practices	i) Multi-disciplinary type or sharing research style	85
	ii) Curiosity driven in all disciplinary research	40
Uniqueness of Nanotech	i) Designing and controlling materials function with many applications	70
	ii) Nano dimension or size	85
Safety and Risks by Nanotech	Safety and risk is normal. People are positive	100

not readily apply. However, the nano dimension requires scientists from different scientific fields, because of its own characteristics, to understand each other's language and to exploit new and much improved applications of materials. In this way, nanotechnology enables people to share one another's expertise and this trend may develop some networks or links across disciplines and domains, helping to boost the efficient outcome possible in science.

Nanotechnology Research Conflation

The so-called characteristics of nanotechnology research of exchanging expertise or knowledge across disciplines can be explained by combinatorial aspects, i.e. fusing of scientific disciplines in a spiral pattern to establish a new platform of innovation, from where multiple technology domains may benefit. It appears from investigation that it seems to be becoming difficult to do nanotechnology research without having multidisciplinary knowledge or a strong connection with multiple disciplines. Multi-disciplinary research practices have appeared as a reality after nano-instruments opened the door to exploring unfocused and undiscovered areas of various aspects of science. Therefore, nanotechnology research conflation strategy represents researchers' keen intention to take advantages of using nano-tools in their fundamental research in order to grasp new opportunities that could begin to address a new realm of possibilities for the gap between the sciences. It can be argued from the analysis that nanotechnology constitutes a combinatorial type of discipline which enables fusion of scientific fields in parallel. A general discipline's research group consists of a variety of experts or researchers – it would include chemists, physicists, engineers, and biologists who are working in parallel, for example, within a scientific discipline, a group of electronic physicist researchers would consist of five sub-groups: one focusing on devices; a

second one concentrating on quantum dots and their formation, integration and assembly; a third working on photonics for photonic crystals and LED; a fourth sub-group would concentrate on nano-scale thin film oxides; and the fifth sub-group would work on simulation. It can be said that through nanotechnology scientific research culture has been changing, moving towards a combination of multi-disciplinary expertise and experiences. Exchange of nano-information between scientific disciplines seems a crucial phenomenon for nanotechnological systems to evolve and to fuse.

Nanotechnology Transfer and Relations to Industry

Technology transfer is always a communication from a researcher to industry engineers. It appears that nanotechnology research transfer from universities is somehow difficult to achieve due to the maintenance of long procedures and time consumption. Some interviewees argued that bureaucracy is responsible for the difficulty in transferring research output to industry. The common reason for difficulties in transferring the output is the conflict arising out of communication between researchers who have something new and industry engineers who do not know much about new or emerging technology, as in the case of nanotechnology. Industry professionals are nearly always interested in more general or common technologies, and their mindset is fundamentally different from a nanotechnologist, as they do not have even preliminary knowledge or information about nanotechnology. However, the stock of nanotechnology literature is still small and an engineer who is working in an industry will certainly have a lack of nano-knowledge. The situation is different in the case of big companies. They have their own R&D set up and usually have a nanotechnology R&D section to look at the opportunities of nanotechnology. It seems that they would not prefer to take up university or public sector research, probably for commercial reasons. In most cases, nanotechnology transfer occurs quite infrequently. The major bottlenecks found in transferring nanotechnology research output are:

- The number of users is not so large at present
- Bureaucracy, i.e. many formalities needed for transferring research output
- Lack of ventures and start up companies compared to Europe
- Less discussion and communication between industry and universities, both inside and outside the institutions
- Limited willingness of large companies to accept nanotechnology research output from university researchers, reproducibility to asses the life cycle of the product

To overcome these difficulties in technology transfer and to improve the industry-academia relationship some recommendations have been made:

- Government should be more open and flexible in their policies related to nanotechnology
- To help or support small start up companies
- Academia needs to interact with industry and government in nanotechnology issues and large companies should be more flexible when considering university research output
- To establish more start ups in the nanotechnology area

NanoSI: The Case of Japan

Nanotechnology appears as a field in the science and technology push, and researchers from the traditional science disciplines explore the technology in three ways: firstly, experiences in nano-scale research can be purely curiosity driven; secondly, much interest from the Japanese

government since they have gradually allocated bigger budgets in competition with the US and EU after the announcement of the National nanotechnology Initiative in the early 2000s. As a result, nanotechnology has been declared one of the key priority areas in Japan; thirdly, nano-instruments that push scientists and researchers to discover new or unfocused area of matter at the nano-scale. Within the NanoSI market and need pull it exists to a lesser extent at present, but is expected to be much influential in this area in the future. In Japan, the role of government is clear and crucial for the smooth functioning of NanoSI. The Japanese government supports public sector research by establishing national nanotechnology infrastructures, for example, '*Spring 8*' in Kobe, through which scientists and researchers can take advantage of using the facilities. As identified, Japan lacks interdisciplinary research centers compared to Europe. The government should initiate more policies to create such interdisciplinary research centers or centers of excellence (COE) in the nanotechnology area in order to accelerate its innovation. Nevertheless, the number of small companies spinning out from universities is comparatively less than in Europe. It also faces a lack of critical mass of expertise compared to other new entrants (e.g. China) in Asia. As described in the previous section, transference of nanotechnology research output is inadequate or only in the pipeline in some cases. Transference to industry has occurred through patent licensing or by direct contract with companies or the technology liaison office[8]. However, the common reason causing the blocking of technology transfer has been identified as bureaucracy. From the community of Japanese nanotechnology scientists and researchers, several suggestions were made to government bodies:

- They should allocate research funding systematically and constantly
- They should identify more application areas and negotiate with medium and small

companies, and support them financially if necessary

- To promote exchange of nano-information and expertise among nanotechnology practitioners across universities, public research institutions and companies
- They should establish more COE and IRC in the nanotechnology area and encourage university scientists to spin out start ups
- Hire a critical mass of expertise

Scientists and researchers believe that the nanotechnology research exploitation system in Japan is at a similar stage with the US, but less effective in focusing on new application areas. An assessment is made through these interviews that Japan is ahead in semiconductors, surface technology and electronic devices sector (i.e. in the top-down approach), while the US is ahead in self-assembly and simulation in the biotechnology area, systems and manufacturing (i.e. in the bottom-up approach), and Europe maintains almost similar strengths in both approaches (e.g., top-down and bottom-up). Nanotechnology R&D is managed by i) the productivity of researchers and their hard credentials in spite of the lack of researchers, and ii) sharing nano-instruments provided by the national nanotechnology infrastructure offered by the government. NanoSI in Japan faces the difficulty of institutional problems in different cases e.g. financing and joint work between universities and industry. Best practices of NanoSI can be enabled by the interaction and inter-exchange among experts in different disciplines from universities, the public sector and large companies. Most of the interviewees believe that although the availability of nanotech researchers is less in Japan, the R&D facilities are advanced enough for achieving nanotechnological breakthroughs. In this sense, it would be possible to train existing researchers to fill the gap in the following ways:

- Taking steps to grow awareness of pre-university or undergraduate level students

and researchers about the benefits and vast opportunities of nanotechnology
- T hire foreign researchers or experts in the relevant field and train Japanese researchers across the general sciences

NANOTECHNOLOGY INNOVATION INFRASTRUCTURES MODEL

Having carried out a detailed analysis of primary data, this study has identified most relevant attributes, similarities and disparities about nanotechnology innovation infrastructure (Table 5).

Similarities:

- Tendency to grasp nanotechnology scientific opportunities and to explore unfocused areas of science due to the rapid development of nano-instruments
- Researchers' strong interests on nanotechnology projects funded by both local and federal government and industry
- Extensive study of new nanomaterials' properties and exploration of its new and improved functions and applications
- Appearance of NanoSI as a hybrid system consisting of multi-disciplinary fields
- Lack of nano-knowledge among industry professionals and lack of communication between academia and industry

Disparities:

- Big company involvement has appeared less in Europe in comparison to small companies and start ups, whereas in Japan large companies are directly involved in nanotechnology R&D while it has weak systems for start ups and ventures
- Bureaucracy of transference of nano-research output to industry is high in Japan, while European policy is more flexible

Table 5. Nanotechnology innovation infrastructures model

	Europe	Japan
Re-labelling Research Topic	High	Low
Curiosity Drive to Grasp Scientific opportunity	Low	High
In-house R&D Projects	Medium	Low
Connection with Industry in terms of Technology Transfer	High	Medium
Financial Support to Technology Transfer	Low	Medium
Bureaucracy of Transferring Nanotechnology Research Output	Low	High
Focusing Nanotechnology Application Areas	High	Low
Big Companies Interest in Nanotechnology R&D	Less	High
Critical Mass of Expertise in Nanotechnology	High	Low
Productivity of Nanotechnology Researchers	Medium	High
Supporting Innovation Infrastructures by Government	Low	High

Note: *Low* – less than 40%; *Medium* – in between 40% to 60%; *High* – more than 60%

- Japan lacks a critical mass of expertise in the nanotechnology area
- NanoSI is managed by national infrastructures supported by the Japanese government, whereas it is managed by several interdisciplinary research programs and research centers in Europe

In summarizing the study, an innovation infrastructure model as illustrated in Table 5 has been constructed, which conveys a message to science & technology policy makers, institutional authorities as well as nanotechnology practitioners worldwide.

DISCUSSIONS AND IMPLICATIONS

This chapter has extensively showed the pattern of nanotechnology innovation infrastructures at the national level in Europe and Japan. Relative to other technologies that generally focus on individual technologies or specific sectors, it can be said that nanotechnology is not a single technology, but rather a constellation of several distinct trajectories of scientific and technological advances. This chapter has suggested that every traditional discipline needs to share nano-information with the others. With the evolution of nanotechnology, the basic research trend has appeared to be to bridge divergent disciplines. In this respect, it would not be possible to continue nanotechnology R&D, if those concerned lacked relevant background knowledge, lacked links with other experts and possessed a lack of learning with multi-disciplinary knowledge. This multi-disciplinary innovation approach breaks down the boundaries of all scientific disciplines. This may have been caused by the sharing of nano-tools for scientific research, helping researchers to grasp nanotechnology opportunities in controlling and manipulating materials with many new and improved applications. Evidence supporting such a hypothesis has important implications for analysts seeking to develop an understanding of the patterns of NanoSI between the East and the West. The findings in this chapter would seem to indicate that nanotechnology shows its heterogeneity where divergent scientific disciplines and technology domains make a bridge which is necessary to establish the emergent NanoSI. Success in NanoSI thus requires scientists and practitioners to acknowledge new multi-disciplinary way of working.

The present study has also reported clearly that strenuous local and international links and teamwork within and outside of institutions would be required to realize the full potential of NanoSI. The existence of interdisciplinary research centers both inside and outside of universities in European countries is a good sign, providing the right environment for the emergence of insights in NanoSI. Japan is strong with its government supported national nanotechnology infrastructures. The nanotechnology R&D system in Europe is stronger than Japan's in terms of fundamental research, but has less impressive results in exploitation. In Europe, small and start up companies are more extensively involved in nanotechnology than large companies. The situation is different in the case of Japan where several well known large companies have been directly involved in looking at the opportunities of nanotechnology, but has only a limited presence in start ups and small firms. The evidence in this chapter has indicated that nanotechnology evolution contributes to innovation studies in a quite unique way. Therefore, it would be useful to adopt policy measures that could facilitate in building a network platform for sharing or exchanging different nano-expertise and knowledge. While basic nanotech research is likely to remain in universities and national laboratories, more applied efforts should involve contributions from industry. Nevertheless, as industry appears less willing to take up university based nanotech research, universities should be more open to non-traditional collaborations to encourage the infusion of industry-specialized knowledge and thereby ease technology transfer. On the other hand, government and industry consortia can support universities as R&D representatives and could fund university purchases of equipment in order to expand the capabilities of local industry.

This chapter has attempted to analyze the pattern of nano-knowledge flow in a type of emergent NanoSI focusing on the science and technology push side. The generalizability of the proposed NanoSI framework needs further empirical research for validation, focusing on the market and need pull side. Therefore, it would be beneficial to examine the relationships between S-T push and M-N pull of NanoSI in future studies.

REFERENCES

Bresnahan, T. F., & Tajtenberg, M. (1995). General Purpose Technologies: Engines of Growth. *Journal of Econometrics*, *65*, 83–108. doi:10.1016/0304-4076(94)01598-T

Carlsson, B., Jacobsson, S., Holmen, M., & Rickne, A. (2002). Innovation systems: analytical and methodological issues. *Research Policy*, *31*, 233–245. doi:10.1016/S0048-7333(01)00138-X

Carlsson, B., & Stankiewicz, R. (1991). On the nature, function and composition of technological systems. *Evolutionary Economics*, *1*, 93–118. doi:10.1007/BF01224915

Davies, A., & Gann, D. (2003). *A Review of Nanotechnology and its Potential Applications for Construction*. London: CRISP, Darby, M. R. & Zucker, L. G. (2003). Grilichesian breakthroughs: inventions of methods of inventing and firms entry in nanotechnology, *NBER Working Paper,* 9825.

Dosi, G. (1982). Technological Paradigms and Technological Trajectories: A Suggested Interpretation of the Determinants and Directions of Technological Change. *Research Policy*, *11*, 147–162. doi:10.1016/0048-7333(82)90016-6

Edquist, C. (1997). Systems of innovation approaches – their emergence and characteristics. In Edquist, C. (Ed.), *Systems of Innovation – Technologies, Institutions and Organizations*. London: Pinter Publishers.

Freeman, C. (1987). *Technology Policy and Economic Performance: Lessons from Japan*. London: Pinter Publishers.

Freeman, C., & Louçã, F. (2001). *As Time Goes By. From the industrial Revolutions to the Information Revolution*. New York: Oxford University Press.

Freeman, C., & Perez, C. (1988). Structural Crisis of Adjustment: Business Cycles and Investment Behaviour. In Dosi, (Eds.), *Technical Change and Economic Theory*. London: Pinter Publishers.

Helpman, E. (1998). *General Purpose Technologies and Economic Growth*. Cambridge, MA: MIT Press.

Ikezawa, N. (2001). Nanotechnology: encounters of atoms, bits and genomes. *NRI Papers* 37.

Islam, N., & Miyazaki, K. (2009). Nanotechnology Innovation System – Understanding Hidden Dynamics of Nanoscience Fusion Trajectories. *Technological Forecasting and Social Change*, 76(1), 128–140. doi:10.1016/j.techfore.2008.03.021

Lundvall, B. A. (Ed.). (1992). *National Systems of Innovation*. London: Pinters Publishers.

Malerba, F. (2002). Sectoral systems of innovation and production. *Research Policy*, 31, 247–264. doi:10.1016/S0048-7333(01)00139-1

Mangematin, V., et al. (2006). *Meeting promises: Public policies and firm strategies in nanotechnologies*. Project proposal for Nanodistrict 2 EU project, PRIME 2006, report. Retrieved from www.nanodistrict.com

Metcalfe, J. S. (1997). Technology systems and technology policy in an evolutionary framework. In Archibuig, D., & Michie, J. (Eds.), *Technology, Globalization and Economic Performance*. Cambridge, UK: Cambridge University Press.

Meyer, M., & Persson, O. (1998). Nanotechnology – interdisciplinarity, patterns of collaboration and differences in application. *Scientometrics*, 42(2), 195–205. doi:10.1007/BF02458355

Nelson, R. (Ed.). (1993). *National Innovation Systems: A Comparative Analysis*. New York: Oxford University Press.

Nelson, R., & Winter, S. (1982). *An Evolutionary Theory of Economic Change*. Cambridge, MA: Harvard University Press.

NSTC [National Science and Technology Council] Report (2006, July). *The National Nanotechnology Initiative: Research and Development Leading to a Revolution in Technology and Industry*.

Perez, C. (2000). Technological Revolutions, Paradigm Shifts and Socio-Institutional Change. In Reinert, E. (Ed.), *Evolutionary Economics and Income Equality*. Aldershot, UK: Edward Elgar.

Porter, A. L., & Cunningham, S. W. (2005). *Tech Mining. Exploiting New Technologies for Competitive Advantage*. New York: Wiley-Interscience. Roco, M. C., & Bainbridge, W.S. (2002). Converging Technologies for Improving Human Performance: Integrating from the nanoscale. *Journal of Nanoparticle Research*, 4(4), 281–295.

Roco, M. C. (2005). International perspective on government nanotechnology funding in 2005. *Journal of Nanoparticle Research*, 7(6), 707–712. doi:10.1007/s11051-005-3141-5

Wonglimpiyarat, J. (2005). The nano-revolution of Schumpeter's Kondratieff cycle. *Technovation*, 25(11), 1349–1354. doi:10.1016/j.technovation.2004.07.002

ENDNOTES

[1]   [*Carbon nanotubes (CNTs)* are extended tubes of rolled graphene sheets, both single-walled and multi-walled types. CNTs have assumed an important role in the context of nanomaterials because of their novel chemical, physical and electrical properties. They are mechanically very strong as stiff

as diamond, flexible about their axis and can conduct electricity extremely well. All of these remarkable properties give CNTs a range of potential applications: for example in reinforced composites, sensors, nanoelectronics and display devices]

[1] [*Fullerenes* called carbon 60, a new class of carbon material, are spherical molecules about 1 nm in diameter comprising 60 carbon atoms arranged as 20 hexagons and 12 pentagons: the configuration of a football]

[2] [The key factors in the identified former 5 Kondratieff's are: 1) cotton for textile innovation, 2) coal and iron for steam power and railway innovation, 3) innovation in industries based on electric power and steel, 4) oil for innovation in automobiles and synthetic materials, and 5) chips (microelectronics) for information, communication and computer networks]

[3] [interview with Professor Anne Ulrich, Institut for Organische Chemie and CFN, University of Karlsruhe; interview with Professor Marcello Baricco, Dipartimento de Chimica IFM and NIS-Centre of Excellence, Universita degli Studi di Torino]

[4] [interview with Professor Kostas Kostarelos, Center for Drug Delivery Research, University of London]

[5] [interview with Dr. Robert Baptist, Directeur de Recherche, CEA (*Commissariat à l'Energie Atomique)* and LETI (*Laboratoire d'Electronique de Technologie et d'Instrumentation*), Grenoble, France]

[6] [interview with Dr. Karl-Heinz Haas, Spokesman of the Fraunhofer Nanotechnology Alliance and Deputy Director for Fraunhofer ISC, Fraunhofer-Gesellschaft]

[7] [interview with Professor John Ryan, Director of IRC Bionanotechnology, University of Oxford]

[8] [interview with Professor Shunri Oda, Quantum Nano-electronics Research Center, Tokyo Institute of Technology]

Compilation of References

A & G Engineering. (n.d.). A & G Engineering. Retrieved from www.agengineering.com.au

Aarons, G. A., & Sawitzky, A. C. (2006). Organisational culture and climate and mental health provider attitudes toward evidence-based practice. *Psychological Services*, *3*(1), 61–72. doi:10.1037/1541-1559.3.1.61

ABC Radio (2008). *From S to M: Small to Medium Businesses in Australia, Lifelong Learning.* Retrieved June 24, 2008, from http://www.abc.net.au/rn/learning/lifelong/features/smallbiz

Abdul-Gafaru, A. (2006). Are multinational corporations compatible with sustainable development? The experience of developing countries. Paper presented at the *MESD 2006 International Research Colloquium.* Atlanta, GA.

Abernathy, W. J., & Clark, K. B. (1985). Innovation: Mapping the winds of creative destruction. *Research Policy*, *14*(1), 3–22. doi:10.1016/0048-7333(85)90021-6

Acar, E., Kocak, I., Sey, Y., & Arditi, D. (2005). Use of information and Communication technologies by small and medium-sized enterprises (SMEs) in building construction. *Construction Management and Economics*, *23*, 713–722. doi:10.1080/01446190500127112

Ackerman, L. S. (1986). Development, Transition or Transformation: The Question of Change in Organizations. *Organizational Development Practitioner*, *December*, 1-8.

Acs, Z. J., Braunerhjelm, P., Audretsch, D. B., & Carlsson, B. (2009). The knowledge spillover theory of entrepreneurship. *Small Business Economics*, *32*(1), 15–30. doi:10.1007/s11187-008-9157-3

Adams, R., Bessant, J., & Phelps, R. (2006). Innovation management measurement: A review. *International Journal of Management Reviews*, *8*(1), 21–47. doi:10.1111/j.1468-2370.2006.00119.x

Adner, R., & Zemsky, P. (2006). A demand-based perspective on sustainable competitive advantage. *Strategic Management Journal*, *27*(3), 215–239. doi:10.1002/smj.513

Agarwal, R., & Bayus, B. L. (2002). The Market Evolution and Sales Takeoff of Product Innovations. *Management Science*, *48*(8), 1024–1041. doi:10.1287/mnsc.48.8.1024.167

Agnihothri, S., Sivasubramaniam, N., & Simmons, D. (2002). Leveraging technology to improve field service. *International Journal of Service Industry Management*, *13*(1), 47–68. doi:10.1108/09564230210421155

Aguilera, R., Rupp, D., Williams, C., & Ganapathi, J. (2007). Putting the "S" back in corporate social responsibility: A multilevel theory of social change in organizations. *Academy of Management Review*, *32*(3), 836–863.

Alexander, J. (1999). The impact of devolution on nonprofits: A multiphase study of social service organizations. *Nonprofit Management & Leadership*, *10*(1), 57–70. doi:10.1002/nml.10105

Alexander, J. (2000). Adaptive strategies of nonprofit human service organizations in an era of devolution and new public management. *Nonprofit Management & Leadership*, *10*(3), 287–303. doi:10.1002/nml.10305

Alexander, V. D. (1998). Environmental constraints and organizational strategies: Complexity, conflict, and coping in the nonprofit sector. In Powell, W. W., & Clemens, E. S. (Eds.), *Private action and the public good* (pp. 272–290). New Haven, CT: Yale University Press.

Alsop, R. (1986, July 10). Companies get on fast track to roll hot new brands. *Wall Street Journal*.

Alter, A. (2005). CIOs Shift: Focus is On Revenue, Not on Saving Money. *CIO Insight.* Retrieved November 27, 2006 from http://www.cioinsight.com/article2/0,1397,1875251,00.asp

Amabile, T. M. (1988). A model of creativity and innovation in organisation. In Shaw, B. M., & Cummings, L. L. (Eds.), *Research in Organisational Behaviour, 10, 123-67.*

Amabile, T. M., Conti, R., Coon, H., Lazenby, J., & Herron, M. (1996). Assessing the work environment for creativity. *Academy of Management Journal, 39,* 1154–1184. doi:10.2307/256995

Ambrosini, V., & Bowman, C. (2001). Tacit knowledge: Some suggestions for operationalization. *Journal of Management Studies, 38*(6), 811–829. doi:10.1111/1467-6486.00260

Amemiya, T. (1973). Regression analysis when the dependent variable is truncated normal. *Econometrica, 41*(6), 997–1016. doi:10.2307/1914031

Anand, N., Gardner, H. K., & Morris, T. (2007). Knowledge-based innovation: Emergence and embedding of new practice areas in management consulting firms. *Academy of Management Journal, 50*(2), 406–428.

Andersen, P. H. (2005). Relationship marketing and brand involvement of professionals through web-enhanced brand communities: The case of Coloplast. *Industrial Marketing Management, 34,* 39–51. doi:10.1016/j.indmarman.2004.07.002

Anderson, J. C., & Gerbing, D. W. (1988). Structural equation modeling in practice: A review and recommended two-step approach. *Psychological Bulletin, 103*(3), 411–423. doi:10.1037/0033-2909.103.3.411

Anderson, N. R., de Dreu, C. K. W., & Nijstad, B. A. (2004). The routinization of innovation research: a constructively critical review of the state-of-the-science. *Journal of Organizational Behavior, 25*(2), 147–174. doi:10.1002/job.236

Anheier, H. K. (2005). *Nonprofit organizations: Theory, management, policy.* London: Routledge.

Ansoff, H. I. (1965). *Corporate strategy.* New York: McGraw-Hill.

Ansoff, I. H. (1957). Strategies for diversification. *Harvard Business Review, 35*(2), 113–124.

APEC Human Resources Development Working Group Capacity Building Network (2007). *Corporate Social Responsibility in the Global Supply Chain: An APEC case book.* Singapore: APEC Secretariat.

Archibugi, D., & Coco, A. (2005). Measuring Technological Capabilities at the Country Level: A Survey and Menu for Choice. *Research Policy, 34,* 175–194. doi:10.1016/j.respol.2004.12.002

Ardichvilia, A., Cardozob, R., & Rayc, S. (2003). A theory of entrepreneurial opportunity identification and development. *Journal of Business Venturing, 18*(1).

Argyris, C. (1990). *Overcoming Organizational Defences: Facilitating Organizational Learning.* Boston: Allyn & Bacon.

Argyris, C., & Schön, D. (1978). *Organizational Learning: A Theory-in-Action Perspective.* Reading, MA: Addison-Wesley.

Argyrous, G. (1993). Emerging exporters: An evaluation. *Journal of Australian Political Economy, 32,* 106–126.

Argyrous, G. (1995). Economic evolution and cumulative causation. In Argyrous, G., & Stilwell, F. (Eds.), *Economics as a Social Science: Readings in Political Economy.* Sydney, Australia: Pluto Press.

Argyrous, G. (2000). The high road and the low road to international trade: Emerging exporters re-visited. *Journal of Australian Political Economy, 45,* 46–67.

Argyrous, G., & Bamberry, G. (2009). Cumulative causation and industrial development: The regional stage. In Berger, S. (Ed.), *The Foundations of Non-Equilibrium*

Economics: The Principle of Circular and Cumulative Causation. London: Routledge.

Argyrous, G., & Sethi, R. (1996). The theory of evolution and the evolution of theory: Veblen's methodology in contemporary perspective. *Cambridge Journal of Economics, 20*, 475–495.

Arias-Aranda, D., Beatriz Minguela-Rata, B., & Rodríguez-Duarte, A. (2001). Innovation and firm size: an empirical study for Spanish engineering consulting companies. *European Journal of Innovation Management, 4*(3), 133–142. doi:10.1108/EUM0000000005671

Arocena, R., & Sutz, J. (2000). Looking at National Systems of Innovation from the South. *Industry and Innovation, 7*(1), 55–75. doi:10.1080/713670247

Arroyabe, J. C. F. D., & Pena, A. N. (1999, 30 August - 2 September). *Technological Cluster Integrated Model for SMEs.* Paper presented at the 3rd International Conference on Technology and Innovation Policy: Assessment, Commercialisation and Application of Science and Technology and Management of Knowledge, Texas, USA.

Asheim, B. T., & Coenen, L. (2006). Contextualising Regional Innovation Systems in a Globalising Learning Economy: On Knowledge Bases and Institutional Frameworks. *The Journal of Technology Transfer, 31*(1), 163–173. doi:10.1007/s10961-005-5028-0

Ashkanasy, N. M., Wilderom, C. P. M., & Peterson, M. F. (2000). *Handbook of Organisational culture and climate.* Thousand Oaks, CA: Sage.

Asia Monitor Resource Centre. (2006). Retrieved August 14, from http://www.amrc.org.hk

Asongu, J. J. (2007). Innovation as an Argument for Corporate social responsibility. *Journal of Business and Public Policy, 1*(3), 1–21.

Atmanand. (2000). *Growth and deregulation of Indian oil industry (post reform analysis).* New Delhi: Excel Books.

Atuahene-Gima, K., & Ko, A. (2001). An empirical investigation of the effect of market orientation and entrepreneurship orientation alignment on product in-novation. *Organization Science, 12*(1), 54–74. doi:10.1287/orsc.12.1.54.10121

Audretsch, D., & Thurik, R. (2004). A model of entrepreneurial economy. *International Journal of entrepreneurship. Education, 2*(2), 143–166.

Australian Bureau of Statistics. (2005). *2005 Year Book Australia.* Canberra, Australia: Australian Government.

Australian Bureau of Statistics. (2005). *Innovation in Australian Business 2003, cat. no. 8158.0.* Canberra, Australia: Australian Government.

Australian Bureau of Statistics. (2006). *Innovation in Australian Business 2005, cat. no. 8158.0.* Canberra, Australia: Australian Government.

Australian Bureau of Statistics. (2008). *Innovation in Australian Business 2006-2007, cat no. 8158.0.* Retrieved April 27, 2009, from http://www.abs.gov.au/AUSSTATS/abs@.nsf/Latestproducts/8158.0Contents2006-07?opendocument&tabname=Summary&prodno=8158.0&issue=2006-07&num=&view=

Axtell, C. M., Holman, D. J., Unsworth, K. L., Wall, T. D., Waterson, P. E., & Harrington, E. (2000). Shopfloor innovation: facilitating the suggestions and implementation of ideas. *Journal of Occupational and Organizational Psychology, 73*, 265–285. doi:10.1348/096317900167029

Backman, E. V., Grossman, A., & Rangan, V. K. (2000). Introduction. *Nonprofit and Voluntary Sector Quarterly, 29*(Supplement), 2–8. doi:10.1177/089976400773746319

Balser, D., & McClusky, J. (2005). Managing stakeholder relationships and nonprofit organization effectiveness. *Nonprofit Management & Leadership, 15*(3), 295–315. doi:10.1002/nml.70

Bamberry, G. (2006). The influence of technology on regional development: Case studies from the Riverina Region. *Australasian Journal of Regional Studies, 12*(2), 173–190.

Bamberry, G. (2006). The significance of linkages for regional manufacturers: A case study of the Riverina Region of New South Wales. In *Proceedings of the Third International Conference on Contemporary Business,*

Leura. Edited by P.K. Basu and G. O'Neill. Charles Sturt University, Bathurst, Australia.

Bamberry, G., & Wickramasekera, R. (1999). *Manufacturing in the Riverina: A report for the Riverina Regional Development Board*. Wagga Wagga, Australia: Charles Sturt University.

Barczak, G., Sultan, F., & Hultink, E. J. (2007). Determinants of IT usage and New Product Performance. *Journal of Product Innovation Management, 24*, 600–613. doi:10.1111/j.1540-5885.2007.00274.x

Barge, K. (2001). Integrating theory, research and practice in select conflict contexts: creating healthy communities through affirmative conflict communication (pp. 92-93). *Conflict Resolution Quarterly, 19*(1), 89–101.

Barney, J. B. (1991). Firm resources and sustained competitive advantage. *Journal of Management, 17*(1), 99–120. doi:10.1177/014920639101700108

Baron, D. P. (2001). Private politics, corporate social responsibility and integrated strategy. *Journal of Economics & Management Strategy, 10*(1), 7–45. doi:10.1162/105864001300122548

Bartunek, J. M. (1993). The Multiple Cognitions and Conflicts Associated with Second Order Organizational Change. In Murnighan, J. K. (Ed.), *Social Psychology in Organizations: Advances in Theory and Research*. Upper Saddle River, NJ: Prentice Hall.

Bateson, G. (1973). *Steps to Ecology of Mind*. London: Palladin.

Bayo-Moriones, A., & Lera-Lopez, F. (2007). A firm-level analysis of determinants of ICT adoption in Spain. *Technovation, 27*, 325–366.

Bayus, B. L. (1992). Have Diffusion Rates Been Accelerating Over Time? *Marketing Letters, 3*(3), 215–226. doi:10.1007/BF00994130

Bayus, B. L. (1994). Are Product Life Cycles Really Getting Shorter? *Journal of Product Innovation Management, 11*, 300–308. doi:10.1016/0737-6782(94)90085-X

Bayus, B. L. (1998). An Analysis of Product Lifetimes in a Technologically Dynamic Industry. *Management Science, 44*(6), 763–775. doi:10.1287/mnsc.44.6.763

Beatson, M. (1995). Labour market flexibility. In *Research Series (No. 48)*. Sheffield: Employment Department.

Becheikh, N., Landry, R., & Amara, N. (2005). Lessons from innovation empirical studies in the manufacturing sector: a systematic review of the literature from 1993-2003. *Technovation, 26*(5-6), 644–663. doi:10.1016/j.technovation.2005.06.016

Beer, A., Bolam, A., & Maud, A. (1994). Beyond the capitals: Urban growth in regional Australia. Canberra, Australia: Commonwealth Department of Housing and Regional Development.

Beer, A., Maud, A., & Pritchard, W. (2003). *Developing Australia's regions: Theory and practice*. Sydney, Australia: University of New South Wales Press.

Beinhocker, E. (2006). The Adaptable Corporation. *The McKinsey Quarterly, 2*, 77–87.

Bekkers, R., Gilsing, V., & van der Steen, M. (2006). Determining factors of IP-based spin-offs. *The Journal of Technology Transfer, 31*, 545–566. doi:10.1007/s10961-006-9058-z

Belderbos, R., Carree, M., & Lokshin, B. (2004). Cooperative R&D and Firm Performance. *Research Policy, 33*, 1472–1477. doi:10.1016/j.respol.2004.07.003

Berger, S. (2008). Circular cumulative causation (CCC) a la Myrdal and Kapp – Political Institutionalism for minimizing social costs. *Journal of Economic Issues, 42*(2), 357–365.

Berger, S., & Elsner, W. (2007). European contributions to evolutionary institutional economics: The cases of cumulative circular causation (CCC) and open systems approach (OSA): Some methodological and policy implications. *Journal of Economic Issues, 41*(2), 529–537.

Bernal, V. (2001). Building Online Communities. *Benton*. Retrieved October 1, 2006 from http://www.benton.org/publibrary/practice/community/assumptions.html

Bessant, J., & Tidd, J. (2007). *Innovation and entrepreneurship*. Chichester, UK: John Wiley & Sons Ltd.

Betz, F. (1987). *Managing technology: Competing through new ventures, innovation, and corporate research*. Englewood Cliffs, NJ: Prentice Hall.

Bevir, M. (2007). *Encyclopedia of governance*. Thousand Oaks, CA: Sage.

Bird, F., & Smucker, J. (2007). The Social Responsibilities of International Business Firms in Developing Areas. *Journal of Business Ethics*, *73*, 1–9. doi:10.1007/s10551-006-9192-4

Birkinshaw, J., & Mol, M. (2006). How Management Innovation Happens. *Management of Technology and Innovation*, *47*(4), 81–88.

Boedker, C., Guthrie, J., & Cuganesan, S. (2005). An integrated framework for visualizing intellectual capital. *Journal of Intellectual Capital*, *6*(4), 510–527. doi:10.1108/14691930510628799

Bontis, N. (1996). There's price on your head: Managing intellectual capital strategically. *Business Quarterly*, *60*(4), 40–47.

Bontis, N. (1998). Intellectual capital: An exploratory study that develops measures and models. *Management Decision*, *36*(2), 63–76. doi:10.1108/00251749810204142

Bontis, N. (1999). Managing organizational knowledge by diagnosing intellectual capital: Framing and advancing the state of the field. *International Journal of Technology Management*, *18*(5-8), 433–462. doi:10.1504/IJTM.1999.002780

Bontis, N., Dragonetti, N. C., Jacobsen, K., & Roos, G. (1999). The knowledge toolbox: A review of the tools available to measure and manage intangible resources. *European Management Journal*, *17*(4), 391–402. doi:10.1016/S0263-2373(99)00019-5

Bontis, N., Keow, W. C. C., & Richardson, S. (2000). Intellectual capital and business performance in Malaysian industries. *Journal of Intellectual Capital*, *1*(1), 85–100. doi:10.1108/14691930010324188

Booz, A. (1982). *New Product Management for the 1980s. New York: Booz*. Hamilton: Allen and Hamilton, Inc.

Bordens, K., & Abbott, B. (1999). *Research design and methods*. Mountain View, CA: Mayfield Publishing.

Borger, F. G., & Kruglianskas, I. (2006). Corporate social responsibility and environmental and technological innovation performance: case studies of Brazilian companies. *International Journal of Technology. Policy and Management*, *6*(4), 399–412.

Borins, S. (2000). Loose cannons and rule breakers, or enterprising leaders? Some evidence about innovative public managers. *Public Administration Review*, *60*(6), 498–507. doi:10.1111/0033-3352.00113

Borzaga, C., & Defourny, J. (2001). Conclusions: Social enterprises in Europe - A diversity of initiatives and prospects. In Borzaga, C., & Defourny, J. (Eds.), *The emergence of social enterprise*. London: Routledge.

Braczyk, H.-J., Cooke, P., & Heidenreich, M. (Eds.). (1998). *Regional Innovation Systems: The Role of Governance in a Globalized World*. London: UCL Press.

Brentani, U. (2001). Innovative versus incremental new business services: Different keys for achieving success. *Journal of Product Innovation Management*, *18*(3), 169–187. doi:10.1016/S0737-6782(01)00071-6

Bresnahan, T. F., & Tajtenberg, M. (1995). General Purpose Technologies: Engines of Growth. *Journal of Econometrics*, *65*, 83–108. doi:10.1016/0304-4076(94)01598-T

Bridge, S., O'Neill, K., & Cromie, S. (1998). *Understanding Enterprise, Entrepreneurship, and Small Businesses*. Manchester, UK: Manchester University Press.

Brock, C. (2008). *Financial crisis hits charities*. Retrieved January 5, 2008, from http://www.mortgageloan.com/financial-crisis-hits-charities-2621

Brockhoff, K. (2003). Customers' perspectives of involvement in new product development. *International Journal of Technology Management*, *26*(5), 464–481. doi:10.1504/IJTM.2003.003418

Brody, P., & Ehrlich, D. (1998). Can Big Companies Become Successful Venture Capitalists. *The McKinsey Quarterly, 2*, 50–63.

Brown, C. J., & Frame, P. (2004). Subjectivity in innovation management. *International Journal of Innovation and Learning, 1*(4), 351–363. doi:10.1504/IJIL.2004.005496

Brown, J., & Duguid, P. (1991). Organization learning and communities-of-practice: Toward a unified view of working, learning, and innovation. *Organization Science, 2*(1), 40–57. doi:10.1287/orsc.2.1.40

Brown, S. L., & Eisenhardt, K. (1998). *Competing on the edge: strategy as structured chaos*. Boston, MA: Harvard Business School Press.

Brusco, S. (1989). A policy for industrial districts. In Goodman, E., & Bamford, J. (Eds.), *Small firms and industrial districts in Italy*. London: Routledge.

Buchele, R., & Christiansen, J. (1999). Employment and productivity growth in Europe and North America: The impact of labour market institutions. *International Review of Applied Economics, 13*(3), 313–332. doi:10.1080/026921799101571

Buckler, S. A., & Zien, K. A. (1996). From Experience: The Spirituality of Innovation: Learning from stories. *Journal of Product Innovation Management, 13*(5), 391–405. doi:10.1016/0737-6782(96)00056-2

Bukh, P. N., Johansen, M. R., & Mouritsen, J. (2002). Multiple integrated performance management systems: IC and BSC in a software company. *Singapore Management Review, 24*(3), 21–33.

Burgelman, R. A., Maidique, M. A., & Wheelwright, S. C. (2001). *Strategic Management of technology and innovation* (3rd ed.). New York: McGraw-Hill/Irwin.

Burgelman, R., & Sayles, L. R. (1986). *Inside corporate innovation*. New York: The Free Press.

Burke, L., & Logsdon, J. (1996). How corporate social responsibility pays off. *Long Range Planning, 29*, 495–502. doi:10.1016/0024-6301(96)00041-6

Burke, W., & Litwin, G. (1992). A Casual Model of Organisational Performance and Change. *Journal of Management, 18*, 523–545. doi:10.1177/014920639201800306

Burns, T., & Stalker, G. M. (1961). *The management of innovation*. London: Tavistock Publication.

Burt, R. S. (1992). *Structural Holes: The Social Structure of Competition*. Cambridge, MA: Harvard University Press.

Bush & Folger. (1994). *The promise of mediation*. San Francisco: Jossey Bass.

Caddy, I., Guthrie, J., & Petty, R. (2001). Managing orphan knowledge: Current Australasian best practice. *Journal of Intellectual Capital, 2*(4), 384–397. doi:10.1108/14691930110409679

Cameron, K. S., & Quinn, R. E. (1999). *Diagnosing and Changing Organisational Culture: Based on the Competing Values Framework*. Reading, MA: Addison Wesley Longman.

Carey, J., & Moss, M. L. (1985). The Diffusion of Telecommunication Technologies. *Telecommunications Policy, 6*, 145–158. doi:10.1016/0308-5961(85)90038-2

Carlsson, B., & Stankiewicz, R. (1991). On the nature, function and composition of technological systems. *Evolutionary Economics, 1*, 93–118. doi:10.1007/BF01224915

Carlsson, B., Jacobsson, S., Holmen, M., & Rickne, A. (2002). Innovation systems: analytical and methodological issues. *Research Policy, 31*, 233–245. doi:10.1016/S0048-7333(01)00138-X

Carmazzi, A., & Aarons, G. A. (2003). Organisational culture and attitudes toward adoption of evidence-based practice. Paper presented at the NASMHPD Research Institute's 2003 Conference on State Mental Health Agency Services Research, Program Evaluation, and Policy, Baltimore, MD.

Carroll, A. (1991). The pyramid of corporate social responsibility: Toward the moral management of organizational stakeholders. *Business Horizons, 34*, 39–48. doi:10.1016/0007-6813(91)90005-G

Carroll, A. B. (1999). Corporate social responsibility: Evolution of a definitional construct. *Business & Society, 38*(3), 268–295. doi:10.1177/000765039903800303

Casalo, L. V., Flavian, C., & Guinaliu, M. (2008). Promoting customer's participation in virtual brand communities: A new paradigm in branding strategy. *Journal of Marketing Communications, 14*(1), 19–36. doi:10.1080/13527260701535236

Casella Wines. (n.d.). Retrieved from www.casellawines.com.au De Bortoli Wines (n.d.). Retrieved from www.debortoli.com.au

Chesbrough, H. (2003). *Open Innovation: The New Imperative for Creating and Profiting from Technology.* Boston: Harvard Business School Press.

Chetkovich, C., & Frumkin, P. (2003). Balancing margin and mission nonprofit competition in charitable versus fee-based programs. *Administration & Society, 35*(5), 564–596. doi:10.1177/0095399703256162

Chia, R. (1996). Teaching paradigm shifts in management education: university business schools and the entrepreneurial imagination. *Journal of Management Studies, 33,* 409–428. doi:10.1111/j.1467-6486.1996.tb00162.x

China Entrepreneurs Survey System. (2007). *Report on Chinese Entrepreneurs Growth and Evolution.* Beijing, China: China Machine Press. (in Chinese)

China Finance Economic Company. (2006). CSR report in China (in Chinese) The annual report of the Chinese Institute of Business Administration, 2005-2006, Beijing, China.

Choo, C. W., & Bontis, N. (Eds.). (2002). *The strategic management of intellectual capital and organizational knowledge.* Oxford, UK: Oxford University Press.

Christensen, C. M. (2003). *The Innovator's Dilemma: The Revolutionary Book that Will Change the Way You Do Business.* New York: Collins.

Christensen, C. M., & Raynor, M. E. (2003). *Innovator's Solution: Creating and sustaining successful growth.* Boston: Harvard Business School Press.

Christensen, C. M., Anthony, S. D., & Roth, E. A. (2004). *Seeing what's next. Using theories of innovation to predict industry change.* Boston: Harvard Business School Press.

Christmann, P., & Taylor, G. (2001). Globalization and the environment: Determinants of firm self-regulation in China. *Journal of International Business Studies, 32*(3), 439–458. doi:10.1057/palgrave.jibs.8490976

Chung, S. (1999, 30 August – 2 September). *Regional Innovation Systems in Korea.* Paper presented at the 3rd International Conference on Technology and Innovation Policy: Assessment, Commercialization and Application of Science and Technology and Management of Knowledge, Texas, USA.

Churchill, G. A. (1979). A paradigm for Developing better measures of Marketing Constructs. *JMR, Journal of Marketing Research, 16*(1), 64–73. doi:10.2307/3150876

Clark, J., & Guy, K. (1998). Innovation and Competitiveness: a Review. *Technology Analysis and Strategic Management, 10*(3), 363–395. doi:10.1080/09537329808524322

Clark, K. (1987). Investment in new technology and competitive advantage. In Teece, D. J. (Ed.), *The competitive challenge* (pp. 59–82). Grand Rapids, MI: Harper & Row.

Clark, K. B. (1985). The Interaction of Design Hierarchies and Market Concepts in Technological Evolution. *Research Policy, 14,* 235–251. doi:10.1016/0048-7333(85)90007-1

Climento, A. (1993). Excellence in Electronics. *The McKinsey Quarterly, 3,* 29–40.

Cohen, J. (2001). When people are the means: negotiating with respect. *The Georgetown Journal of Legal Ethics, 14,* 739–802.

Cohen, W. M., & Levintal, D. A. (1990). Absorptive capacity: A new perspective on learning and innovation. *Administrative Science Quarterly, 35,* 128–152. doi:10.2307/2393553

Cohen, W. M., Levin, R. C., & Mowery, D. C. (1987). Firm size and r&d intensity: A reexamination. *The Journal of Industrial Economics, 35*(4), 543–565. doi:10.2307/2098587

Coleman, J. (1990). *Foundations of Social Theory*. Cambridge, MA: Harvard University Press.

Commonwealth of Australia. (2000). *Business Failure and Change: An Australian Perspective. Staff research paper 2000/12/20*. Canberra, Australia: Australian Productivity Commission.

Conner, K. R. (1995). Obtaining strategic advantages from being imitated: when can encouraging "clones" pay? *Management Science, 41*(2), 209–225. doi:10.1287/mnsc.41.2.209

Constantinos, M. (2006). Disruptive innovation: in need of better theory. *Journal of Product Innovation Management, 23*, 19–25. doi:10.1111/j.1540-5885.2005.00177.x

Constantinos, M., & Geroski, P. A. (2005). Fast Second: how smart companies bypass radical innovation to enter and dominate new markets. San Francisco: Jossey-Bass publication.

Cooper, J., Greenberg, D., & Zuk, J. (2004). Reshaping the funnel: Making innovation more profitable for high-tech manufacturers. *IBM Institute for Business Value*. Retrieved November 11, 2006, from http://www.ibm.com/industries/aerodefense/doc/content/bin/ibv_funnel_1.pdf

Cooper, R. G. (1995). Developing new products on time, in time. *Research Technology Management, 38*(5), 49–58.

Cooper, R. G. (2005). Product leadership: Pathway to profitable innovation (2 ed.). New York: Basic Books.

Cooper, R. G., & Kleinschmidt, E. J. (2007). Winning business in product development: The critical success factors. *Research Technology Management, 50*(3), 52–66.

Cordero, R. (1990). The Measurement of Innovation Performance in the Firm: An Overview. *Research Policy, 19*(2), 185–193. doi:10.1016/0048-7333(90)90048-B

Cornelius, N., Todres, M., Janjuha-Jivraj, S., Woods, A., & Wallace, J. (2008). Corporate social responsibility and the Social Enterprise. *Journal of Business Ethics, 81*, 355–370. doi:10.1007/s10551-007-9500-7

Coutrot, T. (2003). Innovation and job stability. In *Working Paper*. Paris: Centre D'Etudes Prospectives et D'Informations Internationales.

Covin, J. G., & Slevin, D. P. (1989). Strategic management of small firms in hostile and benign environments. *Strategic Management Journal, 10*(1), 75–87. doi:10.1002/smj.4250100107

Coyne, K. P., Hall, S. J. D., & Clifford, P. G. (1997). Is your core competence a mirage? *The McKinsey Quarterly*, 1.

Craig, G., Taylor, M., & Parkes, T. (2004). Protest or partnership? The voluntary and community sectors in the policy process. *Social Policy and Administration, 38*(3), 221–239. doi:10.1111/j.1467-9515.2004.00387.x

Crawford, C. M. (1977). Marketing Research and the New Product Failure Rate. *Journal of Marketing*, (April): 51–61. doi:10.2307/1250634

Crawford, C. M. (1979). New Product Failure Rates - Facts and Fallacies. *Research Management*, (September): 9–13.

Crawford, C. M. (1987). New Product Failure Rates: A Reprise. *Research Management*, (July-August): 20–24.

Cray, D., Mallory, G. R., Butler, R. J., Hickson, D. J., & Wilson, D. C. (1991). Explaining decision processes. *Journal of Management Studies, 28*(3), 227–251. doi:10.1111/j.1467-6486.1991.tb00946.x

Cronqvist, H., Low, A., & Nilsson, M. (2007). Does Corporate Culture Matter for Firm Policies? *A Research Report From Swedish Institute For Financial Research, 48*(2), 1-60. Damanpour, F., & Schneider, M. (2006). Phases of the adoption of innovation in organisations: Effects of environment, organisation and top managers. *British Journal of Management, 17*, 215–236.

Crossan, M., Lane, H., & White, R. (1999). An organizational learning framework: From intuition to institution. *Academy of Management Review, 24*(3), 522–537. doi:10.2307/259140

Cummings, T. G., & Worley, C. G. (1997). *Organization Development and Change* (6th ed.). South-Western College Publishing.

Cutter Consortium. (2005). *Press Release: Software Project Success and Failure*. Retrieved August 24, 2005, from http://www.cutter.com/press/050824.html

Daft, R. L. (1978). A Dual-core model of organizational innovation. *Academy of Management Journal, 21*(2), 193–210. doi:10.2307/255754

Dahan, E., & Hauser, J. R. (2002). The Virtual Customer. *Journal of Product Innovation Management, 19,* 332–353. doi:10.1016/S0737-6782(02)00151-0

Damanpour, F. (1990). Innovation effectiveness, adoption and organizational performance. In West, M. A., & Farr, J. L. (Eds.), *Innovation and Creativity at work: Psychological and Organizational Strategies.* Chichester, UK: Wiley.

Damanpour, F. (1991). A meta-analysis of effects of determinants and moderators. *Academy of Management Journal, 34,* 555–590. doi:10.2307/256406

Damanpour, F. (1991). Organizational innovation: a meta-analysis of effects of determinants and moderators. *Academy of Management Journal, 34*(3), 555–590. doi:10.2307/256406

Damanpour, F., & Evan, W. M. (1984). Organizational innovation and performance: The problem of 'organizational lag'. *Administrative Science Quarterly, 29,* 392–409. doi:10.2307/2393031

Damanpour, F., & Wischnevsky, J. D. (2006). Research on innovation in organizations: Distinguishing innovation-generating from innovation-adopting organizations. *Journal of Engineering and Technology Management, 23*(1), 269–291. doi:10.1016/j.jengtecman.2006.08.002

Dart, R. (2004). The legitimacy of social enterprise. *Nonprofit Management & Leadership, 14*(4), 411–424. doi:10.1002/nml.43

Davies, A., & Gann, D. (2003). *A Review of Nanotechnology and its Potential Applications for Construction.* London: CRISP, Darby, M. R. & Zucker, L. G. (2003). Grilichesian breakthroughs: inventions of methods of inventing and firms entry in nanotechnology, *NBER Working Paper,* 9825.

Davila, T., Epstein, M. J., & Shelton, R. (2006). *Making innovation work - How to manage it, measure it and profit from it.* Upper Saddle River, NJ: Wharton School Publishing.

Davis, G. F., & Thompson, T. A. (1994). A social movement perspective on corporate control. *Administrative Science Quarterly, 39,* 141–173. doi:10.2307/2393497

Day, D. L. (1994). Raising radicals. *Organization Science, 5,* 148–172. doi:10.1287/orsc.5.2.148

Day, G., & Schoemaker, P. J. H. (2000). *Wharton on Managing Emerging Technologies.* New York: Wiley.

De Ridder, J. (1986). Cumulative causation versus comparative advantage. *Journal of Australian Political Economy,* (20), 44-48.

Dean, D., & Dvorak, R. (1995). Do it, then fix it: The power of prototypes. *The McKinsey Quarterly, 4,* 50–61.

Dees, J. G. (1998). Enterprising nonprofits. *Harvard Business Review, 76*(1), 55–69.

Deffeyes, K. S. (2001). *Hubbert's peak: The impending world oil shortage.* Princeton, NJ: Princeton University Press.

Defourny, J. (2001). Introduction: From third sector to social enterprise. In Borzaga, C., & Defourny, J. (Eds.), *The emergence of social enterprise.* London: Routledge.

Deming, W. E. (1986). *Out of the crisis.* Cambridge, MA: MIT Center for Advanced Engineering Study.

Deshpandé, R., Farley, J. U., & Webster, F. E. (1993). Corporate culture, customer orientation and innovativeness in Japanese firms: a quadrad analysis. *JMR, Journal of Marketing Research, 57*(1), 23–37.

Deutsch, M. (1973). *The resolution of conflict: constructive and destructive processes.* New Haven, CT: Yale University Press.

Deutsch, M., & Coleman, P. (2000). *The handbook of conflict resolution: theory and practice.* San Francisco, CA: Jossey-Bass.

Dewar, R. D., & Dutton, J. E. (1986). The adoption of radical and incremental innovations: an empirical analysis. *Management Science, 32,* 1422–1433. doi:10.1287/mnsc.32.11.1422

Dewey, J. (1939). *Theory of Valuation.* Chicago, IL: University of Chicago Press.

Dhodapkar, P. K., Gogoi, A. K., Kalita, P. K., & Medhi, A. (2006). *Technology innovation requirements in an upstream hydrocarbon company*. Retrieved November 21, 2008, from http://www.iamot.org/conference/index.php/ocs/10/paper/viewFile/1750/794

Di Gregerio, D., & Shane, S. A. (2003). Why some universities generate more start-ups than others? *Research Policy, 32*, 209–227. doi:10.1016/S0048-7333(02)00097-5

DiBella, A. J., & Nevis, E. C. (1998). *How Organizations Learn. An Integreted Strategy for Building Learning Capability*. San Francisco: Jossey-Bass Publishers.

Dickson, P., Schneier, W., Lawrence, P., & Hytry, R. (1995). Managing Design in Small High-Growth Companies. *Journal of Product Innovation Management, 12*(5), 406–414. doi:10.1016/0737-6782(95)00056-9

Dillon, T., Lee, R., & Matheson, D. (2005, March-April). Value Innovation: Passport to wealth creation. *Research Technology Management*, 22-37.

DiMaggio, P. J., & Powell, W. W. (1983). The iron cage revisited: Institutional isomorphism and collective rationality in organizational fields. *American Sociological Review, 48*, 147–160. doi:10.2307/2095101

Di-Masi, P. (2006). *Defining Entrepreneurship*. Retrieved January 27, 2006, from http://www.gdrc.org/icm/micro/define-micro.html

Donckels, R. (1991). Education and entrepreneurship experiences from secondary and university education in Belgium. *Journal of Small Business and Entrepreneurship, 9*(1), 35–42.

Dosi, G. (1982). Technological Paradigms and Technological Trajectories: A Suggested Interpretation of the Determinants and Directions of Technological Change. *Research Policy, 11*, 147–162. doi:10.1016/0048-7333(82)90016-6

Dosi, G. (1988). Sources, procedures and microeconomic effects of innovation. *Journal of Economic Literature, 26*, 1120–1171.

Dosi, G., Freeman, C., Nelson, R., Silverberg, G., & Luc Soete. (1988). *Technical change and economic theory*. London: Pinter Publishers.

Dougherty, D., & Hardy, C. (1996). Sustained product innovation in large, mature organizations. *Academy of Management Journal, 39*, 1120–1153. doi:10.2307/256994

Douglas, J. V. (2008, August 28-October 1). Small Business Help. *Business Review Weekly,*, 22.

Dowling, M., & Helm, R. (2006). Product development success through cooperation: A study of entrepreneurial firms. *Technovation, 26*(4), 483–488. doi:10.1016/j.technovation.2005.06.015

Dresner, H. (2006). Business Intelligence: Standardization and Consolidation of Tools. *Hyperion*. Retrieved November 11, 2006, from http://www.hyperion.com/company/overview/thought_leadership/exec_perspectives/BI_Tools.cfm

Driver, M. (2002). The learning organization: Foucauldian gloom or utopian sunshine? *Human Relations, 55*(1), 33–53. doi:10.1177/0018726702055001605

Dröge, C., & Calantone, R. (1996). New product strategy, structure, and performance in two environments. *Industrial Marketing Management, 25*, 555–566. doi:10.1016/S0019-8501(96)00064-8

Drucker, P. F. (1984). The new meaning of corporate social responsibility. *California Management Review, 26*, 53–63.

Drucker, P. F. (1985). *Innovation and entrepreneurship*. New York: Harper and Row.

Drucker, P. F. (2002). The discipline of innovation. *Harvard Business Review, 80*, 77–83.

Druckman, D. (2005). *Doing research: methods of inquiry for conflict analysis*. Thousand Oaks, CA: Sage.

Dubelaar, C., Sohal, A., & Savic, V. (2005). Benefits, impediments, and critical success factors in B2C E-business adoption. *Technovation, 25*, 1251–1262. doi:10.1016/j.technovation.2004.08.004

Dubois, A., & Gadde, L.-E. (2002). The construction industry as a loosely coupled system: implications for productivity and innovation. *Construction Management and Economics, 20*, 621–631. doi:10.1080/01446190210163543

Dulaimi, M. F., Ling, F. Y. Y., & Bajracharya, A. (2003). Organizational motivation and inter-organizational interaction in construction innovation in Singapore. *Construction Management and Economics*, *21*(3), 307–318. doi:10.1080/0144619032000056144

Dundon, E. (2002). *The seeds of innovation: cultivating the synergy that fosters new ideas.* New York: AMACOM.

Dunning, J. (1998). Location and the Multinational Enterprise: A Neglected Factors? *Journal of International Business Studies*, *25*(1), 39–73.

Dwyer, F. R., Shur, P. H., & Oh, S. (1987). Developing buyer-seller relationships. *Journal of Marketing*, *51*(April), 11–27. doi:10.2307/1251126

Dzinkowski, R. (2000). The measurement and management of intellectual capital: An introduction. *Management Accounting*, *78*(2), 32–36.

Easingwood, C. J., & Lunn, S. O. (1992). Diffusion Paths in A High-Tech Environment: Clusters and Commonalities. *R & D Management*, *1*, 69–80. doi:10.1111/j.1467-9310.1992.tb00789.x

Edquist, C. (1997). *Systems of Innovation: Technologies, Institutions and Organizations.* London: Pinter Publisher.

Edquist, C. (2001). Innovation Policy - A Systemic Approach. In D. L. B.-A. Archibugi, (eds) (Ed.), The Globalizing Learning Economy (pp. 220-238). Oxford, UK: Oxford University Press.

Edquist, C. (2005). Systems of Innovation: Perspectives and Challenges. In J. Fagerberg, Mowery, D., and Nelson, R. (eds.). (Ed.), The Oxford Handbook of Innovation (pp. 181-208). Oxford, UK: Oxford University Press.

Edquist, C., & Mckelvey, M. (2000). *Systems of Innovation: Growth, Competitiveness and Employment (Vol. 1-2).* Cheltenham, UK: Edward Elgar Publishing Limited.

Edvinsson, L. (1997). Developing intellectual capital Skandia. *Long Range Planning*, *30*(3), 366–373. doi:10.1016/S0024-6301(97)90248-X

Edvinsson, L., & Malone, M. S. (1997). *Intellectual Capital - The proven way to establish your company's real value by measuring its hidden brainpower.* New York: HarperBusiness.

Egbu, C. O. (2004). Managing knowledge and intellectual capital for improved organizational innovations in the construction industry: an examination of critical success factors. *Engineering, Construction, and Architectural Management*, *11*(5), 301–315. doi:10.1108/09699980410558494

Eisenberg, P. (1997). A crisis in the nonprofit sector. *National Civic Review*, *86*(4), 331–341. doi:10.1002/ncr.4100860409

Eisenberg, P. (2000). The nonprofit sector in a changing world. *Nonprofit and Voluntary Sector Quarterly*, *29*(2), 325–330. doi:10.1177/0899764000292007

Eisenhardt, K. (1989). Building theory from case study research. *Academy of Management Journal*, *14*, 532–550. doi:10.2307/258557

Ekvall, G., & Avrvonen, J. Waldenström-Lindblad's, I. (1983). Creative Organisational climate: Construction and validation of a measuring instrument. Report 2. Stockholm: FA rådet, The Swedish Council for Management and Organisational Behaviour.

Epstein, E. M. (1987). The corporate social policy process: Beyond business ethics, corporate social responsibility and corporate social responsiveness. *California Management Review*, *29*, 99–114.

Erbe, N. (2003) Holding these truths: empowerment and recognition in action (interactive case study curriculum for multicultural dispute resolution. Berkeley, CA: Berkeley Public Policy Press.

Erbe, N. (2004). The global popularity and promise of facilitative adr. *Temple International and Comparative Law Journal*, *18*(2), 345–371.

Erbe, N. (2006). Appreciating mediation's global role in promoting good governance. *Harvard Negotiation Law Review*, *11*, 370–419.

Erbe, N., & Sebok, T. (2008). Shared global interest in skillfully applying ioa standards of practice. *Journal of the International Ombudsman*, *1*, 28–38.

Erbe, N., & Smith, R. (2008, October). *Falling in Love With Teaching and Learning: Proven Activities for Engaging Diverse Students in Collaborative Learning.* Paper presented at the annual meeting of the International Society for Teaching and Learning, Las Vegas, Nevada.

Ernst, H. (2002). Success Factors of New Product Development: A Review of the Empirical Literature. *International Journal of Management Reviews, 4*(1), 1–40. doi:10.1111/1468-2370.00075

Escribano, A., Fosfuri, A., & Tribó, J. A. (2009). Managing external knowledge flows: The moderating role of absorptive capacity. *Research Policy, 38*(1), 96–105. doi:10.1016/j.respol.2008.10.022

Evans, P., & Rauch, J. (1999). Bureaucracy and growth: A cross-national analysis of the effects of "Weberian" state structures on economic growth. *American Sociological Review, 64*, 748–765. doi:10.2307/2657374

Experian (2006). *Failure rate of British Companies.* Retreived April 15, 2006, from http://experian.de/download/2006/companyreport/pdf

Experience and ideas for developing foresight. (2004). *Experience and ideas for developing foresight in a regional innovation strategy context.* Retrieved September 21, 2008, from ftp://ftp.cordis.europa.eu/pub/foresight/docs/blueprint-for-ris.pdf

Falck, O., & Heblich, S. (2007). *Corporate social responsibility: Doing Well by Doing Good.* Business Horizons.

Featherstone, T (2008, September 4-10). Ideas Wanted. *Business Review Weekly,* 58.

Feldman, M. P. (2001). The entrepreneurial event revisited: Firm foundation in a regional context. *Industrial and Corporate Change,* 861–891. doi:10.1093/icc/10.4.861

Fenn, J. (2005). Emerging Trends, 2010-2015. *Gartner.* Retrieved November 11, 2006, from http://www.gartner.com/teleconferences/attributes/attr_135627_115.pdf

Fiet, J. (2001). The pedagogical side of entrepreneurship theory. *Journal of Business Venturing, 16*(2), 101–117. doi:10.1016/S0883-9026(99)00042-7

Filion, L. (1997). From Entrepreneurship to Entreprenology, HEC University of Montreal Business School. Retrieved January 10, 2006, from http://www.usasbe.org/knowledge/proceedings/1997/P207Filion.PDF

Fink, D. (2003). *Creating significant learning experiences.* San Francisco: Jossey-Bass.

Finkelstein, S., & Hambrick, D. (1996). *Strategic leadership: Top executives and their effects on organizations.* Minneapolis, St. Paul: West Publisher.

Fisher, I. (1906). *The nature of capital and income.* New York: Reprints of Economic Classics, Augustus M. Kelley Publisher. Reprinted in 1965

Fisher, R., & Ury, W. (1991). *Getting to yes: negotiating agreement without giving in.* New York: Penguin Books.

Fletcher, A., Guthrie, J., Steane, P., Roos, G., & Pike, S. (2003). Mapping stakeholder perceptions for a third sector organization. *Journal of Intellectual Capital, 4*(4), 505–527. doi:10.1108/14691930310504536

Floyd, S. W., & Lane, P. J. (2000). Strategizing throughout the organization: Managing role conflict in strategic renewal'. *Academy of Management Review, 25*, 154–177. doi:10.2307/259268

Fotion, N., Kashnikov, B., & Lekea, J. K. (2008). *Terrorism: the new world order.* New Delhi, India: Viva-Continuum.

Fowler, A. (2000). NGDOs as a moment in history: Beyond aid to social entrepreneurship or civic innovation? *Third World Quarterly, 21*(4), 637–654. doi:10.1080/713701063

Frances, N. (2008). *The end of charity: Time for social enterprise.* Crows, New South Wales: Allen and Unwin.

Frederick, W. C. (1960). The growing concern over business responsibility. *California Management Review, 2*, 54–61.

Freel, M. (2000). External linkages and product innovation in small manufacturing firms. *Entrepreneurship & Regional Development, 12*, 245–266. doi:10.1080/089856200413482

Freeman, C. (1987). *Technology Policy and Economic Performance: Lessons from Japan*. London: Pinter Publishers.

Freeman, C., & Louçã, F. (2001). *As Time Goes By. From the industrial Revolutions to the Information Revolution*. New York: Oxford University Press.

Freeman, C., & Perez, C. (1988). Structural Crisis of Adjustment: Business Cycles and Investment Behaviour. In Dosi, (Eds.), *Technical Change and Economic Theory*. London: Pinter Publishers.

Freeman, R. E. (1984). *Strategic Management: A Stakeholder Approach*. Boston: Pitman.

Freeman, R. E. (1994). The Politics of Stakeholder Theory: Some Future Directions. *Business Ethics Quarterly, 4*, 409–422. doi:10.2307/3857340

FT Technologies (n.d.). Retrieved from www.ft-tech.net.au

Galunic, C., & Rodan, S. (1998). Resource recombinations in the firm: Knowledge structures and the potential for Schumpeterian innovation. *Strategic Management Journal, 19*(12), 1193–1201. doi:10.1002/(SICI)1097-0266(1998120)19:12<1193::AID-SMJ5>3.0.CO;2-F

Garavan, T., Cinnéide, B., & Fleming, P. (1997). *Entrepreneurship and Business Start-Ups in Ireland*. Dublin, Ireland: Oak Press.

Gargiulo, M., & Benassi, M. (2000). Trapped in your own net? Network cohesion, structural holes, and the adaptation of social capital. *Organization Science, 11*(2), 183–196. doi:10.1287/orsc.11.2.183.12514

Garriga, E., & Melé, D. (2004). *Corporate social responsibility Theories: Mapping the* Territory. *Journal of Business Ethics, 53*(1-2), 51–71. doi:10.1023/B:BUSI.0000039399.90587.34

Gartner, W., & Vesper, K. (1998). Experiments in entrepreneurship education: Success and failures. *Journal of Business Venturing, 9*(2), 179–187.

Gatignon, H., & Xuereb, J.-M. (1997). Strategic Orientation of the firm and new product performance. *JMR, Journal of Marketing Research, 34*(1), 77–90. doi:10.2307/3152066

Gellene, D. (2008, September 10). Study finds left-wing brain, right-wing brain. *Los Angeles Times*.

George, G., & Zahra, S. A. (2002). *Being entrepreneurial and being market-driven: exploring the interaction effect of entrepreneurial and market orientation on firm performance*. Paper presented at the Babson College. Babson Park, MA.

Ghererdi, S., & Nicolini, D. (2001). The Sociological Foundation of Organizational learning. In Dierkes, M., Antal, A. B., Child, J., & Nonaka, I. (Eds.), *Organizational Learning and Knowledge*. Oxford, UK: Oxford University Press.

Gibb, A. (1996). Entrepreneurship and small business management: can we afford to neglect them in the twenty-first century business school? *British Journal of Management, 7*, 309–321. doi:10.1111/j.1467-8551.1996.tb00121.x

Gibb, A. (2002). In pursuit of a new enterprise and entrepreneurship paradigm for learning: creative destruction, new values, new ways of doing things and new combinations of knowledge. *International Journal of Management Reviews, 4*(4), 223–269.

Giffords, E. D., & Dina, R. P. (2004). Strategic planning in nonprofit organizations: Continuous quality performance improvement - A case study. *International Journal of Organization Theory and Behavior, 7*(1), 66–80.

Glass, R. L. (1997, June). Software runaways - some surprising findings. *SIGMIS Database, 28*(3), 16–19. doi:10.1145/272657.272687

Glisson, C., & Hemmelgarn, A. (1998). The effects of Organisational climate and interOrganisational coordination on the quality and outcomes of children's service systems. *Child Abuse & Neglect, 22*(5), 401–421. doi:10.1016/S0145-2134(98)00005-2

Glisson, C., & James, L. R. (2002). The cross-level effects of culture and climate in human service teams. *Journal of Organizational Behavior, 23*, 767–794. doi:10.1002/job.162

Goldense, B. L., & Power, J. R. (2005). Developmental Overload. *Mechanical Engineering (New York, N.Y.), 127*(3), 13A–13A.

Goleman, D. (1997). *Emotional intelligence*. New York: Bantam.

Goold, M. (1997). Institutional advantage: A way into strategic management in not-for-profit organizations. *Long Range Planning, 30*(2), 291–293. doi:10.1016/S0024-6301(96)00001-5

Gopalakrishnan, S., & Santoro, M. D. (2001). Do size and slack matter? Exploring the multi-dimensions of organizational innovation. In *Proceedings, Portland International Conference on Management of Engineering and Technology 2001.* Portland, OR.

Grasenick, K., & Low, J. (2004). Shaken, not stirred: Defining and connecting indicators for the measurement and valuation of intangibles. *Journal of Intellectual Capital, 5*(2), 268–281. doi:10.1108/14691930410533696

Gray, M., Healy, K., & Crofts, P. (2003). Social enterprise: Is it the business of social work? *Australian Social Work, 56*(2), 141–154. doi:10.1046/j.0312-407X.2003.00060.x

Griffin, A., & Hauser, J. R. (1996). Integrating R&D and Marketing: A Review and Analysis of the Literature. *Journal of Product Innovation Management, 13*(3), 191–215.

Grossman, G. M., & Helpman, E. (1991). *Innovation and growth in the global economy*. Cambridge, MA: MIT Press.

Guerrero, I. (2003). How do firms measure their intellectual capital? Defining an empirical model based on firm practices. *International Journal of Management and Decision Making, 4*(2/3), 178–193. doi:10.1504/IJMDM.2003.003503

Guimarães, R. (1998). *Política Industrial e Tecnológica e Sistemas de Inovação*. Oeiras, Portugal: Celta Editora.

Guinet, J. (1999). Libertar o Potencial de Inovação: o Papel do Governo. *Revista Economia & Prospectiva, 10*, 53–80.

Guthrie, J., Petty, R., & Ricceri, F. (2006). The voluntary reporting of intellectual capital: Comparing evidence from Hong Kong and Australia. *Journal of Intellectual Capital, 7*(2), 254–271. doi:10.1108/14691930610661890

Gyampoh-Vidogah, R., & Moreton, R. (2002). Implementing information management in construction: establishing problems, concepts and practice. *Construction Innovation, 3*, 157–173.

Hackman, R. J., & Oldham, G. R. (1975). Development of the Job Diagnostic Survey. *The Journal of Applied Psychology, 60*(2), 159–170. doi:10.1037/h0076546

Hafsi, T., & Thomas, H. (2005). The field of strategy: In search of a walking stick. *European Management Journal, 23*(5), 507–519. doi:10.1016/j.emj.2005.09.006

Halila, F. (2006). Networks as a means of supporting the adoption of organizational innovations in SMEs: The case of environmental management systems (EMSs) based on ISO 14001. *Corporate Social Responsibility and Environmental Management, 14*, 167–181. doi:10.1002/csr.127

Hambrick, D. C., Finkelstein, S., & Mooney, A. C. (2005). Executive job demands: New insights for explaining strategic decisions and leader behaviors. *Academy of Management Review, 30*(3), 472–491.

Hamori, M. (2003). The impact of reputation capital on the career paths of departing employees. *Journal of Intellectual Capital, 4*(3), 304–315. doi:10.1108/14691930310487770

Hampson, K. D., & Brandon, P. (2004). [*A Vision for Australia's Property and Construction Industry*. Brisbane, Australia: CRC for Construction Innovation, Brisbane.]. *Construction (Arlington)*, 2020.

Hanna, V., & Walsh, K. (2002). Small networks: a successful approach to Innovation. *R & D Management, 32*(3), 201–207. doi:10.1111/1467-9310.00253

Hannan, M. T., & Freeman, J. (1984). Structural inertia and organizational change. *American Sociological Review, 49*, 149–164. doi:10.2307/2095567

Hansen, K. (2006, July). - Augst). Project Visualization for Software. *IEEE Software, 23*(4), 84–92. doi:10.1109/MS.2006.111

Hargadon, A. B. (2002). Brokering Knowledge: Linking learning and innovation. *Organizational Behavior, 24*, 41–85. doi:10.1016/S0191-3085(02)24003-4

Harnett, D. L. (1982). *Statistical Methods* (3rd ed.). Reading, MA: Addison Wesley.

Harney, A. (2008). *The China Price*. New York: The Penguin Press.

Hartmann, G. C., Myers, M. B., & Rosenbloom, R. S. (2006). Planning your Firm's R&D Investment. *Research Technology Management, 49*(2), 25–36.

Hauknes, J. (1999). *Innovation Systems and Capabilities*. Paper presented at the Paper prepared within the framework of the "TSER/RISE, Program, for the European Commission (DGXII) STEP Gruppen.

Hedberg, B. (1981). How Organisations Learn and Unlearn. In Nystrom, P. C., & Starbuck, W. H. (eds.), Handbook of Organisational Design. London

Helpman, E. (1998). *General Purpose Technologies and Economic Growth*. Cambridge, MA: MIT Press.

Henderson, R. M. (1993). Underinvestment and incompetence as responses to radical innovation. *The Rand Journal of Economics, 24*, 248–270. doi:10.2307/2555761

Henderson, R. M., & Clark, K. B. (1990). Architectural Innovation. *Administrative Science Quarterly, 35*(March), 9–30. doi:10.2307/2393549

Henig, P. (2004). Thinking Out Loud: Dr. Harry M. Markowitz: When Harry Met Alfred. *CIO Insight*. Retrieved November 27, 2006, from http://www.cioinsight.com/article2/0,1397,1609468,00.asp

Henttonen, K. (2006, 15-17 March). *Innovation in Complex Networks - the State -of-the-Art and propositions for Further Research*. Paper presented at the The Innovation Pressure, International ProAct-Conference, Tampere, Finland.

Herzberg, F. (1968). One more time: how do you motivate employees? *Harvard Business Review, 46*(1), 53–62.

Hill, G., & Rothaermel, F. (2003). The performance of incumbent firms in the face of radical technological innovation. *Academy of Management Review, 28*(2), 257–274.

Hill, T. (1993). *Manufacturing strategy: The strategic management of the manufacturing function* (2nd ed.). London: Macmillan.

Hillman, A., & Keim, G. (2001). Shareholder value, stakeholder management, and social issues: what's the bottom line? *Strategic Management Journal, 22*(2), 125–139. doi:10.1002/1097-0266(200101)22:2<125::AID-SMJ150>3.0.CO;2-H

Hills, (1988). Variations in university entrepreneurship education: An empirical study of an evolving field. *Journal of Business Venturing, 3*(2), 109-122.

Hills, G., & Morris, M. (1998). Entrepreneurship education: a concept model and review. In Scott, M., Rosa, P., & Klandt, H. (Eds.), *Educating Entrepreneurs in Wealth Creation* (pp. 38–58). Aldershot: Ashgate.

Hills, S. B., & Sarin, S. (2003). From market driven to market driving: An alternate paradigm for marketing in high technology industries. *Journal of Marketing Theory and Practice*(summer), 13-24.

Hippel, E. v. (1988). *Sources of innovation*. New York: Oxford University Press.

Hirschman, A. (1959). Investment policies and 'dualism' in underdeveloped countries. *The American Economic Review, 47*, 550–570.

Hitt, M. A., Ireland, R. D., Camp, S. M., & Sexton, D. L. (2001). Strategic entrepreneurship: Entrepreneurial strategies for wealth creation. *Strategic Management Journal, 22*(6/7), 479–491. doi:10.1002/smj.196

Ho, P. (2005). Greening industries in newly industrializing countries: Asian-style leapfrogging? *Int. J. Environmental and Sustainable Development, 4*(3), 209–226. doi:10.1504/IJESD.2005.007738

Hodgson, G. M., & Knudsen, T. (2006). Balancing inertia, innovation, and imitation in complex environments. *Journal of Economic Issues, 40*(2), 287–295.

Hof, R. (1992, June 1). Inside Intel: It's moving at Double-Time to head off competitors. *Business Week*, 86-94.

Hof, R. (1995, February 20). Intel: Far beyond the Pentium. *Business Week*, 88-90.

Hofstede, G. (1987). *Culture and Organizations: Software of the Mind*. New York: McGraw-Hill.

Holditch, S. A. (2007). Tight gas reservoirs. In Warner Jr., H. R. & Lake, L. W. (Eds.), Petroleum engineering handbook vol. VI: Emerging and peripheral technologies (pp 297-351). Richardson, TX: Society of Petroleum Engineers.

Hopkins, J. (2003, February 18). Study: New company failure rate not so high, *USA Today.*

Hoskisson, R. E., Hitt, M. A., Wan, W. P., & Yiu, D. (1999). Theory and research in strategic management: Swings of a pendulum. *Journal of Management, 25*(3), 417–456. doi:10.1177/014920639902500307

Hu, M.-C., & Mathews, J. A. (2005). Innovative capacity in East Asia. *Research Policy, 34*(9), 1322–1349. doi:10.1016/j.respol.2005.04.009

Hudson, M. (1999). *Managing without profit: The art of managing third-sector organizations* (2nd ed.). London: Penguin.

Hult, G. T. M., Hurley, R. F., & Knight, G. A. (2004). Innovativeness: its antecedents and impact on business performance. *Industrial Marketing Management, 33*(5), 429–442. doi:10.1016/j.indmarman.2003.08.015

Humphrey, J., & Schmitz, H. (1995). *Principles for promoting clusters and networks of SMEs.* Retrieved September 17, 2008, from http://www.unido.org/fileadmin/media/documents/pdf/SME_Cluster/Humphrey.pdf

Humphreys, M., & Brown, A. D. (2008). An Analysis of Corporate social responsibility at Credit Line: A Narrative Approach. *Journal of Business Ethics, 80*, 403–418. doi:10.1007/s10551-007-9426-0

Hurst, D. K. (1986). 'Why Strategic Management is Bankrupt'. *Organizational Dynamics, Spring*, 5-27. Garvin, D. A., (1993). Building a Learning Organization. *Harvard Business Review*, (July-August): 78–91.

Husted, B. W., & Allen, D. B. (2007). Strategic corporate social responsibility and value creation among large firms lessons from the Spanish experience. *Long Range Planning, 40*(6), 594–610. doi:10.1016/j.lrp.2007.07.001

Husted, B., & Allen, D. (2006). Corporate social responsibility in the multinational enterprise: Strategic and institutional approaches. *Academy of International Business Studies, 12*, 838–849. doi:10.1057/palgrave.jibs.8400227

Huxham, C., & Vangen, S. (2005). *Managing to collaborate: The theory and practice of collaborative advantage.* London: Routledge.

IBM alphaWorks. (2003). IBM Community Tools. *IBM Corporation.* Retrieved November 21, 2006, from http://www.alphaworks.ibm.com/tech/ict

IBM. (2006). Extreme Blue. *IBM Corporation.* Retrieved November 21, 2006, from http://www.ibm.com/extremeblue/

IBM. (2006). Introducing IBM Lotus Sametime 7.5. *IBM Corporation.* Retrieved November 21, 2006, from ftp://ftp.software.ibm.com/software/lotus/lotusweb/product/sametime/Sametime_7.5_Detailed_View.pdf

Ichniowski, C., & Shaw, K. (1995). Old dogs and new tricks; determinants of the adoption of productivity-enhancing work practices, Brookings Papers: Microeconomics, pp. 1-55.

Ikezawa, N. (2001). Nanotechnology: encounters of atoms, bits and genomes. *NRI Papers* 37.

Indian manufacturing industry. (2005). *Indian manufacturing industry: Technology status and prospects.* Retrieved October 12, 2008, from http://www.unido.org/fileadmin/import/81586_IndManuf1Rep131005.pdf

Inkpen, A., & Tsang, E. (2005). Social capital, networks, and knowledge transfer. *Academy of Management Review, 30*(1), 146–165.

Ishikawa, A., Mako, C., & Warhurst, C. (2006). *Work and Employee Representation: Workers, Firms and Unions. Part 3.* Tokyo, Japan: Chuo University Press.

Islam, N., & Miyazaki, K. (2009). Nanotechnology Innovation System – Understanding Hidden Dynamics of Nanoscience Fusion Trajectories. *Technological Forecasting and Social Change, 76*(1), 128–140. doi:10.1016/j.techfore.2008.03.021

J. M., & Liker, J. K. (2006). The Toyota Product Development System: Integrating People, Process And Technology (1 ed.) Florence, KY:Productivity Press.

Jamali, D., & Keshishian, T. (2009). Uneasy alliances: Lessons learned from partnerships between businesses and NGOs in the context of CSR. *Journal of Business Ethics, 84*(2), 277–295. doi:10.1007/s10551-008-9708-1

Jamison, I. B. (2003). Turnover and retention among volunteers in human service agencies. *Review of Public Personnel Administration, 23*(2), 114–132. doi:10.1177/0734371X03023002003

Janssen, O. (2000). Job demands, perceptions of effort-reward fairness and innovative work behaviour. *Journal of Occupational and Organizational Psychology, 73*, 287–302. doi:10.1348/096317900167038

Janszen, F. (2000). *The Age of Innovation: making business creativity a competence, not a coincidence.* London: Prentice-Hall.

Japanese Foundation Beijing Office (2008). *Corporate Social Responsibility: Philanthropic Activities by Japanese Companies in South China* (in Japanese)

Jaumotte, F. (2006). Maintaining Switzerland's Top Innovation Capacity. *OECD ECO/WKP, 15*(487).

Javed, T., Maqsood, M. E., & Durrani, Q. S. (2004, May). A study to investigate the impact of requirements instability on software defects. *SIGSOFT Software. Engineering Notes, 29*(3), 1–7. doi:10.1145/986710.986727

Jespersen, K. R. (2008). User-driven product development: Creating a user-involving culture (1 ed.). Denmark: Forlaget Samfundslitteratur.

Johannesen, R. (1996). Ethics in human communication (pp. 67-68). Prospect Heights, Il: Waveland Press.

Johnson, J. (1995, July). Creating Chaos, *American Programmer.*

Jones, T. M. (1980). Corporate social responsibility revisited, redefined. *California Management Review*, 59–67.

Judge, T. A., Thoresen, C. J., Bono, J. E., & Patton, G. K. (2001). The job satisfaction-job performance relationship: A qualitative and quantitative review. *Psychological Bulletin, 127*(3), 376–407. doi:10.1037/0033-2909.127.3.376

Kahn, K. B. (2005). The PDMA handbook of new product development (2 ed.). Hoboken, NJ: John Wiley & Sons.

Kaldor, N. (1966). Causes of the slow rate of economic growth in the United Kingdom. In *Further Essays on Economic Theory.* New York: Holmes & Meyer.

Kaldor, N. (1970). The case for regional policies. In *Further Essays on Economic Theory.* New York: Holmes & Meyer.

Kaldor, N. (1972). Advanced technology in a strategy of development. In *Further Essays on Applied Economics.* New York: Holmes & Meyer.

Kanellos, M. (2004). IBM Heeds message to integrate IM, email, *News.com.* Retrieved November 21, 2006, from http://news.com.com/2102-1012_3-5165991.html?tag=st.util.print

Kanne-Urrabazo, C. (2006). Management's role in shaping Organisational culture. *Journal of Nursing Management, 14*(3), 188–194. doi:10.1111/j.1365-2934.2006.00590.x

Kanter, R. M. (1983). *The change masters.* New York: Simon & Schuster.

Kanter, R. M. (1999). From spare change to real change: The social sector as beta site for business innovation. *Harvard Business Review, 77*(3), 122–132.

Kapp, K. W. (1961). *Towards a science of man in society: A positive approach to the integration of social knowledge.* The Hague, The Netherlands: Martinus Nijhoff.

Kaulio, M. A. (1998). Customer, consumer and user involvement in product development: A framework and a review of selected methods. *Total Quality Management, 9*(1), 141–149. doi:10.1080/0954412989333

Kelley, D. (2005). *Corporate entrepreneurship and venturing.* New York: Springer.

Kenny, M., & Burgh, U. (1999). Technology, entrepreneurship and path dependence: Industrial clustering in

Silicon Valley and Route 128. *Industrial and Corporate Change, 8*(3), 67–103. doi:10.1093/icc/8.1.67

Kerlinger, F. N., & Lee, H. B. (2000). *Foundations of behavioral research* (4th ed.). Florence, KY: Wadsworth.

Kim, S. E., & Lee, J. W. (2007). Is mission attachment an effective management tool for employee retention? An empirical analysis of a nonprofit human services agency. *Review of Public Personnel Administration, 27*(3), 227–248. doi:10.1177/0734371X06295791

King, N., & Anderson, N. (2002). *Managing innovation and change: A critical guide for organizations.* Tampa, FL: Thomson.

Kirsner, S. (2000, April). Faster Company, *Fast Company, 43*, 162. Retrieved November 21, 2006, from http://www.fastcompany.com/online/34/ibm.html

Klein, D. A. (Ed.). (1998). *The strategic management of intellectual capital.* Boston: Butterworth-Heinemann.

Kleinknecht, A., Oostendorp, R. M., Pradhan, M. P., & Naastepad, C. W. M. (2006). Flexible labour, firm performance and the Dutch job creation miracle. *International Review of Applied Economics, 20*(2), 171–187. doi:10.1080/02692170600581102

Kleinschmidt, E. J., & Cooper, R. G. (1991). The Impact of Product Innovativeness on Performance. *Journal of Product Innovation Management, 8*, 240–251. doi:10.1016/0737-6782(91)90046-2

Knight, D. J. (1999). Performance measures for increasing intellectual capital. *Planning Review, 27*(2), 22–27.

Knight, K. E. (1967). A descriptive model of the intra-firm innovation process. *The Journal of Business, 40*(4), 478–496. doi:10.1086/295013

Knowles, A., & Wareing, J. (2007). *Economic and social geography.* New Delhi, India: Rupa & Co.

Koehler, C., & Weissbarth, R. (2004, 070704). The Art of Underengineering. *Strategy+Business Magazine.*

Kogut, B., & Singh, H. (1988). The Effect of National Culture on the Choice of the Entry Mode. *Journal of International Business Studies, 19*, 411–432. doi:10.1057/palgrave.jibs.8490394

Kogut, B., & Zander, U. (1993). Knowledge of the firm and the evolutionary theory of the multinational corporation. *Journal of International Business Studies, 24*(4), 625–645. doi:10.1057/palgrave.jibs.8490248

Koivu, T., & Mantyla, K. (2000). Innovation management in the Finnish construction industry. In *Proceedings of the International Conference: Technology Watch and Innovation in the Construction Industry,* (pp. 147-152), Brussels, Belgium.

Kola-Nystrom, S. M. (2005). In search of corporate renewal: how to benefit from corporate venturing? PhD dissertation, Lappeenrannan teknillinen yliopisto, Acta Universitatis.

Kong, E. (2003). *Human capital as a key component of intellectual capital in nonprofit organizations.* Paper presented at the Conference on Challenging the Frontiers in Global Business and Technology (GBATA): Implementation of Changes in Values, Strategy and Policy, Governance and Knowledge Management (GKM), Budapest, Hungary.

Kong, E. (2003). Using intellectual capital as a strategic tool for nonprofit organizations. *International Journal of Knowledge. Culture and Change Management, 3*(1), 467–474.

Kong, E. (2008). The development of strategic management in the nonprofit context: Intellectual capital in social service nonprofit organizations. *International Journal of Management Reviews, 10*(3), 281–299. doi:10.1111/j.1468-2370.2007.00224.x

Kong, E., & Thomson, S. B. (2006). Intellectual capital and strategic human resource management in social service nonprofit organizations in Australia. *International Journal of Human Resources Development and Management, 6*(2-4), 213–231.

Kostova, T., & Roth, K. (2002). Adoption of an organizational practice by subsidiaries of multinational corporations: Institutions and relational effects. *Academy of Management Journal, 45*(1), 215–233. doi:10.2307/3069293

Kostova, T., & Zaheer, S. (1999). Organizational legitimacy under conditions of complexity: The case of the multinational enterprise. *Academy of Management Review*, *24*(1), 64–81. doi:10.2307/259037

Kotler, P. (1996). *Marketing management: Analysis, planning, implementation and control* (9th ed.). Englewood Cliffs, NJ: Prentice Hall.

Kourula, A., & Halme, M. (2008). Types of corporate social responsibility and engagement with NGOs: an exploration of business and societal outcomes. *Corporate Governance*, *8*(2), 557–570. doi:10.1108/14720700810899275

Kristoffersen, L., & Singh, S. (2004). Successful application of a customer relationship management program in a nonprofit organization. *Journal of Marketing Theory and Practice*, *12*(2), 28–42.

Kyro, P. (2000). *Is there a pedagogical basis for entrepreneurship education?* Jyväskylä, Finland: Department of Economics, Jyväskylä University.

Lam, M. L. L. (2000). *Working with Chinese expatriates in business negotiations: Portraits, issues, and applications*. Westport, UK: Quorum Books.

Lam, M. L. L. (2003). Chinese executives' perceptions of United States-Chinese negotiating styles and relationships. In *Proceedings of the 2003 Marketing Management Association Conference*. Chicago.

Lam, M. L. L. (2004). Hong Kong Chinese executives' perceptions of United States-Chinese negotiating styles and relationships. In *Proceedings of the 38th Academy of Marketing Conference*. University of Gloucestershire, Cheltenham, Gloucestershire, U.K.

Lam, M. L. L. (2005). Trust building: Some of the American and Chinese business negotiators' cross-cultural challenges. In *Proceedings of the Academy of International Business Northeast Annual Conference*. Cleveland, OH.

Lam, M. L. L. (2007). A study of the transfer of corporate social responsibility from well-established foreign multinational enterprises to Chinese subsidiaries. In Hooker, J., Hulpke, J., & Madsen, P. (Eds.), *Controversies in international corporate responsibility. International Corporate Responsibility Series* (*Vol. 3*, pp. 343–363). Pittsburgh, PA: Carneige Mellon University.

Lam, M. L. L. (2008). *Proceedings of Academy of Innovation and Entrepreneurship 2008, Tsinghua University*. Beijing, China: Being Innovative by Doing Good.

Lam, M. L. L. (2009) Non-government organizations as the salt and light in the Corporate Social Responsibility movement in China. In *Proceedings of the 2008 Christian Business Faculty Association Annual Conference*. Indianapolis, IN.

Lam, M. L. L. (2009) Sustainable development and corporate social responsibility of multinational enterprises in China. In Ivanaj and McIntyre (Eds.), Multinational Enterprises and the Challenge of Sustainable Development. Cheltenham, UK and Northampton, MA: Edward Elgar.

Lam, M. L. L. (2009). Beyond Credibility of Doing Business in China: Strategies for Improving Corporate Citizenship of Foreign Multinational Enterprises in China. *Journal of Business Ethics*, *86*(1).

Laursen, K., & Foss, N. J. (2003). New Human Resource Management Practices, Complementarities, and the Impact on Innovative performance. *Cambridge Journal of Economics*, *27*(2), 243–263. doi:10.1093/cje/27.2.243

Lee, M.-D. P. (2008). A review of the theories of corporate social responsibility: Its evolutionary path and the road ahead. *International Journal of Management Reviews*, *10*(1), 53–73. doi:10.1111/j.1468-2370.2007.00226.x

Leifer, R., McDermott, C. M., O'Connor, G. C., Peters, L. S., Rice, M. P., & Veryzer, R. W. (2000). *Radical Innovation: How Mature Companies Can Outsmart Upstarts*. Boston: Harvard Business School Press.

Leifer, R., Rice, M., & Veryzer, R. (2000). *Radical innovation: how mature companies can outsmart up-starts*. Boston: Harvard Business School Press.

Leiponen, A. (2008). Control of intellectual assets in client relationships: Implications for innovation. *Strategic Management Journal*, *29*(13), 1371–1394. doi:10.1002/smj.715

Leonard-Barton, D. (1995). *Wellsprings of knowledge: Build and sustaining the sources of innovation.* Boston: Harvard Business School Press.

Letts, C. W., Ryan, W. P., & Grossman, A. (1999). *High performance nonprofit organizations - Managing upstream for greater impact.* New York: John Wiley and Sons, Inc.

Levinthal, D. A., & March, J. G. (1993). The Myopia of Learning. *Strategic Management Journal*, *14*, 95–112. doi:10.1002/smj.4250141009

Lewis, G. (1994). *An illustrative history of the Riverina rice industry.* Leeton, New South Whales: Ricegrowers' Co-operative Limited.

Lewrick, M. (2007). *Changes in Innovation Styles: Comprehensive Study of the changes in innovation styles to identify the causes and effects of different influencing factors and capabilities to create a general innovation pattern.* Edinburgh, Scotland: Napier University Business School.

Lewrick, M. (2007). *Learning from the successful companies in a regional entrepreneurial and innovation system.* Presented at the 2nd International Seminar on Regional Innovation Policies, Oct 2007, pp 26-46

Lewrick, M. (2007). The Innovators Social Network: A cross-sector exploration on the influence of social networks and social capital on innovation and success. *Journal of Technology Management Innovations*, *2*(3), 38–48.

Lewrick, M. (2008). *The Influence of Customers and Competitors on the Market Orientation and Innovators on Start-up and Mature Companies* (Working Paper, RP033/2008), Edinburgh, Scotland: Napier University

Li, H., & Atuahene-Gima, K. (2001). Product innovation strategy and the performance of new technology ventures in China. *Academy of Management Journal*, *44*(6), 1123–1134. doi:10.2307/3069392

Lichtenstein, D. R., Drumwright, M. E., & Braig, B. M. (2004). The effect of corporate social responsibility on customer donations to corporate-supported nonprof-

its. *Journal of Marketing*, *68*(4), 16–32. doi:10.1509/jmkg.68.4.16.42726

Lieberman, M. B., & Asaba, S. (2006). Why do firms imitate each other? *Academy of Management Review*, *31*(2), 366–385.

Lieberman, M. B., & Montgomery, D. B. (1988). First-mover advantages. *Strategic Management Journal*, *9*(Summer), 41–58. doi:10.1002/smj.4250090706

Lieberman, M. B., & Montgomery, D. B. (1998). First-mover (dis)advantages: retrospective and link with the resource-based view. *Strategic Management Journal*, *19*(12), 1111–1125. doi:10.1002/(SICI)1097-0266(1998120)19:12<1111::AID-SMJ21>3.0.CO;2-W

Liebschutz, S. F. (1992). Coping by nonprofit organizations during the Reagan years. *Nonprofit Management & Leadership*, *2*(4), 363–380. doi:10.1002/nml.4130020405

Ling, F. Y. Y. (2003). Managing the implementation of construction innovations. *Construction Management and Economics*, *21*(6), 635–649. doi:10.1080/0144619032000123725

Locke, E. A. (1976). The nature and causes of job satisfaction. In Dunnette, M. D. (Ed.), *Handbook of Industrial and Organisational Psychology* (pp. 1297–1349). Chicago: Rand McNally.

Logsdon, J., & Wood, D. (2005). Global business citizenship and voluntary codes of ethical conduct. *Journal of Business Ethics*, *59*, 55–67. doi:10.1007/s10551-005-3411-2

Lomax, A. (2005). Yahoo!'s Delicious Deal, *The Motley Fool*. Retrieved on April 10, 2009, from http://www.fool.com/investing/general/2005/12/12/yahoos-delicious-deal.aspx

Love, P., Irani, Z., & Edwards, D. (2004). Industry-centric benchmarking of information technology benefits, costs and risks for small-to-medium sized enterprises in construction. *Automation in Construction*, *13*(4), 507–524. doi:10.1016/j.autcon.2004.02.002

Lowe, J., & Miller, P. (2001). Business clustering: Panacea or placebo for regional Australia. In Rodgers, M.F.

& Collins, Y.M.J. (eds.), 2001 The Future of Australia's Country Towns. Melbourne, Australia: La Trobe University, Centre for Sustainable Regional Communities.

Luecke, R., & Katz, R. (2003). *Managing Creativity and Innovation*. Boston: Harvard Business School Press.

Luke, B., & Verreynne, M.-L. (2006). Social enterprise in the public sector. MetService: Thinking beyond the weather. *International Journal of Social Economics, 33*(5/6), 432–445. doi:10.1108/03068290610660698

Lumpkin, G. T., & Dess, G. G. (1996). Classifying the entrepreneurial orientation construct and liking it to performance. *Academy of Management Review, 21*(1), 135–172. doi:10.2307/258632

Lund, D. B. (2003). Organisational culture and job satisfaction. *Journal of Business and Industrial Marketing, 18*(3), 219–236. doi:10.1108/0885862031047313

Lundvall, B.-Å. (1992). *National Systems of Innovation: Towards a Theory of Innovation and Interactive Learning*. London: Pinter Publishers.

Lundvall, B.-Å. (1998). Why Study National Systems and National Styles of Innovation. *Technology Analysis and Strategic Management, 10*(4), 407–421. doi:10.1080/09537329808524324

Lundvall, B.-Å. (1999). National Business Systems and National Systems of Innovation. *International Studies of Management & Organization, 29*(2), 60–77.

Lundvall, B.-Å., Patarapong, I., & Vang, J. (2006). *Asia's Innovation systems in transition*. Cheltenham, UK: Edward Elgar.

Lynn, G. S., Morone, J. G., & Paulson, A. S. (1996). Marketing and Discontinuous Innovation: The Probe and Learn Process. *California Management Review, 38*(3), 8–37.

Lyon, D. (2004). How can you help organizations change to meet the corporate responsibility agenda? *Corporate Social Responsibility and Environmental Management, 11*, 133–139. doi:10.1002/csr.60

Lyons, M. (1999). Service industries: Special article - Australia's nonprofit sector, Year Book Australia: 536-551. Canberra: Australian Bureau of Statistics (ABS).

Lyons, M. (2001). *Third sector: The contribution of nonprofit and co-operative enterprises in Australia*. St. Leonards, New South Wales: Allen and Unwin.

Lyons, M., & Fabiansson, C. (1998). Is volunteering declining in Australia? *Australian Journal on Volunteering, 3*(2), 15–21.

Lyons, W. (2003). Glasgow's failure rate hits 60%, *The Scotmans*. Retrieved June, 2003, from http://thescotsman.scotsman.com/business.cfm?id=516142003

Macher, J., & Richman, B. (2004). Organisational Responses to Discontinuous Innovation: A case study approach. *International Journal of Innovation Management, 8*(1), 87–114. doi:10.1142/S1363919604000939

MacMillan, I., McCaffery, M. L., & Van Wijk, G. (1985). Competitors' responses to easily imitated new products– exploring commercial banking product introductions. *Strategic Management Journal, 6*(1), 75–86. doi:10.1002/smj.4250060106

MacPherson, A. D. (1998). Academic-industry linkages and small firm innovation: evidence from the scientific instrumentations sector. *Entrepreneurship & Regional Development, 10*, 261–275. doi:10.1080/08985629800000015

Maddala, G. S. (1983). *Limited-Dependent and Qualitative Variables in Econometrics*. Cambridge, UK: Cambridge University Press.

Maguire, S., Koh, S. C. L., & Huang, C. (2007). identifying the range of customers listening tools: a logical pre-cursor to CRM? *Industrial Management & Data Systems, 107*(4), 567–586. doi:10.1108/02635570710740706

Mahler, J. (1997). Influences of Organizational Culture on Learning in Public Agencies. *Journal of Public Administration: Research and Theory, 7*(4), 519–541.

Mahmood, I. P., & Rufin, C. (2005). Government's dilemma: the role of government in imitation and innovation. *Academy of Management Review, 30*(2), 338–360.

Mahmood, M. A., Hall, L., & Swanberg, D. L. (2001). Factors Affecting Information Technology Usage: Meta-analysis of Empirical Literature. *Journal of Organizational Computing and Electronic Commerce, 11*(2), 107–130. doi:10.1207/S15327744JOCE1102_02

Majdalani, Z., Ajam, M., & Mezher, T. (2006). Sustainability in the construction industry: a Lebanese case study. *Construction Innovation, 6*(1), 33–46.

Malerba, F. (2002). Sectoral systems of innovation and production. *Research Policy, 31*, 247–264. doi:10.1016/S0048-7333(01)00139-1

Malerba, F., Nelson, R., Orsenigo, L., & Winter, S. (1999). History-friendly models of industry evolution: The computer industry. *Industrial and Corporate Change, 8*(1), 3–40. doi:10.1093/icc/8.1.3

Malveau, R., & Mowbray, T. (2001). *Doing Software Wrong. Software Architect Bootcamp.* Upper Saddle River, NJ: Prentice Hall.

Malveau, R., & Mowbray, T. (2001). *Software Process Background. Software Architect Bootcamp.* Upper Saddle River, NJ: Prentice Hall.

Manfredi, F. (2005). Social responsibility in the concept of the social enterprise as a cognitive system. *International Journal of Public Administration, 28*(9/10), 835–848. doi:10.1081/PAD-200067371

Mangematin, V., et al. (2006). *Meeting promises: Public policies and firm strategies in nanotechnologies.* Project proposal for Nanodistrict 2 EU project, PRIME 2006, report. Retrieved from www.nanodistrict.com

Manley, K., Allan, D., Blayse, A., Coillet, M., Hardie, M., & Hough, R. (2005). *BRITE Innovation Survey.* Brisbane, Australia: CRC for Construction Innovation.

Manring, S. L. (2003). How do you create lasting organizational change? You must first slay Grendel's mother. In Woodman, R. W., & Pasmore, W. A. (Eds.), Research in Organizational Change and Development, 14, 195-224. Greenwich, UK: JAI Press.

Mansfield, E. (1968). *Industrial Research and Technological Innovation; An Econometric Analysis.* London: Longmans, Green & Co.

Mansfield, E., Schwartz, M., & Wagner, S. (1981). Imitation costs and patents: an empirical study. *The Economic Journal, 91*(364), 907–918. doi:10.2307/2232499

Marceau, J., Manly, K., & Sicklen, D. (1997). *The high road and the low road? Alternatives for Australia's future.* Sydney, Australia: Australian Business Foundation.

Markham, S. K., & Griffin, A. (1998). The Breakfast of Champions: Associations between Champions and Product Development Environments, Practices and Performance. *Journal of Product Innovation Management, 15*, 436–454. doi:10.1016/S0737-6782(98)00010-1

Marr, B., & Roos, G. (2005). A strategy perspective on intellectual capital. In Marr, B. (Ed.), *Perspectives on intellectual capital: Multi-disciplinary insights into management, measurement, and reporting.* Amsterdam: Elsevier Butterworth-Heinemann.

Martin de Holan, P., & Phillips, N. (2004). Organizational forgetting as strategy. *Strategic Organization, 2*(4), 423–433. doi:10.1177/1476127004047620

Martin, B. (2000). Knowledge-based organizations: Emerging trends in local government in Australia. *Journal of Knowledge Management Practice, 2*.

Martin, G., Beaumont, P., Doig, R., & Pate, J. (2005). Branding: A new performance discourse for HR? *European Management Journal, 23*(1), 76–88. doi:10.1016/j.emj.2004.12.011

Martin, J. (2006). Why Sametime 7.5 Was Created, *solutions-daily.com.* Retrieved November 21, 2006, from http://lotus.solutions-daily.com/mediafiles/ibm_lagarde.m4a

Martin, R. (1999). The New 'geographical turn' in economics: Some critical reflections. *Cambridge Journal of Economics, 23*, 65–91. doi:10.1093/cje/23.1.65

Martins, E. C., & Terblanche, F. (2003). Building organisational culture that stimulates creativity and innovation. *European Journal of Innovation Management, 6*(1), 64–74. doi:10.1108/14601060310456337

Mason, C., Kirkbride, J., & Bryde, D. (2007). From stakeholders to institutions: The changing face of social enterprise governance theory. *Management Decision*, *45*(2), 284–301. doi:10.1108/00251740710727296

Massa, S., & Testa, S. (2004). Innovation or imitation? Benchmarking: a knowledge-management process to innovate services. *Benchmarking*, *11*(6), 610–620. doi:10.1108/14635770410566519

Massingham, P. (2008). Measuring the impact of knowledge loss: More than ripples on a pond? *Management Learning*, *39*(5), 541–560. doi:10.1177/1350507608096040

Mathews, J. A., & Hu, M.-C. (2007). Enhancing the Role of Universities in Building National Innovative Capacity in Asia: The Case of Taiwan. *World Development*, *35*(6), 1005–1020. doi:10.1016/j.worlddev.2006.05.012

Matten, D., & Moon, J. (2008). "Implicit" and "Explicit" CSR: A conceptual framework for a comparative understanding of corporate social responsibility. *Academy of Management Review*, *33*(2), 404–424.

Matthews, J. (2002). Clusters of innovative firms: Absorptive capacity in larger networks. In *Proceedings of the Sixteenth ANZAM Conference*. Melbourne, Australia: La Trobe University.

Matthyssens, P., Pauwels, P., & Vandenbempt, K. (2005). Strategic flexibility, ridigity and barriers to the development of absorptive capacity in business markets: Themes and research perspectives. *Industrial Marketing Management*, *34*, 547–554. doi:10.1016/j.indmarman.2005.03.004

Maula, M. (1999). *Multinational Companies As Learning and Evolving Systems: A Multiple-case Study of Knowledge-Intensive Service Companies. An application of Autopoiesis Theory*. Helsinki, Finland: Helsinki School of Economics and Business Administration.

McAdam, D., & Scott, W. R. (2005). Organizations and movements. In, Gerald F. Davis, Doug McAdam, W. Richard Scott, and Mayer N. Zald (Eds.), Social movements and organization theory (pp xviii). New York: Cambridge University Press.

McAdam, D., McCarthy, J. D., & Zald, M. N. (1996). Introduction: Opportunities, mobilizing structures, and framing process—toward a synthetic, comparative perspective on social movements. In McAdam, D., McCarthy, J. D., & Zald, M. (Eds.), *Comparative Perspectives on Social Movements* (pp. 1–22). New York: Cambridge University Press.

McAdam, R. (2000). Knowledge management as a catalyst for innovation within organizations: A qualitative study. *Journal of Knowledge and Process Management*, *7*(4), 233–241. doi:10.1002/1099-1441(200010/12)7:4<233::AID-KPM94>3.0.CO;2-F

McCann, J. E. III, & Buckner, M. (2004). Strategically integrating knowledge management initiatives. *Journal of Knowledge Management*, *8*(1), 47–63. doi:10.1108/13673270410523907

McCutcheon, D., & Meredith, J. (1993). Conducting case study research. *Journal of Operations Management*, *11*, 239–256. doi:10.1016/0272-6963(93)90002-7

McEvily, S. K., Das, S., & McCabe, K. (2000). Avoiding competence substitution through knowledge sharing. *Academy of Management Review*, *25*(2), 294–311. doi:10.2307/259015

McGrath, R. G. (2001). Exploratory learning, innovative capacity and managerial oversight. *Academy of Management Journal*, *44*, 118–131. doi:10.2307/3069340

McGrath, R. G., Ferrier, W. J., & Mendelow, A. L. (2004). Real options as engines of choice and heterogeneity. *Academy of Management Review*, *29*, 86–101.

McGregor, D. (1957). An uneasy look at performance appraisal. *Harvard Business Review*, *35*(May/June), 89–94.

McKinsey & Company. (1993). Emerging exporters: Report for the Australian Manufacturing Council. Sydney, Australia.

McMullan, W., & Long, W. (1987). Entrepreneurship education in the nineties. *Journal of Business Venturing*, *2*(3), 261–275. doi:10.1016/0883-9026(87)90013-9

McNamara, C. (n.d.). *Basic Context for Organizational Change*. Free Management Library. Retrieved Janurary 14, 2007, from http://www.managementhelp.org/mgmnt/orgchnge.htm

McWilliam, G. (2000). Building stronger brands thorugh online communities. *Sloan Management Review*, (Spring): 43–54.

McWilliams, A., & Siegel, D. (2001). Corporate social responsibility: A theory of the firm perspective. *Academy of Management Review*, *26*(1), 117–127. doi:10.2307/259398

Metcalfe, J. S. (1997). Technology systems and technology policy in an evolutionary framework. In Archibuig, D., & Michie, J. (Eds.), *Technology, Globalization and Economic Performance*. Cambridge, UK: Cambridge University Press.

Meyer, J. P., & Allen, N. J. (1991). A three-component conceptualization of Organisational commitment. *Human Resource Management Review*, *1*, 61–89. doi:10.1016/1053-4822(91)90011-Z

Meyer, M., & Persson, O. (1998). Nanotechnology – interdisciplinarity, patterns of collaboration and differences in application. *Scientometrics*, *42*(2), 195–205. doi:10.1007/BF02458355

Michie, J., & Sheehan, M. (2003). Labour market deregulation, 'flexibility' and innovation. *Cambridge Journal of Economics*, *27*, 123–148. doi:10.1093/cje/27.1.123

Miles, I. (1988). *Home Informatics. Information technology and the transformation of everyday life*. London: Pinter.

Miles, R. E., Miles, G., & Snow, C. C. (2005). *Collaborative Entrepreneurship: How Communities of Networked Firms Use Continuous Innovation to Create Economic WEalth*. Stanford, CA: Stanford University Press.

Millen, D. R., Feinberg, J., & Kerr, B. (2006). Dogear: Social bookmarking in the enterprise. In *Proceedings of the SIGCHI Conference on Human Factors in Computing Systems* (Montréal, Canada, April 22 - 27, 2006). R. Grinter, T. Rodden, P. Aoki, E. Cutrell, R. Jeffries, and G. Olson, Eds. CHI '06. New York: ACM.

Miller, C. J. M., Packham, G. A., Pickernell, D. G., & McGovern, M. (2004). Building for the future: the potential importance of the construction industry in Welsh economic development policy. *Construction Management*

and Economics, *22*(5), 533–540. doi:10.1080/014461903 10001649128

Miller, D. (1983). The correlates of entrepreneurship in three types of firms. *Management Science*, *29*(7), 770–791. doi:10.1287/mnsc.29.7.770

Miller, D. (1990). *The icarus paradox: How exceptional companies bring about their own downfall*. New York: Harper-Collins.

Miller, D., & Friesen, P. H. (1978). Archetypes of Strategy formulation. *Management Science*, *24*(9), 921–933. doi:10.1287/mnsc.24.9.921

Mintzberg, H. (1973). Strategy-making in three modes. *California Management Review*, *16*(2), 44–53.

Mirvis, P., & Googins, B. (2006). Stage of corporate citizenship. *California Management Review*, *48*(2), 104–126.

Mizik, N., & Jacobson, R. (2003). Trading off between value creation and value appropriation: the financial implications of shifts in strategic emphasis. *Journal of Marketing*, *67*(January), 63–76. doi:10.1509/jmkg.67.1.63.18595

Moenaert, R. K., & Souder, W. E. (1996). Context and Antecedents of information utility at the R&D/Marketing interface. *Management Science*, *42*(11), 1592–1610. doi:10.1287/mnsc.42.11.1592

Moncrief, W., & Cravens, D. (1999). Technology and the changing marketing world. *Marketing Intelligence & Planning*, *17*(7), 329–332. doi:10.1108/02634509910301142

Moorman, C., & Slotegraaf, R. J. (1999). The contingency value of complementary capabilities in product development. *JMR, Journal of Marketing Research*, *36*(May), 239–257. doi:10.2307/3152096

Morgan, R. M., & Hunt, S. D. (1994). The commitment-trust theory of relationship marketing. *Journal of Marketing*, *58*(July), 20–38. doi:10.2307/1252308

Moriarty, R. T., & Kosnik, T. J. (1989). High-tech marketing: concepts, continuity, and change. *Sloan Management Review*, *7*, 7–17.

Morimoto, R., Ash, J., & Hope, C. (2005). Corporate social responsibility Audit: From Theory to Practice.

Journal of Business Ethics, 63, 315–325. doi:10.1007/s10551-005-0274-5

Morone, J. G. (1993). *Winning in high-tech markets: the role of general management*. Boston: Harvard Business School Press.

Morris, M., Lewis, P., & Sexton, D. (1994). Reconceptualizing Entrepreneurship: An Input-Output Perspective. S.A.M. *Advanced Management Journal, 59*(1), 21–31.

Mothe, J. D., & Paquet, G. (2000). *National Innovation Systems and Instituted Processes*. London: Pinter Publishers.

Mouritsen, J. (1998). Driving growth: Economic value added versus intellectual capital. *Management Accounting Research, 9*(4), 461–482. doi:10.1006/mare.1998.0090

Mouritsen, J., & Koleva, G. (2004). The actorhood of organizational capital. *International Journal of Learning and Intellectual Capital, 1*(2), 177–189. doi:10.1504/IJLIC.2004.005070

Mouritsen, J., & Larsen, H. T. (2005). The 2nd wave of knowledge management: The management control of knowledge resources through intellectual capital information. *Management Accounting Research, 16*(3), 371–394. doi:10.1016/j.mar.2005.06.006

Mouritsen, J., Larsen, H. T., & Bukh, P. N. (2005). Dealing with the knowledge economy: Intellectual capital versus balanced scorecard. *Journal of Intellectual Capital, 6*(1), 8–27. doi:10.1108/14691930510574636

Mulhare, E. M. (1999). Mindful of the future: Strategic planning ideology and the culture of nonprofit management. *Human Organization, 58*(3), 323–330.

Mulroy, E. A. (2003). Community as a factor in implementing inter-organizational partnerships: Issues, constraints and adaptations. *Nonprofit Management & Leadership, 14*(1), 47–66. doi:10.1002/nml.20

Mumford, M. D., & Gustafson, S. B. (1988). Creativity syndrome: Integration, application, and innovation. *Psychological Bulletin, 103*, 27–43. doi:10.1037/0033-2909.103.1.27

Mumford, M. D., & Licuanan, B. (2004). Leading for innovation: conclusions, issues and directions. *The Leadership Quarterly, 15*(1), 163–171. doi:10.1016/j.leaqua.2003.12.010

Murdoch, H., & Gould, D. (2004). *Corporate social responsibility in China: Mapping the environment. A study commission by the Global Alliance for Communities and Workers*. Baltimore: GA Publication Series.

Myrdal, G. (1944). *An American dilemma: The Negro problem and modern democracy*. New York: Pantheon.

Myrdal, G. (1957). *Economic theory and underdeveloped regions*. London: Duckworth.

Myrdal, G. (1968). *Asian drama: An inquiry into the poverty of nations*. New York: Pantheon.

Nambisan, S. (2002). Designing virtual customer environments for new product development: Toward a theory. *Academy of Management Review, 28*(3), 392–413. doi:10.2307/4134386

Nanus, B., & Dobbs, S. M. (1999). *Leaders who make a difference: Essential strategies for meeting the nonprofit challenge*. San Francisco: Jossey-Bass Publishers.

Narver, J. C., & Slater, S. F. (1990). The effect of a market orientation on business profitability. *Journal of Marketing, 54*(4), 20–42. doi:10.2307/1251757

National innovation systems. (1997). *National innovation systems*. Retrieved August 14, 2008, from www.oecd.org/dataoecd/35/56/2101733.pdf

Neely, A., Gregory, M., & Platts, K. (2005). Performance measurement system design: A literature review and research agenda. *International Journal of Operations & Production Management, 25*(12), 1228–1263. doi:10.1108/01443570510633639

Neistat, C., & Neistat, V. (2004). *Info about iPod's Dirty Secret*. Retrieved November 21, 2006, from http://www.ipodsdirtysecret.com/message.html

Nelson, K., & McCann, J. E. (2008). Developing intellectual capital and innovativeness through knowledge management. *International Journal of Learning and Intellectual Capital*, *5*(2), 106–122. doi:10.1504/IJLIC.2008.020147

Nelson, R. (1988). Institutions Supporting Technical Change in the United States. In Dosi, G. E. A. (Ed.), *Technical Change and Economic Theory*. London: Pinter Publishers.

Nelson, R. (1993). *National Systems of Innovation: a Comparative Study*. Oxford, UK: Oxford University Press.

Nelson, R. (2000). National Systems of Innovation. In Acs, Z. J. E. (Ed.), *Regional Innovation, Knowledge and Global Change* (pp. 11–26). London, New York: Pinter Publisher.

Nelson, R., & Winter, S. (1982). *An Evolutionary Theory of Economic Change*. Cambridge, MA: Harvard University Press.

Nerkar, A., & Shane, S. (2007). Determinants of invention commercialization: an empirical examination of academically sourced inventions. *Strategic Management Journal*, *28*(11), 1155–1166. doi:10.1002/smj.643

Nguyen, T. T. U. (2007). *Impact of public support on firms' innovation performance Evidence from Luxemburg's firms*. International Network for Studies in Technology, Environment, Alternatives, Development CEPS/INSTEAD – Luxembourg.

Niefert, M., Metzger, G., Heger, D., & Licht, G. (2006). Hightech Gründungen in Deutschland: Trends und Entwicklungsperspektiven, Endbericht ZEW GmbH, Mannheim, Juni 2006 OECD and Eurostat (2005). Oslo Manual: The Measurement of Scientific and Technological Activities. Guidelines for Collecting and Interpreting Innovation Data, 3rd edition, Paris: OECD and Eurostat publication.

Nieman, G. (2003). Growth Strategies and Options. In Nieman, G., Hough, J., & Niewenhuizen, C. (Eds.), *Entrepreneurship: A South African Perspective*. Pretoria, South Africa: Van Schaik.

Nonaka, I., & Takeuchi, H. (1995). *The knowledge-creating company: How Japanese companies create the dynamics of innovation*. New York: Oxford University Press.

Nonaka, I., von Krogh, G., & Voelpel, S. (2006). Organizational knowledge creation theory: evolutionary paths and future advances. *Organization Studies*, *27*(8), 1179–1208. doi:10.1177/0170840606066312

Nørreklit, H. (2000). The balance on the balanced scorecard: A critical analysis of some of its assumptions. *Management Accounting Research*, *11*(1), 65–88. doi:10.1006/mare.1999.0121

North, D. C. (1990). *Institutions, institutional change and economic performances*. Cambridge, UK: Cambridge University Press.

NSTC [National Science and Technology Council] Report (2006, July). *The National Nanotechnology Initiative: Research and Development Leading to a Revolution in Technology and Industry*.

Nutt, P. C., & Backoff, R. W. (1997). Crafting Vision. *Journal of Management Inquiry*, *6*(4), 308–329. doi:10.1177/105649269764007

Nyström, P. C., & Starbuck, W. H. (1984). To Avoid Organizational Crises, Unlearn. *Organizational Dynamics*, (Spring): 53–65. doi:10.1016/0090-2616(84)90011-1

O'Connor, K., Stimson, R., & Daly, M. (2001). *Australia's changing economic geography: A society dividing*. Melbourne, Australia: Oxford University Press.

O'Hara, P. A. (2008). Principal of circular and cumulative causation: Fusing Myrdalian and Kaldorian growth and development dynamics. *Journal of Economic Issues*, *42*(2), 375–387.

O'Reilly, C. A. III, & Tushman, M. L. (1986). *The ambidextrous organization*. Harvard Business Review.

OECD. (1997). *National Innovation System*. Paris: OECD Publications.

OECD. (1998). Science, Technology and Industry Outlook. Paris: Organization for Economic Co-operation and Development.

OECD. (2000). *OECD Guidelines for Multinational Enterprises: 2000 Review*. Retrieved September 15, 2008, from http://www.oecd.org

OECD. (2004). Science, Technology and Industry Outlook. Paris: Organization for Economic Co-operation and Development.

OECD. (2005). Oslo Manual – Guidelines for Collecting and Interpreting Innovation Data" (3rd ed.), Paris: Organization for Economic Co-operation and Development/ European Commission Eurostat.

Olleros, F. (1986). Emerging Industries and the Burnout of Pioneers. *Journal of Product Innovation Management*, *1*, 5–18. doi:10.1016/0737-6782(86)90039-1

Orchard, L. (1998). Managerialism, economic rationalism and public sector reform in Australia: Connections, divergences, alternatives. *Australian Journal of Public Administration*, *57*(1), 19–32. doi:10.1111/j.1467-8500.1998.tb01361.x

Ordóñez de Pablos, P. (2004). The importance of relational capital in service industry: The case of the Spanish banking sector. *International Journal of Learning and Intellectual Capital*, *1*(4), 431–440. doi:10.1504/IJLIC.2004.005993

Organization. (n.d.). *The organization.* Retrieved 09 August, 2008, from http://petroleum.nic.in/affpsus.htm and http://petroleum.nic.in/affothe.htm

Orlitzky, M., Schmidt, F., & Rynes, S. (2003). Corporate social and financial performance: a meta-analysis. *Organization Studies*, *24*(3), 403–441. doi:10.1177/0170840603024003910

Orr, S., & Sohal, A. (1999). Technology and global manufacturing: some German experience. *Management Decision*, *37*(4), 356–363. doi:10.1108/00251749910269401

Ortt, J. R., & Delgoshaie, N. (2008, April 6-10). Why does it take so long before the diffusion of new high-tech products takes off? In *Proceedings of IAMOT (International Association for Management of Technology) conference,* Dubai, UAE

Ortt, J. R., & Schoormans, J. P. L. (2004). The pattern of development and diffusion of breakthrough communication technologies. *European Journal of Innovation Management*, *7*(4), 292–302. doi:10.1108/14601060410565047

Ortt, J. R., & Smits, R. (2006). Innovation management: different approaches to cope with the same trends. *International Journal of Technology Management*, *34*, 296–318. doi:10.1504/IJTM.2006.009461

Ortt, J. R., Shah, C. M., & Zegveld, M. A. (2008). Commercialising breakthrough technologies: Scenarios and strategies. *Management of Technology Innovation and Value Creation*, *13*, 205–220.

Ospina, S., Diaz, W., & O'Sullivan, J. F. (2002). Negotiating accountability: Managerial lessons from identity-based nonprofit organizations. *Nonprofit and Voluntary Sector Quarterly*, *31*(1), 5–31. doi:10.1177/0899764002311001

Owen, L. (1993). *Business growth and export development: Issues for firms in rural areas.* Armidale, Australia: The Rural Development Centre.

Ozer, M. (2000). Information Technology and New Product Development: opportunities and pitfalls. *Industrial Marketing Management*, *29*, 387–396. doi:10.1016/S0019-8501(99)00060-7

Page, A. L. (1993). Assessing new product development practices and performance: Establishing crucial norms. *Journal of Product Innovation Management*, *10*(4), 273–290. doi:10.1016/0737-6782(93)90071-W

Parker, R., & Bradley, L. (2000). Organisational culture in the public sector: Evidence from six organisations. *International Journal of Public Sector Management*, *13*(2), 125–141. doi:10.1108/09513550010338773

Pasinetti, L. (1981). *Structural change and economic growth.* Cambridge, UK: Cambridge University Press.

Patel, P., & Pavitt, K. (1994). *Nature et Importance Économique des Systèmes Nationaux D'Innovations (Vol. 14).* Paris: OCDE.

Patton, M. (1990). *Qualitative evaluation and research methods.* Newbury Park, CA: Sage.

Pavitt, K. (1999). *Technology, Management and Systems of Innovation.* Cheltenham, UK: Edward Elgar.

Pech, R. J. (2003). Memetics and innovation: profit through balanced meme management. *European*

Journal of Innovation Management, 6(2), 111–117. doi:10.1108/14601060310475264

Penmara Wines. (n.d.). Retreived from www.penmarawines.com.au

Pepall, L. (1997). Imitative competition and product innovation in a Duopoly Model. *Economica, 64*(254), 264–279.

Peppard, J., & Rylander, A. (2001). Using an intellectual capital perspective to design and implement a growth strategy: The case of APiON. *European Management Journal, 19*(5), 510–525. doi:10.1016/S0263-2373(01)00065-2

Perez, C. (2000). Technological Revolutions, Paradigm Shifts and Socio-Institutional Change. In Reinert, E. (Ed.), *Evolutionary Economics and Income Equality*. Aldershot, UK: Edward Elgar.

Pérez-Luño, A., Valle Cabrera, R., & Wiklund, J. (2007). Innovation and imitation as sources of sustainable competitive advantage. *Management Research, 5*(2), 67–79. doi:10.2753/JMR1536-5433050201

Peters, T. J., & Waterman, R. H. Jr. (1982). *In Search of Excellence: Lessons from America's best-run companies*. New York: Harper.

Petty, R., & Guthrie, J. (2000). Intellectual capital literature review. Measurement, reporting and management. *Journal of Intellectual Capital, 1*(2), 155–176. doi:10.1108/14691930010348731

Philipp, B. (2006). Multinationals' sustainable supply chains and influence exertion upon suppliers in the U.S. and outside the U.S.: A comparative approach. Paper presented at the *MESD 2006 International Research Colloquium*. Atlanta, GA.

Phillips, B. (1993). The influence of industry and the location on small firms failure rates, in N.C. Churchill, et al. (Eds.), Frontieres of Entrepreneurship Research (pp. 286-301), Wellesley, MA: Babson College.

Phills, J. A., Jr., Deiglmeier, K., & Miller, D. T. (2008). Rediscovering Social Innovation. Stanford, Leland Stanford Jr. University: Social Innovation Review.

Plashka and Welsch (1990). Emerging structures in entrepreneurship education: Curricula designs and strategies. *Entrepreneurship Theory and Practice, 28*, 129-144.

Podsakoff, P. M., Mackenzie, S. B., Paine, J. B., & Bachrach, D. G. (2000). Organizational citizenship behaviors: A critical review of the theoretical and empirical literature and suggestions for future research. *Journal of Management, 26*, 513–563. doi:10.1177/014920630002600307

Polanyi, M. (1966). *The tacit dimension*. London: Routledge.

Pomerantz, M. (2003). The business of social entrepreneurship in a 'down economy'. In Business, 25(2), 25-28.

Pontikakis, D., McDonnell, T., & Geoghegan, W. (2005). *Conceptualising a National Innovation System: Actor, Roles and Incentives*. Unpublished manuscript.

Porter, A. L., & Cunningham, S. W. (2005). *Tech Mining. Exploiting New Technologies for Competitive Advantage*. New York: Wiley-Interscience. Roco, M. C., & Bainbridge, W.S. (2002). Converging Technologies for Improving Human Performance: Integrating from the nanoscale. *Journal of Nanoparticle Research, 4*(4), 281–295.

Porter, M. (1996). Competitive advantage, agglomeration economics, and regional policy. *International Regional Science Review, 19*(1-2), 85–94.

Porter, M. (1998). Clusters and the new economics of competition. *Harvard Business Review*, (Nov-Dec): 77–93.

Porter, M. E. (1980). *Competitive advantage. Techniques for analyzing industries*. New York: The Free Press.

Porter, M. E. (1980). *Competitive strategy: techniques for analyzing industries and competitors*. New York: Free Press.

Porter, M. E. (1985). *Competitive advantage: creating and sustaining superior performance*. New York: Free Press.

Porter, M. E. (1990). *The Competitive Advantage of Nations*. New York: Free Press.

Porter, M. E. (2008). *On Competition*. Boston: Harvard Business School Press.

Porter, M. E., & Kramer, M. R. (2006). Strategy and society: The link between competitive advantage and corporate social responsibility. *Harvard Business Review, 84*(12), 78–92.

Porter, M. E., & Stern, S. (1999). *The New Challenge to America's Prosperity: Finding from the Innovation Index*. New York: Free Press.

Prahalad, C. K., & Hamel, G. (1990). The Core Competence of the Corporation. *Harvard Business Review, 68*(3), 79–92.

Precision Parts. (n.d.). Retrieved from www.precision-parts.com.au

Pressman, S., & Holt, R. P. (2008). Nicholas Kaldor and cumulative causation: Public policy implications. *Journal of Economic Issues, 42*(2), 367–373.

Prime Minister package for north east states. (n.d.). *Prime Minister package for north east states.* Retrieved September 03, 2008, from http://www.mdoner.gov.in/index2.asp?sid=225

Probst, G., & Bücher, B. (1997). *Organizaional Learning. The Competitive Advantage of the Future*. Upper Saddle River, NJ: Prentice Hall.

Probst, G., Buchel, B., & Raub, S. (1998). Knowledge as a strategic resource. In von Krogh, G., Roos, J., & Kleine, D. (Eds.), *Knowing in firms* (pp. 241–252). London: Sage.

Quaak, L., Aalbers, T., & Goedee, J. (2007). Transparency of corporate social responsibility in Dutch Breweries. *Journal of Business Ethics, 76*, 293–308. doi:10.1007/s10551-006-9282-3

Quazi, A. M., & O'Brien, D. (2000). *An empirical test of a cross-national model of corporate social responsibility. Journal of Business Ethics, 2533-51*. The Netherlands: Kluwer Academic Publishers.

Rabino, S., & Wright, R. (1993). Accelerated Product Introductions and Emerging Managerial Accounting Perspectives: Implications for Marketing Managers in the Technology Sector. *Journal of Product Innovation Management, 10*(2), 126–135. doi:10.1016/0737-6782(93)90004-A

Radjou, N. (2005, March). IBM Transforms its Supply Chain to Drive Growth, *Forrester.*

Ramia, G., & Carney, T. (2003). New public management, the job network and nonprofit strategy. *Australian Journal of Labor Economics, 6*(2), 249–271.

Report on evaluation study of the growth centres scheme. (n.d.). *Report on evaluation study of the growth centres scheme.* Retrieved May 21, 2008, from http://planningcommission.nic.in/reports/peoreport/peoevalu/peo_cgs.pdf

Ricoy, C. (1988). Cumulative causation. In Eatwell, J., Milgate, M., & Newman, P. (Eds.), *The new Palgrave: A dictionary of economics*. London: Macmillan.

Riddel, M., & Schwer, K. (2003). Regional Innovative Capacity with Endogenous Employment: Empirical Evidence from the U.S. *The Review of Regional Studies, 33*(1), 73–84.

Rigby, D., & Zook, C. (2002). Open-market innovation. *Harvard Business Review, 80*(10), 80–89.

Rink, D. R., & Swan, J. E. (1979). Product Life Cycle Research: A Literature Review. *Journal of Business Research*, 219–242. doi:10.1016/0148-2963(79)90030-4

Rivkin, J. W. (2001). Reproducing knowledge: replication without imitation at moderate complexity. *Organization Science, 12*(3), 274–293. doi:10.1287/orsc.12.3.274.10106

Roberts, B. (2000). Facilitating industry cluster development. *Regional Policy and Practice, 9*(1), 36–45.

Roberts, E. B., & Berry, C. A. (1985). Entering new businesses: Selecting strategies for success. *Sloan Management Review*, (Spring): 3–17.

Roberts, P., & Amit, R. (2003). The dynamics of innovative activity and competitive advantage: The case of Australian Retail Banking, 1981 to 1995. *Organization Science, 14*(2), 107–122. doi:10.1287/orsc.14.2.107.14990

Robey, D., & Keil, M. (2001). Blowing the whistle on troubled software projects. *Communications of the ACM, 44*(4), 87–93. doi:10.1145/367211.367274

Roco, M. C. (2005). International perspective on government nanotechnology funding in 2005. *Journal of Nanoparticle Research*, 7(6), 707–712. doi:10.1007/s11051-005-3141-5

Rogers, E. M. (1986). *Communication Technology. The New Media in Society*. New York: The Free Press.

Rogers, E. M. (2003). *Diffusion of Innovations* (5th ed.). New York: Free Press.

Romer, P. (1990). Endogenous Technological Change. *The Journal of Political Economy*, 98, S71–S102. doi:10.1086/261725

Rondinelli, D. (2006). Globalization of sustainable development? Principles and practices in transnational corporations. Paper presented at the *MESD 2006 International Research Colloquium*. Atlanta, GA.

Ronen, S., & Shenkar, O. (1985). Clustering Countries on Attitudinal Dimensions: A Review and Synthesis. *Academy of Management Review*, 10(3), 435. doi:10.2307/258126

Roos, G., & Jacobsen, K. (1999). Management in a complex stakeholder organization. *Monash Mt. Eliza Business Review*, 2(1), 83–93.

Roos, J. (1998). Exploring the concept of intellectual capital (IC). *Long Range Planning*, 31(1), 150–153. doi:10.1016/S0024-6301(97)87431-6

Roos, J., Roos, G., Dragonetti, N. C., & Edvinsson, L. (1997). *Intellectual capital: Navigating the new business landscape*. London: Macmillan Press Limited.

Roper, J., & Cheney, G. (2005). Leadership, learning and human resource management: The meanings of social entrepreneurship today. *Corporate Governance*, 5(3), 95–104. doi:10.1108/14720700510604733

Rosenberg, N. (1976). *Perspectives on technology*. Cambridge, UK: Cambridge University Press. doi:10.1017/CBO9780511561313

Rosenstiel, L., & Koch, S. (2001). Change in Socioeconomic values as a trigger of Organisational learning. In Dierkes, M., Antal, A. B., Child, J., & Nonaka, I. (Eds.), *Organisational Learning and Knowledge*. Oxford, UK: Oxford University Press.

Roy, S. (2007). *Macroeconomic policy environment: An analytical guide for managers*. New Delhi, India: Tata-McGraw Hill.

Saint-Onge, H. (1996). Tacit knowledge: The key to the strategic alignment of intellectual capital. *Strategy and Leadership*, 24(2), 10–14. doi:10.1108/eb054547

Salaman, G., & Butler, J. (1999). Why Managers Won't Learn. In Mabey, C., & Iles, P. (eds.), Managing Learning, 34-42, International Thompson Business Press.

Salamon, L. M. (1986). Government and the voluntary sector in an era of retrenchment. *Journal of Public Policy*, 6(1), 1–20. doi:10.1017/S0143814X00003834

Salamon, L. M. (1996). The crisis of the nonprofit sector and the challenge of renewal. *National Civic Review*, 85(4), 3–15. doi:10.1002/ncr.4100850403

Salamon, L. M. (1999). The nonprofit sector at a crossroads: The case of America. *Voluntas: International Journal of Voluntary and Nonprofit Organizations*, 10(1), 5–23. doi:10.1023/A:1021435602742

Sawheny, M., Verona, G., & Prandelli, E. (2005). Collaborating to create: The Internet as a platform for customer engagement in product innovation. *Journal of Interactive Marketing*, 19(4), 4–17. doi:10.1002/dir.20046

Schein, E. H. (2004). *Organisational Culture and Leadership*. New York: John Wiley and Sons.

Schepers, D. (2006). The impact of NGO network conflict on the corporate social responsibility strategies of multinational corporations. *Business & Society*, 45(3), 282–299. doi:10.1177/0007650306289386

Schilling, M. A. (2006). Strategic management of technical innovation (2 ed.). New York: McGraw-Hill.

Schiuma, G., Lerro, A., & Carlucci, D. (2005). An interfirm perspective on intellectual capital. In Marr, B. (Ed.), *Perspectives on intellectual capital: Multidisciplinary insights into management, measurement, and reporting* (pp. 155–169). Amsterdam: Elsevier Butterworth-Heinemann.

Schneider, S., & Barsoux, J.-L. (1997). *Managing Across Cultures*. Upper Saddle River, NJ: Prentice Hall.

Schumpeter, J. (1911). *"Theorie der wirtschaftlichen Entwicklung* (transl. *The Theory of Economic Development: An inquiry into profits, capital, credit, interest and the business cycle*) Leipzig, Verlag von Duncker and Humblot. Internet translation Retrieved from http://findarticles.com/p/articles/mi_m0254/is_2_61/ai_86469065/pg_24

Schumpeter, J. (1934). *The theory of economic development.* Boston: Harvard University Press.

Schumpeter, J. A. (1934/1961). *The theory of economic development: an inquiry into profits, capital, credit, interest, and the business cycle.* New Brunswick, NJ: Transaction Publishers.

Schwab, K. (2008). Global Corporate Citizenship. *Foreign Affairs (Council on Foreign Relations), 87*(1), 107–118.

Scott, S. G., & Bruce, R. A. (1994). Determinants of innovative behaviour: a path model of individual innovation in the workplace. *Academy of Management Journal, 38,* 1442–1465.

Seel, R. (2005). Culture and Complexity: New Insights on Organisational Change. *Organisations and People, 7*(2), 2–9.

Seelos, C., & Mair, J. (2005). Social entrepreneurship: Creating new business models to serve the poor. *Business Horizons, 48*(3), 241–246. doi:10.1016/j.bushor.2004.11.006

Seider, R. (2006). Optimizing Project Portfolios. *Research Technology Management, 49*(5), 43–48.

Selsky, J. W., & Parker, B. (2005). Cross-sector partnerships to address social issues: Challenges to theory and practice. *Journal of Management, 31*(6), 849–873. doi:10.1177/0149206305279601

Senge, P. M. (2006). *The fifth discipline: The art & practice of learning organizations.* London: Random House.

Sethi, R., Pant, S., & Sethi, A. (2003). Web-Based Product Development Systems Integration and New Product Outcomes: A conceptual framework. *Journal of Product Innovation Management, 20,* 37–56. doi:10.1111/1540-5885.201004

Setterfield, M. (1997). History vs equilibrium and the theory of economic growth. *Cambridge Journal of Economics, 21,* 365–378.

Sexton, M., & Barrett, P. (2003). Appropriate innovation in small construction firms. *Construction Management and Economics, 27*(6), 623–633. doi:10.1080/0144619032000134156

Shah, C. M., Zegveld, M. A., & Roodhart, L. (2008). Designing ventures that work. *Research Technology Management, 51*(2), 17–25.

Sharma, A. (1999). Central dilemmas of managing innovation in large firms. *California Management Review, 41,* 146–164.

Sharma, S., & Vredenburg, H. (1998). Proactive corporate environmental strategy and the development of competitively valuable organizational capabilities. *Strategic Management Journal, 19*(8), 729–753. doi:10.1002/(SICI)1097-0266(199808)19:8<729::AID-SMJ967>3.0.CO;2-4

Sherman, J. D., Souder, W. E., & Jenssen, S. A. (2000). Differential Effects of the Primary Forms of Cross Functional Integration on Product Development Cycle Time. *Journal of Product Innovation Management, 17*(4), 257–267. doi:10.1016/S0737-6782(00)00046-1

Shipton, H., West, M. A., Parkes, C., & Dawson, J. F. (2004). *Aggregate job satisfaction, HRM and organizational innovation.* Birmingham, UK: Aston Business School, Aston University.

Siguaw, J. A., Simpson, P. M., & Enz, C. A. (2006). Conceptualizing Innovation Orientation: A framework for study and integration of innovation research. *Journal of Product Innovation Management, 23,* 556–574. doi:10.1111/j.1540-5885.2006.00224.x

Silverthorne, C. (2004). The impact of Organisational culture and person-organisation fit on Organisational commitment and job satisfaction in Taiwan. *Leadership and Organization Development Journal, 25*(7), 592–599. doi:10.1108/01437730410561477

Sink, D. S., & Tuttle, T. C. (1989). *Planning and Measurement in your Organisation of the Future*. Norcross, GA: Industrial Engineering and Management Press.

Sirmon, D. G., Hitt, M. A., & Ireland, R. D. (2007). Managing firm resources in dynamic environments to create value: Looking inside the black box. *Academy of Management Review, 32*(1), 273–292.

Slack, N., Chambers, S., & Johnston, R. (2007). Operations Management (5 ed.): Pearson Education Limited.

Slater, S. F., & Mohr, J. J. (2006). Successful Development and Commercialization of Technological Innovation: Insights Based on Strategy Type. *Journal of Product Innovation Management, 23*, 26–33. doi:10.1111/j.1540-5885.2005.00178.x

Sleeper, B. J., Schneider, K. C., Weber, P. S., & Weber, J. E. (2006). Scale and Study of Students Attitudes Toward Business Education's Role in Addressing Social Issues. *Journal of Business Ethics, 68*(4), 381–391. doi:10.1007/s10551-006-9000-1

Smith, G. P. (2002). *The new leader: bringing creativity and innovation to the workplace, Chart Your Course*. Georgia: Conyers.

Smith, J. (2002). The 40 root causes of troubled IT projects. *Engineering Management Journal, 12*(5), 238–242. doi:10.1049/em:20020506

Snell, R., & Chak, A. M.-Ky. (1998). The Learning Organization: Learning and Empowerment for whom? *Management Learning, 29*(3), 337–364. doi:10.1177/1350507698293005

Solal, P. (1997). Système National d'Innovation, Division du Travail et Territoire: un Retour a F. List et H.C. Carey. *Revue d'Economie Régionale et Urbaine - RERU, 4*, 545-564.

Solomon, G. T., Duffy, S., & Tarabishy, A. (2002). The state of entrepreneurship education in the United States: A nationwide survey and analysis. *International Journal of Entrepreneurship Education, 1*(1), 65–86.

Spear, R. (2001). United Kingdom: A wide range of social enterprises. In Borzaga, C., Defourny, J., Adam, S., &

Callaghan, J. (Eds.), *The emergence of social enterprise*. London: Routledge.

Spencer, J. W. (2003). Firms' knowledge-sharing strategies in the global innovation system: Empirical evidence from the flat panel display industry. *Strategic Management Journal, 24*(3), 217–233. doi:10.1002/smj.290

St. Leon, M. V. (2002). Intellectual capital: Managerial perceptions of organizational knowledge resources. *Journal of Intellectual Capital, 3*(2), 149–166. doi:10.1108/14691930210424743

Stahl, T. (2007). The Rhine-Neckar-Triangle regional development partnership. In Ennals, R., Gustavsen, B., & Nyhan, B. (Eds.), *Learning together for local innovation: Promoting learning regions*. Luxembourg: Cedefop.

Steffens, J. (1994). *New Games: Strategic Competition in the PC Revolution*. New York: Pergamon Press.

Stern, S., Porter, M. E., & Furman, J. L. (2002). The Determinants of National Innovative Capacity. *Research Policy, 31*, 899–993. doi:10.1016/S0048-7333(01)00152-4

Stevens, J. E. (1999). *An Organisational Culture Perspective of Strategic Leadership and Organisational Change: Shaping the Future of the Army*. Study project.

Stewart, T. A. (1997). *Intellectual capital: The new wealth of organizations*. New York: Currency Doubleday.

Stone, M. M., Bigelow, B., & Crittenden, W. E. (1999). Research on strategic management in nonprofit organizations: Synthesis, analysis, and future directions. *Administration & Society, 31*(3), 378–423. doi:10.1177/00953999922019184

Storper, M., & Scott, A. J. (Eds.). (1992). *Pathways to industrialization and regional development*. London: Routledge.

Stringer, R. (2000). How to manage radical innovation. *California Management Review, 40*(4), 70–88.

Suarez-Villa, L. (1990). Invention, Inventive Learning and Innovative Capacity. *Behavioral Science, 35*(4), 290–310. doi:10.1002/bs.3830350404

Suarez-Villa, L. (1997). Innovative Capacity, Infrastructure and Regional Inversion: Is there a Long-term Dynamic? In Bertuglia, S. L. A. P. N. E. C. S. (Ed.), *Innovative Behaviour in Space and Time* (pp. 291–305). Berlin, Heidelberg, New York: Springer-Verlag.

Suarez-Villa, L. (2003). *Innovative Capacity, Networks and the rise of Experimental Firm: Implications for Regional Development and Policy*. Paper presented at the International Workshop on Modern Entrepreneurship, Regional Development and Policy: Dynamic and Evolutionary Perspectives.

Subramaniam, M., & Youndt, M. A. (2005). The influence of intellectual capital on the types of innovative capabilities. *Academy of Management Journal*, *48*(3), 450–463.

Sugarman, B. (2001). A leaning-based approach to organizational change: Some results and Guidelines. *Organizational Dynamics*, *30*(1), 62–67. doi:10.1016/S0090-2616(01)00041-9

Sull, D. N. (2005). Strategy as active waiting. *Harvard Business Review*, *83*(9), 120–129.

Sullivan, P. H. (Ed.). (1998). *Profiting from intellectual capital: Extracting value from innovation*. New York: John Wiley and Sons, Inc.

Sullivan-Mort, G., Weerawardena, J., & Carnegie, K. (2003). Social entrepreneurship: Towards conceptualization. *International Journal of Nonprofit and Voluntary Sector Marketing*, *8*(1), 76–88. doi:10.1002/nvsm.202

Sum, N. L., & Ngai, P. (2005). Globalization and paradoxes of ethical transnational production: Code of conduct in a Chinese workplace. *Competitive & Change*, *9*(2), 181–200. doi:10.1179/102452905X45427

Sunstein, C. R. (2004). Democracy and Filtering. *Communications of the ACM*, *47*(12), 57–59. doi:10.1145/1035134.1035166

Swann, G. N. P., Prevezer, M., & Stout, D. (1998). *The dynamics of industrial clustering: International comparisons in computing and biotechnology*. Oxford, UK: Oxford University Press.

Sweeney, G. (1987). *Innovation, entrepreneurs and regional development*. London: Frances Pinter.

Tamai, T., & Itou, A. (1993). Requirements and design change in large-scale software development: analysis from the viewpoint of process backtracking. In *Proceedings of the 15th international Conference on Software Engineering*. Los Alamitos, CA: IEEE Computer Society Press. Presented at the International Conference on Software Engineering (May 17-21, 1993), Baltimore, MD.

Tang, V., Liu, B., Kellam, B. A., Otto, K. N., & Seering, W. P. (2005). *Enabling factors in successful product development*. Paper presented at the International conference on engineering design.

Tanimoto, K., & Suzuki, K. (2005). *Corporate social responsibility in Japan: Analyzing the participation companies in global reporting initiative*. Working Paper 208.

Tannenbaum, A., Swearingen, C., Cook, J., Bardon, D., & Dong, J. (2006). NotesBuddy: A unified experience for messaging, *IBM Corporation*. Retrieved November 21, 2006, from http://www.ibm.com/easy/page/1979

Targetti, F. (1992). *Nicholas Kaldor: The economics and politics of capitalism as a dynamic system*. Oxford, UK: Oxford University Press.

Tateisi, N. (2004). *Corporate social responsibility leads to sustainable economic growth in China—Observations from the leader of the CBCC Dialogue mission on CSR in the People's Republic of China*. Retrieved September 8, 2006, from http://www.keidanren.or.jp/CBCC/english/report/2004

Taylor, S. J., & Bogdan, R. (1984). *Introduction to qualitative research methods: The search for meaning*. New York: Wiley.

Tchong, M. (2005). The Culture of Innovation, *Fast Company*. Retrieved November 13, 2006, from http://www.fastcompany.com/resources/innovation/tchong/101804.html

Teece, D. J., & Pisano, G. (1994). Dynamic capabilities and strategic management. *Industrial and Corporate Change*, *3*, 537–556. doi:10.1093/icc/3.3.537-a

Tellis, G. J., & Golder, P. N. (1996). First to Market, First to Fail? Real Causes of Enduring Market Leadership. *Sloan Management Review*, (Winter): 65–75.

Teresko, J. (2008). Metrics Matter. *Leaders in manufactoring* Retrieved November, 2008, from http://www.industryweek.com/ReadArticle.aspx?ArticleID=16116

The American Chamber of Commerce People's Republic of China (2006). *Corporate Social Responsibility Initiatives of AmCham-China Member Companies: Partnering for Progress.*

Thirlwall, A. (1987). *Nicholas Kaldor.* Sussex, UK: Wheatsheaf Books.

Thomke, S. H. (2003). *Experimentation Matters. Unlocking the Potential of New Technologies for innovation.* Boston: Harvard Business School Press.

Thompson, J. L. (2002). The world of the social entrepreneur. *International Journal of Public Sector Management*, *15*(5), 412–431. doi:10.1108/09513550210435746

Thompson, J., & Doherty, B. (2006). The diverse world of social enterprise: A collection of social enterprise stories. *International Journal of Social Economics*, *33*(5/6), 361–375. doi:10.1108/03068290610660643

Ticehurst, G. W., & s, A. J. (2000). *Business research methods: A managerial approach.* Frenchs Forest, Australia: Longman.

Tidd, J., Bessant, J., Pavitt, K., Tidd, J., & Bessant, J. R. (1997). *Managing innovation: integrating technological, market and organizational change.* New York: John Wiley & Sons.

Times, F. (2008, October 9). China explores new ways to tackle its environmental challenges. *Financial Times (North American Edition)*, 4.

Tobin, J. (1958). Estimation for relationships with limited dependent variables. *Econometrica*, *26*(1), 24–36. doi:10.2307/1907382

Toner, P. (1998). *Main currents in the theory of circular and cumulative causation: The dynamics of growth and development.* New York: St Martin's Press.

Toner, P. (2000). Manufacturing industry in the Australian economy: Its roles and significance. *Journal of Australian Political Economy*, *45*, 18–45.

Transforming the northeast. (1997). *Transforming the northeast: Tackling Backlogs in Basic Minimum Services and infrastructural needs.* Retrieved November 28, 2008, from http://planningcommission.nic.in/reports/genrep/ne_exe.pdf

Trippl, M. (2006). *Cross-Border Regional Innovation Systems.* Retrieved from http://epub.wu-wien.ac.at

Trott, P. (1998). *Innovation management and new product development.* London: Financial Times.

Trott, P., & Hoecht, A. (2007). Product counterfeiting, non-consensual acquisition of technology and new product development; An innovation perspective. *European Journal of Innovation Management*, *10*(1), 126–143. doi:10.1108/14601060710720582

Trout, J. (2006). *Tales from the marketing wars – Peter Drucker on marketing.* Retrieved December 1, 2007, from http://www.forbes.com/columnists/2006/06/30/jack-trout-on-marketing-cx_jt_0703drucker.html

Tsai, W. (2001). Knowledge transfer in intra-organizational networks: Effects of network position and absorptive capacity on business unit innovation and performance. *Academy of Management Journal*, *44*(5), 996–1004. doi:10.2307/3069443

Tsai, W. (2001). Knowledge transfer in intra-organizational networks: Effects of network position and absorptive capacity on business unit innovation and performance. *Academy of Management Journal*, *44*, 996–1004. doi:10.2307/3069443

Tushman, M. L., & Anderson, P. (1986). Technological Discontinuities and Organizational Environments. *Administrative Science Quarterly*, *31*, 439–465. doi:10.2307/2392832

Tushman, M. L., & Rosenkopf, L. (1992). Organizational Determinants of Technological Change. Towards a Sociology of Technological Evolution. *Research in Organizational Behavior*, *14*, 311–347.

Tushman, M., & O'Reilly, C. (1997). *Winning Through Innovation: A Practical Guide to Leading Organizational Change and Renewal.* Boston: Harvard Business Press.

Ulrich, K. T., & Eppinger, S. D. (2003). Product design and development (3 ed.). New York: McGraw-Hill Education.

UNIDO technology foresight manual. (2005). *UNIDO technology foresight manual vol. 1: Organization and methods.* Retrieved August 22, 2006, from https://www.unido.org/foresight/registration/dokums_raw/volume1_unido_tf_manual.pdf

UNIDO technology foresight manual. (2005). *UNIDO technology foresight manual vol. 2: Technology foresight in action.* Retrieved August 22, 2006, from https://www.unido.org/foresight/registration/dokums_raw/volume2_unido_tf_manual.pdf

University of Cambridge. (2006). The Development Funnel, *Institute for Manufacturing Centre for Economic Policy.* Retrieved November 11, 2006, http://www.ifm.eng.cam.ac.uk/dstools/paradigm/innova.html

Unsworth, K., & Parker, S. (2003). Proactivity and innovation: Promoting a new workforce for the new workplace. In Holman, D., Wall, T., Clegg, C., Sparrow, P., & Howard, A. (Eds.), *The New Workplace: A Guide to the Human Impact of Modern Working Practices.* West Sussex, UK: Wiley.

USA Today (2003). Retrieved June 10, 2008, from http://www.usatoday.com/educate/college/business/casestudies/20030521-entrepreneurs.pdf

Useem, J. (2001, May). The risk taker return. *Fortune Small Business*, 70-72.

Using foresight to improve the science-policy relationship. (2006). *Using foresight to improve the science-policy relationship.* Retrieved August 07, 2008, from http://ec.europa.eu/research/foresight/pdf/21967.pdf

Utterback, J. M., & Brown, J. W. (1972). Monitoring for Technological Opportunities. *Business Horizons*, *15*(October), 5–15. doi:10.1016/0007-6813(72)90042-0

Vaill, P. (2007). Organizational epistemology: Interpersonal relations in organizations and the emergence of

wisdom. In Kessler E. and Bailey J. (eds.), The Handbook of Managerial and Organizational Wisdom (327-355). Thousand Oaks, CA: Sage Publications.

Valle, M. (1999). Crisis, culture and charisma: The new leader's work in public organisations. *Public Personnel Management*, *28*(2), 245–257.

Van de Ven, & Andrew H. (1986). Central Problems in the Management of Innovation. *Management Science*, *32*(5), 590–607. doi:10.1287/mnsc.32.5.590

Van de Zwan, P., Thurik, A. R., & Grilo, I. (2008). (forthcoming). The entrepreneurial ladder and its determinants. *Applied Economics.*

Van den Bulte, C. (2000). New Product Diffusion Acceleration: Measurement and Analysis. *Marketing Science*, *19*(4), 366–380. doi:10.1287/mksc.19.4.366.11795

van Marrewijk, M. (2003). Concepts and definitions of CSR and Corporate Sustainability: Between Agency and Communication. *Journal of Business Ethics*, *44*(2/3), 95–105. doi:10.1023/A:1023331212247

van Rooij, B. (2006). Implementation of Chinese environmental law: Regular enforcement and political campaigns. *Development and Change*, *37*(1), 57–74. doi:10.1111/j.0012-155X.2006.00469.x

van Tulder, R., & van der Zwart, A. (2006). *International business-society management.* Oxford, UK: Routledge.

VanderWerf, P. A., & Mahon, J. F. (1997). Meta-analysis of the impact of research methods on findings of first-mover advantage. *Management Science*, *43*(11), 1510–1519. doi:10.1287/mnsc.43.11.1510

Vang-Lauridsen, J., & Chaminade, C. (2006). *Globalization of Knowledge Production and Regional Innovation Policy: Supporting Specialized Hubs in Developing Countries.* Unpublished manuscript.

Vang-Lauridsen, J., Coenen, L., Chaminade, C., & Asheim, B. (2007). Universities, Regional Innovation Systems and the Bangalore Experience: Towards a Contextual and Evolutionary Perspective. Paper presented at the Managing Total Innovation and Open Innovation in the 21st Century. In *Proceedings of the 5Th international.*

Symposium on Management of Technology (ISMOT'07), Zhejiang, China.

Vassilakis, S. (1987). Learning by doing. In Eatwell, J., Milgate, M., & Newman, P. (Eds.), *The new Palgrave: A dictionary of economics*. London: Macmillan.

Veblen, T. (1898). Why is economics not an evolutionary science? *The Quarterly Journal of Economics, 12*, 373–397. doi:10.2307/1882952

Venkatesh, V., Morris, M. G., Davis, G. B., & Davis, F. D. (2003). User Acceptance of Information Technology: Toward a unified view. *MIS Quaterly, 27*(3), 425–478.

Verburg, R. M., & Hartog, D. (2005). Human Resource Management for advanced technology. In Verburg, R. M., Ortt, J. R., & Dicke, W. M. (Eds.), *Managing Technology and Innovation* (pp. 43–46). London: Routledge.

Verity, J. (1992, November 23). Deconstructing the Computer Industry. *Business Week*, 90-100.

Verloop, J. (2004). *Insight the Innovation: Managing innovation by understanding the laws of innovation*. Amsterdam: Elsevier Science.

Veryzer, R. W. (1998). Key Factors Affecting Customer Evaluation of Discontinuous New Products. *Journal of Product Innovation Management, 15*, 136–150. doi:10.1016/S0737-6782(97)00075-1

Vesper, K., & McMullen, W. (1988). Entrepreneurship: Today courses, tomorrow degrees? *Entrepreneurship Theory and Practice, 13*(1), 7–13.

Von Hippel, E. (2005). *Democraticing Innovation*. Cambridge, MA: MIT Press.

Waddock, S., & Graves, S. (1997). The corporate social performance - financial performance link. *Strategic Management Journal, 18*(4), 303–319. doi:10.1002/(SICI)1097-0266(199704)18:4<303::AID-SMJ869>3.0.CO;2-G

Waddock, S., & Post, J. E. (1991). Social entrepreneurs and catalytic change. *Public Administration Review, 51*(5), 393–401. doi:10.2307/976408

Wallis, J., & Dollery, B. (2005). Leadership and economic theories of nonprofit organizations. *Review of Policy Research, 22*(4), 483–499. doi:10.1111/j.1541-1338.2005.00151.x

Watson, C. (2001). Small business versus entrepreneurship revisited. In Brockhaus, R. (Ed.), *Entrepreneurship education: a global view*. Burlington, UK: Ashgate.

Webster, E. (2000). The growth of enterprise intangible investment in Australia. *Information Economics and Policy, 12*(1), 1–25. doi:10.1016/S0167-6245(99)00024-4

Weerawardena, J., & Sullivan-Mort, G. (2006). Investigating social entrepreneurship: A multidimensional model. *Journal of World Business, 41*(1), 21–35. doi:10.1016/j.jwb.2005.09.001

Wehmeier, S., Hornby, A. S., & McIntosh, C. (Eds.). (2005). *Oxford Advanced Learner's Dictionary of Current English (Vol. 7)*. New York: Oxford University Press.

Weihrich, H. (1982). The TOWS matrix: A tool for situational analysis. *Long Range Planning, 15*(2), 54–66. doi:10.1016/0024-6301(82)90120-0

Weisbrod, B. A. (1997). The future of the nonprofit sector: Its entwining with private enterprise and government. *Journal of Policy Analysis and Management, 16*(4), 541–555. doi:10.1002/(SICI)1520-6688(199723)16:4<541::AID-PAM2>3.0.CO;2-G

Weisbrod, B. A. (Ed.). (1998). *To profit or not to profit: The commercial transformation of the nonprofit sector*. Cambridge, UK: Cambridge University Press. doi:10.1017/CBO9780511625947

Weiss, A. (2005). The power of collective intelligence. *netWorker, 9*(3), 16–23. doi:10.1145/1086762.1086763

Welford, R. (2006). New guidelines for Chinese CSR. *CSR Asia Weekly, 2*(35). Retrieved September 4, 2006, from http://www.csr-asia.com/upload/csrasiaweekly-vol2week35.pdf

West, P. III, & Noel, T. W. (2009). The impact of knowledge resources on new venture performance. *Journal of Small Business Management, 47*(1), 1–22. doi:10.1111/j.1540-627X.2008.00259.x

Westend Estate Wines. (n.d.). Retrieved from www.westendestate.com.au

Wheelright, S. C., & Clark, K. B. (1992). *Revolutionizing product development: Quantum leaps in speed, efficiency, and quality.* New York: Free Press.

White, A. Paper from the Business Roundtable (2000). *Corporate social responsibility in China: Practices by U.S. companies.*

Whitley, R., Parish, T., Dressler, R., & Nicholson, G. (1998). Evaluating R&D performance using the new sales ratio. *Research Technology Management, 41*(5), 20–22.

Wickham, M., & Hanson, D. (2002). Industrial clustering in regional Australia: The role of chance, entrepreneurs and government in the Tasmanian light ships industry. In *Proceedings of the Sixteenth ANZAM Conference.* Melbourne, Australia: La Trobe University.

Wickham, P. (2001). *Strategic Entrepreneurship: A decision-making approach to new venture creation and management* (2nd ed.). Upper Saddle River, NJ: Person Education.

Wickramasekera, R., & Bamberry, G. (2001). Australian wineries: Factors perceived to enhance or inhibit export market expansion. In Gray, S. J., McCaughey, S. L., & Purcell, W. R. (Eds.), *Asia Pacific Issues in International Business.* Cheltenham, UK: Edward Elgar.

Wickramasekera, R., & Bamberry, G. (2003). An overview of a successful export industry from regional Australia. *International Journal of Wine Marketing, 15*(3), 15–27. doi:10.1108/eb008760

Wickramasekera, R., & Bamberry, G. (2003). Exploration of born globals/international new ventures: Some evidence from the Australian wine industry. *Australasian Journal of Regional Studies, 9*(2), 207–219.

Wikipedia (n.d.). *Agile Software Development.* Retrieved November 21, 2006, from http://en.wikipedia.org/wiki/Agile_software_development

Wikipedia. (n.d.). *Innovation.* Retrieved December 13, 2006, from www.en.wikipedia.org/wiki/Innovation

Williams, F., Rice, R. E., & Rogers, E. M. (1988). *Research Methods and the New Media.* New York: The Free Press.

Williamson, O. E. (1996). *The Mechanisms of Governance.* New York: Oxford University Press.

Wilson, M. I., & Larson, R. S. (2002). Nonprofit management students: Who they are and why they enrol? *Nonprofit and Voluntary Sector Quarterly, 31*(2), 259–270. doi:10.1177/08964002031002005

Wiseman, R. M., & Bromiley, P. (1996). Toward a model of risk in declining organizations. An empirical examination of risk, performance and decline. *Organization Science, 7*(5), 524–543. doi:10.1287/orsc.7.5.524

Wolfe, R. A. (1994). Organizational innovation: review, critique and suggested research directions. *Journal of Management Studies, 31*(3), 405–431. doi:10.1111/j.1467-6486.1994.tb00624.x

Wonglimpiyarat, J. (2005). The nano-revolution of Schumpeter's Kondratieff cycle. *Technovation, 25*(11), 1349–1354. doi:10.1016/j.technovation.2004.07.002

Wood, C. H., & Kaufman, A. (2007). The communication of corporate social responsibility (CSR) through the supply chain: an SME perspective. In Gerald I. Susman (ed.), Small and Medium-Sized Enterprises and the Global Economy, 140-153. Cheltenham, UK and Northampton, MA: Edward Elgar.

Wood, D. J. (1991). Social Issues in Management: Theory and Research in Corporate Social Performance. *Journal of Management, 17*(2), 383–406. doi:10.1177/014920639101700206

Workforce sustainability and talent management. (2006). *Workforce sustainability and talent management in the Indian oil and gas upstream industry.* Retrieved April 03, 2008, from http://petrofed.winwinhosting.net/upload/manpowerstudy2006.pdf

World Business Council for Sustainable Development. (2005). *Perspective: Corporate responsibility and business success in China.* Retrieved August 14, 2006 from http://www.wbcsd.org

Wright, P. M., McMahan, G. C., & McWilliams, A. (1994). Human resources and sustained competitive advantage: A resource-based perspective. *International Journal of Human Resource Management, 5*(2), 301–326.

Wright, P., & Ferris, S. (1997). Agency conflict and corporate strategy: the effect of divestment on corporate value. *Strategic Management Journal, 18*(1), 77–83. doi:10.1002/(SICI)1097-0266(199701)18:1<77::AID-SMJ810>3.0.CO;2-R

Wu, W.-Y., Chang, M.-L., & Chen, C.-W. (2008). Promoting innovation through the accumulation of intellectual capital, social capital, and entrepreneurial orientation. *R & D Management, 38*(3), 265–277. doi:10.1111/j.1467-9310.2008.00512.x

Yoogali Engineering. (n.d.). Retrieved from www.yoogaliengineering.com.au

Youndt, M. A., Subramaniam, M., & Snell, S. A. (2004). Intellectual capital profiles: An examination of investments and returns. *Journal of Management Studies, 41*(2), 335–361. doi:10.1111/j.1467-6486.2004.00435.x

Young, A. (1928). Increasing returns and economic progress. *The Economic Journal, 38*(152), 527–542. doi:10.2307/2224097

Young, D. R. (2001). Organizational identity in nonprofit organizations: Strategic and structural implications. *Nonprofit Management & Leadership, 12*(2), 139–157. doi:10.1002/nml.12202

Yu, X. M. (2006*). Putting corporate codes of conduct regarding labor standards in a global-national-local context: A case study of Reebok's athletic footwear supplier factory in China.* Unpublished dissertation, The Hong Kong University of Science and Technology.

Zack, M. H. (2005). The strategic advantage of knowledge and learning. *International Journal of Learning and Intellectual Capital, 2*(1), 1–20. doi:10.1504/IJLIC.2005.006803

Zadek, S. (2004, December). The path to corporate responsibility. *Harvard Business Review*, 125–132.

Zaltman, G., Duncan, R., & Holbek, J. (1973). *Innovations and Organisations.* New York: Wiley.

Zappala, G. (2001). From 'Charity' to 'Social Enterprise': Managing volunteers in public-serving nonprofits. *Australian Journal on Volunteering, 6*(1), 41–49.

Zeithaml, C., & Rice, G. (1987). Entrepreneurship/Small business education in American universities. *Journal of Small Business Management, 25*(1), 44–50.

Zhou, J., & Shalley, C. E. (2003). Research on employee creativity: a critical review and proposal for future research directions. In Martocchio, J. J., & Ferris, G. R. (Eds.), *Research in Personel and Human Resource Managemen.* Oxford, UK: Elsevier.

Zhou, K. Z. (2006). Innovation, imitation, and new product performance: the case of China. *Industrial Marketing Management, 35*, 394–402. doi:10.1016/j.indmarman.2005.10.006

Zhu, K. (2004). The Complementarity of Information Technology Infrastructure and E-Commerce Capacity: A Resource based Assessment of Their Business Value. *Journal of Management Information Systems, 21*(2), 167–202.

Zhu, K., Kraemer, K. L., & Xu, S. (2006). *The Process of Innovation Assimilation by Firms in Different Countries: A Technology Diffusion Perspective on E-Business.* Management.

Zhuang, L. (1995). Bridging the gap between technology and business strategy: a pilot study on the innovation process. *Management Decision, 33*(8), 13–21. doi:10.1108/00251749510093897

Zmud, R. W. (1982). Diffusion of modern software practices: influence of centralization and formalization. *Management Science, 28*(12), 1421–1431. doi:10.1287/mnsc.28.12.1421

About the Contributors

Latif Al-Hakim is the Program Leader of the Supply Chain Management Discipline in the Faculty of Business at the University of Southern Queensland, Australia. His experience spans industry, research and development and academic institutions. He received his first degree in Mechanical Engineering in 1968. His MSc (1977) in Industrial Engineering and PhD (1983) in Management Science were awarded from the University of Wales (UK). He has published extensively in industrial engineering, information management and systems modelling. He is the author and editor of nine books, twelve chapters in books and more than 75 papers in various journals and conference proceedings. He is selected in the editorial board of several research journals and has consulted to a number of major organisations in Australia. Dr Hakim is the editor-in-chief of the International Journal of Information quality and associate editor of the International journal of Networking and Virtual Organisations. In addition, Latif has conducted technology transfer training courses and seminars in various fields of system and information management.

Chen Jin is Deputy Dean for Undergraduate Study, Dean of Research Centre for Science, Technology & Education Policy, and Deputy Director of National Institute for Innovation Management at Zhejiang University, China. Dr Chen was awarded his first degree in 1987 By Zhejiang University and PhD in Engineering Management by the same University in 1994.. In 1998, he was a Visiting Scholar at Alfred Sloan School of Management at MIT (USA). His research areas include technology and innovation management, strategic management, human resource management, sustained development and Chinese S&T policy. Processor Chen supervised numerous number of PhD students in the various field of his research interests. He is a project leader of a variety of research projects in China as well as abroad. Professor Chen has published more than 50 books and more than 180 papers on management of technology and innovation. Journal outlets include IEEE Transition on Engineering Management, Technovation, and R&D Management.

* * *

Ruth Alas is the Vice-Rector for Scientific Affairs and Head of Management Department in Estonian Business School. She has written twenty three management textbooks and more than 100 articles. Her research is focusing on employee attitudes, learning abilities, organisational culture, leadership, crises management, business ethics and corporate social responsibility. Ruth Alas has given lectures about change management in Estonia, China and South Africa Republic. Ruth Alas has organized several international conferences in Estonia, and is Chair of EIASM workshops' series 'Organizational development and change'. Ruth Alas is in editorial boards of nine journals.

Geoff Bamberry, BA Dip Public Admin (QLD) Dip Teach (ASOPA) M.A. (Sussex) PhD (NSW), is Associate Professor of Public Administration in the School of Business at Charles Sturt University, Wagga Wagga Australia. Prior to this he taught in a number of educational institutions in Papua New Guinea. His research and publications are in the area of regional development, including factors influencing the clustering of manufacturing, the development of export markets by regional firms, particularly the wine industry, the impact of technology and telecommunications on regional development, the economic development of small rural towns and the development of tourism.

Ascensão Maria Martins Braga is Adjunct Professor at Polytechnics Institute of Guarda, Portugal, Phd. in Management by the University of Évora, and has a Master's degree in Management by the University of Beira Interior. She teaches Operations Management; New Technologies and Information Systems Management; and Marketing Decision Support Systems. She is also a Research Fellow at *Research Unit for Inland Development* (Portugal). Her main interests include Management, Operations Management and Information Society. She has published articles in international journals such as Journal of the American Academy of Business and in the Journal of Comparative International Management.

Nuka Buck is research assistant at Aarhus School of Business, Department of Marketing and Statistics. Her projects have addressed ICT usage in NPD as well as information processing in NPD.

Stefan Cedergren is an industrial Ph. D. candidate at Level Twenty-one Management and Mälardalen University, Sweden. He received his Licentiate degree from Mälardalen University in 2008 and M. Sc. in Applied physics and Electrical engineering from Linköping University in 2003. Previously he was a development engineer at Bombardier. His research interests are within product innovation and especially how performance can be evaluated, in order to increase the understanding of the relation between technology, process, organization, customer, business, and leadership in large organizations developing complex industrial products.

João Pedro Almeida Couto is Assistant Professor at University of Azores, Phd. in International Business, and as the MBA by the University of Porto. Directs the management section of the Department of Economics and Management and teaches International Business and Strategic Management. He is also Research Fellow at CEEAplA (Portugal). His main interests include International Business, International Marketing and Strategic Management. He has published several articles in international journals such as The Business Review, Multinational Business Review, Journal of the American Academy of Business, Journal of Comparative International Management among others.

Ronald Dekker is assistant professor in the Economics of Innovation department of TU Delft and senior researcher in the institute ReflecT at Tilburg University. He received his MSc in econometrics from Erasmus University Rotterdam and his PhD in labour economics from Tilburg University. He has been a visiting fellow at the Institute for Socio-economic Research at the University of Essex. His research interests are labour and innovation economics.

Prashant Dhodapkar is presently working as Deputy Chief Research Scientist in Oil India Limited (OIL), a national oil company of India His 24 years of experience in OIL includes development of various techniques for solving crude oil production problems and coal liquefaction process. Apart from devel-

338

oping innovations, he was involved in inducting and adopting new technology in the organization and has authored several technical reports and papers. His current assignment is development of enhanced oil recovery method. He is a member of the technology management team of OIL. Dhodapkar holds a M. Sc. degree in Chemistry from Nagpur University, India.

Nancy D. Erbe, J.D., L.L.M. is an associate professor of negotiation and peacebuilding at California State University Dominguez Hills. She is the author of Holding These Truths: Empowerment and Recognition in Action published by Berkeley Public Policy Press and several articles on global process published by Harvard Negotiation Law Review and other internationally recognized journals. A Fulbright specialist, her students and clients to date represent about seventy countries. The collaboration she teaches is a step by step structured creative problem solving process grounded in exemplary communication, analysis and relationship skills. It consistently builds enthusiastic cross cultural relationships resulting in innovation.

Anup Gogoi, SPE, is a Chief Chemist in Oil India Limited (OIL). He has 30 years of experience in the oil industry which includes drilling fluid engineering related to drilling and workover operations as well as in reservoir fluid studies and petrophysical studies of reservoir rocks. His present interests include drilling and workover activities in the North East India and issues related to technology management in OIL. For several years, he has been active in organizational change efforts and worked in different multi-disciplinary teams and committees. Gogoi holds a M. Sc. degree in Chemistry from Gauhati University of India.

Steven Goh is a Lecturer & Consultant in Engineering and Management in the Faculty of Engineering and Surveying at the University of Southern Queensland, where he specializes in materials science, engineering education and engineering management. He joined USQ as an academic staff in 2006 after spending 10 years in industry in various roles including R&D Manager, Business Development Engineer to Managing Director of his own firm, and is currently active in a number of boards. His research interests are in engineering education and management.

Brian Goodman is a Senior Technical Staff Member in IBM's Cloud Computing organization focusing on architecture, development and end-to-end user experience for IBM's cloud services. He leads a catalyst team of architects, developers, designers and user experience professionals based out of New York and California. Prior to that, Mr. Goodman focused on identity, grassroots collaboration and social software leading a skunk works team responsible for designing and developing emerging technology that enriches collaboration and productivity. He was a co-founder and principal architect directing technical enablement for IBM's Technology Adoption Program (TAP), the innovation space accelerating the process of identifying, developing and transitioning innovation from the laboratory to internal applications and customer implementation. He has authored over three-dozen publications and holds forty-two patent filings worldwide. He is a three-time recipient of the IBM Outstanding Technical Achievement Award and holds professional certifications with IBM and The Open Group as a Master IT Architect. Mr. Goodman is a member of the IEEE Computer Society, the Association for Computing Machinery and the Association of Open Group Enterprise Architects. He earned a multi-disciplinary BA degree in computer science, psychology and graphic design from Hampshire College, Amherst, Massachusetts, where his thesis centered on human-computer interface design for early childhood applications.

Amy Hutchins' experience has been focused on applying emerging technology to address strategic business issues. As a co-founder and manager of IBM's Technology Adoption Program (TAP), she and her team nurtured a company-wide passion around introducing a cultural change in IBM to help formally embrace innovation in an open, collaborative manner – not through a traditional approach that relies on voting and governing teams. Drawing on technical strengths from her portal development and deployment experience along with business insights and relationship skills from her assignments as an IBM certified strategy consultant, Amy's leadership earned an Outstanding Innovation Award for TAP's transformational effort. She holds multiple patents in text analytics, an M.B.A. degree from the Johnson School of Management at Cornell University, and a B.A. degree in Economics from Bucknell University. Mrs. Hutchins is currently a Global Strategy Consultant in IBM's Global Technology Services' Maintenance and Technical Support organization.

Nazrul Islam is a Post-doctoral Research Fellow at CUIMRC, Cardiff Business School, UK. He has received his Doctorate degree in the area of innovation management and has two Masters and a Bachelor degree in applied chemistry and chemical technology. His research interests are nanotechnology systems of innovation, technology and innovation management, technological forecasting and roadmapping, development of new concepts and research methods. He has authored over 30 journal and conference papers including several book chapters in these areas. Dr Islam's publications have received academic awards including the Pratt & Whitney Canada: Innovation Management Best Paper Award. He is an associate member of the Institute of Nanotechnology, a member of IAMOT and ISPIM.

Kristina Risom Jespersen is Associate Professor at Aarhus University, School of Economics and Management. Her research is in the field of information and new product development with a special interest in the user involvement competence and the potential of ICT in NPD. Kristina has published in various journals on this topic and she holds several memberships on journal editorial boards as well as conference committees. She teaches innovation management and research methods courses.

Alfred Kleinknecht is Professor in the Economics of Innovation at TU Delft, The Netherlands. Earlier, he was Professor of Industrial Economics at the Free University of Amsterdam. Kleinknecht was earlier connected to the Berlin Wissenschaftszentrum, the two Amsterdam Universities, and the University of Maastricht. In 2006 he was a visiting professor at Università la Sapienza Rome and in 2009 he was visiting professor at Université Panthéon Sorbonne Paris I.

Eric Kong is a Senior Lecturer at the School of Management & Marketing, University of Southern Queensland, Australia. He completed his PhD in Strategic Management at Monash University, Australia. He also holds a Master of Science in Quality Management from the University of Paisley, United Kingdom and a Postgraduate Diploma in Training from the University of Leicester, United Kingdom. Prior to joining the academia, Eric worked in Human Resources and Training & Development in the private sector for 10 years. His current research interests include intellectual capital, knowledge management, non-profit management, strategic management and governance. Eric is a member of Academy of Management (AOM) and Australian and New Zealand Academy of Management (ANZAM).

Michael Lewrick is a graduate of Napier University Edinburgh and holds a MBA from Bristol Business School. His research interests centres on the management issues related to the development and commercialisation of technological and business model innovation. Specific areas of focus include developing capabilities for innovativeness and business success. Currently, he advises companies in developing business strategies, innovation initiatives and the management of change.

Maria Lai-ling Ling is Professor of Business Administration at Malone University, Canton, Ohio, U.S. She holds the degrees of Bachelor of Business Administration, Master of Business Administration, Master of Art in Religion Studies, from the Chinese University of Hong Kong, and a Ph.D. in Business Administration from George Washington University. She has more than twenty years of professional experience in marketing and organization behavior in China business. She is a fellow of International Academy of Intercultural Research; and a member of several professional bodies. She has published one book and several articles. Her research interest is corporate social responsibility development in China, cross-cultural negotiation, and business education.

Maria Manuela Santos Natário is Adjunct Professor at Polytechnics Institute of Guarda, Portugal, Phd. in Economics of Innovation and Competitiveness by University of Évora, and has a Masters degree in Management by the University of Beira Interior. She directs the economic scientific area and she teaches Economics; Innovation and Creativity; Innovation and Competitiveness. She is also a Research Fellow at Research Unit for Inland Development (Portugal). Her main interests include Economy of Innovation, Innovation and Competitiveness. She has published articles in international journals such as Journal of the American Academy of Business and in the Journal of Comparative International Management.

Agadh Medhi is presently working as 'Breakthrough Performance' (BP) Coach for Oil India Limited (OIL). He has been regularly conducting leadership and organizational development programs in OIL. His present work focuses on organizational transformation i.e. to make OIL a vision driven and value governed organization. He is also working on the various issues related to technology management. His 20 years of experience in the oil industry includes various positions in the Production (Natural Gas) department and was responsible for production, compression and utilization of natural gas. Medhi holds a B.E. degree in Mechanical Engineering from Gauhati University, India.

Christer Norström is professor in Computer Science and Engineering at Mälardalen University, Sweden. Previously he was manager for Motion Control and Applications at ABB Robotics. His research interests are design of real-time systems, and architectures, processes and organization for efficient and effective product development of software intensive systems in a global context. He is also very interested in technology transfer from academia to industry which he has manifested through several successful transfers to the automotive industry.

Maktoba Omar (Reader in Marketing) is a graduate of Leeds University Business School and reader in Marketing at Edinburgh Napier University, she has published in a number of national and international academic journals and presented at numerous conferences and workshops. She is also a Research Associate of the China-EU Development & Research Centre and a Visiting Scholar at Harbin University of Commerce. Her main research interests focus on, international strategy, marketing policy, branding, entrepreneurial and innovation. Her current research focus is the study of the emerging markets development in relation to developed countries.

Roland J. Ortt joined the Faculty of Technology Policy and Management at Delft University of Technology, the Netherlands in 2002 and is currently an Associate Professor of Technology Management and R&D Management. His current research interests include the different paths of development and the diffusion of technology. Specifically, he is interested in methods of market and technology analysis to assess the potential of new technologies. He is the author of various articles in journals such as the *Journal of Product Innovation Management*, the *Market Research Society* and the *International Journal of Technology Management*.

Ana Perez-Luño, PhD, is an assistant professor in the Business Administration Department, Universidad Pablo de Olavide (Seville, Spain), where she obtained her doctorate in 2007. She teaches organization theory and business administration to undergraduate students, and entrepreneurship and innovation to MBA and PhD students. Her current work focuses on research innovation, knowledge, competitiveness, etc. She is publishing her research in several Spanish and international journals. Her papers have appeared in CEDE, Human Resource Management, International journal of Entrepreneurship and Innovation Management, International journal of intellectual property management, International journal of Technology Intelligence and Planning, Management Research, etc.

John Rooney is a Program Manager for Collaboration and Innovation in the IBM CIO office. In this role, he is responsible for defining strategy, technical architecture and program offerings to support collaboration and innovation to support IBM's worldwide employee population. During his career at IBM, Mr. Rooney has been able to introduce many new collaborative technologies to IBM employees including instant messaging, blogging, wikis and podcasting. He was co-founder of IBM's Technology Adoption Program (TAP), which allows IBM to engage employees directly in the full cycle of technology innovation, from initial prototype to deployed solution. He has previously been responsible for the technical strategy for the IBM intranet portal and has managed software development teams. He has written numerous articles on software development topics and hold five patents in the area of collaboration technology. Mr. Rooney holds a B.S. degree in Business Administration and Finance from Marist College.

Victor Scholten is Assistant Professor at the Delft University of Technology, the Netherlands, where he joined in 2007 the research group on Technology, Strategy and Entrepreneurship. His current research focuses on high-technology-based start-ups in academic and corporate environments. His is particularly interested in high technology based entrepreneurship, new business venturing and business networks. In 2006 he completed his PhD research on the early growth of Dutch academic spin-offs at the Wageningen University, the Netherlands.

Chintan Shah, A member of Technology & Development group at Bluewater Energy Services, he is responsible for coordinating new product development, developing business case and defining strategy. Chintan is working as a part-time Research Associate at the department of Technology, Strategy and Entrepreneurship at Delft University of Technology (TUD), the Netherlands. His research interests include technology strategy, corporate venturing and managing breakthrough innovations at large firms. Mechanical engineer by background, Chintan received MSc in Management of Technology from TUD.

Wei Sun got PhD from Estonian Business School. She achieved her MBA degree and then worked as a business consultant for her own consulting company. Her research interest is mainly change management in Chinese organizations. Currently she has several papers about change management published in different international journals and her dissertation is focused on behavioral factors of organizational changes in Chinese companies.

David Thorpe is a Senior Lecturer in the Faculty of Engineering and Surveying at the University of Southern Queensland, where he specializes in engineering management and is currently coordinating the delivery of engineering program at the new Springfield campus of the University as well as the post-graduate Master of Engineering program. He has research interests in project and construction management, innovation management, life cycle asset management and engineering education. Prior to joining the University in 2002, he had an extensive civil engineering career in local and state government.

Maria Teresa Borges Tiago is Assistant Professor at University of Azores, Phd. in International Marketing, and as the MBA by the Portuguese Catholic University. Directs the majors section of the Department of Economics and Management and teaches Services Marketing, International Marketing and Marketing Research. She is also Research Fellow at CEEAplA (Portugal). Her main interests include International Marketing, International Business and TIC. She has published several articles in international journals such as International Journal of e-Business Management, The Business Review, Management Research News, Journal of the American Academy of Business, Journal of Electronic Customer Relationship Management.

Ülle Übius has PhD in management science. Theme of her doctoral thesis was: The impact of corporate social responsibility, and organizational and individual factors on the innovation climate. She has done researches mainly in the fields of innovation management, innovation climate, corporate social responsibility and organization culture. She is also lecturer. She gives lectures in the following themes: project management, innovation climate, quality management.

Ramon Valle is a professor of Human Resource Management in the Business Administration Department, Universidad Pablo de Olavide (Seville, Spain). He obtained his doctorate at the Universidad de Sevilla in 1983. His teaching and research interests focus on strategic human resource management and innovation. He is heading several research projects on innovation, organizational capital, and employment relationships, and he is coauthor of several HRM textbooks and papers in international journals. His papers have appeared in The International Journal of Human Resource Management, R & D Management, The Journal of Management Studies, International Journal of Technology Management, Human Resource Management, etc.

Anders Wall is a researcher at ABB Corporate Research. He is also active in the academic community as a researcher at Mälardalen University. He received his M.Sc in Computer Science from Uppsala University in 1994, his Ph.Lic from Uppsala University in September 2000, and his Ph.D. from Mälardalen University in September 2003. Anders has several years of industrial experience from software development of industrial control systems at ABB. His main research interest includes software product development including software architecture, development processes, organization, and business- and strategic aspects of product development. Other areas where Anders has been active academically include component based software engineering for real-time systems and formal methods for real-time systems.

Johan Wiklund is a Professor of Entrepreneurship at both the Syracuse University (USA) and the Jönköping International Business School (Sweden). His research interests include entrepreneurship, growth and competitiveness. His papers have appeared in Strategic Management Journal, Journal of Business Venturing, Journal of Management, Journal of Economic Psychology, Entrepreneurship Theory and Practice, Journal of Management Studies, Swedish Economic Policy Review, etc.

Haibo Zhou is a PhD student in the department of Organization, Strategy and Entrepreneurship in the Erasmus School of Economics, Erasmus University of Rotterdam. She received her Master degree in Management of Technology from TU Delft and a Bachelor degree in Automobile Engineering from Shanghai University of Engineering Science. She is currently working on her PhD about 'Knowledge, Entrepreneurship and Performance', which investigates the relationship between knowledge and entrepreneurship at different levels of aggregation.

Index

A

accountability 97
adhocracy 188
agglomerates 95
ambiguous 154, 159
analytical competencies 81, 86
ancillary 53, 54, 55, 59, 61
ANOVA 98
Ansoff matrix 189
antecedents 76, 77, 78, 81, 82, 85, 87
applied experience 166

B

balanced approach 25
biotechnology 82, 281, 282, 283, 284, 290, 294
Bluetooth 42, 43, 44, 51
bottlenecks 283, 289, 290, 293
brainstorming 220
brand model 41
breakthrough concept 125
breakthrough technologies 36, 44, 45, 46, 49
burnout of the pioneers 38
business case analysis 210
business transformation management system (BTMS) 21, 25

C

campaign system 84
Cannabis 258
capital theory 166
carbon nanotubes 282
case analysis 81
case-study research 127
catalyst 171, 180

causation 1, 2, 3, 4, 5, 6, 9, 12, 13, 14, 15, 16, 17
centers of excellence (COE) 293, 294
centralized funding 25
change type 53, 60
chief information officer (CIO) 19, 20, 24, 29, 31, 32, 33
circumvent 120, 129, 130
cold silence 215
collaboration 76, 79, 80, 88
collaborative conflict resolution 209, 220
collaborative dispute resolution 214
collaborative process 220
collective knowledge 163
commercialization 142, 281, 282, 285, 291
commonality 218, 220, 222
communications theory 212
community-based decision making 24
community innovation survey (CIS) 150
competitive advantages 64, 68, 94, 96, 97
competitive environment 106, 109, 111, 114, 116
competitive reward system 153, 154
competitor orientation 111, 112, 117
complacency 123, 124, 129, 130, 133
complementary solutions 128
conceptual evaluation 135
confirmatory factor analysis (CFA) 70
conflation 285, 287, 288, 292
conflict resolution 209, 212, 213, 219, 221, 222
contextual factors 196
contextual safety 220
contingency theory 65
control variables 65, 70, 71, 72, 154, 155, 156, 157